# Key Readings in Media Today

By combining classic studies of mass communication with contemporary research on media, technology, and culture, *Key Readings in Media Today* will help students to make sense of the rapidly changing media environment. This collection is designed to supplement the 3rd edition of *Media Today: An Introduction to Mass Communication*, but it can also be used independently.

*Key Readings in Media Today* provides both historical and contemporary analyses of each of the major media industries: book, newspaper, magazine, sound recording/radio, motion picture, television, digital media, advertising, and public relations. The volume places an emphasis on convergence, looking at the ways boundaries between these media industries are blurring in surprising new ways. Section introductions and headnotes for each article offer valuable critical and historical context, while review questions after each reading test students' understanding of key concepts. Additional resources on the companion website at **www.routledge.com/textbooks/9780415992053** are designed to spark classroom discussion and connect the readings to the latest contemporary media issues and controversies.

**Contributors:** Chris Anderson, Ben H. Bagdikian, C. Edwin Baker, Yochai Benkler, Brooke Erin Duffy, Stuart Ewen, Mark Fitzgerald, Bob Garfield, Ian Gordon, David Hendy, Janis Ian, Mark Jancovich, Henry Jenkins, Steven Johnson, Eric Klinenberg, Deepa Kumar, Peter Lattman, Paul F. Lazarsfeld, Lawrence Lessig, Matthew P. McAllister, Robert McChesney, Robert King Merton, Philip M. Napoli, Philip Nel, Neil Postman, W. James Potter, Steve Powers, Michael Real, Katherine Sender, Ethan Smith, Gloria Steinem, Inger L. Stole, Gaye Tuchman, Joseph Turow, James B. Twitchell, Janet Wasko

**Brooke Erin Duffy** is pursuing her PhD at the University of Pennsylvania's Annenberg School for Communication.

**Joseph Turow** is Robert Lewis Shayon Professor of Communication at the University of Pennsylvania's Annenberg School for Communication. He has authored eight books, edited five books, and written more than one hundred articles on mass media industries, including the third edition of his textbook *Media Today: An Introduction to Mass Communication*, also published by Routledge.

# Key Readings in

# Media Today

Mass Communication in Contexts

Edited by

## Brooke Erin Duffy and
## Joseph Turow

Routledge
Taylor & Francis Group

NEW YORK AND LONDON

First published 2009
by Routledge
270 Madison Ave, New York, NY 10016

Simultaneously published in the UK
by Routledge
2 Park Square, Milton Park, Abingdon, Oxon OX14 4RN

*Routledge is an imprint of the Taylor & Francis Group, an informa business*

© 2009 Taylor & Francis

Typeset in Perpetua and Bell Gothic by
RefineCatch Limited, Bungay, Suffolk
Printed and bound in the United States of America on acid-free paper by
Sheridan Books, Inc.

*Library of Congress Cataloging-in-Publication Data*
Key readings in media today : mass communication in contexts / edited by Brooke Erin Duffy and
Joseph Turow.
    p.  cm.
    Includes bibliographical references and index.
    1. Mass media.   I. Duffy, Brooke Erin.   II. Turow, Joseph.
    P91.25.K49 2008
    302.23—dc22

                                       2008021845

ISBN10: 0–415–99204–4 (hbk)
ISBN10: 0–415–99205–2 (pbk)

ISBN13: 978–0–415–99204–6 (hbk)
ISBN13: 978–0–415–99205–3 (pbk)

# Contents

# Acknowledgments

The following were reproduced with kind permission. While every effort has been made to trace copyright holders and obtain permission, this has not been possible in all cases. Any omissions brought to our attention will be remedied in future editions.

## Part I: Understanding the Nature of Mass Media

P.F. Lazarsfeld and Robert King Merton, "Mass Communication, Popular Taste and Organized Social Action" from *The Communication of Ideas,* ed. L. Bryson, (pp. 95–118). New York: Harper. Copyright © 1948. Reproduced by permission of The Louis Finkelstein Institute for Religious and Social Studies.

W. James Potter, "Media Literacy Approach" from *Media Literacy: 4th edn* by W.J. Potter, (pp. 11–26). Thousand Oaks, California: Sage Publications. Copyright © 2005. Reproduced by permission of the publisher.

Ben H. Bagdikian, "Common Media for an Uncommon Nation" from *The New Media Monopoly* by Ben Bagdikian, (pp. 233–256). Copyright © 2004 by Ben Bagdikian. Reprinted by permission of Beacon Press, Boston.

Robert McChesney, "Political Problem, Political Solutions" from *The Problem of the Media: U.S. Communication Politics in the 21st Century* by Robert McChesney, (pp. 16–56). New York: Monthly Review Press. Copyright © 2004. Reproduced by permission of the publisher.

C. Edwin Baker, "Not Toasters: The Special Nature of Media Products" from *Media, Markets, and Democracy* by C. Edwin Baker, (pp. 7–19). Cambridge: Cambridge University Press. Copyright © 2002. Reproduced by permission of the publisher.

Lawrence Lessig, "Four Puzzles from Cyberspace" from *Code: Version 2.0* by Lawrence Lessig, (pp. 9–28). New York: New York Basic Books. Copyright © 2006. Reproduced by permission of the publisher.

## Part II: The Print Media

Gaye Tuchman, "Making News: Time and Typifications" Reprinted with the permission of The Free Press, a Division of Simon & Schuster Adult Publishing Group, from *Making News: A Study in the Construction of Reality* by Gaye Tuchman. Copyright © 1978 by the Free Press. All rights reserved.

Eric Klinenberg, "Convergence: News Production in a Digital Age" reprinted by permission from Sage Publications Ltd from *The Annals of the American Academy of Political and Social Science,* January 2005; 597: 48–64. Copyright © Sage Publications, 2005.

Brooke Erin Duffy, "Time Ahead: Digital Challenges Facing Magazines." Printed with permission of the author. Copyright © 2007.

Gloria Steinem, "Sex, Lies, and Advertising" reprinted by permission from East Toledo Productions from *Ms. Magazine,* July/August 1990; 18–28. Copyright © 1990.

Nel, Philip. Is There a Text in This Advertising Campaign?: Literature, Marketing, and Harry Potter. The Lion and the Unicorn 29:2 (2005), 236–267. © The John Hopkins University Press.

Mark Fitzgerald, "Newspapers Rocken Espanol" reprinted by permission from *Editor and Publisher,* March 2004; 137, 26–32. Copyright © 2004.

## Part III: The Electronic Media

"What is News?", from How to Watch TV News by Neil Postman and Steve Powers, copyright © 1992 by Neil Postman and Steve Powers. Used by permission of Viking Penguin, a division of Penguin Group (USA) Inc.

Katherine Sender, "Queens for a Day: *Queer Eye for the Straight Guy* and the Neoliberal Project" reprinted by permission from Taylor and Francis, Ltd from *Critical Studies in Media Communication*, 2006; 23, 2. 131–151. Copyright © Taylor and Francis Ltd, http://www.informaworld.com, 2006.

Philip Napoli, "Deconstructing the Diversity Principle" reprinted by permission from Blackwell Publishing Ltd. from *Journal of Communication*, 1996; 49 (4), 7–34. Copyright © Blackwell Publishing Ltd, 1996.

David Hendy, "Radio in Modernity: Time, Place, and 'Communicative Capacity'" from *Radio in the Global Age* by David Hendy, (pp. 177–193). Cambridge: Polity Press. Copyright © 2000. Reproduced by Permission of the publisher.

Janis Ian (2002, August 1). "Fallout: A Follow Up to the Internet Debacle Online" from http://www.janisian.com, August 1, 2002. Copyright © 2002. Reproduced by permission of the author.

Janet Wasko, "Promoting and Protecting the Industry" from *How Hollywood Works* by Janet Wasko, (pp. 188–220). Thousand Oaks, CA: Sage. Copyright © 2004. Reproduced by permission of the publisher.

Matthew P. McAllister, Ian Gordon, and Mark Jancovich, "Art House Meets Graphic Novel, or Blockbuster Meets Superhero Comic?: The Contradictory Relationship between Film and Comic Art" reprinted by permission from Heldref Publications from *Journal of Popular Film and Television*, 2006; 34 (3), 108–114. Copyright © 2006.

## Part IV: The Digital Media

Chris Anderson (2004, October) "The Long Tail" Copyright © 2004 Conde Nast Publications. All Rights reserved. Originally published in *Wired*. Reprinted by permission.

Yochai Benkler, "Peer Production and Sharing" from *The Wealth of Networks: How Social Production Transforms Markets and Freedom* by Yochai Benkler, (pp. 1–22). Copyright © 2006. New Haven: Yale University Press. Reproduced by permission of the publisher.

Steven Johnson (2005, July). "Your Brain on Video Games: Could They Actually Be Good for You?" reprinted by permission from Paradigm from *Discovery*, July 2005; 27, 7, 38–43. Copyright © 2005.

Michael Real "Sports Online: The Newest Player in Mediasport" from *Handbook of Sports and Media* edited by Arthur A. Raney and Jennings Bryant, (pp. 171–184). Mahwah, NJ: Lawrence Erlbaum Associates. Copyright © 2006. Reprinted by permission of the publisher.

Henry Jenkins, "Quentin Tarantino's Star Wars?: Digital Cinema, Media Convergence, and Participatory Culture" from Thorburn, David, and Henry Jenkins, eds., *Rethinking Media Change: The Aesthetics of Transition*, excerpt from pages 281–315, © 2003 Massachusetts Institute of Technology, by permission of The MIT Press. Reprinted by permission of the publisher.

Ethan Smith & Peter Lattman, "Download This: YouTube Phenom Has a Big Secret" reprinted by permission from Dow Jones, Inc. from the *Wall Street Journal*. Online. www.wsj.com. September 6, 2007. Copyright © 2007.

## Part V: Advertising and Public Relations

James B. Twitchell, "The Work of Adcult" from *Adcult USA: The Triumph of Advertising in American Culture* by James B. Twitchell. (pp. 161–178). Copyright © 1997. New York: Columbia University Press. Reprinted with permission of the publisher.

Bob Garfield, (2005, April 13), "'Chaos Scenario': A Look at the Marketing Industry's Coming Disaster" reprinted with permission from Crain Communications Inc. from *Advertising Age*. Online. www.adage.com. April 13, 2005. Copyright, Crain Communications, Inc. © 2008.

Joseph Turow, "Rethinking Television in the Digital Age" from *Media, Organization, and Identity* edited by Lilie Chouliaraki and Mette Morsing. London: Palgrave. Forthcoming. Printed with permission of the publisher.

Inger Stole, "Philanthropy as Public Relations: A Critical Perspective on Cause Marketing", reprinted by permission from *Critical International Journal of Communication* and the University of Southern California, 2008; 2, 20–40. Copyright © 2008.

Deepa Kumar, "Media, War, and Propaganda: Strategies of Information Management During the 2003 Iraq War", reprinted by permission from Taylor and Francis, Ltd. from *Communication and Critical/Cultural Studies*, 2006; 3, 1, 48–69. Copyright © Taylor and Francis Ltd, http://www.informaworld.com, 2006.

Stuart Ewen, "The Public and Its Problems: Some Notes for the New Millennium" from *PR: A Social History of Spin* by Stuart Ewen, (399–414). New York: Basic Books. Copyright © 1996. Reproduced by permission of the publisher.

# BROOKE ERIN DUFFY

# INTRODUCTION

**I**F YOU WERE TO EMBARK on a study of media today, a television program that is broadcast but once a year might seem an unlikely place to start. That is, of course, unless that program is the Super Bowl. Not only does the game draw an audience of nearly 100 million viewers, but it also attracts big-name advertisers who are willing to shell out close to 3 million dollars to broadcast a 30-second in-game commercial. That's $100,000 *a second*! Perhaps more important, the changing ways in which these audiences and advertisers experience the game reflect significant transformations taking place in the contemporary media world. For example, as fans increasingly tune in to the game from their laptops, mobile phones, and other electronic devices, one may question whether it is even accurate to refer to the Super Bowl as a "television program." Of course, this is not a trend unique to sports broadcasts. As you may know, many popular TV series—including *Grey's Anatomy, The Office*, and *Lost*—make their content freely available online.

The Super Bowl also reveals much about the role of advertisers in an era of digital media. As advertisers pay tremendous sums of money to reach audiences during the event, it is perhaps not surprising that they are eager to extend the life span of each ad. One way they accomplish this is by using new media platforms, most notably the Internet, to get people talking both before and after the game. Advertisers refer to this as word-of-mouth marketing, or "generating buzz." You can probably think of many examples of Super Bowl advertisers who have done just that—whether by tugging at the heartstrings or pushing the limits of good taste.

During the weeks bracketing the 2008 Super Bowl, for example, PepsiCo launched a branded site on Facebook to coincide with its television campaign. Meanwhile, web hosting company Go Daddy tempted football fans to visit their web site to see the racy ads that Fox, that year's Super Bowl broadcaster, rejected. Several other marketers turned to traditional media to generate post-game buzz. Both Doritos and E*Trade placed ads *about their ads* in national newspapers the day after the game. The promotional tactics of these and other Super Bowl advertisers dovetailed with the marketing efforts of online media companies. While YouTube sponsored a contest prompting fans to vote for their favorite ad, MySpace created a Super Bowl "profile" featuring the commercials that ran during the game. Fox, meanwhile, which is owned by the same media conglomerate as MySpace, provided Super Bowl advertisers with the opportunity to buy space on the popular social network site. According to an *Advertising Age* columnist who described this strategy, "The network ran on-air promotions during the game urging viewers to visit [MySpace]. Advertisers were able to offer different perks to those who watch the ads online, including coupons, links to other websites, and the chance to see movie trailers."[1]

These examples from the Super Bowl indicate some of the fundamental changes taking place in the world of media during the first decade of the twenty-first century. Chief among them is the trend among audiences to consume traditional media products on new or different media platforms. This is known as *media convergence* and describes the sort of activities you may engage in on a daily basis: accessing a web browser from your mobile device; watching a streaming television channel online, or downloading an audio clip onto your iPod, among many others.

Media convergence not only impacts the activities of audiences, but also those of media producers and advertisers. Henry Jenkins, a prominent scholar of media studies whose work we return to later, has noted the considerable ways in which the creation of media content is shifting shape in the digital age. According to Jenkins, media producers are feeling the pressure of integrated media industries to create content that "provoke[s] strong audience engagement and investment."[2] This means that companies have to give greater consideration to the types of media products that will successfully cross media boundaries. Superhero comics are a good example of this for they transfer well from the comic book pages to the movie screen; you will read more about this in a later chapter.

The fact that audiences today have more control over *where* (e.g. on television versus online versus mobile phones) they consume media translates into less control for advertisers. So, too, does the fact that audiences are in greater command of *when* they view or listen to a particular program. This is, of course, in response to the spread of digital recording devices and online media players, both of which are commonly referred to as "time-shifting" technologies. Within this context, advertisers are beginning to rethink where and when they can most efficiently reach audiences.

Given such transformations in the behaviors and expectations of media audiences, producers, and advertisers, it is truly an exciting time to study the media of mass communication. To help guide you through this dynamic media landscape, it is valuable to draw on a wide range of perspectives—both traditional and contemporary, both theoretical and practical. Therefore, *Key Readings in Media Today* brings the classic, yet still provocative, writings of Paul Lazarsfeld and Robert Merton, Stuart Ewen, and Gaye Tuchman together with the contemporary scholarship of Henry Jenkins, Robert McChesney, Janet Wasko, and Lawrence Lessig, among others. Those with first-hand experience in the business of media, meanwhile, provide insight from a different stance. They include Mark Fitzgerald, a writer for newspaper trade magazine *Editor and Publisher, Advertising Age* columnist Bob Garfield, *Wired* editor-in-chief Chris Anderson, and Ethan Smith and Peter Lattman, both of whom report for the *Wall Street Journal*. Together, these media scholars, critics, and professionals tackle a wide variety of issues related to mass media and their significance to the contemporary social, economic, and political systems.

Not only does *Key Readings in Media Today* put you in touch with a broad range of debates about media, but it also addresses a diverse array of media products—from video games, women's magazines, and comic books, to Hollywood blockbusters, children's literature, and video-sharing web sites. Before continuing, it's probably a good idea to state what we mean by the term *media*. A *medium*—that's the singular version of the word—is a vehicle for the presentation of messages. You could say that a person is a medium, in the sense that he or she creates messages by speaking or using gestures. Typically, though, we reserve the word medium for a technology that serves as a platform for messages. The technology can be as traditional as the printing press or as cutting-edge as a supermarket video cart that offers shoppers bargains depending on where they are in the store. The messages can be serious or funny, fiction or nonfiction, printed, audio, audiovisual, or a combination of these attributes. Television is an example of a medium; so is the Internet. So, for that matter, are the greeting card, the billboard, and the supermarket coupon.

Media often carry messages that are created by individuals and distributed in a very limited way. Think of a parent creating videos of a new child or a husband and wife communicating over the phone. There are, however, many cases where organizations, not individuals, carry out the production, distribution and exhibition of materials. That happens, for example, when NBC produces its *Nightly News* program, and when Electronic Arts creates Madden football video games. We call this sort of activity *mass communication*. Mass communication is the industrialized production, distribution and exhibition of messages through technological devices.

In recent years, a distinction has emerged between "traditional" and "new" media industries. The former includes books, newspapers, magazines, radio, film, and television. The latter refers to industries that deal with digital media content, such as the Internet, video games, and mobile devices. At first glance, these distinctions seem logical. The more you understand these businesses, though, the more you will realize that it is becoming increasingly difficult to determine where one industry ends and another begins. The "traditional" and "new" industries are bleeding into one another.

For example, if you read an article on sportsillustrated.com, a site related to a "traditional" print magazine firm, is this material from the "Internet industry" or the "magazine industry"? What happens if you watch a video on one of these sites? This site, then, becomes a point of overlap—of *convergence*—among print, online, and electronic media content, not to mention the many ads which are included on these sites! This example raises the issue of whether in an era of media convergence, it is useful to look at media industries separately. This book takes the perspective that it is both useful and necessary. In addition to highlighting the significant differences that distinguish print, electronic, and digital media, such an approach illustrates the unique content and format of each medium. This will also provide a strong foundation for realizing the benefits and challenges of media convergence in the twenty-first century.

The 31 essays in this book are organized into five sections: Understanding the Nature of Mass Media, Print Media, Electronic Media, Digital Media, and Advertising and Public Relations. In many cases, the essays will build upon previous sections and the topics addressed within them. A brief introduction is included with each essay which will help to contextualize the topic and provide you with information about the author(s). Discussion questions are also included and can help spark small-group and classroom discussions. These questions encourage you to apply foundational concepts, debate policy objectives, draw conclusions about the future of media, and compare and contrast the different readings in this book.

One way to compare and contrast these essays is to see how much emphasis they place on the continuities versus changes in media and their relationship to society. By continuities, we mean the tradition and history of a medium along with the idea that there are some media activities and some debates about their social role that cross generations. An emphasis on change, by contrast, means that the author prefers to focus on breaks with the past, how media industries and society at large are being transformed. If you compare Gaye Tuchman's piece on news with Eric Klinenberg's, you'll see how the first reading emphasizes continuities in journalism—she discusses journalism as an activity that has longstanding practices—while the second centers on the many changes moving through the business today. Of course, a writer doesn't have to choose to be concerned with change or with continuity. As you'll see, many of the readings discuss both; they may emphasize one over the other.

The first essay in Understanding the Nature of Mass Media, titled "Mass Communication, Popular Taste, and Organized Social Action," takes us back to an era when scholars were in the early decades of paying attention to media as social phenomena. The authors, pioneering sociologists Paul Lazarsfeld and Robert Merton, identify and examine three major concerns with mass media—their potential power, their effects on audiences, and their detrimental impact on popular taste. Today, more than 60 years after this essay was written, media scholars and activists continue to grapple with these issues. Lazarsfeld and Merton conclude by noting how mass media "have served to cement the structure of our society." Indeed this theme is woven throughout many of the essays that follow.

While Lazarsfeld and Merton sensitize us to broad possible consequences that we should consider when we deal with media, communication professor W. James Potter provides specific guidelines on how to become more media literate. Although scholars have struggled to define this term, Potter articulates media literacy as "a set of perspectives that we actively use to expose ourselves to the media to interpret the meaning of messages we encounter." This means that those who have a higher degree of media literacy can maintain more control over media messages.

This topic of control is an issue that media critic Ben Bagdikian takes up in his essay "Common Media for an Uncommon Nation." Bagdikian, who has been writing about the concentration of media ownership for more than 25 years, finds it alarming that five global media conglomerates (Time Warner, Viacom, Disney, NBC Universal, and Fox) control the majority of U.S. newspapers, magazines, books, film studios, and television stations. In fact, he argues that the power shared by "the Big Five . . . has become a major force in shaping contemporary American life," in part because it limits the diversity of viewpoints to which people are exposed. Bagdikian closes his essay by noting uncertainties that the digital revolution has brought to the media picture. In the few years since this piece was published, Google and Yahoo have had enormous influence on the media landscape. As you'll see, we've added a question after the article that invites you to explore these new powerhouses.

Robert McChesney, a prominent scholar and activist, expands upon Bagdikian's discussion of the relationship between media and the government. His opening argument in "Political Problem, Political Solutions" is that set against the backdrop of a seemingly democratic society, the present media system is considerably antidemocratic: very few political and economic forces shape the majority of media content. McChesney suggests this is the result of government policy decisions that have emerged over the decades. Such policies continue to influence our exposure to and experience with media messages.

The next essay addresses the ways in which media policies are considered by the legal system. In "Not Toasters: The Special Nature of Media Products," communication law expert C. Edwin Baker takes off from a comment by a former Federal Communications Commission Chairman that television sets are like toasters. Baker disagrees, and he argues that traditional economic approaches to government regulation are not relevant when dealing with media. This argument is based on what Baker identifies as several unique features of communication products, including their "public good" value and their dual revenue stream. Dual revenue stream refers to the fact that media receive financial support from audiences (a cable subscription, a movie ticket) and advertisers. Baker uses the example of copyright law, which protects the rights of content creators, to illustrate why the government regulation of media is fundamentally different from other products, including toasters.

The final essay in Part One, Law Professor Lawrence Lessig's "Four Puzzles from Cyberspace," examines the changing relationship between media, society, and regulation in the context of the digital age. Lessig provides an entertaining series of tales to highlight some of the fundamental features of cyberspace. He argues that while in some ways life in cyberspace is similar to material ("real") life, the two worlds cannot be fully mapped on to one another. This awareness leads Lessig to question whether or not the regulatory policies from the physical world can be easily translated into regulation, or code, in the virtual world.

While Part One of *Key Readings in Media Today* provides a bird's eye view of mass media and their role in the social, economic, and political systems, Part Two zooms in on print media. The readings discuss books, newspapers, and magazines. Together, they suggest significant areas of change as well as important continuities within the oldest media industries.

Gaye Tuchman's "Making News: Time and Typifications" is excerpted from a larger research project that she carried out in the late 1970s to understand the practices involved in news production. In this piece, she explores how journalists' timing rhythms—the hours in the workday, the weekly schedule—impact how they think about and present news. She shows, for example, how considerations of when and how a story unfolds impacts whether it gets organized and presented as a "hard news" (e.g. factual and informative), "soft news" (e.g. features, human-interest stories), or "developing." Tuchman's basic insight that ideas about time affect how news is defined and presented is as relevant today as it was when she wrote her piece in 1978.

But certain ways in which journalists' concerns about time shape news may well have changed substantially since then. They now find themselves in a so-called "twenty-four/seven" era of news and information, where news web sites constantly want to post the latest information about events. So while we can undoubtedly find important continuities with Tuchman's findings in today's journalistic work, there has also been a great deal of change since the time of Tuchman's writing.

This is an issue that media scholar and sociologist Eric Klinenberg devotes considerable attention to in his essay "Convergence: News Production in a Digital Age." Reaffirming the importance of timing to news production, Klinenberg describes how news workers today are in the midst of a "news cyclone." This, he explains, is "an information environment in which there is always breaking news to produce, consume, and—for reporters and their subjects—'react against.' " Another theme that Klinenberg addresses is the shift to media convergence. As you well know, many people have turned to the Web or mobile devices to access newspaper content. Klinenberg notes how this puts pressures on journalists to produce news content that can successfully cross media boundaries.

In her essay "Pushing Time Ahead," Brooke Erin Duffy argues that the magazine industry is also facing timing-related challenges in a highly time-sensitive media age. Duffy notes how producers of magazines tend to work on issues months in advance of the publication's cover date. In recent years, the viability of this practice has been questioned as magazine readers and advertisers expect information to be timely in ways current production routines do not allow. While many magazines are responding by increasing the online presence of their magazine brands, this presents a whole new set of challenges as producers struggle to maintain synchronicity between two platforms—print and the Web.

The next two essays examine the role of advertising in print media and, in so doing, raise questions about the extent to which advertising influences media content. Writer-activist Gloria Steinem wrote the article "Sex, Lies, and Advertising" in 1990 to describe the difficulties the feminist magazine *Ms.* faced in trying to attract advertising support. Such difficulties stemmed from the magazine's refusal to comply with requests from marketers to place ads in a "supportive editorial atmosphere." So, for instance, a company advertising a baking product will stipulate that the ad must appear adjacent to a magazine recipe which includes the product. While Steinem argues that practices like these have a long history in women's magazines, they have since extended to almost all other media.

Children's literature has been an especially popular site for the blurring of entertainment and marketing, and Philip Nel turns to an example of this in "Is There a Text in this Advertising Campaign?: Literature, Marketing, and Harry Potter." Nel, an English professor and novelist, takes the position that the highly successful Harry Potter series should be recognized as a literary achievement *and* a marketing phenomenon. Thus, by studying the creation and distribution of Harry Potter products, we can learn a great deal about the commercialization of literature and other products. At the same time, this emphasis on marketing should not eclipse the literary merits, or what Nel playfully refers to as the "magic beyond the marketing."

Part Two concludes with an article on the newspaper industry that points to different elements of change and continuity in print media from the ones covered in the other essays. In "Newspapers Rocken Espanol," *Editor and Publisher* columnist Mark Fitzgerald describes the explosive growth of Spanish-language newspapers as companies aim to capture the increasing population of Hispanics in cities across America. The benefits to newspaper chains seem obvious—increased revenues in the form of circulation and advertising. But, as Fitzgerald warns, newspaper chains must make sure they know they are familiar with the market they are trying to reach. This trend in targeting media products at specific segments of the population is not new; magazine and radio companies have been doing it for decades. What *is* new is the increasing sophistication of these techniques, a topic which receives further consideration in the final section of this book.

We then move to Part Three, which centers on electronic media, including television, radio, sound recording, and motion pictures. Despite the shift to a different set of media, many of the themes discussed in earlier essays—such as communication policy initiatives, the significance of timing, the blurring boundary between advertising and entertainment, and the shift to media convergence—are revived in this section.

In the first essay, Neil Postman and Steve Powers discuss the contemporary state of television news. By questioning, "What is News?" Postman and Powers emphasize the point that news is not simply what happens, but, rather, what gets made into news. Often it is made "on the basis of what the journalist thinks important or what the journalist thinks the audience thinks is important or interesting." Yet the authors make an even more provocative suggestion: that broadcast news, which is funded exclusively by advertisers, essentially serves as a 'filler' to keep people tuned in to the commercials. The desire to keep the audience flowing into commercials also explains, they argue, why television news tends to focus on entertainment reports.

Ideas about reality can come from both news and entertainment, and the way we arrange our viewing may lead both forms of programming to flow together. If you're like most Americans, so-called "reality television" makes up part of that flow. Communication Professor Katherine Sender addresses social issues surrounding a particular form of reality TV—the makeover series—in "Queens for a Day: *Queer Eye for the Straight Guy* and the Neoliberal Project." She focuses on some overlooked elements of the former Bravo makeover show, including the ways in which it presents the experts and candidates. Sender contends that the show encourages heterosexual men to "produce themselves as viable commodities," again blurring the lines between entertainment and advertising. Yet she also points to the significance of this show in challenging conventional stereotypes of gender and sexuality.

The notion of stereotypes leads us into the next essay, "Deconstructing the Diversity Principle," written by media policy expert Philip Napoli. Although Napoli's essay is somewhat complex, it gets to the heart of one of the most important issues in American broadcasting: diversity. In order to address the many facets of diversity, Napoli breaks the concept down into three distinct components: source, content, and exposure diversity. Not only does he describe and provide examples of each of these components, but he also offers suggestions on how they can frame analyses of electronic media. More broadly, Napoli relates the issue of broadcast diversity to the topic of "the marketplace of ideas," which is a key element of the U.S. constitution.

The next essay, "Radio and Modernity: Time, Place, and 'Communicative

Capacity,'" allows us to contrast the nature of broadcasting in the U.S. with that of the U.K. The author, media and cultural historian David Hendy, examines radio through the twin dimensions of time and space, using examples from the British Broadcasting Corporation (BBC) in the U.K. One aspect of time he considers is that of the flow, or programming sequence, of a radio station. The particular flow of a station is what makes its personality. For example, the programming of a radio station aimed at college students might flow from a series of hit songs to a local news update to a contest for a spring break trip. Radio's sense of place, meanwhile, speaks to the ways in which it offers a "virtual coming together." This, to Hendy, suggests an important social function of radio which far surpasses its capacity to communicate. Another significant aspect of Hendy's work is that it allows us to see how much radio has changed since this article was written in 2000. Not only do listeners today construct their own music schedules, much like Hendy foreshadows, but they can also transcend the boundaries of space by accessing radio stations from across the globe.

Intimately connected with the radio industry is that of sound recording, although this relationship is not as strong as it once was. Singer-songwriter Janis Ian explores one of the most significant reasons for this in her essay, "Fallout—A Follow Up to the 'Internet Debacle.'" This piece was written in 2002 in response to another article in which Ian lambasted the recording industry's move to condemn the now-defunct free music sharing site Napster. The original article received staunch criticism from executives of the major recording firms that support the Record Industry Association of America (RIAA). In the second piece, Ian defends her position and, in so doing, raises questions about the role of the music industry, online music, and performers in the new media environment.

The final two essays in Part Three address the motion picture industry and, more specifically, explore the economic potential of blockbuster films. Janet Wasko describes the extensive—and expensive—marketing practices of film companies in her essay "Promoting the Industry." Continuities and changes in the industry's approach are quite clear: the practices range from traditional advertising, publicity, and movie trailers to more recent marketing tactics like product placement deals, event production, and targeted Internet promotions. A recent example of this is the Internet campaign that was developed to promote *Indiana Jones and the Kingdom of the Crystal Skull*. When the trailer for the movie was launched on the Web in February 2008, it was viewed more than 200 million times *in the first week*.

While Wasko addresses how the need to maximize profits impacts the promotion of movies, Matthew McAllister, Ian Gordon, and Mark Jancovich examine how economic considerations also impact content creation. In their essay "Art House Meets Graphic Novel, or Blockbuster Meets Superhero Comic?: The Contradictory Relationship Between Film and Comic Art," they explore a problematic aspect of media convergence. While Hollywood studios have benefited tremendously from superhero blockbusters such as *Batman Begins, Superman Returns*, and *X-Men: The Last Stand*, the story is different for those in the comic book industry. They are often forced to come up with characters and plots that will translate well from the comic book pages to the big screen. This focus on "economic predictability and long time licensing potential," may even result in a loss of creative control.

This discussion of media convergence at the end of Part Three sets up Part Four of *Key Readings in Media Today*, which explores the increasingly interconnected nature of media in the digital age. The essays in this section address the video game, Internet, and mobile industries. While the emphasis is on the new, far from everything about these media businesses is totally novel. The past plays a part in every new media story as industry practitioners struggle to understand how to make money in the face of strong competition. Quite frequently, the business models that they choose reflect at least partly the business models of successful traditional firms that came before them. That's true as much about video games as it is about cable TV, which not too many decades ago was considered a "new" platform.

In the first essay, "The Long Tail," *Wired* magazine editor-in-chief Chris Anderson examines the economic potential for media businesses that shift their focus to the online world. "The Long Tail" is a phrase coined by Anderson to describe the people whom the economics of new digital media platforms make it profitable to pursue. These people can be pictured as those with unusual interests that fall outside the large bump of people with mainstream interests. These non-mainstream individuals make up the "tails"—the outliers—on a normal statistics curve. The cost structures of new media, Anderson says, make it more financially feasible than ever before to cater to these people. He illustrates this with the case of the home video market at the time that he wrote his book. Whereas an offline video store like Blockbuster was carrying fewer than 3,000 titles, the online retailer Netflix was getting a fifth of its rental profits from DVDs outside the top 3,000. According to Anderson, "combine enough non-hits on the Long Tail and you've got a market bigger than the hits." Of course, Blockbuster realized this point, as well, and it has since configured its online business to compete for the "Long Tail" with Netflix.

While Anderson provides guidance on how digital technology can be used to rethink how industrialized media products are sold, Yochai Benkler sees new media as changing the basic ways the media materials are made. Benkler, an expert in communication law, is particularly interested in peer production, or "production systems that depend on individual action that is self-selected and decentralized rather than hierarchically assigned." Although this may sound complicated, peer production is something with which you are probably very familiar. It includes collaborative information web sites like Wikipedia, online worlds such as Second Life, and music sharing services like KaZaa. To Benkler, the popularity of peer production and sharing serves to challenge "our most widely held beliefs about economic behavior."

In "Your Brain on Video Games: Could They Actually be Good for You?" Steven Johnson challenges a commonly held assumption about video games. Johnson, an author whose work brings together technology and society, asserts that games—from *Tetris* and *The Time Machine* to the *Grand Theft Auto* games and *Medal of Honor*—may be highly beneficial to players. His claim is based upon a number of studies that have emerged in recent years to address the effects of video game usage. Particularly significant are findings by James Gee that video games enable players to develop such cognitive skills as "pattern recognition, system thinking, even patience."

Some of the most popular games involve sports, a topic of particular interest to Michael Real, whose academic work focuses on media and public culture. In his essay, "Sports Online: The Newest Player in Mediasport," Real addresses the myriad ways in which the Internet is changing the nature of sports fandom. This includes the popularity of sports webcasts, online gambling, blogging, and fantasy leagues. Real suggests that the world of sports in the twenty-first century can be likened to a "stadium without walls," and it can teach us much about the changing landscape of media. Indeed, in his conclusion, Real addresses many of the themes that we can find throughout this book, including continuity and change, media ownership, convergence, diversity, and the opportunity for audiences to produce media content.

These themes are also reflected in Henry Jenkins's essay, "Quentin Tarantino's *Star Wars*? Digital Cinema, Media Convergence, and Participatory Culture." Jenkins, who was mentioned at the beginning of this chapter, uses the example of *Star Wars* to explore how media today are increasingly convergent and participatory. While *Star Wars* has long generated significant fan activity, Jenkins explains how new media technologies are making it possible for these media *consumers* to become media *producers* through the creation and distribution of amateur fan films. He notes the particular significance of the Internet as "a site of experimentation and innovation, where amateurs test the waters, developing new practices, themes, and generating materials which may well attract cult followings on their own terms."

The emphasis that Benkler and Jenkins place on the audience as producer shouldn't cloud the traditional corporate interest in exerting power over the audience, if only to make money from it. Part Four therefore closes by addressing a very different aspect of amateur media production in the Internet age. In "Download This: YouTube Phenom has a Big Secret," *Wall Street Journal* reporters Ethan Smith and Peter Lattman examine the case of Marié Digby, a young singer-guitarist who was catapulted to fame after a series of 'homemade music videos' appeared on YouTube. While many believed Digby was an amateur whose widespread recognition was made possible by the Internet, information later emerged that she was signed by a record company long before her success on YouTube. In fact, Digby's record company even devised this Internet strategy and consulted with her on the type of songs to post. For Smith and Lattman, this is solid evidence that "traditional media conglomerates are going to new lengths to take advantage of the Internet's ability to generate word-of-mouth buzz."

Word-of-mouth is but one of the many tactics that advertisers are turning to in the present era of interactive digital media. The final section of *Key Readings in Media Today* examines some of these tactics in detail while building upon earlier discussions of the relationship between advertising and media. This section also includes a selection of essays on public relations. Public relations is a multifaceted business that one writer sums up as "information, activities and policies by which corporations and other organizations seek to create attitudes favorable to themselves and their work, and to counter adverse attitudes."[3] While people usually associate the public relations industry with crisis response—for example, after a children's toy manufacturer issues a safety recall—the final three essays of this book reveal the value of strategic communication in other situations.

James Twitchell, an English professor who has written extensively on the culture of

advertising, revives the topic of the Super Bowl in his essay, "The Work of Adcult."
For Twitchell, the Super Bowl—along with the Academy Awards, Valentine's Day,
Spring Break, Grandparent's Day, Halloween, Christmas, and a slew of others—is not
merely a holiday or event, but rather, a "festival of consumption." In fact, all of the
celebrations that Twitchell describes have been profoundly shaped by the influence of
advertisers. The most noteworthy example of this is Christmas, which has evolved
from a day of religious remembrance to what Twitchell describes as a "make-it or
break-it event" upon which Western capitalism depends. A larger theme to emerge
from Twitchell's discussion of "festivals of consumption," is that advertising impacts
culture and society in taken-for-granted ways, including how we think about time and
rituals.

While Twitchell's essay seems to reinforce the constancy of advertising,
*Advertising Age* columnist Bob Garfield believes that marketing today is anything
but stable. The title of his article, " 'Chaos Scenario': A Look at the Marketing
Industry's Coming Disaster," is particularly telling of Garfield's outlook on the future
of advertising. By identifying a number of recent trends in media—including the rise of
digital video recorders, changes in media ownership, and the success of web-streaming
video—Garfield argues that "the collapse of the old media model" of marketing is
imminent. While he goes on to predict what the future model might look like, it will no
doubt raise questions about advertising and its role in media and society.

Like Garfield, media and marketing scholar Joseph Turow believes that digital
technologies are causing a fundamental shift in the current advertising/media system.
In his essay, "Rethinking Television in the Digital Age," Turow argues that the spread
of video recording devices, coupled with the rise of online programming, has helped to
"bring an end to television as we have known it." Television executives and advertisers
have responded with new marketing tactics such as branded entertainment, an extreme
form of product placement in which the product or brand is central to the dialogue of
a TV episode. An example of this is NBC's *Heroes,* which not only features a Nissan
SUV driven by a main character, but has also written comments about another Nissan
model into the script. With an eye toward the future, Turow suggests that television
programming will become increasingly targeted and customized through new methods
of collecting user information.

While Turow's essay illustrates some of the ways in which advertising and
entertainment are merging, the next essay, Inger Stole's "Philanthropy as Public
Relations: A Critical Perspective on Cause Marketing," suggests that marketing and
charity are also coming together. Stole, whose research focuses on communication and
consumer activism, examines the issue of cause marketing, a public relations activity
that has grown tremendously in recent years. Cause marketing is defined as "the practice of pegging consumer purchases to philanthropic donations." It is something with
which you have no doubt come into contact. Some of the most well known examples
are Yoplait's support of Breast Cancer Awareness, Gap (Product) Red's Global Fund
to help eliminate AIDS, and Dove's Campaign for Real Beauty. While many people
believe such examples of corporate philanthropy address pressing social issues, Stole
provides a more critical take on this practice. Perhaps most significant, she argues,
cause marketing allows businesses to enhance their image at the same time that they
disregard more effective means of solving social problems.

Journalism scholar Deepa Kumar, meanwhile, critiques a different aspect of contemporary public relations in his provocative article, "Media, War, and Propaganda: Strategies of Information Management during the 2003 Iraq War." An anti-war activist, Kumar takes the position that mainstream media assisted the U.S. government in justifying war. Not only does Kumar cite the abundance of pro-war media articles as evidence of this, but also the ways in which the media omitted certain information that, he feels, would have portrayed the government support for the war in a particularly bad light. Kumar concludes his article with recognition of some of the ways in which the press was able to restore its credibility. Yet questions remain about the democratic nature of media and their role in "facilitating the widest possible exchange of ideas."

This "marketplace of ideas" concept, which is further discussed in Philip Napoli's essay, is a useful entry point into the final essay in this book, Stuart Ewen's "The Public and Its Problems." Written nearly a decade and a half ago, the piece opens with a short tribute to Edward Bernays, a founding figure in the public relations industry who thought about the nature of "the public" in two contradictory ways. On one hand, Bernays saw the public as a critical and knowledgeable mass; on the other, he saw it as a collectivity that could be manipulated through what he called "the engineering of consent." What does that have to do with now? As Ewen well understands, many continuities with Bernays's media era of public relations remain in the U.S. media system despite the huge changes that have taken place. The desire to "engineer consent" exists today in the PR industry, though perhaps in more sophisticated form than in the past. Ewen wonders how this perspective affects democracy in an era in which the PR-guided modern media of communication "are everywhere and inescapable."

For Ewen, encouraging the public to understand and resist such powerful forces can best be accomplished through education in media and visual literacy. This, of course, brings us full circle to the topics of media research and literacy that began *Key Readings in Media Today*. We hope that after reading the essays in this book, you will be better informed about the nature of mass media and their relationship with our social, economic, and political systems. You will also be able to recognize the ways in which traditional and new media are converging. And you will understand how the boundaries are blurring between advertising and entertainment; between news and politics; and between media production and consumption. Perhaps most important, you will be able to think critically about your own role in the media system, a skill which is at the heart of understanding media today.

## Notes

1    Brian Steinberg. "Super Bowl busts ratings on 'the greatest day' ever for Fox." *Advertising Age*, February 11, 2008.

2    Henry Jenkins. "Quentin Tarantino's *Star Wars*? Digital cinema, media convergence, and participatory culture." In *Media and Cultural Studies*, Meenakshi Gigi Durham and Douglas M. Kellner, eds. Malden, MA: Blackwell, 2006, p. 553.

3    Robert Oskar Carlson. "Public relations." In *The Encyclopedia of Communication*. New York: Oxford University Press, 1989, p. 391.

# PART ONE

# Understanding the Nature of Mass Media

# INTRODUCTION

A S FORMS OF COMMUNICATION, MASS media are not very old. Although the printing press was invented in the 1400s, the development of industries to produce and distribute newspapers, books, magazines, sheet music and other printed materials on a large scale didn't take place until the first half of the 1800s in the U.S. and parts of Europe. The second half of the nineteenth century saw the rise of the phonograph, movie, radio and billboard industries. The advertising and public relations industries also took root during this time. Historians have offered many reasons for these developments. They have, for example, linked the rise of mass media to advances in technology, increases in literacy, the growth of dense population centers (and therefore dense audiences for newspapers) as people left farms for factories, and the increase in leisure time for the growing middle class. The creation of railroads, the spread of postal services, and the growing number of companies interested in advertising their products also make the list of important factors.

What many observers found startling about the new media of the nineteenth and early twentieth centuries was how many people they could reach in such a short period of time. It astounded them that big-city newspapers could reach millions of readers each day. They marveled that movies could bring realistic versions of life to audiences around the world, and that a radio program could reach an entire nation at once. At the same time, the ability of the mass media to reach so many different people so quickly intrigued many observers. Some wondered whether these new instruments of communication such as newspapers and radio could bring the diverse people of a modern populous nation together by focusing their attention on important issues. Others worried that the vivid words, sounds and images of the mass media might be used by corporate and government propagandists to push products and ideas on people that might be harmful. Children, they feared, might be especially vulnerable to the influence of commercials and the violent sounds or images from radio, the movies, comic books and (later) television.

Academics who studied these issues systematically in the U.S. beginning after World War I concluded that the mass media were not as influential in changing people as many nervous observers believed; people's prior beliefs and their relationships with others often led them to interpret media presentations through their own value systems. Yet researchers also recognized that children might be more susceptible to media influences than others. That is partly because their value systems haven't taken hold, and possibly because the youngest have not yet developed the ability to understand important media distinctions—the difference, for example, between the story in a program and the commercial message surrounding it. Many intellectuals also realized that despite reams of research articles about the effects of media on individuals, questions about the larger consequences of the mass media for society as a whole were much more difficult to address. Are the mass media raising the level of critical taste in society, or dumbing it down? Do media play a major role in reinforcing the politically and economically powerful institutions in a society? If so, is that always the case, or are there times when groups advocating radical social change can use the media to push their agendas? Should the government become involved in making sure that a diversity of voices have access to powerful media that use public airwaves, and if yes, how? And if media are so powerful in some circumstances or with some groups (such as children), can teaching people how the media operate provide them with an awareness that will make them less susceptible to media messages?

In asking these questions about the roles that media play in the political, economic and cultural life of society, observers of the nineteenth and twentieth centuries emphasized the huge numbers of people that media industries could reach through their technologies and so influence society. By contrast, observers in the twenty-first century note that the Internet, mobile phones, and even the newest forms of television can both reach huge numbers with the same messages and target individuals with messages customized to them. Moreover, mass media are no longer just one-way instruments that provide people with content they can experience but not change. To the contrary, today's media firms increasingly create digital platforms that allow—even encourage—audience members (now often called "users") to interact with the content. Readers of newspapers in 1915 and 1995 could discuss with others the stories they read and ads they saw, and they could write a letter to the paper if they disagreed with something. Today's newspaper readers in most cases can do far more. If they read the "paper" online, they can comment immediately on articles so that others might read the comments. They might also be able to create journals—blogs—that are linked to the paper's home pages so that their comments become part of the continual stream of ideas associated with the paper. Newspapers encourage these activities because they bring people to their sites. That, in turn, allows the papers to serve ads to them, ads that are now not shared by everyone but are customized to what the paper knows about the specific reader.

The new digital media, then, are changing the way audiences interact with media as well as the ways media approach audiences. Still, the questions above that writers in the twentieth century asked about mass media remain very relevant. Alongside them are new issues that come from people's ability to interact with a company's material, copy it, and circulate it without permission. The recording industry is the media sector that is struggling most with this challenge.

The readings in Part I introduce many of the enduring and new issues relating to media, society and power that observers have struggled with over the decades. The thinkers in this section cover a lot of bases—from concerns about media's effect on people's tastes to the power of media conglomerates, to the proper role of government regulation to the peculiar challenges of the digital environment ("cyberspace"). When you read them, ask yourself how you relate to the questions they raise. Think about how their points relate to the media you use. Don't hesitate to disagree, to point out contradictions, to demand more evidence. The aim here is to bring you into the media debate.

# Chapter 1

# PAUL F. LAZARSFELD AND ROBERT K. MERTON

# MASS COMMUNICATION, POPULAR TASTE AND ORGANIZED SOCIAL ACTION

PUBLISHED INITIALLY IN 1948, THIS essay has been reprinted many times because, despite its age, it is filled with helpful ideas about the roles that mass media play in society. Paul Lazarsfeld and Robert Merton were highly influential Professors of Sociology at Columbia University. They worked together on a series of projects during the 1930s and 1940s that tried to understand the power of media to persuade individuals to change their behavior. In this article, Lazarsfeld and Merton focus not on whether the media can influence an individual's actions but on broader issues of the media's power in society. They suggest that the real power of the media may not be in causing people to make major changes in their lives; that rarely happens. Rather, say the authors, we can see media power in the prestige that they bestow on individuals and groups by covering them as well as in their reinforcement (rather than their change) of the basic lines of cultural, political, and business power in the society. As you read this piece, see if you always agree with the authors' understanding of the media's power—and why or why not.

Problems engaging the attention of men change, and they change not at random but largely in accord with the altering demands of society and economy. If a group such as those who have written the chapters of this book had been brought together a generation or so ago, the subject for discussion would in all probability have been altogether different. Child labor, woman suffrage or old age pensions might have occupied the attention of a group such as this, but certainly not problems of the media of mass communication. As a host of recent conferences, books and articles indicate, the role of radio, print and film in society has become a problem of interest to many and a source of concern to some. This shift in public interest appears to be the product of several social trends.

## Social Concern with the Mass Media

Many are alarmed by the ubiquity and potential power of the mass media. A participant in this symposium has written, for example, that "the power of radio can be compared only with the power of the atomic bomb." It is widely felt that the mass media comprise a powerful instrument which may be used for good or for ill and that, in the absence of adequate controls, the latter possibility is on the whole more likely. For these are the media of propaganda and Americans stand in peculiar dread of the power of propaganda. As the British observer, William Empson, recently remarked of us: "They believe in machinery more passionately than we do; and modern propaganda is a scientific machine; so it seems to them obvious that a mere reasoning man can't stand up against it. All this produces a curiously girlish attitude toward anyone who might be doing propaganda. 'Don't let that man come near. Don't let him tempt me, because if he does I'm sure to fall.' "

The ubiquity of the mass media promptly leads many to an almost magical belief in their enormous power. But there is another and, probably, a more realistic basis for widespread concern with the social role of the mass media; a basis which has to do with the changing types of social control exercised by powerful interest groups in society. Increasingly, the chief power groups, among which organized business occupies the most spectacular place, have come to adopt techniques for manipulating mass publics through propaganda in place of more direct means of control. Industrial organizations no longer compel eight year old children to attend the machine for fourteen hours a day; they engage in elaborate programs of "public relations." They place large and impressive advertisements in the newspapers of the nation; they sponsor numerous radio programs; on the advice of public relations counsellors they organize prize contests, establish welfare foundations, and support worthy causes. Economic power seems to have reduced direct exploitation and turned to a subtler type of psychological exploitation, achieved largely by disseminating propaganda through the mass media of communication.

This change in the structure of social control merits thorough examination. Complex societies are subject to many different forms of organized control. Hitler, for example, seized upon the most visible and direct of these: organized violence and mass coercion. In this country, direct coercion has become minimized. If people do not adopt the beliefs and attitudes advocated by some power group—say, the National Association of Manufacturers—they can neither be liquidated nor placed in concentration camps. Those who would control the opinions and beliefs of our society resort less to physical force and more to mass persuasion. The radio program and the institutional advertisement serve in place of intimidation and coercion. The manifest concern over the functions of the mass media is in part based upon the valid observation that these media have taken on the job of rendering mass publics comformative to the social and economic *status quo*.

A third source of widespread concern with the social role of mass media is found in their assumed effects upon popular culture and the esthetic tastes of their audiences. In the measure that the size of these audiences has increased, it is argued, the level of esthetic taste has deteriorated. And it is feared that the mass media deliberately cater to these vulgarized tastes, thus contributing to further deterioration.

It seems probable that these constitute the three organically related elements of our great concern with the mass media of communication. Many are, first of all, fearful of the ubiquity and potential power of these media. We have suggested that this is something of an indiscriminate fear of an abstract bogey stemming from insecurity of social position and tenuously held values. Propaganda seems threatening.

There is, secondly, concern with the present effects of the mass media upon their enormous audiences, particularly the possibility that the continuing assault of these media may lead to the unconditional surrender of critical faculties and an unthinking conformism.

Finally, there is the danger that these technically advanced instruments of mass communication constitute a major avenue for the deterioration of esthetic tastes and popular cultural standards. And we have suggested that there is substantial ground for concern over these immediate social effects of the mass media of communication.

A review of the current state of actual knowledge concerning the social role of the mass media of communication and their effects upon the contemporary American community is an ungrateful task, for certified knowledge of this kind is impressively slight. Little more can be done than to explore the nature of the problems by methods which, in the course of many decades, will ultimately provide the knowledge we seek. Although this is anything but an encouraging preamble, it provides a necessary context for assessing the research and tentative conclusions of those of us professionally concerned with the study of mass media. A reconnaissance will suggest what we know, what we need to know, and will locate the strategic points requiring further inquiry.

To search out "the effects" of mass media upon society is to set upon an ill defined problem. It is helpful to distinguish three facets of the problem and to consider each in turn. Let us, then, first inquire into what we know about the effects of the existence of these media in our society. Secondly, we must look into the effects of the particular structure of ownership and operation of the mass media in this country, a structure which differs appreciably from that found elsewhere. And, finally, we must consider that aspect of the problem which bears most directly upon policies and tactics governing the use of these media for definite social ends: our knowledge concerning the effects of the particular contents disseminated through the mass media.

## The Social Role of the Machinery of Mass Media

What role can be assigned to the mass media by virtue of the fact that they exist? What are the implications of a Hollywood, a Radio City, and a Time-Life-Fortune enterprise for our society? These questions can of course be discussed only in grossly speculative terms, since no experimentation or rigorous comparative study is possible. Comparisons with other societies lacking these mass media would be too crude to yield decisive results and comparisons with an earlier day in American society would still involve gross assertions rather than precise demonstrations. In such an instance, brevity is clearly indicated. And opinions should be leavened with caution. It is our tentative judgment that the social role played by the very existence of the mass media has been commonly overestimated. What are the grounds for this judgment?

It is clear that the mass media reach enormous audiences. Approximately seventy million Americans attend the movies every week; our daily newspaper circulation is about forty-six million, and some thirty-four million American homes are equipped with radio, and in these homes the average American listens to the radio for about three hours a day. These are formidable figures. But they are merely supply and consumption figures, not figures registering the effect of mass media. They bear only upon what people do, not upon the social and psychological impact of the media. To know the number of hours people keep the radio turned on gives no indication of the effect upon them of what they hear. Knowledge of consumption data in the field of mass media remains far from a demonstration of their net effect upon behavior and attitude and outlook.

As was indicated a moment ago, we cannot resort to experiment by comparing contemporary American society with and without mass media. But, however tentatively, we can compare their social effect with, say, that of the automobile. It is not unlikely that the invention of the automobile and its development into a mass owned commodity has had a significantly greater effect upon society than the invention of the radio and its development into a medium of mass communication. Consider the social complexes into which the automobile has entered. Its sheer existence has exerted pressure for vastly improved roads and with these, mobility has increased enormously. The shape of metropolitan agglomerations has been significantly affected by the automobile. And, it may be submitted, the inventions which enlarge the radius of movement and action exert a greater influence upon social outlook and daily routines than inventions which provide avenues for ideas—ideas which can be avoided by withdrawal, deflected by resistance and transformed by assimilation.

Granted, for a moment, that the mass media play a comparatively minor role in shaping our society, why are they the object of so much popular concern and criticism? Why do so many become exercised by the "problems" of the radio and film and press and so few by the problems of, say, the automobile and the airplane? In addition to the sources of this concern which we have noted previously, there is an unwitting psychological basis for concern which derives from a socio-historical context.

Many make the mass media targets for hostile criticism because they feel themselves duped by the turn of events.

The social changes ascribable to "reform movements" may be slow and slight, but they do cumulate. The surface facts are familiar enough. The sixty hour week has given way to the forty hour week. Child labor has been progressively curtailed. With all its deficiencies, free universal education has become progressively institutionalized. These and other gains register a series of reform victories. And now, people have more leisure time. They have, ostensibly, greater access to the cultural heritage. And what use do they make of this unmortgaged time so painfully acquired for them? They listen to the radio and go to the movies. These mass media seem somehow to have cheated reformers of the fruits of their victories. The struggle for freedom for leisure and popular education and social security was carried on in the hope that, once freed of cramping shackles, people would avail themselves of major cultural products of our society, Shakespeare or Beethoven or perhaps Kant. Instead, they turn to Faith Baldwin or Johnny Mercer or Edgar Guest.

Many feel cheated of their prize. It is not unlike a young man's first experience in the difficult realm of puppy love. Deeply smitten with the charms of his lady love, he saves his allowance for weeks on end and finally manages to give her a beautiful bracelet. She finds it "simply divine." So much so, that then and there she makes a date with another boy in order to display her new trinket. Our social struggles have met with a similar denouement. For generations, men fought to give people more leisure time and now they spend it with the Columbia Broadcasting System rather than with Columbia University.

However little this sense of betrayal may account for prevailing attitudes toward the mass media, it may again be noted that the sheer presence of these media may not affect our society so profoundly as is widely supposed.

## Some Social Functions of the Mass Media

In continuing our examination of the social role which can be ascribed to the mass media by virtue of their "sheer existence," we temporarily abstract from the social structure in which the media find their place. We do not, for example, consider the diverse effects of the mass media under varying systems of ownership and control, an important structural factor which will be discussed subsequently.

The mass media undoubtedly serve many social functions which might well become the object of sustained research. Of these functions, we have occasion to notice only three.

*The Status Conferral Function*. The mass media *confer* status on public issues, persons, organizations and social movements.

Common experience as well as research testifies that the social standing of persons or social policies is raised when these command favorable attention in the mass media. In many quarters, for example, the support of a political candidate or a public policy by *The Times* is taken as significant, and this support is regarded as a distinct asset for the candidate or the policy. Why?

For some, the editorial views of *The Times* represent the considered judgment of a group of experts, thus calling for the respect of laymen. But this is only one element in the status conferral function of the mass media, for enhanced status accrues to those who merely receive attention in the media, quite apart from any editorial support.

The mass media bestow prestige and enhance the authority of individuals and groups by *legitimizing their status*. Recognition by the press or radio or magazines or newsreels testifies that one has arrived, that one is important enough to have been singled out from the large anonymous masses, that one's behavior and opinions are significant enough to require public notice. The operation of this status conferral function may be witnessed most vividly in the advertising pattern of testimonials to a product by "prominent people." Within wide circles of the population (though not within certain selected social strata), such testimonials not only enhance the prestige of the product but also reflect prestige on the person who provides the testimonials. They give public notice that the large and powerful world of commerce regards him as possessing sufficiently high status for his opinion to count with many people. In a word, his testimonial is a testimonial to his own status.

The ideal, if homely, embodiment of this circular prestige-pattern is to be found in the Lord Calvert series of advertisements centered on "Men of Distinction." The commercial firm and the commercialized witness to the merit of the product engage in an unending series of reciprocal pats on the back. In effect, a distinguished man congratulates a distinguished whisky which, through the manufacturer, congratulates the man of distinction on his being so distinguished as to be sought out for a testimonial to the distinction of the product. The workings of this mutual admiration society may be as non-logical as they are effective. The audiences of mass media apparently subscribe to the circular belief: "If you really matter, you will be at the focus of mass attention and, if you *are* at the focus of mass attention, then surely you must really matter."

This status conferral function thus enters into organized social action by legitimizing selected policies, persons and groups which receive the support of mass media. We shall have occasion to note the detailed operation of this function in connection with the conditions making for the maximal utilization of mass media for designated social ends. At the moment, having considered the "status conferral" function, we shall consider a second: the enforced application of social norms through the mass media.

*The Enforcement of Social Norms.* Such catch phrases as "the power of the press" (and other mass media) or "the bright glare of publicity" presumably refer to this function. The mass media may initiate organized social action by "exposing" conditions which are at variance with public moralities. But it need not be prematurely assumed that this pattern consists *simply* in making these deviations widely known. We have something to learn in this connection from Malinowski's observations among his beloved Trobriand Islanders. There, he reports, no organized social action is taken with respect to behavior deviant from a social norm unless there is *public* announcement of the deviation. This is not merely a matter of acquainting the individuals in the group with the facts of the case. Many may have known privately of these deviations—*e.g.*, incest among the Trobrianders, as with political or business corruption, prostitution, gambling among ourselves—but they will not have pressed for public action. But once the behavioral deviations are made simultaneously public for all, this sets in train tensions between the "privately tolerable" and the "publicly acknowledgeable."

The mechanism of public exposure would seem to operate somewhat as follows. Many social norms prove inconvenient for individuals in the society. They militate against the gratification of wants and impulses. Since many find the norms burdensome, there is some measure of leniency in applying them, both to oneself and to others. Hence, the emergence of deviant behavior and private toleration of these deviations. But this can continue only so long as one is not in a situation where one must take a public stand for or against the norms. Publicity, the enforced acknowledgment by members of the group that these deviations have occurred, requires each individual to take such a stand. He must either range himself with the non-conformists, thus proclaiming his repudiation of the group norms, and thus asserting that he, too, is outside the moral framework or, regardless of his private predilections, he must fall into line by supporting the norm. *Publicity closes the gap between "private attitudes" and "public morality."* Publicity exerts pressure for a single rather than a dual morality by preventing continued evasion of the issue. It calls forth public reaffirmation and (however sporadic) application of the social norm.

In a mass society, this function of public exposure is institutionalized in the mass media of communication. Press, radio and journals expose fairly well known deviations to public view, and as a rule, this exposure forces some degree of public action against what has been privately tolerated. The mass media may, for example, introduce severe strains upon "polite ethnic discrimination" by calling public attention to these practices which are at odds with the norms of non-discrimination. At times, the media may organize exposure activities into a "crusade."

The study of crusades by mass media would go far toward answering basic questions about the relation of mass media to organized social action. It is essential to know, for example, the extent to which the crusade provides an organizational center for otherwise unorganized individuals. The crusade may operate diversely among the several sectors of the population. In some instances, its major effect may not be so much to arouse an indifferent citizenry as to alarm the culprits, leading them to extreme measures which in turn alienate the electorate. Publicity may so embarrass the malefactor as to send him into flight as was the case, for example, with some of the chief henchmen of the Tweed Ring following exposure by *The New York Times*. Or the directors of corruption may fear the crusade only because of the effect they anticipate it will have upon the electorate. Thus, with a startlingly realistic appraisal of the communications behavior of his constituency, Boss Tweed peevishly remarked of the biting cartoons of Thomas Nast in *Harper's Weekly:* "I don't care a straw for your newspaper articles: my constituents don't know how to read, but they can't help seeing them damned pictures."[1]

The crusade may affect the public directly. It may focus the attention of a hitherto lethargic citizenry, grown indifferent through familiarity to prevailing corruption, upon a few, dramatically simplified, issues. As Lawrence Lowell once observed in this general connection, complexities generally inhibit mass action. Public issues must be defined in simple alternatives, in terms of black and white, to permit of organized public action. And the presentation of simple alternatives is one of the chief functions of the crusade. The crusade may involve still other mechanisms. If a municipal government is not altogether pure of heart, it is seldom wholly corrupt. Some scrupulous members of the administration and judiciary are generally intermingled with their unprincipled colleagues. The crusade may strengthen the hand of the upright elements in the government, force the hand of the indifferent and weaken the hand of the corrupt. Finally, it may well be that a successful crusade exemplifies a circular, self-sustaining process, in which the concern of the mass medium with the public interest coincides with its self-interest. The triumphant crusade may enhance the power and prestige of the mass medium, thus making it, in turn, more formidable in later crusades, which, if successful, may further advance its power and prestige.

Whatever the answer to these questions, mass media clearly serve to reaffirm social norms by exposing deviations from these norms to public view. A study of the particular range of norms thus reaffirmed would provide a clear index of the extent to which these media deal with peripheral or central problems of the structure of our society.

*The Narcotizing Dysfunction.* The functions of status conferral and of reaffirmation of social norms are evidently well recognized by the operators of mass media. Like other social and psychological mechanisms, these functions lend themselves to diverse forms of application. Knowledge of these functions is power, and power may be used for special interests or for the general interest.

A third social consequence of the mass media has gone largely unnoticed. At least, it has received little explicit comment and, apparently, has not been systematically put to use for furthering planned objectives. This may be called the narcotizing dysfunction of the mass media. It is termed *dys*functional rather than functional on the assumption that it is not in the interest of modern complex society to have large masses of the population politically apathetic and inert. How does this unplanned mechanism operate?

Scattered studies have shown that an increasing proportion of the time of Americans is devoted to the products of the mass media. With distinct variations in different regions and among different social strata, the outpourings of the media presumably enable the twentieth century American to "keep abreast of the world." Yet, it is suggested, this vast supply of communications may elicit only a superficial concern with the problems of society, and this superficiality often cloaks mass apathy.

Exposure to this flood of information may serve to narcotize rather than to energize the average reader or listener. As an increasing meed of time is devoted to reading and listening, a decreasing share is available for organized action. The individual reads accounts of issues and problems and may even discuss alternative lines of action. But this rather intellectualized, rather remote connection with organized social action is not activated. The interested and informed citizen can congratulate himself on his lofty state of interest and information and neglect to see that he has abstained from decision and action. In short, he takes his secondary contact with the world of political reality, his reading and listening and thinking, as a vicarious performance. He comes to mistake *knowing* about problems of the day for *doing* something about them. His social conscience remains spotlessly clean. He *is* concerned. He *is* informed. And he has all sorts of ideas as to what should be done. But, after he has gotten through his dinner and after he has listened to his favored radio programs and after he has read his second newspaper of the day, it is really time for bed.

In this peculiar respect, mass communications may be included among the most respectable and efficient of social narcotics. They may be so fully effective as to keep the addict from recognizing his own malady.

That the mass media have lifted the level of information of large populations is evident. Yet, quite apart from intent, increasing dosages of mass communications may be inadvertently transforming the energies of men from active participation into passive knowledge.

The occurrence of this narcotizing dysfunction can scarcely be doubted, but the extent to which it operates has yet to be determined. Research on this problem remains one of the many tasks still confronting the student of mass communications.

## The Structure of Ownership and Operation

To this point we have considered the mass media quite apart from their incorporation within a particular social and economic structure. But clearly, the social effects of the media will vary as the system of ownership and control varies. Thus to consider the social effects of American mass media is to deal only with the effects of these media as privately owned enterprises under profit oriented management. It is general knowledge that this circumstance is not inherent in the technological nature of the mass media. In England, for example, to say nothing of Russia, the radio is to all intents and purposes owned, controlled and operated by government.

The structure of control is altogether different in this country. Its salient characteristic stems from the fact that except for movies and books, it is not the magazine reader nor the radio listener nor, in large part, the reader of newspapers who supports the enterprise, but the advertiser. Big business finances the production and distribution of mass media. And, all intent aside, he who pays the piper generally calls the tune.

## Social Conformism

Since the mass media are supported by great business concerns geared into the current social and economic system, the media contribute to the maintenance of that system.

This contribution is not found merely in the effective advertisement of the sponsor's product. It arises, rather, from the typical presence in magazine stories, radio programs and newspaper columns of some element of confirmation, some element of approval of the present structure of society. And this continuing reaffirmation underscores the duty to accept.

To the extent that the media of mass communication have had an influence upon their audiences, it has stemmed not only from what is said, but more significantly from what is not said. For these media not only continue to affirm the *status quo* but, in the same measure, they fail to raise essential questions about the structure of society. Hence by leaning toward conformism and by providing little basis for a critical appraisal of society, the commercially sponsored mass media indirectly but effectively restrain the cogent development of a genuinely critical outlook.

This is not to ignore the occasionally critical journal article or radio program. But these exceptions are so few that they are lost in the overwhelming flood of conformist materials. The editor of this volume, for example, has been broadcasting a weekly program in which he critically and rationally appraises social problems in general and the institution of radio in particular. But these fifteen minutes in which Mr. Bryson addresses himself to such questions over one network constitute an infinitesimally small drop in the weekly flood of materials from four major networks, from five hundred and seventy or so unaffiliated stations, from hundreds of magazines and from Hollywood.

Since our commercially sponsored mass media promote a largely unthinking allegiance to our social structure, they cannot be relied upon to work for changes, even minor changes, in that structure. It is possible to list some developments to the contrary, but upon close inspection they prove illusory. A community group, such as the PTA, may request the producer of a radio serial to inject the theme of tolerant race attitudes into the program. Should the producer feel that this theme is safe, that it will not antagonize any substantial part of his audience, he may agree, but at the first indication that it is a dangerous theme which may alienate potential consumers, he will refuse, or will soon abandon the experiment. Social objectives are consistently surrendered by commercialized media when they clash with economic gains. Minor tokens of "progressive" views are of slight importance since they are included only by grace of the sponsors and only on the condition that they be sufficiently acceptable as not to alienate any appreciable part of the audience. Economic pressure makes for conformism by omission of sensitive issues.

## Impact Upon Popular Taste

Since the largest part of our radio, movies, magazines and a considerable part of our books and newspapers are devoted to "entertainment," this clearly requires us to consider the impact of the mass media upon popular taste.

Were we to ask the average American with some pretension to literary or esthetic cultivation if mass communications have had any effect upon popular taste, he would doubtlessly answer with a resounding affirmative. And more, citing abundant instances, he would insist that esthetic and intellectual tastes have been depraved by the flow of trivial formula products from printing presses, radio stations and movie studios. The columns of criticism abound with these complaints.

In one sense, this requires no further discussion. There can be no doubt that the women who are daily entranced for three or four hours by some twelve consecutive "soap operas," all cut to the same dismal pattern, exhibit an appalling lack of esthetic judgment. Nor is this impression altered by the contents of pulp and slick magazines, or by the depressing abundance of formula motion pictures replete with hero, heroine and villain moving through a contrived atmosphere of sex, sin and success.

Yet unless we locate these patterns in historical and sociological terms, we may find ourselves confusedly engaged in condemning without understanding, in criticism which is sound but largely irrelevant. What is the historical status of this notoriously low level of popular taste? Is it the poor remains of standards which were once significantly higher, a relatively new birth in the world of values, largely unrelated to the higher standards from which it has allegedly fallen, or a poor substitute blocking the way to the development of superior standards and the expression of high esthetic purpose?

If esthetic tastes are to be considered in their social setting, we must recognize that the effective audience for the arts has become historically transformed. Some centuries back, this audience was largely confined to a selected aristocratic elite. Relatively few were literate. And very few possessed the means to buy books, attend theaters and travel to the urban centers of the arts. Not more than a slight fraction, possibly not more than one or two per cent, of the population composed the effective audience for the arts. These happy few cultivated their esthetic tastes, and their selective demand left its mark in the form of relatively high artistic standards.

With the widesweeping spread of popular education and with the emergence of the new technologies of mass communication, there developed an enormously enlarged market for the arts. Some forms of music, drama and literature now reach virtually everyone in our society. This is why, of course, we speak of *mass* media and of *mass* art. And the great audiences for the mass media, though in the main literate, are not highly cultivated. About half the population, in fact, have halted their formal education upon leaving grammar school.

With the rise of popular education, there has occurred a seeming decline of popular taste. Large numbers of people have acquired what might be termed "formal literacy," that is to say, a capacity to read, to grasp crude and superficial meanings, and a correlative incapacity for full understanding of what they read.[2] There has developed, in short, a marked gap between literacy and comprehension. People read more but understand less. More people read but proportionately fewer critically assimilate what they read.

Our formulation of the problem should now be plain. It is misleading to speak simply of the decline of esthetic tastes. Mass audiences probably include a larger number of persons with cultivated esthetic standards, but these are swallowed up by the large masses who constitute the new and untutored audience for the arts. Whereas yesterday the elite constituted virtually the whole of the audience, they are today a minute fraction of the whole. In consequence, the average level of esthetic standards and tastes of audiences has been depressed, although the tastes of some sectors of the population have undoubtedly been raised and the total number of people exposed to communication contents has been vastly increased.

But this analysis does not directly answer the question of the effects of the mass media upon public taste, a question which is as complex as it is unexplored. The answer can come only from disciplined research. One would want to know, for example, whether mass media have robbed the intellectual and artistic elite of the art forms which might otherwise have been accessible to them. And this involves inquiry into the pressure exerted by the mass audience upon creative individuals to cater to mass tastes. Literary hacks have existed in every age. But it would be important to learn if the electrification of the arts supplies power for a significantly greater proportion of dim literary lights. And, above all, it would be essential to determine if mass media and mass tastes are necessarily linked in a vicious circle of deteriorating standards or if appropriate action on the part of the directors of mass media could initiate a virtuous circle of cumulatively improving tastes among their audiences. More concretely, are the operators of commercialized mass media caught up in a situation in which they cannot, whatever their private preferences, radically raise the esthetic standards of their products?

In passing, it should be noted that much remains to be learned concerning standards appropriate for mass art. It is possible that standards for art forms produced by a small band of creative talents for a small and selective audience are not applicable to art forms produced by a gigantic industry for the population at large. The beginnings of investigation on this problem are sufficiently suggestive to warrant further study.

Sporadic and consequently inconclusive experiments in the raising of standards have met with profound resistance from mass audiences. On occasion, radio stations and networks have attempted to supplant a soap opera with a program of classical music, or formula comedy skits with discussions of public issues. In general, the people supposed to benefit by this reformation of program have simply refused to be benefited. They cease listening. The audience dwindles. Researches have shown, for example, that radio programs of classical music tend to preserve rather than to create interest in classical music and that newly emerging interests are typically superficial. Most listeners to these programs have previously acquired an interest in classical music; the few whose interest is initiated by the programs are caught up by melodic compositions and come to think of classical music exclusively in terms of Tschaikowsky or Rimsky-Korsakow or Dvorak.

Proposed solutions to these problems are more likely to be born of faith than knowledge. The improvement of mass tastes through the improvement of mass art products is not as simple a matter as we should like to believe. It is possible, of course, that a conclusive effort has not been made. By a triumph of imagination over the current organization of mass media, one can conceive a rigorous censorship over all media, such that nothing was allowed in print or on the air or in the films save "the best that has been thought and said in the world." Whether a radical change in the supply of mass art would in due course reshape the tastes of mass audiences must remain a matter of speculation. Decades of experimentation and research are needed. At present, we know conspicuously little about the methods of improving esthetic tastes and we know that some of the suggested methods are ineffectual. We have a rich knowledge of failures. Should this discussion be reopened in 1976, we may, perhaps, report with equal confidence our knowledge of positive achievements.

At this point, we may pause to glance at the road we have traveled. By way of introduction, we considered the seeming sources of widespread concern with the place of mass media in our society. Thereafter, we first examined the social role ascribable to the sheer existence of the mass media and concluded that this may have been exaggerated. In this connection, however, we noted several consequences of the existence of mass media: their status conferral function, their function in inducing the application of social norms and their narcotizing dysfunction. Secondly, we indicated the constraints placed by a structure of commercialized ownership and control upon the mass media as agencies of social criticism and as carriers of high esthetic standards.

We turn now to the third and last aspect of the social role of the mass media: the possibilities of utilizing them for moving toward designated types of social objectives.

## Propaganda for Social Objectives

This final question is perhaps of more direct interest to you than the other questions we have discussed. It represents something of a challenge to us since it provides the means of resolving the apparent paradox to which we referred previously: the seeming paradox arising from the assertion that the significance of the sheer existence of the mass media has been exaggerated and the multiple indications that the media do exert influences upon their audiences.

What are the conditions for the effective use of mass media for what might be called "propaganda for social objectives"—the promotion, let us say, of non-discriminatory race relations, or of educational reforms, or of positive attitudes toward organized labor? Research indicates that, at least, one or more of three conditions must be satisfied if this propaganda is to prove effective. These conditions may be briefly designated as (1) monopolization (2) canalization rather than change of basic values and (3) supplementary face to face contact. Each of these conditions merits some discussion.

## Monopolization

This situation obtains when there is little or no opposition in the mass media to the diffusion of values, policies or public images. That is to say, monopolization of the mass media occurs in the absence of counter propaganda.

In this restricted sense, monopolization of the mass media is found in diverse circumstances. It is, of course, indigenous to the political structure of authoritarian society, where access to the media of communication is wholly closed to those who oppose the official ideology. The evidence suggests that this monopoly played some part in enabling the Nazis to maintain their control of the German people.

But this same situation is approximated in other social systems. During the war, for example, our government utilized the radio, with some success, to promote and to maintain identification with the war effort. The effectiveness of these morale building efforts was in large measure due to the virtually complete absence of counter propaganda.

Similar situations arise in the world of commercialized propaganda. The mass media create popular idols. The public images of the radio performer, Kate Smith, for example, picture her as a woman with unparalleled understanding of other American women, deeply sympathetic with ordinary men and women, a spiritual guide and mentor, a patriot whose views on public affairs should be taken seriously. Linked with the cardinal American virtues, the public images of Kate Smith are at no point subject to a counter propaganda. Not that she has no competitors in the market of radio advertising. But there are none who set themselves systematically to question what she has said. In consequence, an unmarried radio entertainer with an annual income in six figures may be visualized by millions of American women as a hard working mother who knows the recipe for managing life on fifteen hundred a year.

This image of a popular idol would have far less currency were it subjected to counter propaganda. Such neutralization occurs, for example, as a result of preelection campaigns by Republicans and Democrats. By and large, as a recent study has shown, the propaganda issued by each of these parties neutralizes the effect of the other's propaganda. Were both parties to forego their campaigning through the mass media entirely, it is altogether likely that the net effect would be to reproduce the present distribution of votes.

This general pattern has been described by Kenneth Burke in his *Attitudes Toward History* ". . . businessmen compete with one another by trying to *praise their own commodity* more persuasively than their rivals, whereas politicians compete by slandering the *opposition*. When you add it all up, you get a grand total of absolute praise for business and grand total of absolute slander for politics."

To the extent that opposing political propaganda in the mass media are balanced, the net effect is negligible. The virtual monopolization of the media for given social objectives, however, will produce discernible effects upon audiences.


## Canalization

Prevailing beliefs in the enormous power of mass communications appear to stem from successful cases of monopolistic propaganda or from advertising. But the leap from the efficacy of advertising to the assumed efficacy of propaganda aimed at deeprooted attitudes and ego involved behavior is as unwarranted as it is dangerous. Advertising is typically directed toward the canalizing of preexisting behavior patterns or attitudes. It seldom seeks to instil new attitudes or to create significantly new behavior patterns. "Advertising pays" because it generally deals with a simple psychological situation. For Americans who have been socialized in the use of a toothbrush, it makes relatively little difference which brand of toothbrush they use. Once the gross pattern of behavior or the generic attitude has been established, it can be canalized in one direction or another. Resistance is slight. But mass propaganda typically meets a more complex situation. It may seek objectives which are at odds with deeplying attitudes. It may seek to reshape rather than to canalize current systems of values. And the successes of advertising may only highlight the failures of propaganda. Much of the current propaganda which is aimed at abolishing deep-seated ethnic and racial prejudices, for example, seems to have had little effectiveness.

Media of mass communication, then, have been effectively used to canalize basic attitudes but there is little evidence of their having served to change these attitudes.


## Supplementation

Mass propaganda which is neither monopolistic nor canalizing in character may, nonetheless, prove effective if it meets a third condition: supplementation through face to face contacts.

A case in point will illustrate the interplay between mass media and face to face influences. The seeming propagandistic success achieved some years ago by Father Coughlin does not appear, upon inspection, to have resulted primarily from the propaganda content of his radio talks. It was, rather, the product of these centralized propaganda talks *and* widespread local organizations which arranged for their members to listen to him, followed by discussions among themselves concerning the social views he had expressed. This combination of a central supply of propaganda (Coughlin's addresses on a nationwide network), the coordinated distribution of newspapers and pamphlets and locally organized face to face discussions among relatively small groups—this complex of reciprocal reinforcement by mass media and personal relations proved spectacularly successful.

Students of mass movements have come to repudiate the view that mass propaganda in and of itself creates or maintains the movement. Nazism did not attain its brief moment of hegemony by capturing the mass media of communication. The media played an ancillary role, supplementing the use of organized violence, organized distribution of rewards for conformity and organized centers of local indoctrination. The Soviet Union has also made large and impressive use of mass media for indoctrinating enormous populations with appropriate ideologies. But the organizers of indoctrination saw to it that the mass media did not operate alone. "Red corners," "reading huts" and "listening stations" comprised meeting places in which groups of citizens were exposed to the mass media in common. The fifty-five thousand reading rooms and clubs which had come into being by 1933 enabled the local ideological elite to talk over with rank and file readers the content of what they read. The relative scarcity of radios in private homes again made for group listening and group discussions of what had been heard.

In these instances, the machinery of mass persuasion included face to face contact in local organizations as an adjunct to the mass media. The privatized individual response to the materials presented through the channels of mass communication was considered inadequate for transforming exposure to propaganda into effectiveness of propaganda. In a society such as our own, where the pattern of bureaucratization has not yet become so pervasive or, at least, not so clearly crystallized, it has likewise been found that mass media prove most effective in conjunction with local centers of organized face to face contact.

Several factors contribute to the enhanced effectiveness of this joining of mass media and direct personal contact. Most clearly, the local discussions serve to reinforce the content of mass propaganda. Such mutual confirmation produces a "clinching effect." Secondly, the central media lessen the task of the local organizer, and the personnel requirements for such subalterns need not be as rigorous in a popular movement. The subalterns need not set forth the propaganda content for themselves, but need only pilot potential converts to the radio where the doctrine is being expounded. Thirdly, the appearance of a representative of the movement on a nationwide network, or his mention in the national press, serves to symbolize the legitimacy and significance of the movement. It is no powerless, inconsequential enterprise. The mass media, as we have seen, confer status. And the status of the national movement reflects back on the status of the local cells, thus consolidating the tentative decisions of its members. In this interlocking arrangement, the local organizer ensures an audience for the national speaker and the national speaker validates the status of the local organizer.

This brief summary of the situations in which the mass media achieve their maximum propaganda effect may resolve the seeming contradiction which arose at the outset of our discussion. The mass media prove most effective when they operate in a situation of virtual "psychological monopoly," or when the objective is one of canalizing rather than modifying basic attitudes or when they operate in conjunction with face to face contacts.

But these three conditions are rarely satisfied conjointly in propaganda for social objectives. To the degree that monopolization of attention is rare, opposing propagandas have free play in a democracy. And, by and large, basic social issues involve more than a mere canalizing of preexistent basic attitudes; they call, rather, for substantial changes in attitude and behavior. Finally, for the most obvious of reasons, the close collaboration of mass media and locally organized centers for face to face contact has seldom been achieved by groups striving for planned social change. Such programs are expensive. And it is precisely these groups which seldom have the large resources needed for these expensive programs. The forward looking groups at the edges of the power structure do not ordinarily have the large financial means of the contented groups at the center.

As a result of this threefold situation, the present role of mass media is largely confined to peripheral social concerns and the media do not exhibit the degree of social power commonly attributed to them.

By the same token, and in view of the present organization of business ownership and control of the mass media, they have served to cement the structure of our society. Organized business does approach a virtual "psychological monopoly" of the mass media. Radio commercials and newspaper advertisements are, of course, premised on a system which has been termed free enterprise. Moreover, the world of commerce is primarily concerned with canalizing rather than radically changing basic attitudes; it seeks only to create preferences for one rather than another brand of product. Face to face contacts with those who have been socialized in our culture serve primarily to reinforce the prevailing culture patterns.

Thus, the very conditions which make for the maximum effectiveness of the mass media of communication operate toward the maintenance of the going social and cultural structure rather than toward its change.

## Questions for Consideration

1   Lazarsfeld and Merton suggest that compared to the automobile and its development in society, the mass media play a "minor role in shaping our society." Do you agree? Why or why not?

2   Lazarsfeld and Merton argue that the enforcement of social norms is one important power of the mass media. Do you agree that media still enforce social norms? Explain your answer with an example.

3   "To the extent that the media of mass communication have had an influence upon their audiences, it has stemmed not only from what is said, but more significantly from what is not said." What do Lazarsfeld and Merton mean by this statement? How does it relate to the media's relationship to political and economic power, and to the term *status quo*?

## Notes

1. James Bryce, *The American Commonwealth,* Volume 2. Copyright 1898 by Macmillan and Company; 1910, 1914 by The Macmillan Company; 1920 by The Right Honorable Viscount Bryce.

2. *Ibid.*, Part IV, Chapter LXXX, James Bryce perceived this with characteristic clarity: "That the education of the masses is nevertheless a superficial education goes without saying. It is sufficient to enable them to think they know something about the great problems of politics: insufficient to show them how little they know. The public elementary school gives everybody the key to knowledge in making reading and writing familiar, but it has not time to teach him how to use the key, whose use is in fact, by the pressure of daily work, almost confined to the newspaper and the magazine. So we may say that if the political education of the average American voter be compared with that of the average voter in Europe, it stands high; but if it be compared with the functions which the theory of the American government lays on him, which its spirit implies, which the methods of its party organization assume, its inadequacy is manifest." *Mutatis mutandis*, the same may be said of the gap between the theory of "superior" cultural content in the mass media and the current levels of popular education.

# Chapter 2

# W. JAMES POTTER

# THE DEFINITION OF MEDIA LITERACY

W. JAMES POTTER IS AMONG a small number of academics—Renee Hobbs is another—who have made it their goal to encourage people to think about what they are doing when they use media. In this brief piece from his book on media literacy, Potter presents a concise definition of the term and provides some reasons why becoming media literate can be useful. In an earlier portion of the book, Potter emphasizes his belief that he does not fall into the camp of writers who believe that the purpose of media literacy is primarily to help people "be mindful during their media exposures so that they can argue against faulty messages and thereby protect themselves from harm." While he agrees that media literacy should help people understand how and when media are trying to manipulate them, he emphasizes that learning how to best understand the media can help audiences increase their enjoyment of what they watch, hear and read.

## What Is Media Literacy?

Many people have written about media literacy. These writings share two characteristics. First, they criticize the mass media and emphasize their harmful nature. Second, they suggest that people need to be more mindful during their media exposures so they can argue against faulty messages and thereby protect themselves from harm. In these writings, the purpose of media literacy is to remind people to be mindful and take an oppositional stance to the practices of media companies and media messages.

I break with that perspective and present an alternative perspective that is more balanced. It takes a more personal approach to media literacy. And it provides strategies for developing media literacy that are more realistic and attainable.

As for the first characteristic of criticizing the media, this book's perspective is that the mass media are not all bad; they also offer many, many positive effects. Think about all the information you have learned from the media that have helped you live a better life. Think about all the pleasure the mass media have given you through music, movies, television shows, and so on. I am not arguing that all media effects are good or that the mass media do not deserve criticism at times. Instead, I am arguing that we need to take a more balanced approach if we are to become media literate. We need to appreciate the good as well as criticize the bad.

As for the characteristics of protecting ourselves from harmful media effects through mindful exposures, it is unrealistic to believe that we will be able to do much of this. We encounter almost all media messages in an automatic state and pay attention to perhaps only 1%. It is not possible for people to encounter all media messages in a state of concentrated awareness—there are just are too many messages to be able to do this. Also, it is a foolhardy task to encourage people to pay attention to, say, 2% of all messages rather than 1% and expect this to make a difference in media literacy. People who try to follow this advice will inevitably fail and feel that media literacy is an impossible goal. Instead, my perspective is that if we learn how to see things differently in that 1% of media messages we really attend to, we will learn how to reprogram our mental code. By making changes in our mental code, we will end up processing the other 99% differently when our minds are running on automatic pilot. To get ourselves in a position to do this, we need to acquire some building blocks.

## The Three Building Blocks of Media Literacy

There are three essential building blocks of media literacy. These are your personal locus, knowledge structures, and skills. These three are necessary to build a person's wider set of perspectives on the media. Your personal locus is the energy and your plan. The knowledge structures are the raw materials. The skills are the tools.

### *Personal Locus*

Your personal locus is composed of goals and drives. The goals shape the information-processing tasks by determining what gets filtered in and what gets ignored. The more you are aware of your goals, the more you can direct the process of information seeking. And the stronger your drives for information are, the more effort you will expend to attain your goals. However, when your locus is weak (you are not aware of particular goals and your drive energy is low), you will default to media control; that is, you allow the media to exercise a high degree of control over exposures and information processing.

The more you know about this locus and the more you make conscious decisions to shape it, the more you can control the process. The more you pay conscious attention to your locus, the more you control the process of information acquisition and usage. The more you engage your locus, the more you will be increasing your media literacy. Being media literate, however, does not mean that the locus is always fully engaged. This is an impossible task because no one can maintain that high a degree of concentration continuously. Media literacy is a process, not a product. Therefore, becoming more media literate means that a person uses the locus more (thus less time with mindless exposures) and uses it more actively.

The locus operates in two modes: conscious and unconscious. When the locus operates in the conscious mode, you are aware of options and can exercise your will in making decisions. In contrast, when the locus operates in the unconscious mode, the decisions are made outside of your awareness and control. In both modes, knowledge structures can get formed and elaborated. However, when you are consciously using your locus, you are in control of the information processing and meaning making, but when your locus is operating in the unconscious mode, the media exert their most powerful effect. The locus is in the unconscious mode when we follow the default model and are in a state of automaticity.

## Knowledge Structures

Knowledge structures are sets of organized information in a person's memory. Knowledge structures do not occur spontaneously; they must be built with care and precision. They are not just a pile of facts; they are made by carefully crafting pieces of information into an overall design. To perform such a task, we rely on a set of skills. These skills are the tools. We use these tools to mine through the large piles of facts, so that we can uncover the particular facts we need and brush away the rest. Once we have selected the facts we need, we shape those facts into information and carefully fit those pieces of information into their proper places in a structure. The structure helps us see the patterns. We use these patterns as maps to tell us where to get more information and also where to go to retrieve information we have previously crafted into our knowledge structure.

Information is the essential ingredient in knowledge structures. But not all information is equally useful to building a knowledge structure. Some information is rather superficial, such as the names of television shows or the melodies of popular music. If all a person has is the recognition of surface information such as lyrics to television show theme songs, names of characters and actors, settings for shows, and the like, he or she is operating at a low level of media literacy because this type of information addresses only the question of "what." The more useful information comes in the form of the answers to the questions of "how" and "why." But remember that you first need to know something about the "what" before you can delve deeper into the questions of how and why.

In everyday language, the terms *information* and *knowledge* are often used as synonyms, but they have meanings very different from one another. Information is piecemeal and transitory, whereas knowledge is structured, organized, and of more enduring significance. Information resides in the messages, whereas knowledge resides in a person's mind. Information gives something to the person to interpret, whereas knowledge reflects that which has already been interpreted by the person.

Information is composed of facts. Facts by themselves are not knowledge any more than a pile of lumber is a house. Knowledge requires structure to provide context and thereby exhibit meaning. Think of messages as the raw materials and skills as the tools you use to do something with the raw materials. That "something" is in the service of attaining the goal of pulling the information out of the messages and turning that information into knowledge, that is, to reconstruct the information so that it will contribute to our knowledge structures. A characteristic of higher media literacy is the ability and habit of transforming information into knowledge structures.

While I'm on the topic of distinguishing information from knowledge, I also need to define a few terms related to the idea of information: *message, factual information*, and *social information*. Messages are those instruments that deliver information to us. Information is the content of those messages. Messages can be delivered in many different media—television, radio, CDs, video games, books, newspapers, magazines, Web sites, conversations, lectures, concerts, signs along the streets, labels on the products we buy, and so on. They can be large (an entire Hollywood movie) or small (one utterance by one character in a movie).

Messages are composed of two kinds of information: factual and social. A fact is something raw, unprocessed, and context free. For example, when you watch the news and hear messages about terrorism, those messages are composed of facts, such as the following: *The World Trade Center in New York City was destroyed on September 11, 2001. On that day, the United States declared war on terrorism. The person suspected of planning the attack on the World Trade Center was Osama bin Laden.* These statements are facts. Facts are discrete bits of information, such as names (of people, places, characters, etc.), definitions of terms, formulas, lists, and the like.

Social information is composed of accepted beliefs that cannot be verified by authorities in the same way factual information can be. This is not to say that social information is less valuable or less real to people. Social information is composed of techniques that people learn from observing social interactions. Examples of social information are rules about how to dress, talk, and act to be considered attractive, smart, athletic, hip, and so forth.

With media literacy, we need strong knowledge structures in five areas: media effects, media content, media industries, the real world, and the self. With knowledge in these five areas, people are much more aware during the information-processing tasks and are therefore more able to make better decisions about seeking out information, working with that information, and constructing meaning from it that will be useful to serve their own goals. The information that makes these awarenesses possible resides in knowledge structures.

People who have had a wider range of experiences in the real world have a broader base from which to appreciate and analyze media messages. For example, those who have helped someone run for political office can understand and analyze press coverage of political campaigns to a greater depth than those who have not had any real-world experience with political campaigns. People who have played sports will be able to appreciate the athletic accomplishments they see on television to a greater depth than those who have not physically tested themselves on those challenges. People who have had a wide range of relationships and family experiences will have a higher degree of understanding and more in-depth emotional reactions to those portrayals in the media.

Knowledge structures provide the context we use when trying to make sense of new media messages. The more knowledge structures we have, the more confident we can be in making sense of a wide range of messages. For example, you may have a very large, well-developed knowledge structure about a particular television series. You may know the names of all the characters in that TV show. You may know everything that has happened to those characters in all the episodes. You may even know the names and histories of the actors who play the characters. If you have all of this information well organized so that you can recall any of it at a moment's notice, you have a well-developed knowledge structure about that television series. Are you media literate? Within the small corner of the media world where that one TV show resides, you are. But if this were the only knowledge structure you had developed, you would have little understanding of the content produced by the other media. You would have difficulty understanding trends about who owns and controls the media, how the media have developed over time, why certain kinds of content are never seen while other types are continually repeated, and what effects that content may be having on you. With many highly developed knowledge structures, you could understand the entire span of media issues and therefore be able to "see the big picture" about why the media are the way they are.

## Skills

Skills are tools that people develop through practice. They are like muscles; the more you exercise them, the stronger they get. Without practice, skills become weaker.

The skills most relevant to media literacy are analysis, evaluation, grouping, induction, deduction, synthesis, and abstraction. These skills are not exclusive to media literacy tasks; instead, we use these skills in all sorts of ways in our everyday lives. We all have some ability with each of these skills, so the media literacy challenge is not to acquire these skills; rather, our challenge is to get better at using each of these skills as we encounter media messages. In the remainder of this section, I will define each of these skills and show how they are applied in a media literacy context.

*    *    *

*Analysis* is the breaking down of a message into meaningful elements. As we encounter media messages, we can simply accept these messages on the surface or we can dig deeper into the message itself by breaking them down into their components and examining the composition of the elements that make up the message. For example, with a news story, we can accept what a journalist tells us or we can analyze the story for completeness. That is, we can break the story down into its who, what, when, where, why, and how to determine if the story is complete or not.

*Evaluation* is making a judgment about the value of an element. This judgment is made by comparing a message element to some standard. When we encounter opinions expressed by experts in media messages, we could simply memorize those opinions and make them our own. Or we could take the information elements in the message and compare them to our standards. If those elements meet or exceed our standards, we conclude that the message—and the opinion expressed there—is good, but if the elements fall short of our standard, it is unacceptable.

There is a lot of evidence that people simply accept the opinions they hear in media messages without making their own evaluations. One example of this is the now widespread opinion that in the United States, the educational system is not very good, and a big reason for this is that children now spend too much time with the media, especially TV. There are many media stories that present this opinion. One example is the Third International Mathematics and Science Study; the test, which is administered to eighth graders in 41 countries, revealed that American students rank 28th in math and 17th in science in the world ("The Learning Lag," 1996). The 1998 National Assessment of Educational Progress, administered nationally by a group established by Congress, reported that one third of high school seniors lack even a basic understanding of how the American government is run, and only 26% of seniors were considered well versed enough in civics to make reasonable, well-informed choices during elections (McQueen, 1999). The National Assessment of Educational Progress (NAEP) reports that only about one quarter of American schoolchildren have achieved the proficiency standard in writing (Wildavsky, 1999). Reports such as this have led many conscientious parents to accept the opinion that it is bad for their young children to watch television. They believe that TV somehow will make their children's minds lazy, reduce their creativity, and turn them into lethargic entertainment junkies. If this happens, children will not value achievement and will not do well in school.

This belief is faulty because it blames the media, not the child or the parent, for poor academic performance. It also focuses only on the negative effect and gives the media no credit for potentially positive effects. However, when we look carefully at the research evidence, we can see that the typically reported finding is wrong, and when we look more carefully, there are several effects happening simultaneously (see W. J. Potter, 1987a). For example, the typically reported finding is that television viewing is negatively related to academic achievement. And a fair amount of research reports this conclusion. What makes this faulty is that this relationship is explained better by something else—IQ. School achievement is overwhelmingly related to IQ. Also, children with lower IQs watch more television. So it is IQ that accounts for lower achievement and higher television viewing. Research analyses that take a child's IQ into account find that there is no overall negative relationship; instead, there is a much more interesting pattern. The negative relationship does not show up until the child's viewing has passed the threshold of 30 hours per week. Beyond that 30-hour point, the more television children watch, the lower their academic achievement, and that effect gets stronger with the more hours they watch beyond that threshold. This means that academic achievement goes down only after television viewing starts to cut into study time and sleep. But there is no negative effect for less than 30 hours of viewing per week. In fact, at the lowest levels of television viewing, there is actually a positive effect; that is, a child who watches none or only a few hours a week is likely to do less well academically than a child who watches a moderate amount (around 12 to 15 hours per week). Thus, the pattern is as follows: Children who are deprived of the source of information that television provides do less well in school than children who watch a moderate amount of television; however, when a child gets to the point where the amount of television viewing cuts into needed study time, academic performance goes down.

When we pose the question, "What effect does viewing television have on a child's academic performance?" we could give the simple, popular answer: There is a negative effect. But now you can see that this answer is too simple—it is simpleminded. It is also misleading because it reinforces the limited belief that media effects are negative and polarized and that the media are to blame. This conclusion is not so simple as to lend itself easily to a short sound bite or flashy image, so it is not likely to be presented in the mass media.

The reason faulty beliefs are such a dangerous trap is because they are self-reinforcing. By this, I mean that as people are continually exposed to faulty information, they feel even more secure that their faulty beliefs are accurate. They feel less and less motivation to challenge them. When someone points out that the information on which their beliefs are based is faulty, they do not accept this criticism because they are so sure that they are correct. Thus, over time, they are not only less likely to examine their beliefs but also less tolerant of other beliefs having the possibility of being correct.

*Grouping* is determining which elements are alike in some way—determining how a group of elements is different from other groups of elements. The key to doing this well is determining a classification rule. The media tell us what classification rules are, so if we accept their classification rules, we will end up with the groups they want us to use. But if we make the effort to determine which classification rules are the best ways for us to organize our perceptions of the world, we will end up with groups that have more meaning and more value for us.

*Induction* is inferring a pattern across a small number of elements, then generalizing the pattern to all elements in the larger set. When we examine the result of public opinion polls, we can see that many people are using elements in media stories to infer patterns about real life, and this creates faulty beliefs about real life. For example, when people are asked about health care in this country, 90% of adults say that the health care system is in crisis; this is what many news stories and pundits tell the public. But when people are asked about their own health care, almost 90% feel that their health care is of good quality. About 63% of people think other people's doctors are too interested in making money, but only 20% think their own doctor is too interested in making money. People are using elements they have learned in media messages to dominate their perception of a pattern in real life. They accept a faulty belief because they do not take their own real-life experience into account when inferring a pattern; that is, they do not use induction well, instead preferring to use elements from mass media stories and not the elements from their own lives when inferring a pattern.

This faulty use of induction also shows up in other beliefs. For example, in public opinion polls about crime, only 17% of people think crime is a big problem in their own community, whereas 83% of Americans think crime is a big problem in society (Whitman & Loftus, 1996). People think this way because most do not experience crime in their own lives and therefore do not think it is a big problem where they live. However, they are convinced that it is a big problem in society. Where could the public get such an idea? From the media's fixation on deviance in the news. Also the news media prefer to present *sensationalized* events rather than *typical* events. So when a crime is reported, it is usually a violent crime, following the news ethic of "if it bleeds, it leads." Watching evening newscasts with their highlighting of crime and violence leads us to infer that there must be a high rate of crime and that most of it is violent assaults. But in reality, less than 20% of all crime is violent. More than 80% of all crime is property crime, with the victim not even present (U.S. Bureau of the Census, 2000). Furthermore, the rate for violent crime has been declining in this country since the mid-1980s, yet very few people are aware of this decline (Whitman & Loftus, 1996). Instead, most people believe that violent crime is increasing because they continually see crime stories and gory images in the media. They have fashioned their opinions on sensationalized events, and this type of information provides no useful basis to infer an accurate picture about crime. As for education, 64% give the nation's schools a grade of C or D, but at the same time, 66% give their public school a grade of A or B. As for religion, 65% say that religion is losing its influence on American life, whereas 62% say religion is becoming a stronger influence in their own lives. As for responsibility, almost 90% believe that a major problem with society is that people don't live up to their commitments, but more than 75% say they meet their commitments to families, kids, and employers. Nearly half of the population believes it is impossible for most families to achieve the American Dream, whereas 63% believe they have achieved or are close to the American Dream. And 40% to 50% think the nation is currently moving in the wrong direction, but 88% of Americans think their own lives and families are moving in the right direction (Whitman, 1996).

*Deduction* is using general principles to explain particulars. When we have faulty general principles, we will explain particular occurrences in a faulty manner. One general principle that most people hold to be true is that the media, especially television, have a very strong negative effect on other people. They have an unrealistic opinion that the media cause other people to behave violently. Some believe that if you allow PSAs (public service announcements) on TV about using condoms, children will learn that it is permissible and even a good thing to have sex. This is clearly an overestimation. At the same time, people *under*estimate the influence the media have on them. When they are asked if they think the media have any effect on them personally, 88% say no. These people argue that the media are primarily channels of entertainment and diversion, so they have no negative effect on them. The people who believe this say that they have watched thousands of hours of crime shows and have never shot anyone or robbed a bank. Although this may be true, this argument does not fully support the claim that the media have no effect on them; this argument is based on the false premise that the media only trigger high-profile, negative, behavioral effects that are easy to recognize. But there are many more types of effects, such as giving people the false impression that crime is a more serious problem than it really is or that most crime is violent.

*Synthesis* is assembling elements into a new structure. This is the primary skill we use when building our knowledge structures. As we take in new information, we must analyze it or break it down into useful elements. Then we evaluate the elements to determine which are useful, credible, and interesting. The elements that are evaluated positively need to be grouped along with the elements already in our existing knowledge structures; this will often require us to create new groups and look for new patterns. Thus, the process of synthesis is using our new media messages to keep reformulating, refining, and updating our existing knowledge structures.

*Abstracting* is creating a brief, clear, and accurate description capturing the essence of a message in a smaller number of words than the message itself. Thus, when we are describing a media message to someone else or reviewing the message in our own minds, we use the skill of abstracting. The key to using this skill well is to be able to capture the "big picture" or central idea of the media message in as few words as possible.

## The Definition of Media Literacy

Now that I have laid the foundation for media literacy by setting out its three major building blocks, it is time to present its formal definition. *Media literacy is a set of perspectives that we actively use to expose ourselves to the media to interpret the meaning of the messages we encounter.* We build our perspectives from knowledge structures. To build our knowledge structures, we need tools and raw material. These tools are our skills. The raw material is information from the media and from the real world. Active use means that we are aware of the messages and are consciously interacting with them.

What is a perspective? Let's illustrate this with an analogy. Let's say you wanted to learn about Earth. You could build a 100-foot-tall tower, climb up to the top, and use that as your perspective to study Earth. That would give you a good perspective that would not be blocked by trees so that you could see for perhaps several miles in any direction. If your tower were in a forest, you would conclude that Earth is covered with trees. But if your tower were in a suburban neighborhood, you would conclude that Earth is covered with houses, roads, and shopping centers. If your tower were inside the New Orleans Superdome stadium, you would conclude something quite different. Each of these perspectives on Earth would give you a very different set of perceptions. None of these perspectives is better than any other. The key to understanding Earth is to build lots of these towers so you have many different perspectives to enlarge your understanding about what Earth is. And not all of these towers need to be 100 feet tall. Some should be very short so that you can better see what is happening between the blades of grass in a lawn. And others should be hundreds of miles away from the surface so that you can tell that Earth is a sphere and that there are large weather formations constantly churning around the globe.

To illuminate this idea of media literacy further, I need to describe two of its most important characteristics. First, media literacy is a multidimensional concept with many interesting facets. Therefore, we need to view it from many different perspectives to appreciate all it has to offer. Second, media literacy is a continuum, not a category.

*Media Literacy Is Multidimensional.* When we think of information, we typically think of sets of facts such as from a textbook, a newspaper, or a magazine article. But this is only one type of information—cognitive. Media literacy requires that we acquire information and build knowledge in more than just the cognitive dimension but also to consider information from emotional, aesthetic, and moral dimensions. Each of these four dimensions focuses on a different domain of understanding. The cognitive domain refers to factual information—dates, names, definitions, and the like. Think of cognitive information as that which resides in the brain.

The emotional domain contains information about feelings, such as love, hate, anger, happiness, and frustration. Think of emotional information as that which lives in the heart—feelings of happy times, moments of fear, instances of embarrassment. Some people have very little ability to experience an emotion during exposure to the media, whereas others are very sensitive to cues that generate all sorts of feelings in them. For example, we all have the ability to perceive rage, fear, lust, hate, and other strong emotions. Producers use easy-to-recognize symbols to trigger these, so they do not require a high degree of literacy to perceive and understand. But some of us are much better than others at perceiving the more subtle emotions such as ambivalence, confusion, wariness, and so on. Crafting messages about these emotions requires more production skill from writers, directors, and actors. Perceiving these subtle emotions accurately requires a higher degree of literacy from the audience.

The aesthetic domain contains information about how to produce messages. This information gives us the basis for making judgments about who are great writers, photographers, actors, dancers, choreographers, singers, musicians, composers, directors, and other kinds of artists. It also helps us make judgments about other products of creative craftsmanship, such as editing, lighting, set designing, costuming, sound recording, layout, and so forth. This appreciation skill is very important to some scholars (Messaris, 1994; Silverblatt, 1995; Wulff, 1997). For example, Messaris (1994) argues that viewers who are visually literate should have an awareness of artistry and visual manipulation. By this, he means an awareness about the processes by which meaning is created through the visual media. What is expected of sophisticated viewers is some degree of self-consciousness about their role as interpreters. This includes the ability to detect artifice (in staged behavior and editing) and to spot authorial presence (style of the producer/director).

Think of aesthetic information as that which resides in our eyes and ears. Some of us have a good ear for dialogue or musical composition. Some of us have a good eye for lighting, photographic composition, or movement. The more information we have from this aesthetic domain, the finer discriminations we can make between a great actress and a very good one, between a great song that will endure and a currently popular "flash in the pan," between a film director's best and very best work, between art and artificiality.

The moral domain contains information about values. Think of moral information as that which resides in your conscience or your soul. This type of information provides us with the basis for making judgments about right and wrong. When we see characters make decisions in a story, we judge them on a moral dimension, that is, the characters' goodness or evilness. The more detailed and refined our moral information is, the more deeply we can perceive the values underlying messages in the media and the more sophisticated and reasoned are our judgments about those values. It takes a highly media-literate person to perceive moral themes well. You must be able to think past individual characters to focus your meaning making at the overall narrative level. You are able to separate characters from their actions—you might not like a particular character, but you like his or her actions in terms of fitting in with (or reinforcing) your values. You do not focus your viewing on only one character's point of view but try to empathize with many characters so you can vicariously experience the consequences of their actions throughout the course of the narrative.

Your media literacy perspective needs to include information from all four of these domains. For example, you may be able to be highly analytical when you watch a movie and quote lots of facts about the history of the genre, the director's point of view, and the underlying theme. But if you cannot evoke an emotional reaction, you are simply going through a dry, academic exercise.

*Media Literacy Is a Continuum, Not a Category*. Media literacy is not a category—like a box—where either you are in the category or you are not. For example, either you are a high school graduate or you are not; either you are an American citizen or you are not. In contrast, media literacy is best regarded as a continuum—like a thermometer—where there are degrees.

We all occupy some position on the media literacy continuum. There is no point below which we could say that someone has no literacy, and there is no point at the high end where we can say that someone is fully literate—there is always room for improvement. People are positioned along that continuum based on the strength of their overall perspective on the media. The strength of a person's perspective is based on the number and quality of knowledge structures. And the quality of knowledge structures is based on the level of a person's skills and experiences. Because people vary substantially on skills and experiences, they will vary on the number and quality of their knowledge structures. Hence, there will be a great variation of media literacy across people.

People operating at lower levels of media literacy have weak and limited perspectives on the media. They have smaller, more superficial, and less organized knowledge structures, which provide an inadequate perspective to use in interpreting the meaning of a media message. These people are also habitually reluctant or unwilling to use their skills, which remain underdeveloped and therefore more difficult to employ successfully.

*     *     *

## Advantages of Developing a Higher Degree of Media Literacy

What are the advantages of developing a higher degree of media literacy? I will emphasize three. First, media literacy grows one's appetite for a wider variety of media messages. Second, it gives people knowledge about how to program their own mental codes. And third, it provides people with more control over the media.

### *Appetite for Wider Variety of Media Messages*

The media offer an incredible array of choices. The Internet contains Web sites on every topic that humans can conceive. Books are published each year on an extremely wide range of topics. Magazines are a bit more narrow in focus, but the 10,000 titles published each year offer a much wider range than any one person can consume. Cable television is a bit more narrow still, but with 500-plus channels from most cable TV providers, the choice is much wider than any one person can keep up with. However, the mass media continually try to direct our choices to a smaller set. For example, with magazines, although there are about 10,000 magazines published in this country, even a large bookstore is likely to have only about 300 on its magazine shelves. You don't want to have to scan through all 300 magazines, so you rely on your automatic filtering to narrow your choice down to about a dozen magazines that you have found interesting in the past—that is, the media have conditioned you to like these magazines. Your choice is then to buy one or two from this smaller list of 12. Do you have a choice? Yes, of course. But see how the media—first through the bookstore buyer, then through media conditioning—have narrowed your choice down to 12? In other words, the decision you made was determined 99.88% by factors other than you. The media have programmed you to think that you have choices when in fact, the degree of choice is greatly limited. It is rather like a parent laying out two pairs of dress pants—one black and the other dark blue—for his or her 4-year-old son and giving him the total power to choose what he is to wear today. Whether you regard this as a real choice depends on how much you know about the real range of options. If the boy knows about jeans, cargo pants, skater shorts, bathing trunks, and football pants, then he will not think the two dress pants is much of a choice. But what if he only knows about dark dress pants? In this case, he believes he does have a big choice between black and dark blue.

The mass media continually try to constrain your choices so they can condition you into habitual exposure of a few types of media vehicles. This makes you more predictable from a marketing point of view, and this predictability increases mass media companies' ability to reduce their business risk.

However, the choices are still there for you to take advantage of, but most of us prefer our habitual patterns of exposure. Most of us do not explore much of the range in media messages.

The media literacy perspective asks you to be more adventurous and explore a wider range of messages. When you do so, you will likely find many of those messages are not interesting or useful to you. But you will also likely find a few types of messages that are highly useful, and this will expand your exposure repertoire.

### More Self-Programming of Mental Codes

The purpose of media literacy is to empower individuals to control media programming.

When I use the term *programming* in this sense, I do not mean television programs or media messages. An individual by himself or herself will not have much influence on altering how the mass media craft or schedule their messages. An individual will never be able to exercise much control over what gets offered to the public. However, a person can learn to exert a great deal of control over the way one's mind gets programmed. Thus, the purpose of media literacy is to show people how to shift control from the media to themselves. This is what I mean when I say that the purpose of media literacy is to help people control media programming.

The first step in shifting control away from the media to the individual is for individuals to understand how the media program them. This programming by the media continually takes place in a two-phase cycle that repeats over and over again. One of these phases of the cycle is the constraining of choices, and the second phase is the reinforcing of experience.

### More Control Over Media

The mass media are composed of businesses that are very sophisticated in knowing how to attract your attention and condition you for repeat exposures. The media are very successful in using you to achieve their business goals. Often, the media's business goals and your personal goals are the same, so it is a win-win situation. But there are also many times when your personal goals are different from the media's goals; when this occurs, you need to break away from your media-conditioned habits to follow your own goals. The media literacy perspective will help you recognize this divergence of goals and help you take alternative steps. Thus, you are more likely to treat media messages as tools to reach your own goals.

\* \* \*

### Questions for Consideration

1 Potter says that it's great to be analytical when you watch a movie, "but if you cannot evoke an emotional reaction, you are simply going through a dry, academic exercise." What does he mean? Bring an example from your experience.

2 Do you think it pays to take the time to be highly media literate? Why or why not?

# Chapter 3

# BEN H. BAGDIKIAN

# COMMON MEDIA FOR AN UNCOMMON NATION

BEN BAGDIKIAN IS A PULITZER-PRIZE winning journalist who was also the dean of the University of California—Berkeley's Graduate School of Journalism. This reading comes from the 2004 edition of his book *The New Media Monopoly*. The first edition was published in 1983, and in it Bagdikian railed against 50 firms that he said were controlling the American media system. By the time he got to this edition, the number of corporations controlling most daily newspapers, magazines, radio and TV stations, book publishers and movie companies had dropped to five. As you'll see, this situation deeply angers Bagdikian, who sees the Big 5 firms as reflecting big business over the needs of individual Americans and steadfastly supporting conservative elements of the government. At the time he was writing the book, Google had not yet become the political and cultural power that it would shortly become. Yet despite the arrival of the relatively new names of Google and Microsoft to the top ranks of U.S. media firms, Time Warner, News Corporation, Disney, Viacom and Bertelsmann are still dominant. The key to media power today, Bagdikian notes, is influence across media boundaries, and these firms have such power in spades.

*New York Times, February 20, 2003 . . . Senator Byron Dorgan, Democrat of North Dakota, had a potential disaster in his district when a freight train carrying anhydrous ammonia derailed, releasing a deadly cloud over the city of Minot. When the emergency alert system failed, the police called the town radio stations, six of which are owned by the corporate giant, Clear Channel. According to news accounts, no one answered the phone at the stations for more than an hour and a half. Three hundred people were hospitalized, some partially blinded by the ammonia. Pets and livestock were killed.*

*Anhydrous ammonia is a popular fertilizer that also creates a noxious gas, irritating the respiratory system and burning exposed skin. It fuses clothing to the body and sucks moisture from the eyes. To date, one person has died and 400 have been hospitalized.*

(www.ucc.org/ucnews/mayo2/train.htm)

Clear Channel, referred to by Senator Dorgan, is the largest radio chain in the United States. It owns 1,240 radio stations with only 200 employees. Most of its stations, including the six in Minot, North Dakota, are operated nationwide by remote control with the same prerecorded material.[1]

The United States, as said so often at home with pride and abroad with envy or hostility, is the richest country in the world. A nation of nineteen thousand cities and towns is spread across an entire continent, with the globe's most diverse population in ethnicity, race, and country of origin. Its people live in regional cultures as different as Amherst is from Amarillo. In contrast to other major nations whose origins go back millennia, the United States is a new country, less than three hundred years old. Consequently, it has not inherited the baggage of centuries of monarchs, czars, and religious potentates who had held other populations powerless with absolute authority. From its birth, the United States' most sacred principle has been government by consent of the governed.

But the United States has always been in a state of constant change. Today it is living through one of the most sweeping technological innovations in its history. The speed with which the digital revolution has penetrated an entire society has been breathtaking. The computer and Internet, added to one of the world's largest quantity of mass media outlets, have altered the way millions live their daily lives. The new technology has almost miraculous functions that at their best have led to the betterment of numberless aspects of life, like science, scholarship, and medicine.

The country is unique in yet another way. It has left to each community control of its own schools, its own land use, its own fire and police, and much else, functions that in other developed countries are left solely to nationwide agencies. Given the United States' unique dependence on local civic decision making and its extraordinary multiplicity of local self-governing units and hundreds of media outlets, a rational system for a nation with such a vast diversity of people and places would be hundreds of individual local media owners, each familiar with the particular needs of his or her own community. It would be a reasonable assumption that only then would an American community recieve the media programming it needs.

It would be a reasonable assumption. But it would be wrong.

Five global-dimension firms, operating with many of the characteristics of a cartel, own most of the newspapers, magazines, book publishers, motion picture studios, and radio and television stations in the United States. Each medium they own, whether magazines or broadcast stations, covers the entire country, and the owners prefer stories and programs that can be used everywhere and anywhere. Their media products reflect this. The programs broadcast in the six empty stations in Minot, North Dakota, were simultaneously being broadcast in New York City.

These five conglomerates are Time Warner, by 2003 the largest media firm in the world; The Walt Disney Company; Murdoch's News Corporation, based in Australia; Viacom; and Bertelsmann, based in Germany. Today, none of the dominant media companies bother with dominance merely in a single medium. Their strategy has been to have major holdings in all the media, from newspapers to movie studios. This gives each of the five corporations and their leaders more communications power than was exercised by any despot or dictatorship in history.

*     *     *

No imperial ruler in past history had multiple media channels that included television and satellite channels that can permeate entire societies with controlled sights and sounds. The leaders of the Big Five are not Hitlers and Stalins. They are American and foreign entrepreneurs whose corporate empires control every means by which the population learns of its society. And like any close-knit hierarchy, they find ways to cooperate so that all five can work together to expand their power, a power that has become a major force in shaping contemporary American life. The Big Five have similar boards of directors, they jointly invest in the same ventures, and they even go through motions that, in effect, lend each other money and swap properties when it is mutually advantageous.

It is not necessary for a single corporation to own everything in order to have monopoly power. Nor is it necessary to avoid certain kinds of competition. Technically, the dominant media firms are an oligopoly, the rule of a few in which any one of those few, acting alone, can alter market conditions. The most famous global cartel, OPEC (the Organization of Petroleum Exporting Countries), has had brutal shooting wars between some of its members, and there are mutual jealousies among others. But when it comes to the purpose of their cartel—oil—they speak with one voice.

Thus, Time Warner, the largest media firm in the group, competes against another member of the Big Five, Bertelsmann, the largest publisher of English-language books in the world. But in Europe, AOL Time Warner is a partner with both Bertelsmann and News Corporation in the European cable operation, Channel V. According to the Securities and Exchange Commission (SEC), in 2001 AOL Time Warner needed to inflate AOL ad sales figures quickly for stock market reasons. So, in a complex set of transactions, Bertelsmann agreed to buy $400 million worth of advertising in its "competitor," AOL Time Warner, in return for AOL Time Warner transferring to Bertelsmann additional shares in a European firm in which they were already partners. Thus, Bertelsmann, according to the SEC, helped its "competitor" look healthier than it really was.

The Big Five "competitors" engage in numerous such cartel-like relations. News Corporation, for example, has a joint venture with the European operations of Paramount Pictures, which belongs to Viacom, another of its "competitors" in the Big Five. According to French and American securities agencies, Vivendi, the disintegrating French media conglomerate, had agreed to place $25 million worth of advertising in AOL media in return for AOL giving the French firm a share of one of its operations in France.[2]

Some competition is never totally absent among the Big Five media conglomerates. The desire to be the first among many is as true for linked corporations as it is for politicians and nations. It was true two decades ago when most big media companies aspired to command market control in only one medium, for example, Gannett in newspapers; Time, Incorporated in magazines; Simon & Schuster in books; the three TV networks in radio; CBS in television; Paramount in motion pictures. But completion of that process fed an appetite for expansion toward a new and more powerful goal, a small group of interlocked corporations that now have effective control over all the media on which the American public says it depends.

## Free Markets or Free Lunches?

Corporate life and capitalist philosophy are almost synonymous, and at the heart of capitalism is competition, or the contemporary incantation, "the free market." If the dominant media corporations behaved in accordance with classical capitalist dogma, each would experiment to create its own unique product. In the media world, *product* means news, entertainment, and political programs. It would mean offering differing kinds of programs that reflect the widely different tastes, backgrounds, and activities of the American population. To compete outright would mean unique products and the goal of a winner-take-all victory. Instead, the Big Five indulge in mutual aid and share investments in the same media products. They jointly conform to the periodic ratings that presume to show what kinds of programs have fractionally larger audiences, after which "the competitors" then imitate the winners and take slightly varying shares of the total profits.

One result of this constricted competition is that the thousands of media outlets carry highly duplicative content. Another result is that an innovative newcomer can hope to become a significant participant in the industry only as one of the many subsidiaries of the billion-dollar established giants. It is only in legends that David beats Goliath. In the history of modern media, if two experimenters in a garage create an ingenious invention that could revolutionize their industry, ultimately they have limited choices: sell their device for millions or billions to a dominant firm, [sic] risk a hostile takeover, or being crushed by the vast promotion and financial resources of a threatened Goliath. In the end, Goliath wins.

Practitioners of current American capitalism do not reflect Adam Smith's eighteenth-century image of an all-out rivalry in which merchants compete by keeping prices lower and quality higher than their fellow merchants. That classical mythology would create a final battlefield with one victor and four companies reduced to leftovers or worse. No dominant media firm, given its size and wealth, wishes to risk such a loss. The Ford Motor Company and General Motors do not compete to the death because each has too much to lose in an all-or-nothing rivalry. Similarly, the major media maintain their cartel-like relationships with only marginal differences among them, a relationship that leaves all of them alive and well—but leaves the majority of Americans with artificially narrowed choices in their media. It is the small neighborhood stores and restaurants that truly compete in products, price, and quality, and are willing to risk failure in the process.

The narrow choices the dominant firms offer the country are not the result of a conspiracy. Dominant media members do not sit around a table parceling out market shares, prices, and products, as is done literally by OPEC. The five dominant media firms don't need to. They share too many of the same methods and goals. But if a new firm will strengthen their ability to promote the companies they already own, they will compete with each other to add it to their collections.

The possibilities for mutual promotion among all their various media is the basic reason the Big Five have become major owners of all kinds of media. For example, actors and actresses in a conglomerate's wholly owned movie studio can appear on the same company's television and cable networks, photographs of the newly minted celebrities can dominate the covers of the firm's wholly owned magazines, and be interviewed on the firm's wholly owned radio and television talk shows. The conglomerate can commission an author from its wholly owned book publishing firm to write a biography or purported autobiography of the new stars, which in turn are promoted on the firms' other media.

In addition to jousting for fractional points in broadcast ratings, each of the Big Five wants its shares on the stock market higher than the others (which also increases the value of shares and stock options owned by top executives). Although if one conglomerate is momentarily ahead, it is tolerable for the others because being a momentary "loser" still allows prodigious profits. Television stations, for example, regard 30 percent profit a year as "low" (being a "loser") because the more successful TV stations that may be Number One at the moment, can make 60 percent profit a year. As one of the executives in their trade, Barry Diller, once said of TV stations, "This is a business where if you are a birdbrain you have a thirty-five percent margin. Many good broadcasters have a forty-to-sixty-percent margin."[3]

Though not a literal cartel like OPEC, the Big Five, in addition to cooperation with each other when it serves a mutual purpose, have interlocking members on their boards of directors. An interlock exists when the same board member sits on the board of more than one corporation (this is illegal only if the interlocked firms would form a monopoly if they merged). According to a study by Aaron Moore in the March/April 2003 *Columbia Journalism Review,* News Corporation, Disney, Viacom, and Time Warner have forty-five interlocking directors.

It is a more significant cooperation that closely intertwines all five into a mutual aid combine. The dominant five media conglomerates have a total of 141 joint ventures, which makes them business partners with each other. To cite only one example, News Corporation shares a financial interest with its "competitors" in 63 cable systems, magazines, recording companies, and satellite channels in the United States and abroad. All five join forces in one of Washington's most powerful lobbies, the National Association of Broadcasters, to achieve the laws and regulations that increase their collective power over consumers. In 2000, for example, the National Association of Broadcasters spent $2.5 million lobbying on communications issues, using 24 of its own lobbyists plus four independent lobbying firms, and that year made 64 percent of its campaign contributions to Republicans and 36 percent to Democrats. This is in addition to the lobbying and campaign money spent by the major media corporations on their own.[4]

The media conglomerates are not the only industry whose owners have become monopolistic in the American economy. But media products are unique in one vital respect. They do not manufacture nuts and bolts: they manufacture a social and political world.

New technology has expanded the commercial mass media's unprecedented power over the knowledge and values of the country. In less than a generation, the five intertwined media corporations have enlarged their influence in the home, school, and work lives of every citizen. Their concentrated influence exercises political and cultural forces reminiscent of the royal decrees of monarchs rejected by the revolutionists of 1776.

The Five have become major players in altering the politics of the country. They have been able to promote new laws that increase their corporate domination and that permit them to abolish regulations that inhibit their control. Their major accomplishment is the 1996 Telecommunications Act. In the process, power of media firms, along with all corporate power in general, has diminished the place of individual citizens. In the history of the United States and in its Constitution, citizens are presumed to have the sole right to determine the shape of their democracy. But concentrated media power in news and commentary, together with corporate political contributions in general, have diminished the influence of voters over which issues and candidates will be offered on Election Day.

Conservative policies have traditionally been preferred by all large corporations, including the large media conglomerates. The country's five dominant media corporations are now among the five hundred largest corporations in the world.[5] These five corporations dominate one of the two worlds in which every modern person is destined to live.

It is still true, of course, that the face-to-face, flesh-and-blood environment continues to be the daily reality for human beings. It is part of human evolution and if it has any order and social principles it is the result of the millennia of insights, conventions, and experiences of the human race.

In contrast, the mass media world began in earnest only two hundred fifty years ago. Many of its most dramatic and influential elements have emerged within the lifetimes of the present generation. The media world—newspapers, magazines, books, radio, television, movies, and now the Internet—occupies a major role in the commerce and private life of the entire population.

## New Media in a New World

Media corporations have always possessed the power to affect politics. That is not new in history. But the five dominant corporations—Time Warner, Disney, News Corporation, Viacom, and Bertelsmann—have power that media in past history did not, power created by new technology and the near uniformity of their political goals. The political and social content projected by these media to the country's population has had real consequences: the United States has the most politically constricted voter choices among the world's developed democracies. That raises fundamental questions about how and by whom the nature of democracy shall be determined.

The magnitude of the change may be more readily understood by looking back from today's twenty-first century. In retrospect, the awesome power of the contemporary mass media has in one generation been a major factor in reversing the country's progressive political, social, and economic momentum of the twentieth century. As a result, in the United States, the twenty-first century inherited a new, more extreme brand of conservative policies.

Twentieth-century politics began with a Republican president, Theodore Roosevelt (1901–1909), at a time when every city of any size had five or more competing newspapers with a broad range of politics, right, center, and left. With the support of a number of influential periodicals and a portion of its newspapers, Theodore Roosevelt initiated historic conservation of natural resources and dismantled huge interlocked corporate conglomerates, then called *trusts*. The control of trusts in writing laws, bribing officials, and damaging the social welfare had been exposed month after month by some of the country's leading writers in its most influential periodicals—Lincoln Steffens, Owen Wister, Ida Tarbell, Louis Brandeis (sixteen years before he became a member of the U.S. Supreme Court), Upton Sinclair, and many others. Their investigative articles appeared in major media—newspapers published by Joseph Pulitzer, E.W. Scripps, and the early Hearst. Articles asking for reform were centerpieces of influential national magazines like *Harper's, Atlantic, Cosmopolitan, McClure's*, and *Century*.

That fundamental period of confronting the urgent new needs of industrial democracy ended when J. P. Morgan and John D. Rockefeller decided to buy *Harper's* and *Atlantic* and other angry financiers paid high salaries to the most skilled editors to take positions more compatible with the vision of Wall Street banking houses. That, along with World War I, ended the period of reform.[6]

A similar period of reform repaired the chaos created by the wildly uninhibited free markets of the 1920s. Franklin Roosevelt's New Deal (1932–1945) established new social and regulatory agencies after the Great Depression's corporate breakdowns. The New Deal also established immediate jobs and agencies for housing and feeding the country's poor and middle-class families. While Franklin Roosevelt, unlike his cousin Theodore, had no overwhelming media support before his election, the newspapers, which were the only medium that really counted at the time, had lost much of their credibility. They had glorified the failed policies that produced the shambles of the Wall Street Crash of 1929 and the Great Depression that followed. By the time that Franklin Roosevelt ran for president in 1932, desperate unemployment, and murmurings of popular revolt were ominous. Fear led many of the once-conservative or neutral newspapers and magazines to moderate opposition to the election of Roosevelt.

Roosevelt created what were, for that period, radical reforms, like the Securities and Exchange Commission to monitor corporations that sold shares to the public, Social Security to create old age pensions for much of the population, and laws that prevented banks from speculating in the stock market with their depositors' money. The uninhibited free market had created the wild euphoria of every-man-a-millionaire in the 1920s, which then led to the chaos. This had a temporary chastening effect on the main media's normal philosophy of "leave business alone."

In contrast, the presidencies of Ronald Reagan (1981–1988) and of the Bushes—George H.W. Bush (1989–1993), the forty-first president, and his son, George W. Bush, the forty-third president, who took office in 2000—again created an abrupt reversal. After his ascendancy to the presidency in 2000, the younger Bush engaged in a systematic reversal or cancellation of earlier natural resource conservation plans, reduced welfare, and adopted economic policies that hastened the flow of wealth to the most rich. The theory espoused by President Reagan had been that the wealth at the top would trickle down to create jobs for middle-class and poor workers. It was a long-discredited theory characterized by John Kenneth Galbraith: "if you feed the horse with enough oats, sooner or later it will leave something behind for the sparrows."

Any dynamic democracy inevitably changes political direction as conditions and public desires evolve. The radical changes of the late twentieth century obviously reflected universal alterations in technology, world economics, and other underlying tides. But the contemporary power of mass media imagery controlled by a small number of like-minded giant corporations played a powerful role. The media of that period, particularly broadcasters, were compliant with requests of the Reagan White House, for example, to limit access of reporters to the president himself.[7] The former actor's folksy personality distracted much of public attention from the disastrous consequences that followed an expanded national debt. What happened after the 1990s in the American economy was an eerie echo of the wild storms of the 1920s that brought the crash of 1929.

There are multiple reasons for the politics of any country to change, but with growing force the major media play a central role in the United States. In the years after 1980, conservatives began the chant of "get the government off our backs" that accelerated the steady elimination of a genuinely progressive income tax. They adopted the goal of uninhibited corporate power. Political slogans advocating a shrinking government and arguments involving that idea filled the reportorial and commentary agendas of most of the country's major news outlets. It was the beginning of the end of government-as-protector-of-the-consumer and the start of government-as-the-protector-of-big-business. And the news industry, now a part of the five dominant corporations, reflected this new direction.

By the time Bush the Younger had become president, the most influential media were no longer the powerful *Harper's, Century*, and other influential national organs of one hundred years earlier that had helped to expose abuses and campaigned to limit the power of massive corporations. In sharp contrast to the major media that led to Theodore Roosevelt's reforms, the most adversarial media in 2000, both in size of audience and political influence, were the right-wing talk shows and a major broadcast network, the Murdoch News Corporation's Fox network, with its overt conservatism. Murdoch went further and personally created *The Weekly Standard*, the intellectual Bible of contemporary American conservatism and of the administration of Bush the Younger. Murdoch's magazine is delivered each week to top-level White House figures. The office of Vice President Cheney alone receives a special delivery of thirty copies.[8]

It is not simply a random artifact in media politics that three of the largest broadcast outlets insistently promote bombastic far-right political positions. Murdoch's Fox radio and television have almost unwavering right-wing commentators. The two largest radio groups, Clear Channel and Cumulus, whose holdings dwarf the rest of radio, are committed to a daily flood of far-right propagandistic programming along with their automated music. Twenty-two percent of Americans polled say their main source of news is radio talk shows.[9] In a little more than a decade, American radio has become a powerful organ of right-wing propaganda. The most widely distributed afternoon talk show is Rush Limbaugh's, whose opinions are not only right wing but frequently based on untruths.[10]

Dominant media owners have highly conservative politics and choose their talk show hosts accordingly. Editor Ron Rodriques of the trade magazine *Radio & Records* said "I can't think of a single card-carrying liberal talk show syndicated nationwide."[11] The one clearly liberal talk show performer, Jim Hightower of ABC, was fired in 1995 by the head of Disney, Michael Eisner, the week after Eisner bought the Disney company, which owns ABC.

The political content of the remaining four of the Big Five is hardly a counter to Fox and the ultraconservatism and bad reporting of dominant talk shows. American television viewers have a choice of NBC (now owned by General Electric), CBS (now owned by one of the Big Five, Viacom), and ABC, now owned by another of the Big Five, Disney. Diversity among the tens of thousands of United States media outlets is no longer a government goal. In 2002, the chairman of the Federal Communications Commission, Michael Powell, expressed the opinion that it would not be so bad if one broadcast giant owned every station in an entire metropolitan area.[12]

The machinery of contemporary media is not a minor mechanism. The 280 million Americans are served, along with assorted other small local and national media, by 1,468 daily newspapers, 6,000 different magazines, 10,000 radio stations, 2,700 television and cable stations, and 2,600 book publishers.[13] The Internet gave birth to a new and still unpredictable force, as later portions of this book will describe. Though today's media reach more Americans than ever before, they are controlled by the smallest number of owners than ever before. In 1983 there were fifty dominant media corporations; today there are five. These five corporations decide what most citizens will—or will not—learn.[14]

During these years the political spectrum of American politics has been shifted far to the right. What was the far right forty years ago is now the center. What was liberal is now seen by the dominant party as radical and even unpatriotic. The shift does not reflect the political and social values of the American public as a whole. A recent Harris poll showed that 42 percent of Americans say they are politically moderate, middle-of-the-road, slightly liberal, liberal, or extremely liberal, compared to 33 percent for the same categories of conservatives, with 25 percent saying "Don't know or haven't thought about it."[15]

## Dollars versus Votes

One force creating the spectrum change has been, to put it simply, money—the quantities of cash used to gain office. Spontaneous national and world events and the accidents of new personalities inevitably play a part in determining a country's legislation and policies. But in American politics, beyond any other single force, money has determined which issues and candidates will dominate the national discourse that, in turn, selects the issues and choices available to voters on Election Day.

The largest source of political money has come from corporations eager to protect their expanded power and treasure. The country's massive media conglomerates are no different—with the crucial exception that they are directly related to voting patterns because their product happens to be a social-political one. It is, tragically, a self-feeding process: the larger the media corporation, the greater its political influence, which produces a still larger media corporation with still greater political power.

The cost of running for office has risen in parallel with the enlarged size of American industries and the size of their political contributions to preferred candidates and parties.

In 1952, the money spent by all candidates and parties for all federal election campaigns—House, Senate, and presidency—was $140 million (sic). In 2000, the races spent in excess of $5 billion. Spending in the 2000 presidential campaign alone was $1 billion.[16]

The growth of money in politics is multiplied by what it pays for—the growth of consultants skilled in, among other things, the arts of guile and deception that have been enhanced by use of new technology in discovering the tastes and income of the public.

Television political ads are the most common and expensive campaign instrument and the largest single expenditure in American political campaigns. Typically, the commercials are brief, from a few seconds to five minutes, during which most of the content consists of slogans and symbols (waving Americans flags are almost obligatory), useless as sources of relevant information. Television stations and networks are, of course, the recipients of most of the money that buys air time. This is why the country's political spectrum is heavily influenced by which candidate has the most money.

Incumbents always have an advantage in attracting money from all sources because even conservative business leaders want influence with whoever happens to vote for legislation, even if it is a liberal. Nevertheless, if one eliminates incumbents, the big spenders have almost always been the winners. Beginning in 1976, candidates who spent more than $500,000 were increasingly Republicans.[17] Conservatives perpetually accuse Democrats of bowing to *special interests*. In the conservative lexicon, these are code words for labor unions. And, indeed, labor unions in 2000, for example, gave Democrats $90 million and Republicans only $5 million. But in the 1990s, corporate and trade association Political Action Committees have given Republicans twice as much money as they have to Democrats and in quantities many multiples of labor union political contributions.[18] In the crucial midterm 2002 elections, when control of the Senate depended on a few votes, Democrats spent $44 million and Republicans $80 million. Republicans gained control of Congress, undoubtedly helped by President Bush, who, two months before the election, suddenly declared that the country would go to war against Iraq and that opponents would be seen as supporters of Saddam Hussein's tyranny. That alone took domestic economic troubles off the front pages and out of TV news programs.

Increasingly, House and Senate candidates have spent their own money on campaigns, a choice available only to multimillionaires. Thus, the money both of the wealthy and of corporate interests has come to dominate American politics in the single generation during which the country's political spectrum has shifted far to the right.

## The View from the Top

The major news media overwhelmingly quote the men and women who lead hierarchies of power. Powerful officials are a legitimate element in news because the public needs to know what leaders in public and private life are saying and doing. But official pronouncements are only a fraction of the realities within the population. Complete news requires more. Leaders, whether in public or private life and whatever their personal ethical standards, like most human beings seldom wish to publicize information that discloses their mistakes or issues they wish to keep in the background or with which they disagree. Officials do not always say the whole truth.

Citizen groups issuing serious contrary studies and proposals for mending gaps in the social fabric get only sporadic and minimal attention in the major media. Consequently, some of the country's most pressing problems remain muted. Unless powerful official voices press for attention and remedies for those missing issues, the pressing problems remain unresolved.

It is not rare to have speakers and large organizations to complain publicly that it is shameful for the richest and most powerful country in the world to have increasing numbers of citizens homeless, that the United States is the only industrial country in the world without universal health care, or that its rhetorical support of education seems to believe that this requires no additional money from the federal government—even though it is the federal government that requires local schools to meet higher standards. Or that the country withdrew unilaterally from previous treaties to protect the planetary environment. Or that, despite agreement to restrict existing stocks of Russian and American nuclear weapons, President Bush the Younger announced that he would consider military action against countries initiating nuclear weapons research while simultaneously announcing that the United States would restart its own nuclear weapons research.

These issues are not absent from major news media. They are reported but then they are dropped, though national stories about a distant kidnapped child can continue on front pages and television news for weeks. There is nothing harmful and often some good in persistent stories about individual human tragedies. But in the national news agenda, there is no such media persistence with problems that afflict millions. It is an unrelenting tragedy that more than 41 million Americans remain without health care, that millions of young people are jammed into inadequate classrooms with inadequate teaching staffs, that deterioration threatens Planet Earth as a human habitat, or that a similar threat is growth of nuclear weaponry in the United States and the rest of the world. Or that preemptive war as a permanent policy is the law of the jungle.

News executives claim periodically that no one's really interested in unmet domestic needs, or people are tired of bad news, or we had a story on that. This is the same industry that is proud of its ability to be artful and ingenious in making any kind of story interesting, that many of the same editors pursue the "lost child story" that, in fact, interests only part of the audience and is ignored by the rest. Every reader of a newspaper or viewer of television will pay close attention and absorb copious detail on an issue that affects that reader personally, whether it is a jobless bookkeeper on the national prospects for the unemployed or a family member desperate for possible treatments for Alzheimer's disease.

The major news media fail to deal systematically with the variety of compelling social needs of the entire population. Those needs remain hidden crises, obscured in the daily flood of other kinds of news. Yet the weight of most reputable surveys shows that, in the late twentieth and early twenty-first century, most Americans were deeply concerned with systematic lack of funds for their children's education, access to health care, the growing crises in unemployment, homelessness, and steady deterioration of city and state finances.

But these issues are not high priorities among the most lavish contributors to political candidates and parties. Corporations have other high-priority issues. There is a world of wealth, stratospheric in its imperial heights, which is so beyond the life of most Americans that it is barely imaginable.

*     *     *

## A Built-in Imbalance

Most of the more conventionally wealthy families are able to buy private services that ordinary families can obtain only in a publicly funded school or other community and national facilities that suffer from budget cuts made, among other reasons, to provide tax cuts for the wealthy.

The many decades of only passing treatment to the major needs of most people have produced hopelessness about the possibility for change. Consequently, masses of potential voters have become resigned to the assumption that what the major media tell them is the norm and now unchangeable. In the first edition of this book, I observed twenty years ago, "media power is political power." The five dominant media firms, now among the largest in the world, have that power and use it to enhance the values preferred by the corporate world of which they are a part.

The imbalance between issues important to corporate hierarchies and those most urgent to the population at large is obscured by the neutralist tone of modern news.

The right-ward impact of modern news is not in the celebrated inflamed language that once characterized nineteenth-century sensationalist headlines and language. Today the imbalance is in what is chosen—or not chosen—for print or broadcast. Media politics are reflected in the selection of commentators and talk show hosts. It is exercised powerfully in what their corporations privately lobby for in legislation and regulations, the contributions they and their leaders make to political parties and candidates. It is the inevitable desire of most large corporations to have a political environment that is friendly to weakening minimum standards for public service and safety in order to produce maximum corporate profit levels and lower the corporate share of city, state, and federal taxes. But these seldom provide comparable benefits for the common good, like health care, safe environments, and properly funded public education.

In the last twenty-five years, the media world has experienced accelerated inventions and with them conflicts and uncertainties about which media will survive and which will die off. Yet again, newspeople agonize whether a new method of communication that distracts the country's youths might condemn the daily newspaper to an early death. Similar questions have arisen about other traditional media, like magazines and books, to be dealt with later.

As Gutenberg's movable type was in his day, the new electronic media as a social force remain in a still-uncertain balance. Today, massive demonstrations protesting a government policy have been gathered solely by marshaling sympathizers by Internet. At the same time, the digital revolution has made ambiguous the privacy within one's home because a government official, or anyone else with enough skill, can enter the citizen's computer from a remote location and thereby end the historic assumption that "my home is my castle."

That question hovers over the extraordinary but unpredictable innovations of the electronic media and the transformations that are continuing in our time.

## Questions for Consideration

1   Bagdikian argues that American media are failing the local communities of the U.S. What does he mean? Do you agree?

2   Bagdikian contends that major media firms that seem to be competitive with one another are really in many respects cooperating. According to him, why do they do that, and how?

3   Bertlesmann is privately held and so does not have to release an annual report. Time Warner, News Corporation, Disney, and Viacom do release annual reports, though, and they provide fascinating insight into the breadth of the firms' holdings and cross-media activities. Choose one of the firms and examine its holdings and cross-media activities through the most recent annual report.

## Notes

Citations to the *New York Times* refer to the national edition.

1.  *New York Times*, 24 March 2003, 15.
2.  http://media.guardian.co.uk/news/story/0,7541,941565,00.html
3.  *The New Yorker*, 9 November 1998, 34.
4.  Opensecrets.org, Center for Responsive Politics, for 2000.
5.  *Fortune 500*, 2002, and *Fortune Global 500*, 2002, www.fortune.com
6.  Harvey Swados, ed., *Years of Conscience: The Muckrakers* (Cleveland: Meridian Books, 1962).
7.  Mark Hertsgaard, *On Bended Knee* (New York: Farrar Straus Giroux, 1988).
8.  *Vanity Fair*, July 2003, 14.
9.  *Index of Free Expression*, www.indexonline.org/news/ 20030319_unitedstates.shtml
10. S. Rendall, J. Naureckas, and J. Cohen, *The Way Things Aren't: Rush Limbaugh's Reign of Error* (New York: New Press, 1995).
11. *New York Times*, 8 December 2002, sec. 4, 7.
12. *National Journal Technology Daily*, 19 September 2002.
13. *Statistical Abstract of the United States, 2001*, 121st ed. (Washington, D.C.: U.S. Census Bureau, 2001), table 1121.
14. Ben H. Bagdikian, *The Media Monopoly*, 1st ed. (Boston: Beacon Press, 1983).
15. www.dsmarketing.com/usgov_amph.htm
16. www.thisnation.com/question/028.html;www.historylearningsite.co.uk/finance.htm
17. American Enterprise Institute, "Vital Statistics on Congress," 1984–85 ed. (Washington, D.C.: American Enterprise Institute, 1985), 67,74, tables 3–7 and 3–5.
18. Center for Responsive Politics, http://opensecrets.org/overs /blio.aspCycle=2000

# Chapter 4

# ROBERT McCHESNEY

# POLITICAL PROBLEM, POLITICAL SOLUTIONS

**I**N THIS PROVOCATIVE EXCERPT FROM his 2004 book *The Problem of the Media: U.S. Communication Politics in the Twenty-First Century*, Robert McChesney challenges the generally held assumption in the U.S. that marketplace competition is the best way to ensure a healthy media system. He argues that "even if one accepts that the U.S. economy functions more effectively with a highly commercialized media system, it does not mean that democracy is best served by such a system." He adds that strong government media policies should be put in place to encourage a media structure that, in turn, encourages a healthy democracy. The tremendous changes taking place in media now provide the opening, he says, for informed and vigorous public discussions on what such government policies should be. McChesney, a professor at the University of Illinois, has been encouraging just such a discussion through the organization he founded called Free Press. See www.freepress.net

Mention "the problem of the media" and most people think of poor or inadequate media content that negatively affects our culture, politics, and society. If the media were doing a commendable job, there would be no problem. But there is another meaning for the word *problem*; its first definition in *Webster's Dictionary* is "a question raised for inquiry, consideration, or solution." Media systems of one sort or another are going to exist, and they do not fall from the sky. The policies, structures, subsidies, and institutions that are created to control, direct, and regulate the media will be responsible for the logic and nature of the media system. Whether their content is good, bad, or a combination, the media therefore present a political problem for any society, and an unavoidable one at that. In other words, the first problem with the media deals with its content; the second and larger problem deals with the structure that generates that content. Understood this way, the manner in which a society decides how to structure the media system, how it elects to solve the problem of the media in the second sense, becomes of paramount importance. Such policy debates will often determine the contours and values of the media system that then produces the media content that is visible to all.

The problem of the media exists in all societies, regardless of their structure, but the range of available solutions for each society is influenced by its political and economic structures, cultural traditions, and communication technologies, among other things. In dictatorships and authoritarian regimes, those in power generate a media system that supports their domination and minimizes the possibility of effective opposition. The direct link between control over the media and control over the society is self-evident. But in democratic societies, the same tension exists between those who hold power and those who do not, only the battle assumes different forms. Media are at the center of struggles for power and control in any society, and they are arguably even more vital players in democratic nations.

The political nature of the problem of the media in democratic societies is well-known; virtually all theories of self-government are premised on having an informed citizenry, and the creation of such an informed citizenry is the media's province. The measure of a media system in political terms is not whether it creates a viable democratic society—that would be too much of a burden to place upon it. Instead, the measure is whether the media system, on balance and in the context of the broader social and economic situation, challenges antidemocratic pressures and tendencies or reinforces them. Is the media system a democratic force? Much less understood is the importance of the media to economics; this relationship with economics goes a long way toward shaping the media's political role and their relationship with the dominant political and economic forces in society. In the United States the starting point for grasping the problem of the media is seeing where the media system fits in the broader capitalist economic system. The crucial tension lies between the role of the media as profit-maximizing commercial organizations and the need for the media to provide the basis for informed self-government. It is this tension that fuels much of the social concern around media and media policy making.

In this chapter I will present a framework for understanding the problem of the media in the second, broader definition of the word *problem*. Only then can we make sense of problems with content. I will debunk the myths that the U.S. media are inherently the province of the "free market" and that the modern commercial media system is the result of informed debate. In doing so, I will look at the origins of the U.S. press system in the late eighteenth and early nineteenth centuries and the role media policies made in crafting it. I will also explore the public debate surrounding radio broadcasting in the 1930s and that battle's consequences that shape our media policy making to this day. This analysis leads directly to an overview of the corrupt and decrepit state of media policy making as it has evolved over the twentieth century. The United States has not satisfactorily addressed the problem of the media in recent generations. As a result, the media system has been set up to serve the interests of those who make the policies behind closed doors—large profit-driven media corporations—while the broad and vital interests of the population have been largely neglected. This system has contributed to a political crisis of the highest magnitude and unless it is confronted directly will severely limit our ability to make progress on any of the other major social and political problems that face the nation. On balance, the media system has become—ironically, in view of the freedom of the press clause in the First

Amendment—a significantly antidemocratic force. It is a political problem that requires a political solution.

## Media, Markets, and Policies

The operating assumption in most discussions of the U.S. media system is that media are a natural province of the market. From this perspective, when governments regulate these markets, they represent an outside intervening force. To the pro-corporate political right this is dogma. As one *Wall Street Journal* columnist put it, "Man's natural instinct is to choose free enterprise and free markets," so government regulation certainly violates nature and, quite possibly, the intent of God.[1] But even among liberals the same position holds, although the prospect of government regulation can be more readily justified.[2] By this logic, much of media policy making or regulation, to the extent it exists, is merely to protect property rights in the free market systems that have naturally and inexorably emerged.

This framework is ideologically loaded. Looking at the situation from the classical liberal and democratic assumption that society selects the manner in which it wishes to regulate social behavior, the procedure by which a society chooses from a range of options may be democratic, autocratic, plutocratic, or some combination, but it is a decision that a society makes. Thus, enacting laws, setting regulations, and using markets ultimately become policy decisions. Private property and markets are employed to the extent that they are seen as superior regulatory mechanisms to other alternatives. In contemporary society, we can regulate social behavior through four general paths: markets, laws, architecture, and cultural norms.[3] Each has its strengths and weaknesses, and none can lay claim to being the natural or "default" position. It is from this palette that people create the world in which they live. The more democratic a society, the more likely the decisions about how best to regulate social life will be the result of widespread informed debate. The less democratic a society, the more likely those decisions will be made by powerful self-interested parties with a minimum of popular participation.

This dispute, then, is not about whether the market is the *natural* manner to organize media—and all of social life for that matter. It is about whether the market is the *superior* means, or *a* superior means among others, to regulate media. Just as capitalism is not the "natural" social system for humanity, so commercial media are not Nature's creation either. Our social system and our media system both require aggressive and explicit government activity to exist. Media policy, then, is a far broader and more significant historical phenomenon than that found in the conventional wisdom, which depicts it as something inherently tedious drawn up by bespectacled policy wonks and government bureaucrats addressing obscure technical issues. To the contrary, the U.S. media system—even its most "free market" sectors—is the direct result of explicit government policies and in fact would not exist without those policies. Most dominant media firms exist because of government-granted and government-enforced monopoly broadcasting licenses, telecommunication franchises, and rights to content (a.k.a. copyright). Competitive markets in the classic sense are rare; they were established or strongly shaped by the government.

So the real struggle is over whose interests the regulation will represent. And this is where media policy making, rather than being dull and tedious, oozes with the excitement of politics at its most enthralling. In this context, the term *deregulation* becomes somewhat misleading; it means, more often than not, government regulation that advances the interests of the dominant corporate players. To the dominant firms, when government allocates to them lucrative monopoly licenses or regulates on their behalf, it is not considered regulation. But to society, it is a serious form of control, and one that results from explicit media policies made in the public's name.

For a concrete example of the misuse of the term *deregulation* in media, consider radio broadcasting. In 1996 the Telecommunications Act eliminated the cap on the number of radio stations a single company could own nationally. It had been 40 prior to that, and for decades it had been much lower than that. Radio, it was said, was now "deregulated." The vast majority of U.S. radio stations were sold after 1996 and a few massive firms came to dominate the industry. Clear Channel alone soon owned more than 1,200 stations. So does it make sense, as is regularly proclaimed, to depict radio broadcasting as deregulated—or is it simply regulated differently for different ends serving different interests? For a test of the deregulation hypothesis, one need only go out and commence broadcasting a signal on an AM or FM frequency used by an existing broadcaster. Immediate arrest and possible incarceration would result. That is serious regulation. The government is still granting monopoly licenses to radio and TV channels and still enforcing those monopoly licenses. It is not open season for anyone to begin using the airwaves. The only difference the Telecommunications Act made is that today the largest corporations can possess more of these monopoly licenses than they could before. (It is worth noting that these firms do not pay the government a single penny for the right to have monopoly access to these valuable and scarce channels of the publicly owned spectrum.) There is every bit as much regulation by the government as before, only now it is more explicitly directed to serve large corporate interests.

Although there is no mandatory connection between having a profit-driven economy and having a profit-driven media system, it is understandable why one would make that assumption. In the past hundred years, media have become an important location for profit making. This process has been ongoing in the United States but the decisive era came in the early twentieth century when the modern capitalist film, music, advertising, and broadcasting industries emerged. This growth of the commercial media sector was part and parcel of the rise of modern corporate-based capitalism in the United States. The integration of media into the commanding heights of U.S. capitalism has only increased in recent decades. In terms of sales, the eight or nine largest media firms now rank among the two or three hundred largest corporations in the world. Less than thirty years ago, only two media companies were among the three hundred largest firms in the United States, not to mention worldwide.[4] In terms of market value, eleven of the world's two hundred largest corporations are media firms, another three do significant media business, and many more on the list are in the related software, Internet, and telecommunications industries.[5] Today the United States has a media system dominated by a small number of very large vertically integrated corporations.

Looking at lists of wealthiest Americans from the nineteenth century to the present time provides some sense of the change. It was well into the second half of the twentieth century before more than one or two media magnates rated among the thirty richest Americans or families. By 1992—before the media explosion of the late 1990s—nine of the largest thirty fortunes were made in media, and a couple others on the list had closely related holdings, such as software.[6] Since the early 1990s and through 2001, commercial media have become one of the three fastest-growing industries in the

United States. Studies suggest that media may not remain among the top three but will still grow well above the national average deep into the first decade of the twenty-first century.[7] Put another way, media spending per household grew at twice the rate of inflation throughout the 1990s.[8] And in 2002, *Forbes* magazine calculated that over *one-third* of the fifty wealthiest Americans generated the preponderance of their fortunes through media and related industries.[9]

Our media, then, far from being on the sidelines of the capitalist system, are among its greatest beneficiaries. Research links media corporations with the largest investment banks and demonstrates how often media corporation board members sit on other Fortune 500 companies' boards.[10] The interconnection of media and capitalism grows that much stronger when one considers the role of advertising, which provides around one-third of all media revenues. The very largest corporations generate the preponderance of advertising.[11] Investment in media and expenditures on media appear to be central to macroeconomic growth in the overall economy.[12]

These connections suggest considerable tension if the media are also supposed to grease the wheels of democratic self-governance. A central issue in democratic theory has been how to reconcile social and economic inequality with political equality. For most of the nation's founders this was a vexing issue, and, perhaps because they were the beneficiaries of the existing unequal distribution of resources, many favored restricting the franchise to white male property owners to prevent social turmoil. Benjamin Franklin and Thomas Paine were the most radical and argued that democracy must trump inequality. Franklin supported a clause in the Pennsylvania constitution warning that "an enormous Proportion of Property vested in a few Individuals is dangerous to the Rights, and destructive of the Common Happiness, of Mankind; and therefore every free State hath a Right by its Laws to discourage the Possession of such Property."[13] Battles to extend suffrage were central to U.S. politics until well into the twentieth century. Invariably these were fights between the haves and the have-nots.[14] The media system, in democratic theory, was charged with providing information equally so that even poor citizens would have the capacity to be effective citizens, despite their unequal access to resources. As I will discuss shortly, policies put in place in the early republic made it far more likely that the press would not be dominated by the wealthy and powerful but would be accessible and of value to broad segments of the population.

The emergence of modern corporate capitalism alters the initial equation. For a variety of reasons, universal adult suffrage arises alongside it in the United States. But at the same time, without discounting the ways in which capitalism can promote self-government, it also by its very nature tends to generate social and economic inequality. To the extent that the contemporary media system answers to investors first and foremost, it may become a weaker democratic force. Commercial media also may be useful to capitalism in generating a political culture that is more enthusiastic about capitalism and suspicious of capitalism's critics. In short, a cursory analysis of the U.S. media industries suggests troubling implications for the classic notion of a free press—and therefore for democracy—in which everyone has a realistic opportunity to communicate with others. We would expect, instead, a media system that would serve the interests of the wealthy and denigrate the interests of those at the bottom of the social pecking order.

Hence, even if one accepts that the U.S. economy functions more effectively with a highly commercialized media system, it does not mean that democracy is best served by such a system. In liberal and democratic theory, democracy must be in the driver's seat, and the type of media system and economy that develop can be justified only to the extent that they best meet the needs of the people, not vice versa. Ultimately, one must hold to the conviction that the media system that best serves democratic values will contribute to generating an economic system most responsive to the genuine needs of the population. At the same time, if one accepts that it is proper for a society's economy to be capitalistic, commercial control of media might sound more acceptable, especially if there is little awareness of policy alternatives. In a capitalist society, the requirements of political democracy do not compete on an equal basis with the exigencies of the market. Rather, there is a bias toward the market.

But this bias in policy debates toward the existing economic structure does not mandate the turn to market control over media any more than it mandates market control over education systems, electoral systems, or religion. Even more important for our purposes, different shades of market-regulated media systems exist based upon different choices in policies. The very nature of markets is influenced, if not explicitly determined, by government policies. Capitalist economies have coexisted with media systems that have had significant noncommercial and nonprofit elements over the years. In many nations they have cohabited—if not exactly had a successful marriage— through a good portion of the twentieth century. Even in the context of contemporary capitalism, significant changes in the media system would not require a radical change in the economy's structure. While it may be self-evident that a socialist or a critic of capitalism would have severe reservations about media policies that generate a profit-driven media system, one can be a proponent of capitalism and deplore rabidly "pro-capitalist" media policies. The British actor John Cleese observes that "capitalism is the best system" only if its profit-obsessed logic is constrained. Cleese points to contemporary media as a prime example of "inferior" damn-the-torpedoes capitalism: "I would rather live in Czechoslovakia under Dubcek than work for a newspaper run by Rupert Murdoch."[15]

We need to bury the notions that media are "naturally" commercial and that government has been and is an innocent bystander (or nonproductive intruder) in the process of creating media systems. Moreover, if media are necessary institutions for a healthy democracy and if the nature and logic of the media system result from explicit government policies, then debates over the fundamental nature of media policies will determine the caliber of the media system. Therefore, I am as concerned with the caliber and nature of the public debates surrounding media policies as I am with the policies themselves.

In particular, I will devote most of the attention in this chapter to what are termed *critical junctures*, those historical moments when the policy-making options are relatively broad and the policies put in place will set the media system on a track that will be difficult to reroute for decades, even generations.[16] Critical junctures are another way to say that society holds a "constitutional convention" of sorts to deal with the problem of the media. At these points there tends to be much greater public criticism of media systems and policies and much more organized public participation than during less tumultuous periods. Critical junctures can come about when important new media technologies emerge, when the existing media system enters a crisis, or when the political climate changes sufficiently to call accepted policies into question or to demand new ones. When two or all three factors kick in, there is a high probability of a critical juncture; at these historical moments, opportunities to recast the media that would be nearly impossible under normal circumstances can materialize.

## U.S. Media System Not "Naturally" Profit Driven

It is one thing to assert that the U.S. media system is not naturally the province of large profit-driven corporations; it is another thing to demonstrate it. History indicates that the idea that this nation was founded on what is erroneously called a "libertarian" theory of the press—that government should let business run media to maximize profit—does not hold up under scrutiny. Media policy making has always been of paramount importance in the United States. The Constitution and the Bill of Rights contain numerous passages that still directly and indirectly create and shape our media system, either on their own or through the legislation, regulations, and court decisions that were later made on their basis. Media-related concerns permeate the political discourse of the revolutionary and constitutional era, and many politicians of those times—most notably, Madison and Jefferson—understood the vital importance of astute media policies for laying the foundation for a viable republic. Three constitutional provisions in particular provide blueprints for the media system's construction.

First, Article 1, Section 8 of the Constitution authorizes Congress to establish copyright "to promote the Progress of Science and the useful Arts, by securing for limited Times to Authors and Inventors the exclusive Right to Distribute Writings and Discoveries."[17] Copyright addresses the "public good" nature of media property that distinguishes it from all other industries. When one consumes a public good, it does not diminish the ability of others to consume it as well. If I read a book, someone else can read the same book, or a copy of it, and we can both enjoy it. Such is not the same for an automobile or a hamburger. In this context, the problem was that if anyone could publish a book without the author's permission, the price would be low and the public would benefit, but the author would not receive much or any compensation, so there would be no incentive to write books. Copyright was an explicit government intervention—an artificial government-created and government-enforced anti-free market mechanism—to give authors (or publishers) a legal monopoly over their books for a "limited" time period to ensure the incentive to produce books. In its best light, copyright was a policy implemented not just to throw a bone to authors but rather to benefit society by encouraging cultural production. In fact, commercial publishers were eager to see copyright put in place and provided a strong force behind its adoption. It is difficult to imagine how book publishing and many subsequent media industries could have existed as commercial institutions without copyright protection.[18]

Second, whereas copyright was a somewhat obscure topic in the Constitution until recently, the same cannot be said for what is generally understood as the main media policy plank in the Constitution's Bill of Rights, the First Amendment: "Congress shall make no law respecting an establishment of religion, or prohibiting the free exercise thereof; or abridging the freedom of speech, or of the press; or the right of people peaceably to assemble, and to petition the government for a redress of grievances." In the context of the late eighteenth century, this was a revolutionary policy statement concerning liberal freedoms and democratic society; such freedoms were barely given even rhetorical support anywhere in the world at the time. Indeed, it remains a revolutionary statement in the twenty-first century. Numerous great thinkers have been so taken by the powerful ideas embedded in the First Amendment that they have proclaimed themselves First Amendment "absolutists." The question then becomes what is it, exactly, that the First Amendment absolutely protects? This is arguably most difficult when attempting to decipher the meaning of the free press clause, one of the five core freedoms listed in the First Amendment.

A common contemporary "absolutist" notion of the free press argues that the Founders meant that the government should never be involved with media, commercial or otherwise. A core problem that plagues much contemporary thinking about the free press clause is that the terms *free speech* and *free press* are used interchangeably.[19] And in this union of free speech with free press, the former gets almost all the attention, while the conclusions are often applied without qualification to the latter. In a representative example, a classic text on the First Amendment collapses its discussion of freedom of the press into its chapter on freedom of speech and never even mentions the press.[20] So if one holds that the government should not stop a person from speaking on a street corner, then, ipso facto, the government should not stop commercial media from doing whatever they wish to do. What these positions tend to neglect is that while free speech and free press are similar or even interchangeable on some matters, they are quite distinct on others. Unique problems accompany constitutional protection of a free press, its political economy if you will, and these tend to be shunted aside when the discussion is framed solely in terms of free speech. Both are separate concerns, otherwise *there would have been no need for both to be included in the First Amendment.*

Specifically, engaging in the free press (using the media) is typically an industrial enterprise requiring considerable resources. Unlike speech, it has not been open to everyone. Also unlike speech, how the press system is structured will go a long way toward determining what ideas get heard and what ideas get silenced, even before a government commissar brings down the heavy hand of censorship. The legal scholar Michael Kent Curtis calls these institutional factors "the second constitution" in view of their centrality for a free press.[21] It is difficult to extrapolate from the Constitution a sense of what "free press" means because the press system of the 1790s was so radically different from ours. But it is clear that the Founders understood the importance of industrial structure and subsidy to the formation of a viable free press. This was not an area to be left to the whims of investors or the market or, more broadly, to an unregulated, nongovernmental sector.

To be blunt, the press in the early republic was not seen as an engine of capital accumulation, as merely one of many areas in which investors might put their capital to generate maximum returns in the marketplace. The press was highly partisan and integrally linked to the political process. Government printing contracts were for generations used by federal and state governments explicitly to subsidize the dominant partisan newspapers in Washington, D.C., and across the nation. It was not until the establishment of the U.S. Government Printing Office in 1860 that the practice ended. Likewise, the U.S. State Department was authorized by Congress to issue printing contracts to as many as three newspapers in every state and territory, for the purpose of publishing the federal laws.[22] This program stopped only in the 1870s.

Even this capsule history does not do justice to the way in which the press system was consciously subsidized as a fourth estate in the first several generations of the republic. In many respects "newspaper politics" were the heart and soul of all politics in the first few generations of U.S. history.[23] By the 1790s, and for decades thereafter, editors were seen as politicians and were treated accordingly. The popular political movements of the period depended upon printing contracts to subsidize their presses. When Jefferson assumed office in 1801, he aggressively coordinated both federal and state printing contracts to subsidize a press to counteract the Federalists. He arranged for printing subsidies for Samuel Harrison Smith to establish the *National Inteligencer,* which would become the *New York Times* and *Washington Post* of its day, though expressly committed to support Jeffersonian politics. Entering the White House in 1829, Andrew Jackson "elevated patronage of the press to a new level." He devoted $25,000 per year to the editor of his Washington-based newspaper and assigned fifty-nine editors to "plush political appointments."[24]

This episode in U.S. press history is important for two reasons. First, the freedom of the press clause appears more directly concerned with a functioning democracy. If the party in power could outlaw the opposition press, it would effectively terminate its opposition. This was not an abstract concern. During the Adams administration, the Federalists used the Alien and Sedition Acts to muzzle the Jeffersonian press. Second, ordinary Americans, at least those of the literate white male variety, were unusually interested in politics compared to other eras. Perhaps the nature of the press system had something to do with that. Its success hinged on a variety of well-subsidized viewpoints, not just those of the party in power, and new political groups had a chance to enter the fray. The historian of the *National Intelligencer* concluded that the subsidized system produced a caliber of journalism "that in many ways has not since been equaled on an intellectual level."[25]

Recent research has again and again repudiated the notion that the intent of the free press clause in the First Amendment was to empower individuals in the marketplace to do as they pleased, regardless of the implications for society as a whole. Such a notion violated the tenor of the times *in toto.* "A mountain of historical research," the leading historian of the free press tradition in Colonial and Revolutionary America observes, "finds in early American political discourse a stress on civic virtue and public, rather than private, good." All who argued for press liberty "defended the right to press liberty not for individual expression in our current, increasingly self-indulgent sense but rather so that the community might hear and judge the merit of others' views."[26] Akhil Reed Amar suggests that the First Amendment, especially the free press clause, was motivated by popular opposition to the preponderantly antidemocratic nature of the federal government, as devised in the Constitution.[27]

The writings of Jefferson and Madison attest to the distinct social function of the free press.[28] Jefferson, in particular, saw freedom of the press as the foundation of popular democracy and as protection against elite rule. "If once they [the people] become inattentive to the public affairs," he wrote his friend Edward Carrington, "you and I, and Congress and Assemblies, Judges and Governors, shall all become wolves." Ironically, Jefferson's letter to Carrington is sometimes taken as arguing that the government should let private interests rule the press and let the chips fall where they may. Here is the most cited passage, but I include the follow-up sentence, which is sometimes omitted. "The basis of our governments being the opinion of people," Jefferson wrote, "the very first object should be to keep that right; and were it left to me to decide whether we should have a government without newspapers, or newspapers without government, I should not hesitate a moment to prefer the latter. *But I should mean that every man should receive those papers, and be capable of reading them.*" The implication of this final sentence is that it is not enough to negatively protect the press system. Active promotion is necessary to ensure universal distribution of public information to competent citizens. In other words, the public's right to hear a variety of voices and properly digest their messages is the central platform of a democracy.[29] On another occasion, Jefferson remarked, "An enlightened citizenry is Indispensable for the proper functioning of a republic."[30] As Madison famously put it, "A popular Government without popular information or the means of acquiring it, is but a Prologue to a Farce or a tragedy or perhaps both." And such a free press, they argued, came as the result of explicit government policies and subsidies that would create it; to think otherwise was nonsensical.

More broadly, as Richard John, the leading historian of government communication policy in the eighteenth and nineteenth centuries has emphasized, only in the 1840s did discussion of "private enterprise" become widespread in U.S. political discourse. The notions of entrepreneurs and free markets were almost entirely absent in the early republic, as was the idea that the press was or should be a commercial activity set up solely to meet the needs of press owners. It was an unthinkable idea. As John concludes, "A commitment to energetic government in service of the public good has long been recognized as one of the principal legacies of the American Revolution."[31]

My point is not to argue about the "original intent" of the First Amendment and urge the Supreme Court to radically revise its interpretation of the free press clause on that basis. My point is to discredit the position that freedom of the press means strictly the right of private individuals to do as they please in the realm of media—regardless of the social implications—to suit their own (invariably) commercial interests. That notion has almost nothing to do with the Founders' intent or with our press system's evolution. The turn to a more market-based notion of a "free press" came gradually with the emergence of powerful private, profit-driven media. Nothing in the First Amendment mandated this interpretation. Had the United States evolved in a different manner, we would have no doubt had a different interpretation of the First Amendment. Yet while freedom of the press is a malleable policy, it is not Silly Putty. Even today the First Amendment is not widely interpreted in the purely commercial terms that corporate media and its advocates proclaim. In the Supreme Court's seminal 1927 *Whitney v. California* case, Justice Louis Brandeis concluded: "Those who won our independence believed that the final end of the State was to make men free to develop their faculties; . . . that the greatest menace to freedom is an inert people; that public discussion is a political duty; and that this should be a fundamental principle of American government."[32] Jefferson and Madison live, even if it appears at times that they are on life support.

The commercial interpretation of a free press has been in ascendance for much of the past quarter century, if not longer. Proponents assert that this right is absolute, because the First Amendment says "no law." Therefore capitalists can do as they please in the realm of media and they need answer only to their bottom lines; the market will prove to be a superior regulator of the press. If the journalism is atrocious and the culture hyper-commercialized, if the public is uninformed or misinformed, if self-governance is a sham, the fault is not the press system but the moronic citizens who demand such fare and reward those who provide it. The government can't do a damned thing about it except indirectly, through improving education so that the next generation will not be composed of idiots. (Yet advocates of this commercial version of the First Amendment tend to correlate highly with those who are opposed to expanding and enhancing education, so it is largely a rhetorical point.) From this perspective, the connection between a free press and democracy, which inspired this nation's founders, is dead.

This commercial interpretation of the free press clause does not go unchallenged. A much more progressive interpretation of the First Amendment has held its ground, inspired by the work of people such as Alexander Meiklejohn and Supreme Court Justice Hugo Black. Black was a legendary First Amendment "absolutist," but he was no commercialist when it came to a free press. Government censorship was not the only threat to a free press, and it was not the only legitimate public concern. In his famous opinion in the 1945 *Associated Press v. U.S.* case, Black defended the government's right to regulate media ownership: "The First Amendment, far from providing an argument against application of the Sherman Act, here provides powerful reasons to the contrary. That Amendment rests on the assumption that the widest possible dissemination of information from diverse and antagonistic sources is essential to the welfare of the public, that a free press is a condition of a free society. . . . Freedom to publish means freedom for all and not for some."[33] According to the progressive perspective, then, the right to a free press is a social right to a diverse and effective press system enjoyed by all Americans, not just media corporations or wealthy owners of commercial media. The First Amendment thus not only permits but indeed *requires* positive government activities to promote a free press, much as it has done with postal and printing subsidies.[34] As constitutional law professor Burt Neuborne puts it, otherwise you are left with a "First Amendment for the rich."[35] Prior restraint by the government should be opposed—and proponents of this perspective take a backseat to no one in their opposition to government censorship—but it is not to be seen as the sole government activity concerning the press.

Two distinct interpretations of the First Amendment for media have emerged over the course of the twentieth century. In the realm of broadcasting, the progressive interpretation holds; in 1969 the Supreme Court ruled in *Red Lion Broadcasting Co. v. FCC* that the First Amendment is a social right of the entire population to have a radio and television system that best serves its democratically determined needs. The First Amendment privileges of the commercial broadcasters are secondary and they must meet publicly determined public interest standards to keep their monopoly broadcasting licenses. With regard to print and most other media, the commercialist position is increasingly influential and treats the First Amendment as a license for the media to do as they please. A concerted campaign by progressives in the Meiklejohnian tradition to extend the social interpretation of the First Amendment from broadcasting to newspapers in the 1970s failed in the 1974 case *Miami Herald v. Tornillo*. Since then, commercial broadcasters have been working the court system to see that they get accorded the same First Amendment privileges as other media. That would, in effect, privatize the broadcast spectrum, remove broadcasting from public control, and constitute a gift of tens, even hundreds, of billions of dollars in public property to a small number of large private firms. Seen that way, the First Amendment becomes a policy with significant economic as well as political implications.

## Subsidizing the Press

The third pertinent section of the Constitution regarding media policy gave Congress the power "to establish Post Offices and Post Roads." The resulting Post Office Act of 1792 was arguably one of the most significant pieces of legislation in the nation's history; as Richard R. John observes, the post office was "rapidly transformed into a dynamic institution that would exert a major influence on American commerce, politics, and political thought."[36] Theda Skocpol notes that "the postal system was the biggest enterprise of any kind in the preindustrial United States."[37] As John puts it, "For the vast majority of Americans, the postal system was the central government." It was the largest single employer in the country.

What makes this crucial for our discussion, and what is striking upon review, is that the post office was primarily a medium of mass communication. In 1794 newspapers made up 70 percent of post office traffic; by 1832 the figure had risen to well over 90 percent. The crucial debate in the 1792 Congress was how much to charge newspapers to be sent through the mails. All parties agreed that Congress should permit newspapers to be mailed at a price well below actual cost—to be subsidized—to encourage their production and distribution. Postal subsidies of newspapers would become perhaps the largest single expenditure of the federal government. In Congress, the range of debate was between those who wished to charge newspapers a nominal fee for postage and those who wanted to permit newspapers the use of the mails absolutely free of charge. The latter faction was supported by Benjamin Franklin's grandson, the editor Benjamin Bache, who argued that any postal charge would open the door to commercial pressures that would be unacceptable because they would "check if not entirely put a stop to the circulation of periodical publications." James Madison wrote to Thomas Jefferson that even a token fee for postage was a "tax" on newspapers that was "an insidious forerunner of something worse."[38]

Although those favoring free delivery did not prevail, pressure from both printers and the citizenry made the only relevant issue for Congress for subsequent generations whether to eliminate the postal charge. It was seen as a public subsidy for democracy. As John C. Calhoun put it, "the mail and the press are the nerves of the body politic."[39] Abolitionists and dissident political groups led the fight to maintain and extend the postal subsidy of newspapers. In 1851, Congress granted free postal privileges to weekly newspapers within its home county. Within a year 20 percent of newspapers being mailed qualified for free postage.[40] A version of this policy continued into the twentieth century, and postal rates on newspapers were never raised during the nineteenth century.

By the middle of the nineteenth century the consequences of the large postal subsidy—the fee was "trifling," even to Bache—had been the "almost illimitable circulation of newspapers through the mails," as one journalist remarked in 1851. As John concludes, the 1792 act "transformed the role of the newspaper press in American public life."[41] In his *Democracy in America,* Alexis de Tocqueville wrote with astonishment of the "incredibly large" number of periodicals in the United States.[42] This had nothing to do with some notion of a laissezfaire, commercially driven newspaper market—presumed by modern-day absolutists as the sine qua non of the Founders' notion of a free press. As Timothy Cook concludes, "Public policy from the outset of the American Republic focused explicitly on getting the news to a wide readership, and chose to support news outlets by taking on costs of delivery and, through printers' exchanges, of production."[43] This was enlightened democratic policy making, and it was successful. As with the First Amendment, the United States was leading the world.

The post office regulatory model was challenged when the telegraph became a competitor of sorts in the 1840s and 1850s. The idea that the postal service should be "privatized" was rejected categorically.[44] At first there was considerable public demand that telegraphy be made a government monopoly like the mails, but those favoring market regulation won the day. It was a measure, to some extent, of the increasing power of capital and notions of private enterprise in the political culture. By the end of the Civil War, however, telegraphy had gone from a competitive industry to a booming private monopoly under the control of Western Union. The private monopoly control over telegraphy was one of the most incendiary issues of the Gilded Age: between 1866 and 1900 some seventy bills were proposed to reform the industry, usually calling for some sort of nationalization.[45] This private control, as opposed to the systems in Europe in which the government operated the monopoly telegraph service, meant that Western Union could use its "natural monopoly" to favor more lucrative accounts from large business customers over smaller businesses and individuals. As such, economic historians regard the growth of Western Union as a major factor in the dominance of big business in American life.[46] For radicals, populists, socialists, and labor, nationalizing the telegraph was right up there with nationalizing the railroads as a core demand. Telegraphy faded in importance with the rise of radio and, especially, telephony in the early twentieth century. A similar public outcry greeted the private monopoly of telephony under the aegis of AT&T in the early twentieth century. After decades of political struggle, a compromise of sorts was reached: the telephone system was a private monopoly but one that was, unlike Western Union, theoretically held to strict government regulation.

The control and regulation of telecommunication systems like telegraphy and telephony are important and underrated components of media policy making. As with the post office, they have significantly affected the press system. Western Union was instrumental in revolutionizing journalism, the media system, and the broader political economy. It used its monopoly power to collaborate in the development of the Associated Press, a monopoly news service run in cooperative fashion by the largest newspaper publishers. This relationship was mostly unknown to the public. With exclusive access to the wires—Western Union refused to let potential competitors use its wires—AP became the only wire news service in the nation. So as not to offend any of its thousands of clients, it encouraged a journalism that was seemingly nonpartisan—hence it contributed heavily to the rise of journalistic "objectivity." Because newspapers without access to the AP were at a decided competitive disadvantage, it also discouraged competition in local markets. Likewise, the AP had extraordinary influence in the way it covered national politics because it served as the main voice for most major newspapers. Needless to say, it invariably presented a voice that took the side of business interests.[47]

Not surprisingly, the news coverage provided by AP and the major newspapers of the late nineteenth century strongly advocated keeping telegraphy a private and unregulated monopoly.[48] Western Union's interests were well taken care of by major U.S. newspapers. It was the first clear example of how concentrated press power could shape public debates over media and communication policy. It also highlights how much the press had moved from being a feisty fourth estate in service to democracy—or, less grandly, a political institution devoted to a variety of partisan causes—to a commercial institution dedicated to the rule of big business. Some members of Congress who opposed Western Union noted the monopoly's effect on newspaper concentration and content and went so far as to characterize the struggle for a publicly owned or regulated telegraph system as a battle to preserve a free press.[49] Dan Schiller's pioneering research reveals the broad-based and radical movement between the 1880s and the 1910s for reconstructing the corporate telecommunications systems; a core organizing principle was to break the "infernal bondage" imposed by Western Union and the AP.[50]

One can only imagine how the telegraph might have influenced the media system and journalism differently if it had been a national monopoly like the post office and had people like James Madison been in Congress arguing for a well-subsidized diverse press. Along similar lines in the 1920s, AT&T's telephone network was instrumental in getting the NBC national radio network off the ground. The implication of having a single monopoly control telephony and national radio broadcasting was such that AT&T was required by the government to divest its broadcasting interests.

Although it does not appear in the U.S. Constitution, one other crucial policy was common in state constitutions, and prescribed by Jefferson and John Adams: public education. The Northwest Ordinance of 1787 provided the sentiment, even the wording, for many state constitutions concerning state-funded public education: "Being necessary to good government and the happiness of mankind, schools and the means of education shall forever be encouraged" by the state legislatures.[51] In spirit, one can see the strong link between public education and a free press as democratic institutions. Moreover, public schools formed an important market for books by creating literate citizens. Public libraries, also funded by state government, offered another avenue for individual education. The commercial publishing industries would have been a shadow of themselves—and much of it would not have existed—without these massive public subsidies.[52]

These subsidies point to another crucial manner in which governments shape and influence media systems: as purchasers and as advertisers. During the 1950s and 1960s, aggressive purchasing by the federal government of nonfiction books for its overseas libraries subsidized a veritable golden age of book publishing. Controversial and experimental work that would never have met market criteria otherwise was published. The sharp decline in library purchases of university press books in the past decade—due in part to monopoly control of academic journals that has driven their prices beyond the means of university libraries—threatens to eliminate the publication of significant scholarly work that was routinely published in the past.[53] Furthermore, since its inception the government has developed into a major purchaser of many forms of commercial media content, not just books. During World War II, for example, federal government purchases counted for some 90 percent of the Disney Corporation's sales.[54] The government has also become a major advertiser.

In the twentieth century, government media policies and subsidies provided the basis for much of commercial and corporate media's growth. The value of monopoly licenses to scarce broadcast channels, monopoly cable TV franchises, and copyright protection—all granted and enforced by the government and all provided at no charge to commercial interests—runs into the hundreds of billions of dollars. This is no "natural" free market. It is a market created and shaped by the government.

Understood this way, the crucial issue then becomes how these media policies and subsidies are generated. What is the nature of the policy-making process? In the first generations of the republic, these policies were subject to relatively widespread informed public participation and debate. The resulting policies reflected such public involvement. Over the course of the nineteenth century and certainly by the twentieth century, as large commercial interests began to dominate media markets, the public's role began to shrink. Nevertheless, the transition to a corporate-controlled, advertising-supported media system was not seamless; at certain moments core policy fights burst onto the political stage. The most important juncture was the emergence of radio broadcasting.

## The Rise of Broadcasting

In the United States, as elsewhere, controlling and structuring radio broadcasting posed an immediate and unavoidable political problem. The pro-commercial policy model deployed for other new media, like national magazines or motion pictures or recorded music, was simple and followed the "small *c*" conservative impulse: Let commercial interests figure out how to make the most money and then write laws and regulations to protect their system. Policy making, from this perspective, should not protect public interests. But this approach was a nonstarter for radio broadcasting. Even a stridently pro-market policy required explicit, aggressive regulation by the government, and there was no consensus even among business interests about how to do it. In broadcasting, the rhetorical notion of laissez-faire media policy making was reduced to the absurd.

Four factors explain why broadcasting, far more than any other new medium, generated such a critical juncture for policy that set the terms for much of media policy making for subsequent generations. First and foremost, there were a limited number of frequencies for broadcasting. Only a small portion of those who would like to broadcast would be able to do so. When more than one broadcaster used the same frequency in the same region it created interference and static that made reception difficult, even impossible. The spectrum was in the public domain, and there was no sentiment, even among capitalists, to privatize it, even if that was possible. It fell upon governments, whether they liked it or not, to determine who would be able to secure monopoly rights to the scarce number of frequencies and who would not. Second, when broadcasting emerged, there was still no consensus that private companies seeking to maximize their profits regardless of the social implications rightfully and unquestionably should dominate. A rich legacy of serving the public, not owners, still prospered. (Commercial broadcasters would acknowledge this sentiment in their self-regulation codes.) Third, the preceding concerns were magnified by the *power* of radio broadcasting. This revolutionary medium could bring voices from around the world into people's homes at all hours of the day. Space and time collapsed as had never been imagined. Fourth, the federal government's other concerns affected radio. The U.S. Navy in particular had been instrumental in developing the technology and public subsidies had fueled its invention. The government also wanted to use radio for its own purposes, such as military communication.

I have written a detailed history of this critical juncture elsewhere.[55] For our purposes the following is worth noting. The pioneers of U.S. radio broadcasting in the early 1920s included many nonprofit institutions. At this time there was no sense that radio broadcasting could be profitable. Government policy making never authorized commercial broadcasting because it did not yet exist. The Radio Act of 1927 was emergency legislation that established the Federal Radio Commission (FRC) to bring order to the airwaves. Because many more broadcasters were operating than the spectrum could possibly accommodate, the FRC was supposed to award licenses on the basis of the vague admonition to select those applicants that best served the "public interest." By the late 1920s the two main national networks, NBC and CBS, began to see potential profit in creating national chains of stations supported by the sale of advertising. The new FRC, acting with minimal oversight by Congress, basically implemented a plan drafted by commercial broadcasting engineers and lawyers to turn almost all of the best channels over to commercial broadcasters, especially those affiliated with NBC and CBS, and to acknowledge advertising as the only legitimate form of support for broadcasters. In just a few years, network commercial broadcasting became an enormous and highly profitable industry in the United States—during the Great Depression, no less. Nonprofit and noncommercial broadcasting, which accounted for roughly half the stations in 1924 or 1925, basically fell off the map. By 1934 nonprofit broadcasters had virtually ceased to exist for most Americans.

The Radio Act of 1927 was temporary legislation and the FRC had to be renewed by Congress annually, so these issues were debated until the passage of the Communications Act of 1934, which established the Federal Communications Commission (FCC) as a permanent regulatory body. During these seven years a feisty broadcast reform movement composed of displaced educational broadcasters, religious groups, organized labor, farmers, women's groups, journalists, and civil libertarians like the ACLU coalesced. Its existence reflected the profound public dissatisfaction with advertising-drenched radio broadcasting. The movement bitterly complained that commercial broadcasting demonstrated a grotesque misuse of a scarce and valuable public resource. Commercial interests had hijacked radio broadcasting. A genuine public debate about the radio broadcasting system was required. Proponents assumed that any public debate would inevitably lead to a system with a powerful non-profit and noncommercial broadcasting sector and in which commercial broadcasters would play a subordinate role. The reformers were inspired by the British Broadcasting Corporation (BBC), which showed what well-funded public broadcasting could accomplish, though few favored a centralized and exclusively noncommercial radio system. The reformers were also inspired by a similar reform movement in Canada that halted a purely commercial radio system and forced the establishment of the public Canadian Broadcasting Corporation (CBC) in 1932.

Commercial broadcasters responded to this challenge as if their very lives were in danger. In the early 1930s advocates for nonprofit broadcasting got major reform bills to the floor of the House or the Senate, where they had significant support. Broadcasters wielded all their political skills to undercut their adversaries and became obsessed with minimizing or eliminating public participation in or awareness of broadcast policy debates. While they loudly spoke of the public's love of commercial radio, they knew they could not let the public express this love in a debate over how the industry should be structured. Indeed, the radio lobby was adamant that radio regulation was so "complex" that only experts, not even members of Congress, should be permitted to make policy. They argued that FRC members—many of whom would go on to lucrative careers in commercial broadcasting—should be solely permitted to make broadcasting a viable profit-generating industry. Through their trade association, the National Association of Broadcasters (NAB), the industry developed an elaborate public relations campaign to promote commercial broadcasting as an inherently democratic and American system. It would be difficult to exaggerate the power of the NAB as a lobby; in addition to having money it also controlled access to the airwaves for politicians.

The crucial political development came in December 1933 when the NAB reached an agreement with the American Newspaper Publishers Association: the broadcasters would not compete in providing news if the publishers would not support the broadcast reformers on Capitol Hill and, tacitly, in their pages. With the passage of the Communications Act and the formation of the FCC in 1934, the NAB accomplished its mission. Congress no longer debated the propriety of commercial broadcasting; it was now a system to be regulated by the FCC outside the light of public attention. With no sense of irony, as soon as the law passed and the system was entrenched, in a 180-degree reversal, the NAB began to characterize any government regulation as a violation of broadcasters' First Amendment rights. Commercial broadcasters, who received what would eventually total in the hundreds of billions of dollars in value through the grant of monopoly broadcast licenses at no charge, went from statists to libertarians almost overnight.

This outcome set the pattern for subsequent debates over new media technologies. FM radio, shortwave, and television all presented innovations threatening to engender a critical juncture, a public reappraisal of broadcasting that could lead to its reformation. But in each case only a whisper of the radio broadcasting policy debate resulted; policy makers simply assumed that the logic of the existing commercial broadcasting system would naturally dominate the new technologies. To the general public, not to mention members of Congress, there was no sense that a debate was even possible, so the matter was given no thought.[56] The FCC's plan for the development of television was a particularly shameful episode. FCC chairman Charles Denny pushed for a plan that basically gave NBC and CBS near monopoly control, and six months later Denny left the FCC to triple his salary as an NBC executive.[57] Later, cable television became a regulated monopoly service in local communities. The handful of firms that came to own most of the cable TV systems were able to parlay this market power into the eventual ownership of many successful cable TV channels.[58] To this day, most of the largest media firms have been built around government monopoly licenses to either broadcast channels or cable franchises.

If anything, the government played an even larger role in subsidizing subsequent communication technologies. The development of the Comsat communication satellite system by the government in the late 1950s and early 1960s was a monumental accomplishment; after the government had assumed all the risk and had gotten it off the ground, its takeover by private interests behind closed doors and with the assistance of government regulators reeked of corruption.[59] It barely raised an eyebrow in Washington, however, because it followed the pattern established in 1934.

But the Communications Act of 1934 did not totally deregulate and privatize broadcasting and telecommunication. To the contrary, the law made it clear that government monopoly rights to broadcasting and telecommunication licenses were to be granted with the condition that the commercial recipient serve the "public interest." In theory, recipients of these licenses were not to be regarded as pure profit-motivated firms but rather as public service firms. Broadcasters were therefore required to include some programming they would have ordinarily avoided if they were strictly profit-maximizing, and it was this less commercially viable public service programming that justified their possession of the valuable monopoly broadcast license. Cable TV systems, in a similar manner, were expected to make concessions to the public interest to justify their monopoly franchises, usually by setting aside channels for public access and noncommercial use.[60]

The caliber and intensity of public interest regulation of commercial broadcasters depended very much on the political temper of the times. During a brief period in the 1940s, when Clifford Durr was on the FCC and Dallas Smythe was its chief economist, the FCC proposed an aggressive regulatory regime typified by a report demanding real public service programming by commercial broadcasters, called *The Blue Book*.[61] Over the years consultants such as Charles Siepmann and FCC members such as Frieda

Hennock, Newton Minow, and Nicholas Johnson used what leverage they could to up the public service ante for commercial broadcasters.[62] But the private and commercial domination of the broadcast system was inviolable. After the 1940s, the high water mark for broadcast regulation came in the late 1960s and early 1970s, when public interest groups associated with the likes of Ralph Nader began to work the corridors of regulatory agencies with mild success.

The FCC did place some regulations on commercial broadcasters. The most notable public service requirement was the Fairness Doctrine, inspired by *The Blue Book*, which required commercial broadcasters to give ample time to matters of public importance and to provide a range of viewpoints on controversial issues.[63] In addition, ownership restrictions limited the number of radio and television stations that a single broadcaster could own. The theory went that it would be improper to let individual firms possess too many of these monopoly licenses or use the profits generated from having a broadcast license to gobble up all the other non-broadcast media. While the commercial basis of the industry was beyond reproach, the FCC had political and popular support to keep ownership relatively diverse. (These policies also had the support of many advertisers as well as small station owners, who knew they would have a dubious future if ownership caps were lifted.) In 1975 the FCC prohibited a single firm from owning both a daily newspaper and a broadcast station in the same market.[64] Likewise, firms were not permitted to own a TV station and be the monopoly cable TV system provider in the same community. To prevent broadcast networks from using their monopoly power to dominate TV show production, the FCC adopted the "financial interest and syndication rules" that prevented the networks from owning prime-time programs, hence fostering an independent TV production sector.[65] Foreign ownership of U.S. broadcast stations is also prohibited, on national security grounds.[66]

With the exception of the ownership restrictions, broadcast regulation in the public interest has largely been a failure in the United States, even in the relatively enlightened 1940s and 1970s. The Fairness Doctrine, for example, was never enforced to require commercial broadcasters to do ample public affairs and controversial programming; instead, broadcasters used its provision to include more than one side of an issue as an excuse to offer as little public affairs programming as possible.[67] The reason for broadcast regulation's failure is obvious: for the system to work effectively, the FCC would have to review licenses rigorously when they came up for renewal and assign them to different applicants if the existing licensee was found to have been negligent in the provision of public service or to superior applicants even if the existing broadcaster had been adequate. This penalty was almost never leveled against a commercially successful broadcaster and was *never* used to punish a licensee for failing to meet the standards of the Fairness Doctrine.[68]

In a classic example of just how reluctant the FCC has been to tamper with commercial broadcast licensees, in the 1960s it refused to withdraw the license of an explicitly white supremacist station in Jackson, Mississippi, which had a 45 percent African American population. Finally, the U.S. District Court in the District of Columbia overturned the FCC, leaving Judge Warren Burger, later to be chief justice, to comment that the FCC was "beyond repair."[69] By 2003 FCC member Michael Copps characterized the license renewal process as a "farce," noting that it amounts to little more than mailing in a postcard.[70] The reason for this deplorable state was equally clear: commercial broadcasters represented such a powerful lobbying force that each effort by the FCC to enforce strict regulation—and there were only a few such cases—was met by howls of protest on Capitol Hill. Because there was no threat of losing a license for noncompliance, there was no reason to comply. It seemed far better for the NAB to trumpet the public service that stations provided voluntarily, almost none of which affected the stations' operations or bottom line in any appreciable manner.[71]

Today public service has degenerated into tragicomedy. By 2002, a study revealed that much of the do-gooder "public service" advertising—all that remained of broadcasters' public service activity—was relegated to the "wee hours of the night," when audiences were minuscule and it was impossible to sell much commercial advertising anyway.[72] An October 2003 survey of local TV stations in six markets determined that less than one-half of 1 percent of the programming went toward covering local public affairs, despite the fact that commitment to "localism" is considered a primary mechanism for broadcasters to serve the public interest. The survey concluded: "There is a near blackout of local public affairs."[73] When soliciting investors or doing business, on the other hand, even lip service about public service has ceased. "We're not in the business of providing news and information," Clear Channel CEO Lowry Mays told a business publication in 2003. "We're not in the business of providing well-researched music. We're simply in the business of selling our customers' products."[74]

The FCC has become the classic "captured" regulatory agency. The public, even Congress, is largely unaware of its activities, which receive little or no press attention except in the business pages as issues of interest to investors and managers. Most FCC members go on to lucrative careers with those they had been ostensibly regulating previously. As more than one skeptic has noted, when a commercial firm's executive comes before the FCC, the members do not know whether to regard him as someone to be regulated or as a possible future employer. Much of the data used by the FCC to make its policies have been spoon-fed to them by the broadcasting industry—data that is often "of very questionable verisimilitude," according to a public interest advocate.[75] While the rhetoric of regulation remains ensconced in public interest terminology, the logic of regulation has turned to the reality of making broadcasters profitable. In the minds of the broadcasters, this has always been the proper role of regulation and government media policy making. The "public interest" perspective has gravitated from striving for what would be best for the public and creating a system that best produces those results to what would be best for the public after the dominant firms maximize their profits. Their happiness is the starting point for all that follows, and it cannot be challenged. The system was structured in such a way that the public is nowhere to be found in the day-to-day functioning of the FCC.

But it would be misleading to dismiss the FCC as a meaningless puppet of the NAB. It is also a referee, arbitrating fights between the broadcasting, cable, and telecommunication sectors.[76] William Kennard recalled his education when he assumed the chair of the FCC in President Clinton's second term: "I came to the job feeling very strongly that the agency had become captive of corporate interests and was really not connecting to its core mission." Kennard asked several former FCC chairs to join him for lunch and explain to him how he could best do his new job. One pulled him aside and confided, "Bill, You have to realize that when you are chairman of the FCC, you're basically a referee of big money fights and they are fights between the rich on the one hand, and the very wealthy on the other. The key to being a successful chairman is to keep the power in equilibrium. So if you give something to one powerful lobby one week, you better balance it out by giving their opponents something the next week."

Kennard remarked that "after having lunch with him" he felt almost unspeakably "depressed." But his years at the FCC only reinforced the accuracy of that previous chair's assessment.[77] His successor, Michael Powell, acknowledged the same situation: "A day in the life of the FCC is listening to company after company argue for policy changes in their self-interest." Powell, though, seemed untroubled by this job description.[78]

It should be noted that even in the warped world of broadcast regulation, advocates of the public interest—that is, those not representing self-interested commercial organizations—have had some influence with the FCC and on Capitol Hill. But to be taken seriously—the ante for admission on Capitol Hill and at the FCC—these groups had to accept the commercial basis of the broadcasting system. The reformers could then only tweak the system to generate marginally better results. As a consequence, their range of legitimate options was often quite small, and their proposals were hardly dramatic enough to capture the public's imagination and support. It also did not help matters that press coverage was almost nonexistent. To have any hope for success, reformers have had to ally themselves with one corporate sector against another corporate sector. So it is that public interest groups tend to work with small TV and radio station owners to combat the networks and large station-owning groups.

Perhaps the most prominent public interest initiatives have been brought by civil rights and feminist groups to protest the lack of people of color or women in important media positions, the homogeneity of media owners, and the portrayal of race and gender issues in commercial journalism and entertainment programming. In particular, in the wake of the massive political movements of the 1960s and 1970s, groups pushed the FCC to become more aggressive in the review of licenses because all had been doled out between the 1920s and 1940s when anyone other than white men were essentially excluded from owning them.[79] Because these initiatives did not coincide with a critical juncture for the media, structural change and core media policies remained off-limits. Boycotting and otherwise pressuring the commercial interests were the only options for change.[80]

To most people and in most moments of history, the media system appears natural and immutable. Policy debates focus on marginal and tangential issues because core structures and policies are off-limits to criticism. In this environment, policy debates tend to gravitate to the elite level and public participation virtually disappears. After all, for most people, minor media policy issues are far down on the list of important topics. Sweeping media reform is unthinkable—and politically impossible. The public's elimination from the process is encouraged by the corruption of the U.S. political system, in which politicians tend to be comfortable with the status quo and not inclined to upset powerful commercial media owners and potential campaign contributors. The dominant media firms enjoy the power to control news coverage of debates over media policies; this is a power they have used shamelessly to trivialize, marginalize, and distort opposition to the status quo.

In the second half of the twentieth century, media policy making came to resemble the scene from *The Godfather II* in which Michael Corleone, Hyman Roth, and the heads of the U.S. gangster families meet on a patio in Havana to "divide" up pre-Communist Cuba. Roth ceremonially gives each gangster a piece of Cuba as he slices his birthday cake, which has the outline of Cuba on it. As Roth doles out the slices he applauds the Batista government for favoring private enterprise—that is, letting the gangsters plunder the country. The gangsters fight among themselves to get the biggest slice of

Cuba—indeed, the film revolves around this theme—but they agree that they alone should own Cuba. So it is with media policy making in the United States. Massive corporate lobbies duke it out with each other for the largest share of the cake, but it is their cake.

## The Neoliberal Period

Antidemocratic tendencies in media policy making have grown more powerful over the past quarter century. The period has signaled upheaval in U.S. media regulation, far more so than in any period since the critical juncture of the 1920s and 1930s. But the main story of the final two decades of the twentieth century has been the decisive increase in the business domination of media policy making. The rather extensive coterie of public interest activist groups that formed in the late 1960s and early 1970s to get public interest media regulation enhanced in Congress and at the FCC drifted for the most part into obscurity when it became clear that the possibility of achieving anything more than the smallest victory was close to zero. These groups were soon overshadowed by another wave of policy activists, often very well funded by comparison, who began working to see that public interest regulation was reduced and ultimately discontinued.[81]

This rigorous drive for so-called deregulation is based upon the "neoliberal" view that markets and profit making should be allowed to regulate every aspect of social life possible. By the late 1970s, broadcasting's traditional regulatory regime had begun to unravel. On the one hand, the existing public interest regulation was clearly ineffectual, and even political liberals were becoming disillusioned with the status quo. They did not like the commercial broadcasting system, but they were increasingly willing to accept that the regulatory process was as much the problem as any sort of solution. The case of airline deregulation was similar, and liberal Ted Kennedy of Massachusetts and President Jimmy Carter were instrumental in putting that in place. On the other hand, commercial media interests pushed ahead with their campaign to dismantle public interest regulation, arguing that markets could do a better job of regulation than government bureaucrats could. This campaign emphasized that new technologies—then cable and satellite broadcasting, later the Internet—eliminated the scarcity rationale for public interest regulation. The market could accomplish seamlessly and without coercion what the government could do only clumsily and inefficiently. The campaign was in part a well-financed public relations operation to promote and widely disseminate pro-deregulation arguments and to discredit and marginalize opposing views as akin to the flat-earth society worldview or totalitarianism. But it also was a big-ticket political juggernaut, working the court system, Congress, the White House, and the FCC simultaneously to reduce or eliminate the legal basis for public interest regulation of commercial media.

In theory, this impasse and the emergence of new digital communication technologies could have led to a critical juncture. The new technologies certainly offered the promise of a media world with far less dependence upon advertising, for example, and a much wider range of economically viable media producers. In a different political climate, change might have been possible. But with the 1980 election of Ronald Reagan, the neoliberal moment had commenced. Neoliberal ideology became hegemonic not only among Republicans but also in the Democratic Party of Bill Clinton, Al Gore, and

Joseph Lieberman. Differences remained on timing and specifies, but on the core issues both parties agreed that business was the rightful ruler over society.[82] It was a return to the 1920s, if not the Gilded Age of the late nineteenth century.

Few industries seized the neoliberal high ground as quickly or as firmly as the media and communication industries. A new generation of economists, with scholarly tomes published by the leading presses, trumpeted the value of applying market principles to all communication policy matters; as one of them put it, the *ancien régime* was "often dominated by ad hoc prescriptions premised on shaky economics applied to dubious histories."[83] These tended to be circular arguments—if you start from the presupposition that the market is infallible and appropriate to regulate media, it is awfully hard to justify anything that interferes with the market. Proper appreciation for free market competition and new technologies eliminated the need for public interest regulation, the industry argued, and such regulation certainly violated the free press and free speech clauses of the First Amendment. On these grounds the FCC eliminated the Fairness Doctrine in the 1980s, invoking the most eloquent phrases from the opinions of Supreme Court Justice William O. Douglas to do so. (Ironically, Douglas himself was a strong proponent of broadcast regulation in the public interest.)[84] Everyone from broadcasters to cable companies to advertisers claimed that any regulation of their affairs violated their First Amendment rights.[85]

Behind the mighty rhetoric, the stakes were clear. These corporations knew that if they were granted absolutist First Amendment protection, their existence and operations "would be placed beyond the reach of majorities," as Justice Robert Jackson once described the purpose of the Bill of Rights. Putting their legitimacy in question, even regulating them, would become vastly more difficult.[86] Or, as Herbert I. Schiller put it, the commercial "expansion" of the First Amendment protections to giant, monopolistic corporations led directly to the shrinking of democracy.[87]

Listen to the rhetoric and read the proclamations of the commercial broadcasters since the 1980s and one might think that as soon as onerous regulations like the Fairness Doctrine were eliminated companies could proceed unencumbered on their free market way. The truth of neoliberalism, however, is that while the rhetoric extols small government, free markets, competition, and entrepreneurial risk-taking, the reality is that a large government is doling out crucial contracts, monopoly licenses, and subsidies to huge firms in highly concentrated industries. Indeed, in the neoliberal environment, the only thing that changes aside from the market-worship rhetoric is that Washington is even *more* of an open trough filled with billions of dollars worth of goodies. Neo-liberalism simply reduces or eliminates the *idea* that government should represent the public interest vis-à-vis the corporate interest. There is no longer a meaningful conflict between the public and the corporate sector—public service is bunk—so politicians and regulators can serve corporations with impunity.

The corruption in media policy making culminated in the passage of the 1996 Telcommunications Act, arguably one of the most important pieces of U.S. legislation. The law rewrote the regulatory regime for radio, television, telephony, cable television, and satellite commuication—indeed, all of electronic communication including the Internet. It laid down the core values for the FCC to implement for generations. The operating premise of the law was that new communication technologies combined with an increased appreciation for the genius of the market rendered the traditional regulatory model moot. The solution therefore was to lift regulations and ownership restrictions from commercial media and communication companies, allow competition in the marketplace to develop, and reduce the government's role to that of protecting private property. There was virtually no dissent whatsoever to this legislation from either political party; the law sailed through both houses of Congress and was signed by a jubilant President Clinton in February 1996. Corporate CEOs regarded the bill as their "Magna Carta," and humanity was soon to enter an era of permanent and unprecedented economic growth and human happiness. The rhetoric of neoliberalism was at its most optimistic and flowery; as Thomas Frank remarked, thanks to the competition, deregulation, entrepreneurial genius, and the Internet, we were indeed becoming "One Market under God."[88] In actuality, however, the law merely amended the 1934 Communications Act; the statutory commitment to regulation in the public interest remained.

The details of how this law was drafted and passed have been chronicled elsewhere; herein the following points are worth noting.[89] The emergence of new communication technologies *did* require Congress to revisit the issue of regulation; the ability to use cable broadcasting wires and telephone wires to provide one another's services, to cite one example, would eventually undermine the technological rationale for having different regulatory systems for each system.[90] This was a critical juncture for media requiring a fundamental rethinking of communication regulation. According to democratic theory, it deserved the widespread and informed participation of as much of the political culture as possible. Ideally, it would have been the subject of contentious debate between political parties. Behind the lofty neoliberal platitudes, however, the drafting of the law was as corrupt and as antidemocratic as one could imagine. The world's most powerful lobbies squared off secretly to get the best concessions; free-market rhetoric notwithstanding, this was a mad dash to get government support for business, and the stakes were in the tens of billions of dollars. In a dramatic instance of collusion between media sectors, there was almost no press coverage—except in the business and trade press. Not surprisingly, Americans were uninformed on the law's consequences. One survey has found, for example, that only three Americans in ten understand that the public owns the airwaves, and only one American in ten knows that commercial broadcasters use the airwaves at no charge from the government.[91] The general public contributed to the legislation not at all; even the Washington-based public interest lobbying groups were kept out. This was high-stakes corruption, and penny-ante players were not invited.

When conflicts between the massive lobbies over which firms and sectors would get the best perks threatened to derail the bill in early 1996, the sides agreed to unite to pass the bill and then let the FCC work out the "deregulation" details. Their concern was that a gadfly like Ross Perot might make a political issue of the matter if it remained in Congress during the 1996 election. Once the law was in the safe hands of the FCC, the debates could be hidden from public view. Congress held no floor debate on the bill's core; most members had little or no idea of the law's contents when they voted for it. The notion that the Telecommunications Act was about promoting genuine competition was dubious from the outset—why would these powerful lobbies ram through a bill if it threatened their profitability?—although this point eluded members of Congress, not to mention the minuscule number of reporters who covered it. In truth, the bill promised the worst of both worlds: more concentrated ownership over communications with less possibility for regulation in the public interest. Accordingly, both the cable and the telecommunication industries have become significantly more concentrated since 1996, and customer complaints about lousy service have hit all-time highs. Cable industry rates for consumers have also shot up, increasing some 50 percent between 1996 and 2003.[92]

One of the more contentious areas during the backroom slugfests over the Telecommunications Act was media ownership. This was not exactly a neoliberal coming-out party. Large media owners despise these restrictions for self-evident reasons. As they get larger they enjoy economies of scale, face less competition, and increase profits. For years they have lobbied incessantly to get these ownership restrictions relaxed, if not eliminated. They faced significant opposition from small broadcast and independent media owners, who understood that they would be unable to compete if the caps were lifted. To the extent the public weighed in, there was no support for concentrated media ownership. In the 1980s and 1990s, under neoliberalism, ownership caps were gradually relaxed. With the 1996 Telecommunications Act, the big media companies went in for the kill, arguing that the caps were an outdated relic from a bygone era. In the age of the Internet and multichannel television, they claimed, the market could regulate media more efficiently and fairly than ownership policies could. In the world of converging media, it was unfair for the government to tie the hands of broadcast and cable-owning companies with ownership regulations while their competitors faced no similar handicaps.

The corporate campaign for eliminating media ownership rules flopped. Smaller media and members of Congress who did not like the idea of media concentration offered too much opposition. Indeed, going against the neoliberal flow, Senator Byron Dorgan nearly got majority support for an amendment to *tighten* TV station ownership regulations. The one media sector that had its media ownership caps significantly relaxed in the Telecom Act was radio. Big media companies had convinced enough small station owners that they would be better off with ownership "deregulation" and thereby minimized their opposition. The Telecom Act otherwise turned the matter over to the FCC, requiring it to reevaluate all of its media ownership rules every two years and change them if conditions had changed sufficiently to warrant such action. The crucial remaining rules were limits on the number of TV stations a single firm could hold in a single market or nationally, the limit on the number of cable TV systems a firm could own nationally, and bans on cross-ownership of cable TV systems and broadcast outlets in the same community or newspaper and broadcast outlets in the same community.[93]

The range of legitimate debate in the FCC after the passage of the 1996 Telecommunications Act remained locked in a neoliberal paradigm through the Clinton years. The Democratic FCC head William Kennard endorsed the notion that new technologies and competition eliminated the need for public interest regulation; he differed from hardcore neoliberals mostly on the question of timing. Kennard thought that ownership deregulation needed to be brought along slowly, to make sure that it actually led to some semblance of competition and not to monopolies.[94] During these years, crucial areas of concern for public interest advocates—areas that had widespread popular support to the extent that people knew about them, like increasing educational TV programs to children—continued to flounder. A 1999 University of Pennsylvania study concluded that one-fifth of all programs billed as educational for children had "little or no educational value." Hence, many broadcasters thereby failed to meet the FCC's requirement of three hours of children's educational programming per week, yet nothing was done.[95] A longtime public interest advocate who had worked for years on policy matters with the FCC characterized the Kennard years as "a real failure."[96] It was no particular surprise that after leaving the FCC Kennard accepted a high-paying job brokering wireless deals for the Carlyle Group. In view of the generous treatment Kennard had given Carlyle client SBC Communications before the FCC, the hire reeked of corruption and cronyism, or, in other words, business as usual at the FCC.[97]

In fairness to Kennard, he did try to enact positive change during his tenure as FCC chair. He was deeply concerned about the drop in minority radio station owners following the 1996 Telecommunications Act and developed low-power FM radio as a means to address this problem. He also attempted to push through free TV airtime for political candidates to offset the obvious problems with access to paid commercial time. But here Kennard faced the historic problem any FCC reformer faces: the relevant committees in Congress remained under the thumb of corporate lobbies. The NAB was resolutely opposed to free airtime, and many members of Congress informed Kennard in no uncertain terms to back off. As Kennard explains: "When I first started talking to people about free airtime for political candidates, some of my oldest and closest friends in Washington took me to breakfast, and they said, 'Bill, don't do this, it's political suicide, you know. You're just going to kill yourself.' " Eventually Kennard abandoned his campaign for free airtime. He learned an important lesson, one that no FCC member ever acted on before 2003: "In order to do things that are in the public interest, where you have no powerful lobby behind you, the only way that you can garner support for it is to reach outside Washington, get outside the Beltway and build coalitions with people who will speak to their legislatures at the grass roots."[98]

Kennard's run-in with Congress could have been predicted. Congressional committee members are well lubricated in cash and goodies from the media lobbies. A 2000 study by Charles Lewis and the Center for Public Integrity revealed that the fifty largest media firms and the four media trade organizations spent $111 million on lobbying between 1996 and 2000, and the number of media-related lobbyists increased from 234 to 284. In the same time span, media firms paid for 118 members of Congress and their senior staff to take 315 junkets, with a total value of $455,000. Rep. Billy Tauzin, chair of the House Commerce Committee that oversees the FCC, was the champion recipient of corporate largesse. He and his staff accounted for fully 42 of the junkets, and, in 1999, Tauzin and his wife enjoyed a six-day $18,910 junket to Paris courtesy of Time Warner and Instinet. Tauzin's daughter Kimberly worked as a lobbyist for the NAB in the late 1990s as well. This might have been purely coincidental, but Tauzin became the number-one promoter of corporate media interests in Washington during these years, with a slavish devotion to their cause. And he was not alone. Between 1993 and 2000 the same corporations gave $75 million in campaign contributions to candidates for federal office and spread the money to politicians on both sides of the aisle.[99] Sure, there were fights between the various corporate media sectors over who got the largest slice of cake, but on core issues, corporate media interests owned the policy debate in Washington. In 2000, large media firms were major contributors to both Bush and Gore, and Time Warner donated large sums to both sides.[100] As one media CEO euphorically remarked in 2000 when asked which candidate would best serve the interest of corporate media owners, "Bush? Gore? It doesn't matter!"[101]

The trajectory of this chapter is admittedly bleak. The consequences of corrupt policy making are apparent all around us. But as the unprecedented protest over media concentration in 2003 demonstrates, the future of media policy making is not necessarily doomed to be a repetition of its ignominious past. When the public is informed about how policy is created and what options for change are actually available—rather than the limited few the profit-driven media typically herald—a critical juncture may open again that will allow for revelation, debate, and democracy.

---

## Questions for Consideration

1   McChesney writes, "In contemporary society, we can regulate social behavior through four general paths: markets, laws, architecture, and cultural norms." Explain how these four "paths" can regulate social behavior, and give an example for each.

2   After learning McChesney's position on the need to rethink media regulation in the U.S., do you agree? Why or why not?

---

## Notes

1.   George Melloan, " 'Limits to Growth': A Dumb Theory That Refuses to Die," *Wall Street Journal Online*, 27 August 2002.
2.   Patricia Aufderheide, *Communications Policy and the Public Interest: The Telecommunications Act of 1996* (New York: Guilford Press, 1999), p. 5.
3.   For an enlightening discussion of this point, see Lawrence Lessig, *Code and Other Laws of Cyberspace* (New York: Basic Books, 1999), ch. 7.
4.   "The World's 500 Largest Corporations," *Fortune*, 21 July 2003, pp. 105–12; "The Forbes Sales 500," *Forbes*, 15 May 1975, pp. 159–65.
5.   "The World's Top 200 Companies," *Business Week*, 14 July 2003, pp. 61–62.
6.   See Kevin Phillips, *Wealth and Democracy* (New York: Broadway Books, 2002), chap. 2.
7.   Jane L. Levere, "A Forecaster Predicts a Recovery in the Media Sector, but Not of the Vigor Seen in the Past," *New York Times*, 5 August 2002; "Lights! Camera! No Profits!" *The Economist*, 18 January 2003, pp. 11–12.
8.   Michael J. Wolf, "These Are Not the Dark Ages for Media's Brightest Lights," *Wall Street Journal Online*, 23 July 2002.
9.   "2002 Forbes 400 List," www.hollywoodreporter.com, 13 September 2002.
10.   Janet Wasko, *Movies and Money: Financing the American Film Industry* (Norwood, N.J.: Ablex, 1982); Aron Moore, "Entangling Alliances," *Columbia Journalism Review*, March–April 2003.
11.   AdAge.com, "100 Leading National Advertisers Ranked by Total U.S. Advertising Spending in 2001," http://www. adage.com/page.cms?pageId=913.
12.   See Bernard Miege, *The Capitalization of Cultural Production* (New York: International General, 1989).
13.   Cited in Robin Blackburn, "The Bourgeois Revolutionary," *The Nation*, 4/11 August 2003, p. 34.
14.   Alexander Keyssar, *The Right to Vote: The Contested History of Democracy in the United States* (New York: Basic Books, 2000).
15.   Andrew Davidson, "A Tall Order," *Financial Times*, 31 August 31–1 September 2002, p. 3.
16.   For an elaboration of this notion, see Ruth Berins Collier and David Collier, *Shaping the Political Arena: Critical Junctures, the Labor Movement, and Regime Dynamics in Latin America* (Princeton, N.J.: Princeton University Press, 1991).
17.   See Ithiel de Sola Pool, *Technologies of Freedom* (Cambridge, Mass.: Belknap Press, 1983), pp. 16–17.
18.   For a discussion of copyright and the political economy of communication, see Ronald V. Bettig, *Copyrighting Culture: The Political Economy of Intellectual Property* (Boulder, Colo.: Westview, 1996).

19. Some of the most influential and outstanding works on the First Amendment and democracy in recent times have accordingly emphasized free speech, though they suggest clear implications for free press. See Steven H. Shiffrin, *The First Amendment, Demcocracy, and Romance* (Cambridge, Mass.: Harvard University Press, 1990); David M. Rabban, *Free Speech in Its Forgotten Years* (New York: Cambridge University Press, 1990).

20. See Milton R. Konvitz, *Fundamental Liberties of a Free People: Religion, Speech, Press, Assembly* (New Brunswick, N.J.: Transaction Press, 2003). First published by Cornell University Press in 1957.

21. Michael Kent Curtis, *Free Speech, "The People's Darling Privilege": Struggles for Freedom of Expression in American History* (Durham, N.C.: Duke University Press, 2000).

22. See Culver H. Smith, *Press, Politics, and Patronage: The American Government's Use of Newspapers, 1789–1875* (Athens, Ga.: University of Georgia Press, 1977).

23. See Jeffrey L. Pasley, *"The Tyranny of Printers": Newspaper Politics in the Early American Republic* (Charlottesville, Va.: University Press of Virginia, 2001).

24. Timothy E. Cook, *Governing with the News: The News Media as a Political Institution* (Chicago: University of Chicago Press, 1998), pp. 26–32.

25. William E. Ames, *A History of the National Intelligencer* (Chapel Hill, N.C.: University of North Carolina Press, 1972), p. 345.

26. Robert W.T. Martin, *The Free and Open Press: The Founding of American Democratic Press Liberty, 1640–1800* (New York: New York University Press, 2001), pp. 8, 168.

27. Akhil Reed Amar, *The Bill of Rights* (New Haven: Yale University Press, 1998), chap. 2.

28. For several of these quotes, see Robert W. McChesney and John Nichols, *Our Media, Not Theirs: The Democratic Struggle Against Corporate Media* (New York: Seven Stories Press, 2002).

29. Adrienne Koch and William Peden, eds., *The Life and Selected Writings of Thomas Jefferson* (New York: Modern Library, 1944), p. 412. Quote taken from a letter to Edward Carrington, 16 January 1787.

30. Cited in Jay Inslee, "Media Mergers Endanger Democracy, Diversity of News," *Seattle Times*, 7 March 2003.

31. Richard R. John, "Private Enterprise, Public Good? Communications Deregulation as a National Political Issue, 1839–1851," unpublished paper, January 2002.

32. *Whitney v. California*, 274 U.S. 357 (1927), cited in Gene Kimmelman, "Deregulation of Media: Dangerous to Democracy," text of speech given at University of Washington Law School, Seattle, Wa., 6 March 2003.

33. Cited in Harold L. Nelson and Dwight L. Teeter Jr., eds., *Law of Mass Communications* (Mineola, N.Y.: Foundation Press, 1969), p. 488.

34. C. Edwin Baker is perhaps the most articulate in this regard. See his *Media, Markets and Democracy* (New York: Cambridge University Press, 2001).

35. Burt Neuborne, "First Amendment for the Rich?" *The Nation*, 9 October 2000, p. 25.

36. Richard R. John, *Spreading the News: The American Postal System from Franklin to Morse* (Cambridge, Mass.: Harvard University Press, 1995).

37. Theda Skocpol, "The Tocqueville Problem: Civic Engagement in American Democracy," *Social Science History* 21(4) (1997): 455–79.

38. Cited in Richard B. Kielbowicz, *News in the Mail: The Press, Post Office, and Public Information, 1700–1860s* (Westport, Conn.: Greenwood Press, 1989), p. 35.

39. Pool, *Technologies of Freedom*, P. 77.

40. Cook, *Governing with the News*, pp. 40–44.

41. John, *Spreading the News*, chap. 2.

42. Alexis de Tocqueville, *Democracy in America* (New York: Signet Classic, 2001), p. 93.

43. Cook, *Governing with the News*, p. 44.

44. John, "Private Enterprise, Public Good?"

45. Dan Schiller, *Theorizing Communication: A History* (New York: Oxford University Press, 1996).

46. See Richard Du Boff, "The Rise of Communications Regulation: The Telegraph Industry, 1844–1880," *Journal of Communication* 34, no. 2 (Summer 1984): 52–66; Richard B. Du Boff, "The Telegraph and the Structure of Markets in the United States, 1845–1890," in *Research in Economic History: A Research Annual*, vol. 8, ed. Paul Uselding (Greenwich, Conn.: JAI Press, Inc., 1983), pp. 253–277.

47. Menahen Blondheim, *News Over the Wires: The Telegraph and the Flow of Public Information in America, 1844–1897* (Cambridge, Mass.: Harvard University Press, 1994).

48. Richard B. Du Boff, "The Telegraph in Nineteenth-Century America: Technology and Monopoly," *Comparative Studies in Society and History* 26, no. 4 (October 1984): 571–86.

49. Ibid., p. 582.

50. Dan Schiller, "Telecommunications and the Cooperative Commonwealth: The Challenge from Below and Its Containment, 1894–1919," unpublished manuscript, 2003, part of longer book project.http://leep.lis.uiuc.edu/publish/dschille/Telecommunications_And_The_Cooperative_Commonwealth.pdf.

51. Harry G. Good and James D. Teller, eds., *A History of American Education*, 3rd ed. (New York: Macmillan, 1973), chap. 3; quotation, p. 85.

52. See Sarah Mondale and Sarah B. Patton, *School: The Story of American Public Education* (Boston: Beacon Press, 2001).

53. Willis G. Regier, "5 Problems and 9 Solutions for University Presses," *The Chronicle of Higher Education*, 13 June 2003.

54. Janet Wasko, *Understanding Disney* (Cambridge, Mass.: Polity. 2001), p. 19.

55. See Robert W. McChesney, *Telecommunications, Mass Media, and Democracy: The Battle for the Control of U.S. Broadcasting, 1928–1935* (New York: Oxford University Press, 1993). All of the material in this particular discussion is drawn from this book.

56. See Vincent Mosco. *Broadcasting in the United States* (Norwood, N.J.: Ablex, 1979).

57. See Gerd Horten, *Radio Goes to War. The Cultural Politics of Propaganda During World War II* (Berkeley: University of California Press, 2002), p. 181.

58. "Who Owns Who in Cable," *Electronic Media*, 24 January 2000, p. 112.

59. See Michael E. Kinsley, *Outer Space and Inner Sanctums: Government, Business, and Satellite Communication* (New York: John Wiley & Sons, 1976); Dallas Smythe, *Counterclockwise: Perspectives on Communication*, ed. Thomas Guback (Boulder, Colo.: Westview, 1994), chap. 10.

60. William Kennard, " 'What Does $70 Billion Buy You Anyway?': Rethinking Public Interest Requirements at the Dawn of the Digital Era," speech delivered at Museum of Television and Radio, New York, N.Y., 10 October 2000.

61. "The Blue Book: Public Service Responsibility of Broadcast Licensees," in *Documents of American Broadcasting*, 3rd ed. (Englewood Cliffs, N.J.: Prentice-Hall, 1978), pp. 132–216.

62. See, for example, Charles A. Siepmann, *Radio, Television, and Society* (New York: Oxford University Press, 1950); Susan L. Brinson, *Personal and Public Interests: Frieda B. Hennock and the Federal Communications Commission* (Westport, Conn.: Praeger, 2002).

63. "The Fairness Doctrine: In the Matter of Editorializing by Broadcast Licensees," in *Documents of American Broadcasting*, ed. Frank J. Khan (Englewood Cliffs, N.J.: Prentice-Hall, 1978), pp. 217–31; Ford Rowan, *Broadcast Fairness: Doctrine, Practice, Prospects* (New York: Longman, 1984); William B. Ray, *FCC: The Ups and Downs of Radio–TV Regulation* (Ames, Iowa: Iowa State University Press, 1990), chap. 4.

64. Douglas Gomery. *The FCC's Newspaper–Broadcast Cross-Ownership Rule: An Analysis* (Washington, D.C.: Economic Policy Institute, 2002).

65. Steve McClellan, "Fin-Syn;" *Broadcasting & Cable*, 24 January 2000. pp. 30–36.

66. See Charles Goldsmith, "U.S. Is Unlikely to Copy U.K. Move to Ease Media Ownership Controls," *Wall Street Journal Online*, 13 May 2002.

67. See Charles H. Tillinghast, *American Broadcast Regulation and the First Amendment: Another Look* (Ames, Iowa: Iowa State University Press, 2000).

68. Erwin G. Krasnow, Lawrence D. Longley, and Herbert A. Terry, *The Politics of Broadcast Regulation*, 3rd ed. (New York: St. Martin's Press, 1982), chap. 8.

69. Michael J. Copps, "Remarks," Everett Parker Ethics in Communications Lecture, Washington, D.C., 24 September 2002.

70. Todd Shields, "Copps Criticizes Broadcast License Renewals," www. mediaweek.com, 23 July 2003.

71. Paige Albinek, "Service with an $8B Smile," *Broadcasting & Cable*, 10 April 2000, p. 24.

72. David Hatch, "Report: PSA's Air in Worst Daypart," *Electronic Media*, 25 February 2002, p. 6.

73. "All Politics Is Local, But You Wouldn't Know It by Watching Local TV," Report of the Alliance for Better Campaigns, October 2003; see also Jennifer Harper, "Study Finds 'Near Blackout' of Local Public Issues on TV," *Washington Times*, 28 October 2003.

74. Christine Y. Chen, "The Bad Boys of Radio," *Fortune*, March 3, 2003, p. 119.

75. Bill McConnell, "Merger-Modeling Debut," *Broadcasting & Cable*, 10 June 2002, p. 22.

76. See, for example, James C. Foust, *Big Voices of the Air: The Battle Over Clear Channel Radio* (Ames, Iowa: Iowa State University Press, 2000).

77. Robert W. McChesney interview with William Kennard, February 2001. For a small section of the interview, see Robert W. McChesney, "Kennard, the Public, and the FCC," *The Nation*, 14 May 2001, pp. 17–20.

78. Julie Wakefield, "Telecom's Man of the Moment," *Scientific American*, February 2002.

79. For a good overview of this episode, see Erwin G. Krasnow, Lawrence D. Longley, and Herbert A. Terry, *The Politics of Broadcast Regulation*, 3rd ed. (New York: St. Martin's Press, 1982), pp. 206–20.

80. See, for a related example, Ira Tienowitz, "Black Leaders Turn Up Heat," *Advertising Age*, 16 September 2002, p. 4.

81. See Milton Mueller, "Reinventing Media Activism: Citizen Activism as a Socio-Economic and Political Phenomenon," unpublished paper, 2003.

82. For an excellent treatment of this subject, see Robert Pollin, *Contours of Descent: U.S. Economic Fractures and the Landscape of Global Austerity* (New York: Verso, 2003).

83. Quotation of Professor Thomas W. Hazlett, a leading figure in the movement to have free market principles guide communications policy making. Taken from the back cover of Peter Huber, *Law and Disorder in Cyberspace: Abolish the FCC and Let Common Law Rule the Telecosm* (New York: Oxford University Press, 1997). See also Bruce M. Owen, *The Internet Challenge to Television* (Cambridge, Mass.: Harvard University Press, 1999).

84. Lee C. Bollinger, *Images of a Free Press* (Chicago: University of Chicago Press. 1991), p. 121.

85. David Hatch, "Independents Fight the Good Fight," *Electronic Media*, 29 January 2001, p. 3; Doug Halonen, "FCC Sets Its Sights on 'Total Carriage,'" *Electronic Media*, 19 August 2002, p. 1A.

86. Cited in Lucas A. Powe Jr., *The Fourth Estate and the Constitution* (Berkeley: University of California Press, 1991).

87. Herbert I. Schiller, *Culture, Inc.: The Corporate Takeover of Public Expression* (New York: Oxford University Press, 1989), chap. 3.

88. Thomas Frank, *One Market Under God: Extreme Capitalism, Market Populism, and the End of Market Democracy* (New York: Doubleday, 2000).

89. See Robert W. McChesney, *Rich Media, Poor Democracy: Communication Politics in Dubious Times* (New York: New Press, 2000). Also see Patricia Aufderheide, *Communications Policy and the Public Interest: The Telecommunications Act of 1996* (New York: Guilford Press, 1999).

90. See, for example, Matt Richtel, "Time Warner to Use Cable Lines to Add Phone to Internet Service," *New York Times*, 9 December 2003; Matt Richtel, "Phone Service Over Internet Revives Talk of Regulation," *New York Times*, 15 December 2003.

91. Poll conducted by Pew Research Center for the People and the Press, May 2002. See www.people-press.org.

92. "Consumer Group Says Deregulation of Cable Industry Hasn't Cut Rates," *Wall Street Journal Online*, 24 July 2002; Jon Groat, "Cable Not Competitive, Congress Told," http://cbs.market-watch.com, 6 May 2003.

93. Several exceptions to the cross-ownership prohibition existed, such as News Corporation owning the *New York Post* as well as having a Fox TV station in New York. Likewise the *Chicago Tribune* owned WGN radio and television stations in Chicago.

94. Juliana Ratner, "Regulator Steps Out Into the Market," *Financial Times*, 22 August 2002, p. 8.

95. Meg James, "TV Networks Find Ways to Stretch Educational Rules," *Los Angeles Times*, 23 February 2003.

96. Doug Halonen, "Watchdogs Label Kennard a 'Failure,'" *Electronic Media*, 17 July 2000, p. 3.

97. Dab Briody, *The Iron Triangle: Inside the Secret World of the Carlyle Group* (Hoboken, N.J.: John Wiley & Sons, 2003), pp. 106–10; Tim Shorrock, "Crony Capitalism Goes Global," *The Nation*, 1 April 2002, pp. 11–15.

98. McChesney, "Kennard, the Public, and the FCC."

99. Charles Lewis, "Media Money," *Columbia Journalism Review*, September/October 2000, pp. 20–27.

100. Derrick Wetherell, "The Bush/Gore Scorecard," *Columbia Journalism Review*, September/October 2000, p. 23.

101. Mark Fitzgerald, "Bush? Gore? It Doesn't Matter!" *Editor & Publisher*, 5 June 2000, p. 12.

# Chapter 5

# C. EDWIN BAKER

# NOT TOASTERS
## The Special Nature of Media Products

**C**. EDWIN BAKER IS THE Nicholas F. Gallacchio Professor of Law at the University of Pennsylvania Law School. In this chapter from his book *Media Concentration and Democracy*, he presents four features of communication products that, he argues, make them different from typical industrial output such as cars and toasters. Baker's overall point is that "each of these four special features of media products can lead to results contrary to what the audience wants—what it would pay for." He demonstrates this by looking at fascinating implications of copyright law for the marketplace.

Economics-oriented critics of government intervention in the media realm typically rely on oversimplified economics. Under certain purportedly normal circumstances, the market provides firms with an incentive to produce and sell the product as long as the product's cost (e.g., its cost of production and distribution) is less than the purchaser will pay, that is, as long as marginal costs are less than marginal price. The market thereby leads to a preference-maximizing production and distribution. This I call the "standard model."

The standard model is subject to a host of general critiques mostly related to why the market will fail or will be dysfunctional.[1] As one example of the latter, note that market competition creates an incentive for a market enterprise (e.g., capital holders) *to gain power* in relation to other resource owners (e.g., labor or other competitors) as much as it creates an incentive *to produce goods efficiently*. The power struggles between stakeholders, however, are primarily over distribution and do not produce any goods. As such, they waste resources as well as often generating unjust distributions.[2]

Of course, no one ever claims that the market works perfectly. Still, despite its problems, many find the standard model relatively adequate, at least enough so that it provides a presumptive reason to rely on "free" markets. For present purposes, I assume that the market *generally* works relatively well—for example, it effectively and efficiently leads to roughly the right production and distribution of cars or can openers. My claim is that, whatever the validity of general critiques of the market, the standard model applies especially badly to media products.

The standard model's persuasiveness depends on the following assumptions. (1) Products are sold in competitive markets and are sold at their marginal cost. (This will mean that their market price will equal their marginal cost, which will equal their average cost, which implicitly requires that at this point their marginal cost is rising.) (2) Product's production and normal use create relatively few serious externalities (i.e., relatively few major benefits not captured by or costs not imposed on the seller-producer). (3) The most significant policy concern is satisfying market-expressed preferences.

Even if these assumptions are true enough in general, my claim is that they do not apply so well to certain categories of products of which the media are an example. Media products are unlike the hypothesized "typical" product, such as a car or can opener, in four ways that are relevant here. Each difference complicates any economic claim concerning the wisdom of reliance on markets.

## Four Features of Communication Products

First, media products have significant "public good" aspects. A public good is an item for which one person's use of or benefit from the product does not affect its use by or benefit to another person. National defense or public parks are goods that, once provided, many can use without interfering with others' use.[3] Similarly, many can watch the same broadcast or read the same poem once it is created. Economic definitions of "public good" usually emphasize two aspects: "nonrivalrous use," which is the aspect that I am primarily concerned with here, and "nonexcludability."[4] Typically, utilities or other "natural" monopolies exhibit this "nonrivalrous use" public-good quality in their infrastructure, for example, in the gas lines, water mains, or telephone lines (other than the final connection to the house). Multiple consumers can use this infrastructure with no or very modest extra expense. To the extent that adding an additional customer does not increase the cost of this infrastructure, which is usually true until crowding requires larger lines or mains, the infrastructure exists as a public good. If this infrastructure is a major part of the delivered product's cost, the marginal cost of serving that additional consumer will predictably be substantially less than the average cost. That is, the marginal cost of supplying the new user could approach zero while the average cost of the infrastructure to each user, that is, its total cost divided by the number of users, stays much higher.

This situation creates a problem. If the product is priced at its average cost (or priced higher if a seller exercises monopoly power), some consumers will be unwilling (or unable) to pay that price, even though they want the products and would be willing to pay the added cost created by their usage. Charging the average cost results in underproduction. On the other hand, charging the marginal cost, as efficiency considerations normally recommend, fails to produce enough revenue (selling price times the number of purchasers) to cover the product's cost. The market will not support production if the seller must provide the product or service to all customers at the marginal cost of supplying the last customer. At that price, the seller would not recover the cost of the required infrastructure.

To gather, write, and edit news or to create and produce video entertainment, the media incur huge "first-copy costs." This economically significant element of media products' cost is like the utility's infrastructure or, better, is like national defense. There is no limit to how many can benefit from the producer's expenditure on first-copy costs or analogous costs, such as the expense of broadcasting.[5] Writing the story or sending out the broadcast signal costs the same no matter how many people "tune in." Adding a marginal consumer does not affect these costs. As long as these public-good costs are a large enough part of the media's total cost,[6] charging potential audience members the average cost leads to inefficient exclusions. Charging the average cost excludes people who would pay more for the story or broadcast than it actually costs to include them among the recipients. Alternatively, setting the price at the marginal cost, that is, the cost of supplying it to the last purchaser, creates insufficient incentives to produce the media product.

Firms sometimes avoid these consequences by engaging in "price discrimination"— charging different purchasers different prices and thereby tapping the "consumer surplus" that some consumers would receive if they were charged only the marginal costs. Whether there are sufficient opportunities for price discrimination to lead to a value-maximizing level of production (hopefully without producing monopoly profits) is an empirical matter that will vary with the product and market in question. I assume in much of the discussion that follows that providers of media products cannot uniformly engage in sufficient price discrimination to eliminate this problem. Moreover, even when reasonably adequate levels of production could be achieved because of the availability of relatively costless price discrimination, price discrimination introduces an additional policy-based fairness issue. When and why should some consumers have to pay more than others for the same good, thereby reducing or eliminating their potential "consumer surplus," in order to achieve distribution to others who willingly pay the marginal cost but would not pay the higher price necessary to cover infrastructure or first-copy costs? This is a central issue in many rate-setting disputes. It can obviously also raise controversial issues in the media context—for example, was it fair for an early Congress to charge some mail users a price higher than the cost of serving them in order to subsidize the cost of communication for other users, namely newspapers?

Second, media products often produce extraordinarily significant positive and negative externalities. Externalities typically refer to the value some item has to someone who does not participate in the transaction. If one or more persons, often numerous unorganized people, would potentially pay to have the transaction occur, then the externality is positive; it is negative if they would potentially pay to have it not occur. For example, people care whether their reputation is ruined or advanced, whether people they meet are boring or cultured, and whether they are murdered or aided by the person they pass on the street—and these are among the phenomena whose occurrence can be significantly influenced by *other people's* media consumption. Likewise, many people value a well-functioning democracy. They are affected by whether the country goes to war, establishes parks, or provides for retirement and medical care—and hence can be greatly benefited by other people's consumption of quality media or harmed by others' ignorance or apathy produced by inadequate consumption or consumption of misleading, distortive, and demobilizing media. Furthermore, the political or corporate corruption that the threat of media exposure deters is a benefit that the press cannot effectively capture—there is no story—to sell to consumers. In each case, people other than the direct media consumers would pay if necessary to have the beneficial effect occur or to avoid the harmful effects. Later I suggest that many media policies, ranging from libel laws to reporters' privileges or postal subsidies given to newspapers or direct grants for public broadcasting—and much, much more— can be understood as in part designed to increase positive or to reduce negative externalities.

Third, media products are unusual in that often two very different purchasers pay for the transfer of media content to its audience. The media enterprise commonly sells media products to audiences and sells audiences to advertisers. Of course, multiple parties being "affected" by a transaction, each thus being a potential but often not an actual payee or purchaser, is not an unusual phenomenon—that basically defines an "externality." However, in the media context this multiple set of purchasers represents not merely potential purchasers; and the payment from advertisers in return for what is sold or delivered to audiences plays an unusually large and relatively routinized role. Selling to both audiences and advertisers has especially significant consequences and adds special complexities. For example, what is the right level of production of television programming? The "value" of a television broadcast is its combined value for the audience and the advertiser—in economic terms, the amount they would be willing to pay. To the extent that the broadcaster only collects from the advertiser, the broadcaster apparently receives an inadequate incentive to spend money on programming. From this observation, some economists conclude that our society drastically underinvests in television broadcasting.[7]

Having multiple purchasers creates other issues. For example, advertisers in effect pay the media firm to gain an audience by providing the audience with something the audience wants, although not necessarily what the audience most wants. A portion of the advertisers' payment often goes to having the editorial content better reflect the advertisers' interests. There is a potential conflict between advertisers' and audiences' interests in the media content.[8] A century ago many papers routinely accepted "reading matter," material prepared by advertisers that promoted their products (or sometimes their political goals) but that was not identified as advertising. Advertisers wanted this material presented as if it were editorial content, not advertising, while (presumably) the public would have preferred identification of the source. Typically the public wants and expects the news and editorial content in the news media to embody the journalists' and editors' independent professional judgment. The market brings this audience interest to bear on the journalistic enterprise to the extent that the enterprise can better sell its publication if it gains a reputation for independence. However, in the case of "reading matter," the market did not suffice to induce source identification or to create journalistic independence. In 1912 Congress responded by prohibiting the practice for any paper receiving second-class mail privileges.[9]

A fourth aspect of the media relevant to media economics involves why or how audiences value media products. In the standard economic model just presented, people seek products that satisfy various existing preferences. When people purchase media products—as when they seek education or advice from psychological, legal, or spiritual advisors—they are often seeking information or guidance for the very purpose of forming preferences. People often want a media product for what I call "edification," which includes education, exposure to wisely selected information, or wise opinion and good argument. This feature of media is difficult to embody fully within the terms of standard economic analysis. Even if a market can properly allocate resources to fulfill preferences for preference formation activities, a market for this type of product will have unusual features. When a person wants to develop "better" preferences, values, or outlooks, she puts her present outlook or preferences into question without a clearly formulated alternative to put in their place. Thus, her own preferences do not give her a complete standard by which to measure whether her purchases provide the right thing. Her preference might well be to choose a context in which she expects to get the best guidance—a context that may or may not be consistent with market purchases.

This dilemma is not entirely resolvable. How does a person know whether the person she became after seeing the psychologist is who she wants to be or whether her changes would have been better with a different psychologist? Furthermore, from what perspective does she evaluate—from the views she now has, those she had earlier when she chose the psychologist, or the views she would have had if she had chosen a different psychologist? The answers may very well not be the same, so which perspective should she privilege? Of course, even when people do not know precisely what they want, they can still have rules of thumb for guessing whether they are likely to get it. They may know the seller's or producer's general reputation for expertise. In addition, they may have reasons to presume the seller or producer exercises independent judgment and to believe that this supplier uses this independence to try to serve the purchaser's interests—reasons purportedly underwritten by professionalism in education, law, psychology, or the priesthood. These concerns provide a catalyst for the press to portray itself as independent and an explanation for most people's outrage at any evidence that advertisers influence media's editorial content. In addition, some people may also use as a rule of thumb indications that the seller shares or, at least, has familiarity with and responsiveness to the purchaser's basic values or perspectives. This sharing supports the hope that she will receive desirable guidance in formulating new preferences and values. In the media context, this might lead to preference for media with a particular partisanship. Moreover, one response that a person could rationally choose is to have society (government) create nonmarket methods of providing these edifying products.

Finally, people value media products for various reasons. Audiences want media products (sometimes the same media product) for entertainment or for specific information, as well as for "edification." Attributes that make a media product good for one purpose may not be those that make it good for another. This diversity in functions introduces complications for the notion of the audience getting what it wants, complications that are often exacerbated due to the multiple purchasers—audiences and advertisers. Audience members' knowledge about how well a media product serves differing purposes often varies. Advertisers, on the other hand, may wish to control—or have a veto over—particular attributes. For example, an advertiser may be interested in a movie's or story's transformative and informative roles, especially the product's slant and its capacity to persuade on issues related to the advertiser's corporate interests. In contrast, the audience may evaluate the media content mostly in terms of its potential to entertain. This focus might make some sense if the audience is best situated to evaluate this characteristic. In consequence, the advertiser may pay for, say, a pro-Pepsi informational slant, about which the audience is unaware or unconcerned as long as the slant does not affect the movie's entertainment value. Thus, predictably, advertisers pay for "product placements" where their products are presented within the apparently nonadvertising content.

More generally, when content serves multiple functions to different degrees but where the audience members' ability to assess its contribution varies from one function to another, a person is likely to choose on the basis of functions about which her ability to assess its contribution is better. In this circumstance, the market creates increased opportunities for manipulative or ideologically distorted content. If the audience values both the media's entertainment and edification roles strongly, but if information in respect to a program's contribution to edification is harder to obtain or evaluate, the audience may choose a media product on the basis of its entertainment value in the hope that the different dimensions correlate. This audience strategy reduces the cost to the advertiser in having its editorial choices prevail. For example, tobacco companies might "pay" (i.e., threaten to withdraw advertising) for the editorial slant they wanted in popular women's magazines—no negative stories about smoking. Their capacity to pursue this strategy increases if the slant did not overly influence the magazine's fulfilling the role most easily and actively evaluated by the audience. However, such payment is, in effect, censorship.

The point is merely that the combination of multiple purchasers (audience plus advertiser) creates multiple allegiances. Influence tends to flow in particular directions—toward the larger purchaser, the purchaser with greater knowledge of how well the media are serving its interests, and the purchaser whose purchase is most sensitive to how well the media serve its interest in relation to the specific issue in question. Having an audience that values the product in multiple ways but with different degrees of knowledge about how well it performs each is a context that enhances the opportunity for the other purchaser, the advertiser, to influence content away from what the audience wants in the dimensions about which the audience finds knowledge most difficult to obtain.

In sum, each of these four special features of media products can lead to results contrary to what the audience wants—what it would pay for.

## Copyright: an Illustration

Drawing out policy implications of these four attributes of communicative products could explain much of copyright law. I do not attempt that here, but some examination of how copyright responds to these attributes is useful later on and serves as an illustration of some of their implication.

Once produced, media content is a public good. No one's consumption (e.g., reading, viewing, discussing) prevents anyone else from consuming the same content. Maximum value results from allowing consumption without charge for the content, although a consumer should pay for any marginal cost involved in access. The problem is that if content were *freely* appropriable by any consumer, although this pricing (i.e., a zero price) would not exclude any audience members who value the content, this regime would provide no economic incentive for creation and would fail to encourage production.

Enter the regime of intellectual property, probably the most overt legal response to the public-good aspect of media content. Copyright law creates private property rights in content so that authors and creators will receive a reward adequate to induce production. Complexities of copyright law are (or, at least, are supposed to be) a response to its utilitarian aim of influencing both production and distribution in a manner that maximizes the availability and valued use of intellectual content. The Constitution gives Congress the power to grant rights in intellectual creations not in order to recognize some asserted natural right of authorship but in order "to promote the Progress of Science and useful Arts."[10] Copyright properly aims to recognize private property rights only to the extent that they "contribute" more to production of valuable content than they "cost" in terms of restricting access to and use of that content. This goal explains, at least in part, copyright doctrines such as "fair use." Ideally, fair use benefits audiences by allowing free use whenever free use adds more value than it "costs" in terms of reduced incentives to create and distribute. Similar economic balancing of gains and losses due to propertizing intellectual content can explain why copyright only attempts to protect the "unique expression" of the idea and not the idea (or fact) itself.

Thus, arguably, copyright's maximizing policy is relatively nonideological in merely aiming to efficiently promote "science and the useful arts," that is, to make more content more widely available. On closer examination, however, it turns out to be significantly more complicated. Specifics of copyright law favor the production of some types and some ways of producing content over others and affect who has access to it. Whether copyright favors creating and distributing the content that society most values—whether it maximizes value—is often unclear. Despite the standard economic argument for intellectual property rights, economic arguments opposed to all restrictive rights and in favor of zero pricing are imaginable and, depending on circumstantially variable empirical factors and people's values, could be persuasive. Much commercial production of content would continue without legal protection of intellectual property rights. Moreover, the commercial production for which copyright provides an incentive, that is, production for profit, competes to a degree with noncommercially produced content (e.g., ideological speech that people spread for political reasons or amateur productions where the joy or pride of expression provides a primary motive for production). Possibly, the absence of copyright, by dispensing with the advantage it gives commercial production, would encourage a culture in which noncommercial communications were more dominant. The policy issue is whether this culture would by any relevant measures be richer than the existing commercial culture created by the mass media. The problem is how to compare and evaluate the worlds that would be produced by the alternative legal regimes.[11]

Different content creators line up on both sides of a debate about extending or limiting copyright protection. All creative works borrow from potentially copyrighted past creations. Often noncommercial creative "borrowers" favor less restrictions on their partial appropriations, whereas most commercial producers favor greater protection in order to maximize their return on content they own.[12] Still, because a prime role of copyright is to create effective distribution channels, sometimes even audience-oriented, non-profit-seeking creators have an interest in a commercially effective copyright. A writer or advocate may be personally unconcerned with economic rewards, wanting to make her creation maximally available out of a desire for influence or fame, but still want an effective copyright in order to induce a publisher or distributor to make her work available.

Copyright not only favors commercialization but also tilts production toward particular types of content. First Amendment lawyers will recognize this as troublesome. Copyright is a speech-related law that involves content discrimination.[13] Here, however, I want to examine the bias in terms of the policy issues that copyright's lack of neutrality raises. Existing copyright law allows privatization of only some aspects of content. It covers, for example, only the "unique expression," not facts or ideas. If privatization serves its intended purpose of creating production incentives, this coverage means that copyright directly encourages investment in creating and distributing "unique expressions" while only incidentally and presumably less effectively encouraging investment in uncovering, developing, or communicating "facts or ideas" (although, admittedly, patent and trade-secret law encourage investment in developing some commercially relevant categories of new information). This bias is potentially dramatic. For example, the distinction could encourage greater investment in unique entertainment content (expression) and less investment in news content (facts). Of course, other factors may be more central, but this bias is illustrated by media expenditures. In 1995, the annual newsroom budget of the *Washington Post*, the paper that brought us Watergate, was reportedly about $70 million, while the quite forgettable 1995 movie, *Waterworld*, reportedly cost about $175 million, although this figure includes more than just content creation (e.g., an approximately $30 million marketing budget).[14]

Even within news production, copyright rules influence expenditures. They favor unique or flashy presentation as opposed to expenditures on gathering hard news, especially news that is expensive to obtain. It should not be surprising that market competition leads television stations to advertise the images of, and pay high salaries to, appealing "anchorpersons." These personalities, like the copyrightable words, are a "unique" element that an owner can exploit commercially. Then, as newscasters' salaries increase, the networks fire senior professionals and generally engage in cutting the costs of news production.[15] And this bias favoring anchor personalities has additional consequences. James Fallows has forcefully attacked the deleterious effect on democracy of the media's constant cynical emphasis on the competitive, horse-race aspects of politics rather than on its substantive aspects. He concludes that having a star personality "report" on the top current story twists the content of news in a way that contributes to this misdirected media focus because, usually, this star figure does not have expertise or reportorial knowledge of the specific issue but has general expertise on issues such as how the issue will play politically.[16]

Although 40 percent of viewers report that the anchorperson is their reason for viewing a particular network news program,[17] that does not necessarily mean that the bias toward expenditures on anchorpersons rather than news represents audience preferences, much less that a democratic society would self-consciously choose to promote this tilt. Rather their report may result from competitive factors created by the existing legal and market structure. First, the anchorperson may be their reason for choosing among programs, not their reason for watching the news. As for it being a determinative factor in that choice, this may reflect the extent of broadcaster expenditures both on making this element appealing and on advertising to promote viewer interest in this element. These broadcaster efforts may, in turn, make "economic" sense. Anchorperson personalities and their expressive delivery, not facts and ideas that other stations can freely appropriate, are the station's unique goods. The station or network's exclusive position in respect to a given anchorperson gives it a reason to promote the merits or appeal of its anchor as a reason to "tune in." This incentive replicates the peculiarities of the legal order's privatization rules. Unsurprisingly, systems operating under different copyright rules, as well as systems where broadcasters are less driven by market pursuit of profit, are likely to make very different choices of what type of content—anchor personality or informative factual material—to emphasize and to spend money on creating.

Privatizing facts or ideas in order to encourage their discovery or development is hardly an appropriate corrective. Although in special circumstances this is arguably acceptable (e.g., with patents, although here only certain commercial uses are privatized), generally most people rightly see ownership of ideas and facts as offensive. Because a person comes up with an idea or uncovers facts hardly suggests that she should be able to stop another from independently doing the same and then telling others about it. Even when the second person learns something from the originator, the notion that she cannot then repeat it, or reformulate it and then include it in her own messages, is contrary to how thinking and discussion occur and contrary to how cultures develop. Granting the originator control over "copying" and repetition gives her a virtual property right in the recipient's mind and speech. Of course, a person may agree or contract to keep a confidence. The default rule, however, is and should be that repetition is limited only by discretion, not by law.[18] Economic arguments, ranging from avoiding enforcement costs to reducing transaction costs in making efficient use of information, also argue against routine privatization of facts and ideas.

Various responses by media entities or government can reduce the negative consequences and underproduction related to lack of copyright protection for facts and ideas. The media may successfully nurture desires for speedy news and, more important, for reliable news. They may be able to teach audiences to correlate these attributes with news organizations that themselves engage in (some) investigations. This process of individualization of media entities would give these entities some incentive to spend money on finding facts and developing ideas. Or the government (and others) could heavily subsidize development of desired information and ideas, which then could be communicated by the media. Government-supported research universities, prestige-based reward systems within those universities, direct government sponsorship of research, and noncopyrightability of governmentally produced intellectual works serve as examples. Public officials' news conferences and press releases, and similar techniques used by various private sources, create and make available considerable information without concern for the lack of copyright protection—although with obvious, questionable content tilts.[19]

Still, the basic points remain. Communications can often be cheaply provided for everyone after being originally produced, but this provides insufficient incentives for production. The intellectual property regime responds to this problem but inefficiently restricts access. It also encourages production of some content more than other. Responses to differential underproduction provide only partial cures, and the cures contain their own tilts. Inevitably, the audience gets what the law encourages, not some "uncontaminated" version of what it wants. No "free market" could provide otherwise.

**Questions for Consideration**

1   Choose two of Baker's four features and bring your own examples of how they apply in a media industry of your choosing.

2   What are the pros and cons of the current copyright regime? From what Baker writes, do you think that American society is better with or without this copyright regime?

## Notes

1.   For example, (1) reliance on market allocation accepts the existing distribution of wealth as a given when it should be changed or is contested; (2) the market stimulates undesirable desires precisely because they can be profitably fulfilled; (3) the market encourages (rewards) undesirable interpersonal behavior and undesirable personality traits; and (4) the market promotes optimal preference satisfaction only if, contrary to reality, most goods are made available at their marginal cost; moreover, too much production of a good properly priced at its marginal cost will occur when it improperly substitutes for a good improperly priced above its marginal cost and too little will occur when the properly priced good is replaced by a good priced below its marginal cost. These problems suggest a more modest policy-making role for traditional economic analysis, especially for the standard model described here, than many of its practitioners recognize.

2.   See, e.g., Richard C. Edwards, *Contested Terrain: The Transformation of the Workplace in the Twentieth Century* (New York: Basic Books, 1979).

3.   The point is somewhat overstated. Many goods function like public goods only within limits. For example, more users eventually interfere with the quality of the park—the crowd begins detracting from others' enjoyment or otherwise imposes marginal costs, like extra cleanup or wear-and-tear costs. Still, once goods like defense of national borders or media content are produced, multiple people can consume them without significant increased costs.

4.   I make little direct use of nonexcludability, although the concept could apply to (positive) externalities. In common usage, nonexcludability as an aspect of a public good usually refers to situations where any purchaser and each nonexcluded beneficiary get roughly the same type of benefit from the good, whereas the concept of externalities is most commonly used where the benefit or burden on nonexcluded third parties is of a different sort than that which enticed the purchaser.

5.   Economists often identify this factor as the cause of the current dominance of one-newspaper towns. A monopoly newspaper pays only one set of first-copy costs (and requires a single infrastructure) in serving the whole city. By adding customers, it constantly reduces its average cost. See James N. Rosse & James N. Dertouzos, *Economic Issues in Mass Communication Industries* (Stanford: Department of Economics, Stanford U., 1978), 55–78. Any competitive equilibrium would be unstable, usually requiring two papers roughly equal in circulation. See Randolph E. Bucklin et al., "Games of Survival in the US Newspaper Industry," *Applied Economics* 21 (1989): 631, 636. Despite this theoretical account, until a long-term decline began just before the end of the nineteenth century, competition generally prevailed among local daily newspapers. Thus, Rosse more precisely suggests that the "fundamental long-run cause of newspaper failure is loss of effective market segmentation." James E. Rosse, "The Decline of Direct Newspaper Competition," *Journal of Communications* 30 (1980): 65, 67. Although Rosse does not explain this loss, the decline in effective segmentation could result from the changed incentives that occur when advertisers become the primary purchaser of newspapers' efforts—that is, as they become the paper's primary source of revenue and profit. To the extent that daily newspapers' primary product

becomes readers sold to advertisers rather than product sold to readers, the main product differentiation for daily newspapers selling to mostly local advertisers will be geographically rather than content based. See C. Edwin Baker, *Advertising and a Democratic Press* (Princeton: Princeton U. Press, 1994), ch. 1.

6.   The claim here is that this public-good element in media products is sufficiently large and its significance sufficiently variable among media products that economic and policy analyses ought to take it explicitly into account. The difference here between media products and other goods is at most a matter of degree. Virtually all mass-produced products include what I here call a "public-good" element—most obviously, the "design cost." This always creates some tension in the standard competitive market model. The market encourages efficient amounts of research on practices or product design only to the extent that the research is aimed at creating products over which the researcher will have something approaching monopoly power—for example, if it obtains a patent or trade secret—and will have an ability to price discriminate in its sale. This helps explain, for example, why the market encourages research expenditures on drug therapies *even if* the marginal improvement of health, say the marginal reduction of death from cancer or heart disease, would be much greater from research dollars spent on developing non-patentable "public health" or environmental health methods (although this is only one cause of the skewing of research expenditures). One solution is to socialize research—providing government funding, often times within a university.

7.   An early study calculated that the value to Americans of free over-the-air television was at least $20 billion, which was roughly ten times the advertising revenue then produced. See Roger G. Noll et al., *Economic Aspects of Television Regulation* (Washington, D.C.: Brookings Institution, 1973), 23. The authors concluded that "by traditional criteria of consumer welfare, not only another network but a very large expansion of television is warranted." Ibid., 30.

8.   See C. Edwin Baker, *Advertising and a Democratic Press* (Princeton: Princeton U. Press, 1994), ch. 2.

9.   See Linda Lawson, *Truth in Publishing: Federal Regulation of the Press's Business Practices, 1880– 1920* (Carbondale: Southern Illinois U. Press, 1993). The requirement that advertising be identified may have conformed to the competitive economic interests of some, especially the quality, papers. The law also required papers to publish the identity of their owners in the expectation that public knowledge of ownership would allow greater ability to resist manipulation. In both respects, the law required some editors to print what they would prefer not to print. See *Lewis Publ'g Co. v. Morgan*, 229 U.S. 288, 296 (1913) (upholding the law against a First Amendment challenge); cf. *Miami Herald Publ'g Co. v. Tornillo*, 418 U.S. 241, 254–55 (1974) (invalidating a Florida statute requiring newspapers that attack a political candidate's character to print the candidate's reply).

10.   U.S. Constitution, Art. I, Sec 8. The Court repeatedly emphasizes this point. Copyright "is a means by which an important public purpose may be achieved." The right is created "in order to benefit the public." It "is intended to increase and not to impede the harvest of knowledge" and "serve[s] its intended purpose [by] inducing the creation of new material." *Harper & Row, Publishers v. Nation*, 471 U.S. 539 U.S. 539, 545–46 (internal quotes from *Sony v. Universal Studios*, 464 U.S. 417, 429, 477) (opinions of Stevens for the Court and Blackmun, dissenting).

11.   Yochai Benkler, "Free as the Air to Common Use: First Amendment Constraints on Enclosure of the Public Domain," *New York University Law Review* 74 (1999): 354.

12.   See James Boyle, *Shamans, Software and Spleens: Toward the Construction of the Information Society* (Cambridge: Harvard U. Press, 1996), 51–60.

13.   The Supreme Court claims to invalidate most content discriminations involving protected speech content. But see C. Edwin Baker, "Turner Broadcasting: Content Regulation of Persons and Presses," *Supreme Court Review* (1994): 54. Whether copyright is a content-based regulation is an issue that has troubled some commentators. The best formulation is Brennan's. He claims that the traditional approach is: "any restriction on speech, the application of which turns on the content of the speech, is a content-based restriction." *Boos v. Barry*, 485 U.S. 312, 335–36 (Brennan and Marshall, concurring in part and concurring in the judgment). Obviously, one cannot know whether a writing violates another's copyright

without looking at its content. Thus, copyright rules are content-discriminatory on their face. Even if that were not recognized, clearly copyright's purpose is to protect the copyrighted content and thereby to favor creation of such content over any content whose value copyright does not protect (or content whose creation copyright prohibits absent permission by some copyright holder). And the Supreme Court treats facially content-neutral laws as content-based if the law has any purpose to affect content. See *Turner Broadcasting System v. FCC*, 512 U.S. 622, 642–43 (1994).

14. See Dan Cox, "Soaring Star Salaries Induce Labor Pains," *Variety* (Sept. 11, 1995): 1; Richard Harwood, "Extinct Stained Wretches?" *Washington Post* (Nov. 2, 1995): A31.

15. See Leo Bogart, *Commercial Culture: The Media System and the Public Interest* (New York: Oxford U. Press, 1995), 182.

16. See James Fallows, *Breaking the News* (New York: Pantheon Books, 1996), 157–59.

17. Bogart, *Commercial Culture*, 186.

18. *Cohen v. Coles Media*, 501 U.S. 63 (1991). This raises interesting issues in the context of current debates about privacy and the Internet. Cf. Jerry Kang, "Information Privacy in Cyberspace Transactions," *Stanford Law Review* 50 (1998): 1193. I believe the key step is to see that regulation of how commercial enterprises other than the press obtain, use, and sell information poses problems largely outside the concern of the First Amendment.

19. See Edward S. Herman & Noam Chomsky, *Manufacturing Consent: The Politics of the Mass Media* (New York: Pantheon Books, 1988), 18–25.

# Chapter 6

# LAWRENCE LESSIG

# FOUR PUZZLES FROM CYBERSPACE

IN HIS BOOK *CODE*, PROFESSOR Lawrence Lessig of Stanford Law School points out that "cyberspace"—the Internet and its related technologies—"demands a new understanding of how regulation works." Rather than focus on laws or norms, suggests Lessig, we have to focus on the "code"—the basic assumptions that are built into the programming that creates and guides the system. This reading from the second edition of his book presents four "puzzles" that bring out ideas about the importance of code in deciding what to regulate and how to regulate in the new media world.

Everyone who is reading this book has used the Internet. Some have been in "cyberspace." The Internet is that medium through which your e-mail is delivered and web pages get published. It's what you use to order books on Amazon or to check the times for local movies at Fandango. Google is on the Internet, as are Microsoft "help pages."

But "cyberspace" is something more. Though built on top of the Internet, cyberspace is a richer experience. Cyberspace is something you get pulled "into," perhaps by the intimacy of instant message chat or the intricacy of "massively multiple online games" ("MMOGs" for short, or if the game is a role-playing game, then "MMORPGs"). Some in cyberspace believe they're in a community; some confuse their lives with their cyberspace existence. Of course, no sharp line divides cyberspace from the Internet. But there is an important difference in experience between the two. Those who see the Internet simply as a kind of Yellow-Pages-on-steroids won't recognize what citizens of cyberspace speak of. For them, "cyberspace" is simply obscure.

Some of this difference is generational. For most of us over the age of 40, there is no "cyberspace," even if there is an Internet. Most of us don't live a life online that would qualify as a life in "cyberspace." But for our kids, cyberspace is increasingly their second life. There are millions who spend hundreds of hours a month in the alternative worlds of cyberspace—later on we will focus on one of these worlds, a game called

"Second Life."[1] And thus while you may think to yourself, this alien space is nothing I need worry about because it's nowhere I'll ever be, if you care to understand anything about the world the next generation will inhabit, you should spend some time understanding "cyberspace."

That is the aim of two of the stories that follow. These two describe cyberspace. The other two describe aspects of the Internet more generally. My aim through these four very different stories is to orient by sometimes disorienting. My hope is that you'll come to understand four themes that will recur throughout this book. At the end of this chapter, I come clean about the themes and provide a map. For now, just focus on the stories.

## Borders

It was a very ordinary dispute, this argument between Martha Jones and her neighbors.[2] It was the sort of dispute that people have had since the start of neighborhoods. It didn't begin in anger. It began with a misunderstanding. In this world, misunderstandings like this are far too common. Martha thought about that as she wondered whether she should stay; there were other places she could go. Leaving would mean abandoning what she had built, but frustrations like this were beginning to get to her. Maybe, she thought, it was time to move on.

The argument was about borders—about where her land stopped. It seemed like a simple idea, one you would have thought the powers-that-be would have worked out many years before. But here they were, her neighbor Dank and she, still fighting about borders. Or rather, about something fuzzy at the borders—about something of Martha's that spilled over into the land of others. This was the fight, and it all related to what Martha did.

Martha grew flowers. Not just any flowers, but flowers with an odd sort of power. They were beautiful flowers, and their scent entranced. But, however beautiful, these flowers were also poisonous. This was Martha's weird idea: to make flowers of extraordinary beauty which, if touched, would kill. Strange no doubt, but no one said that Martha wasn't strange. She was unusual, as was this neighborhood. But sadly, disputes like this were not.

The start of the argument was predictable enough. Martha's neighbor, Dank, had a dog. Dank's dog died. The dog died because it had eaten a petal from one of Martha's flowers. A beautiful petal, and now a dead dog. Dank had his own ideas about these flowers, and about this neighbor, and he expressed those ideas—perhaps with a bit too much anger, or perhaps with anger appropriate to the situation.

"There is no reason to grow deadly flowers," Dank yelled across the fence. "There's no reason to get so upset about a few dead dogs," Martha replied. "A dog can always be replaced. And anyway, why have a dog that suffers when dying? Get yourself a pain-free-death dog, and my petals will cause no harm."

I came into the argument at about this time. I was walking by, in the way one walks in this space. (At first I had teleported to get near, but we needn't complicate the story with jargon. Let's just say I was walking.) I saw the two neighbors becoming increasingly angry with each other. I had heard about the disputed flowers—about how their petals carried poison. It seemed to me a simple problem to solve, but I guess it's simple only if you understand how problems like this are created.

Dank and Martha were angry because in a sense they were stuck. Both had built a life in the neighborhood; they had invested many hours there. But both were coming to understand its limits. This is a common condition: We all build our lives in places with limits. We are all disappointed at times. What was different about Dank and Martha?

One difference was the nature of the space, or context, where their argument was happening. This was not "real space" but virtual space. It was part of what I call "cyberspace." The environment was a "massively multiple online game" ("MMOG"), and MMOG space is quite different from the space we call real.

Real space is the place where you are right now: your office, your den, maybe by a pool. It's a world defined by both laws that are man-made and others that are not. "Limited liability" for corporations is a man-made law. It means that the directors of a corporation (usually) cannot be held personally liable for the sins of the company. Limited life for humans is not a man-made law: That we all will die is not the result of a decision that Congress made. In real space, our lives are subject to both sorts of law, though in principle we could change one sort.

But there are other sorts of laws in real space as well. You bought this book, I trust, or you borrowed it from someone who did. If you stole it, you are a thief, whether you are caught or not. Our language is a norm; norms are collectively determined. As our norms have been determined, your "stealing" makes you a thief, and not just because you took it. There are plenty of ways to take something but not be thought of as a thief. If you came across a dollar blowing in the wind, taking the money will not make you a thief; indeed, not taking the money makes you a chump. But stealing this book from the bookstore (even when there are so many left for others) marks you as a thief. Social norms make it so, and we live life subject to these norms.

Some of these norms can be changed collectively, if not individually. I can choose to burn my draft card, but I cannot choose whether doing so will make me a hero or a traitor. I can refuse an invitation to lunch, but I cannot choose whether doing so will make me rude. I have choices in real life, but escaping the consequences of the choices I make is not one of them. Norms in this sense constrain us in ways that are so familiar as to be all but invisible.

MMOG space is different. It is, first of all, a virtual space—like a cartoon on a television screen, sometimes rendered to look three-dimensional. But unlike a cartoon, MMOG space enables you to control the characters on the screen in real time. At least, you control your character—one among many characters controlled by many others in this space. One builds the world one will inhabit here. As a child, you grew up learning the physics that governed the world of Road Runner and Wile E. Coyote (violent but forgiving); your children will grow up making the world of Road Runner and Wile E. Coyote (still violent, but maybe not so forgiving). They will define the space and then live out the story. Their choices will make the laws of that space real.

This is not to say that MMOG space is unreal. There is real life in MMOG space, constituted by how people interact. The "space" describes where people interact—much as they interact in real space no doubt, but with some important differences. In MMOG space the interaction is in a virtual medium. This interaction is "in" cyberspace. In 1990s terms, people "jack" into these virtual spaces, and they do things there. And "they" turns out to be many many people. As Edward Castronova estimates, "an absolute minimum figure would be 10 million [but my] guess is that it is perhaps 20 to

30 million" participating in these virtual worlds.[3] The "[t]ypical user spends 20–30 hours per week inside the fantasy. Power users spend every available moment."[4] As one essay estimates, "assuming just average contact time among these 9.4 million people, subscribers to virtual worlds could be devoting over 213 million hours per week to build their virtual lives."[5]

The things people do there are highly varied. Some play role-playing games: working within a guild of other players to advance in status and power to some ultimate end. Some simply get together and gab: They appear (in a form they select, with qualities they choose and biographies they have written) in a virtual room and type messages to each other. Or they walk around (again, the ambiguity is not a slight one) and talk to people. My friend Rick does this as a cat—a male cat, he insists. As a male cat, Rick parades around this space and talks to anyone who's interested. He aims to flush out the cat-loving sorts. The rest, he reports, he punishes.

Others do much more than gab. Some, for example, homestead. Depending on the world and its laws, citizens are given or buy plots of undeveloped land, which they then develop. People spend extraordinary amounts of time building a life on these plots. (Isn't it incredible the way these people waste time? While you and I spend up to seventy hours a week working for firms we don't own and building futures we're not sure we'll enjoy, these people are designing and building things and making a life, even if only a virtual one. Scandalous!) They build houses—by designing and then constructing them—have family or friends move in, and pursue hobbies or raise pets. They may grow trees or odd plants—like Martha's.

MMOG space grew out of "MUD" or "MOO" space.[6] MUDs and MOOs are virtual worlds, too, but they are text-based virtual worlds. There are no real graphics in a MUD or MOO, just text, reporting what someone says and does. You can construct objects in MOO space and then have them do things. But the objects act only through the mediation of text. (Their actions are generally quite simple, but even simple can be funny. One year, in a MUD that was part of a cyberlaw class, someone built a character named JPosner. If you poked JPosner, he muttered, "Poking is inefficient." Another character was FEasterbrook. Stand in a room with FEasterbrook and use the word "fair," and FEasterbrook would repeat what you said, substituting the word "efficient." "It's not fair" became "You mean, it's not efficient.")

Although it was easy for people who liked texts or who wrote well to understand the attraction of these text-based realities, it was not so easy for the many who didn't have that same fondness. MMOG space lifts that limit just a bit. It is the movie version of a cyberspace novel. You build things here, and they survive your leaving. You can build a house, and people walking down the street see it. You can let them come in, and in coming into your house, they see things about you. They can see how you construct your world. If a particular MMOG space permits it, they might even see how you've changed the laws of the real world. In real space, for instance, people "slip and fall" on wet floors. In the MMOG space you've built, that "law" may not exist. Instead, in your world, wet floors may make people "slip and dance."

The best example of this space today is the extraordinary community of Second Life. In it, people create both things and community, the avatars are amazingly well crafted, and their owners spend hundreds of thousands of hours building things in this space that others see, and some enjoy. Some make clothes or hair styles, some make machines that make music. Whatever object or service the programming language allows, creators in Second Life are creating it. There are more than 100,000 residents of Second Life at the time of this writing. They occupy close to 2,000 servers housed in downtown San Francisco, and suck 250 kilowatts of electricity just to run the computers—about the equivalent of 160 homes.

But here we get back to Martha and Dank. In their exchange—when Martha blamed Dank for having a dog that died with pain—they revealed what was most amazing about that particular MMOG. Martha's remarks ("Why do you have a dog that suffers when dying? Get yourself a pain-free-death dog, and my petals will cause no harm") should have struck you as odd. You may have thought, "How weird that someone would think that the fault lay not in the poisonous petals but in a dog that died with pain." But in this space, Dank did have a choice about how his dog would die. Maybe not a choice about whether "poison" would "kill" a dog, but a choice about whether the dog would "suffer" when it "died." He also had a choice about whether a copy of the dog could be made, so that if it died it could be "revived." In MMOG space, these possibilities are not given by God. Or rather, if they are defined by God, then the players share the power of God. For the possibilities in MMOG space are determined by the code—the software, or architecture, that makes the MMOG space what it is. "What happens when" is a statement of logic; it asserts a relationship that is manifested in code. In real space we don't have much control over that code. In MMOG space we do.

So, when Martha said what she said about the dog, Dank made what seemed to me an obvious response. "Why do your flowers have to stay poisonous once they leave your land? Why not make the petals poisonous only when on your land? When they leave your land—when, for example, they are blown onto my land—why not make them harmless?"

It was an idea. But it didn't really help. For Martha made her living selling these poisonous plants. Others (ok not many, but some) also liked the idea of this art tied to death. So it was no solution to make poisonous plants that were poisonous only on Martha's property, unless Martha was also interested in collecting a lot of very weird people on her land.

But the idea did suggest another. "Okay," said Dank, "why not make the petals poisonous only when in the possession of someone who has 'purchased' them? If they are stolen, or if they blow away, then let the petals lose their poison. But when kept by the owner of the plant, the petals keep their poison. Isn't that a solution to the problem that both of us face?"

The idea was ingenious. Not only did it help Dank, it helped Martha as well. As the code existed, it allowed theft.[7] (People want reality in that virtual space; there will be time enough for heaven when heaven comes.) But if Martha could modify the code slightly so that theft[8] removed a plant's poison, then "theft" would also remove the plant's value. That change would protect the profit in her plants as well as protect Dank's dogs. Here was a solution that made both neighbors better off—what economists call a pareto superior move. And it was a solution that was as possible as any other. All it required was a change of code.

Think for a second about what's involved here. "Theft" entails (at minimum) a change in possession. But in MMOG space "possession" is just a relation defined by the software that defines the space. That same code must also define the properties that possession yields. It might, like real space, distinguish between having a cake and eating it. Or it might erase that distinction, meaning you can "eat" your cake, but once it's "eaten," it magically reappears. In MMOG space you can feed a crowd with five loaves and two fishes, and it isn't even a miracle.[9]

So why not craft the same solution to Martha and Dank's problem? Why not define ownership to include the quality of poisonousness, and possession without ownership to be possession without poison? If the world is designed this way, then it could resolve the dispute between Martha and Dank, not by making one of them change his or her behavior, but by changing the laws of nature to eliminate the conflict altogether.

My claim is that both "on the Internet" and "in cyberspace," we will confront precisely the questions that Martha and Dank faced, as well as the questions that their solution raised. Both "on the Internet" and "in cyberspace," technology constitutes the environment of the space, and it will give us a much wider range of control over how interactions work in that space than in real space. Problems can be programmed or "coded" into the story, and they can be "coded" away. And while the experience with gamers so far is that they don't want virtual worlds to deviate too far from the real, the important point for now is that there is the capacity to make these worlds different. It is this capacity that raises the question: What does it mean to live in a world where problems can be coded away? And when, in that world, should we code problems away, rather than learn to work them out, or punish those who cause them?

It is not MMOG space that makes these questions interesting problems for law; the very same problems will arise outside of MMOG space, and outside MUDs and MOOs. The problems of these spaces are problems of the Internet in general. And as more of our life becomes wired (and weird), in the sense that more of our life moves online, these questions will become more pressing.

But I have learned enough in this business to know that I can't convince you of this with an argument. (I've spent the last 12 years talking about this subject; at least I know what doesn't work.) If you see the point, good for you. If you don't, I must show you. So my method for readers of the second sort must be more indirect. Proof, for them, will come in a string of stories, which aim to introduce and disorient. That, again, is the purpose of this chapter.

Let me describe a few other places and the oddities that inhabit them.

## Governors

A state—call it "Boral"—doesn't like its citizens gambling, even if many of its citizens do like gambling. But the state is the boss; the people have voted; the law is as it is. Gambling in the state of Boral is illegal.

Then along comes the Internet. With the Net streaming into their homes through phones or cable lines, some citizens of Boral decide that Internet gambling is the next "killer app." A citizen of Boral sets up a "server" (a computer that is accessible on the Internet) that provides access to online gambling. The state doesn't like it. It tells this citizen, "Shut down your server or we will lock you up."

Wise, if evasive, the gambling Boralian agrees to shut his server down—at least in the state of Boral. But he doesn't choose to leave the gambling business. Instead, he rents space on a server in an "offshore haven." This offshore web server hums away, once again making gambling available on the Net and accessible to the people of Boral via the Internet. Here's the important point: Given the architecture of the Internet (at least as it was circa 1999), it doesn't really matter where in real space the server is. Access doesn't depend on geography. Nor, depending on how clever the gambling sorts are, does access require that the user know anything about who owns, or runs, the real server. The user's access can be passed through anonymizing sites that make it practically impossible in the end to know *what* went on *where* and with whom.

The Boral attorney general thus now faces a difficult problem. She may have moved the server out of her state, but she hasn't succeeded in reducing Boralian gambling. Before the Net, she would have had a group of people she could punish—those running gambling sites, and those who give those places custom. Now, the Net has made them potentially free from punishment—at the least because it is more difficult to know who is running the server or who is gambling. The world for this attorney general has changed. By going online, the gamblers moved into a world where this behavior is no longer *regulable*.

By "regulable" I mean simply that a certain behavior is capable of regulation. The term is comparative, not absolute—in some place, at some time, a certain behavior will be more regulable than at another place and in another time. My claim about Boral is simply that the Net makes gambling less regulable there than it was before the Net. Or at least, in a sense that will become clearer as the story continues, with the architecture of the Net as it originally was, life on the Net is less regulable than life off the Net.

## Jake's Communities

If you had met Jake at a party in Ann Arbor (were Jake at a party in Ann Arbor), you would have forgotten him.[10] If you didn't forget him, you might have thought, here's another quiet, dweeby University of Michigan undergraduate, terrified of the world, or, at least, of the people in the world.

You wouldn't have figured Jake for an author—indeed, quite a famous short-story author, at least within his circles. In fact, Jake is not just a famous author, he was also a character in his own stories. But who he was in his stories was quite different from who he was in "real" life—if, that is, after reading his stories you still thought this distinction between "real life" and "not real life" made much sense.

Jake wrote stories about violence—about sex as well, but mainly about violence. They seethed with hatred, especially of women. It wasn't enough to rape a woman, she had to be killed. And it wasn't enough that she was killed, she had to be killed in a particularly painful and tortured way. This is, however unfortunate, a genre of writing. Jake was a master of this genre.

In real space Jake had quite successfully hidden this propensity. He was one of a million boys: unremarkable, indistinguishable, harmless. Yet however inoffensive in real space, the harmfulness he penned in cyberspace was increasingly well known. His stories were published in USENET, in a group called alt.sex.stories.

USENET isn't itself a network, except in the sense that the personal ads of a national newspaper are part of a network. Strictly speaking, USENET is the product of a protocol—a set of rules named the network news transfer protocol (NNTP)—for exchanging messages intended for public viewing. These messages are organized into "newsgroups," and the newsgroups are organized into subjects. Most of the subjects are quite technical, many are related to hobbies, and some are related to sex. Some messages newsgroups come with pictures or movies, but some, like Jake's, are simply stories.

There are thousands of newsgroups, each carrying hundreds of messages at any one time. Anyone with access to a USENET server can get access to the messages (or at least to the ones his administrator wants him to read), and anyone with access can post a message or respond to one already posted. Imagine a public bulletin board on which people post questions or comments. Anyone can read the board and add his or her own thoughts. Now imagine 15,000 boards, each with hundreds of "threads" (strings of arguments, each tied to the next). That, in any one place, is USENET. Now imagine these 15,000 boards, with hundreds of threads each, on millions of computers across the world. Post a message in one group, and it is added to that group's board every-where. That, for the world, is USENET.

Jake, as I said, posted to a group called alt.sex.stories. "Alt" in that name refers to the hierarchy that the group sits within. Initially, there were seven primary hier-archies.[11] "Alt" was created in reaction to this initial seven: Groups are added to the seven through a formal voting process among participants in the groups. But groups are added to "alt" based solely on whether administrators choose to carry them, and, generally, administrators will carry them if they are popular, as long as their popularity is not controversial.

Among these groups that are carried only on demand, alt.sex.stories is quite popular. As with any writing space, if stories are "good" by the standards of the space—if they are stories that users of the space demand—they are followed and their authors become well known.

Jake's stuff was very valuable in just this sense. His stories, about kidnapping, torturing, raping, and killing women, were as graphic and repulsive as any such story could be—which is why Jake was so famous among like-minded sorts. He was a supplier to these people, a constant and consistent fix. They needed these accounts of innocent women being violated, and Jake supplied them for free.

One night in Moscow, a sixteen-year-old girl read a story by Jake. She showed it to her father, who showed it in turn to Richard DuVal, a Michigan alum. DuVal was shocked at the story, and angry that it bore the tag "umich.edu" on the story's header. He called his alma mater and complained. They took the complaint seriously.[12]

The university contacted the police; the police contacted Jake—with handcuffs and a jail cell. A slew of doctors examined him. Some concluded that he was a threat. The local prosecutors agreed with these doctors, especially after his computer was seized and e-mails were discovered between Jake and a Canadian fan who was planning to re-enact in real space one of the stories Jake published in cyberspace. At least, that's what the e-mails said. No one could tell for certain what the two men really intended. Jake said it was all pure fiction, and indeed, there was no evidence to prove otherwise.

Nonetheless, federal charges were brought against Jake for the transmission of a threat. Jake said that his stories were only words, protected by the First Amendment to the U.S. Constitution. A month and a half later, a court agreed. The charges were dropped,[13] and Jake returned to the special kind of obscurity that had defined his life before.

I don't care so much just now about whether Jake Baker's words should have been protected by the Constitution. My concern is Jake Baker himself, a person normed into apparent harmlessness in real space, but set free in cyberspace to become the author of this violence. People said Jake was brave, but he wasn't "brave" in real space. He didn't express his hatred in classes, among friends, or in the school newspaper. He slithered away to cyberspace, and only there did his deviancy flourish.

He did this because of something about him and something about cyberspace. Jake was the sort who wanted to spread stories of violence, at least if he could do so without public account. Cyberspace gave Jake this power. Jake was in effect an author and publisher in one. He wrote stories, and as quickly as he finished them he published them—to some thirty million computers across the world within a few days. His potential audience was larger than twice that for the top fifteen best-selling novels combined, and though he made nothing from his work, the demand for it was high. Jake had discovered a way to mainline his depravity into the veins of a public for whom this stuff was otherwise quite difficult to find. (Even *Hustler* wouldn't publish the likes of this.)

Of course, there were other ways Jake could have published. He could have offered his work to *Hustler*, or worse. But no real-world publication would have given Jake a comparable audience. Jake's readership was potentially millions, stretching across country and continent, across culture and taste.

This reach was made possible by the power in the network: Anyone anywhere could publish to everyone everywhere. The network allowed publication without filtering, editing, or, perhaps most importantly, responsibility. One could write what one wanted, sign it or not, post it to machines across the world, and within hours the words would be everywhere. The network removed the most important constraint on speech in real space—the separation of publisher from author. There is vanity publishing in real space, but only the rich can use it to reach a broad audience. For the rest of us, real space affords only the access that the publishers want to give us.

Thus cyberspace is different because of the reach it allows. But it is also different because of the relative anonymity it permits. Cyberspace permitted Jake to escape the constraints of real space. He didn't "go to" cyberspace when he wrote his stories, in the sense that he didn't "leave" Ann Arbor. But when he was "in" cyberspace, it allowed him to escape the norms of Ann Arbor. He was free of real-life constraints, of the norms and understandings that had successfully formed him into a member of a college community. Maybe he wasn't perfectly at home; maybe he wasn't the happiest. But the world of the University of Michigan had succeeded in steering him away from the life of a psychopath—except when it gave him access to the Net. On the Net he was someone else.

As the Internet has grown, it has produced many more opportunities for Jake-like characters—characters that do things in the virtual world that they would never do in the real world. One of the most popular MMOGs is a game called "Grand Theft Auto." In this game, one practices committing crimes. And one of the most troubling uses of video chat is the practice of virtual-prostitution by children. As the *New York Times* recently reported, thousands of children spend hundreds of hours prostituting themselves online. Sitting in the "privacy" of their own bedroom, using the iSight camera their parents gave them for Christmas, a 13-year-old girl or boy enacts the sexual behavior demanded by the audience. The audience gets their fix of sexual perversion. The kid gets money, and whatever psychological baggage this behavior creates.[14]

It is impossibly difficult to look across this range of Jake-like characters and not think that, at some point, the virtual has crossed over into something real. Or, at least, the virtual has real effects—either on those who live it, or on those who live with them.[15] When Jake was prosecuted, many First Amendment defenders argued his words, however vivid, never crossed into reality. And no doubt, there is a difference between writing about rape and raping, just as there is a difference between an actor enacting rape and actually raping someone. But I take it that all concede a line is crossed somewhere as we move across this range of Jake-like characters. If a parent was untroubled by the virtual prostitution of her son in his bedroom, we would not understand that to be principled free speech activism, even if the only "prostitution" was the son describing in text how he was molested by those in the chat.

But my point is not to draw lines between the acceptable virtual dual-lives and the unacceptable. It is instead to remark that this space enables more of this duality. And though part of this duality is always "only virtual," and sometimes "only words," real-space regulators (whether parents or governments) will feel compelled to react. The Net enables lives that were previously impossible, or inconvenient, or uncommon. At least some of those virtual lives will have effects on non-virtual lives—both the lives of the people living in the virtual space, and the lives of those around them.

## Worms That Sniff

A "worm" is a bit of computer code that is spit out on the Net and works its way into the systems of vulnerable computers. It is not a "virus" because it doesn't attach itself to other programs and interfere with their operation. It is just a bit of extra code that does what the code writer says. The code could be harmless and simply sit on someone's machine. Or it could be harmful and corrupt files or do other damage that its author commands.

Imagine a worm designed to do good (at least in the minds of some). Imagine that the code writer is the FBI and that the FBI is looking for a particular document belonging to the National Security Agency (NSA). Suppose that this document is classified and illegal to possess without the proper clearance. Imagine that the worm propagates itself on the Net, finding its way onto hard disks wherever it can. Once on a computer's hard disk, it scans the entire disk. If it finds the NSA document, it sends a message back to the FBI saying as much. If it doesn't, it erases itself. Finally, assume that it can do all this without "interfering" with the operation of the machine. No one would know it was there; it would report back nothing except that the NSA document was on the hard disk.

Is this an unconstitutional worm? This is a hard question that at first seems to have an easy answer. The worm is engaging in a government-initiated search of citizens' disks. There is no reasonable suspicion (as the law ordinarily requires) that the disk holds the document for which the government is searching. It is a generalized, suspicionless search of private spaces by the government.

From the standpoint of the Constitution—the Fourth Amendment in particular— you don't get any worse than that. The Fourth Amendment was written against the background of just this sort of abuse. Kings George II and George III would give officers a "general warrant" authorizing them to search through private homes looking for evidence of a crime.[16] No suspicion was needed before the officer ransacked your house, but because he had a warrant, you were not able to sue the officer for trespass. The aim of the Fourth Amendment was to require at least suspicion, so that the burden of the search fell on a reasonably chosen class.[17]

But is the worm really the same as the King's general search? One important difference is this: Unlike the victims of the general searches that the Framers of our Constitution were concerned about, the computer user never knows that his or her disk is being searched by the worm. With the general search, the police were breaking into a house and rummaging through private stuff. With the worm, it is a bit of computer code that does the breaking, and (I've assumed) it can "see" only one thing. And perhaps more importantly, unlike the general search, the worm learns little and leaves no damage after it's finished: The code can't read private letters; it doesn't break down doors; it doesn't interfere with ordinary life. And the innocent have nothing to fear.

The worm is silent in a way that King George's troops were not. It searches perfectly and invisibly, discovering only the guilty. It does not burden the innocent; it does not trouble the ordinary citizen; it captures only what is outside the protection of the law.

This difference complicates the constitutional question. The worm's behavior is like a generalized search in that it is a search without suspicion. But it is unlike the historical generalized search in that it creates no disruption of ordinary life and "discovers" only contraband. In this way, the worm is like a dog sniff—which at least at airports is constitutionally permissible without probable cause[18]—but better. Unlike the dog sniff, the worm doesn't even let the computer user know when there is a search (and hence the user suffers no particularized anxiety).

Is the worm, then, constitutional? That depends on your conception of what the Fourth Amendment protects. In one view, the amendment protects against suspicionless governmental invasions, whether those invasions are burdensome or not. In a second view, the amendment protects against invasions that are burdensome, allowing only those for which there is adequate suspicion that guilt will be uncovered. The paradigm case that motivated the framers does not distinguish between these two very different types of protections, because the technology of the time wouldn't distinguish either. You couldn't—technically—have a perfectly burdenless generalized search in 1791. So they didn't—technically—express a view about whether such a search should be consti-tutionally proscribed. It is instead we who must choose what the amendment is to mean.

Let's take the example one step further. Imagine that the worm does not search every machine it encounters, but instead can be put on a machine only with judicial authorization—say, a warrant. Now the suspicionless-search part of the problem has been removed. But now imagine a second part to this rule: The government requires that networks be constructed so that a worm, with judicial authorization, could be placed on any machine. Machines in this regime, in other words, must be made worm-ready, even though worms will be deployed only with judicial warrant.

Is there any constitutional problem with this? I explore this question in much greater detail, but for now, notice its salient feature. In both cases, we are describing a regime that allows the government to collect data about us in a highly efficient man-ner—inexpensively, that is, for both the government and the innocent. This efficiency is made possible by technology, which permits searches that before would have been far too burdensome and invasive. In both cases, then, the question comes to this: When the ability to search without burden increases, does the government's power to search increase as well? Or, more darkly, as James Boyle puts it: "Is freedom inversely related to the efficiency of the available means of surveillance?" For if it is, as Boyle puts it, then "we have much to fear."[19]

This question, of course, is not limited to the government. One of the defining features of modern life is the emergence of technologies that make data collection and processing extraordinarily efficient. Most of what we do—hence, most of what we are—is recorded outside our homes. When you make telephone calls, data are recorded about whom you called, when, how long you spoke, and how frequently you made such calls.[20] When you use your credit cards, data are recorded about when, where, what, and from whom you made purchases. When you take a flight, your itinerary is recorded and possibly profiled by the government to determine whether you are likely to be a terrorist.[21] If you drive a car in London, cameras record your license plate to determine whether you've paid the proper "congestion tax." No doubt Hollywood's image of counter-terrorist units—where one person sitting behind a terminal instantly tracks the life of another—is wrong. But it need not be terribly wrong for much longer. It may not be easy to imagine systems that follow an individual wherever he goes, but it is easy to imagine technologies that gather an extraordinary amount of data about everything we do and make those data accessible to those with the proper authorization. The intrusiveness would be slight, and the payoff could be great.

Both private and public monitoring in the digital age, then, have the same salient feature: monitoring, or searching, can increase without increasing the burden on the individual searched. Both present a similar question: How should we think about this change? How should the protection the framers gave us be applied to a world the framers couldn't even imagine?

## Themes

Four stories, four themes, each a window into one aspect of cyberspace that will be central in all that follows. I thus end this chapter with a map of the four.

### Regulability

"Regulability" is the capacity of a government to regulate behavior within its proper reach. In the context of the Internet, that means the ability of the government to regulate the behavior of (at least) its citizens while on the Net. The story about Boral was thus a story about regulability, or more specifically, about the changes in regulability that cyberspace brings. Before the Internet, it was relatively easy for the attorney general of Boral to control commercial gambling within her jurisdiction; after the Internet, when the servers moved outside of Boral, regulation became much more difficult.

For the regulator, this is just a particular instance of a much more general story. To regulate well, you need to know (1) who someone is, (2) where they are, and (3) what they're doing. But because of the way the Internet was originally designed (and more on this below), there was no simple way to know (1) who someone is, (2) where they are, and (3) what they're doing. Thus, as life moved onto (this version of) the Internet, the regulability of that life decreased. The architecture of the space—at least as it was—rendered life in this space less regulable.

Can we imagine a more regulable cyberspace? Is this the cyberspace we are coming to know?

## Regulation by Code

The story about Martha and Dank is a clue to answering this question about regulability. If in MMOG space we can change the laws of nature—make possible what before was impossible, or make impossible what before was possible—why can't we change regulability in cyberspace? Why can't we imagine an Internet or a cyberspace where behavior can be controlled because code now enables that control?

For this, importantly, is just what MMOG space is. MMOG space is "regulated," though the regulation is special. In MMOG space regulation comes through code. Important rules are imposed, not through social sanctions, and not by the state, but by the very architecture of the particular space. A rule is defined, not through a statute, but through the code that governs the space.

This is the second theme of this book: There is regulation of behavior on the Internet and in cyberspace, but that regulation is imposed primarily through code. The differences in the regulations effected through code distinguish different parts of the Internet and cyberspace. In some places, life is fairly free; in other places, it is more controlled. And the difference between these spaces is simply a difference in the architectures of control—that is, a difference in code.

If we combine the first two themes, then, we come to a central argument: The regulability described in the first theme depends on the code described in the second. Some architectures of cyberspace are more regulable than others; some architectures enable better control than others. Therefore, whether a part of cyberspace—or the Internet generally—can be regulated turns on the nature of its code. Its architecture will affect whether behavior can be controlled. To follow Mitch Kapor, its architecture is its politics.[22]

And from this a further point follows: If some architectures are more regulable than others—if some give governments more control than others—then governments will favor some architectures more than others. Favor, in turn, can translate into action, either by governments, or for governments. Either way, the architectures that render space less regulable can themselves be changed to make the space more regulable. (By whom, and why, is a matter we take up later.)

This fact about regulability is a threat to those who worry about governmental power; it is a reality for those who depend upon governmental power. Some designs enable government more than others; some designs enable government differently; some designs should be chosen over others, depending upon the values at stake.

## Latent Ambiguity

The worm tells a different story still. Though it is a technology for searching, the worm's function differs from "searching" in real space. In real space, a search carries costs: the burdens of the search, the insecurities it might create, the exposure it might make possible to invasions beyond a legitimate reach.[23] The worm erases those costs: The burden is gone, the search is (practically) invisible, and the searching technology is programmed to find only what is illegal. This raises a question about how such a search should, under the Constitution, be understood.

A fair view of the Constitution's protections could go in either of two ways. It may be that we see the worm's invasion as inconsistent with the dignity that the amendment was written to protect,[24] or it may be that we see the invasion of the worm as so unobtrusive as to be reasonable. The answer could be either, which means that the change reveals what I will call "a latent ambiguity" in the original constitutional rule. In the original context, the rule was clear (no generalized search), but in the current context, the rule depends upon which value the Constitution was meant to protect. The question is now ambiguous between (at least) two different answers. Either answer is possible, depending upon the value, so now we must choose one or the other.

You may not buy my story about the worm. You may think it is pure science fiction. But . . . I will convince you that there are any number of cases in which a similar ambiguity troubles our constitutional past. In many of them our Constitution yields no answer to the question of how it should be applied, because at least two answers are possible—in light of the choices that the framers actually made and given the technologies of today.

For Americans, this ambiguity creates a problem. If we lived in an era when courts felt entitled to select the value that produced an answer that made the most sense in the context, there would be no problem. Latent ambiguities would be answered by choices made by judges—the framers could have gone either way, but our judges choose to go *this* way.

But we don't live in such an era, and so we don't have a way for courts to resolve these ambiguities. As a result, we must rely on other institutions. My claim is a dark one: We have no such institutions. If our ways don't change, our constitution in cyberspace will be a thinner and thinner regime.

Cyberspace will present us with ambiguities over and over again. It will press this question of how best to go on. We have tools from real space that will help resolve the interpretive questions by pointing us in one direction or another, at least some of the time. But in the end the tools will guide us even less than they do in real space and time. When the gap between their guidance and what we do becomes obvious, we will be forced to do something we're not very good at doing—deciding what we want, and what is right.

## Competing Sovereigns

But regulation by whom? For the rules are different in one place versus another.

This was one important issue raised by Jake Baker. Jake lived in Ann Arbor, Michigan. His life there was subject to the norms of Ann Arbor, and he apparently adapted to these norms reasonably well. The authority of that space governed Jake, and, as far as anyone knew, it appeared to govern him exclusively.

But in cyberspace, Jake's behavior changed, in part because the norms of the space were different. That created the problem. For when Jake "went to" cyberspace, he didn't leave real space. In particular, he never left Ann Arbor. While sitting in a dorm at the University of Michigan, he was able to teleport himself—in the only normatively significant sense—to a different world where the norms of civility and decency that governed outside his dorm room did not reign. Cyberspace gave Jake the chance to escape Ann Arbor norms and to live according to the norms of another place. It created a competing authority for Jake and gave him the chance to select between these competing authorities merely by switching his computer on or off.

Again, my point is not that no similar possibility exists in real space—it plainly does. There is no doubt a Jake living in Hackensack, New Jersey (a suburban town with suburban values), who drives every night into lower Manhattan and lives for a few hours according to the "rules" of lower Manhattan. Those rules are not the rules of Hackensack; that life is different. Like Ann Arbor Jake, the Hackensack Jake lives under competing authorities. But between the lives of these two Jakes, there is a difference in degree that ripens into a difference in kind: It is at least conceivable that the Ann Arbor Jake raises a more significant problem for Ann Arbor than the Hackensack Jake raises for Hackensack. The differences could well be greater, and the effect more pervasive.

Nor should we think too narrowly about the competing normative communities into which a Jake might move. "Escape" here can be good or bad. It is escape when a gay teen in an intolerant small town can leave the norms of that town through a gay chat room on America Online;[25] it is escape when a child predator escapes the norms of ordinary society and engages a child in online sex.[26] Both escapes are enabled by the architecture of cyberspace as we now know it. Our attitudes about each, however, are very different. I call the first escape liberating and the second criminal. There are some who would call both escapes criminal, and some who would call both liberating. But the question isn't about name-calling, it's about the consequences of living in a world where we can occupy both sorts of space at the same time. When 50 people from 25 jurisdictions around the world spend 2,000 hours building a virtual community in Second Life that is housed on servers in San Francisco, what claim should real world jurisdictions have over that activity? Which of the 25 jurisdictions matters most? Which sovereign should govern?

Regulation in cyberspace can help us see something important about how all regulation works. That's the lesson of the first theme, "regulability." It will also introduce a regulator ("code") whose significance we don't yet fully understand. That's the second theme, "Regulation by Code." That regulation will render ambiguous certain values that are fundamental to our tradition. Thus, the third theme, "latent ambiguity." That ambiguity will require us, the United States, to make a choice. But this choice is just one among many that many sovereigns will have to make. In the end the hardest problem will be to reckon these "competing sovereigns," as they each act to mark this space with their own distinctive values.

I explore these four themes against a background that, as I said at the start, has changed significantly since the first edition of this book. When I first wrote the book, two ideas seemed to dominate debate about the Net: first, that the government could never regulate the Net, and second, that this was a good thing. Today, attitudes are different. There is still the commonplace that government can't regulate, but in a world drowning in spam, computer viruses, identity theft, copyright "piracy," and the sexual exploitation of children, the resolve against regulation has weakened. We all love the Net. But if some government could really deliver on the promise to erase all the bads of this space, most of us would gladly sign up.

Yet while attitudes about the Net have progressed, my own views have not. I still believe the Net can be regulated. I still believe that the obvious consequence of obvious influences will be to radically increase the ability of governments to regulate this Net. I also still believe that, in principle, this is not a bad thing. I am not against regulation, properly done. I believe regulation is essential to preserving and defending certain fundamental liberties. But I also still believe that we are far from a time when our government in particular can properly regulate in this context. This is both because of a general skepticism about government—grounded in a disgust about the particular form of corruption that defines how our government functions—and a particular skepticism about government—that it has not yet fully recognized just how regulation in the digital age works.

No doubt this particular mix of views will continue to puzzle some. How can I believe in regulation and yet be so skeptical about government? But it doesn't take much imagination to understand how these apparently conflicting views can go together. I take it we all believe in the potential of medicine. But imagine your attitude if you were confronted with a "doctor" carrying a vial of leeches. There's much we could do in this context, or at least, that is my view. But there's a very good reason not to want to do anything with this particular doctor.

## Questions for Consideration

1  Earlier in his book, Lessig states that "code is law." What does he mean?
2  Which of Lessig's "four puzzles" most intrigues or concerns you? Why?
3  Lessig states that "Regulation in cyberspace can help us see something important about how all regulation works." What do you think he means? Give an example from another media industry.

## Notes

1.  Second Life—"What is Second Life?". The currently leading game, World of Warcraft, claims more than five million alone.
2.  It is also hypothetical. I have constructed this story in light of what could be, and in places is. I'm a law professor; I make up hypotheticals for a living.
3.  Edward Castronova, *Synthetic Worlds: The Business and Culture of Online Games* (Chicago: University of Chicago Press, 2005), 55.
4.  Ibid., 2.
5.  John Crowley and Viktor Mayer-Schoenberger, "Napster's Second Life?—The Regulatory Challenges of Virtual Worlds" (Kennedy School of Government, Working Paper No. RWP05–052, 2005), 8.
6.  "MUD" has had a number of meanings, originally Multi-User Dungeon, or Multi-User Domain. A MOO is a "MUD, object-oriented." Sherry Turkle's analysis of life in a MUD or MOO, *Life on the Screen: Identity in the Age of the Internet* (New York: Simon and Schuster, 1995), is still a classic. See also Elizabeth Reid, "Hierarchy and Power: Social Control in Cyberspace," in *Communities in Cyberspace*, edited by Marc A. Smith and Peter Kollock (New York: Routledge, 1999), 107. The father—or god—of a MUD named LambdaMOO is Pavel Curtis. See his account in "Mudding: Social Phenomena in Text-Based Virtual Realities," in Stefik, *Internet Dreams*, 265–92. For two magical pages of links about the

history of MUDs, see Lauren P. Burka, "The MUDline"; and Lauren P. Burka, "The MUDdex."

7.    This is not a rare feature of these spaces. It is indeed quite common, at least within role-playing games. Julian Dibbell described to me a "parable" he recognized within Ultima Online: As he calls it, the "case of the stolen Bone Crusher."

> "I got two offers for a Bone Crusher, which is a powerful sort of mace for bopping monsters over the head. I started dealing with both of them. At a certain point I was informed by one of them that the Bone Crusher had been stolen. So I said, 'I'll go buy it from the other guy. But, by the way, who was it that stole the Bone Crusher, do you know?' He said the name of the other guy. I was faced with this dilemma of was I going to serve as a fence for this other guy knowingly. And so, I turned to my mentor in this business, the guy who had been doing this for years and makes six figures a year on it, and, you know, I thought of him as an honest guy. So I sort of thought and maybe even hoped that he would just say just walk away. We don't do these kinds of deals in our business. We don't need that, you know, blah, blah, blah. But he said, 'Well, you know, thieving is built into the game. It is a skill that you can do. So fair is fair.' It is in the code that you can go into somebody's house and practice your thieving skills and steal something from them. And so, I went ahead and did the deal but there was this lingering sense of, 'Wow, in a way that is completely arbitrary that this ability is in the code here whereas, you know, if it wasn't built into the code it would be another story; they would have stolen it in another way.' . . ."
>
> "But in Ultima Online, it is very explicitly understood that the code allows you to steal and the rules allow you to steal. For me what was interesting was that there remains this gray area. It made it an interesting game, that you were allowed to do something that was actually morally shady and you might have to decide for yourself. I'm not sure that now, going back to the deal, I would have taken the fenced item. I've been stolen from in the game, according to the rules, and it feels like shit."
>
> (Audio Tape: Interview with Julian Dibbell (1/6/06) (on file with author))

8.    And only theft. If you transferred the property for a different purpose—say, sold the property—then the feature wouldn't change.

9.    Compare Susan Brenner, "The Privacy Privilege: Law Enforcement, Technology and the Constitution," *Journal of Technology Law and Policy* 7 (2002): 123, 160. ("Pool tables in cyberspace do not require legs in this place where gravity does not exist"), citing Neal Stephenson, *Snow Crash* (New York: Bantam, 1992), 50 (in the Metaverse, tables only have tops, not legs).

10.   Jake Baker's given name was Abraham Jacob Alkhabaz, but he changed his name after his parents' divorce. See Peter H. Lewis, "Writer Arrested After Sending Violent Fiction Over Internet," *New York Times*, February 11, 1995, 10.

11.   The seven are comp, misc, news, rec, sci, soc, and talk. See Henry Edward Hardy, "The History of the Net, v8.5," September 28, 1993.

12.   I have drawn from Jonathan Wallace and Mark Mangan's vivid account in *Sex, Laws, and Cyberspace* (New York: M&T Books, 1996), 63–81, though more interesting variations on this story circulate on the Net (I'm playing it safe).

13.   See *United States v. Baker*, 890 FSupp 1375, 1390 (EDMich 1995); see also Wallace and Mangan, *Sex, Laws, and Cyberspace*, 69–78.

14.   See Kurt Eichenwald, "Through His Webcam, a Bot Joins a Sordid Online World," *New York Times*, December 19, 2005, A1.

15.   See C. Anderson and B. Bushman, "Effects of Violent Video Games on Aggressive Behavior, Aggressive Cognition, Aggressive Affect, Physiological Arousal, and Prosocial Behavior: A Meta-Analytic Review of the Scientific Literature," *Psychological Science* 12(5) (2001): 353–359, available at link #8; Jonathan L. Freedman, *Media Violence and Its Effect on Aggression* (Toronto: Toronto University Press, 2002).

16.    See William J. Stuntz, "The Substantive Origins of Criminal Procedure," *Yale Law Journal* 105 (1995): 393, 406–7.

17.    See, for example, Thomas K. Clancy, "The Role of Individualized Suspicion in Assessing the Reasonableness of Searches and Seizures," *University of Memphis Law Review* 25 (1995): 483, 632. "Individualized suspicion . . . has served as a bedrock protection against unjustified and arbitrary police actions."

18.    See *United States v. Place*, 462 US 693, 707 (1983).

19.    James Boyle, *Shamans, Software, and Spleens: Law and the Construction of the Information Society* (Cambridge, Mass.: Harvard University Press, 1996), 4.

20.    See Susan Freiwald, "Uncertain Privacy: Communication Attributes After the Digital Telephony Act," *Southern California Law Review* 69 (1996): 949, 951, 954.

21.    Cf. John Rogers, "Bombs, Borders, and Boarding: Combatting International Terrorism at United States Airports and the Fourth Amendment," *Suffolk Transnational Law Review* 20 (1997): 501, n.201.

22.    See Mitchell Kapor, "The Software Design Manifesto"; David Farber, "A Note on the Politics of Privacy and Infrastructure," November 20, 1993, "Quotations"; see also Pamela Samuelson et al., "A Manifesto Concerning the Legal Protection of Computer Programs," *Columbia Law Review* 94 (1994): 2308. Steven Johnson powerfully makes a similar point: "All works of architecture imply a worldview, which means that all architecture is in some deeper sense political"; see *Interface Culture: How New Technology Transforms the Way We Create and Communicate* (San Francisco: Harper Edge, 1997), 44. The Electronic Frontier Foundation, originally cofounded by Mitch Kapor and John Perry Barlow, has updated Kapor's slogan "architecture is politics" to "architecture is policy." I prefer the original.

23.    Jed Rubenfeld has developed most extensively an interpretive theory that grounds meaning in a practice of reading across time, founded on paradigm cases; see "Reading the Constitution as Spoken," *Yale Law Journal* 104 (1995): 1119, 1122; and "On Fidelity in Constitutional Law," *Fordham Law Review* 65 (1997): 1469. See also Jed Rubenfeld, *Freedom and Time; A Theory of Constitutional Government* (New Haven: Yale University Press, 2001).

24.    See *Minnesota v. Dickerson*, 508 US 366, 380 (1993) (Justice Antonin Scalia concurring: "I frankly doubt . . . whether the fiercely proud men who adopted our Fourth Amendment would have allowed themselves to be subjected, on mere suspicion of being armed and dangerous, to such indignity. . . .").

25.    See Steve Silberman, "We're Teen, We're Queer, and We've Got E-Mail," *Wired* (November 1994): 76, 78, 80, reprinted in *Composing Cyberspace: Identity, Community, and Knowledge in the Electronic Age*, edited by Richard Holeton (Boston: McGraw-Hill, 1998), 116.

26.    Cf. *United States v. Lamb*, 945 F.Supp 441 (NDNY 1996). (Congress's intent in passing the Child Protection Act was to regulate child pornography via computer transmission, an interest legitimately related to stemming the flow of child pornography.)

PART TWO

# The Print Media

# INTRODUCTION

YOU PROBABLY NOTICE IT IN your own life: print media in America are facing tremendous challenges in the digital age. Daily newspapers have long been losing readers, but that loss is accelerating as people turn to the Web to read news. Advertisers have been leaving the papers to follow the readers, and while many of the readers (and some advertisers) have turned to those papers' web sites, the gain in online advertising has not yet made up for the losses on the print side. The situation is more varied in the magazine industry. Many magazines have been hit hard by the movement of readers and advertisers online, though many others have managed to hold on to their print readers and advertisers. The more general question magazine publishers have faced in recent years is how much of their printed material to post online, and whether they should charge readers for that material. Most have recently concluded—as most newspaper publishers concluded years ago—that they should open all articles to free online reading and try to make money by selling advertisers the right to reach those audiences. At the same time, newspaper and magazine publishers alike have found that their understandings of their print and online periodicals have had to change. A printed version may come out once a day or once a month, while readers may expect an online version to change all the time, as circumstances demand. That requires a rethinking of what it means to produce a newspaper and a magazine.

The book industry has not yet been as profoundly impacted by the digital world, but important changes are taking place. You may have seen the digital readers that Sony and Amazon have been selling. These are portable devices that allow people to download dozens of books for immediate access. Textbook companies have also been selling digital copies for use on laptops by high school and college students. So far, these developments cannot be called huge successes, but the technology is quite new, and it is likely to become even more advanced in the coming decades.

All this is taking place in an American society that itself is being altered dramatically, by immigration that is transforming the population, by energy costs, and by a gap between the upper class and working class that is widening. Newspaper, magazine, and book publishers have tried to adapt to these changes as well. The readings in this section cannot cover them all, but we have chosen pieces that will give you a sense of the challenges that they face. And, because continuities exist among even remarkable changes, we have included decades-old pieces about making news and making advertisements that point to issues around print media that have been around for a long time.

# Chapter 7

## GAYE TUCHMAN

## MAKING NEWS
## Time and Typifications

T HE WORLD CAN BE A confusing place, and we all have to make sense of it in
order to get our work done and keep our lives reasonably predictable. Sociologists
sometimes use the term *typification* to describe the tags or classifications that people
develop to make sense of the world. For Gaye Tuchman, the need for typifications helps
explain the ways journalists think about news. She points out that the way they understand the worlds of soft, hard, spot, developing, and continuing news has much to do
with the demands of their jobs and the time schedules in which they and the people
they cover work. Despite the changes roiling through journalism, the terms *soft*, *hard*,
*spot*, *developing*, and *continuing* news are as much a part of reporters' understanding
of the world today as in 1978, when *Making News*, the book from which this reading
comes, was published. Tuchman helps us understand why.

As competent members of society, we all commonsensically know of the intertwining
of time and space. We speak of a family hour, a time when people gather in the same
space for a common activity. We measure space in temporal terms when we indicate
that some place is within a two-minute drive or a ten-minute walk. We use a spatial
metaphor when we speak of a "length of time." Specialists in the study of time-use
affirm that we measure distances temporally. They inform us that diverse societies
regulate the time it takes to get from home to work, regardless of the distance. That
is, people who drive to work in the United States average the same amount of time
in transit as do people who use public transportation in some European societies
(Robinson, Converse, and Szalai, 1972).

Yet, the metaphor of "spatialized time" is profound, for it emphasizes that the social
ordering of time and space stands at the heart of organized human activity. A few
sociologists have written on this theme of the social generation of time measurement.
In a monograph reminiscent of Thomas Mann's *Magic Mountain* (1946), Roth (1963)
considers the generation of timetables by patients at a tuberculosis sanitarium. Even

earlier, in a classic article, Sorokin and Merton (1937) point out that the calendar is a social artifact geared to the rhythm of collective activity. Surveying a variety of societies, they find "weeks" of assorted lengths. For agricultural societies, they note, the number of days in the week is related to the frequency of market day. Bringing produce to a central location marks a break in the routine chores of day-to-day agricultural existence. Furthermore, Zerubavel (1977) finds that the generation of a calendar to coordinate social activities requires its legitimation by institutions. He points out that the French Republic successfully instituted the metric system of measures and weights but failed in its attempt to impose a rational metric calendar. Although legally introduced, its chronological framework and subdivisions of the day could not replace social rhythms associated with church life, and so the "logical" calendar was ultimately discarded.

The interwining of time and space as social phenomena is implicit in both the Sorokin and Merton (1937) and the Zerubavel (1977) discussions. The week of non-Christian agricultural communities was set off by physical movement from farm to market place. The week of active French Christians was marked by bodily movement to church services. Indeed, in some religious communities, gatherings with special spatial characteristics also mark the division of the day into discrete units. For instance, Heilman (1976) tells us, members of an Orthodox Jewish synagogue signify their religiosity by gathering to pray together morning and evening. At these morning and evening gatherings they disperse through the sanctuary in a different pattern from that used at the main Sabbath service.

A similar intertwining of time and space is found in the anchoring of the news net.[1] Consider some examples mentioned in the earlier discussion of the spatial dispersion of reporters and the activities of editors. First, I suggested that editorial conferences are held because editors are not necessarily aware of occurrences unfolding simultaneously in others' geographic territories, even though those occurrences collectively compete for inclusion in the news product. Second, I suggested, the managing editor keeps track of what's happening or is expected to happen, and where, so that he can revise plans for the daily news product should an important occurrence arise unexpectedly. Similarly, the City Hall bureau chief of one New York newspaper was said to keep tabs on the number of "his" reporters in the City Hall area in case a story requiring the services of many reporters should break. In Schutz' (1962: 69) terms, such temporal planning characterizes social action as project. That is, social action is carried out in the future perfect tense. Action is cast into the future in order to accomplish acts that will have happened, should everything go as anticipated.

Other examples of the intertwining of social time and social space also illustrate news as accomplished project.[2] Until the mid-1970s, the London bureau of the *New York Times* edited European and African copy because its location enabled copy to have been edited before the New York workday began (Adler, 1971). To mix metaphors of time and space, that work could be done in the time zone (geographic location) of the London bureau meant that New York copy editors had some of their work "already out of the way" before their workday formally began. One may generalize that the news media carefully impose a structure upon time and space to enable themselves to accomplish the work of any one day and to plan across days. As is the case with the spatial news net, the structuring of time influences the assessment of occurrences as news events.

## The Rhythm of Newsmaking

### The Daily Tempo

Just as reporters seek central spatial locations to find potential news events, so, too, reporters are temporally concentrated. At morning papers, most reporters come to work between 10:00 and 11:00 A.M., after offices likely to generate news have geared up for the day. Most reporters leave between 6:00 and 7:00 P.M., after news sources have closed their offices. One or two reporters check in at 8:00 A.M. at metropolitan dailies "in case something should happen" before the others arrive. A skeletal staff remains until 11:00 P.M. or midnight, anticipating any unscheduled contingencies. Then, usually an assistant city editor holds down the "lobster shift"[3] to revise late editions of the paper and to summon reporters to work if necessary. At 8:00 A.M. the editor on the lobster shift is relieved by an assistant city editor, whose other colleagues arrive at about 10:00 A.M. to start again the news rhythm of the day.

This matching of the news organization's dispersion of reporters to the office hours of institutions extends to weekend scheduling. Then, less than half the desks in the city room are occupied, and some of those are being used by reporters normally assigned to outside beats. The City Hall bureau of one New York daily provides a good example of this temporal synchronization. Monday through Friday, eight or nine reporters sit at bureau desks, including a constant cadre of seven who have weekends off. One of the nine spends Tuesday through Friday at the City Hall bureau and Saturday at the city room; another, Monday through Thursday at the bureau and Sunday at the city room. Since City Hall is closed on weekends, the shifting spatial location of the last two reporters and the temporal arrangement of all nine captures the rhythm of the work week of City Hall politicians.

One consequence of synchronized working hours is that few reporters are available to cover stories before 10:00 A.M. or after 7:00 P.M. on weekdays, and even fewer at those times on weekends. This social arrangement influences the assessment of occurrences as potential news events. According to one New York reporter, anyone wishing coverage for an evening occurrence had better have a "damned good story."[4] For the few reporters available are held in reserve to cover any emergency that might be thought to require their presence. As the New York reporter put it, "They're there in case someone plants a bomb at La Guardia Airport." Sending a reserve reporter to an evening occurrence depletes the news organization's ability to handle a major story, the very contingency that has determined the reporter's working hours.

Variant rhythms, but similar principles, govern the hours of television reporters. When I first observed news processing at NEWS, I surmised that news was potentially limited to occurrences happening between 10:00 A.M. and 4:00 P.M., the deadline for feeding film into the developer in order to have footage edited by the 6:00 P.M. telecast.[5]

Having available staff also influences the assessment of occurrences during periods when reporters are temporally concentrated. A story justifying the presence of a reporter at 11:00 A.M. might not justify assigning one late in the afternoon. By 3:00 P.M., the few reporters left without assignments are being held in reserve for emergencies, their time filled with writing obituaries and small items, such as rewrites of news releases, that can be handled from the office by making a few telephone calls. And unless the news organization has been alerted in advance that a "good story" will occur late in the day, a high-status reporter will not be available to cover it. By noon, those reporters have received their assignments or enterprised their stories for the day.[6]

Similarly, Gieber (1956) found that the internal scheduling of newswork influences the wire-service editor's assessment of stories to be included in the newspaper. At a morning paper the wire-service editor selects copy in the evening. Using the wire services' budgets, he quickly sets about filling the columns made available to him. The later the hour, the less space he has left to fill. Accordingly, an occurrence late in the evening must present special competitive merits to be included as a story in the daily news product.

## Planning Across Days

Finally, to project work into time and so to control work, the news media plan across days. Consider the following example, a memo addressed to the city editor by a court reporter. It was written in mid-November:

> The grand larceny trial of nursing home owner Bernie Bergman and his son Stanley and accountant Sandak is now scheduled to begin with jury selection January 5. Pretrial motions . . . get under way December 15 before Manhattan Supreme Court. . . . And the federal tax-evasion trial of the Bergmans will follow shortly upon the completion of the state trial.
>
> The grand-larceny trial is expected to be lengthy and time consuming for the reporter. For those reasons, it would be advantageous for the desk to decide in the near future who it wants to provide trial coverage. My view is that the assigned reporter should be free from other responsibilities during the duration of the trial so as not to downgrade the quality of our daily beat coverage.

Or consider the weekly plan of the City Hall reporter whose days off were Fridays and Saturdays. Every Thursday he sought to find a story to file on Thursday and another to write for Sunday, when he worked in the city room, and when it would be more difficult to locate occurrences qualifying as news. Of course, this reporter's foresight meant that to become news, an item found on Sunday would have to be competitive with the item located on Thursday. Otherwise, the reporter would not alter his allocation of his time; he would not change "his" story.

Ultimately, the anchoring of the news net in time and space means that reporters and news organizations suffer from a "glut of occurrences" with which to fill the news product. Having reporters assigned to beats and bureaus means that they each interpret their task as "filing [at least] a daily story" (Roshco, 1975) about occurrences at their various locations. Some reporters seek to file more, often commenting to colleagues about how many they've written that day. A multitude of stories means that each one cannot be disseminated; choices must be made. The multitude of news releases arriving at reporters' and editors' desks—perhaps fifty a day at New York's City Hall bureau alone—also requires careful winnowing of the use of reporters across time. The process of planning to handle this glut results in a system of classifying occurrences as news events.

## Time and the Glut of Occurrences

I [already] emphasized the need to locate potential news stories to fill the daily product. Now I argue that the news net produces more stories than can be processed. Each one of these is a potential drain upon the news organization's temporal and staff resources. For each occurrence can claim to be idiosyncratic—a particular conjunction of social, economic, political, and psychological forces that formed an occurrence into "this particular occurrence" and not any other existing or having existed in the everyday world.

Accepting this claim for all occurrences is an organizational impossibility. Like any other complex organization, a news medium cannot process idiosyncratic phenomena. It must reduce all phenomena to known classifications, much as hospitals "reduce" each patient to sets of symptoms or diseases, and as teachers view individual students in terms of categories pertinent to learning. Any organization that sought to process each and every phenomenon as a "thing in itself" would be so flexible that it would be unrecognizable as a formal organization. Some means between flexibility and rigidity must be attained (March and Simon, 1958).

Concentrating reporters' working hours does not necessarily provide time to handle the idiosyncrasy of occurrences. A comparison makes this clearer. Providing more doctors than usual in a hospital's emergency room on weekend and holiday nights does not guarantee that the seriously ill and wounded will receive adequate medical treatment, even though that provision takes into account the everyday rhythm of work and recreation. (More accidents arrive in hospitals on weekends because of bar brawls and family disputes engendered by extended intensive interaction.) To facilitate adequate treatment, hospitals institute special routines. For instance, they may schedule all elective surgery before 5:00 P.M. on weekdays. Operating-room schedules also take into account the amount of time customarily required for the expected surgical procedures. What a patient sees as a personal medical emergency is thus rendered routine by the hospital so that it may plan the use of both personnel and physical resources and thus control the flow of work. When allocating resources each week, some hospitals even check lists of critical patients to estimate the kind and amount of work to be expected by the morgue's personnel (Sudnow, 1967).

Just as hospital personnel differentiate among diseases according to their demands for organizational resources, news personnel must anticipate the claims of potential occurrences upon their resources. To control work, newsworkers have developed typifications of occurrences as news stories.[7] (Typifications are classifications arising from practical purposive action.) Anchored or embedded in the use of time, the news typifications characterize stories, much as the anchorage of the news net in space characterizes and constitutes newsworthiness.

The anchoring or embeddedness of typifications in time shares two other important characteristics with the anchoring of newsworthiness in the spatial news net. That is, both news typifications and the assignment of newsworthiness are relatively content free. We have seen that newsworthiness is a negotiated phenomenon rather than the application of independently derived objective criteria to news events. So too, typifications of kinds of news draw upon the *way* occurrences happen, not upon *what* is happening. The typifications are only relatively content free, because some sorts of occurrences are likely to happen one way while others have a different temporal rhythm. For instance, a hospital may generally preplan a specific cesarean delivery; a news organization may preplan coverage of a particular trial. Neither organization can specifically anticipate the work associated with a particular four-alarm fire.

Just as newsworkers claim that there are specific criteria of content against which news is assessed (i.e., how many people are affected by the event), so, too, newsworkers insist that their categorization of news depends upon a story's content.

## Newsworkers on Categories of News

At work, reporters and editors refer to five categories of news: hard, soft, spot, developing, and continuing. Journalism texts and informants explain that these terms differentiate kinds of news content or the subject of events-as-news. Asked for definitions of their categories, newsworkers fluster, for they take these categories so much for granted that they find them difficult to define.[8] To specify definitions, newsworkers offer examples of the stories that fall within a given category. They tend to classify the same stories in the same manner. Some stories are cited with such frequency that, viewed as prototypes, they are incorporated in the following discussion.

### Hard News Versus Soft News

The newsworkers' main distinction is between hard news and its antithesis, soft news. As they put it, hard news concerns occurrences potentially available to analysis or interpretation, and consists of "factual presentations" of occurrences deemed news-worthy. When pressed, informants indicated that hard news is "simply" the stuff of which news presentations are made. For instance, asked for a definition of hard news, a television editor offered the following catalog of basic news stories: "Hard news is the gubernatorial message to the legislature, the State of the Union Address to Congress, the train-truck accident or the murder, the bank holdup, the legislative proposal . . . and the fire tomorrow."

This editor and other informants voluntarily contrasted hard news with soft news, also known as feature or human-interest stories (cf. Hughes, 1940). Some examples of soft-news stories are: an item about a big-city bus driver who offers a cheery "good morning" to every passenger on his early morning run; a feature about a lonely female bear; a story about young adults who rent a billboard for a month to proclaim "Happy Anniversary Mom and Dad."

Newsworkers distinguish between these two lists by saying that a hard-news story is "interesting to human beings" and a soft-news story is "interesting because it deals with the life of human beings" (Mott, 1952: 58). Or they state that hard news concerns information people should have to be informed citizens and soft news concerns human foibles and the "texture of our human life" (Mott, 1952: 58). Finally, newsworkers may simply summarize: Hard news concerns important matters and soft news, interesting matters.

These separate yet similar attempts to distinguish between hard and soft news present the same classificatory problem; the distinctions overlap. Frequently it is difficult, if not impossible, to decide whether an event is interesting or important or is both interesting and important. Indeed, the same event may be treated as either a hard- or a soft-news story. During a two-year period, the observed television station presented as feature stories some events that its primary television competition presented as hard news, and vice versa.

### Spot News and Developing News

Difficulties also appear in the newsworkers' distinctions between spot news and developing news. The most important problem is that the newsworkers partially abandon their claim that the categories are based upon the content or subject matter of events-as-news.

Asked to discuss spot news, newsworkers replied that it is a type (subclassification) of hard news. They cited fires as a prototypical example of spot news. (Occasionally informants added a second example, such as a robbery, murder, accident, tornado, or earthquake.) The subject matter of all examples was conflict with nature, technology, or the penal code.

Asked about developing news (another subclassification of hard news), the newsworkers cited the same examples. Asked, then, to distinguish between spot and developing news, informants introduced a new element, the amount of information that they have about an event-as-news at a given moment. When they learned of an unexpected event, it was classed "spot news." If it took a while to learn the "facts" associated with a "breaking story," it was "developing news." It remained "developing news" so long as "facts" were still emerging and being gathered. When I pointed to previous statements asserting that the subject of the story determined that story's classification, the newsworkers insisted that both statements were correct. In essence, they countered, the subject matter of certain kinds of event-as-news had a tendency to occur in specific ways (fires break out unexpectedly, whereas many demonstrations are pre-planned). And so, newsworkers happen to learn of them in certain ways.

### Continuing News

Asked to define continuing news, newsworkers reverted to discussing the subject matter of an event-as-news. As the newsworkers put it, continuing news is a series of stories on the same subject based upon events occurring over a period of time. As a prototype, the newsworkers cited the legislative bill. The passage of a bill, they explained, is a complicated process occurring over a period of time. Although news of the bill's progress through the legislative maze may vary from day to day, all stories about the bill deal with the same content—the bill's provisions and whether they will be enacted. In this sense, they said, the story about the legislative bill continues as news. (Other examples cited by informants included trials, election campaigns, economics, diplomacy, and wars. Almost all examples were confrontations within or among recognized institutions, and all are produced by complex organizations.)

Then, once again, the newsworkers partially modified their statements. Maintaining that certain kinds of news content tend to fall under the rubric "continuing news," they added that certain kinds of content (stories about legislative bills and trials, for example) "simply" tend to occur over an extended period of time.

## Typifications of News

### From Category to Typification

Unfortunately, the newsworkers' definitions of their categories are difficult to apply, even though the definitions, prototypical examples, and lists of stories decrease the variability of the occurrences as the raw material of news, and so reduce their idiosyncrasy. More important, discussing spot, developing, and continuing news, the newsworkers introduce a seemingly extraneous element mentioned in the comparison of hospitals and news organizations: certain kinds of event-as-news tend to happen in certain ways. And so, reporters and editors "just happen" to be alerted to the need to process them in different ways.

The notion of news as frame, particularly the recognition that organizations perform work upon the everyday world to make sense of daily experience, enables the realization that the classificatory scheme is grounded in the rhythm of time use. Schutz' interpretive sociology suggests that the newsworkers' classifications are typifications rather than categories. "Category" refers to the classification of objects according to one or more relevant characteristics ruled salient by the classifiers, frequently by what anthropologists term a "formal analysis." The use of "category" connotes a request for definitions from infomants and a sorting of those definitions along dimensions specified by the researcher. "Typification" refers to classification in which the relevant characteristics are central to the solution of practical tasks or problems at hand and are constituted and grounded in everyday activity. The use of "typification" connotes an attempt to place informants' classifications in their everyday context, for typifications are embedded in and take their meaning from the settings in which they are used, and the occasions that prompt their use.[9]

Embedded in practical tasks, the newsworkers' typifications draw on the synchronization of their work with the likely schedule of potential news occurrences. As summarized in table 7.1, the newsworkers' distinctions between hard and soft news reflect questions of scheduling. Distinctions between spot and developing news pertain to the allocation of resources across time, and vary in their application according to the technology being used. And the typification "continuing news" is embedded in predicting the course of events-as-news.

### Hard News: The Flow of Newswork and Scheduling

Because news is a depletable consumer product, newsworkers claim that "quickening urgency" is the "essence of news" (H.M. Hughes, 1940:58; Roshco, 1975). If newsworkers do not act quickly, the hard-news story will be obsolete before it can be distributed in today's newscast or tomorrow's paper. To quote Robert Park (Park and Burgess, 1967), old news is "mere information."

In contrast, soft-news stories need not be "timely." The Sunday newspaper is padded with feature stories about occurrences earlier in the week. Concerned with "timeliness," newsworkers make fine distinctions. They explain that some kinds of content (hard-news stories) become obsolete more quickly than others (soft-news items). This distinction is based upon the distribution of nonscheduled, prescheduled, and unscheduled events as hard and soft news.

Table 7.1  Practical issues in typifying news*

| Typification | How is event scheduled? | Is dissemination urgent? | Does technology affect perception? | Are future predictions facilitated? |
|---|---|---|---|---|
| Soft news | Nonscheduled | No | No | Yes |
| Hard news | Unscheduled and prescheduled | Yes | Sometimes | Sometimes |
| Spot news | Unscheduled | Yes | No | No |
| Developing news | Unscheduled | Yes | Yes | No |
| Continuing news | Prescheduled | Yes | No | Yes |

* As McKinney and Bourque (1972: 232) note, typifications are flexible and undergo continual transformation. Theoretically, then, as noted by Lindsey Churchill (personal communication), recording typifications in this manner transforms them into components of a typology, for it separates them from the ongoing situations in which they are embedded.

A *non*scheduled event-as-news is an occurrence whose date of dissemination as news is determined by the newsworkers. A *pre*-scheduled event-as-news is an occurrence announced for a future date by its convenors; news of it is to be disseminated the day it occurs or the day after. An *un*scheduled event-as-news is one that occurs unexpectedly; news of it is to be disseminated that day or the day after. The type of scheduling characteristic of an event-as-news affects the organization of work.

Most hard-news stories concern prescheduled events (a debate on a legislative bill) or unscheduled events (a fire). Newsworkers do not decide when stories about prescheduled events and unscheduled events-as-news are to be disseminated. Nor do they decide when to gather "facts" and to disseminate accounts and explanations of nonscheduled hard-news stories. Nonscheduled hard-news stories often involve investigative reporting. The publication of the *Pentagon Papers* by the *New York Times* is an example of a nonscheduled hard-news story. The *Times* held the papers for several months before it published extracts, digests, and analyses of them. Processing nonscheduled stories, the news organization copes with the timing and flow of work.

Members of the news enterprise almost always control the timing and flow of work required to process soft-news stories. Few soft-news stories concern unscheduled events, as indicated by the previous list of feature stories. Another example is the "Man in the News" series run by the *New York Times*. Like the obituaries of famous men and women, the "facts" can be, and often are, gathered, written up, and edited in anticipation of future dissemination. Prescheduled soft news also includes such annual "February stories" as items appropriate for Washington's and Lincoln's birthdays and for Valentine's Day. A reporter may be assigned to these stories days in advance, and the specific information to be included in the story may be gathered, written, and edited days before its eventual dissemination.

Of course, there are exceptions to these rules. But news organizations handle those exceptions in a manner that conserves personnel and retains control of the flow of newswork. For instance, "facts" to be used in a feature story about the atmosphere at an important trial cannot be gathered in advance. Nor can feature information about an unscheduled event, such as a fire, be gathered in advance. However, the impact of these events-as-feature stories upon the allocation of personnel is minimal. In the first case, a reporter may be assigned to write the "feature angle" of the trial several days in advance, his name struck from the roster of reporters available to cover the fast-breaking news of the day. In the second case, the same person generally reports both the hard-news fire and its soft-news angle, so that the news organization can conserve reporters.

## Spot News: Allocating Resources and Dealing with Technology

As in the case of the hospital, governing the flow of newswork involves more than scheduling. It also involves the allocation of resources and the control of work through prediction. The distinctions among spot news, developing news, and continuing news are occasioned by these practical tasks.

Spot-news events are unscheduled; they appear suddenly and must be processed quickly. The examples offered by informants indicate that spot news is the *specifically* unforeseen event-as-news. For instance, although the staff may anticipate the probability of a fire, they cannot specifically predict where and when a fire will start. This inability to make a definite prediction concerning some events affects the flow of newswork. If a three-alarm fire starts close to deadline, information must be gathered and edited more quickly than usual. If a major fire starts fifty miles from the city room, transportation problems influence the time needed to gather and process "facts" and so influence the allocation of resources to cover the fire.

Some events that newsworkers nominate for membership in the typification "spot news" are of such importance that newsworkers try to create a stable social arrangement to anticipate them—even if the probability that the event will occur is minute. The city desk of most major dailies is staffed around the clock in case a spot-news event should occur. For example, the president of the United States is covered twenty-four hours a day in case something should happen to him. Continually creating stable social arrangements such as these requires both extended allocation of resources (assigning a staff member to sit at the city desk all night) and immediate reallocation of resources (pulling a reporter off another story) if and as necessary.

The different news technologies each have their own varying time rhythms. Film can be shot, edited, and aired in an hour; print technology is more cumbersome and time consuming. Accordingly, as might be expected from the finding that technology influences the organization of work (Hage and Aiken, 1969; Perrow, 1967; Thompson, 1967), as well as my argument that time rhythms influence typifications, a television station's allocation of resources differs from that of a newspaper. The print technology is labor intensive; electronic technology is not. At the *Seaboard City Daily* at least three of the twenty-person staff of general reporters and rewriters sat in the city room from 10:00 A.M. until midnight doing minor but necessary tasks. The observed television station had few reserve reporters and no reserve cameramen, except from 4:00 to 6:00 P.M. and from 9:30 to 11:00 P.M. At these times, reporters and cameramen, bringing their film to be processed, had generally returned from their assignments. They would wait either to cover a spot-news story or to go off shift. Should a specifically unforeseen event occur at any other time of day, the station had to: pay overtime; pull a reporter and a cameraman from a less important story they were already covering; pull a cameraman from a "silent film story" he was covering by himself; hire a free-lance cameraman; pull a staff announcer from his routine duties, such as reading station identification; or assign a newswriter to act as reporter after gaining permission from the appropriate unions. The alternative(s) chosen depended upon the specific situation—the existing dispersion of both film crews and occurrences in time and space at that moment of that day.

### Developing News: Technology and the Perception of Events

Practical problems of dealing with a technology and its rhythms are so important that they even affect the newsworker's perception of a spot-news story, especially whether the typification "developing news" will be applied to an event-as-story. In the case of developing news, technology provides a lens through which events-as-news are perceived.[10]

Developing news concerns "emergent situations." A plane crashes. Although this occurrence is unexpected, there are, nonetheless, limitations on the "facts" it can possibly contain. Editors would not expect to run a story stating that those reported dead had come to life. Nor would they expect to run a report of an official denial that a crash occurred. The "facts" of the news story are: A plane crashed at 2:00 P.M. in Ellen Park when an engine caught fire and another went dead, killing eight people, injuring an additional fifteen persons, and damaging two houses. All else is amplification. Since this *specific* plane crash was unexpected, reporters were not present to record "facts" "accurately." "Facts" must be reconstructed, and as more information becomes known, the "facts" will be more "accurate." Although the actual occurrence remains the same, the account of it changes, or, as the newsworkers put it, "the story develops." Ongoing changes of this sort are called "developing news."[11]

Most spot-news stories are developing news. Since both present interrelated work demands, newspaper staffs tend to use the terms interchangeably. Television workers use the term "developing news" in a more restricted sense, identifying some stories as spot news that print journalists term "developing news."[12] Again, technology acts as a key in their formulations, each technology being associated with a different rhythm in the centralized services feeding the news net. The process of covering the death of Martin Luther King, an occurrence that raised different practical problems for the two New England media, illustrates this variation.[13]

At the local newspaper, King's injury and subsequent death were labeled "developing news." A continual flow of updated copy needed editing and "demanded" constant revision of the planned format. The assistant managing editor learned of the attempted assassination and plotted a format for the front page. When King's condition was reported as grave by the wire services, the editor drew another format that affected other stories above the fold on page one. When a wire-service bulletin reported King to be dead, all other stories were relegated below the fold. Every story on page one needed a new headline of different-sized type, and lead paragraphs of some stories had to be reset in smaller type. Inside pages were also affected.

The television network, with which NEWS is affiliated, reported on King's condition as a developing story. Periodically, it interrupted programs to present bulletins.

But this was a spot-news story for the local television station's personnel. Obviously, the format of the 11:00 P.M. newscast was modified early in the evening. Because of the network's bulletins, the story about King (whatever it might turn out to be) had to be the program's lead. At the newspaper, the production manager and compositors bemoaned the need to lay out the front page three times, each reset accompanying a major development in the story. All production staff worked overtime. At the television station, readjustments in production plans meant less work, not more. By prearrangement, the network preempted the first few minutes of the late-evening newscast to tell the story, just as it had preempted the same five minutes some months earlier to report the death of three astronauts.[14]

## Continuing News: Controlling Work Through Prediction

Spot news and developing news are constituted in work arrangements intended to cope with the amount of information specifically predictable before an event occurs. This information is slight or nonexistent, because the events are unscheduled. In contrast, continuing news *facilitates* the control of work, for continuing news events are generally prescheduled. Prescheduling is implicit in the newsworkers' definition of continuing news as a "series of stories on the same subject based upon events occurring over a period of time."[15] This definition implies the existence of prescheduled change. For instance, the account of the progress of a legislative bill through Congress is an account of a series of events following one another in a continual temporal sequence. An event occurring at any specific point in the sequence bears consequences for anticipated events.

Because they are prescheduled, continuing news stories help newsworkers and news organizations regulate their own activities by freeing staff to deal with the exigencies of the specifically unforeseen. Take that legislative bill. It is to be channeled through the House, the Senate, and the executive office. To cover this series of events-as-news, the reporters must be familiar with the legislative process. Such familiarity may even be viewed as part of a "professional stock of knowledge at hand" (see Schutz, 1964: 29 ff.). The reporter knows the sentiments of pertinent committee members, as well as the distribution of power within both the various House and Senate committees and the House and the Senate themselves. In addition, the reporter also knows the progress being made by other legislative bills. With this cumulative stock of knowledge at hand, the reporter may not only predict the bill's eventual disposition, including the specific route through the legislative process (this bill will be bogged down in the House Ways and Means Committee), but may also weigh the need to cover this bill on any one day against the need to cover another bill about which there is comparable information. That "expert" or "professional" stock of knowledge at hand permits this reporter, other reporters and editors, and the news organization to control work activities.

The continuing news story is a boon to the reporter's ability to control his or her own work, to anticipate specifically, and so to dissipate future problems by projecting events into a routine. Indeed, newsworkers seek out continuing stories because they are predictably and readily covered. The news organization's ability to process continuing stories routinely by predicting future outcomes enables the organization to cope with unexpected events. At the very least, it enables a city editor to state, "Joe Smith will not be available to cover spot-news stories a week from Tuesday because he will be covering the Bergman trial."

## One Consequence of Typifications

Thus far, the examination of time and typifications suggests that newsworkers use typifications to transform the idiosyncratic occurrences of the everyday world into raw materials that can be subjected to routine processing and dissemination. Typifications are constituted in practical problems, including those posed by the synchronization of newswork with how occurrences generally unfold. They impose order upon the raw material of news and so reduce the variability (idiosyncrasy) of the glut of occurrences. They also channel the newsworkers' perceptions of the everyday world by imposing a frame upon strips of daily life.

Yet we do not know whether typifications, as components of the news frame, carry significant consequences when they key occurrences from one multiple reality to another, from the everyday world to the world preferred by the news product. Why do typifications matter? Are they of more than theoretical interest?

Following Schutz (1962, 1964, 1966, 1967), Berger and Luckman (1967) tell us that knowledge may be objectified by institutions. Instead of existing as formulations subject to continual revision and reconstitution, objectified ideas may elicit set ways of dealing with the world. As the product of the intertwining of news time and the news net, the news typifications have become part of the reporter's professional stock of knowledge-at-hand. That is, being a professional reporter capable of coping with idiosyncratic occurrences means being able to use typifications to invoke appropriate reportorial techniques. Again, there is a medical parallel.[16] Being a doctor means having the professional knowledge needed to typify symptoms as diseases and to process patients according to appropriate hospital procedures governing the allocation of resources. Reporters explain their classificatory system as objective categories, as objectifications.[17] Doctors objectify symptoms as defined (categorized) diseases. [O]ne example of the objectification of professional knowledge arising from the use of typification must suffice. For objectification of knowledge may result in errors, much as applying stereotypes about a "criminal appearance" may result in incorrectly labeling someone as criminal or untrustworthy. And in some cases, professional errors in prediction influence the assessment of the newsworthiness of a story.

Put formally, if objectified, typifications can be seductive. Faced with the need to predict and to plan, newsworkers may be seduced into applying what everyone knows—that is, what all newsworkers collectively agree upon. Having a collective stock of knowledge-at-hand concerning how occurrences unfold and a system of typification partially based in the utility of known-in-detail prediction, newsworkers may predict inaccurately. The Wilson–Heath and Dewey–Truman elections are classic examples of such inaccurate prediction.[18]

Inaccurately predicted events-as-news require major unplanned alterations in work processes. Like spot news, they are unscheduled and specifically unforeseen. Like developing news, they are perceived through the frame of a specific technology. Like continuing news, they involve both prediction and postdiction of an event as a member of a chain of events. They challenge knowledge and routines that reporters and editors take for granted.

Reporters and editors cope with the problems of inaccurately predicted events by invoking a special typification: "What-a-story!" This typification is constituted in the unusual arrangements that are routinely made to cope with a "what-a-story!" That newsworkers typify these events emphasizes the centrality of typification in their work and the degree to which typifications are constituted in their work.

Symbolically, the degree to which this typification is itself routine is captured by the almost stereotypical manner in which verbal and nonverbal gestures accompany the pronunciation of "*what*-a-story!" "What" is emphasized. The speakers I observed provided additional emphasis by speaking more slowly than usual, adding yet more emphasis by nodding their heads slowly, smiling, and rubbing their hands together, or by enthusiastically touching colleagues.

The extent to which unusual arrangements are routinely made to cope with a "what-a-story" is illustrated by the reaction of the staff of the *Seaboard City Daily* to President Johnson's speech of March 31, 1968. Learning of Johnson's announcement that he would not run for re-election, the newsworkers immediately instituted taken-for-granted routines to handle the what-a-story, and referred to similar situations in the past.

Johnson's speech was prescheduled. The newspaper, like other news media, had an advance copy of the text that omitted, of course, Johnson's "surprise announcement" that he would not run for reelection. As Johnson spoke on television of the deescalation of American bombing, the editors awaited companion stories concerning reactions of political leaders to the so-called bombing halt. These were to be supplied by the wire services. A preliminary format had been drawn for page one. The lead story about the military situation (slugged "bombing halt") had been headlined and edited and was being set into type. Page one was also to include a political story, not placed prominently, about the coming election. Several other assessments of the political situation had already been set into type, including columnists' analyses of the 1968 presidential election to be printed on the editorial page and the page opposite the editorial page; a political cartoon showing Johnson speaking on the telephone and saying "Yes, Bobby"; and a small story speculating whether Robert Kennedy would join Eugene McCarthy in challenging the president as a candidate for the Democratic nomination. The newspaper was in good shape for the first-edition deadline, 11:00 P.M.

And then it happened: bedlam. A prescheduled announcement concerning the continuing "Vietnam problem" and warranting a limited amount of political speculation turned into a major surprise of military, political, and diplomatic importance. An assistant city editor had been watching the speech on the television set of the news-paper's entertainment critic. Excited, he ran, shouting, into the city room. The editor's reaction was perhaps more unprecedented than the president's announcement.[19] The telephone of the assistant managing editor rang. The managing editor was calling to discuss coverage of the speech. Although the managing editor had already made his nightly telephone check, the assistant managing editor automatically said "Hello, Ted," before he had even heard the voice on the other end.[20]

It would be impossible to describe the amount of revision accomplished in a remarkably brief time as reporters summoned by telephone, volunteering editors, and mounds of wire-service copy poured into the newsroom. But the comments of editors and reporters are significant. Lifting their heads to answer telephones, bark orders, and then clarify them, the editors periodically announced, "*What* a story! . . . The story of the century. . . . What a night, what a night! . . . Who would have believed it? . . . There's been nothing like it since Coolidge said, 'I will not run.' "

These remarks are telling. First, they reveal that typification is also based upon taken-for-granted assumptions. The paper's top political reporter, when covering the New Hampshire primary, had offered to bet anyone that Johnson would not run for reelection. Few had accepted his challenge, because it would have been like "taking money from a baby."[21]

Second, the remarks emphasize the degree to which work routines can be routinely altered. Johnson's speech of March 31 was said to require reassessing the military situation in Vietnam, the diplomatic situation, especially the possibility of successful peace talks, and the political situation in the United States. The managing and assistant managing editors specifically alerted the copyboys to watch the news services carefully for analyses of these topics. Before any notification came the editors "knew to expect" analyses of these topics. In addition, handling the story required a substantial amount of revision and readjustment of the allocation of resources. Significantly, all the editors took for granted the nature of those readjustments. No discussion was required to decide which political reporters would come back to work. Only minor discussion was required to decide which of the general reporters would be asked to return to work from their homes.

Third, the analogy to Coolidge (the editor who mentioned him thought the others might be too young to remember) alerted the staff to an unusual routine. That is, rules governing the coverage of a what-a-story were invoked by citing another what-a-story. Indeed, the invocation of Coolidge involves an implicit call to reduce the variability of events as the raw material of news, for it states that this event-as-news is "like" that one from years ago.

Fourth, the degree to which an individual what-a-story is typified and thus made routine is indicated by the assistant managing editor's reference to previous what-a-story(ies). He rejected an offer of help from another editor, recalling that that editor had been more of a hindrance than a help in processing a previous what-a-story. Some months later, trying to decide the size of type to be used for a headline about Robert Kennedy's death, he thought back to Christmas and explained, "What a year! What a year! . . . The Tet offensive, Johnson's speech, King's death . . . now this."[22]

Finally, City Hall reporters describe their coverage of the announcement of New York's fiscal crisis and the possibility of default as the "natural" invocation of routines associated with spot coverage, not with those of continuing political coverage. Their daily routines were altered; other modes of coverage were invoked. According to one City Hall bureau chief, "We covered it the way we would cover a disaster—like a hurricane or earthquake. We were [systematically] scattered all over the place," rather than centralized in City Hall.[23] Said the reporter who broke the story for a Long Island paper, "What a story!" Proudly, he explained that he was the reporter who first learned New York's budget was awry. Reporters at neighboring desks firmly attested that they all knew "what to do," how to respond to a story that contravened their professional expectations, how to disperse and what to look for.

In short, as professionals, they knew how to institute routines associated with the rhythm of newswork. And, as professionals, they were familiar with the news organization's need to generate stories and to control the idiosyncrasies of the glut of occurrences by dispersing reporters in a news net flung through time and space.

## Questions for Consideration

1   Tuchman states that "news media carefully impose a structure upon time and space." What does she mean? Can you see how you do the same thing in your work as a student?

2   What difference does it make for the news audience that reporters classify a story they are covering as either soft, hard, spot, developing, and continuing news? Do you see one type of news classification as more "professional" than another?

3   Tuchman's use of journalists' understandings of time to make sense of the way they construct news stories pretty much holds up today. More generally, though, the idea of time has changed dramatically for journalism. The relatively new phrase, *24/7 news cycle*, particularly reflects this change. Using periodicals databases such as Nexis or Factiva, try to track down when the phrase *24/7 news cycle* came into use and why.

## Notes

1.   The examples just discussed suggest that in everyday life, social actors work to link the temporal and spatial characteristics of social activities. This work is accomplished both in everyday talk and thought (as in "It's ten minutes from here") and in observable behavior (for example, the dispersion in the synagogue). Newsworkers as social actors also work at such linkages. Additionally, the news net institutionalizes such linkages as it routinizes newswork. Occurrences that may qualify as news events are not only expected to occur at specific locations, but they are expected to occur at those places at specific times. Or, at least, the rhythm of newswork is designed to catch those occurrences that happen at the appropriate time in the appropriate place. Time and space are accordingly objectified or given solidity by these organizational arrangements.

2.   "Accomplished project" has a technical meaning. First, Schutz views action as a project (or projection) of present concerns and past experiences into the future. "Project" thus implies the intentionality of consciousness. Second, as used by the ethnomethodologists, the term "accomplished" refers to the project as a human achievement.

3.   "Lobster" is a reference to the red eyes of tired newsworkers as they come off the night shift.

4.   Coverage of evening stories is even more difficult for television stations. If they use film cameras rather than portable videotape packs to cover the story, the film must be developed. Using either technology, footage must be processed quickly for presentation. Television stations are now using live coverage from new small remote cameras for events occurring during the news program, but problems associated with live coverage have to be ironed out. For instance, passersby may run in front of the camera or harass the reporter.

5.   Epstein (1973) argues that news is also spatially limited. At the time of his study, the networks found it easier to cover stories in Los Angeles, Chicago, New York, and Washington than in other cities because of the placement of connecting cables. Additionally, stories from Vietnam had to have a timeless quality, since the film had to be flown from Saigon to New York for editing. New technologies have created somewhat greater flexibility.

6.   The familiarity of politicians and public relations officers with the rhythm of newswork enables them to manipulate newsworkers and news organizations now and then. A New

York political reporter recalls Governor Hugh Carey's and Mayor Abraham Beame's joint announcement of their proposal for the Municipal Assistance Corporation. They unexpectedly called an emergency news conference, scheduling it shortly before the deadlines of morning newspapers and 6:00 P.M. newscasts. The setting, a midtown Manhattan hotel suite, lacked telephones. The timing and lack of telephones accomplished two things: The reporters did not have ample time to check the claims made by the politicians, because the story was rushed to meet the deadline. Without phones, the reporters could not inform their editors about the substance of the story. Had the reporters been able to do so, the editors could have assigned additional reporters to double-check the officials' interpretation of the fiscal crisis, and that information could have been available in time to meet the deadline. Reporters both dislike and distrust news promoters who manipulate them too often.

7.  I am claiming that newsworkers develop typifications to control the flow of work in organizations. Generally, though, that aspect of "control" is credited to organizational processes, not professional practices. However, there is theoretical justification for my usage. Zimmerman concludes: "It appears that the 'competent use' of a given [organizational] rule or set of rules is founded upon members' practiced grasp of what particular actions are necessary on a given occasion to provide for the regular reproduction of a normal state of affairs [1970: 237]."

8.  See Giddens (1976) for a discussion of informants' inability to articulate objectified taken-for-granted classificatory systems.

9.  In recent years researchers (Zimmerman, 1970; Cicourel, 1968; Emerson, 1969; Emerson and Messinger, 1977; Sudnow, 1967) have discussed the relationship of typification to practical tasks in people-processing organizations. Examining the production of typifications has enabled labeling theorists to highlight the moral and occupational assumptions underpinning the treatment of deviants. It has enabled them to locate the *practical* considerations that families, police, judges, doctors, and social workers rely on to lable offenders and clients (see Emerson and Messinger, 1977). As Schutz (1962) pointed out, typifications help to routinize the world in which we live. They epitomize the routine grounds of everyday life; they enable us to make limited predictions (projections) and thus to plan and act. Schutz's use of the term "typification" is, however, slightly different from that used here. In some contexts Schutz uses the term "category" to apply to social-science constructs. At other times he refers to categories as a subtype of typification whose application depends upon the specificity of the phenomenon being typed (see also McKinney, 1970).

10. To a great extent, these comments about technology and perception are based on my observations, not the comments of the observed reporters. But they are informed by newsworkers' accounts of encounters with one another, including a NEWS reporter's tale that the "ink" reporters started to treat him respectfully when he joined them in the boring task of waiting for a jury to report its verdict, after having sat through the trial hour after hour, day after day. (Frequently, television stations identify such assignments as wasting the reporter as a resource, for the reporter could cover another story in the morning and "do" the trial in the afternoon.) An ex-wire-service reporter resigned from the writing staff of NEWS (despite improved pay) to rejoin his old wire service. He announced that he missed the excitement of perpetual deadlines designed to feed copy to morning and afternoon newspapers scattered in different time zones. In both cases the association of variant rhythms with different media were at issue.

11. Although newsworkers single out only this type of news as being subject to ongoing change, interpretive theories would insist that this process is ongoing for all kinds of news at all times. Suffice it to say that developing news provides a particularly clear example of indexicality (see pp. 188–91).

12. Howard Epstein (personal communication) notes an additional problem that developing news poses for newspapers: the point at which to "break" a story for successive editions. For instance, should one hold the mail edition for fifteen minutes to include the beginning of a speech, or should one hold the story for inclusion in the later, home-delivery edition? Competition with television makes this decision more difficult and somewhat "meaningless," because whatever the newspaper editors decide to do, the television newscast may carry the speech first.

13.  I observed coverage of King's death at the *Seaboard City Daily*. Activities at NEWS are reconstructed from conversations with the staff held within three days of the assassination.

14.  Used to compare the local media, the concept technology is a gloss, containing the idea that each medium also has different resources associated with its attachment to the national news net. Obviously, as the source of the feed to local stations, the network experienced King's death as developing news.

15.  See Fishman (1977) for a discussion of how newsworkers constitute "sameness" and a critique of my analysis of news typifications.

16.  The parallel is not exact, for doctors reign supreme in hospitals and claim the license to control how other members of the medical team do their work. Newsworkers do not "control" the activities of the editorial, advertising, or production staff (see Engwall, 1976; Freidson, 1971).

17.  The process of objectification raises two additional issues. At what point and how does objectification become reification? At what point and how do objectified typifications become stereotypes?

18.  It is tempting to identify inaccurate predictions as mistakes. "Mistake" is a lay term (E.C. Hughes, 1964). As Stelling and Bucher (1973) argue, this notion is cast aside in the course of professional socialization, to be replaced by concepts emphasizing the process of doing work. Given evidence of inaccurate *collective* predictions, the newsworkers essentially argue that they are specialists in knowing, gathering, and processing "general knowledge" (Kimball, 1967). If and when their predictions are collective, they are necessarily accurate, for they are based upon shared expertise. The newsworkers argue that since their stock of knowledge is necessarily correct, the *situation* is in "error." That is, the situation changed in a way they could not anticipate. The post-hoc explanation of Heath's "surprise victory" over Wilson, as offered in the daily press, supports this interpretation: Confident of victory, Wilson did not campaign sufficiently. Spurred by accounts that he was the underdog, Heath made a special effort to win. A similar process, dependent upon knowledge in detail, might also explain the ability of Agnes, a transsexual claiming to be an intersexed person, to con her doctors (Garfinkel, 1967: 116–185, 285–288). Given their stock of knowledge at hand, the doctors assumed it was impossible for a boy to self-administer the correct dosages of the correct hormones at just the right time to interfere with "normal" sexual development. As a lad, Agnes had done this by taking hormones prescribed for his mother.

19.  The newsworkers were particularly proud of the quiet that prevailed in the newsroom. One editor, who had worked at the *New York Times*, claimed that the news of D-Day had spread through the *Times'* city room in whispers.

20.  Neither this incident nor the previous one was witnessed. They were reported to me by five different newsworkers as the evening progressed.

21.  Similar stories concerning the assumptions about Johnson's candidacy made by newsmen based in Washington, D.C., have circulated in the mass media. A question asked by Kurt H. Wolff (personal communication) prompts a more technical interpretation of the what-a-story. One might say that the content of the what-a-story challenges the newsworkers' taken-for-granted notions of the social world so much that it threatens their ability to maintain the "natural attitude." The routines used to process a what-a-story may then be seen as the process through which the staff work to reestablish the natural attitude. Another approach is also possible. The five typifications previously discussed enable the workers to process other people's emergencies. When faced with a what-a-story, newsworkers are themselves placed in a state of emergency. That they immediately invoke routines to handle the what-a-story again stresses the use of typification grounded in routine to accomplish practical tasks. In this case, the task might be simultaneously processing information and working one's way out of an organizational emergency.

22.  King's death was retrospectively treated as a what-a-story. At the time, newsworkers greeted it with head shaking devoid of glee, and some quietly discussed the racism of other staff members. How much a what-a-story is subject to routine is forcefully indicated by an incident at the television station on the day of Robert Kennedy's death. Most newsworkers were called to work at 6:00 A.M. Several were not, so that they would still be fresh for the

11:00 P.M. newscast. Coming to work in the midafternoon, one on-camera reporter asked an early-morning arrival, "Did we gather the usual reaction [stories]?" Then, indicating his realization that this question would seem crass to an outsider, he asked me not to include his question in my field notes.

23. Dahlgren (1977) points out that economic forces and processes are reified by news, that is, treated as though they were natural phenomena.

# References

ADLER, RUTH
   1971 *A Day in the Life of the "New York Times."* New York: Lippincott.
BERGER, PETER, AND THOMAS LUCKMANN
   1967 *The Social Construction of Reality*. Garden City, N. Y.: Doubleday Anchor.
CICOUREL, AARON V.
   1968 *The Social Organization of Juvenile Justice*. New York: Wiley.
DAHLGREN, PETER
   1977 "Network TV News and the Corporate State: The Subordinate Consciousness of the Citizen-Viewer." Ph.D. dissertation. The Graduate Center, City University of New York.
EMERSON, ROBERT M.
   1969 *Judging Delinquents: Context and Process in Juvenile Court*. Chicago: Aldine.
——, AND SHELDON MESSINGER
   1977 "The Micro-Politics of Trouble." *Social Problems* 25: 121–34.
ENGWALL, LARS
   1976 *Travels in Newspaper Country*. Manuscript. University of Uppsala, Department of Business Administration.
FISHMAN, MARK
   1977 "Manufacturing the News: the Social Organization of Media News Production." Ph.D. dissertation. University of California, Santa Barbara.
FREIDSON, ELIOT
   1971 *Profession of Medicine: A Study in the Sociology of Applied Knowledge*. New York: Dodd, Mead.
GARFINKEL, HAROLD
   1967 *Studies in Ethnomethodology*. Englewood Cliffs, N.J: Prentice Hall.
GIDDENS, ANTHONY
   1976 *New Rules of Sociological Method*. New York: Basic Books.
GIEBER, WALTER
   1956 "Across the Desk: A Study of 16 Telegraph Editors." *Journalism Quarterly* 33 (Fall): 423–32.
HAGE, JERALD, AND MICHAEL AIKEN
   1969 "Routine Technology, Social Structure and Organizational Goals." *Administrative Science Quarterly* 14 (3): 366–78.
HEILMAN, SAMUEL
   1976 *Synagogue Life*. Chicago: University of Chicago Press.
HUGHES, EVERETT C.
   1964 *Men and Their Work*. New York: Free Press.
HUGHES, HELEN MACGILL
   1940 *News and the Human Interest Story*. Chicago: University of Chicago Press.
KIMBALL, PENN
   1967 "Journalism: Art, Craft or Profession?" Pp. 242–60 in Kenneth S. Lynn and the editors of *Daedalus*, eds., *The Professions in America*. Boston: Beacon Press.
MARCH, JAMES, AND HERBERT SIMON
   1958 *Organizations*. New York: Wiley.

McKinney, John C.
  1970 "Sociological Theory and the Process of Typification." in John C. McKinney and Edward Tiryakian, eds., *Theoretical Sociology*. New York: Appleton-Century-Crofts.
——, and Linda Bourque
  1972 "Further Comments on 'the Changing South': A Response to Sly and Weller." *American Sociological Review* 37 (April): 230–36.
Mott, Frank Luther
  1952 *The News in America*. Cambridge, Mass.: Harvard University Press.
Park, Robert, and Ernest Burgess
  1967 *The City*. Chicago: University of Chicago Press.
Perrow, Charles
  1967 "A Framework of the Comparative Analysis of Organizations." *American Sociological Review* 32 (April): 194–208.
Robinson, John P., Philip Converse, and Alexander Szalai
  1972 "Everyday Life in Twelve Countries." Pp. 113–44 in Alexander Szalai, ed., *The Use of Time*. The Hague: Mouton.
Roshco, Bernard
  1975 *Newsmaking*. Chicago: University of Chicago Press.
Roth, Julius
  1963 *Timetables: Structuring the Passage of Time in Hospital Treatment and Other Careers*. New York: Bobbs-Merrill.
Schutz, Alfred
  1962 *Collected Papers, Volume I: The Problem of Social Reality*. The Hague: M. Nijhoff.
——
  1964 *Collected Papers, Volume II: Studies in Social Theory*. The Hague: M. Nijhoff.
——
  1966 *Collected Papers, Volume III: Studies in Phenomenological Philosophy*. The Hague: M. Nijhoff.
——
  1967 *The Phenomenology of the Social World*. Evanston, Ill.: Northwestern University Press.
Sorokin, Pitrim A., and Robert K. Merton
  1937 "Social Time: A Methodological and Functional Analysis." *American Journal of Sociology* 42 (5): 615–29.
Sudnow, David
  1967 *Passing On: The Social Organization of Death and Dying*. Eaglewood Cliffs, N.J.: Prentice-Hall.
Thompson, James
  1967 *Organizations in Action*. New York: McGraw-Hill.
Zerubavel, Eviatar
  1977 "The French Revolutionary Calendar: A Case Study in the Sociology of Time," Paper presented at the meetings of the Eastern Sociological Society, New York City, March.
Zimmerman, Don H.
  1970 "Record-keeping and the Intake Process in a Public Welfare Organization." Pp. 319–54 in Stanton Wheeler, ed., *On Record: Files and Dossiers in American Life*. New York: Russell Sage.

# Chapter 8

## ERIC KLINENBERG

# CONVERGENCE
## News Production in a Digital Age

THE TENSIONS INVOLVED IN THE transformation of today's newsroom
are captured in this 2005 piece by New York University sociologist Eric Klinenberg. Lamenting the virtual absence of close sociological studies of news work since
their heyday in the 1970s (see Tuchman's piece in this book), Klinenberg reports on
his attempt to understand how journalism is changing under the pressures of conglomerates (see the Bagdikian and McChesney readings) and new digital media. What
he finds in his study of a major corporation's newsroom is a tension-filled environment
where the need to create television and Internet reports generates new demands on
print journalists, and where commercial pressures affect editors more explicitly than in
the past.

A paradox of contemporary sociology is that the discipline has largely abandoned the
empirical study of journalistic organizations and news institutions at the moment when
the media has gained visibility in political, economic, and cultural spheres; when other
academic fields have embraced the study of media and society; and when leading
sociological theorists—including Bourdieu (1998), Habermas (1989), Castells (1996),
and Luhmann (2000)—have broken from the disciplinary cannon to argue that the
media are key actors in modern life. Herbert Gans (1972) called attention to this
"famine in media research" in a review article in the *American Journal of Sociology*.
Yet—with the notable exceptions of a few landmark studies conducted in the 1970s
(Tuchman 1978; Gans 1979; Fishman 1980)—in the past thirty years American
sociologists have largely stayed out of newsrooms and ignored the conditions of journalistic production. Although a few studies are emerging of digital technologies in
newsrooms (see especially Boczkowski 2004), and of labor issues for journalists (see
Majoribanks 2000), the media scholar Timothy Cook (1998, x) noted that "it is as if a
virtual moratorium were placed on further studies" of newsrooms. The sociology of
news organizations is all but dead.

Ironically, studies of media are flourishing elsewhere in the academy. Today, most major universities have developed schools, departments, and programs dedicated to media and communications. Political scientists consider the news organization a political institution (or "fourth estate"), and most government agencies employ public relations specialists to manage their representations in the public sphere. Economists attribute fluctuations in the market to reports and opinions broadcast in the specialized business media, and financial analysts pay close attention to the way media pundits cover various industries and companies. Anthropologists have discovered the centrality of media as a source of imagination, migration, and the articulation of identity, and they are observing sites of production, reception, and circulation in diverse settings (Appadurai 1996; Ginsburg, Abu-Lughod, and Larkin 2002). Recent sociological accounts of news have been either historical, most notably the work of Michael Schudson (1978, 1995) and Paul Starr (2004); cultural, as in debates over the various public spheres (Calhoun 1993; Jacobs 2000); political, such as "media effects" studies; or theoretical. Todd Gitlin (2002), for example, argued that contemporary experience is "supersaturated" with a torrent of images and information so pervasive that most people take it for granted. Similarly, Manuel Castells (1996, 333) claimed that the media have reconstituted time and space, fundamentally altering the symbolic substratum of social life. Variants of these claims are surely familiar to anyone familiar with social scientific and humanities research today.

If, indeed, there is consensus that media products are central to the operations of different fields of action, it is surprising that sociologists have stopped examining how organizations responsible for producing the news and information work. Research in other disciplines often emphasizes the importance of sociological studies of news institutions, only to cite work that is several decades old and no longer reliable to explain how newsrooms work. Lacking current research, critics are left to guess about the strategies, practices, and interests that shape major news corporations; determine the content of news products; and produce the "symbolic power" (Bourdieu 1994) of publicly defining, delimiting, and framing key issues and events. Communications scholars, for example, often rely on anecdotal evidence for their assessments of how changes in the media industry have affected conditions of news production. Within sociology, social problems scholars typically do careful work to *show that* journalists selectively frame public issues; yet they rarely follow up by going inside newsrooms and asking reporters and editors how they constructed their stories, instead *speculating about why* the coverage takes certain forms.[1]

There has been no shortage of activity and change within media institutions and the journalistic field since the 1970s. The past thirty years has been a revolutionary period in the news media, which have experienced

- the advent of cable television, the beginning of a twenty-four-hour news cycle, and the steady decline of newspaper readership levels (though not a decline in newspaper profitability);

- the introduction of advanced communications technologies, such as satellites, the Internet, desktop publishing, and, most important, computers, which were rarely used in the newsrooms of the 1970s;

- the demise of family-owned news organizations with special interests in supporting journalistic principles with lower revenues and the emergence of chain papers and multimedia production companies;

- the rise of conglomerate media giants that use synergistic production and distribution strategies (in which different branches of the company share and cross-promote each others' resources and services);
- the related destruction of legendary divisions between managerial and editorial operations, the mythical church and state of the journalistic field;
- the birth of new forms and formats, such as the television news magazine, dramatized news footage, and product-driven news sections;
- the deregulation of media markets, and specifically of restrictions on ownership of multiple media outlets in the same city; and
- a crisis of legitimacy for journalists, who often complain that new conditions of production undermine their capacity to meet their own standards, struggle with the emergence of a polarized labor force including a celebrity class of journalistic elites, and consistently rank at the bottom of opinion polls rating the popularity of various professions (Gans 2003).

These transformations are pervasive: in 1945, for example, roughly 80 percent of American daily papers were independently owned. By 2000, about 80 percent were owned and operated by publicly traded chains, and major media corporations were actively building lines of vertical and horizontal integration to link everything from news production to entertainment to advertising in-house (Dugger 2000). Yet in the United States, little ethnographic work penetrates these organizations to describe or explain how they work.

This article examines the point of journalistic production in one major news organization and shows how reporters and editors manage constraints of time, space, and market pressure under regimes of convergence news making. I describe how news organizations, like firms in other American industries during the recent phase of "flexible accumulation," have downsized their staffs while imposing new demands that workers become skilled at multitasking with new technologies. Digital systems for reporting, writing, file sharing, and printing facilitate this flexibility. I consider the implications of these conditions for the particular forms of intellectual and cultural labor that journalists produce, drawing connections between the political economy of the journalistic field, the organizational structure of multimedia firms, new communications technologies, and the qualities of content created by news workers.

This article grows out of a multiyear ethnographic project based on case studies of news organizations that began as print media but now use advanced technologies to produce and distribute content across platforms. Here, I draw upon fieldwork to show how changes in the journalistic field, particularly the rise of new technologies and the corporate integration of news companies, have led to a double fragmentation: first, for newsmakers, whose daily work has been interrupted and rearranged by additional responsibilities and new pressures of time and space; second, for news audiences, whom marketers have segmented into narrow units and who are encouraged to forge symbolic or imagined communities on the basis of market concerns. This article focuses on one particular but also particularly important case: Metro News, an emerging second-tier media corporation that is broadly considered an industry model organization for integrating different forms of media work.[2] Recently Metro News won *Fortune* magazine's survey for "most admired news company" several years in a row, the industry's leading publications routinely feature it as an exemplary case, and international firms visit often for tours of the facility. In the late 1990s I spent three weeks inside the Metro News newsroom, where I observed journalists and editors in action as they worked on stories, conducted formal editorial meetings, and searched for news. I also conducted and taped interviews with twenty-five reporters, editors, and managers. When I began the project, the news editor not only allowed me to sit in on meetings and interrupt his busy reporters. He also let me occupy an unused office in the corner of the main news floor, and I could bring reporters back into my private room and give them space to speak openly about their work.

## Convergence and the New Media Market

Metro News has been a major player in the American politics and society since the mid-nineteenth century. For the first fifty years of its life, the Metro News company devoted its energy to local news and politics, and at the turn of the twentieth century, its editor gained attention by arguing that the mission of an urban paper is to acculturate and integrate new immigrants to local as well as American national culture. In the next decades, the company grew with the times, establishing a new paper in New York after World War I, a local radio station in the 1920s, and an affiliated television station in 1948. Still, the core of the company was its main paper, so when readership began to decline in the 1970s, Metro News, like most other newspaper companies, had to refashion its mission. Its new managers decided that a great newspaper could not survive unless it was embedded in a great news and entertainment network. This is the moment of rebirth for the Metro News and for other media organizations. Unfortunately, the classic sociological studies of news work were conducted just before this renaissance.

From 1975 until today, major media companies such as Metro News have evolved through four key development strategies: First, *taking companies out of private hands* (usually ending the control of wealthy families who held long ties to the news profession), *raising capital with public stock offerings* (Metro News, for example, went public in the early 1980s), and *reforming the corporate mission* to meet the bottom-line demands of stockholders. Second, and related, is *bringing in new corporate managers to streamline production systems in the newsroom* and to reduce labor costs. Third, *making massive investments in digital communications technologies* and remaking the corporate infrastructure. Fourth, *establishing lines of horizontal integration in the company*, which meant acquiring or merging with other content providers and distributors, such as television stations, Internet companies, and magazines, and linking the marketing as well as the news divisions across subsidiary firms. Metro News began aggressively purchasing new papers and local TV stations in the 1970s, and today its holdings include more than a dozen city newspapers, with major dailies in the largest urban markets. It owns a national television superstation, a share of another national network, and more than two dozen local TV stations. Finally, it operates a fleet of radio stations in leading markets, a book publisher, several television production companies, massive digital media investments, a professional sports franchise, and local cable television news stations that broadcast local news around the clock.

For the company, ownership of such diverse operations is the key to a *synergistic* mode of production (Auletta 1998), whereby each media outlet uses the products of the others to enhance its offerings and, to use the language of the industry, to *cross-promote its brands*. On the business side, synergy allows big news companies to integrate their advertising sales work and create special packages for clients; this gives them a major competitive advantage over smaller media companies and also increases the efficiency of their marketing projects. At the organizational level, the Metro News's acquisitions of newspapers in California, New York, and Florida allow the corporation to cut and streamline its slate of domestic and international bureaus. Local reporters in Los Angeles, Chicago, or New York City are both city and national correspondents because their work is used by different papers. Similarly, one foreign bureau can provide news and photography for several papers at once. And freelancers—who are increasingly popular with news companies—can broker deals with a corporate network rather than a single outlet. Digital communications infrastructures are crucial for this level of convergence since they allow for immediate circulation of content and distribute information in easily editable formats.

But this is only the beginning of synergy. Metro News also uses each branch of its operation to produce content for several media at once, and it has turned its company into a flexible producer. Within any single metropolitan news agency, the main news-room is increasingly likely to contain a television studio, Internet production facilities, radio equipment, sophisticated graphics machines, and hundreds of computer terminals for print journalists. There are separate staffs for the different media, but workers in the various departments have frequent contact with each other, in part because they all produce material for many platforms.

Just what these cultural workers produce is the subject of major debate inside Metro News and the profession more broadly. Reporters and professional observers complain that the corporate management has classified their product as "content," a category that suits any story, image, or other form of intellectual property, rather than journalism (see Auletta 1998). According to journalists and editors, the craft distinctions between different genres of news work that historically organized the field are beginning to blur. Media managers argue that their staff should be able to tell stories across platforms, and many reporters are increasingly worried about bottom-line-driven assaults on their vocational techniques and professional values. Although the news media was born as a commercial medium and has always been deeply entangled with corporate, profit-driven interests, insiders fear that the logic of the market has penetrated to unprecedented depths of the modern newsroom (Underwood 1993; Downie and Kaiser 2001). In response, journalists are making use of the language of the professions, mobilizing the image of the professional journalist who is independent, specially trained, skeptical, and objective to defend their status from incursions by the market and new players in the field.

## The New Newsroom

The organizational transformation of Metro News has produced major changes in the physical and social space of its offices. Reporters and editors can see powerful signs of their industry's transformation in their work spaces, which have been completely redesigned so that journalists can move freely between print, television, radio, and Internet outlets and meet the demands of the new media environment. The most striking difference in the newsroom is that in 1999 the company placed a television news studio at the physical and symbolic center of the office, directly in front of the editor's door, so that the editorial staff orbits around the studio. This is, of course, hardly an innocent move since journalists have fierce internal battles about the ways that television news culture—with its emphasis on video, sound bites, and soft features—threatens the integrity of other reporting practices.

For much of the newspaper staff, the emergence of television as the centerpiece of the organization signals the rise of a different journalistic mission, one determined by the production values of TV news. But then there is another, more seductive side of television: everyone, including print reporters, recognizes the power of TV to reach a massive audience, and for reporters, television represents a route to celebrity, wealth, and influence. In fact, one adviser to the company told me that the introduction of television into the newsroom had been "the biggest non-story of the year. It turns out," he explained, "that print reporters want to be on TV just as much as everyone else."

Perhaps the deepest source of the journalists' frustration is their perception that the new environment has forced them to take on additional responsibilities in the same work period, which has particularly severe consequences for cultural production that requires serious, independent thinking. Of course, there is nothing new about either deadlines or news cycles. Modern journalists have always worked against the clock to meet their rigid production and distribution schedules, and news stories are necessarily written in haste. During the 1970s, national television news programs were broadcast once a day, in the early evening, which gave the production team a clear twenty-four-hour span to cover "breaking news." Most major newspapers were published in the early morning or afternoon, and with the contemporary printing technologies, reporters had to file their stories several hours in advance.

The time cycle for news making in the age of digital production is radically different: the regular news cycle has spun into an erratic and unending pattern that I characterize as a *news cyclone*. The advent of twenty-four-hour television news and the rapid emergence of instant Internet news sites have eliminated the temporal borders in the news day, creating an informational environment in which there is always breaking news to produce, consume, and—for reporters and their subjects—react against. In the new media world, a Metro News writer says, "There's a writing process that's just *constant, constant, constant* . . . in everything we're doing we're dealing with the clock. *Bang. Bang. Bang. Bang. Bang.* And that clock just goes on."

## Synergy and Digital Systems

So, just how has Metro News managed to meet the new time pressures and to increase the efficiency and productivity of its already busy staff? This is the deeper story of synergy, and it is also the place where digital technologies enter the picture. In the new media newsroom, journalists have to become *flexible laborers*, reskilled to meet demands from several media at once. And as companies break down the division of news labor, reporters experience a time compression that they make sense of through the language of stress and pressure. As one reporter explains,

> Metro News is a multimedia company. . . . Increasingly, there are pressures to put reporters who are covering stories on television, and there are other demands that you have as a reporter for other ways of covering stories. Let me be specific. There have been pressures to participate in cyberspace . . . they put your stuff on cyberspace and they

ask you to do other things, provide links, [create] other kinds of information. There's [also] an emphasis in journalism now, much more than ever, on graphics. So some of the time that you're writing the story has to be spent with the graphics team talking to them about what we're doing, so that their graphics can add to what we're doing and not simply repeat. But also you are providing some reporting information for graphics, which is a whole new layer. [All of this] requires conversations with other people in the newsroom, and that requires time taken away from just the story. . . . [After describing other responsibilities involved in television and internet she concludes:] Very recently . . . one of the things that they decided to try was having reporters write conceptual headlines for their stories. . . . I think to some people it's like, just another thing to do. You know, we've already got graphics, we've already got ties to photo, sometimes we have to appear on TV and do cyberspace. *And now we're going to have to make suggestions for headlines too?*

For Metro News, such coordinated news-making activities keep labor costs down and increase the output and efficiency of the production process. For reporters, though, the new regime creates real professional challenges: the more they work with different media, for example, the more they realize that content does not move easily from one medium to the next, and therefore they must develop techniques for translating work across platforms. It is no surprise, then, that the new journalism textbooks and curricular programs emphasize developing news skills that work in several media. Many veteran journalists worry that if television becomes the most valuable and important medium for major news companies, then being telegenic will become the most important journalistic skill and a criterion for entry-level reporting jobs. What is more immediately worrisome for journalists is that the new responsibilities also reduce the editorial staff's time to research, report, and even to think about their work. Time matters in special ways for cultural producers since incursions into the working schedule undermine one's ability to perform a craft (see Bourdieu 2000). The greatest fear among print journalists is that the production routines for daily television news will become normative in their medium as well. In a discussion with me, one reporter explained that

some people are very concerned about the redesign of our newsroom and how our TV station is going to have a presence on the desk. Digital is going to be on the desk. And on the other hand, I think that it's all to the good and that the more we get integrated and familiar with these other areas, the more likely we will be in the future to be prepared for whatever happens in the future, rather than be isolated and out of print.

EK: Are you asked to take any other responsibilities?

So far I haven't been. I mean, I was asked one time to lead a chat room on ethnic issues by our digital folks. But there are a lot of other people who are constantly being asked to get on TV and talk about their stories. I just haven't really done that. I was on the television news for a project I did on National earlier this year on the elections. . . . So I haven't really been affected by that push. But I know of folks in Washington . . . I think they have pretty heavy TV duties in Washington, a lot of live stories on what they're covering. And that takes up a lot of their time. They have to write the scripts. OK, so they write their news stories and then they write their scripts and they don't get paid for that and it takes a lot of time. And I don't know if that's going to be coming for us as well.

I guess my only concern is that right now we have for many years been the source for TV news. You know, they read us and then they go out and do their stories. So if having news television in here means that we'll get to do . . . I mean I would rather do my story for both mediums than have somebody scarf up my story and do it, and kind of steal it from me after I did all the work. So there's sort of two ways to look at it.

Editors have related concerns: they have to sustain a certain level of journalistic quality to maintain the company's reputation. Indeed, it is important to have Pulitzer Prize–winning investigations, and in the past several years, the Metro News has had many. But it achieves this system by introducing a new system of stratification inside the newsroom, with elite reporters given ample time to do large projects and a large staff of second-tier journalists responsible for much of the daily workload. This hierarchical arrangement is similar to those emerging in other cultural fields, including the academy.

In their most extreme forms, concerns about efficiency can push journalists to forgo traditional kinds of reporting and to rely, instead, on the most easily accessible information: news that is available online. In recent years, several leading professional news publications have run stories about the industry's most dangerous computer virus, whose symptoms include staying at the desk and using material from the Web for reporting that is faster and easier than work in the streets. There are several well-known cases in which journalists relying on Web-based information used faulty statistics as the basis for published stories. Reporters, particularly when they are working against the clock, are susceptible to Internet misinformation. Online reporting practices are unlikely to displace traditional reporting techniques, as some of the most concerned critics worry. But media organizations are learning that the same digital systems that improve journalists' ability to do research in the office can also have perverse effects.

The responsibility to produce content that can be used across platforms also places a different kind of pressure on editors and business managers. For them, directing a multimedia company requires ensuring that a sufficient level of content meets the needs of each medium, and this means that reporters assigned to key beats or stories have to produce even if they want more time to explore. According to one reporter, "Being productive means you're gathering information that is short order. . . . Everything, all the incentives, come down to producing for tomorrow." One effect of this imperialism of the immediate is that Metro News, long renowned for serious and time-consuming investigative reports, has reduced the number of investigative stories. Between 1980 and 1995, the newspaper cut the number of investigative stories by 48 percent. One reporter explains his view of the change as follows: "The whole idea of giving reporters time and space to explore just doesn't seem like an efficient way to do business." The core city reporting staff no longer has enough time to penetrate into the deep pockets of urban life and come up with surprising stories. Crime, local scandals, entertainment, all the events that are easy to cover have become more prominent in the city news. As one city editor told me,

The best way to blanket the city, and the most efficient way to blanket the city, is to cover the [big] institutions [with beats]. So, it's hard to justify, from a resource standpoint, a more burdensome way of getting information, which is out on the streets. It's not efficient at all. There are no press releases, no spokespeople, and if there are, there is a bunch of spokespeople [saying different things]. And to sort through that and weave through that and get a clear picture is just time-consuming and it's harder to devote the resources to doing that.

## Target Marketing and Media Segmentation

One of the most economically significant characteristics of digital news systems is that they have enabled media organizations to push the principles of target marketing to new levels, to make specialized information and entertainment products that appeal to narrow groups of consumers but that can be sold by one advertising staff (see Turow 1998). Competition within the American media market has fragmented the mass audience on which network television stations and major newspapers built their fortunes. According to one major media executive, "People want to know what their neighbors are up to. People want to know what's going on in their block. People want information that touches their lives" (quoted in Lieberman 1998). Today the strategy of most news companies is to locate and target affluent audiences. For many city papers, the major impact of new digital technologies (especially publishing technologies) is that they enable companies to target coverage to the suburban areas that contain most of the affluent readers whom advertisers want to reach. Using digital technologies, Metro News has expanded its system of zoned newspaper production and distribution so that it prints not only a special section for each of the zoned regions in the metropolitan area but occasionally different front pages, with special headlines, photos, and stories, as well. One reporter expressed her frustration with this system of target marketing:

> Something might go on page one in the city and then something else will go in the suburbs in the suburban papers. . . . Oftentimes, we have stories that have been like page one in *USA Today* or the *Wall Street Journal*, but could only get read by people in one zone. So nobody saw the story if they lived in the suburbs, until they read it two weeks later on the front page of the *USA Today*, or until they saw it on TV because TV picked it up. So that's really frustrating from the point of view of the reporter who thinks they've got a nicely written story, to not get play because the editors think that won't be of interest to people in Dixon County. And then my argument to that is well these white people in Dixon County will be mighty interested when these Mexican people get pushed out and soon they'll be on their door-step. (Laughs,) And he said, well we can change the lead. "In a move that made white residents of Dixon County uneasy . . ."

Yet there is an important exception to the rise of target-marketed news: it is not available to people who live in poor neighborhoods or suburbs and lack a strong base of desirable professionals for advertisers to target. As a former *Chicago Tribune* editor explains, "By reducing circulation efforts among low-income, minority readers, newspapers actually improve the overall demographic profile of their audiences, which they then use to justify raising advertising rates" (Squires 1993).

The Internet, rather than television or print, offers the most exciting possibilities for creating new forms of journalism with advanced technology and convergence production. The Internet is the ideal medium for deepening coverage with interactive links to video, text, and graphics, and the spatial constraints are relatively loose online. (In theory, of course, Internet reporting need not be bound by any spatial constraints. But many editors still try to sharpen their stories so that they conform to conventional narrative forms from print media.) Yet by 2003, few news organizations had developed a business model that generated profits for news Web sites, and particularly after the collapse of the dot-com industry, news companies were reluctant to invest significant resources in the most innovative kinds of online media production. A former editor who developed the new media offerings in one major Florida newspaper told me that

> in most companies, the real convergence action involves putting print reporters on television, and that's just not the way to make convergence work. One thing is that it doesn't take advantage of the medium. There's nothing journalistically or technologically interesting about putting a print reporter on TV—it just uses personnel in a more flexible way, getting more out of them. The real innovations in convergence journalism are going to come on the web, or eventually on interactive television, where you can produce new kinds of content. Now the problem is that no one knows how to make a web-based business model that works for journalism. So although the internet is the best place to combine text, video, graphics, and interactivity—all the things that make multimedia production exciting—there's not much corporate interest in doing it because it's not really profitable, and it's not clear that it will be. And you can't get support for innovative news production if there's not a business model that works.

Some participants in convergence projects argue that other, less visible journalistic benefits come from convergence production. Sharing resources and staff helps both television and newspaper companies expand the scope of their reporting, allowing them to cover stories that they would otherwise miss. A study by the Project for Excellence in Journalism found that convergence production systems can help improve the quality of television news since TV staffs are comparably small and print reporters bring depth to their offerings. But several newspaper reporters complain that the stories and sources from television tend to focus on crime and violence issues since those are major topics on local TV news.[3] Many print journalists believe that the greatest influence of television news practices on newspapers is to promote this visual information at the expense of textual depth, and they are anxious that the norms and forms of television will take over the paper.

## Conclusion: Newsrooms in an Age of Digital Production

From the late nineteenth century, when American urban newspapers announced their project of integrating and acculturating new immigrants to local and national culture, journalists and social scientists have argued that news organizations "not only serve but create their communities" by providing raw materials for collective social and political life (Fuller 1996, 228). In recent years, cultural critics and sociologists have grown so interested in global circuits of information and the possibilities for cosmopolitan uses of news that they have scarcely recognized how media companies use the Internet and other advanced communication technologies to alter their local coverage.[4] According to the *Columbia Journalism Review*, from 1985 to 1995, space for international news fell in each of the major American weekly news magazines: from 24 to 14 percent at *Time*, from 22 to 12 percent at *Newsweek*, and from 20 to 12 percent at *U.S. News and World Report*. Network television news programs, which devoted 45 percent of their broadcasts to foreign affairs in the 1970s, gave 13.5 percent of their time to international news in 1995 (Hickey 1998). According to Downie and Kaiser (2001), after September 11, the American news media exhibited an increased interest in foreign affairs and heightened international coverage. Yet one year later, in the new Afterward to the paperback edition of the same book (2002), they reported that soon after the disaster most news organizations returned to their pre–September 11 patterns of coverage. The optimism about the future of foreign reporting they expressed in the first edition seems unwarranted (also see Alterman 2003, 263–64).

When news organizations do cover national and international events, editors and managers encourage journalists to "localize" the stories, that is, to illustrate why news far from home is relevant to the local community. One prominent media consultant told me that "if you want to write a story about the war in Kabul, you're better off tying it to the Kabul House restaurant in town." In theory, news audiences can use advanced communications technologies to obtain enormous amounts of information about the world. In practice, as advertisers and news executives know, most people use the news to gain a world of information about their personal interests, their hometown, and themselves. Target marketing and convergence production techniques have helped to create informational islands of communities whose segregation in physical space is increasingly joined and reinforced by the differentiation of specialized news products. As Cass Sunstein (2001) argued, new media and digital technologies have played important roles in this segmenting process.

The consequences of the emergent journalistic and managerial practices described here are already visible. Convergence news companies expect their journalistic staff to be flexible and fast, and both editors and corporate managers are already revaluing their workers, considering multimedia skills in their story assignments as well as in hiring and retention decisions. Many journalists and media critics complain that the additional labor demands and the work speedup required for convergence have undermined the conditions of news production, mainly by reducing the time available to report, research, write, and reflect on stories. Convergence companies contest these claims, pointing to various awards won by staff in television, print, and the Internet as evidence that multimedia production enriches their offerings and improves their staff. Journalists respond by pointing to an emerging stratification of the labor force, in which major companies support a small elite corps of reporters who are able to conduct serious investigations and long-term projects, and the remaining majority who have more responsibilities than ever. Yet it is notoriously difficult to reliably appraise the overall quality of reporting across fields and themes. Instead of attempting a normative evaluation of whether the new conditions of production are good or bad for journalism, I conclude by explaining how convergence regimes and corporate managerial strategies affect various qualities of news content and features of news work.

The penetration of market principles and marketing projects into the editorial divisions of news organizations is one of the most dramatic changes in the journalistic field, and there is no question the mythical walls separating the editorial and advertising are mostly down. When Gans (1979) studied news organizations in the 1960s and 1970s, he found that editors would occasionally grant access to political officials and listen to their input for various stories and issues, but—as a matter of journalistic principle—not to advertisers or corporations. In the late 1990s, Times Mirror CEO and *Los Angeles Times* publisher Mark Willes generated professional outrage by announcing that advertisers should play a key role in shaping journalistic content. In the early 2000s, editorial meetings with advertisers and the internal marketing staff are routine, and the editors I met unabashedly reported that they worked hard to produce more marketable and profitable products. At the *Chicago Tribune*, architects integrated the famously separate elevator banks for management and journalists, symbolically eliminating the historical markers of journalism's sacred and profane sides. In 2003, managers at the *Dallas Morning News* even began handing out $100 bills to reporters who memorized the company's five business goals and could recite them on demand (Celeste 2003).

It is important to note that news companies have long been driven by bottomline considerations and that media moguls from William Randolph Hearst to Rupert Murdoch have built enormous fortunes through aggressive capitalist management. Yet in recent years, several high-ranking editors, including James Squires from the *Chicago Tribune*, James Fallows from *U.S. News and World Report*, and Leonard Downie Jr. and Robert Kaiser from *The Washington Post*, have argued that corporate managers and advertisers are now active participants in editorial decision making and that their interests now structure the form and content of news to an unprecedented degree (Squires 1993; Downie and Kaiser 2001).

The most notable examples of advertisers taking part in editorial decision making include the case of the *Los Angeles Times* sponsoring the Staples Center, sharing revenue on a 168-page magazine produced by the editorial staff and inserted into the Sunday paper in 1999; the new special sections determined by advertising and dedicated to mutual funds, communications and computer technologies, and home and gardening in most major newspapers; and the rise of service-oriented "news you can use," human interest, health, and entertainment reporting and of news beats such as "malls," "shopping," and "car culture" (Underwood 1993). Contemporary news organizations conduct extensive and expensive research to learn what kinds of content consumers want, too, and they have made important qualitative changes in their offerings to meet market demand. Several new media forms express the strength of market logic in the newsrooms: television newsmagazines, dramatized television news footage and musical scores for news, newspaper "advertorials," niche tabloids for young urban consumers (such as Chicago's *Red Streak* and *Red Eye*, produced by the *Sun-Times* and the Tribune Company, respectively), and Internet reports with ads linked to stories on related products and services. Newspapers' increasing emphasis on color graphics, weather packages, business reporting, and cross-promotional packages are part of the same trend.

The market's pressures transforming the journalistic field have changed other fields as well, including the academy, the medical profession, and publishing. Identifying these shifts in the media as features of broader political economic forces in contemporary societies, as many critics do, is a necessary but insufficient part of sociological analysis. The internal dynamics of any given field always absorb and refract the exogenous forces that enter and alter it, and fieldwork inside media organizations and the industry's social space helps to specify how change happens in this particular sphere. One surprising feature of the journalistic field is that news organizations harness advanced communications technology to speed up and extend the work process for reporters and to enhance their local offerings to suburban markets.

The most exciting innovations in journalistic forms, particularly those involving multimedia packages disseminated through the Internet, have received little support from news organizations because they are not profitable. Moreover, the celebrated genres of the American journalistic craft, particularly investigative reporting, long-term projects, and penetrating urban affairs work, have lost corporate support in all but the most elite publications because of their inefficiencies and the costs of production. One editor of a midsized newspaper told a *Columbia Journalism Review* editor, "If a story needs real investment of time and money, we don't do it anymore"; and a television newsman reports, "Instead of racing out of the newsroom with a camera crew when an important story breaks, we're more likely now to stay at our desks and work the phones, rewrite the wire copy, hire a local crew and a free-lance producer to get pictures at the scene, then dig out some file footage, maps, or still photos for the anchor to talk in front of, or maybe buy some coverage from a video news service like Reuters, AP, or World Television News" (quoted in Hickey 1998).

Digital technologies have changed journalistic production in newsrooms, but not according to journalists' preferences. When conglomerates and publicly traded companies took over news organizations and entered the journalistic field, they imported corporate managerial techniques and developed new strategies to increase the productivity, efficiency, and profitability of news businesses (Squires 1993; Underwood 1993; Dugger 2000; Downie and Kaiser 2001). Media executives and managerial-minded editors not only downsized their journalistic staffs, they also invented new regimes of convergence production to expand their offerings across media (Auletta 1998). They designed applications of digital technologies to facilitate the process of multimedia work and increase their capacity to repackage articles from one newspaper to another or one platform to another (Harper 1998; Pavlik 2001) and invested lightly in innovations to basic journalistic forms, offering little support for multimedia offerings that take full advantage of the Internet's affordances. Digital systems in major news companies remain in embryonic stages of development, and it is difficult to predict how they will develop. But the political economy, cultural conventions, and regulatory restrictions governing the news industry will play powerful roles in determining how advanced communications technologies enter the matrix of journalistic production, just as they did before the digital age.

## Questions for Consideration

1   Klinenberg says that the company he studied is involved in a synergistic mode of production. What does he mean by that? Can you think of non-journalistic media organizations that use that approach?

2   Klinenberg notes journalists have to become "flexible laborers, reskilled to meet demands from several media at once." Do you think that the difficulty he noted among journalists who tried to carry this out might be due to the newness of the phenomenon and their lack of training, or is there a basic problem with the idea of placing cross-media demands on journalists?

3   Klinenberg presents a list of eight major developments that have affected the news media during the past 30 years. Choose one of them and conduct research to find out how it affects the creation and distribution of news.

## Notes

1.   A notable exception is Gilens (1999), who showed that major American news magazines vastly overrepresented African Americans in photographs of poor people, particularly the "undeserving" or unsympathetic poor. He then conducted interviews with photography editors to ask why they used these images and if they recognized their own patterns of representation.

2.   Metro News is a pseudonym.

3.   Downie and Kaiser (2001, 170) reported, "An exhaustive 1999 study of 590 local newscasts on fifty-nine stations in nineteen cities . . . found that nine of every ten local stories on those newscasts came 'from either the police scanner or scheduled events.' Fewer than one in ten stories came from the reporter's own initiatives."

4.   Many scholars invoke Arjun Appadurai's (1996) language of "scapes" and "flows" to portray a floating world of hypermobility, fast action, and congenital rootlessness. Yet in *Modernity at Large*, Appadurai was centrally concerned with "the place of locality" amidst global flows. His theoretical writing called attention to the various cultural processes and institutions that shape local subjects and local knowledge, to the ways that situated communities operate as both *contexts* and *producers of contexts* in contemporary life. Appadurai recounted many familiar techniques for the spatial production of locality, "the building of houses, the organization of paths and passages, the making and remaking of fields and gardens" (p. 180). Yet he paid little attention to how local news organizations contribute to this process.

## References

Alterman, Eric. 2003. *What liberal media? The truth about bias and the news*. New York: Basic Books.

Appadurai, Arjun. 1996. *Modernity at large: Cultural dimensions of globalization*. Minneapolis: University of Minnesota Press.

Auletta, Ken. 1998. Synergy city. *American Journalism Review*, May. http://www.ajr.org/article_printable.asp?id=2446/.

Boczkowski, Pablo. 2004. *Digitizing the news: Innovation in online newspapers*. Cambridge, MA: MIT Press.

Bourdieu, Pierre. 1994. *Language and symbolic power*. Cambridge, MA: Harvard University Press.

——. 1998. *On television*. New York: New Press.

——. 2000. *Pascalian meditations*. Standford, CA: Standford University Press.

Calhoun, Craig, ed. 1993. *Habermas and the public sphere*. Cambridge, MA: MIT Press.

Castells, Manuel. 1996. *The rise of the network society*. Oxford, UK: Blackwell.

Celeste, Eric. 2003. Snooze alarm. *Dallas Observer*, February 13.

Cook, Timothy. 1998. *Governing with the news: The news media as a political institution*. Chicago: University of Chicago Press.

Downie, Leonard, Jr., and Robert Kaiser. 2001. *The news about the news: American journalism in peril*. New York: Knopf.

——. 2002. *The news about the news: American journalism in peril*. New York: Vintage.

Dugger, Ronnie. 2000. The corporate domination of journalism. In *The business of journalism*, ed. William Serrin, 27–56. New York: New Press.

Fishman, Mark. 1980. *Manufacturing the news*. Austin: University of Texas Press.

Fuller, Jack. 1996. *News values: Ideas for the information age*. Chicago: University of Chicago Press.

Gans, Herbert. 1972. The famine in American mass-communications research: Comments on Hirsch, Tuchman, and Gecas. *American Journal of Sociology* 77:697–705.

——. 1979. *Deciding what's news: A study of CBS Evening News, NBC Nightly News, Newsweek, and Time*. New York: Pantheon.

——. 2003. *Democracy and the news*. New York: Oxford University Press.

Gilens. Martin. 1999. *Why Americans hate welfare: Race, media, and the politics of antipoverty policy*. Chicago: University of Chicago Press.

Ginsburg, Faye, Lila Abu-Lughod, and Brian Larkin, eds. 2002. *Media worlds: Anthropology on new terrain*. Berkeley: University of California Press.

Gitlin, Todd. 2002. *Media unlimited: How the torrent of images and sounds overwhelms our lives*. New York: Metropolitan Books.

Habermas, Jurgen. 1989. *The structural transformation of the public sphere*. Cambridge, MA: MIT Press.

Harper, Chrstopher. 1998. *And that's the way it will be: News and information in a digital world*. New York: New York University Press.

Hickey, Neil. 1998. Money lust: How pressure for profit is perverting journalism. *Columbia Journalism Review*, July/August. http://archives.cjr.org/year/98/4/moneylust.asp/.

Jacobs, Ronald. 2000. *Race, media, and the crisis of civil society*. Cambridge: Cambridge University Press.

Lieberman, David. 1998. The rise and rise of 24-hour local news. *Columbia Journalism Review*, November/December http://archives.cjr.org/year/98/6/tvnews.asp/.

Luhmann, Niklas. 2000. *The reality of the mass media*. Stanford, CA: Stanford University Press.

Majoribanks, Tim. 2000. *News corporation, technology, and the workplace*. Cambridge: Cambridge University Press.

Pavlik, John. 2001. *Journalism and new media*. New York: Columbia University Press.

Schudson, Michael. 1978. *Discovering the news: A social history of American newspapers*. New York: Basic Books.

——. 1995. *The power of news*. Cambridge, MA: Harvard University Press.

Squires, James. 1993. *Read all about it: The corporate takeover of America's newspapers*. New York: Random House.

Starr, Paul. 2004. *The creation of the media: Political origins of modern communications*. New York: Basic Books.

Sunstein, Cass. 2001. *Republic.com*. Princeton, NJ: Princeton University Press.

Tuchman, Gaye. 1978. *Making news: A study in the construction of reality*. New York: Free Press.

Turow, Joseph. 1998. *Breaking up America: Advertisers and the new media world*. Chicago: University of Chicago Press.

Underwood, Doug. 1993. *When MBAs rule the newsroom*. New York: Columbia University Press.

# Chapter 9

# BROOKE ERIN DUFFY

## TIME AHEAD
### Digital Challenges Facing Print Magazines

THE PRESENT "TWENTY-FOUR/SEVEN" ERA of news and information poses a dilemma for those in the magazine industry. Because of tradition and technology, they typically work on issues several *months* before they reach readers' mailboxes. In her recent essay, Brooke Erin Duffy explores the difficulties magazine producers face as they confront the new timing demands of the digital age. Duffy suggests that as producers increasingly turn to the Web to provide more regularly updated content, they face the additional challenge of maintaining synchronicity between the print and online versions.

In August 2005, while the devastating events of Hurricane Katrina were unfolding across the Gulf Coast, the October issue of *Shape* magazine was already in press. When the issue hit newsstands just a few weeks later, its "Sin City Shapeovers" feature on New Orleans seemed painfully ironic.[1] That same year, *Glamour* published a short news piece commemorating the 50th anniversary of Rosa Parks's landmark act of civil disobedience. Yet while the article referred to Parks as "now ninety-two and living in Detroit," she had passed away two months before the issue's December cover date.[2] More recently, the November 2006 issue of *Success Magazine Ltd.* featured on its cover "Congressman" John Sweeney. Unfortunately, the issue didn't reach readers until a day after Sweeney was defeated for reelection.[3]

Although fate plays no small role in such instances of poor timing, the schedule on which the magazine industry operates is also at fault. Producers of women's monthly magazines, for example, typically work on editorial content several months ahead of time.[4] This enables them to distribute issues weeks—sometimes months—before the cover date. Freelance writer Abigail Green suggests that this practice is not unique to women's magazines and that some magazine companies plan their editorial line-up more than a year in advance. This forward-looking schedule led Green to remark, "Who [else], besides Santa and seriously organized people, starts thinking about Christmas in July?"[5]

Underpinning the magazine industry's production schedule is a desire to keep time with their advertisers and readers, both of whom the industry depends on for financing and other resources. For example, the fact that advertisers have historically planned their campaigns far in advance has led magazine companies to release their annual editorial calendars (January–December) the preceding fall. This enables advertisers to buy space in those issues and near articles that most closely align with their message.[6] Readers, too, "want advice on things going forward . . . before it happens," as one magazine publisher put it.

Yet because of the technological constraints of magazine publishing—the printing and distribution processes take up to two months—producers have adopted practices to make their content seem more timely. For one, they shift the date on the cover such that a July issue may reach readers as early as the first week of June. Magazine historian Theodore Peterson explains how the roots of this practice can be traced back to the 1870s, when publishers first realized readers would likely not buy a magazine after the date on its cover had passed.[7] Another way producers make content seem timelier is by filling their pages with future-oriented content. This, as one executive explains, provides readers with "freshness and anticipation." The fashion director of another women's publication added, "The magazine that is the most forward-thinking will attract the greatest audience because it will give its readers a leg up on the Joneses."

The dawn of the twenty-first century, however, brought with it a number of technological changes that seemed to clash with the magazine industry's longstanding timing practices. Particularly significant is the rise of a "twenty-four-seven" era of mass communication as digital media—computers, mobile phones, and more—are making textual and pictorial information available in real time. This is leading readers and advertisers to develop new expectations about the timing of media materials, and in turn, poses a significant challenge to those in the magazine industry. Before examining this challenge and the extent to which magazine producers are responding, it is important to bring the topics of time and media production into conversation and to explore some of the social implications of their interrelationship.

## The Timing–Content Link in Media Materials

More than three decades ago, sociologist Gaye Tuchman conducted a study of news organizations that revealed how journalists' daily work rhythms fundamentally guided how they thought about and wrote about news. For example, during the overnight hours when few reporters are available, an event had better be a "damned good story" in order to merit journalistic coverage. To Tuchman, this was just one instance of how timing and social rhythms "influence the assessment of occurrences of potential news events."[8] What emerged from Tuchman's writing, then, was an important link between time and news content which had important implications for the ways in which people learned about the world.

Production considerations within the magazine industry not only suggest that this link still exists 30 years after Tuchman's writing, but also that these findings are applicable to those media organizations that produce information and entertainment. A few examples from the women's magazine industry can help to shed light on the timing–content link. Over the years, magazine producers have developed production routines to ensure that material seems timely and relevant regardless of when it was actually produced. For one, the types of features that take precedence in their publications are described as "timely, but not dependent on time," or even "evergreen." Evergreen refers to content that is always fresh (seasonal content, how-to and advice columns, "soft" features) and is a marked contrast to newsworthy items (breaking news, technological/medical developments, tabloid gossip) which have a more fleeting presence. Indeed, editors admittedly shun the latter for they are more likely to lead to timing accidents.

These timing considerations within the magazine industry influence not just *what* gets written, but also *how* it gets written. To provide just one example, a popular fashion magazine was doing a cover story on a famous singer who was allegedly planning to divorce her husband. Although the celebrity insisted everything was fine with her marriage, the editor admitted to pulling some of the quotes to deemphasize the star's marriage. This would ensure that even if the couple divorced after the issue went to press, it would still seem fresh to readers. At times, however, these timing routines can have significant implications for readers. The editor of one magazine said that they chose to omit research findings on Sudden Infant Death Syndrome, fearing that by the time the information reached readers, it could make the publication seem outdated.

## Timing-Related Challenges

These examples bring the timing challenges associated with magazine production into stark relief. Indeed, the future-oriented schedule has long been perceived as problematical to those in the industry. Perhaps not surprising, it is difficult for staff members to think and work so far into the future. During an interview conducted on a hot summer day, the beauty editor of one women's monthly quipped, "It's 90 degrees out, and I'm sweating, but I have to write a [winter holiday] gift guide and keep in mind what happens to your nails in the winter and how dry your hair gets." Yet a more difficult challenge associated with dating issues in advance is the perishability of information.

Although this is by no means unique to the magazine industry, it is especially complicated given the two-month window between an issues' closing and cover date. Not only can material seem outdated by the time it reaches readers, but it can be devastatingly ill timed, as the following example makes clear. In spring 2006, *Marie Claire* did a photo shoot and interview with singer Ashlee Simpson—several weeks before she underwent highly publicized plastic surgery. Unable to halt production, *Marie Claire's* July issue came out featuring a pre-nose job Simpson on the cover. Inside she was quoted as saying, "Everyone is made differently, and that's what makes us beautiful and unique. I want girls to look in the mirror and feel confident."[9]

What's more, the challenges of such a future-oriented schedule seem to be escalating in the digital age. James Gleick has pointed out that with the Web's rapid success as a mass publishing medium, "the slower media—annual journals, monthly magazines, daily newspapers, even radio and television—agonize over the disruption of their traditional cycles."[10] More broadly, the emergence of new communication platforms has led to a shift toward what one media producer describes as a "have-it-now Internet culture" where people expect everything new and fresh.[11] As such, magazine readers may be growing less accepting of the sort of accidents that were long considered inevitable in publishing. Following the Ashlee Simpson fiasco described above, *Marie Claire* editors received several hundred reader complaints.

Yet it is not just magazine producers and readers who are growing increasingly frustrated with the industry's current timing schedule. Advertisers, too, have expressed their discontent with the inflexible timing of magazines. According to media consultant Valerie Muller, magazine publishers need to be more agile and be "as quick as television in accountability and faster than the two month lead time that many magazines require to place an ad."[12] This issue has only intensified in recent years as ubiquitous Internet and mobile communication allow advertisers to place and update ads in a very short period of time.

## Timing-Related Responses

Given both implicit and explicit pressures from readers and advertisers, magazine producers are beginning to reconsider how they think about time within their organizations—and within their publications. According to a magazine editor with more than 15 years experience in the business, the production schedule of her magazine had undergone dramatic shifts in just the last few years. In the past, she explained, magazine creators would come up with dozens of story ideas which would be written and edited right away and placed into a story inventory until it was time to edit a particular edition. Today, she continued, this inventory system has all but disappeared and writing and editing doesn't begin until much closer to the deadline. In this way, she commented, monthlies "operate much more like newsweeklies." Technologies, too, are improving the production processes as information can be electronically communicated between writers, editors, and publishers.

To this end, many magazines are taking advantage of digital platforms, and particularly the Internet, to deal with timing challenges. Undoubtedly magazine companies are turning to the Web to remain competitive with online content providers. At the same time, the Web's flexible timing is perceived as highly advantageous. One magazine producer noted how the Web can function as a "news updater" in the event that a story becomes outdated by the time it reaches print readers. Others, meanwhile, see the Internet as an opportunity to provide more regularly updated content that can complement the monthly print version. In early 2008, dozens of magazine companies announced new initiatives to provide more timely features. The periodicals include *The Atlantic* ("daily digital essays on news and current events"); *Elle* (live coverage of FashionWeek), *Popular Science* (an interactive, live content management system), *BusinessWeek* ("new content will be published Monday through Friday, featuring articles, blogs lists, videos and more"), among many others.[13]

Of course, the timing challenges of magazine production have not fully disappeared. For one, most magazine companies are still relying on the same production and distribution schedule for their print-bound versions. A recent initiative launched by the Magazine Publishers of America (MPA) reaffirmed this organizational inertia. "Despite time-saving advances in the communication between publishers and printers and the digital delivery of ads and editorial," an MPA report explained, "most official schedules in these areas have not changed substantially for decades."[14]

What's more, as magazines increasingly provide more time-sensitive content on the Web, they are facing the new challenge of balancing the temporalities of the print and online editions. There is great fear among those in the industry that their web site will "scoop" the print magazine, giving readers no reason to spend money on print versions. Some producers have also noted how the presence of magazine companion sites has complicated their organizational dynamics. Few magazines employ staff members who deal exclusively with online content, and accordingly, "members of the print staff are thinking about online content whenever they start planning [a print feature]."

## Conclusion

Like other "traditional" media organizations looking toward a future in an increasingly digital media environment, the magazine industry is at the brink of a grand transition. The industry's future will no doubt be guided by the ways producers think about time as it relates to their organizations, readers, and advertisers. Already, it seems, magazine publishers are beginning to rethink their production practices to be more responsive to the timing demands of the digital age. Some have fully embraced technologies that make it possible to provide regularly updated and interactive content. For instance, in *Self* magazine's May 2007 "Editor's Letter," editor-in-chief Lucy Danziger wrote:

> If I like something, I want it more than once a month: a catchy song, my favorite ice cream, my go-to-shoes. I also want to experience my favorite magazine more than once a month. That's the idea behind *Self*'s decision to record our fitness stories and celebrity photo shoots on video and put them up on self.com. That way, you and I can enjoy the beautiful locations, effective moves and load of inspiration any time, all month long.[15]

Not only does Danziger's quote suggest how magazines are beginning to adapt their schedules, but also how they are repositioning themselves in an era of intense competition. In fact, the title of the piece, "More than just a magazine," reflects a larger shift among magazine companies to promote themselves as cross-platform brands. *Vogue*'s launch of ShopVogue.com, Time Inc.'s development of the home and garden portal MyHomeIdeas.com, *Spin*'s partnership with MySpace, and *Portfolio*'s partnerships with Google, Facebook, and LinkedIn are but a few example of convergence between the magazine and digital media industries. One consequence of this trend is that the definition of a magazine becomes increasingly complicated.[16]

Perhaps a more pressing issue is the way in which and extent to which organizational considerations of timing influence how we learn about and experience the world. While timing concerns clearly impact the media's presentation of news, these patterns are also apparent in those industries that guide society's entertainment and information agendas. For example, magazine producers emphasize timeless, evergreen content so that they can successfully convince readers and advertisers that monthly publications are relevant. Even more significant than the fact that this process influences what gets *included* in issues is that it impacts what gets *excluded*, particularly anything that might become outdated by the time it reaches readers. In an era in which the timing of media materials has been thrust to the fore, the timing–content link and its implications are worthy of careful consideration.

## Questions for Consideration

1    Duffy focuses much of her attention on women's magazines. To what extent do you think her findings would apply to other types of magazines? To which do you think they would apply, and to which do you think they wouldn't?

2    What are some of the benefits and challenges associated with moving the content from a "traditional" medium to the Web?

## Notes

1.    John Rosenthal and Lisa Renaud, "Sin City Shapeovers," *Shape*, October 2005.

2.    Sarah Robbins et al. "The Woman Who Rocked Racism," *Glamour*, December 2005, p. 205.

3.    Michael DeMasi, "Defeated Congressman Sweeney on Cover of 'Success' Magazine," *The Business Review*, Friday, November 10, 2006, www.bizjournals.com/albany/stories/2006/11/06/daily38.html

4.    Much of the data in this study comes from a total of 32 interviews I conducted with highly placed staff members from ten fashion and lifestyle magazine publishing companies. The interviews were conducted in two waves, fall 2005 and fall 2007.

5.    Abigail Green, "The Secret Language of Editors: 'Lead Time' Writers on the Rise," April 17, 2007, http://writersontherise.wordpress.com/2007/04/17/learn-the-secret-language-of-editors-%E2%80%93-lead-time/

6.    Mary Ellen Zuckerman, *A History of Women's Magazines in the United States, 1792–1995* (Westport, CT: Greenwood Press, 1998), p. 39.

7.    Theodore Peterson, *Magazines in the Twentieth Century*, 2nd ed. (Urbana: University of Illinois Press, 1967), pp. 100–103.

8.    Gaye Tuchman, *The Making of News: A Study in the Construction of Reality* (New York: The Free Press, 1978), p. 42.

9.    Dennis Hensley, "Ashlee Simpson's Body Language," *Marie Claire*, July 2006, pp. 50–54. For a description of reader complaints, see Katherine Seelye, "Ashlee's Nose Job Is Last Straw for New Editor of *Marie Claire*," *New York Times*, July 31, 2006, www.nytimes.com/2006/07/31/business/media/31marie.html?_r=1&oref=slogin

10.    James Gleick, *Faster: The Acceleration of Just About Everything* (New York: Pantheon Books, 1999), pp. 69–70.

11.    Joann Klimkiewicz, "Cruel Summer: It's Open Season as Catalogs Roll out Fall Fashions," *Hartford Courant*, July 24, 2007, www.proquest.com

12.    "Agencies Blast Publishers, Move Follows Mag Industry Kvetching," *MediaPost Publications*, October 29, 2003. http://publications.mediapost.com

13.    "Magazine Digital Initiative: 2008," Magazine Publishers of America. Accessed 3/10/2008. www.magazine.org

14.    Magazine Publishers of America, "The Immediacy Initiative—Update," December 2004, www.magazine.org/content/Files/Immed%2011%2018%2004.pdf

15.    Lucy Danziger, "Editor's Letter: More than Just a Magazine," *Self*, May 2007, p. 30.

16.    Similarly, Grindstaff and Turow question the changing definition of television in Laura Grindstaff and Joseph Turow, "Video Cultures: Television Sociology in the 'New TV' Age," *Annual Review of Sociology* 32 (2006): pp. 103–125, 119.

# Chapter 10

# GLORIA STEINEM

# SEX, LIES, AND ADVERTISING

THIS FASCINATING 1990 MEMOIR BY Gloria Steinem recalls her days as the founding editor of *Ms. Magazine* in 1982. As she explains it, the idea of sponsoring a magazine that explored women's issues seriously struck many advertisers as exceedingly strange. Although the stories she tells may seem bizarre and unlikely to happen today, that is not the case. Magazine editors know, for example, that if they want food advertising, they need to publish recipes. They also know that advertisers will get angry if editorial material that might reflect badly on them shows up in an issue in which they advertise. In fact, one could make a case that the financial pressures on magazines today are so profound that the pressures to appeal to advertisers are greater than ever.

About three years ago, as *glasnost* was beginning and *Ms.* seemed to be ending I was invited to a press lunch for a Soviet official. He entertained us with anecdotes about new problems of democracy in his country. Local Communist leaders were being criticized in their media for the first time, he explained, and they were angry.

"So I'll have to ask my American friends," he finished pointedly, "how more subtly to control the press." In the silence that followed, I said, "Advertising."

The reporters laughed, but later, one of them took me aside: How dare I suggest that freedom of the press was limited? How dare I imply that his newsweekly could be influenced by ads?

I explained that I was thinking of advertising's mediawide influence on most of what we read. Even news-magazines use "soft" cover stories to sell ads, confuse readers with "advertorials," and occasionally self-censor on subjects known to be a problem with big advertisers.

But, I also explained, I was thinking especially of women's magazines. There, it isn't just a little content that's devoted to attracting ads, it's almost all of it. That's why advertisers—not readers—have always been the problem for *Ms.* As the only women's magazine that didn't supply what the ad world euphemistically describes as "supportive editorial atmosphere" or "complementary copy" (for instance, articles that praise food/ fashion/beauty subjects to "support" and "complement" food/fashion/beauty ads), *Ms.* could never attract enough advertising to break even.

"Oh, *women's* magazines," the journalist said with contempt. "Everybody knows they're catalogs—but who cares? They have nothing to do with journalism."

I can't tell you how many times I've had this argument in 25 years of working for many kinds of publications. Except as moneymaking machines—"cash cows" as they are so elegantly called in the trade—women's magazines are rarely taken seriously. Though changes being made by women have been called more far-reaching than the industrial revolution—and though many editors try hard to reflect some of them in the few pages left to them after all the ad-related subjects have been covered—the magazines serving the female half of this country are still far below the journalistic and ethical standards of news and general interest publications. Most depressing of all, this doesn't even rate an exposé.

If *Time* and *Newsweek* had to lavish praise on cars in general and credit General Motors in particular to get GM ads, there would be a scandal—maybe a criminal investigation. When women's magazines from *Seventeen* to *Lear's* praise beauty products in general and credit Revlon in particular to get ads, it's just business as usual.

## I

When *Ms.* began, we didn't consider not taking ads. The most important reason was keeping the price of a feminist magazine low enough for most women to afford. But the second and almost equal reason was providing a forum where women and advertisers could talk to each other and improve advertising itself. After all, it was (and still is) as potent a source of information in this country as news or TV and movie dramas.

We decided to proceed in two stages. First, we would convince makers of "people products" used by both men and women but advertised mostly to men—cars, credit cards, insurance, sound equipment, financial services, and the like—that their ads should be placed in a women's magazine. Since they were accustomed to the division between editorial and advertising in news and general interest magazines, this would allow our editorial content to be free and diverse. Second, we would add the best ads for whatever traditional "women's products" (clothes, shampoo, fragrance, food, and so on) that surveys showed *Ms.* readers used. But we would ask them to come in *without* the usual quid pro quo of "complementary copy."

We knew the second step might be harder. Food advertisers have always demanded that women's magazines publish recipes and articles on entertaining (preferably ones that name their products) in return for their ads; clothing advertisers expect to be surrounded by fashion spreads (especially ones that credit their designers); and shampoo, fragrance, and beauty products in general usually insist on positive editorial coverage of beauty subjects, plus photo credits besides. That's why women's magazines look the way they do. But if we could break this link between ads and editorial content, then we wanted good ads for "women's products," too.

By playing their part in this unprecedented mix of all the things our readers need and use, advertisers also would be rewarded: ads for products like cars and mutual funds would find a new growth market, the best ads for women's products would no longer be lost in Oceans of ads for the same category; and both would have access to a laboratory of smart and caring readers whose response would help create effective ads for other media as well.

I thought then that our main problem would be the imagery in ads themselves. Car-makers were still draping blondes in evening gowns over the hoods like ornaments. Authority figures were almost always male, even in ads for products that only women used. Sadistic, he-man campaigns even won industry praise. (For instance, *Advertising Age* had hailed the infamous Silva Thin cigarette theme, "How to Get a Woman's Attention: Ignore Her," as "brilliant.") Even in medical journals, tranquilizer ads showed depressed housewives standing beside piles of dirty dishes and promised to get them back to work.

Obviously *Ms.* would have to avoid such ads and seek out the best ones—but this didn't seem impossible. *The New Yorker* had been selecting ads for aesthetic reasons for years, a practice that only seemed to make advertisers more eager to be in its pages. *Ebony* and *Essence* were asking for ads with positive black images, and though their struggle was hard, they weren't being called unreasonable.

Clearly, what *Ms.* needed was a very special publisher and ad sales staff. I could think of only one woman with experience on the business side of magazines–Patricia Carbine, who recently had become a vice president of *McCall's* as well as its editor in chief–and the reason I knew her name was a good omen. She had been managing editor at *Look* (really *the* editor, but its owner refused to put a female name at the top of his masthead) when I was writing a column there. After I did an early interview with Cèsar Chávez, then just emerging as a leader of migrant labor, and the publisher turned it down because he was worried about ads from Sunkist, Pat was the one who inter-vened. As I learned later, she had told the publisher she would resign if the interview wasn't published. Mainly because *Look* couldn't afford to lose Pat, it was published (and the ads from Sunkist never arrived).

Though I barely knew this woman, she had done two things I always remembered: put her job on the line in a way that editors often talk about but rarely do, and been so loyal to her colleagues that she never told me or anyone outside *Look* that she had done so.

Fortunately Pat did agree to leave *McCall's* and take a huge cut in salary to become publisher of *Ms.* She became responsible for training and inspiring generations of young women who joined the *Ms.* ad sales force, many of whom went on to become "firsts" at the top of publishing. When *Ms.* first started, however, there were so few women with experience selling space that Pat and I made the rounds of ad agencies ourselves. Later the fact that *Ms.* was asking companies to do business in a different way meant our saleswomen had to make many times the usual number of calls–first to convince agencies and then client companies beside–and to present endless amounts of research. I was often asked to do a final ad presentation, or see some higher decision-maker or speak to women employees so executives could see the interest of women they worked with. That's why I spent more tine persuading advertisers than editing or writing for *Ms.*, and why I ended up with an unsentimental education in the seamy underside of publishing that few writers see (and even fewer magazines can publish).

Let me take you with us through some experiences, just as they happened:

■ Cheered on by early support from Volkswagen and one or two other car companies, we scrape together time and money to put on a major reception in Detroit. We know U.S. car-makers firmly believe that women choose the upholstery not the car, but we are armed with statistics and reader mail to prove the contrary: a car is an important purchase for women, one that symbolizes mobility and freedom.

But almost nobody comes. We are left with many pounds of shrimp on the table, and quite a lot of egg on our face. We blame ourselves for not guessing that there would be a baseball pennant play-off on the same day, but executives go out of their way to explain they wouldn't have come anyway Thus begins ten years of knocking on hostile doors, presenting endless documentation, and hiring a full-time saleswoman in Detroit; all necessary before *Ms.* gets any real results.

This long saga has a semihappy ending: foreign and, later, domestic carmakers eventually provided *Ms.* with enough advertising to make cars one of our top sources of ad revenue. Slowly, Detroit began to take the women's market seriously enough to put car ads in other women's magazines, too, thus freeing a few pages from the hot-house of fashion-beauty-food ads.

But long after figures showed a third, even a half, of many car models being bought by women, U.S. makers continued to be uncomfortable addressing women. Unlike foreign carmakers, Detroit never quite learned the secret of creating intelligent ads that exclude no one, and then placing them in women's magazines to overcome past exclusion. (*Ms.* readers were so grateful for a routine Honda ad featuring rack and pinion steering, for instance, that they sent fan mail.) Even now, Detroit continues to ask, "Should we make special ads for women?" Perhaps that's why some foreign cars still have a disproportionate share of the U.S. women's market.

■ In the *Ms.* Gazette, we do a brief report on a congressional hearing into chemicals used in hair dyes that are absorbed through the skin and may be carcinogenic. Newspapers report this too, but Clairol, a BristolMyers subsidiary that makes dozens of products—a few of which have just begun to advertise in *Ms.*—is outraged. Not at newspapers or newsmagazines, just at us. It's bad enough that *Ms.* is the only women's magazine refusing to provide the usual "complementary" articles and beauty photos, but to criticize one of their categories—*that* is going too far.

We offer to publish a letter from Clairol telling its side of the story. In an excess of solicitousness, we even put this letter in the Gazette, not in Letters to the Editors where it belongs. Nonetheless—and in spite of surveys that show *Ms.* readers are active women who use more of almost everything Clairol makes than do the readers of any other women's magazine—*MS.* gets almost none of these ads for the rest of its natural life.

Meanwhile, Clairol changes its hair coloring formula, apparently in response to the hearings we reported.

Our saleswomen set out early to attract ads for consumer electronics: sound equipment, calculators, computers, VCRs, and the like. We know that our readers are determined to be included in the technological revolution. We know from reader surveys that *Ms.* readers are buying this stuff in numbers as high as those of magazines like *Playboy*; or "men 18 to 34," the prime targets of the consumer electronics industry. Moreover, unlike traditional women's products that our readers buy but don't need to read articles about, these are subjects they want covered in our pages. There actually is a supportive editorial atmosphere.

"But women don't understand technology," say executives at the end of ad presentations. "Maybe not," we respond, "but neither do men—and we all buy it."

"If women do buy it," say the decision-makers, "they're asking their husbands and boyfriends what to buy first." We produce letters from *Ms.* readers saying how turned off they are when salesmen say things like "Let me know when your husband can come in."

After several years of this, we get a few ads for compact sound systems. Some of them come from JVC, whose vice president, Harry Elias, is trying to convince his Japanese bosses that there is something called a women's market. At his invitation, I find myself speaking at huge trade shows in Chicago and Las Vegas, trying to persuade JVC dealers that showrooms don't have to be locker rooms where women are made to feel unwelcome. But as it turns out, the shows themselves are part of the problem. In Las Vegas, the only women around the technology displays are seminude models serving champagne. In Chicago, the big attraction is Marilyn Chambers, who followed Linda Lovelace of Deep Throat fame as Chuck Traynor's captive and/or employee. VCRs are being demonstrated with her porn videos.

In the end, we get ads for a car stereo now and then, but no VCRs; some IBM personal computers, but no Apple or Japanese ones. We notice that office magazines like *Working Woman* and *Savvy* don't benefit as much as they should from office equipment ads either. In the electronics world, women and technology seem mutually exclusive. It remains a decade behind even Detroit.

■ Because we get letters from little girls who love toy trains, and who ask our help in changing ads and box-top photos that feature little boys only, we try to get toy-train ads from Lionel. It turns out that Lionel executives have been concerned about little girls. They made a pink train, and were surprised when it didn't sell.

Lionel bows to consumer pressure with a photograph of a boy *and* a girl—but only on some of their boxes. They fear that, if trains are associated with girls, they will be devalued in the minds of boys. Needless to say, *Ms.* gets no train ads, and little girls remain a mostly unexplored market. By 1986, Lionel is put up for sale.

But for different reasons, we haven't had much luck with other kinds of toys either. In spite of many articles on child-rearing an annual listing of nonsexist, multiracial toys by Letty Cottin Pogrebin; Stories for Free Children, a regular feature also edited by Letty; and other prizewinning features for or about children, we get virtually no toy ads. Generations of *Ms.* saleswomen explain to toy manufacturers that a larger proportion of *Ms.* readers have preschool children than do the readers of other women's magazines, but this industry can't believe feminists have or care about children.

*       *       *

■ When *Ms.* begins, the staff decides not to accept ads for feminine hygiene sprays or cigarettes: they are damaging and carry no appropriate health warnings. Though we don't think we should tell our readers what to do, we do think we should provide facts so they can decide for themselves. Since the antismoking lobby has been pressing for health warnings on cigarette ads, we decide to take them only as they comply.

Philip Morris is among the first to do so. One of its brands, Virginia Slims, is also sponsoring women's tennis and the first national polls of women's opinions. On the other hand, the Virginia Slims theme, "You've come a long way, baby," has more than a "baby" problem. It makes smoking a symbol of progress for women.

We explain to Philip Morris that this slogan won't do well in our pages, but they are convinced its success with some women means it will work with *all* women. Finally, we agree to publish an ad for a Virginia Slims calendar as a test. The letters from readers are critical—and smart. For instance: Would you show a black man picking cotton, the same man in a Cardin suit, and symbolize the antislavery and civil rights movements by smoking? Of course not. But instead of honoring the test results, the Philip Morris people seem angry to be proven wrong. They take away ads for *all* their many brands.

This costs *Ms.* about $250,000 the first year. After five years, we can no longer keep track. Occasionally, a new set of executives listens to *Ms.* saleswomen, but because we won't take Virginia Slims, not one Philip Morris product returns to our pages for the next 16 years.

Gradually, we also realize our naivéte in thinking we could decide against taking cigarette ads. They became a disproportionate support of magazines the moment they were banned on television, and few magazines could compete and survive without them; certainly not *Ms.*, which lacks so many other categories. By the time statistics in the 1980s showed that women's rate of lung cancer was approaching men's, the necessity of taking cigarette ads has become a kind of prison.

■ General Mills, Pillsbury Carnation, DelMonte, Dole, Kraft, Stouffer, Hormel, Nabisco: you name the food giant, we try it. But no matter how desirable the Ms. readership, our lack of recipes is lethal.

We explain to them that placing food ads only next to recipes associates food with work. For many women, it is a negative that works against the ads. Why not place food ads in diverse media without recipes (thus reaching more men, who are now a third of the shoppers in supermarkets anyway), and leave the recipes to specialty magazines like *Gourmet* (a third of whose readers are also men)?

These arguments elicit interest, but except for an occasional ad for a convenience food, instant coffee, diet drinks, yogurt, or such extras as avocados and almonds, this mainstay of the publishing industry stays closed to us. Period.

■ Traditionally, wines and liquors didn't advertise to women: men were thought to make the brand decisions, even if women did the buying. But after endless presentations, we begin to make a dent in this category. Thanks to the unconventional Michel Roux of Carillon Importers (distributors of Grand Mamier, Absolut Vodka, and others), who assumes that food and drink have no gender, some ads are leaving their men's club.

Beermakers are still selling masculinity. It takes *Ms.* fully eight years to get its first beer ad (Michelob). In general, however, liquor ads are less stereotyped in their imagery–and far less controlling of the editorial content around them–than are women's products. But given the underrepresentation of other categories, these very facts tend to create a disproportionate number of alcohol ads in the pages of *Ms.* This in turn dismays readers worried about women and alcoholism.

■ We hear in 1980 that women in the Soviet Union have been producing feminist *samizdat* (underground, self-published books) and circulating them throughout the country. As punishment, four of the leaders have been exiled. Though we are operating on our usual shoe-string, we solicit individual contributions to send Robin Morgan to interview these women in Vienna.

The result is an exclusive cover story that includes the first news of a populist peace movement against the Afghanistan occupation, a prediction of *glasnost* to come, and a grassroots, intimate view of Soviet women's lives. From the popular press to women's studies courses, the response is great. The story wins a Front Page award.

Nonetheless, this journalistic coup undoes years of efforts to get an ad schedule from Revlon. Why? Because the Soviet women on our cover *ore not wearing makeup.*

■ Four years of research and presentations go into convincing airlines that women now make travel choices and business trips. United, the first airline to advertise in Ms., is so impressed with the response from our readers that one of its executives appears in a film for our ad presentations. As usual, good ads get great results.

But we have problems unrelated to such results. For instance: because American Airlines flight attendants include among their labor demands the stipulation that they could choose to have their last names preceded by "Ms." on their name tags–in a long-delayed revolt against the standard, "I am your pilot, Captain Rothgart, and this is your flight attendant, Cindy Sue"–American officials seem to hold the magazine responsible. We get no ads.

There is still a different problem at Eastern. A vice president cancels subscriptions for thousands of copies on Eastern flights. Why? Because he is offended by ads for lesbian poetry journals in the *Ms.* Classified. A "family airline," as he explains to me coldly on the phone, has to "draw the line somewhere."

It's obvious that *Ms.* can't exclude lesbians and serve women. We've been trying to make that point ever since our first issue included an article by and about lesbians, and both Suzanne Levine, our managing editor, and I were lectured by such heavy hitters as Ed Kosner, then editor of *Newsweek* (and now of *New York Magazine*), who insisted that Ms. should "position" itself *against* lesbians. But our advertisers have paid to reach a guaranteed number of readers, and soliciting new subscriptions to compensate for Eastern would cost $150,000 plus rebating money in the meantime.

Like almost everything ad-related, this presents an elaborate organizing problem. After days of searching for sympathetic members of the Eastern board, Frank Thomas, president of the Ford Foundation, kindly offers to call Roswell Gilpatrick, a director of Eastern. I talk with Mr. Gilpatrick, who calls Frank Borman, then the president of Eastern. Frank Borman calls me to say that his airline is not in the business of censoring magazines: *Ms.* will be returned to Eastern flights.

■ Women's access to insurance and credit is vital, but with the exception of Equitable and a few other ad pioneers, such financial services address men. For almost a decade after the Equal Credit Opportunity Act passes in 1974, we try to convince American Express that women are a growth market–but nothing works.

Finally a former professor of Russian named Jerry Welsh becomes head of marketing. He assumes that women should be cardholders, and persuades his colleagues to feature women in a campaign. Thanks to this 1980s series, the growth rate for female cardholders surpasses that for men.

For this article, I asked Jerry Welsh if he would explain why American Express waited so long. "Sure," he said, "they were afraid of having a 'pink' card."

■ Women of color read *Ms.* in disproportionate numbers. This is a source of pride to *Ms.* staffers, who are also more racially representative than the editors of other women's magazines. But this reality is obscured by ads filled with enough white women to make a reader snowblind.

Pat Carbine remembers mostly "astonishment" when she requested African American, Hispanic, Asian, and other diverse images. Marcia Ann Gillespie, a *Ms.* editor who was previously the editor in chief of *Essence*, witnesses ad bias a second time:

having tried for *Essence* to get white advertisers to use black images (Revlon did so eventually, but L'Oréal, Lauder, Chanel, and other companies never did), she sees similar problems getting integrated ads for an integrated magazine. Indeed, the ad world often creates black and Hispanic ads only for black and Hispanic media. In an exact parallel of the fear that marketing a product to women will endanger its appeal to men, the response is usually, "But your [white] readers won't identify."

In fact, those we are able to get—for instance, a Max Factor ad made for *Essence* that Linda Wachner gives us after she becomes president—are praised by white readers, too. But there are pathetically few such images.

■ By the end of 1986, production and mailing costs have risen astronomically, ad income is flat, and competition for ads is stiffer than ever. The 60/40 preponderance of edit over ads that we promised to readers becomes 50/50; children's stories, most poetry, and some fiction are casualties of less space; in order to get variety into limited pages, the length (and sometimes the depth) of articles suffers; and, though we do refuse most of the ads that would look like a parody in our pages, we get so worn down that some slip through. . . . Still, readers perform miracles. Though we haven't been able to afford a subscription mailing in two years, they maintain our guaranteed circulation of 450,000.

Nonetheless, media reports on *Ms.* often insist that our unprofitability 'must be due to reader disinterest.' The myth that advertisers simply follow readers is very strong. Not one reporter notes that other comparable magazines our size (say, *Vanity Fair* or *The Atlantic*) have been losing more money in one year than *Ms.* has lost in 16 years. No matter how much never-to-be-recovered cash is poured into starting a magazine or keeping one going, appearances seem to be all that matter. (Which is why we haven't been able to explain our fragile state in public. Nothing causes ad-flight like the smell of non-success.)

My healthy response is anger. My not-so-healthy response is constant worry. Also an obsession with finding one more rescue. There is hardly a night when I don't wake up with sweaty palms and pounding heart, scared that we won't be able to pay the printer or the post office; scared most of all that closing our doors will hurt the women's movement.

Out of chutzpah and desperation, I arrange a lunch with Leonard Lauder, president of Estee Lauder. With the exception of Clinique (the brainchild of Carol Phillips), none of Lauder's hundreds of products has been advertised in *Ms.* A year's schedule of ads for just three or four of them could save us. Indeed, as the scion of a family-owned company whose ad practices are followed by the beauty industry, he is one of the few men who could liberate many pages in all women's magazines just by changing his mind about "complementary copy."

Over a lunch that costs more than we can pay for some articles, I explain the need for his leadership. I also lay out the record of *Ms.*: more literary and journalistic prizes won, more new issues introduced into the mainstream, new writers discovered, and impact on society than any other magazine; more articles that became books, stories that became movies, ideas that became television series, and newly advertised products that became profitable; and, most important for him, a place for his ads to reach women who aren't reachable through any other women's magazine. Indeed, if there is one constant characteristic of the ever-changing *Ms.* readership, it is their impact as leaders. Whether it's waiting until later to have first babies, or pioneering PABA as sun protection in cosmetics, whatever they are doing today a third to a half of American women will be doing three to five years from now. It's never failed.

But, he says, *Ms.* readers are not *our* women. They're not interested in things like fragrance and blush-on. If they were, *Ms.* would write articles about them.

On the contrary, I explain, surveys show they are more likely to buy such things than the readers of, say, *Cosmopolitan* or *Vogue*. They're good customers because they're out in the world enough to need several sets of everything—home, work, purse, travel, gym, and so on. They just don't need to read articles about these things. Would he ask a men's magazine to publish monthly columns on how to shave before he advertised Aramis products (his line for men)?

He concedes that beauty features are often concocted more for advertisers than readers. But *Ms.* isn't appropriate for his ads anyway, he explains. Why? Because Estee Lauder is selling "a kept-woman mentality."

I can't quite believe this. Sixty percent of the users of his products are salaried, and generally resemble *Ms.* readers. Besides, his company has the appeal of having been started by a creative and hardworking woman, his mother, Estee Lauder.

That doesn't matter, he says. He knows his customers, and they would *like* to be kept women. That's why he will never advertise in *Ms.*

In November 1987, by vote of the *Ms.* Foundation for Education and Communication (*Ms.*'s owner and publisher, the media subsidiary of the *Ms.* Foundation for Women), *Ms.* was sold to a company whose officers, Australian feminists Sandra Yates and Anne Summers, raised the investment money in their country that *Ms.* couldn't find in its own. They also started *Sassy* for teenage women.

In their two-year tenure, circulation was raised to 550,000 by investment in circulation mailings, and, to the dismay of some readers, editorial features on clothes and new products made a more traditional bid for ads. Nonetheless, ad pages fell below previous levels. In addition, *Sassy*, whose fresh voice and sexual frankness were an unprecedented success with young readers, was targeted by two mothers from Indiana who began, as one of them put it, "calling every Christian organization I could think of." In response to this controversy, several crucial advertisers pulled out.

Such links between ads and editorial content was a problem in Australia, too, but to a lesser degree. "Our readers pay two times more for their magazines," Anne explained, "so advertisers have less power to threaten a magazine's viability."

"I was shocked," said Sandra Yates with characteristic directness. "In Australia, we think you have freedom of the press—but you don't."

Since Anne and Sandra had not met their budget's projections for ad revenue, their investors forced a sale. In October 1989, *Ms.* and *Sassy* were bought by Dale Lang, owner of *Working Mother*, *Working Woman*, and one of the few independent publishing companies left among the conglomerates. In response to a request from the original *Ms.* staff—as well as to reader letters urging that *Ms.* continue, plus his own belief that *Ms.* would benefit his other magazines by blazing a trail—he agreed to try the ad-free, reader-supported *Ms.* you hold now and to give us complete editorial control.

## II

Do you think, as I once did, that advertisers make decisions based on solid research? Well, think again. "Broadly speaking" says Joseph Smith of Oxtoby-Smith Inc., a consumer research firm, "there is no persuasive evidence that the editorial context of an ad matters."

Advertisers who demand such "complementary copy," even in the absence of respectable studies, clearly are operating under a double standard. The same food companies place ads in *People* with no recipes. Cosmetic companies support the *New Yorker* with no regular beauty columns. So where does this habit of controlling the content of women's magazines come from?

Tradition. Ever since *Ladies Magazine* debuted in Boston in 1828, editorial copy directed to women has been informed by something other than its readers' wishes. There were no ads then, but in an age when married women were legal minors with no right to their own money, there was another revenue source to be kept in mind: husbands. "Husbands may rest assured," wrote editor Sarah Josepha Hale, "that nothing found in these pages shall cause her [his wife] to be less assiduous in preparing for his reception or encourage her to 'usurp-station' or encroach upon prerogatives of men."

Hale went on to become the editor of *Godey's Lady's Book*, a magazine featuring "fashion plates": engraving of dresses for readers to take to their seamstresses or copy themselves. Hale added "how to" articles, which set the tone for women's service magazines for years to come: how to write politely, avoid sunburn, and–in no fewer than 1,200 words–how to maintain a goose quill pen. She advocated education for women but avoided controversy. Just as most women's magazines now avoid politics, poll their readers on issues like abortion but rarely take a stand, and praise socially approved lifestyles, Hale saw to it that *Godey's* avoided the hot topics of its day: slavery abolition, and women's suffrage.

What definitively turned women's magazines, into catalogs, however, were two events: Ellen Butterick's invention of the clothing pattern in 1863 and the mass manufacture of patent medicines containing everything from colored water to cocaine. For the first time, readers could purchase what magazines encouraged them to want. As such magazines became more profitable, they also began to attract men as editors. (Most women magazines continued to have men as top editors until the feminist 1970s.) Edward Bok, who became editor of *The Ladies' Home Journal* in 1889, discovered the power of advertisers when he rejected ads for patent medicines and found that other advertisers canceled in retribution. In the early 20th century, *Good Housekeeping* started its Institute to "test and approve" products. Its Seal of Approval became the grandfather of current "value added" programs that offer advertisers such bonuses as product sampling and department store promotions.

By the time suffragists finally won the vote in 1920, women's magazines had become too entrenched as catalogs to help women learn how to use it. The main function was to create a desire for products, teach how to use products, and make products a crucial part of gaining social approval, pleasing a husband, and performing as a homemaker. Some unrelated articles and short stories were included to persuade women to pay for these catalogs. But articles were neither consumerist nor rebellious. Even fiction was usually subject to formula: if a woman had any sexual life outside marriage, she was supposed to come to a bad end.

In 1965, Helen Gurley Brown began to change part of that formula by bringing "the sexual revolution" to women's magazines, but in an ad-oriented way. Attracting multiple men required even more consumerism, as the Cosmo Girl made clear, than finding one husband.

In response to the workplace revolution of the 1970s, traditional women's magazines–that is, "trade books" for women working at home–were joined by *Savvy*, *Working Woman*, and other trade books for women working in offices. But by keeping the fashion/beauty/entertaining articles necessary to get traditional ads and then adding career articles besides, they inadvertently produced the antifeminist stereotype of Super Woman. The male-imitative, dress-for-success woman carrying a briefcase became the media image of a woman worker, even though a blue-collar woman's salary was often higher than her glorified secretarial sister's, and though women at a real briefcase level are statistically rare. Needless to say, these dress-for-success women were also thin, white, and beautiful.

In recent years, advertisers' control over the editorial content of women's magazines has become so institutionalized that it is written into "insertion orders" or dictated to ad salespeople as official policy. The following are recent typical orders to women's magazines:

■ Dow's Cleaning Products stipulates that ads for its Vivid and Spray 'n Wash products should be adjacent to "children or fashion editorial"; ads for Bathroom Cleaner should be next to "home furnishing/family" features; and so on for other brands. "If a magazine fails for 1/2 the brands or more," the Dow order warns, "it will be omitted from further consideration."

■ Bristol-Myers, the parent of Clairol, Windex, Drano, Bufferin, and much more, stipulates that ads be placed next to "a full page of compatible editorial."

■ S.C. Johnson & Son, makers of Johnson Wax, lawn and laundry products, insect sprays, hair sprays, and so on, orders that its ads "should not *be opposite extremely controversial fratures or material antithetical to the nature/copy of the advertised product.*" (Italics theirs.)

■ Maidenform, manufacturer of bras and other apparel, leaves a blank for the particular product and states: "The creative concept of the _____ campaign, and the very nature of the product itself appeal to the positive emotions of the reader/consumer. Therefore, it is imperative that all editorial adjacencies reflect that same Positive tone. The editorial must not be negative in content or lend itself contrary to the product imagery/message (*e.g. editorial relating to illness, disillusionment, large size fashion,* etc.)." (Italics mine.)

■ The De Beers diamond company, a big seller of engagement rings, prohibits magazines from placing its ads with "adjacencies to hard news or anti/love-romance themed editorial."

■ Procter & Gamble, one of this country's most powerful and diversified advertisers, stands out in the memory of Anne Summers and Sandra Yates (no mean feat in this context): its products were not to be placed in *any* issue that included *any* material on gun control, abortion, the occult, cults, or the disparagement of religion. Caution was also demanded in any issue covering sex or drugs, even for educational purposes.

Those are the most obvious chains around women's magazines. There are also rules so clear they needn't be written down: for instance, an overall "look" compatible with beauty and fashion ads. Even "real" nonmodel women photographed for a woman's magazine are usually made up, dressed in credited clothes, and retouched out of all reality. When editors do include articles on less-than-cheerful subjects (for instance, domestic violence), they tend to keep them short and unillustrated. The point is to be "upbeat." Just as women in the street are asked, "Why don't you smile, honey?" women's magazines acquire an institutional smile.

Within the text itself, praise for advertisers' products has become so ritualized that fields like "beauty writing" have been invented. One of its frequent practitioners explained seriously that "It's a difficult art. How many new adjectives can you find? How much greater can you make a lipstick sound? The FDA restricts what companies can say on labels, but we create illusion. And ad agencies are on the phone all the time pushing you to get their product in. A lot of them keep the business based on how many editorial clippings they produce every month. The worst are products," like Lauder's as the writer confirmed, "with their own name involved. It's all ego."

Often, editorial becomes one giant ad. Last November, for instance, *Lear's* featured an elegant woman executive on the cover. On the contents page, we learned she was wearing Guerlain makeup and Samsara, a new fragrance by Guerlain. Inside were full-page ads for Samsara and Guerlain antiwrinkle cream. In the cover profile we learned that this executive was responsible for launching Samsara and is Guerlam's director of public relations. When the *Columbia Journalism Review* did one of the few articles to include women's magazines in coverage of the influence of ads, editor Frances Lear was quoted as defending her magazine because "this kind of thing is done all the time."

Often, advertisers also plunge odd-shaped ads into the text, no matter what the cost to the readers. At *Woman's Day*, a magazine originally founded by a supermarket chain, editor in chief Ellen Levine said, "The day the copy had to rag around a chicken leg was not a happy one."

Advertisers are also adamant about where in a magazine their ads appear. When Revlon was not placed as the first beauty ad in one Hearst magazine, for instance, Revlon pulled its ads from *all* Hearst magazines. Ruth Whitney, editor in chief of *Glamour*, attributes some of these demands to "ad agencies wanting to prove to a client that they've squeezed the last drop of blood out of a magazine." She also is, she says, "sick and tired of hearing that women's magazines are controlled by cigarette ads." Relatively speaking, she's right. To be as censoring as are many advertisers for women's products, tobacco companies would have to demand articles in praise of smoking and expect glamorous photos of beautiful women smoking their brands.

I don't mean to imply that the editors I quote here share my objections to ads: most assume that women's magazines have to be the way they are. But it's also true that only former editors can be completely honest. "Most of the pressure came in the form of direct product mentions," explains Sey Chassler, who was editor in chief of *Redbook* from the sixties to the eighties. "We got threats from the big guys, the Revlons, blackmail threats. They wouldn't run ads unless we credited them.

"But it's not fair to single out the beauty advertisers because these pressures came from everybody. Advertisers want to know two things: What are you going to charge me? What *else* are you going to do for me? It's a holdup. For instance, management felt that fiction took up too much space. They couldn't put any advertising in that. For the last ten years, the number of fiction entries into the National Magazine Awards has declined.

"And pressures are getting worse. More magazines are more bottom-line oriented because they have been taken over by companies with no interest in publishing.

"I also think advertisers do this to women's magazines especially" he concluded, "because of the general disrespect they have for women."

Even media experts who don't give a damn about women's magazines are alarmed by the spread of this ad-edit linkage. In a climate *The Wall Street Journal* describes as an unacknowledged depression for media, women's products are increasingly able to take their low standards wherever they go. For instance: newsweeklies publish uncritical stories on fashion and fitness. The *New York Times Magazine* recently ran an article on "firming creams," complete with mentions of advertisers. *Vanity Fair* published a profile of one major advertiser, Ralph Lauren, illustrated by the same photographer who does his ads, and turned the lifestyle of another, Calvin Klein, into a cover story. Even the outrageous *Spy* has toned down since it began to go after fashion ads.

And just to make us really worry, films and books, the last media that go directly to the public without having to attract ads first, are in danger, too. Producers are beginning to depend on payments for displaying products in movies, and books are now being commissioned by companies like Federal Express.

But the truth is that women's products—like women's magazines—have never been the subjects of much serious reporting anyway. News and general interest publications, including the "style" or "living" sections of newspapers, write about food and clothing as cooking and fashion, and almost never evaluate such products by brand name. Though chemical additives, pesticides, and animal fats are major health risks in the United States, and clothes, shoddy or not, absorb more consumer dollars than cars, this lack of information is serious. So is ignoring the contents of beauty products that are absorbed into our bodies through our skins, and that have profit margins so big they would make a loan shark blush.

## III

What could women's magazines be like if they were as free as books? As realistic as newspapers? As creative as films? As diverse as women's lives? We don't know.

But we'll only find out if we take women's magazines seriously. If readers were to act in a concerted way to change traditional practices of *all* women's magazines and the marketing of *all* women's products, we could do it. After all, they are operating on our consumer dollars; money that we now control. You and I could:

■ write to editors and publishers (with copies to advertisers) that we're willing to pay *more* for magazines with editorial independence, but *will not* continue to pay for those that are just editorial extensions of ads;

■ write to advertisers (with copies to editors and publishers) that we want fiction, political reporting, consumer reporting—whatever is, or is not, supported by their ads;

■ put as much energy into breaking advertising's control over content as into changing the images in ads, or protesting ads for harmful products like cigarettes;

■ support only those women's magazines and products that take us seriously as readers and consumers.

Those of us in the magazine world can also use the carrot-and-stick technique. For instance: pointing out that, if magazines were a regulated medium like television, the demands of advertisers would be against FCC rules. Payola and extortion could be punished. As it is, there are probably illegalities. A magazine's postal rates are determined by the ratio of ad to edit pages, and the former costs more than the latter. So much for the stick.

The carrot means appealing to enlightened self-interest. For instance: there are many studies showing that the greatest factor in determining an ad's effectiveness is the credibility of its surroundings. The higher the rating of "editorial believability," concluded a 1987 survey by the *Journal of Advertising Research*, "the higher the rating of the advertising." Thus, an impenetrable wall between edit and ads would also be in the best interest of advertisers.

Unfortunately, few agencies or clients hear such arguments. Editors often maintain the false purity of refusing to talk to them at all. Instead, they see ad salespeople who know little about editorial, are trained in business as usual, and are usually paid by commission. Editors might also band together to take on controversy That happened once when all the major women's magazines did articles in the same month on the Equal Rights Amendment. It could happen again.

It's almost three years away from life between the grind-stones of advertising pressures and readers' needs. I'm just beginning to realize how edges got smoothed down—in spite of all our resistance.

I remember feeling put upon when I changed "Porsche" to "car" in a piece about Nazi imagery in German pornography by Andrea Dworkin–feeling sure Andrea would understand that Volkswagen, the distributor of Porsche and one of our few supportive advertisers, asked only to be far away from Nazi subjects. It's taken me all this time to realize that Andrea was the one with a right to feel put upon.

Even as I write this, I get a call from a writer for *Elle*, who is doing a whole article on where women part their hair. Why, she wants to know, do I part mine in the middle?

It's all so familiar. A writer trying to make something of a nothing assignment; an editor laboring to think of new ways to attract ads; readers assuming that other women must want this ridiculous stuff; more women suffering for lack of information, insight, creativity, and laughter that could be on these same pages.

I ask you: Can't we do better than this?

## Questions for Consideration

1  Which (if any) of Steinem's anecdotes startled you most? Why?
2  Steinem asks "What could women's magazines be like if they were as free as books? as realistic as newspapers? as creative as films?" Why might someone suggest that she is being naïve about the independence that creators in those media have?

# Chapter 11

**PHILIP NEL**

# IS THERE A TEXT IN THIS ADVERTISING CAMPAIGN?
## Literature, Marketing, and Harry Potter

IN THIS EXCERPT FROM A 2005 article, Philip Nel surveys the extensive marketing campaigns and licensing activities that have surrounded the Harry Potter books. He notes that many people have concluded that all this commercialism means that in the end Harry Potter is "about" capitalism, pure and simple. For his part, Nel believes that the books can and should be separated from the marketing hype, and that author J. K. Rowling has tried hard to do that. Nevertheless, as this article shows, when advertising and public relations move full-steam ahead, even literature can get lost in the process.

In July 2000, *The Boston Globe*'s Dan Wasserman drew a cartoon that predicted what would become the most prominent threat to Harry Potter's literary legacy. Several months ahead of the beginning of the Harry Potter marketing bonanza and more than a year before the release of the first Potter film, Wasserman's cartoon shows two children walking down a city street. One child holds a Harry Potter novel; and everywhere they look, advertisements announce all variety of Harry merchandise. A shop's sign offers "Harry Wares." A restaurant offers "Potter Pies," "Wizard Fries," and "Happy Harry Meals!" An eyeglass store proclaims "Just In—Harry Frames." A poster (located, perhaps appropriately, on a trash can) invites them to "Visit the Harry Potter Theme Park." And a store's display, window reminds passers-by that "We carry a full line of Harry schlock!", including robes, wands, and "muggle mugs." One child says to the other, "I can already see how it ends—the dark forces win" (Wasserman). In July 2000, such a cartoon was a satirical comment on the culture industry. Less than two years later, it became merely descriptive.

The aggressive marketing predicted by this cartoon also describes a critical problem: the novels and the hype become intertwined, resulting in analyses that fail to take into account the full complexity of either. Because Harry Potter is both a marketing phenomenon and a literary phenomenon, critical conflation of the two does not really advance the understanding of the marketing apparatus or the books themselves. Author J. K. Rowling herself appears to be aware of this problem, as June Cummins has observed. Citing Rowling's charitable work and critical comments about Potter merchandise, Cummins notes that the Harry Potter author "seems determined to separate the books from the aggressive marketing pursued by Scholastic, Warner Brothers, and Mattel." Cummins then asks, "But is her goal realistic? I say it is not" (20). I, however, would argue that it is both realistic and necessary to separate the books from the marketing. First of all, conflating the books with the marketing fails to produce a sufficiently sophisticated analysis of the latter. Second, such critical conflation leads some critics to overlook the novels' considerable literary achievements.

Consider the marketing side of the question first. Jack Zipes, Andrew Blake, and John Pennington correctly underscore Harry Potter as a contemporary capitalist phenomenon. In his essay "From Elfland to Hogwarts, or the Aesthetic Trouble with Harry Potter," John Pennington provides the most succinct version of this idea: "So what are the Potter books really about, then? Well, monetary success primarily" (92). Pennington has a point. It is difficult to talk about Harry Potter and to ignore the marketing. You can see the movies, you can buy the movies, you can buy Legos, action figures, stickers, notebooks, a card game, a board game, puzzles, address books, calendars, Band Aids, toothbrushes, toothpaste, t-shirts, sweatshirts, mugs, trading cards, greeting cards, Bertie Bott's Every Flavour Beans, a Nimbus 2000 broomstick, a Harry Potter wallet, wizarding-world money, and even piña colada-flavored "Dementor's Kisses." Much of the Harry Potter merchandising must make even the most ardent fan cringe just a little bit. And it is difficult to applaud the ways in which these Potter spin-off products encourage consumption for its own sake.

However, to say that the books are only about monetary success ignores the late capitalist conditions of their production. Zipes and Blake offer more nuanced versions of Pennington's claim. As the reason for Harry Potter's success, Zipes cites:

> The conditions under which literature for the young have been transformed through institutional corporate conglomerates controlling the mass media, and market demands. Phenomena such as the Harry Potter books are driven by commodity consumption that at the same time sets the parameters of reading and aesthetic taste. Today the experience of reading for the young is mediated through the mass media and marketing so that the pleasure and meaning of a book will often be prescribed or dictated by convention.
>
> (172)

Judiciously placing his comments in the context of the changing children's literature industry, Zipes points to "institutional corporate conglomerates," and to the role of marketing in selling children's literature. As Zipes explains in *Sticks and Stones: The Troublesome Success of Children's Literature from Slovenly Peter to Harry Potter*, the children's-book industry has grown more interested in creating marketable products than in nurturing good-quality books (51–2, 59). Andrew Blake's *The Irresistible Rise of Harry Potter*, a Potter-themed critique of Tony Blair's New Labour party, offers a version of this argument in the context of how Harry Potter has boosted the financial fortunes of Rowling's British publisher, Bloomsbury. According to Blake, "Capitalism is, as the truism has it, global; certainly, the much-translated Harry has repeated his Bloomsbury trick for child-consumer capitalism the world over" (88). As Gary Cross's *Kids' Stuff: Toys and the Changing World of American Childhood*, Stephen Kline's *Out of the Garden: Toys, TV, and Children's Culture in the Age of Marketing*, and Marsha Kinder's *Playing with Power in Movies, Television, and Video Games: From Muppet Babies to Teenage Mutant Ninja Turtles* have all pointed out, there has been a proliferation of child-targeted marketing over the last few decades. In the US, this phenomenon began to flourish in the 1980s, inspired by the deregulation of children's television (Cross 198; Kline 139, 278, 317; Kinder 40). Though these marketing practices began on TV, characters from children's books have with increasing regularity also been transformed into corporate pitchmen, selling all manner of "tie-in" products. Harry Potter is but part of a trend: Curious George appears in advertisements for Altoids (in the ad, the phrase "The Curiously Strong Mints" puns on George's name), and Winnie-the-Pooh sells his own brand of cereal, "Hunny B's." Following the 2000 release of Ron Howard's *Grinch* film, even the Grinch began selling credit cards, candy, and cereal; Dr. Seuss's original *How the Grinch Stole Christmas!* (1957) actively criticized commercial exploitation of the holiday. When the Grinch can change from anticonsumerist grouch to enthusiastic salesman, we know that Harry Potter is not alone. Harry Potter, then, may be seen as a very prominent example of current business practices in children's literature and culture.

However, it seems to me that citing mass media-controlled "institutional corporate conglomerates" as the primary reason for Harry Potter's success has the unfortunate effect of limiting one's analysis. If we share Zipes's concerns about corporate influences on children's literature (and I do), then we might find a critically productive approach to this problem where business and the entertainment industry meet: intellectual property law. Not coincidentally, the oldest case currently on file in Los Angeles' Superior Court involves intellectual property and children's literature: The heirs of A. A. Milne's literary agent are suing the Walt Disney Company for cheating them on the royalties for Winnie-the-Pooh merchandise (Toobin 58).

In the background of Wasserman's cartoon (mentioned at the begining of this essay), a bus's billboard advertises "Harry Potter: The Movie." While Scholastic and Bloomsbury did promote the Harry Potter books in the US and the UK, respectively, the proliferation of mass-marketing Harry Potter tie-ins begins with Warner Brothers. Warner Brothers relies upon merchandising to help make back some of the extra-ordinary expense of making a film. If Rowling had not agreed to allow her characters to be merchandised, then the Harry Potter films might not have been made at all. Given Chris Columbus's rather tepid film versions of the first two books and all of their associated products, an absence of Harry Potter films may have been a good thing. However, since three films have been released and more are on the way, Warner Brothers' role must be addressed.

Warner Brothers markets such a wide variety of Harry Potter products because the American entertainment industry relies more on trademark law than on copyright law. It does so because it regards trademark as stronger than copyright, and the difference between these laws helps to explain why. Copyright law protects authors and artists, but trademark law protects products and the marks attached to those products. So, copyright protects the book *Harry Potter and the Chamber of Secrets*, but trademark protects a Ron Weasley action figure or a Hedwig plush toy. Why, then, is trademark stronger? Two reasons. The first is that trademarks last as long as they remain in use, although they need to be renewed every ten years if granted on or after November 16, 1989 (as the Potter trademarks would have been). In contrast, copyright lasts for a fixed period of time. As per the Sonny Bono Copyright Term Extension Act of 1998, copyright on works published after 1978 now lasts for the author's life plus seventy years (US Copyright Office). The catch here is that trademarks *must* be attached to a product: in other words, for Rowling's work to gain protection under trademark law, she must enter into licensing agreements, allowing others to make spin-off products like hats, notebooks, toothpaste, and so on.

A second reason why trademark is regarded as stronger than copyright can be traced to a landmark case in entertainment law. As Jane M. Gaines points out in her *Contested Culture: The Image, the Voice, and the Law*, since the 1954 Sam Spade case entertainment lawyers have favored trademark over copyright. The case started because Warner Brothers owned the movie rights to Dashiell Hammett's *The Maltese Falcon*, but Hammett wanted to make sequels using Sam Spade, the novel's main character. The Sam Spade case—officially known as *Warner Brothers, Inc. v. Columbia Broadcasting Co.*— "turned on whether Warner Brothers' motion picture rights to the novel *The Maltese Falcon* included the right to enjoin author Dashiell Hammett from using the character in sequels" (Gaines 211). The court allowed Hammett "to continue to use his literary creation," but it also decided that characters were "mobile pieces in relation to the *work*, the wholeness and totality of which is crucial to copyright law" (211). The result was that the "Characters—the 'mere chessmen,' devices, or vehicles for telling the story— were now seen as less protectable as authorial creations than the work itself" (211–12). Where copyright law failed to protect the characters or title of a work, trademark, "with its emphasis on source, origin, and sponsorship, not authorship, protected both title and character" (212). To maintain protection under trademark law, one needs to enter into licensing agreements, permitting the creation of spin-off products.

These spin-off products—such as the Harry Potter paraphernalia—are symptoms of a legal system that has, in effect, reversed trademark law. As Gaines explains, trademark law is supposed to protect the public, guaranteeing that "the buyer could expect, from the source behind the goods, the same values and qualities received with the last purchase" (211). However, "the inversion of this principle in American common law" means that "the trademark comes to ensure *not* that the public is protected against fraud but that the merchant-owner of the mark is protected against infringers" (211). This "inversion" of trademark law leads to the increased production of mass-marketed Harry Potter merchandise. So, while one might reasonably be skeptical of Harry Potter as a manifestation of corporate marketing, Harry is an effect and not the cause.

Like the characters of Dr. Seuss, A. A. Milne, and H. A. and Margret Rey, Harry Potter has become a symptom of a legal system designed to benefit capitalism more than moral or artistic values. One practical consequence of this fact is that, should we wish to diminish the power that corporations have over children's literature, then the law is one place to begin. As I argue in *Dr. Seuss: American Icon*, were the United States to uphold the provisions of the Berne Convention, then we would remove the need for artists to seek legal protection under trademark law.[1] The Berne Convention recognizes the moral rights of the author over his or her creation, *even after* the copyright has been transferred to another party. For this reason, the copyright page of Bloomsbury's *Harry Potter and the Philosopher's Stone*—and, indeed, the copyright page of virtually every book published in Britain—includes the following sentence: "The moral right of the author has been asserted." No such sentence appears on the copyright page of the American edition, *Harry Potter and the Sorcerer's Stone*, nor does it appear on any other book published in the United States, because in the United States authors do not have moral rights. If authors and artists did have moral rights in the US, then intellectual property law would not rely so heavily upon trademark law. Another legal solution would be to change trademark law so that a trademark need not be constantly in use in order to remain enforceable. As Gaines reports, "American trademark law gives an emphasis to 'use' that it doesn't have in other countries, where, for instance, it is not necessary to demonstrate 'use' [. . .] *before* registering a mark. Whereas in other countries, first registration guarantees the monopoly [. . .] in the U.S., 'use' stakes out the owner's claim" (223). In other words, if US trademark law operated more like British trademark law, then Warner Brothers would need only *register* these Harry Potter items; it need not actually produce them.

While Rowling has followed standard entertainment law in permitting such merchandising, she has also taken the less common step of placing some restrictions on how her characters can be used. Though The Coca-Cola Company has a licensing agreement with Warner Brothers, Rowling has refused to allow her characters to be shown drinking Coca-Cola, so Coke instead agreed to sponsor a reading initiative. In cooperation with Reading is Fundamental, Coca-Cola underwrites "Live the Magic," providing "10,000 Classroom Library Collections for at-risk schools," and "Ingenuity Grants to help explore innovative ways to encourage children to embrace reading" ("Reading Is Fundamental"). In a *60 Minutes* TV interview prior to the production of the Potter toys, Rowling said, "I can only say now to all of the parents out there that if the action figures are horrible, just tell the kids: don't buy them!" She paused, then added, "Sorry, Warner's" (Stahl). In response to Rowling's concern that action figures may promote violent play, Mattel agreed to call its action figures "collectible characters" (Barnes). Changing a name from "action figure" to "collectible character" may not diminish the product's capacity to promote violent play. Similarly, Rowling's publicly expressed skepticism may not dissuade people from buying these products. However, she deserves credit for her attempts to control a marketing apparatus perpetuated by the American legal system.

Indeed, given that changing the American legal system is a rather tall order, another of Rowling's responses—focusing on how the money is used—may be a more effective approach to what we might call late capitalist children's culture. While Seuss, Milne, and the Reys are no longer among the living, Rowling is very much alive and actively involved in managing the profits generated by Harry Potter, donating large amounts to charitable causes. So it seems a bit of an oversimplification to say, as John Pennington does, that Harry Potter is only about "monetary success" or, "If Rowling is out simply to make a buck, then she has succeeded spectacularly" (92). Capitalism is amoral, but what people do with their capital does not have to be. Rowling's depiction of the Dursleys, the Malfoys, and Harry exemplifies precisely this point: all three have sufficient money to live comfortably, but the Dursleys and Malfoys like to lord their socioeconomic status over other people. The Dursleys go out into their front yard "to admire Uncle Vernon's new company car (in very loud voices, so that the rest of the street would notice it too)" (*Prisoner of Azkaban* 8); similarly, Lucius and Draco Malfoy never tire of displaying their wealth to the Weasley family. In contrast, Harry uses his money to buy treats for his friends and gives his Triwizard Tournament winnings to Fred and George Weasley, making them promise that they will use some of the money to buy Ron new dress robes, and use the rest as an investment in their joke shop (*Chamber of Secrets* 48; *Goblet of Fire* 635–6). As Karin E. Westman observes in "Specters of Thatcherism: Contemporary British Culture in J. K. Rowling's Harry Potter Series," "An outsider to the Dursleys' materialism, Harry comes to embody all that his relations are not: he is unselfish, compassionate and good-hearted" (310). Similarly, what Rowling has done with her money shows her to be an ally of Harry, not of the Dursleys or the Malfoys.

While Harry Potter functions as an agent of multinational capitalism, Rowling does her best not to. In September 2000, she donated £500,000 to Britain's National Council for One Parent Families, and has taken on the role of being the organization's ambassador, giving speeches on its behalf and even writing a foreword to the organization's *Families Just Like Us: the One Parent Families good book guide*. In 2001, she wrote *Quidditch Through The Ages* and *Fantastic Beasts and Where to Find Them*—the two "Harry Potter Schoolbooks"—and donated all proceeds to Comic Relief UK, raising £15.6 million for fighting poverty and social injustice in Britain, Africa, and around the world ("Harry's Books"). She also has helped to raise thousands of pounds for Maggie's Centre, an Edinburgh organization that provides information and support for people suffering from cancer (McGinty, "The legacy of Harry"). In 1990, at the age of forty-five, Rowling's mother died from multiple sclerosis. In addition to supplying Harry's feelings of loss for his own parents, her mother's death motivated Rowling to donate to the MS Society of Scotland in 2001, and to underwrite "a senior fellowship in MS research at Aberdeen University" (McGinty). For *MS Matters*, the magazine of the UK MS Society, Rowling wrote an autobiographical article titled "I Miss My Mother So Much," in which she described her mother's decline and called for more government funding for both MS research and drugs that help MS patients live longer and healthier lives. That article was published in 2001; thanks to her advocacy, by 2002 Britain's National Health Service began prescribing disease-modifying drugs for people with MS (Reeves). So, while "commodity consumption" and a mass media controlled by "corporate conglomerates" do fuel the success of Harry Potter, the market forces that motivate the sales of Potter and his merchandise are *not* the same forces that motivate Rowling.

Another way in which Rowling has responded to the marketplace has been to include her own critique of conspicuous consumption within the Harry Potter books themselves. As Westman notes, when Harry is tempted to buy a Firebolt, his response offers a subtle critique of consumption for its own sake (311). Although he needs "to exercise a lot of control not to spend the whole lot [of his money] at once," Harry manages to be thrifty, recognizing that "he had five years to go at Hogwarts" and would need his money for school supplies (*Prisoner* 43). As he says to himself, "what was the point in emptying his Gringotts vault for the Firebolt, when he had a very good broom already?" (44). As Westman observes, "While the wizarding world offers a fantasy of consumer purchases, Harry remains wary of the conspicuous and selfish consumption embodied by the Dursleys he has left behind" (311).

While Rowling is by no means critical of all such commerce (she presents the enterprising Weasley twins' joke shop with an affectionate wink), she does remind readers that the pleasures of mass-produced tie-in products are often short-lived. The rapid decline of the green rosettes that Ron, Harry, and Seamus buy is a case in point. When it is new, a rosette keeps "squeaking" the names of the Irish National Quidditch Team: "*Troy—Mullet—Moran!*" (*Goblet* 97). However, the magic of a rosette soon wears off, and it becomes just an annoying little gimmick. When they meet Seamus on the Hogwarts Express a week after the Quidditch World Cup, he is "still wearing his Ireland rosette." However, "[s]ome of its magic seemed to be wearing off now; it was still squeaking '*Troy! Mullet! Moran!*', but in a very feeble and exhausted sort of way" (149). Rowling's (fictional) rosette seems a gentle parody of some of the (real) plastic gadgets spawned by the Harry Potter merchandising industry. If we listen closely, her rosette does not squeak Quidditch players' names; rather, it whispers "caveat emptor."

So, although Harry Potter is a capitalist juggernaut promoted by corporate conglomerates, it is also too complex to be written off as *only* that. If we take into account the legal context of the merchandising, the charitable uses to which Rowling directs some of the profits, and the anticonsumerist messages in the books themselves, the Harry Potter phenomenon cannot be seen only as an example of corporations' latest attempts to sell stuff to children. Also, it is easy to forget that the film deals came well before Harry Potter became an international phenomenon and Rowling one of the wealthiest women in Britain. *Harry Potter and the Philosopher's Stone* was published in the UK in June 1997; by July, Hollywood studios had already approached her with the idea of making a film out of her novel (Glaister). By 7 October 1998, reports from the Frankfurt Book Fair indicated that "Warner Brothers had paid 'a heavy seven-figure' sum to acquire the two books for at least one major film" (Alberge). At the time, the first Potter novel had sold 70,000 copies in the UK, the second novel had been released—promptly going to the top of the bestseller charts in the UK—and the first book had just been published in America. In December, the book began its ascent up the *New York Times'* list of hardcover bestsellers. In 1999, Harry Potter and Rowling would become superstars. However, when she began entertaining offers, the first book had only just been published, and when she sold the film rights, Rowling was only a few years away from being on public assistance. When considered in this context, her decision to agree to these marketing arrangements seems a very practical, responsible choice; after several years of scraping by, she found financial security for herself and her daughter.

It may also be worth mentioning here that, while it is now hard to imagine Harry without the hype, the books caught on well before the hype began. The marketing didn't really take over until 1999; the products didn't appear until the latter half of 2000; and the first movie (accompanied by its many tie-in products) didn't appear until November 2001. At first, the novel caught on because of strong reviews of two kinds: those in newspapers, and reviews by children themselves. By word of mouth, children told each other about Harry simply because they thought it was a good book. Even though it certainly contributes to the books' current popularity, hype alone is not a sufficient explanation for Harry's appeals.

Turning, then, to the second half of my argument, approaching the Harry Potter books solely as a contemporary capitalist phenomenon tends to cause even scholars of children's literature to overlook the literary merits of Rowling's series. As Lana A. Whited aptly observes, "the cloud of commercialism encircling the books" leads us away from "the serious discussion we ought to be having about the literary merits of J.K. Rowling's Harry Potter novels" (12). For example, reasoning that "For anything to become a phenomenon in Western society, it must become *conventional*," Zipes claims that the novels "are easy and delightful to read, carefully manicured and packaged, and they sell extraordinarily well precisely because they are so cute and ordinary" (175). Making a similar argument, Philip Hensher claims that the Harry Potter "books virtually read themselves," but warned that we "shouldn't confuse the success of the pedagogic tool with literary merit" ("crowd-pleaser"). Echoing Hensher's remarks, Zipes suggests that the "Harry Potter books [. . .] will help children become functionally literate, for they are part of the eternal return to the same and [. . .] part of the success and process by which we homogenize our children" (188). Pennington is more direct: "Rowling

[. . .] seems to purchase her marvelous assorted creatures from the Sears catalogue of fantasy clichés" (82). Or, as Suman Gupta puts it, the novels "often refer back to a shimmering vista of folklore, fairy tale and myth drawn indiscriminately from a range of sources and contexts" (97).

*    *    *

There is much in the Harry Potter novels to make us pensive, too, should we take the time to read slowly and to think as we read. In promoting the pleasures of slow contemplation, the Harry Potter novels can pull readers away from the consumerist pleasures of the Harry Potter merchandising industry. While it is true that, unless borrowed from a library or a friend, many will first need to purchase the books in order to read them, it is equally true that by rewarding rereading, the series may encourage us to enjoy what we already have, instead of spending more money on books, video games, or action figures.

Even the money in Harry Potter's world has symbolic significance. In Harry's very first visit into the wizarding world (which occurs during the "Diagon Alley" chapter of book one), he learns its monetary system: there are 29 Knuts to a Sickle, and 17 Sickles to a Galleon (*Philosopher's Stone* 58). Twenty-nine and seventeen are both prime numbers, and the chapter is full of prime numbers: James Potter used an eleven-inch wand, Harry's wand is eleven inches also; he pays "seven gold Galleons" for the wand, and gives the owl "five Knuts" for delivering a letter (*Philosopher's Stone* 63, 65, 50). Eleven, seven, and five are primes. Why all the prime numbers? As I suggest in my *J. K. Rowling's Harry Potter Novels: A Reader's Guide* (2001), some people consider prime numbers to be mystical; so, the many prime numbers introduce the novel's themes of magic and the supernatural (31–3). When discussing the fact that there will be seven books in the series, Rowling has observed, "Seven is a magical number, a mystical number" (Mehren).

If the "magic" of prime numbers is one reference here, another is money itself. Rowling is poking fun at the British monetary system prior to 1971. Twenty-nine Knuts to a Sickle and seventeen Sickles to a Galleon means that there are 493 Knuts to a Galleon. Before 1971, there were twelve pence to a shilling, and twenty shillings to a pound, which translates to two hundred forty pence to a pound. Today, there are one hundred pence to a pound—just as there are one hundred cents in a dollar. But the British system of coinage used to be quite complicated. Rowling, who was born in 1965, would have been familiar with the older British monetary system because the coins remained in circulation through the early 1980s. Whether the Sickles, Knuts, and Galleons make magical allusions or satirize an overly elaborate currency, numbers are some of the details that make rereading these novels fun. Rereading reveals other layers, changing the ways we think about the novels.

Her inventiveness notwithstanding, many have faulted Rowling's prose style, Pennington claiming that it fails to "induce wonder" (85), and Robert McCrum calling it "as flat (and as English) as old beer" (3). Offering a more diplomatically phrased version of this comment, Tucker says that the *Potter* books have been "[w]ritten up in good, workman-like prose with no frills attached" (228). Zipes observes, more critically, that "[t]here is nothing exceptional about Rowling's writing in comparison with that of many other gifted writers of children's and young adult literature," and he offers his own list of "gifted writers": Lloyd Alexander, Natalie Babbitt, Diana Wynne Jones, Francesca Lia Block, Philip Pullman, Jane Yolen, Donna Jo Napoli, and "many others who are constantly experimenting in innovative ways" (174–5). Claims of literary merit are closely linked to individual taste and therefore nearly impossible to prove. Admitting, then, that my own comments will be as subjective as those just mentioned, I would argue that Rowling compares favorably to most of the writers Zipes mentioned, though she may be surpassed by a few of them. At its best, Block's lyrical imagery exceeds that of Rowling, and Pullman's gift for writing beautiful sentences is unmatched by Rowling or any writer on Zipes's list. Pullman's *His Dark Materials* trilogy has both a more finely crafted style and a greater intellectual depth than does Rowling's series.

Tucker makes a good point in describing Rowling's style as "workman-like," but I would instead argue that she is an efficient writer, skilled at choosing each detail for maximum effect, and consequently able to create an extremely visual experience without indulging in long descriptive passages. Her skill at telling an engaging story allows readers to forget that she often tells by showing. In this sense, Pennington's claim that Rowling "tells but does not show" (83) is a natural assumption to make after experiencing Rowling's prose. However, upon closer examination, the showing is there, but it is all in the service of telling the tale. In *Prisoner of Azkaban*, when Harry and Hermione mount Buckbeak so that they may fly up to Hogwarts' West Tower and rescue Sirius, Rowling's narrative tells us, "Buckbeak soared straight into the dark air. Harry gripped his flanks with his knees, feeling the great wings rising powerfully beneath them" (302). These sentences create an image synechdotally, selecting strong details to suggest the larger picture. Having fully described the Hippogriff on many previous occasions, Rowling here uses "flanks" and "great wings rising powerfully" to highlight Buckbeak's defining features. Referring to the flesh between ribs and hip, the word "flanks" remind us that Hippogriffs have the "bodies, hind legs and tails of horses"; the "great wings rising powerfully" remind us that they have the "wings and heads of [. . .] giant eagles" (87). That is, "flanks" and "wings" say just enough to convey each half of the horse-and-eagle combination. These details are sufficient because Harry and Hermione have spent the last ten pages with Buckbeak, during which time Rowling has Buckbeak breaking into a "trot" (294), "digging his beak into the ground, apparently searching for worms" (298), "cantering along behind them," and "fold[ing] his wings contentedly" (299). When she tells us that "Buckbeak soared straight into the dark air," we should already have a clear picture of the Hippogriff. The words "soared straight" convey his abrupt lift-off, and "dark air" frames the Hippogriff and his riders in black space, creating a sharp contrast between them and the surrounding night sky. In sum, Rowling writes sentences that are both vividly descriptive and actively propelling the plot forward. Every detail tells; nothing's superfluous.

This rescue of Buckbeak and Sirius calls attention to Hermione's centrality to the Potter epic: the combination of her intelligence and Harry's quick thinking are vital to the success of their mission. Harry realizes that they must rescue Buckbeak and fly him to Flitwick's office, rescuing Sirius; Hermione, who understands the seriousness of meddling with time, makes sure that they do not exceed Dumbledore's mandate of "sav[ing] more than one innocent life tonight" (*Prisoner* 288). She also ensures that they time their actions carefully, moving Buckbeak after the executioner Macnair has seen him, but before Macnair leaves Hagrid's hut to do the execution (*Prisoner* 291–3). Despite Hermione's evident importance, Tucker and Zipes, Christine Schoefer, and Donna Harrington-Lueker all fault Rowling for her representations of girls. "Gender roles are stereotyped," says Tucker, "with boys out for action and the one salient girl character forever urging caution" (229); "the girls are always left to gawk and gaze at Harry's stunning prowess," observes Zipes (179).

As the title character, Harry Potter will of necessity be the series' main hero, but Hermione is the intellectual hero and possesses sufficient bravery—that defining Gryffindor trait—to break the school rules, to help Sirius escape, to protect the Philosopher's Stone, and to fight a band of Death Eaters. She does urge caution, but when she does, she is always right. In *Philosopher's Stone*, she's correct to warn Harry that Malfoy's challenge to a duel is a trap: it is, as we learn when Malfoy fails to turn up, but Filch does, nearly catching Harry. In *Order of the Phoenix*, she's correct to encourage Harry to study Occlumency; had he done so, Voldemort would not have been able to lure him to the Ministry. Her intelligence frequently saves the trio. At the end of *Philosopher's Stone*, only she knows how to stop the Devil's Snare from strangling them, and only she can solve the logic puzzle (202, 207–08). In *Goblet of Fire*, Hermione discovers the Four-Point Spell that helps Harry navigate the maze (608). In *Chamber of Secrets*, Hermione solves the mystery of the Chamber of Secrets (189, 215–16). Hermione is so well read that Rowling has appointed her the historian of the series. That is, whenever Rowling needs to introduce some of Hogwarts' history, she gives the job to Hermione. Rowling even makes a joke of this narrative tendency:

> "Honestly, am I the *only* person who's bothered to read *Hogwarts, A History?*" said Hermione [. . .]
> "Probably," said Ron. "why?"
>
> > (*Azkaban* 123)

It is true that Hermione is made fun of for being a know-it-all, but it is equally true that Harry and Ron would have died several times over without her assistance. As Lupin tells her, "You're the cleverest witch of your age I've ever met, Hermione" (*Prisoner* 346). As Eliza Dresang demonstrates in her thorough analysis of gender in the Potter series, "Rowling's Hermione is a strong, intelligent, thoughtful, compassionate female who is not only assisting the males with whom she has an interdependent relationship but also working to become her own agent as well as a catalyst for social change" (242).

The Potter novels do have an activist spirit to them, but the agency of the books themselves—the way in which they act upon the reader—grows out of Rowling's provocative use of ambiguity. Far from describing "a world of simple heroics and moral absolutes" (Tucker 229),[2] the Potter novels endow all but the most villainous characters with a mixture of admirable and distasteful qualities; these complexities can prompt reflection, as readers are forced to think about what they read. Snape, the classic example of such a character, is neither the villain he at first appears to be, nor a particularly likeable fellow. Though a former Death Eater, he is also a member of the Order of the Phoenix; though cruel to Harry, he also saves his life. *Order of the Phoenix* gives us even more reasons for thinking about Snape; the memory of being bullied by James Potter elicits our sympathy, even as Snape continues to delight in bullying Harry and friends. As Rowling told a reader who inquired about Snape, "Keep an eye on him" (Barnes and Noble Chat).

I would suggest readers keep an eye on the Harry Potter phenomenon. It is, like Snape, more complex than it at first may seem. Harry is a marketing juggernaut, the most visible example of the least admirable trends in today's children's literature industry. However, we should be wary of conflating the Harry Potter novels with the

Harry Potter hype. Although Rowling, Harry, and Warner Brothers may be complicit with the legal and market forces that create the Harry Potter phenomenon, Rowling and her books—to the degree that they can—do offer a limited resistance. Further, while reasonable people may disagree about the novels' artistic merits, the books have sufficient textual richness to warrant further study. As if to confirm this fact, three collections of critical essays have been published in the last three years: Lana Whited's *The Ivory Tower and Harry Potter: Perspectives on a Literary Phenomenon*, Elizabeth E. Heilman's *Harry Potter's World: Multidisciplinary Critical Perspectives*, and Giselle Liza Anatol's *Reading Harry Potter: Critical Essays*.

Given the appearance of these collections and of the many other books and scholarly essays on Harry Potter, the hypercommercialization of the Harry Potter franchise has not obscured the appeals of the books. In a scene often cited approvingly as a description of the Harry Potter novels' magical effect on readers, Ron warns Harry about an enchanted "book that you could never stop reading." As he explains, "You just had to wander around with your nose in it, trying to do everything one-handed" (*Chamber* 172). When Rowling wrote Ron's admonition against bewitched texts, Harry Potter was not the massive capitalist enterprise he is now, so the metaphor of the enchanted book seemed to represent the power of Rowling's literary art, how her words held readers' attention, making them reluctant to put the books down. Today, some look around at all the hype and say, reasonably, that the metaphor of the enchanted book dramatizes how people have been bewitched by advertising, lured into reading a popular but second-rate series. The confluence of cultural, fiscal, and legal forces in which Harry Potter is enmeshed may foster the belief that Harry's "magic" is nothing more than savvy marketing, but there *is* a magic beyond the marketing—the magic of good storytelling. Most of the literary criticism to date confirms this perception. That said, even if there comes a time when we are no longer bombarded with all manner of Harry Potter merchandise, the books will never be able to be severed from the vast commercial enterprise of which they are a part. However, the literary magic should never be confused with the marketing magic: if we are to fully understand either aspect of the Harry Potter phenomenon, the literary text and the marketing campaign must be given their due.

## Questions for Consideration

1   With whom do you agree—those who cite marketing as the reason for Harry Potter's success or those who insist that the books themselves are primarily the cause? Why?

2   The copyright on works published after 1978 now lasts for the author's life plus seventy years. What are the pros and cons of this long-lasting protection? Use library books and online databases such as Nexis and Factiva to help you answer the question.

## Notes

1.  The United States signed the Berne Convention in 1988, but did so in a way that exempts itself from upholding it. See Nel. *Dr. Seuss: American Icon* (166–7). See also Nancy Updike's "Green Eggs and Lawsuits."
2.  Tucker echoes some of Wilson's criticisms of Tolkien. Of *The Lord of the Rings*, Wilson writes, "The hero has no serious temptations; is lured by no insidious enchantments, perplexed by few problems. What we get is a simple confrontation—in more or less the traditional terms of the British melodrama—of the Forces of Evil with the Forces of Good" (343).

## Works Cited

Alberge, Dalya. "Grown-ups are going potty for kids' stuff." *The Times* (London) 8 Oct. 1998. Sec. Books. 44–5.

Alexander, Lloyd. *The Black Cauldron*. New York: Holt, Rinehart and Winston, 1965.

——. *The Book of Three*. New York: Holt, Rinehart and Winston, 1964.

——. *The Castle of Llyr*. New York: Holt, Rinehart and Winston, 1966.

——. *The High King*. New York: Holt, Rinehart and Winston, 1968.

——. *Taran Wanderer*. New York: Holt, Rinehart and Winston, 1967.

Anatol, Giselle Liza, ed. *Reading Harry Potter: Critical Essays*. Westport and London: Praeger, 2003.

Austen, Jane. *Emma*. 1816. Ed. James Kinsley. Introduction by David Lodge. New York: Oxford UP, 1992.

——. *Mansfield Park*. 1814. Ed. with an introduction by Tony Tanner. New York: Penguin, 1985.

Barnes, Julian E. "Dragons and Flying Brooms: Mattel Shows Off Its Line of Harry Potter Toys." *New York Times* 1 March 2000: Cl. <http://www.nytimes.com>.

Barnes and Noble Chat with J.K. Rowling. 20 Oct. 2000. <http://www.hpnetwork.f2s.com/jkrowling/jkrbnchat.html>.

Blake, Andrew. *The Irresistible Rise of Harry Potter*. New York and London: Verso, 2002.

Bloom, Harold. "Can 35 Million Book Buyers Be Wrong? Yes." *Wall Street Journal* 11 July 2000: A26.

*Buffy the Vampire Slayer*. Created by Joss Whedon. Perf. Sarah Michelle Gellar. Mutant Enemy Inc./20th Century Fox Television, 1997–2003.

Byatt, A. S. "Harry Potter and the Childish Adult." *New York Times* 7 July 2003: A13 <http://www.nytimes.com>.

Cooper, Susan. *The Boggart*. 1993. London: Puffin, 1994.

——. *The Dark Is Rising*. 1973. New York: Simon & Schuster, 1986.

——. *Greenwitch*. 1974. New York: Simon & Schuster, 1986.

——. *The Grey King*. 1975. New York: Simon & Schuster, 1986.

——. *Over Sea, Under Stone*. 1965. New York: Simon & Schuster, 1989.

——. *Silver on the Tree*. 1977. New York: Simon & Schuster, 1986.

Cross, Gary. *Kids' Stuff: Toys and the Changing World of American Childhood*. Cambridge: Harvard UP, 1997.

Cummins, June. "Read between the lines for a lesson in consumer coercion." *New York Times Higher Education Supplement* 21 Dec. 2001: 20+.

Dahl, Roald. *James and the Giant Peach*. 1961. Puffin, 1988.

——. *Matilda*. 1988. Puffin, 1990.

Dresang, Eliza. "Hermione Granger and the Heritage of Gender." *Harry Potter and the Ivory Tower*. Ed. Lana A. Whited. Columbia: U Missouri P, 2002. 211–42.

Fielding, Sarah. *The Governess; or Little Female Academy*. 1749. Ed. and with Introduction by Jill E. Gray. London: Oxford UP, 1968.

Freud, Clement. *Grimble*. Illus. by Frank Francis. London: Collins, 1968.

Gaines, Jane M. *Contested Culture: The Image, the Voice, and the Law*. Chapel Hill: U of North Carolina P, 1991.

Gallico, Paul. *Manxmouse*. Illus. Janet and Anne Grahame-Johnstone. London: Heinemann, 1968.

Glaister, Dan. "Debut Author and Single Mother Sells Children's Book for 100,000 Pounds." *The Guardian* (London) 8 July 1997: 4.

Goudge, Elizabeth. *The Little White Horse*. 1946. New York: Puffin Books, 2001.

Gupta, Suman. *Re-Reading Harry Potter*. New York: Palgrave MacMillan, 2003.

Harrington-Lueker, Donna. "'Harry Potter' lacks for true heroines." *USA Today* 11 July 2000: 17A.

"Harry's Books." 10 July 2003. *Comic Relief UK*. <http://www.comicrelief.com/harrysbooks/>.

Heilman, Elizabeth E., ed. *Harry Potter's World: Multidisciplinary Critical Perspectives*. New York: RoutledgeFalmer, 2003.

Hensher, Philip. "A crowd-pleaser but no classic." *The Spectator* 12 July 2003: <http://www.spectator.co.uk>

——. "Harry Potter, give me a break." *The Independent* (London) 25 Jan. 2000: 1.

Highfield, Roger. *The Science of Harry Potter: How Magic Really Works*. 2002. New York: Penguin, 2003.

Holden, Anthony. "Why Harry Potter doesn't cast a spell over me." *Observer* 25 June 2000. Review pages, p. 1.

Hughes, Thomas. *Tom Brown's Schooldays*. 1857. Illus. by Arthur Hughes. 1869. Ed. and with an Introduction and Notes by Andrew Sanders. New York: Oxford UP, 1999.

"J. K. Rowling's Bookshelf." *O Magazine* Jan. 2001: 155.

"JK Rowling Transcript." *Comic Relief: Official site of red nose day—Comicrelief. org.uk*. 12 March 2001. 9 Dec. 2001. <http://www.comicrelief.com/harrysbooks/pages/transcript.shtml>.

Kinder, Marsha. *Playing with Power in Movies, Television, and Video Games: From Muppet Babies to Teenage Mutant Ninja Turtles*. Berkeley: U of California P, 1991.

Kline, Stephen. *Out of the Garden: Toys, TV, and Children's Culture in the Age of Marketing*. London: Verso, 1993.

LeGuin, Ursula K. *The Farthest Shore*. 1972. Bantam, 1984.

——. *The Tombs of Atuan*. 1971. Bantam, 1984.

——. *A Wizard of Earthsea*. 1968. Bantam, 1984.

"Magic, Mystery, and Mayhem: An Interview with J. K. Rowling." Amazon.com 15 May 1999. 4 April 2003. <http://www.amazon.com>.

McCrum, Robert. "Plot, plot, plot that's worth the weight." *The Observer* 9 July 2000: 3.

McGinty, Stephen. "The legacy of Harry: The JK Rowling Story—Part III." *The Scotsman* 18 June 2003 <http://www.news.scotsman.com>.

Mehren, Elizabeth. "Upward and onward toward book seven—her way." *Los Angeles Times* 25 Oct. 2000: El+.

Natov, Roni. "Harry Potter and the Extraordinariness of the Ordinary." *The Lion and the Unicorn* 25.2 (2001): 310–27.

Nel, Philip. *Dr. Seuss: American Icon*. New York and London: Continuum, 2004.

——. *J. K. Rowling's Harry Potter Novels: A Reader's Guide*. New York and London: Continuum, 2001.

Nesbit, E. *Five Children and It*. 1902. Puffin, 1996.

——. *The Phoenix and the Carpet*. 1904. Puffin, 1994.

——. *The Story of the Amulet*. 1906. Puffin, 1996.

——. *The Story of the Treasure-Seekers*. 1899. Puffin, 1994.

Pennington, John. "From Elfland to Hogwarts, or the Aesthetic Trouble with Harry Potter." *The Lion and the Unicorn* 26.1 (2002): 78–97.

Phillips, Mark. "Pure magic." *CBS Sunday Morning* 26 Sept. 1999.

Pullman, Philip. *The Amber Spyglass*. London: Scholastic, 2000.

——. *Northern Lights*. 1995. London: Scholastic, 1998.

——. *The Subtle Knife*. 1997. London: Scholastic, 1998.

Randall, Jessy. "Wizard Words: The Literary, Latin, and Lexical Origins of Harry Potter's Vocabulary." *Verbatim: The Language Quarterly* 26.2 (Spring 2001): 1, 3–7.

"Reading Is Fundamental." *Coca-Cola Youth Partnership*. <http://www.youth development.coca-cola.com/ach_reading.html>. 10 July 2003.

Reeves, Debbie. "Getting Disease-Modifying Drugs in the U.K." *Inside MS*. Summer 2002. 10 July 2003. <http://www.nationalmssociety.org>.

Rowling, J. K. Foreword. *Families Just Like Us: the One Parent Families good book guide*. Young Book Trust and National Council for One Parent Families, 2000.

——— . *Harry Potter and the Chamber of Secrets*. London: Bloomsbury, 1998.

——— . *Harry Potter and the Goblet of Fire*. London: Bloomsbury, 2000.

——— . *Harry Potter and the Order of the Phoenix*. London: Bloomsbury, 2003.

——— . *Harry Potter and the Philosopher's Stone*. London: Bloomsbury, 1997.

——— . *Harry Potter and the Prisoner of Azakaban*. London: Bloomsbury, 1999.

——— . "I Miss My Mother So Much." *Inside MS*. Repr. from *MS Matters*, 2001. Summer 2002. 10 July 2003. <http://www.nationalmssociety.org>.

——— . "Let me tell you a story." *Sunday Times* (London) 21 May 2000. Lexis-Nexis 14. May 2004. <http://www.lexis-nexis.co>.

Scamander, Newt [J. K. Rowling]. *Fantastic Beasts and Where to Find Them*. London: Bloomsbury and Obscurus Books, 2001.

Schoefer, Christine. "Harry Potter's Girl Trouble." *Salon* 13 Jan. 2000: <http:// www.salon.com/books/feature/2000/01/13/potter/index.html? CP=SAL&DN =650>.

Stahl, Lesly. Profile of J. K. Rowling. *60 Minutes*. CBS. 12 Sept. 1999.

Steege, David K. "Harry Potter, Tom Brown, and the British School Story: Lost in Transit?" *Harry Potter and the Ivory Tower*. Ed. Lana A. Whited. Columbia: U Missouri P, 2002. 140–58.

Tolkien, J. R. R. *The Lord of the Rings, Part One: The Fellowship of the Ring*. 1956. Rev. Ed. 1965. New York: Ballantine, 1982.

——— . *The Lord of the Rings, Part Two: The Two Towers*. 1956. Rev. Ed. 1965. New York Ballantine, 1982.

——— . *The Lord of the Rings, Part Three: The Return of the King*. 1956. Rev. Ed. 1965. New York: Ballantine, 1982.

Toobin, Jeffrey. "Silly Old Bear v. Mouse." *New Yorker* 22 and 29 Dec. 2003: 58.

Tucker, Nicholas. "The Rise and Rise of Harry Potter." *Children's Literature in Education* 30.4 (Dec. 1999): 221–34.

Updike, Nancy. "Green Eggs and Lawsuits." *LA Weekly* 20–26 July 2001: 19 June 2002. <http://www.laweekly.com>.

US Copyright Office. "Questions Frequently Asked in the Copyright Office Public Information Section." 5 Dec. 2001. 6 Feb. 2002. <http://www.loc.gov/ copyright/faq.html>.

Wasserman, Dan. "I can already see how it ends—the dark forces win." *Washington Post National Weekly Edition* 24 July 2000: 28.

Westman, Karin E. "Specters of Thatcherism: Contemporary British Culture in J. K. Rowling's Harry Potter Series." *The Ivory Tower and Harry Potter: Perspectives on a Literary Phenomenon*. Ed. Lana A. Whited. Columbia: U Missouri P, 2002. 305–28.

Whisp, Kennilworthy [J. K. Rowling]. *Quidditch Through the Ages*. London: Bloomsbury and WhizzHard Books, 2001.

White, T. H. *The Once and Future King*. 1965. New York: Ace Books, 1996.

Whited, Lana A. "Harry Potter: From Craze to Classic?" *The Ivory Tower and Harry Potter: Perspectives on a Literary Phenomenon*. Ed. Lana A. Whited. Columbia: U Missouri P, 2002. 1–12.

Wilson, Edmund. "Oo, Those Awful Orcs!" *The Nation* 14 April 1956: 312–14.

Zipes, Jack. *Sticks and Stones: The Troublesome Success of Children's Literature from Slovenly Peter to Harry Potter*. New York: Routledge, 2001.

# Chapter 12

## MARK FITZGERALD

# NEWSPAPERS ROCKEN ESPANOL

**H**ISPANICS ARE THE FASTEST-GROWING ethnic minority in the United States. Advertisers have recognized that and some media firms are pursuing Hispanics as well, with the hope of bringing in that advertising revenue. In this 2004 article for the newspaper trade magazine *Editor and Publisher*, Mark Fitzgerald describes the gold rush mindset of many newspaper firms and the mistakes that they have been making along the way.

To introduce readers in Racine, Wis., to the first-ever Spanish-language page in *The Journal Times*, Editor Randolph Brandt chose an admittedly unusual but, he figured, appropriate salutation: Guten Tag!

His point was that Racine had a long tradition of publishing newspapers in the language of new immigrants. This city along Lake Michigan was once home to the German-language *Racine Volksblatt*, the Slovenian-language *Slovan Amerikansky*, and a host of papers in Norweigan and Danish. Little Racine once published the biggest Bohemian-language newspaper in America, Brandt reminded readers.

Now people from the Mexican state of Oaxaca were arriving in big numbers in Racine, and creating a burgeoning commercial strip in the traditional "second downtown" along Douglas Avenue. So running a full page of news in Spanish with an English-language summary seemed a natural way to serve the latest group in this city of immigrants.

This would be more than just a feel-good project, too. Local advertisers were clamoring for a Spanish-language vehicle, Brandt says. And looking beyond Racine, the *Journal Times* saw that some of the smartest chains in the newspaper industry—Knight Ridder, BeIo, Tribune Co., MediaNews Group Inc., and Freedom Communications—are betting on a strategy of publishing in Spanish.

And why wouldn't they? The Hispanic population exploded by at least 58% to 35.3 million between 1990 and 2000. In roughly the same period, ad revenues for

Spanish-language and Hispanic papers soared 565%, according to figures from the National Association of Hispanic Publications. The chains that made America's family-owned hometown paper an endangered species are now targeting a market that until recently was served largely by precariously financed Mom-and-Pop operations.

In fact, so many chain-owned papers have jumped into Spanish-language print that they are beginning to compete not just with established Latino newspapers, but each other. In the Dallas/Fort Worth Metroplex, Beio's *AlDia* contends with Knight Bidder's *La Estrella*. This week in Los Angeles, Tribune Co.'s *Hoy* kicks off a three-way competition with MediaNews Group Inc.'s free-distribution weekly *Impacto USA* and Impremedia LLC's *La Opinion*. (The Los Angeles-based *La Opinion* remains the leading Spanish-language daily in the United States.) This fight for Hispanic readers is now happening in the toniest neighborhoods. In West Palm Beach, Fla., *The Palm Reach Post*'s brand-new *La Palma*, launched on Feb. 6, already has competition from the South Florida *Sun-Sentinel*, which began home delivery in Palm Beach County of its weekly *El Sentinel* the day after *La Palrna* launched. This spring, two Spanish-language weeklies will contend in Southampton, one of Long Island, N.Y.'s most exclusive communities.

Daily newspapers beset by declining readership and changing market demographics are increasingly exploring the Spanish language market. They look with envy on the success mainstream papers have achieved with Spanish-language papers. *El Nuevo Herald* in Miami became the fastest-growing newspaper in the Knight Ridder chain when it was loosed from *The Miami Herald*. Tribune Co.'s *Hoy*, based in New York, in just four years grew to be America's secondbiggest Spanish-language daily, and that was before launches in Chicago and Los Angeles—let alone the seven other heavily Hispanic markets the tabloid intends to conquer.

And while it may seem that established dailies—desperate to stem circulation losses—should be trying to bring readers directly to their papers, a recent study suggests separate ethnic papers reinforce their flagships. Latinos, like other immigrants, will eventually come to the English-language paper, concludes a major study of San Francisco Bay area ethnic media by Rufus Browning, a professor at San Francisco State University.

Latino immigrants rapidly increase their use of general media the longer they have been in the United States, Browning wrote. Released in December, the Ford Foundation study concludes that relying solely on the news media in their own language is a "temporary condition" for new immigrants. "The other good news is that [ethnic papers] don't isolate groups, but bring them into the American mainstream," Browning said in a phone interview.

But there are reasons for caution. Consider the Racine experience.

Latino populations are growing fast in places never before considered Hispanic, such as Nebraska, Georgia, North Carolina—and Racine County. There, the *Journal Times*, a Lee Enterprises paper, figured there were at least 5,000 households in its circulation area where Spanish was the first language. "We knew for some time that we wanted to serve this market, we just weren't sure what form it would take," Editor Brandt says. Publishing a page of news in Spanish labeled "El Mundo Latino" three times a week plus a page of community events on Saturday seemed like a modest start.

But when "El Mundo Latino" debuted Jan. 14, it was a sensation—for all the wrong reasons. "Some readers really hated it," Brandt says with considerable understatement.

Not all readers, of course: One high school Spanish class sent 26 fan letters. But in the fraying-blue-collar town with a high unemployment rate and an inchoate resentment of illegal immigrants, the sudden transformation of the "A" section's second page from English to Spanish unnerved—even unhinged—some longtime readers when it first appeared.

"We anticipated some complaints. What we didn't anticipate was that the reaction would be so vociferous," Brandt says. Scores of readers threatened to cancel their subscriptions. A couple of dozen actually did, and it began to look like the cancellations would continue every time the page ran. Not only was the test failing to expand readership, it jeopardized the rest of the paper, Brandt says.

"El Mundo Latino" was cancelled eight days after it began.

## Miami Advice

The *Journal Times'* pursuit of its local Latino market isn't over and may yet have a happy ending, but it is also a cautionary tale for the many daily newspapers who now face the increasingly common strategic decision: How to target a new and rapidly growing audience that seems to have no interest in reading the English-language newspaper.

As Racine's experience shows, the Field of Dreams strategy ("If you build it, they will come") does not work. The good news, though, is that mainstream dailies now have enough experience under their belts to know what works and what doesn't in reaching Spanish readers. Newspapers as widely diverse as *The Orange County (Calif.) Register* and *The Daily Citizen* in Dalton, Ga., are boosting revenues and readership with Spanish-language products.

The first paper to show the way was the *Miami Herald*. If the movement of mainstream newspapers into Spanish-language publishing has a godfather, it is *Herald* Publisher Alberto Ibarguen, who in 1998 showed that a mainstream newspaper's Spanish-language paper could thrive outside the cocoon of its English-language flagship.

"We've been publishing in Spanish for the last 30 years, roughly," Ibarguen says. "We've tried just about everything and we've made just about every mistake—but we also have had some spectacular success."

It was not, however, an overnight success. The *Herald* dipped its toe into the Spanish market some three decides ago in the same way that many papers are starting now, with a couple of pages in the language. That became a section called *El Herald* and that grew into what Ibarguen calls "almost a newspaper in the newspaper" called *El Miami Herald*.

Another redesign, another relaunch—this time as *El Nuevo Herald*, but the paper remained hidden inside the fat *Miami Herald*, "a pound of English covering a quarter-pound of Spanish," Ibarguen says. When he arrived in Miami, Ibarguen roamed the stores and sidewalk counters dispensing Cuban coffee in Little Havana and saw the business consequences of forcing that combined "sale."

"The customer was taking the Spanish-language paper out of the *Herald*, putting the English-language paper back and leaving a quarter on the counter—at a time when the Herald cost 35 cents. The store owner pockets the quarter and we give him credit for an unsold paper," Ibarguen says. The market, he adds dryly, had spoken in favor of a separate paper.

But just separating the papers was not enough, Ibarguen says now. *El Nuevo Herald* did not really take off until Ibarguen convinced the legendary designer Carlos Castaneda to reprise the magic that made *El Nuevo Dia* a hit in Puerto Rico. "My one instruction was to give me a newspaper that could not be confused with the *Miami Herald*" Ibarguen says. "And he sure did."

The lesson, Ibarguen says, is almost too obvious to underscore: "The first thing you've got to do is look at what your market really is. Looking at the market through a rearview mirror as it used to be or as you wished it were and reluctantly, almost grudgingly, making changes in your paper . . . will not work." Knowing your market means knowing where the local Hispanics come from, and, especially, in what language they learned to read: "The newspaper is an intimate pleasure, and people don't really want to work that hard at a pleasure."

Another lesson is that the Hispanic market itself can change, as it has in Miami. Once solidly Cuban, the city attracted a growing population of Nicaraguans, Colombians, and other Latin Americans. So the newspaper changed from emphasizing news of Cuba to becoming a more "pan-American" paper.

Now, *El Nuevo Herald* is changing again. This month it will become more focused on local news of metropolitan Miami, Ibarguen says, because its readers are increasingly putting down permanent roots in the city and suburbs.

## G-o-o-o-o-o-o-a-l-l-l!

For all his success, Ibarguen says he has one regret about *El Nuevo Herald*: "I wish we had changed (the name) to almost anything else. Though we changed the paper, the name of the publication suggests something that it is not. This is not "the new *Herald*; this is something completely different."

Tribune Co., he says, did it right by naming their paper *Hoy*: "It's not '*El Newsday*' or '*El [Chicago] Tribune*' or '*El [Los Angeles] Times*.' "

It couldn't be, explains Louis Sito, who came up with the idea of a separate tabloid Spanish-language daily when he was executive senior vice president of sales for Newsday. Like *USA Today*, *Hoy* is made to look the same in all markets. Publisher and CEO Sito, who last year became Tribune Publishing's first vice president/Hispanic media, says *Hoy* succeeds because it has a clear business goal.

"Our mantra is that *Hoy* is a national brand that is easily recognizable and that is very easy for advertisers to access," says Sito.

The five-year-old *Hoy* became truly national last fall when it launched an edition in Chicago, which Sito says is surpassing expectations. The Chicago *Hoy* will report a paid daily circulation of about 20,000 copies in the Audit Bureau of Circulations FAS-FAX for March 31, he says. A Los Angeles version of *Hoy* launches this week. Sito won't talk about the timing of future launches—"L.A. is a big nut to swallow," he notes—but it's a good bet they will accelerate.

Sito does talk freely about where *Hoy* is going, though: The tabloid will be published in the top 10 Hispanic markets that together cover 75% of American Hispanics. That leaves Miami, San Francisco, Houston, San Antonio, Dallas, and San Diego among the markets that sooner or later can expect to see the distinctive blue and yellow *Hoy* newsboxes on their street corners.

So far, *Hoy* has only launched where *Tribune* already publishes a daily. That, Sito says, will change: "We may partner with a paper, but if not we'll create our own infrastructure." In fact, *Hoy* is already creating a structure independent of its *Tribune* siblings.

## Deep in the Heart of Tejas

Right from the start, Sito says, *Hoy* was never going to be anything less than a daily, mostly because it started in New York which was already served by two daily Spanish-language dailies, most notably the venerable *El Diario La Prensa*: "If we really were serious in establishing a relationship with this community, we couldn't do it one day a week in a market with two dailies."

There was no daily Spanish-language competition in *The Dallas Morning News'* market back in 2001 when it folded a direct-mail product called *La Fuente* and formed a team to come up with an editorially driven product. But the *Morning News*, too, concluded daily publication was the best way to reach its market, says Vice President and Executive Editor Gilbert Bailon, who headed the project: "The number [of Spanish-speakers] plus the level of sophistication of the market convinced us that we needed to offer daily, timely news."

The launch of *Al Dia* demonstrates another lesson for papers looking to publish in Spanish: It isn't necessarily cheap. Belo has committed to invest some $4 million in the paper in the next year and a half. That's on top of the separate newsroom of 32 and an *Al Dia*-only sales staff of 11. Bailon says, "In a city approaching almost 40% [Hispanic] population, we've got to make this work, because there are too many people who are not reading the *Dallas Morning News* in English."

Just before *Al Dia* launched with a circulation of 40,000, the Fort Worth Star-Telegram, aided by help from its Knight Ridder sibling paper *El Nuevo Herald*, relaunched its twice-weekly *La Estrella* as a daily named *Diario La Estrella*.

There's good news for both new dailies and for their parents, according to research released Jan. 30 by Dallas-based Rincon & Associates. By a rate of 12.7% to 6.3%, *Diario La Estrella* is rated better in covering "Latino people and events" than *Al Dia*, but both papers have an equal reach of 19% so far, while *Al Dia* is read more frequently than *Diario La Estrella*. Those gains are not coming at the expense of Latino readership of the English-language dailies, the papers found. However, the corporate-owned *Al Dia*, and *Diario La Estrella* are already cutting into the readership of other area Spanish-language papers, Rincon found.

## Spending for an "Impacto"

Like the *Star-Telegram*'s *Diario La Estrella*, some mainstream chains are already into a second generation of Spanish-language papers.

For more than a decade, MediaNews Group used rack and store drops to distribute 100,000 copies of a free tabloid weekly called *El Economico* in Long Beach and other parts of Los Angeles. "We always had a problem with the name. People would see it and think it was a financial paper," says Publisher Fernando Paramo.

In January, MediaNews relaunched it as a broadsheet called *Impacto USA*, and expanded its distribution to 250,000 Hispanic households in four zones. Using a distribution model of the Latino Newspaper Network, the paper is delivered to households with a minimum income of $35,000 in blocks that are at least 85% Hispanic and located within five miles of a major shopping area, Paramo says.

He acknowledges it was not a cheap move: "Going into direct targeting increased our costs tremendously—perhaps 10 times as much as rack distribution." But the payoff, Paramo adds, is worth the cost: "This positions us as the number-one home-delivered Spanish-language product in the nation."

What's true in the nation's largest Hispanic market is also true in the smaller but fast-growing Latino pockets around the nation, says Jimmy Espy, executive editor of *The Daily Citizen* in Georgia. Five years ago, the 13,492-circulation Community Newspaper Holdings Inc. (CNHI) paper created the free tabloid weekly *El Informador* to serve the rapidly growing number of Mexicans working at the town's carpet mills. Last year, *El Infarmador* made the biggest contribution to the bottom line of any of the paper's operations, including the *Daily Citizen*, Espy says. The paper is attracting ads not only from the local car dealers and Mexican grocery stories, but Budweiser, Coca-Cola and other national advertisers.

Because of *El Infomador*'s success, Espy says, "I get calls from editors all over the country, and almost every time it seems they are trying to do it so cheaply and on the margins that I think it's bound to fail." In his neck of the woods in northwest Georgia, numerous thinly capitalized papers have failed in the past five years, many after only an issue or two.

The same thing has happened in Nebraska, where Mexicans and other Latin Americans working in meat-packing factories and other agribusiness have tripled the Latino population of some rural counties. Nebraska Press Association Executive Director Alien Beermann says several attempts with "some pretty good products" have failed because there was not enough Spanish-language readership or businesses. "They'd last for a few months, maybe a year, and they just kind of ran out of money."

That's why some papers faced with new Hispanic populations take it slow. Utah's third-biggest daily, the *Standard-Examiner* in Ogden, tried a bilingual page a few years ago that failed in part because of resentment by English-language readers. But this Christmas it tested a seasonal product called *El Estandar* that did quite well. "Advertisers wanted to jump on the bandwagon for this niche, and once the *Standard-Examiner* was involved, why, they'd say, 'We want to be involved,' " says Publisher W. Scott Trundle.

The paper figures to launch a weekly product sometime this spring—with one condition: "It may start at a loss," Trundle says, "but it won't stay at a loss very long."

## Racine Redux

In Racine, Wis., the *Journal Times* is still determined to make a go of it. Just days after canceling the regular Spanish-language page, it launched a four-page Spanish section that runs on Thursdays. There is more ad support for the section than there was for the page, Editor Randy Brandt says, although he worries that readership might not be as strong with only a weekly product. Handling the section is Steve Lovejoy, the paper's editorial page editor, and Guadalupe Rendon, a former Racine cop who trained at the Freedom Forum's Diversity Institute.

"We're hoping this takes off and gets a revenue stream going so we can expand the staff a little," Brandt says. "Because we know we need to do this."

## Questions for Consideration

1   Some observers would argue that the "Hispanic" market is really a variety of markets with quite different audiences. How does Fitzgerald's article support this contention?

2   According to Fitzgerald, what did the Tribune Company do right when it created *Hoy*?

3   Although there are two major Spanish-language television networks in the U.S. and some smaller ones, the English-language TV networks have been explicitly adding Hispanic characters to their programs and even incorporating Spanish into some of their shows. Using Nexis, Factiva or other periodical databases, try to explore why they are doing it and how successful they are at it.

# PART THREE

# The Electronic Media

# INTRODUCTION

**T**HINK ABOUT THE LAST TIME you listened to radio. Where were you—at home, in your car, inside a restaurant or shopping mall? Were you listening on a traditional radio receiver or a newer platform such as the Web or a mobile device? Did you hear any commercials while listening? Were you tuned in to an AM/FM station, to HD radio, or to a channel offered through a the XM or Sirius subscription satellite service? Finally, do you know where the station or service you were hearing is located?

Many of these questions wouldn't make much sense if they were asked just a decade and a half ago. The Web as we know it didn't exist; neither did HD or satellite radio. And the notion that you could get streaming music on your mobile phone would probably have been considered absurd. The variety of possibilities for what some would still call "radio" but might as well be named something else (streaming audio?) is emblematic of the escalating options that face Americans in other electronic media. For example, there are so many ways to receive movies nowadays—in the theater, in a hotel, on an airplane, on DVDs from a video store or a mail-in service, via the Web, on a mobile phone. Think, too, of the options for receiving television shows and recorded music. Many young people today are as likely to watch network television shows on their computers as they are to view them on the traditional box. And the recording industry is going through traumas because so many people are using the Internet to share songs with one another rather than to pay for them.

While these examples shed light on the large-scale transformations taking place in the technologies and business of electronic media, it is also important to consider the ways in which the *content* is changing. In the television industry, for example, the successful launches of *Survivor* and *Big Brother* in 2000 marked the birth of a new (well, not entirely new, as you will read about later) programming genre. Today, nearly a decade later, reality television continues to thrive, in part because it's much cheaper for producers to create shows without having to employ big-budget actors and writers. An additional explanation for reality television's continuing success is that it provides a favorable environment for product placement. *The Apprentice, Extreme Makeover: Home Edition*, and *American Idol* are but a few examples of reality shows that prominently feature products or brands. In many ways, it becomes difficult to tell who has the control of the shows—the producers or the advertisers.

In this section, we encourage you to think about these and other examples of the changing nature of radio, television, recordings, and motion pictures. Some of the readings delve deep into a particular format or genre; others situate one or another electronic-media industry within a larger social context. As you'll see, most of the authors worry about how changes in the electronic media relate to broad social issues including the meaning and process of democracy, social unity, and creative control. We hope that the essays will encourage you to think about where you stand on these important topics.

# Chapter 13

# NEIL POSTMAN AND STEVE POWERS

# WHAT IS NEWS?

T HIS READING BY NEIL POSTMAN and Steve Powers comes from a book that they co-wrote called *How to Watch TV News*. Although published in 1992, the book remains helpful in understanding that financial and organizational considerations have a major influence on what gets placed into television news programs and what doesn't. In the chapter excerpted here, Postman (then a professor at New York University) and Powers (at the time a Fox television anchor) argue that an objective definition of news is impossible. More important than a definition, they say, is the need to think about, and discuss, what definitions of news—electronic or print— might be best for society.

All this talk about news—what is it? We turn to this question because unless a television viewer has considered it, he or she is in danger of too easily accepting someone else's definition—for example, a definition supplied by the news director of a television station; or, even worse, a definition imposed by important advertisers. The question, in any case, is not a simple one and it is even possible that many journalists and advertisers have not thought deeply about it.

A simplistic definition of news can be drawn by paraphrasing Justice Oliver Wendell Holmes's famous definition of the law. The law, Holmes said, is what the courts say it is. Nothing more. Nothing less. In similar fashion, we might say that the news is what news directors and journalists say it is. In other words, when you turn on your television set to watch a network or local news show, whatever is on is, by definition, the news. But if we were to take that approach, on what basis would we say that we haven't been told enough? Or that a story that should have been covered wasn't? Or that too many stories of a certain type were included? Or that a reporter gave a flagrantly biased account?

If objections of this kind are raised by viewers, then they must have some conception of the news that the news show has not fulfilled. Most people, in fact, do have such a conception, although they are not always fully conscious of what it is. When people are asked "What is the news?" the most frequent answer given is that the news is "what happened that day." This is a rather silly answer since even those who give it can easily be made to see that an uncountable number of things happen during the course of a day, including what you had for breakfast, that could hardly be classified as news by any definition. In modifying their answer, most will add that the news is "important and interesting things that happened that day." This helps a little but leaves open the question of what is "important and interesting" and how that is decided. Embedded somewhere in one's understanding of the phrase "important and interesting events" is one's definition of "the news."

Of course, some people will say that the question of what is important and interesting is not in the least problematic. What the President says or does is important; wars are important, rebellions, employment figures, elections, appointments to the Supreme Court. Really? We doubt that even the President believes everything he says is important. (Let us take, for example, President Bush's remark that he doesn't like broccoli.) There are, as we write, more than forty wars and rebellions going on somewhere in the world. Not even *The New York Times*, which claims to be the "newspaper of public record," reports on all of them, or even most. Are elections important? Maybe. But we doubt you'd be interested in the election in Iowa's Third Congressional District—unless you happen to live there. Some readers will remember the famous comedy routine of the 2,000-Year-Old Man who was discovered in the imaginations of Carl Reiner and Mel Brooks. Upon being asked what he believed to be the greatest invention of humankind during his life span, the 2,000-Year-Old Man replied unhesitatingly, "Saran Wrap." Now, there is a great deal to be said for Saran Wrap. We suspect that in the long run it may prove more useful to the well-being of most of us than a number of inventions that are daily given widespread publicity in the news media. Yet it is fair to say that no one except its manufacturer knows the date of Saran Wrap's invention, or even cares much to know. Saran Wrap is not news. The color of Liz Taylor's wrap is. Or so some people believe.

On the day Marilyn Monroe committed suicide, so did many other people, some of whose reasons may have been as engrossing as, and perhaps more significant than, Miss Monroe's. But we shall never know about these people or their reasons; the journalists at CBS or NBC or *The New York Times* simply took no notice of them. Several people, we are sure, also committed suicide on the very day in 1991 when the New York Giants won the Super Bowl. We shall never learn about these people either, however instructive or interesting their stories may have been.

What we are driving at is this: "importance" is a judgment people make. Of course, there are some events—the assassination of a president, an earthquake, etc.—that have near-universal interest and consequences. But most news does not inhere in the event. An event *becomes* news. And it becomes news because it is selected for notice out of the buzzing, booming confusion around us. This may seem a fairly obvious point but keep in mind that many people believe that the news is always "out there," waiting to be gathered or collected. In fact, the news is more often *made* rather than gathered. And it is made on the basis of what the journalist thinks important or what the journalist thinks the audience thinks is important or interesting. It can get pretty complicated. Is a story about a killing in Northern Ireland more important than one about a killing in Morocco? The journalist might not think so but the audience might. Which story will become the news? And once selected, what point of view and details are to be included?

After all, once a journalist has chosen an event to be news, he or she must also choose what is worth seeing, what is worth neglecting, and what is worth remembering or forgetting. This is simply another way of saying that every news story is a reflection of the reporter who tells the story. The reporter's previous assumptions about what is "out there" edit what he or she thinks is there. For example, many journalists believe that what is called "the intifada" is newsworthy. Let us suppose that a fourteen-year-old Palestinian boy hurls a Molotov cocktail at two eighteen-year-old Israeli soldiers. The explosion knocks one of the soldiers down and damages his left eye. The other soldier, terrified, fires a shot at the Palestinian that kills him instantly. The injured soldier eventually loses the sight of his eye. What details should be included in reporting this event? Is the age of the Palestinian relevant? Are the ages of the Israeli soldiers relevant? Is the injury to the soldier relevant? Was the act of the Palestinian provoked by the mere presence of Israeli soldiers? Was the act therefore justified? Is the shooting justified? Is the state of mind of the shooter relevant?

The answers to all of these questions, as well as to other questions about the event, depend entirely on the point of view of the journalist. You might think this is an exaggeration, that reporters, irrespective of their assumptions, can at least get the facts straight. But what are "facts"? In A. J. Liebling's book *The Press*, he gives a classic example of the problematic nature of "facts." On the same day, some years ago, both the *Wall Street Journal* and the now-defunct *World Telegram and Sun* featured a story about the streets of Moscow. Here is what the *Wall Street Journal* reporter wrote:

> The streets of central Moscow are, as the guide-books say, clean and neat; so is the famed subway. They are so because of an army of women with brooms, pans, and carts who thus earn their 35 rubles a month in lieu of "relief"; in all Moscow we never saw a mechanical street-sweeper.

Here is what the *World Telegram and Sun* reporter wrote:

> Four years ago [in Moscow] women by the hundreds swept big city streets. Now you rarely see more than a dozen. The streets are kept clean with giant brushing and sprinkling machines.

Well, which is it? Can a dozen women look like an army? Are there giant machines cleaning the streets of Moscow or are there not? How can two trained journalists see events so differently? Well, one of them worked for the *Wall Street Journal*, and when these stories were written, it was the policy of the *Journal* to highlight the contrast between the primitive Russian economy and the sophisticated American economy. (It still is.) Does this mean the reporter for the *Journal* was lying? We doubt it. Each of our senses is a remarkably astute censor. We see what we expect to see; often, we focus on what we are paid to see. And those who pay us to see usually expect us to accept their notions not only of what is important but of what are important details.

That fact poses some difficult problems for those of us trying to make sense of the news we are given. One of these problems is indicated by a proposal, made years ago, by the great French writer Albert Camus. Camus wished to establish "a control newspaper." The newspaper would come out one hour after all the others and would contain estimates of the percentage of truth in each of their stories. In Camus's words: "We'd have complete dossiers on the interests, policies, and idiosyncrasies of the owners. Then we'd have a dossier on every journalist in the world. The interests, prejudices, and quirks of the owner would equal Z. The prejudices, quirks, and private interests of the journalist Y. Z times Y would give you X, the probable amount of truth in the story" (quoted in *The Press* by A. J. Liebling, p. 22n).

Camus was either a reckless mathematician or else he simply neglected to say why and how multiplying Z and Y would tell us what we need to know. (Why not add or divide them?) Nor did he discuss the problem of how to estimate the reliability of those doing the estimating. In any case, Camus died before he had a chance to publish such a newspaper, leaving each one of us to be our own "control center." Nonetheless, we can't help thinking how Camus's idea might be applied to television. Imagine how informative it would be if there were a five-minute television program that went on immediately after each television news show. The host might say something like this: "To begin with, this station is owned by Gary Farnsworth, who is also the president of Bontel Limited, the principal stockholder of which is the Sultan of Bahrain. Bontel Limited owns three Japanese electronic companies, two oil companies, the entire country of Upper Volta, and the western part of Romania. The anchorman on the television show earns $800,000 a year; his portfolio includes holdings in a major computer firm. He has a bachelor's degree in journalism from the University of Arkansas but was a C+ student, has never taken a course in political science, and speaks no language other than English. Last year, he read only two books—a biography of Cary Grant and a book of popular psychology called *Why Am I So Wonderful?* The reporter who covered the story on Yugoslavia speaks Serbo-Croatian, has a degree in international relations, and has had a Neiman Fellowship at Harvard University."

We think this kind of information would be helpful to a viewer although not for the same reason Camus did. Such information would not give an estimate of the "truth probability" of stories but it would suggest possible patterns of influence reflected in the news. After all, what is important to a person whose boss owns several oil companies might not be important to a person who doesn't even have a boss, who is unemployed. Similarly, what a reporter who does not know the language of the people he or she reports on can see and understand will probably be different from the perceptions of another reporter who knows the language well.

What we are saying is that to answer the question "What is news?" a viewer must know something about the political beliefs and economic situation of those who provide the news. The viewer is then in a position to know why certain events are considered important by those in charge of television news and may compare those judgments with his or her own.

But here's another problem. As we have implied, even oil magnates and poorly prepared journalists do not consult, exclusively, their own interests in selecting the "truths" they will tell. Since they want people to watch their shows, they also try to determine what audiences think is important and interesting. There is, in fact, a point of view that argues against journalists imposing their own sense of significance on an audience. In this view, television news should consist only of those events that would interest the audience. The journalists must keep their own opinions to themselves. The response to this is that many viewers depend on journalists to advise them of what is important. Besides, even if journalists were mere followers of public interest, not all members of the audience agree on what they wish to know. For example, we do not happen to think that Liz Taylor's adventures in marriage were or are of any importance whatsoever to anyone but her and Michael Wilding, Nicky Hilton, Mike Todd, Eddie Fisher, Richard Burton, John Warner, Larry Fortensky, and, of course, Debbie Reynolds and Sybil Burton. Obviously, most people don't agree, which is why an announcement of her intention to marry again is featured on every television news show. What's our point? A viewer must not only know what he or she thinks is significant but what others believe is significant as well.

It is a matter to be seriously considered. You may conclude, for example, that other people do not have a profound conception of what is significant. You may even be contemptuous of the taste or interests of others. On the other hand, you may fully share the sense of significance held by a majority of people. It is not our purpose here to instruct you or anyone else in what is to be regarded as a significant event. We are saying that in considering the question "What is news?" a viewer must always take into account his or her relationship to a larger audience. Television is a mass medium, which means that a television news show is not intended for you alone. It is public communication, and the viewer needs to have some knowledge and opinions about "the public." It is a common complaint of individuals that television news rarely includes stories about some part of the world in which those individuals have some special interest. We know a man, for example, who emigrated from Switzerland thirty years ago. He is an American citizen but retains a lively interest in his native land. "Why," he asked us, "are there never any stories about Switzerland?" "Because," we had to reply, "no one but you and a few others have any interest in Switzerland." "That's too bad," he replied. "Switzerland is an interesting country." We agree. But most Americans have not been in Switzerland, probably believe not much happens in Switzerland, do not have many relatives in Switzerland, and would much rather know about what some English lord has to say about the world's economy than what a Swiss banker thinks. Maybe they are right, maybe not. Judging the public mind is always risky.

And this leads to another difficulty in answering the question "What is news?" Some might agree with us that Liz Taylor's adventures in marriage do not constitute significant events but that they ought to be included in a news show precisely for that reason. Her experiences, they may say, are amusing or diverting, certainly engrossing. In other words, the purpose of news should be to give people pleasure, at least to the extent that it takes their minds off their own troubles. We have heard people say that getting through the day is difficult enough, filled with tension, anxiety, and often disappointment. When they turn on the news, they want relief, not aggravation. It is also said that whether entertaining or not, stories about the lives of celebrities should be included because they are instructive; they reveal a great deal about our society—its mores, values, ideals. Mark Twain once remarked that news is history in its first and best form. The American poet Ezra Pound added an interesting idea to that. He defined literature as news that *stays* news. Among other things, Pound meant that the stuff of literature originates not in stories about the World Bank or an armistice agreement but in those simple, repeatable tales that reflect the pain, confusion, or exaltations that are constant in human experience, and touch us at the deepest levels. For example, consider the death of Michael Landon. Who was Michael Landon to you, or you to Michael Landon that you should have been told so much about him when he died? Here is a possible answer: Michael Landon was rich, decent, handsome, young, and successful. Suddenly, very nearly without warning, he was struck down at the height of his powers and fame. Why? What are we to make of it? Why him? It is like some Old Testament parable; these questions were raised five thousand years ago and we still raise them today. It is the kind of story that *stays* news, and that is why it must be given prominence. Or so some people believe.

What about the kind of news that doesn't stay news, that is neither the stuff of history nor literature—the fires, rapes, and murders that are daily featured on local television news? Who has decided that they are important, and why? One cynical answer is that they are there because viewers take comfort in the realization that *they* have escaped disaster. At least for that day. It doesn't matter who in particular was murdered; the viewer wasn't. We tune in to find out how lucky we are, and go to sleep with the pleasure of knowing that we have survived. A somewhat different answer goes this way: it is the task of the news show to provide a daily accounting of the progress of society. This can be done in many ways, some of them abstract (for example, a report on the state of unemployment), some of them concrete (for example, reports on particularly gruesome murders). These reports, especially those of a concrete nature, are the daily facts from which the audience is expected to draw appropriate conclusions about the question "What kind of society am I a member of?" Studies conducted by Professor George Gerbner and his associates at the University of Pennsylvania have shown that people who are heavy television viewers, including viewers of television news shows, believe their communities are much more dangerous than do light televi-sion viewers. Television news, in other words, tends to frighten people. The question is, "Ought they to be frightened?" which is to ask, "Is the news an accurate portrayal of where we are as a society?" Which leads to another question, "Is it possible for daily news to give such a picture?" Many journalists believe it is possible. Some are skeptical. The early-twentieth-century journalist Lincoln Steffens proved that he could create a "crime wave" anytime he wanted by simply writing about all the crimes that normally occur in a large city during the course of a month. He could also end the crime wave by not writing about them. If crime waves can be "manufactured" by journalists, then how accurate are news shows in depicting the condition of a society? Besides, murders, rapes, and fires (even unemployment figures) are not the only way to assess the progress (or regress) of a society. Why are there so few television stories about symphonies that have been composed, novels written, scientific problems solved, and a thousand other creative acts that occur during the course of a month? Were television news to be filled with these events, we would not be frightened. We would, in fact, be inspired, optimistic, cheerful.

One answer is as follows: these events make poor television news because there is so little to show about them. In the judgment of most editors, people *watch* television. And what they are interested in watching are exciting, intriguing, even exotic pictures. Suppose a scientist has developed a new theory about how to measure with more exactitude the speed with which heavenly objects are moving away from the earth. It is difficult to televise a theory, especially it if involves complex mathematics. You can show the scientist talking about his theory but that would not make for good television and too much of it would drive viewers to other stations. In any case, the news show could only give the scientist twenty seconds of air time because time is an important commodity. Newspapers and magazines sell space, which is not without its limitations for a commercial enterprise. But space can be expanded. Television sells time, and time cannot be expanded. This means that whatever else is neglected, commercials cannot be. Which leads to another possible answer to the question "What is news?" News, we might say, may be history in its first and best form, or the stuff of literature, or a record of the condition of a society, or the expression of the passions of a public, or the prejudices of journalists. It may be all of these things but in its worst form it can also be mainly a "filler," a "come-on" to keep the viewer's attention until the commercials come. Certain producers have learned that by pandering to the audience, by eschewing solid news and replacing it with leering sensationalism, they can subvert the news by presenting a "television commercial show" that is interrupted by news.

All of which leads us to reiterate, first, that there are no simple answers to the question "What is news?" and second, that it is not our purpose to tell you what you ought to believe about the question. The purpose of this chapter is to arouse your interest in thinking *about* the question. Your answers are to be found by knowing what you feel is significant and how your sense of the significant conforms with or departs from that of others, including broadcasters, their bosses, and their audiences. Answers are to be found in your ideas about the purposes of public communication, and in your judgment of the kind of society you live in and wish to live in. We cannot provide answers to these questions. But you also need to know something about the problems, limitations, traditions, motivations, and, yes, even the delusions of the television news industry. That's where we can help you to know how to watch a television news show.

---

### Questions for Consideration

1   Postman and Powers mention "the delusions of the television news industry" as one of the considerations you need to know if you want to understand why television news is the way it is. What do you think they mean by "the delusions of the television news industry"? How might you learn what some of these are?

2   Postman and Powers contend that television news presents so few stories about "symphonies that have been composed, novels written, scientific problems solved, and a thousand other creative acts" because "there is so little to show about them"—that is, because they are not visual enough. Do you agree that this is an important reason? Why or why not? Based on what you can learn from reading about the concerns that go into making a TV news program, what might be other reasons that stories such as these surface so infrequently?

# Chapter 14

# KATHERINE SENDER

## QUEENS FOR A DAY
### *Queer Eye for the Straight Guy* and the Neoliberal Project

**A**LTHOUGH MANY VIEWERS BELIEVE REALITY TV is largely considered to be a twenty-first century programming trend, the origins of the genre can be traced back to the earliest days of television. Yet Katherine Sender, a professor of communication at the Annenberg School for Communication, makes it clear that the new generation of unscripted television is fundamentally different from that of the 1950s and 1960s. In this 2006 article, Sender examines how the former Bravo makeover series *Queer Eye for the Straight Guy* reflects themes about our social, economic, and political systems. Her insights help us see the many ways in which media and the broader culture are interrelated and often converge around the issue of consumption.

"Would *you* like to be *Queen* for a *Day*?" Jack Bailey asked viewers of the popular prototype of television makeover shows, *Queen for a Day*, each week from 1956 to 1964. This show pitted women from the audience against each other in a competition for whose life history was most miserable. Bailey offered the winner not only her requested prize (a housekeeper to take care of seven children during her surgery, educational toys for a son with a brain tumor) but also an avalanche of other gifts (a washer-dryer, clothes, cigarettes, a trip to Hawaii, even a kitten and a year's supply of cat food). But the main prize was being "Queen for a Day": being treated like a person of an entirely different class for "24 hours that a Queen will remember." Fifty years later, Bravo's makeover show, *Queer Eye for the Straight Guy*, invites domestically challenged heterosexual men to adopt gay men's perspective on style, grooming, cuisine, and manners—to be "queens for a day." From early morning until the evening's "reveal" to friends and family, the straight guy is trained to see himself with the same critical eye as his gay hosts; somewhat paradoxically, he is encouraged to adopt gay male consumption habits in order to become a better heterosexual. *Queen for a Day* and *Queer Eye for the Straight Guy* offer contrasting narratives of transformation: Both promise a reversal of fortune, but make very different assumptions about who is considered a worthy recipient of a makeover, who is the appropriate catalyst for transformation, and what this transformation is intended to accomplish. Most critiques of *Queer Eye* have focused on stereotyping, in particular whether the show's hosts, the "Fab Five," are "good for gay visibility." Yet the significance of the show is far broader than this focus on gay representations allows: *Queer Eye for the Straight Guy* puts gay style expertise to work to reform a heterosexual masculinity compatible with neoliberalism.

The appeal of personal transformation emerged in the earliest days of broadcasting. *Queen for a Day* began in 1945 as a weekly radio show; when it moved to television in 1956, it became the top-rated game show (Schwartz, Ryan, & Wostbrock, 1999). On television's first makeover show, host Bailey interviewed five women from the audience about what problems they needed to solve—usually caused by poverty, ill health, absent husbands, and general bad luck. In addition to winning product placement prizes, the reigning Queen was driven in a gold Cadillac from the hairdresser to a Hollywood studio tour, to dinner and a show at a Los Angeles "top establishment." *Queen for a Day*'s Cinderella fantasy proved popular with advertisers, who provided products as prizes, sponsored product mentions throughout the show, and paid for advertising spots during commercial breaks.

Like *Queen for a Day* before it, *Queer Eye* has proven remarkably popular by cable channel standards, winning Bravo record audience ratings. Including goods and services as product placements on the show yielded huge increases in sales (Florian, 2004). The show's U.S. popularity precipitated a slew of franchises across the globe and a U.S. spin-off: *Queer Eye for the Straight Girl*. And if not only imitation but satire is the best form of flattery, *Queer Eye* has received no small measure of compliments: Comedy Central's *Straight Plan for the Gay Man* taught flamboyantly gay guys to pass as straight. An episode of *South Park* showed the Fab Five transforming the town's dumpy menfolk into "metrosexuals": "Our cup runneth over," gasped resident gay character Mr. Garrison.

Predictably, *Queer Eye*'s success was met with religious commentators' umbrage. The Parents Television Council, for example, railed that gay TV images "may be acceptable for that element in our culture that's already earning an advanced degree in Sin Acceptance," but was shocked that NBC would agree to broadcast even a pared-down version of *Queer Eye* (Weinraub & Rutenberg, 2003, p. 133). But criticism also came from gay writers:

> *Queer Eye for the Straight Guy* is execrable—a catalog of homosexual stereotypes, played to a throbbing, techno-disco beat, that also systematically denies its gay stars their complexity and their sexuality. From first scene to last, they trill and fuss, displaying their talents at traditionally effeminate domestic tasks.
>
> (Kelly, 2003)

The show was seen as a form of gay "minstrelsy" (Sawyer, 2003), in which "gay TV has become the spectacle of gay men acting out for the amusement of straight people" (Stasi, 2003). Critics complained that the Fab Five perpetuated stereotypes that gay men "possess fabulous taste and deliver the best catty one-liners at any party" (Sawyer, 2003), shifting the image of the "superficial and sex-driven" to the "superficial and image-obsessed" gay man (Lowry, 2003). And despite the larger-than-life presence of the five gay hosts during the makeover process, some commentators have noted that they are ultimately marginalized within the dominant narrative of heterosexual romance. In a "creepy case of self-ghettoization," the Fab Five "literally have to watch the climax of the show from the margins. . . . They can't even stay to take their bows" (Kelly, 2003). Further, the show reproduces these stereotypes and power dynamics for no greater gain than promoting products, making "*Queer Eye* . . . the single most shameless corporate tramp on television" (Sawyer, 2003).

Well-intentioned as debates about stereotyping might be, they are less interesting than an investigation into the cultural conditions that enable acknowledgement of gay-specific style expertise in the heterosexual male makeover. As Henderson (2003) notes, *Queer Eye* cannot be so easily dismissed by the "commercial sexual repressive hypothesis": the assumption, after Michel Foucault's "repressive hypothesis," that commercial media production *only* represses sexual expression and diversity. *Queer Eye* does not just represent gay men (in stereotypic ways, or not), but uses them in a renewed attempt to solve the "problem" of the male consumer, a problem that has plagued advertisers and media producers at least since the debut of *Esquire* magazine in 1933 (Breazeale, 1994). With few exceptions—classically, electronics, cars, tools, and pornography—white, heterosexual men have proven hard to train as consumers, especially of "intimate" goods usually associated with women. If *Queen for a Day* brought poor and working class women into an idealized fold of middle-class consumerism in the 1950s and 1960s, *Queer Eye* entices heterosexual men into a gay-inflected contemporary sphere of intimate consumption. The social, economic, and cultural changes of the intervening half century help to explain the radical revision of the makeover project: its experts, candidates, and strategies of transformation.

*   *   *

## "All Things Just Keep Getting Better"

*Queer Eye*'s title song "All things just keep getting better" hints at the promise of both *Queen for a Day* and *Queer Eye*: consumption facilitates positive change. Yet the premise and the mode of transformation in each show are very different. *Queen for a Day*'s contestants were poor and working-class women who were victims of circumstance. Their makeovers required very little intervention on their own behalf, beyond telling the tale of woe that was their bid for the prize. The transformation of bad luck to good took place exclusively through the consumption of (placed) products, which were represented as both the vehicle for and evidence of a change in fortune. *Queen for a Day*'s contestants appeared to be passive and grateful beneficiaries of a fleeting moment of middle-class comfort and material security.

*Queer Eye for the Straight Guy* is also a makeover facilitated by placed products. Yet here the lower-middle- and middle-class makeover candidates are exhorted to actively work on themselves, to become self-making men. The show's hosts renovate the straight guy's home and clothing, but the real work must be accomplished by the guy himself. After he is instructed to work on his grooming, domestic skills, and self-esteem he must demonstrate that he has learned his lessons by producing a dinner party or romantic meal under the careful surveillance of the show's hosts. Most episodes' missions refer to heterosexual romance either explicitly ("Operation Eligible Dad") or implicitly ("Dance the Night Away"). In order to fulfill this mission, five gay men "come to your house, belittle your wardrobe and decor, and proceed to turn both into a brighter reflection of the real you" (Goldstein, 2003). The makeover experts are "food and wine connoisseur" Ted Allen, "grooming guru" Kyan Douglas, "design doctor" Thom Filicia, "fashion savant" Carson Kressley, and "culture vulture" Jai Rodriguez. These unabashedly gay hosts bring a camp sensibility and homoerotic flirtation into the lives of the straight guys, whose responses range from gleeful pleasure to overt discomfort. The program suggests that after seeing themselves through borrowed queer eyes, these reformed heterosexuals will have had just enough training in romantic, female-friendly, hygienic living to function effectively in the straight world.

The shift from the *Queen for a Day* contestants' dependence on the beneficence of a television show to the *Queer Eye* candidates' active involvement in their personal transformation reflects profound social and cultural changes in the second half of the twentieth century as a result of shifts towards more "flexible" forms of capitalism (Andrejevic, 2004). In both the United States and Western Europe industrial manufacturing gave way to the digital age. This necessitated much greater adaptability to the demands of consumers, a knowledge economy for elite workers, a service economy for unskilled labor, the internationalization of manual labor, and a lack of job security for everyone. This economic phase demands its ideological helpmeet: neoliberalism. Liberalism here is not a "doctrine or a practice of government" (liberalism versus conservatism) but critique of government itself in order to govern *less*, to govern "at a distance" (Barry, Osborne, & Rose, 1996, p. 8). Welfare liberalism characterized mid-twentieth century public policy in the U.K. and much of Europe, and (with a less socialist philosophy) the New Deal of the 1930s through the Great Society of the 1960s in the U.S. Welfare liberalism involved greater government intervention in a range of activities hitherto believed to be the domain of private industry (such as energy production) and an expansion of programs and reforms that aimed to provide a social safety net. However, welfare liberalism came under attack from critics both on the left, who considered its social programs too interventionist in citizens' lives, and on the right, who argued that it posed too great an economic burden on both taxpayers and industry, and hindered entrepreneurial initiative (Rose, 1996).

The dismantling of welfare-oriented provisions in the U.K. and in the U.S. (however insipid these were, even at their height) that began in the 1980s marks a new version of liberal philosophy: neoliberalism. This involves shifts from authoritarian government to individual responsibility; from injunction to expert advice; and from centralized government to quasi-governmental agencies and media, including television, as sources of information, evaluation, and reproach. Proponents of neoliberalism framed welfare liberalism as burdening citizens with a dependency on and obligations to the state, contrasting this burden with the benefits of choice—especially consumer choice—and individual fulfillment.

\*     \*     \*

*Queer Eye*, then, emerged as part of a larger response to the cultural needs and economic opportunities of flexible capitalism. "With social welfare programs all but dismantled, and with lifelong marriage and lifelong professions increasingly anachronistic, it is no longer sufficient to be married or employed; rather it is imperative that one remains marriagable and employable" (McGee, 2005; p. 12). The cultivation of style and intimate relationships has traditionally been seen as facilitating upward social mobility more for women than for men, who are assumed to climb the social ladder through industry alone. Whereas *Queen for a Day* contestants were impoverished, unlucky women, *Queer Eye* candidates are middle class, incompetent, immature men.

*Queen for a Day*'s paternalistic, apparently heterosexual male host awarded material prizes; *Queer Eye*'s makeover team provides a specifically gay expertise. *Queen for a Day* overwhelmed its winners with a fleeting moment of material abundance; *Queer Eye* trains its candidates in a life of responsible and fulfilling citizenship through consumption. *Queer Eye* thus radically departs from the traditions of gendered self-improvement through its choice of experts, its candidates, and the project the show is designed to accomplish.

## The Experts

Neoliberalism has been characterized as involving a shift from injunction to advice, where the authority hitherto exercised over citizens by governmental agencies "gives way to the private counsellor, the self-help manual and the telephone helpline, as practices whereby each individual binds themselves to expert advice as a matter of their own freedom" (Rose, 1996, p. 58). The Fab Five's expertise comes in part from their work backgrounds. For example, fashion advisor Carson Kressley formerly worked for Polo Ralph Lauren, and cooking expert Ted Allen was a food writer for *Esquire* magazine (Y. Cole, 2003). Yet these career trajectories are less important in constructing the Fab Five's authority as style experts than the fact that they are openly and recognizably gay—in their speech and behavior, but most especially in their taste. *Queer Eye* thus makes explicit the long association between gay men and the design, fashion, and grooming industries. In one episode Carson admires a former marine's ceremonial garb, asking, "Who says there are no gays in the military? *Someone* designed this uniform."

*Queer Eye*'s open recognition of gay style expertise reflects, first, the increasing visibility of gay and lesbian characters on U.S. television, and especially in reality television shows. Gross (2005) observes:

> Whereas, as recently as the early 1990s, the inclusion of a gay character would typically be the focus of some dramatic "problem" to be resolved, today, particularly for programs that aim at coveted younger viewers, it seems that the presence of gay people is a necessary guarantor of realism.
>
> (p. 520)

Second, *Queer Eye* capitalizes on the development of the gay market since the 1970s (Sender, 2004). The show deploys gay men's longstanding reputation as affluent and as having great taste in order to court both gay consumers and heterosexuals who want to be associated with the positive attributes of the gay market.

Although all of *Queer Eye*'s heterosexual candidates welcome their gay hosts' consumer expertise, some are nonetheless ambivalent about adopting what they perceive to be gay tastes, an ambivalence that provides much of the show's frisson. In one episode, food expert Ted Allen instructs Staten Island cop John Verdi how to make an Italian torta for a picnic with his girlfriend. After Ted describes a torta as "like a quiche," John appears to recoil. When his mother makes quiche he won't eat it. Evoking, if unintentionally, the 1980s satirical guide to manhood, "Real Men Don't Eat Quiche" (Feirstein, 1982), the show suggests that for John to eat—let alone cook—quiche would intolerably compromise his masculinity. Ted reassures John that "it's not a quiche, it's an Italian quiche, a manly quiche . . . a quiche with balls." Here Ted frames the feminized dish within a hypermasculine version of John's ethnic identity to redeem the quiche from effeminacy.

John's masculinity is bolstered not only by his Italianness but by his working class background. Yet it is precisely this class position that compromises the potential for the makeover; according to the hosts, he needs to "elevate himself" to be a match for his "impossibly hot" girlfriend. Arguing that makeover shows in general dramatize "class mobility through proper consumption," Gamson (2005) points out that in *Queer Eye* this class mobility is assured through the association with gay upper-class status: "[I]f you become 'gayer,' you will become 'classier'" (p. 14). Shaun Cole, fashion historian, traces the link between the upper classes, aestheticism, and same-sex passion back to Oscar Wilde (S. Cole, 2000). Wealthy men were freer than working class men to be publicly gay in the nineteenth and early twentieth centuries, so homosexuality and affluence are associated. More recently, this association has been consolidated by inaccurate market research data that over-represent affluent gay respondents (Badgett, 1998).

*Queer Eye* is a show less about class privilege, however, than class mobility. None of the Fab Five comes from a privileged family background; rather, the hosts elevated themselves from modest beginnings by virtue of their gay tastes, and can instruct heterosexual men in those tastes to effect a similar class trajectory. Nowhere is this class instruction more apparent than in the ubiquitous advice to "jhooz"—the show's trademark neologism. According to the *Queer Eye* book, jhoozing "means taking something and tweaking it, fluffing it, nudging or finessing it to be a little more fabulous and fun" (Allen et al., 2004, p. 11). But, jhoozing has a serious side. Fussell (1983/1992) notes:

> [L]aboring to present yourself as scrupulously clean and neat suggests that you're worried about status slippage and that you care terribly what your audience thinks, both low [class] signs. The perfect shirt collar, the too neatly tied necktie knot, the anxious overattention to dry cleaning— all betray the wimp.
>
> (p. 58)

As part of this unstudied look, jhoozing protects *Queer Eye*'s lower-middle- and middle-class candidates from displaying their class position and aspirations toward upward mobility.

In contrast to the hosts' nuanced instruction in class signifiers, *Queer Eye*'s handling of racial difference seems awkward. Three men of color have appeared on the Fab Five team: James Hannaham, an African American who appeared only in the pilot episode; Blair Boone, also African American, who was replaced after two episodes; and Jai Rodriguez, a Latino who replaced Boone. So prevalent is the value of multiculturalism within GLBT politics that the show was duty bound to cast at least one person of color as a host, yet Hannaham, Boone, and Rodriguez have all been cast as the "culture" expert. Advising the makeover candidates on matters of culture is arguably the most difficult of all the Fab Five's areas of expertise: "The other guys on the show have it easy," Rodriguez complains, whereas his job is complicated: "You can fix a guy's hair and tell him what clothes will enhance his physique, but how do you know what's happening inside? I've got to burrow into our straight guy's skull and figure out where his tastes could use some improving" (Allen et al., 2004, p. 209). The culture expert's primary function seems to be buying new CDs to replace the taste-deficient straight guy's Billy Joel collection, or dispensing tickets to the opera or Broadway shows. Muños (2005) asserts that *Queer Eye* "assigns queers of color the job of being inane culture mavens, while the real economic work is put into the able hands of the white gays, who shop" (p. 102). The role of the culture expert is marginalized because it is amorphous, hard to define, and arguably impossible to accomplish successfully.

The Fab Five affirm the ethnic backgrounds of white candidates in food, mostly, but also in decor, clothes, and family relationships. Yet Black and Latino candidates are instructed to follow predominantly white norms. In one episode, the hosts admire Jamaican American Rob Munroe's dreadlocks but mock his clothes. Commenting that a dashiki, lovingly stored in a dry cleaner's bag, "looks like a bridesmaid's dress from the 1970s," Carson observes, "The point is that you've got some great ethnic pieces that I want to work into an everyday wardrobe." Jai concurs: "He's got this cool cultural sensibility, but there's too much of it all at the same time." Too much "cultural sens-ibility" apparently means that this sensibility is too specifically "ethnic." Rob's "ethnic pieces" survive Carson's fashion makeover only in some pieces of mud cloth glued into a belt buckle and sewn into a jacket yoke.

In matters of interior decor, Rob's taste is too specifically Jamaican. While buying furniture, Thom tells Rob:

> A lot of this stuff [in the store], unlike your house, is from all over. There are things from Sri Lanka, the Philippines, Africa, all mixed in. . . . I want to bring together your photography, your love of ethnic furniture, and your respect for culture. I don't want you to get trapped in one area.

The anxiety about being "too ethnic" or "too Jamaican" does not extend to food, however. Ted teaches Rob to make a spicy Caribbean fish stew to lubricate the first meeting between his beloved godmother and his new girlfriend. The show's disavowal of Rob's "ethnic" tastes in decor and dress, compared with its ready adoption of Caribbean cuisine, makes sense within the show's two rationales: to sell tastes and things to audiences, and to remake the candidate into a more "presentable" straight guy. Whereas the audience may enjoy experimenting with "ethnic" food as a fleeting pleasure, and can thus be sold the fish stew recipe, they are less likely to adopt Rob's distinctively Afrocentric style in dress and decor. Such a racially marked style implies a retrograde identification with places and cultures past, hindering the progressive impulse towards the implicitly white cultural norms of self-improvement that the show demands.

*Queer Eye*'s radical departure from the norms of the makeover genre was to deploy gay men's skills, cultivated through decades of employment in the style trades, in making over straight men. The hosts' class-specific and largely white expertise affirms ethnic differences among white candidates but is less respectful of the cultural tastes of people of color. However, because the potency of the Fab Five's expertise comes from the long-standing association between gayness and high culture, affluence, and upper-middle-class taste, *Queer Eye* represents a significant cultural shift in the relations between experts and subjects in need of reform. After a long history in which gayness was considered medically and criminally pathological, here gay sexuality is not the problem that needs advice and adjustment. On the contrary, the Fab Five's gay taste and consumer expertise is precisely what qualifies them as makeover experts. The problem is that heterosexual masculinity no longer equips straight guys to court successfully.

## The Candidates

*Queen for a Day*'s makeover candidates epitomized the welfare liberal subject: impoverished women whose bad luck and poor choices thrust them on the mercy not of the state but of a television show. *Queer Eye* presents very different makeover candidates: men, usually young and lower-middle class, who have failed to produce an adult self able to function in the world of heterosexual romance. In neoliberalism, subjects' "self-responsibility and self-fulfilling aspirations have been deformed by the dependency culture, [their] efforts at self-advancement have been frustrated for so long that they suffer from 'learned helplessness,' [and their] self-esteem has been destroyed" (Rose, 1996, p. 59). They do not need welfare handouts but "a whole array of programmes for their ethical reconstruction as active citizens" (p. 60). The subject in welfare liberalism is implicitly feminine, either women like those on *Queen for a Day*, or emasculated men dependent on the "nanny" state and for whom reform depends on a virile claiming of a self-authoring life.

Much of the Fab Five's task involves identifying the makeover candidate's domestic shortcomings. The candidates' apartments are so messy or dirty that they are too embarrassed to invite dates over. The Fab Five gleefully point out "DNA" on the sheets, pull pornography from under the couch, observe bathtub grime thick enough to write a name in. When Thom declares, "This is all the culture you have in your home, right here," he is referring to mold on a shower curtain. The candidates' limitations are also manifested in their appearance. Their clothes are scruffy, cheap, ill-fitting, or old-fashioned; their skin needs cleansing, exfoliating, and moisturizing; they have back hair, nose hair, and monobrows. Moreover, their romantic skills need buffing up. One straight guy is blamed for the "monogamy decline" after three years of living with his girlfriend; another hasn't remembered his wife's birthday in years.

The candidates' domestic and romantic shortcomings are diagnosed as largely a result of inadequate consumption. This leads to endless product placement sequences in which the hosts teach the usually baffled candidate not only what to buy, but how to use this dazzling array of new products. *Queer Eye*'s training in correct consumption is ideally suited for the endless expansion of markets. As one journalist observed, straight men's "lack of sophistication may frustrate women and mystify gay men, but it surely drives the style industry nuts. We just don't primp, preen, moisturize or accessorize enough to open up new markets or boost bottom lines" (Shott, 2003).

What is striking here is that it is heterosexual *men* who need training. The plethora of fashion, grooming, domestic, and self-help advice available to women in print and electronic media demonstrates how extensively women have been held responsible both for relationship maintenance and for consumption. *Queer Eye* is notable because it turns this set of expectations onto men. Goldstein (2003) argues that the show only makes sense because of "the newfound power of the female gaze. Now, it's not just women who dress to please; everyone is subject to objectification." For some critics, the culprit of this recent demand that men pay attention to themselves is feminism, which shifted gender roles and, consequently, standards of attractiveness. "Blame the feminists, or the idea that women don't need men anymore. Oh, they still want them, but the days when a woman's survival was intrinsically wrapped up in a man's attentions are long gone" (McQuaid, 2003, p. 19). McQuaid's is a particularly bitter interpretation of the rise of independent, postfeminist women characterized in *Sex and the City*, for example, who show that women no longer need men economically (in the early seasons, at least, they all had well-paying jobs), socially (they have each other), or sexually (they have the Rabbit vibrator). Many *Queer Eye* episodes acknowledge the threat of newly independent women to the candidates' romantic marketability: the Fab Five must turn John Barge-man, who has no specific career, from "Mr. Right Now" to "Mr. Right" by elevating him to his MBA student girlfriend's "level of sophistication."

*Queer Eye*'s gay hosts offer their expertise not only for the heterosexual male candidates but for the benefit of the women who love them. The Fab Five's role as *women*'s best friends reflects long-standing associations between gay men and straight women, for whom gay men are better "boyfriends" than their heterosexual counterparts can ever be (Bordo, 1999). The Fab Five bond with the straight women directly— taking them shopping and confiding that "your boyfriend's working my last gay nerve." Strikingly, however, the Fab Five accomplish what the girlfriends cannot: "A funda-mental premise of the show is that women cannot teach straight guys the things they need to know in order to be with women. . . . It is as crucial that the Fab Five are gay *men* as that they are *gay* men" (Torres, 2005, p. 96). Coming from women, this make-over advice would be nagging; from the Fab Five it is brotherly counsel.

*Queer Eye* addresses the challenges the new gender economy poses to heterosexual men, whose romantic prospects are no longer as assured as they had hitherto imagined. This subject is the ideal makeover candidate, since he provides the rationale for a television show whose content is almost entirely concerned with how to consume more products, in a genre that relies on product placement to sell goods to viewers. But underlying this training in consumption is a more fundamental project: reworking straight guys into more effectively self-monitoring citizens.

## The Project

While *Queer Eye*'s project is ostensibly to improve basic life skills—how to shop, cook, dress, make a woman feel loved—the show simultaneously appeals to an ethics of self-transformation that is bound up with the production of an adult, responsible, worker-citizen. The show promotes technologies of the self with which candidates can engineer better, more fulfilling lives, including "responsibilization" (Burchell, 1996, p. 29) and the internalization of surveillance. Like other makeover shows, *Queer Eye* embodies the neoliberal imperative to cultivate an autonomously calibrating self within a framework that privileges consumer choice over other modes of citizenship.

Inculcating maturity is a fundamental feature of *Queer Eye*'s makeovers. Looking at John Verdi's list of "Things to Do," Thom finds a series of goals: "Lose belly for summer," "Pay off debt," and, contradictorily, "Buy a motorcycle." Thom grabs the pen and writes at the top of the list: "GROW UP." The straight guys' immaturity comprom-ises their prospects as romantic partners. Philly Rojas wants to reunite with his ex-wife Laurie, who says, "If he wants me to take him more seriously, he needs to get his act together." The hosts frequently take the candidates to task for being dependent on mothers or girlfriends: George Katsigiannis lives in the same apartment building as his mother, who decorated his apartment and cooks for both of them. Other episodes blame a more general failure to mature on bad mothering. After viewers watch a catalog of the Bravo twins' truly revolting personal hygiene violations, their mother laments, "What can I say? I've failed as a mother." Inadequate tutelage by mothers or an inability or unwillingness to take responsibility must be corrected in order to produce mature boyfriends, husbands, and fathers.

The Fab Five's role sometimes is to reveal the candidate's real self. One episode's mission is to "Uncover the Real Richard": Richard Miller's wife and children have never seen his bald head. After removing his toupee, Ted concludes that Richard "looks like himself only better." All he needs to do now is to develop confidence as a bald man. *Queer Eye* thus endorses neoliberalism's therapeutic ethos, in which being authentic is a self-affirming accomplishment. But appeals to realness also signal that the makeover is intended to reveal the straight guy's "real self," which is significantly not a "gay self." The show's producers emphasize that what the Fab Five accomplish are not make*overs* but "make-*betters*" (Fonseca, 2003, p. 24). The Fab Five reassure their audience:

> A little hair gel and some pants that fit aren't going to set off anybody's gaydar, people. Women know who's gay and who isn't, and gay men *definitely* know. If tomorrow morning you shave correctly and wear a shirt that's actually your size, gay men aren't all of a sudden going to start palming your ass on the sidewalks.
>
> (Allen et al., 2004, p. 12)

*Queer Eye*'s dominant technology for producing this real, mature self is surveillance, a fundamental characteristic of reality TV. Technological developments in camera and audio equipment allow the hosts, producers, and audiences to observe the makeover candidate's most intimate gestures. But reality television also fosters an internalized mode of surveillance: *Queer Eye* exhorts participants to adopt the gaze of educators, trainers, and other experts. What makes these figures of surveillance so effective is shame: "to feel shame is to feel *seen* in a painfully diminished sense" (Kaufman, 1989, p. 17). Whereas guilt comes from feeling bad about what one has *done*, resulting in anxiety about punishment for a specific transgression, shame is feeling bad about who one *is*, with an attendant anxiety about rejection as a whole person. Makeover shows mobilize shame not only to exhort participants to modify their behavior but to recalibrate their selves according to new rules of subjecthood. Through both the camera's monitoring gaze and the scrutiny of the Fab Five, participants learn to see themselves as strange—as lacking in shared cultural mores. And whereas in infancy shame is a relational response to the reactions of a caregiver (anger, withdrawal), maturing children learn to internalize the monitoring gaze to reduce the risk of further shame. *Queer Eye*'s candidates must "grow up" by internalizing the shaming gaze of childhood.

Felski (2000) considers shame in class terms. She observes that the lower middle classes, especially, have been portrayed as "driven by the fear of shame, tortured by a constant struggle to keep up appearances on a low income" (p. 37). She adds that "the opportunities for experiencing shame increase dramatically with geographic and social mobility, which provide an infinite array of chances for failure, for betraying by word or gesture that one does not belong in one's new environment" (p. 43). *Queer Eye* mobilizes class shame in order to prompt upward class mobility, while also helping candidates accommodate that mobility. If neoliberalism involves both self-monitoring and increased adaptability in new economic and geographical circumstances, shame could be seen as the quintessential neoliberal affect, offering a highly efficient means to govern at a distance.

Significantly, the show's monitoring eye is a queer one. In the opening credit sequence the camera ultimately penetrates Carson's right eye; through this lens the audience will see as Carson, the quintessential queer, will see. The queer eye, however, has an ambiguous status in the narrative of the show. Because of the long association between gay men and the style trades, the queer eye is the expert eye, coolly assessing fashion violations and bad taste. But the queer eye is also the marginalized eye. Having done their work, the Fab Five are ejected from the reveal, the site of heterosexual rebonding, only to observe the fruits of their labor by video screen. Rollins' (1985) ethnography of black women domestics shows that marginalized social positions allow access to the intimate habitus of the powerful, affording a freedom to observe from an invisible position. *Queer Eye* builds this contradiction into the very structure of the show: the homosexual gaze, marginalized both historically and within the narrative of the show, is nevertheless granted access to the heterosexual family's private sphere. Unlike that of domestics, however, this homosexual gaze is granted institutional authority by the show's marketing and media apparatus.

If shame is the show's stick, improved self-esteem is the carrot. "Feeling better about yourself" is the reward for developing an internalized, self-monitoring gaze. The "self-esteem movement," fashionable especially in the 1980s, blamed a range of social problems on subjects' lack of self-esteem, not on poverty, bad housing, or unemployment (Cruikshank, 1996). *Queer Eye* represents low self-esteem not as an understandable response to depressing life circumstances but as a moral failing. En route to meet Philly Rojas, the Fab Five discuss how Philly tore a ligament in his leg, stopped working out, and was dumped by his wife. One host comments, "It sounds like it affected his self-esteem," to which another responds, "We are going to crash his pity party." In another episode, perhaps one of the most painful of the first season, Alan Corey needs a makeover because he's pathologically cheap: he buys his clothes at thrift stores and retrieves furniture from the street on trash day. The Fab Five make him over with products compatible with his thrifty sensibility. The one luxury is a beautiful vintage cocktail set. Left to prepare for the arrival of his parents, his girlfriend, and her parents, Alan is a disaster: panicking and bathed in sweat, the simple prosciutto and parmesan canapés Ted taught him to make seem impossibly complicated. The climax comes when he knocks the cocktail set to the floor, precipitating a self-hating diatribe as he sweeps up the glass: "That was the coolest thing in the world . . . That's why I don't buy nice things. 'Alan, don't buy nice things. You will break them.'" The root of Alan's cheapness is revealed: not a pragmatic thriftiness but a critical parental voice that tells him he does not deserve nice things. This is one of the few episodes that the hosts considered a failure, given Alan's inability to recalibrate his low self-esteem.

In *Queer Eye* the crisis of masculinity is framed not in terms of financial, professional, or relational pressures on men, but as a failure to grow up, to see the self as others do, and to have positive self-regard. Like other makeover shows, *Queer Eye* articulates templates of adult, responsible, self-realized subjecthood to consumer choice as the quintessential model for cultural participation. The show teaches straight guys to be better consumers and more girl-friendly boyfriends—in short, to be metrosexuals. Coined by British journalist Mark Simpson (1994), "metrosexual" described a male "commodity fetishist, a collector of fantasies about the male sold to him by advertising" (p. 22). Not necessarily gay or straight, the metrosexual was "the single man living in the metropolis, and taking himself as his own love object." By the time the term became articulated with *Queer Eye*, however, "metrosexual" had been straightened out, adopted by marketers and lost some of its bite. One journalist described the metrosexual as "a straight guy who loves to shop, cook, primp and preen. . . . He exfoliates and emulsifies. He does yoga and cardio. He just won't do 'that' " (Morris, 2003). Uses of the term tend to emphasize a feminized consumption while distancing heterosexual men from gay sex. From its origins as an ironic term to describe any male narcissistic consumer, "metrosexual" has since become a more positive description of a sensitive, girl- and gay-friendly straight man, a description embraced by marketers oblivious to its critical origins.

## The Metrosexual Man in the New Labor Economy

*Queer Eye* presents the male makeover as a privilege: in an increasingly progressive sexual environment, men are finally free to explore their "inner girlie guy" (Sitt, 2003, p. C1). What is underplayed, however, is the work involved in this transformation. Andrejevic (2004) has discussed "the work of being watched" on reality shows from two perspectives. First, participants labor for usually less than the minimum wage for media corporations, which can make huge profits on this cheap programming. The makeover candidates on *Queer Eye* are not paid but do receive significant compensation in product placement goods. The Fab Five are paid, but much less than writers and actors on fictional shows (they earned $3,000 per episode in the first season). The second form of labor is performed by audiences. As with all commercial media, when people watch reality shows they are being sold as a product to advertisers; profit accrues to media companies when they can sell this audience for more than the cost of the programming. Audiences thus also work when they watch advertising and product placements.

While focusing on the labor of working for reality television, however, most critics have not addressed how makeover shows, especially, serve the labor economy beyond the television environment. *Queer Eye* trains participants to be better workers, endorsing "the spread of self-fashioning as a requirement of personal and professional achievement through the US middle-class labor force" (Miller, 2005, p. 112). Many episodes involve direct interventions in the candidates' professional lives. Philly Rojas, for example, has been in the same position at his graphic design company for four years, and his colleagues won't show clients around the office because they think he looks unprofessional. Kyan observes, "It sounds like he's not taking his professional life very seriously." The Fab Five get to work: Carson aims for a "dressed up hip hop [look] so you still look cool . . . but also so you are sophisticated at work so people give you credit." Ted teaches Philly the finer points of selecting wine and recommending dishes, not for pleasure but for professional development: "A great deal of business in American culture is done over dinner tables, and I think this should be part of your bag of tricks." These efforts are rewarded at a dinner party, where Philly's boss enthuses, "I think the sky's the limit as far as your career [goes]—I think you see it. I'm glad you are focused; it's great to see you confident." What is at stake here, then, is not Philly's competence as a graphic designer, which is never in question, but his self-presentation as someone who "takes his professional life seriously."

Embedded in *Queer Eye*'s preoccupations with heterosexual romance is a sustained narrative about class mobility in an increasingly uncertain world of work.

Whereas in industrial capitalism work was seen as necessarily alienating for most people, now workers (or, at least, skilled workers) are expected to invest themselves in their jobs (Gee, 1996). Success in this "new work order" depends less on the kinds of skills workers have than on how adeptly they have absorbed a work ethic attentive to self-presentation and self-management. Miller (2005) observes that between the early 1970s and the late 1990s, far greater proportions of men reported dissatisfaction with their appearance, in part because "the middle-class US labor market now sees wage discrimination by beauty among men as well as among women, and major corporations frequently require executives to tailor their body shapes to the company ethos" (p. 113). The metrosexual appears at a particularly uncertain moment for heterosexual men, not only in relation to women, but also as employees.

Faludi (1999) argues that increased numbers of women in the labor force precipitated a "crisis of masculinity" for men on two fronts: greater competition with women for jobs, and decreased family stability as women's economic independence grew. She notes, however, that the narrowing of the pay gap between women and men in the past 30 years "reflected not an improvement in women's wages but a decline in men's real earnings" (p. 263). To blame the crisis of masculinity on women and on feminism overlooks the extent to which flexible capitalism both allowed and demanded gender shifts in the workforce. *Queer Eye*'s emphasis on a *gender* crisis, which requires the Fab Five's intervention into the romantic lives of the show's straight guys, effaces the extent to which the straight guys also face a *class* crisis caused by lower annual earnings.

*Queer Eye*'s emphasis on heterosexual romance is not independent of neoliberalism's requirement to reshape the male labor force, but inherent to it. Coupled relationships privatize "the costs of social reproduction, along with the care of human dependency needs, through personal responsibility exercised in the family and civil society—thus shifting costs from state agencies to individuals and households" (Duggan, 2003, p. 14). Insofar as flexible capitalism has helped destabilize the nuclear family in the past thirty years, its survival simultaneously depends upon the family as a form of privatized welfare in the post-welfare era.

The de-racing of the men of color in the show—making Jamaican American Rob Monroe "less ethnic," Puerto Rican Philly Rojas "less hip hop"—may be a response to the even more precarious labor conditions faced by Black and Lation men than by white, lower-middle-class men. In a labor economy where the unemployment rate for African Americans is more than double the rate for Caucasians, racial signifiers may be dangerously associated with not "fitting" in the workplace.[1] If white men have to grow up and take responsibility in order to be both employable and good marriage material, men of color must additionally temper their ethnic style.

Much of the criticism leveled at *Queer Eye* focused on its gay male hosts and the perpetuation of gay stereotypes, overlooking the extent to which the show's joke is on its makeover candidates: now straight white guys have to work harder, in the ways women and gay men have had to work, in order to get and keep their mate, their job, their class position. Men of color must work harder still. The turn of the twenty-first century is not the first time that men have faced the crisis of authority that comes from being unable to provide for a family, but whereas during the Great Depression of the 1930s economic hardship was seen as resulting from forces beyond men's control, the current neoliberal ethos frames such hardship as a personal failing. And if it is a personal failing, it is also a personal responsibility to fix it, through the ministrations of experts such as *Queer Eye*'s Fab Five.

## The Camp Eye

*Queer Eye*, then, looks like a project for heterosexual dupes. But *Queer Eye* seems to exploit gay men too, as they make straight guys more marriageable at a time when same-sex marriage is not a constitutional right in the U.S., make them more employable when GLBT people have no federal employment protection, and expand consumer markets in the service of large corporations that may or may not care about their GLBT employees and consumers. Yet *Queer Eye*'s queerness cannot be so easily folded into the grinding functionalism of a neoliberal analysis. As Henderson (2003) notes, the show's queer sensibility cannot be subsumed into a critique that emphasizes only exploitation and marginalization. The irony is that the queer eye that is the show's source of expertise is also the camp eye that undermines values fundamental to its project: class aspiration, gender conformity, and heteronormativity. *Queer Eye*'s signature campness performs in excess of its pedagogical purpose, which helps to account both for its delightful effervescence and its progressive politics.

Richard Dyer defines camp less as a property of people, objects, or texts, than as a "way of looking at things" (Dyer, 2002, p. 52). Nothing in the straight guys' homes is protected from camp deconstruction: Kyan dons chintz curtains as a robe and turban to offer "mystic" advice on poker night; Carson takes pink feathers from a fly fisherman to decorate a tiara. Camp lifts the lid off bourgeois respectability, airing the dirty laundry. As John Verdi feeds his girlfriend chocolate sauce from his finger, Carson comments, "In our community that's frowned upon, when you have a big brown wad. . . . Get rid of that." And if the Fab Five bring to light the unseemly underside of bourgeois respectability, they also ridicule its pretensions. Thom devises a game in Jeff Toale's house that involves the family finding as many dried flower arrangements as they can in the shortest possible time. The pleasure in revealing the distance between the ideal and the real is not only afforded to the hosts but to *Queer Eye*'s editor, too. During a lesson on fake tanning, the editor places the text, "AIR BRUSH TAN: emphasizes muscle definition" over the straight guy's flabby belly.

The camp eye also sees that "roles, and, in particular, sex roles, are superficial—a matter of style" (Babuscio, 1984, p. 44). In a hilarious moment of butch drag, Carson takes a waxing strip, covered with a candidate's copious back hair, and tucks it into his shirt to fashion a hairy chest. The show is also replete with moments that deconstruct the boundary between the apparently heterosexual and the possibly gay. Steven Smith asks whether the shoes he is trying on will "make me gay." As Carson leans around him to help him with the shoes he retorts, "No, but this will," his pelvis in close proximity to Steven's ass. Contrary to an essentialized view of gender and sexuality, *Queer Eye* flirts with such cut and dried distinctions in ways that both the straight guys (for the most part) and the Fab Five seem to enjoy.

Camp also tempers the sober neoliberal emphasis on becoming a responsible adult. The Fab Five often present themselves as playful and childlike, disrupting domestic order, trying on clothes, and playing with kids' toys. Camp distinguishes the straight guys' pathetic immaturity from the Fab Five's joyous playfulness. As Sontag (1966) writes, "Camp is playful, anti-serious. More precisely, Camp involves a new, more complex relation to 'the serious.' One can be serious about the frivolous, frivolous about the serious" (p. 288). The Fab Five are not immature, even if they are at times childlike, because they know the "real adult" rules and when to apply them. "Rebuilding a better straight man" is important labor indeed; the straight guys' love lives and careers depend upon it. But delivering training in playful ways is precisely what makes the training bearable and the show watchable. The Fab Five are playful in the serious task of the makeover, but they are also serious about what is conventionally held to be frivolous. Engaging in the frivolous is now a necessity, not only for women and queers, but for straight men too.

The camp eye thus dislocates the straight guy's usual perspective, forcing him to see himself from a different point of view. The hosts capitalize on this shift in order to improve relations between straight and gay men. Co-producer David Collins has remarked: "Gay guys, straight guys, they may do things a little different in the bedroom, but in the end, they're just guys. They just want to feel good about themselves, and confident" (Morago, 2003). Importantly, the realm of consumption is situated in the show as the ideal place to enact this new kind of male bonding. Kyan and Andrew Lane discuss the possibilities of gay–straight male friendship while having their nails done. Kyan assures Andrew: "It's fun—building bridges, one manicure at a time." By "building bridges" between heterosexual and gay men through new forms of consumption, the Fab Five reverse the homophobic hostilities of the schoolyard—not for their own benefit, but because straight men need them to.

*Queer Eye* promotes a very different personal transformation from the *Queen for a Day* model. The earlier makeover show features the paternalistic attentions of a heterosexual male host, prizes, overwhelmed women, the transitory nature of the promotion to "queen," and the overarching frame of luck (bad and good). In contrast, *Queer Eye*'s Fab Five offer brotherly advice and placed products to help incompetent heterosexual men become "entrepreneurs of themselves" (Rose, 1990, p. 230). Through a lifetime of self-monitoring, self-improvement, and consumption, the straight guys produce themselves as viable commodities on the labor and marriage markets. Yet along with the constitution of better boyfriends, better consumers, and better workers, the show promotes changing ideas about gender and sexuality, and especially about relations between gay and straight men, that cannot be collapsed into a functionalist neoliberal critique. *Queer Eye* nevertheless leaves assumptions about upward class mobility and the benefits of consumption firmly in place. The show suggests that the appropriate place to negotiate gender and sexual politics is the commercial realm, leaving its progressive message vulnerable to the vagaries of audience ratings and marketers' patronage. The popularity of *Queer Eye* waned in the fall of 2004, with its ratings dropping by 40 percent compared with 2003 (Wallenstein, 2004). Bravo's gay programming may prove fragile in a commercial television marketplace in which sizable and sellable audiences are the nonnegotiable bottom line. *Queer Eye* asserts that to be a queen for a day offers training for a lifetime of fulfilling self-surveillance and shopping, but the moment for a progressive politics that this neoliberal project affords might be fleeting indeed.

## Questions for Consideration

1   Do you agree with Sender that we are living in a "neoliberal moment"? Why or why not?
2   Do you think that television game shows such as *The Price is Right* are part of what Sender calls the neoliberal project? Why or why not?

## Note

1.   In 2004, 11.1% of the African American labor force was unemployed, compared with 4.8% of the Caucasian labor force (United States Department of Labor, 2004).

## References

Allen, T., Douglas, K., Filicia, T., Kressley, C., & Rodriguez, J. (2004). *Queer eye for the straight guy: The Fab 5's guide to looking better, cooking better, dressing better, behaving better, and living better*. New York: Clarkson Potter.

Andrejevic, M. (2004). *Reality TV: The work of being watched*. New York: Rowman & Littlefield.

Babuscio, J. (1984). Camp and the gay sensibility. In R. Dyer (Ed.), *Gays and film* (pp. 40–57). New York: Zoetrope.

Badgett, M. V. L. (1998). *Income inflation: The myth of affluence among gay, lesbian, and bisexual Americans*. New York/Amherst MA: The Policy Institute of the National Gay and Lesbian Task Force and the Institute for Gay and Lesbian Strategic Studies.

Barry, A., Osborne, T., & Rose, N. (Eds.). (1996). *Foucault and political reason: Liberalism, neo-liberalism and rationalities of government*. Chicago: University of Chicago Press.

Bordo, S. (1999). *The male body: A new look at men in public and in private*. New York: Farrar, Strauss and Giroux.

Breazeale, K. (1994). In spite of women: Esquire magazine and the construction of the male consumer. *Signs, 20*(1), 1–22.

Burchell, G. (1996). Liberal government and techniques of the self. In A. Barry, T. Osborne, & N. Rose (Eds.), *Foucault and political reason: Liberalism, neo-liberalism and rationalities of government* (pp. 19–35). Chicago: University of Chicago Press.

Cole, S. (2000). *Don we now our gay apparel: Gay men's dress in the twentieth century*. New York: Berg.

Cole, Y. (2003). *"Queer eye for the straight guy": Americans love to watch them but don't want them to marry*. Retrieved September 5, 2003, from http://www.diversityinc.com

Cruikshank, B. (1996). Revolutions within: Self-government and self-esteem. In A. Barry, T. Osborne, & N. Rose (Eds.), *Foucault and political reason: Liberalism, neo-liberalism and rationalities of government* (pp. 231–251). Chicago: University of Chicago Press.

Duggan, L. (2003). *The twilight of equality? Neoliberalism, cultural politics, and the attack on democracy*. Boston: Beacon Press.

Dyer, R. (2002). It's being so camp as keeps us going. In R. Dyer (Ed.), *The culture of queers* (pp. 49–62). New York: Routledge.

Faludi, S. (1999). *Stiffed: The betrayal of the American man*. New York: William Morrow.

Feirstein, B. (1982). *Real men don't eat quiche: A guidebook to all that is truly masculine*. New York: Summit.

Felski, R. (2000). Nothing to declare: Identity, shame, and the lower middle class. In R. Felski (Ed.), *Doing time: Feminist theory and postmodern culture* (pp. 33–54). New York: New York University Press.

Flocker, M. (2003). *The metrosexual guide to style: A handbook for the modern man*. Cambridge, MA: Da Capo Press.

Florian, E. (2004, February 9). Queer Eye makes over the economy! *Fortune*, 38.

Fonseca, N. (2003, August 8). They're here! They're queer! And they don't like your end tables! The straight dope on how the gayest show on TV (sorry, Will) became this summer's breakout hit. *Entertainment Weekly*, 24.

Fussell, P. (1992). *Class: A guide through the American status system*. New York: Touchstone. (Original work published 1983)

Gamson, J. (2005). The intersection of Gay Street and Straight Street: Shopping, social class, and the new gay visibility. *Social Thought and Research, 26*(1&2), 3–18.

Gee, J. P. (1996). *The new work order: Behind the language of the new capitalism*. Boulder, CO: Westview Press.

Goldstein, R. (2003, July 23). What Queer Eye? Are the Fab Five a breakthrough or a stereotype? *Village Voice*. Retrieved October 13, 2005, from http://villagevoice.com

Gross, L. (2005). The past and the future of gay, lesbian, bisexual, and transgender studies. *Journal of Communication, 55*, 508–528.

Hay, J. (2005). *Overhaulin' TV and government (Thoughts on the political campaign to Pimp Your Ride)*. Retrieved May 18, 2005, from http://www.flowtv.org

Henderson, L. (2003, November). *Sexuality, cultural production and Foucault/conjunctures*. Paper presented at the Sexuality After Foucault Conference, Manchester, UK.

Illouz, E. (2003). *Oprah Winfrey and the glamour of misery: An essay on popular culture*. New York: Columbia University Press.

Kaufman, G. (1989). *The psychology of shame: Theory and treatment of shame-based syndromes*. New York: Springer Publishing.

Kelly, C. (2003, August 17). Gay TV comes out, but who's proud? *Fort Worth Star Telegram*. Retrieved October 13, 2005, from NewsBank database.

Lowry, B. (2003, August 27). It's profitable to be a little bit gay. *Los Angeles Times*. Retrieved October 13, 2005, from NewsBank database.

McCarthy, A. (2005). *The republic of Tyra*. Retrieved May 18, 2005, from http://www.flowtv.org

McGee, M. (2005). *Self-help Inc.: Makeover culture in American life*. Oxford: Oxford University Press.

McQuaid, P. (2003, September 7). Forget the metrosexual movement: Looking good starts with finding yourself and accepting your limits—and getting a little advice from those in the know. *Los Angeles Times Magazine*, 19.

Miller, T. (1993). *The well-tempered self: Citizenship, culture, and the postmodern subject*. Baltimore: John Hopkins University Press.

Miller, T. (2005). A metrosexual eye on "Queer Guy". *GLQ: A Journal of Gay and Lesbian Studies, 11*(1), 112–117.

Miller, T., & McHoul, A. (1998). Helping the self. *Social Text, 57* (Winter), 127–155.

Morago, G. (2003, July 14). Gay style for straights. *Hartford Courant*. Retrieved October 13, 2005, from NewsBank database.

Morris, W. (2003, August 3). Beyond "Queer Eye": Is a vast national sex change underway? *Boston Globe*. Retrieved October 13, 2005, from LexisNexis database.

Muños, J. E. (2005). Queer minstrels for the straight eye. *GLQ: A Journal of Gay and Lesbian Studies, 11*(1), 101–102.

Ouellette, L. (2004). "Take responsibility for yourself": *Judge Judy* and the neoliberal citizen. In S. Murray & L. Ouellette (Eds.), *Reality TV: Remaking television culture* (pp. 231–250). New York: New York University Press.

Rimke, H. M. (2000). Governing citizens through self-help literature. *Cultural Studies, 14*(1), 61–78.

Rollins, J. (1985). *Between women: Domestics and their employers*. Philadelphia: Temple University Press.

Rose, N. (1990). *Governing the soul: The shaping of the private self*. New York: Routledge.

Rose, N. (1996). Governing "advanced" liberal democracies. In A. Barry, T. Osborne, & N. Rose (Eds.), *Foucault and political reason: Liberalism, neo-liberalism and rationalities of government* (pp. 37–64). Chicago: University of Chicago Press.

Sawyer, T. (2003). *Hail the Prada-worshipping queer.* Retrieved July 24, 2003, from http://www.alternet.org

Schwartz, D., Ryan, S., & Wostbrock, F. (1999). *The encyclopedia of TV game shows.* New York: Checkmark Books.

Sender, K. (2004). *Business, not politics: The making of the gay market.* New York: Columbia University Press.

Shott, B. (2003, July 24). Straight slobs unite! Resist the "Queer Eye". *San Francisco Chronicle.* Retrieved October 13, 2005, from http://www.sfgate.com

Simpson, M. (1994, November 15). Here come the mirror men. *Independent,* p. 22.

Sitt, P. (2003, November 6). Guys belly up to counter for grooming products. *Seattle Times,* p. Cl.

Sontag, S. (1966). Notes on camp. In S. Sontag (Ed.), *Against interpretation and other essays* (pp. 275–292). New York: Delta.

Stasi, L. (2003, August 26). Flame out! Linda isn't happy with how gay TV turned out. *New York Post.* Retrieved October 13, 2005, from LexisNexis database.

Torres, S. (2005). Why can't Johnny shave? *GLQ: A Journal of Gay and Lesbian Studies, 11*(1), 95–97.

United States Department of Labor. (2004). *Employment status of the civilian noninstitutional population by age, sex, and race, 2004.* Retrieved March 1, 2005, from http://www.bls.gov/cps/cpsaat3.pdf

Wallenstein, A. (2004, September 10). Ratings not so fab as "Queer Eye" fad fades. *Hollywood Reporter.* Retrieved Oct 13, 2005, from LexisNexis database.

Weinraub, B., & Rutenberg, J. (2003, July 29). Gay-themed TV gaining a wider audience. *New York Times,* p. A1.

# Chapter 15

## PHILIP M. NAPOLI

# DECONSTRUCTING THE DIVERSITY PRINCIPLE

DOES THE U.S. ELECTRONIC MEDIA system uphold the standards of press diversity built into the U.S. constitution? Fordham University professor Philip Napoli argues that before we can address such a complex question, we must first have a shared understanding of what diversity is and how it can best be analyzed. His essay addresses these issues by establishing a typology for diversity and suggesting directions for future analyses. Napoli wrote this article in 1999, several months after the Federal Communication Commission launched an initiative to assess the nature of diversity in media programming and ownership. The distance in time allows us to consider the extent to which this initiative has been realized in the decade since Napoli's writing.

\*     \*     \*

Diversity has been one of the foundation principles in communications policy (Napoli, in press-a). It has become a fundamental principle underlying evaluations of the performance of mass media systems and the objectives of communications policymaking (Levin, 1971). Diversity has been described as one of the "paramount goals of broadcast regulation in America" (Owen, 1978, p. 43). The inherent value of diversity has also been a foundation of much of the Supreme Court's First Amendment jurisprudence (Bhagwat, 1995). According to McQuail (1992a), "Diversity has come to acquire the status of an end in itself . . . a broad principle to which appeal can be made on behalf of both neglected minorities and of consumer choice, or against monopoly and other restrictions" (p. 142).

Recently, the Federal Communications Commission (FCC) initiated an empirical inquiry into the nature of diversity in the electronic media. FCC Chairman William Kennard (1998) noted that the Commission is

> studying the relationship between gender diversity of licensees and the nature of programming presented to the viewers. We are also launching a

variety of other studies designed to establish a constitutionally sound record to reinstate designed initiatives to foster female and minority ownership.

(p. 4)

In the end, the Commission hopes to "prove the link" between diversity of sources of information and diversity of content (p. 4). What is perhaps most important about this statement by Chairman Kennard is that it reflects a shift in emphasis in the Commission's approach to diversity. Specifically, the Commission appears willing to approach diversity as a tangible and empirically assessable construct rather than a justification for policy initiatives. This shift in orientation is a product of a series of judicial repudiations of FCC diversity policies, based in part on a lack of empirical support.

The Commission's research plan is fraught with challenges because, despite diversity's status as a foundation principle in communications policy, policymakers, scholars, and policy analysts have seldom agreed on what constitutes adequately defining or measuring this rather ambiguous concept (Entman & Wildman, 1992; LeDuc, 1982; Owen, 1977, 1978). Indeed, diversity is a concept with multiple dimensions, means of assessment, and underlying assumptions. However, the FCC's recent empirical commitment to the concept reestablishes diversity research as a major priority in communications policy analysis.

In this essay I outline the various aspects of the diversity principle to establish an analytical framework from which future diversity research can develop. In keeping with the FCC's line of jurisdiction, the primary focus here will be on diversity in the U.S. electronic media. However, many of the conceptual and methodological points discussed are applicable to other media industry contexts (e.g., print, music) in which diversity has been valued (Bagdikian, 1997; Lacy, 1991; Peterson, 1994; Rothenbuhler & Dimmick, 1982), as well as to issues of diversity policy in international contexts (Blumler, 1992; McQuail, 1992b). Also, in the spirit of the FCC's recent inquiry, I approach diversity from an empirical standpoint, highlighting its various components, means of assessment, and the hypothesized relationships requiring empirical attention. This deconstruction of the diversity principle can serve as a useful guide for future assessments of diversity in the communications policy arena and stimulate an expansion and reorientation of diversity-policy analysis.

In the first section I place the diversity principle within the larger context of the "marketplace of ideas." Diversity is a central component of the broader principle of a robust marketplace of ideas that has historically guided policymakers and the courts. Only when diversity is placed within the context of the marketplace of ideas metaphor, and the specific social and political objectives that a robust marketplace of ideas is presumed to achieve, do the theoretical justifications for diversity policies become clear. The assumptions underlying the marketplace of ideas metaphor help define the various components of diversity and the presumed relationships among them. In the second section I outline the three central components of diversity (along with their subcomponents), the relationships that are often hypothesized to exist between them, and the various empirical approaches to these components that have been employed. Drawing upon the marketplace of ideas metaphor, the three primary components of diversity are (a) souce diversity, (b) content diversity, and (c) exposure diversity. Although these three components appear rather simple on the surface, they possess numerous subcomponents. These important subcomponents will be outlined here as well. As will become clear, important relationships among diversity dimensions have been consistently neglected in empirical research. This empirical neglect has undermined many policy initiatives. In addition, despite the centrality of exposure diversity to the ideals inherent in the marketplace of ideas metaphor, the source and content components of diversity have received far more attention from policymakers and policy analysts than the exposure component. In the concluding section I summarize the theoretical and empirical gaps in diversity policy to date and argue for more multidimensional approaches to diversity research.

## The Marketplace of Ideas and Diversity

It is first important to review the relationship between diversity as a policy objective and the broader objective of achieving a robust marketplace of ideas. The marketplace of ideas metaphor provides the underlying theoretical justification for most diversity policies. Indeed, though diversity is often perceived as the central objective of communications policy decisions, it is best perceived as a key subcomponent (along with competition) of an effectively functioning marketplace of ideas. The emphasis on diversity as a policy objective grows directly out of the First Amendment tradition that stresses the "widest possible dissemination of information from diverse and antagonistic sources" (*Associated Press v. United States*, 1945, p. 1424) in an effort to promote goals such as informed decision-making, cultural pluralism; citizen welfare, and a well-functioning democracy (see Bloustein, 1981; Glasser, 1984; Meiklejohn, 1948/1960, 1948/1972; Redish, 1982). This is the essence of the marketplace of ideas concept. It is the mechanism by which First Amendment freedoms are translated into effective democracy. The key is to recognize that a robust marketplace of ideas—and the diversity components that grow out of it—are intended to achieve broader social objectives. As Oliver Wendell Holmes stated in his famous dissent in *Abrams v. United States* (1919), "the ultimate good desired is better reached by free trade in ideas. . . . That at any rate is the theory of our Constitution" (p. 630).

Thus, the marketplace of ideas has been conceived by the courts, legal scholars, and policymakers as a key dimension of First Amendment freedoms, in which citizens are free to choose from a wide range of ideas (content diversity), delivered from a wide range of sources (source diversity). The citizens then partake of this diversity (exposure diversity) to increase their knowledge, encounter opposing viewpoints, and become well-informed decision-makers who are better capable of fulfilling their democratic responsibilities in a self-governing society. Thus, within the marketplace of ideas framework, source, content, and exposure diversity are integrated contributors to the process of developing well-informed citizens and enhancing the democratic process.

The marketplace of ideas concept has served as a guiding principle for a number of (intended) diversity-enhancing policies, including ownership regulations (1998 Biennial Regulatory Review, 1998) and the Fairness Doctrine (Complaint of Syracuse Peace Council, 1988; Handling of Public Issues, 1974). The linkage between the marketplace of ideas and diversity policy is particularly well illustrated in a 1993 Memorandum Opinion and Order released by the FCC regarding its decision to relax, and ultimately eliminate, the Financial Interest and Syndication (Fin-Syn) rules. These rules, initially adopted in 1970, were designed to limit the participation of the three big television

**Table 15.1** Diversity components, subcomponents, and assumed relationships

| Source diversity | Content diversity | Exposure diversity |
|---|---|---|
| 1. Ownership<br>　a. Programming<br>　b. Outlet<br>2. Workforce | 1. Program-Type Format<br>2. Demographic<br>3. Idea/Viewpoint | 1. Horizontal<br>2. Vertical |

networks in the off-network syndication business and to limit the degree to which the networks could have a financial interest in the programming they aired (Amendment of Part 73, 1970). The intermediate goals of these policies included enhancing the profitability of program producers and restraining or diminishing network bargaining power (Besen, Krattenmaker, Metzger, & Woodbury, 1984). However, the ultimate goal was to "limit network control over television programming and thereby encourage the development of a diversity of programs through diverse and antagonist sources of program services" (Evaluation of the Syndication, 1993b, p. 1454). Here we see an explicit adoption of the marketplace of ideas language used by Justice Black in the *Associated Press v. United States* (1945) decision. In sum, it should be clear how the marketplace of ideas metaphor, as a guiding principle for communications policy-makers, has motivated the development of policies specifically designed to enhance diversity.

## Dimensions of Diversity

Academics and policymakers have long debated about what exactly constitutes diversity (Entman & Wildman, 1992; Krattenmaker & Powe, 1994; McQuail, 1992a). Here, the focus will be on those components that have the greatest relevance to communications policymakers. Any neglected dimensions are generally beyond policymakers' range of concern. It should also be noted that this discussion of the primary dimensions of diversity uses Glasser's (1984) distinction between diversity and variety. Variety refers to the raw number of outlets or content choices available, whereas diversity focuses both on the number of choices and the differences among them (e.g., in terms of content or ownership characteristics). Certainly, increasing variety may also be an important policy objective (e.g., Fowler & Brenner, 1982; Owen, 1975), particularly given that increases in the number of outlets can potentially lead to increases in diversity (Owen & Wildman, 1992). Thus, to the extent that variety is related to diversity, it is relevant to the various dimensions of diversity. However, variety alone does not fall within the boundaries of the diversity principle as it is discussed here.

At the general level, the primary components of diversity include (a) source diversity, (b) content diversity, and (c) exposure diversity. More specific subcategories fall under each of these three larger categories. As important as the individual categories (perhaps more so), however, are the relationships that have often been assumed to exist between the categories. Table 15.1 provides an outline of the primary dimensions of diversity, their corresponding subcomponents, and their presumed relationships. As the table illustrates, diversity in the sources of information has frequently (though not always)[1] been assumed to be causally related to the diversity of content that is available. In addition, particularly within the context of the marketplace of ideas metaphor, it has often been assumed that an increase in the diversity of available content leads to an increase in the diversity of content consumed by audiences. I will discuss these relationships in greater detail below.

## Source Diversity

The assumption that optimum citizen decision-making arises from the consideration of information from "diverse and antagonistic sources" (*Associated Press v. United States*, 1945, p. 1424) is implicit within the marketplace of ideas metaphor. Consequently, communications policymakers have long concerned themselves with increasing the diversity of sources available to media audiences. However, even such a superficially straightforward concept as source diversity contains distinct subcomponents. Specifically, source diversity has traditionally been conceptualized by policymakers in three separate ways: (a) in terms of the diversity of ownership of content or programming, (b) in terms of the diversity of ownership of media outlets, and (c) in terms of the diversity of the workforce within individual media outlets. Each of these subcomponents is described below, with categories *a* and *b* both described under the broader heading of "ownership diversity."

### Ownership Diversity (Content and Outlet)

The two categories of ownership diversity are content ownership and outlet ownership, though they are not necessarily mutually exclusive. Sometimes, there are even multiple levels within these two categories. For example, when assessing ownership diversity in cable television, it is possible to focus on the owners of the cable systems (outlets). On the other hand, it is possible to focus on the owners of the individual channels that are carried on the cable systems (a second level of outlet). It is also possible to focus on the producers of the programs that run on the individual cable channels (content owners).

This distinction between content ownership and outlet ownership is not absolute, however, given that television stations and cable channels also produce their own content and can simultaneously qualify as both content and outlet owner. It is also important to recognize that outlets are not passive in their distribution activities. Outlets such as cable television systems and broadcast stations actively decide which sources of programming will receive distribution. Thus, outlets are active programmers who may favor certain program owners over others. Consequently, although there is a valid distinction between content (program) and outlet ownership, the separation is in some ways artificial, because, to a large degree, the available diversity in program ownership rests with the decisions made by the owners of the distribution outlets. This helps explain why the FCC's concern with source diversity has typically focused on the local level (1998 Biennial Regulatory Review, 1998). That is, the Commission has traditionally been most concerned with source diversity at the final stage in the distribution process. Along these lines, the FCC has placed national and within-market limits on broadcast station ownership and restricted broadcast station-cable system and broadcast station-newspaper cross-ownership (see 1998 Biennial Regulatory Review, 1998).

*Assessing ownership diversity.* Clearly, the degree to which ownership diversity has been a central policy objective necessitates that there be an effective means of assessing ownership diversity. There is a long tradition of research that has empirically assessed ownership diversity within both the print and electronic media (e.g., Bagdikian, 1997; Chan-Olmsted, 1991; Compaine, Sterling, Guback, & Noble, 1982). Typically, such assessments involve counting the number of separately owned outlets or sources of programming within particular markets or industries, or examining the distribution of audiences or market shares among market participants (using economic measures of concentration such as the Herfindahl-Hirschman index, see Department of Justice, 1992). Operationalizing source diversity strictly in terms of the number of market participants provides a useful indicator of the degree to which a diversity of sources of information is available. However, this approach does not account for the possibility that the marketplace is structured in a way that prevents all sources from having reasonable access to the audience. Operationalizing source diversity in terms of the distribution of market shares provides a better indication of possible structural inequities and simultaneously addresses the exposure diversity component of the diversity principle (see below).[2]

The FCC typically distinguishes between diversity in program producers (generally using the broad term "source" diversity for this category) and diversity in outlets (see Evaluation of the Syndication, 1993a). According to the Commission, source diversity is a measure of the number of program originators, whereas outlet diversity is a measure of the number of independent transmission systems delivering programming to the public (Evaluation of the Syndication, 1993a, p. 3302). Thus, television stations would be categorized as outlets, and program producers would be categorized as sources.

The appropriate unit of analysis for assessing ownership diversity is not always clear-cut. Consider, for instance, the FCC's decision to sunset the Fin-Syn Rules (Evaluation of the Syndication, 1993a, 1993b). During an inquiry into the continued necessity of the Fin-Syn rules, a controversy arose over the appropriate methodology for measuring diversity of program sources. One commenting party, the Coalition to Preserve the Financial Interest and Syndication Rules, argued that the appropriate measure of source diversity was the number of individuals presenting program ideas to the networks and creating programs. Consequently, the Coalition advocated focusing on the number of different executive producers of network programs as the true measure of source diversity (see Evaluation of the Syndication, 1993a, p. 3296). The FCC, however, disagreed, concluding that the more appropriate measure was the number of different copyright holders, as the copyright holders have the "ultimate control over the programming project" (Evaluation of the Syndication, 1993a, p. 3311). This was also the measurement standard advocated by the broadcast networks, who vigorously opposed the Fin-Syn rules.

The controversy was particularly important given that, under the executive producer measurement methodology, concentration in the program production industry appeared to have declined over the years. In contrast, under the copyright holder methodology, concentration had increased. Thus, under one measurement standard the Fin-Syn rules had been effective in achieving one of their primary goals—reducing ownership concentration in the program production industry. According to another measurement standard, the Fin-Syn rules had been a failure. Thus, the ultimate decision about the utility of the Fin-Syn rules rested heavily upon the choice of measurement standard used for assessing diversity in program ownership.

The FCC ultimately relied on the copyright holder methodology and has generally been consistent through the years in focusing on copyright holders as its measure of program sources. The FCC has provided strong support for this strategy by pointing out that the number of executive producers for individual programs has proliferated in recent years for reasons irrelevant to diversity concerns (e.g., increases in the number of half-hour programs, increases in the number of made-for-TV movies; Evaluation of the Syndication, 1993a). This particular controversy highlights the need for such measures to be well-thought-out from the beginning and to be applied in a consistent manner over time, in order to facilitate the most rigorous and thorough longitudinal analyses possible.

## Workforce Diversity

Regulations designed to enhance the diversity of sources of information have not been limited to the owners of media outlets or media programming. Policymakers also have been concerned with enhancing the diversity of the entire workforce within media outlets. The prime example of efforts to achieve "workforce diversity" can be found in the FCC's Equal Employment Opportunity (EEO) regulations for broadcast licensees. These rules encouraged broadcast stations to have a personnel mix that reflected the diversity of their market area. Specifically, these regulations forbade stations to discriminate against any person because of race, color, religion, national origin, or gender. These regulations also required stations to adopt affirmative action EEO programs targeted to minorities and women in an effort to increase the degree to which the personnel composition of broadcast stations reflected the demographics of the surrounding market (*Lutheran Church-Missouri Synod v. Federal Communications Commission*, 1998).

These rules obviously reflect a broader interpretation of the term "source" than is reflected in the ownership diversity component discussed above. Within the context of workforce diversity, all personnel, ranging from management to secretarial and custodial staff, are considered components of the source of information and thus all fall under the purview of the diversity principle.

*Assessing workforce diversity.* As with the assessment of ownership diversity, there have been different approaches to assessing workforce diversity. The FCC's initial assessment approach involved determining whether qualified women and minorities were employed in "some reasonable relationship to the numbers in the local labor market" (Nondiscrimination, 1975, p. 360). Unfortunately, the Commission did not define "reasonable relationship." Obviously, from an assessment standpoint, this approach contained an enormous amount of ambiguity.

Consequently, in 1977 the Commission adopted explicit quantitative standards for operationalizing workforce diversity. Specifically, broadcast stations with more than 10 full-time employees would have their license applications reviewed if minorities were not employed at a ratio of 50% of their overall availability in the labor force and 25% in the upper four job categories (see *Lutheran Church-Missouri Synod v. Federal Communications Commission*, 1998). This operationalization of sufficient workforce diversity grew more stringent in 1980, when the percentage of minority representation in the upper four job categories was raised to 50% of their availability in the labor force (Equal Employment Opportunity, 1980). The case of workforce diversity represents an instance in which, from an assessment standpoint, the FCC moved from an ambiguous and highly subjective operational approach to a more explicit quantitative operational-ization. However, as the following section will illustrate, these quantitative measures were never effectively employed in assessing the EEO policy's ultimate objectives.

### The Source-Content Relationship Within the Policy Arena

Policies designed to enhance source diversity (be it ownership or workforce diversity) are not implemented purely for the sake of enhancing source diversity. The assumption that a greater diversity of sources leads to a greater diversity of content has been implicit in virtually all these source diversity policies.[3] This assumption has been prominent among policymakers and prevalent in judicial decision-making. In many instances, the FCC and the courts have used ownership diversity as a proxy for content diversity, adopting a "reasonable expectation" that content diversity would stem from ownership diversity (Kleiman, 1991, p. 413; Wilson, 1988). For instance, although the immediate objective of the FCC's EEO regulations was to enhance source diversity, the ultimate objective was to foster diverse program content (*Lutheran Church of Missouri-Synod v. FCC*, 1998). The Commission's operating assumption in promulgating these policies was that a more diverse workforce would lead to more diverse programming.

It is important to recognize that diverse programming was the ultimate objective of these policies, because it is questionable whether the FCC even has the authority to promulgate straightforward antidiscrimination regulations. As the D.C. Circuit Court of Appeals has noted, "the FCC is not the Equal Employment Opportunity Com-mission" (*Bilingual Bicultural Coalition on Mass Media, Inc. v. FCC*, 1978, p. 628). The Commission itself refused to claim that the EEO policies had any antidiscrimination motivation whatsoever, recognizing the potential vulnerability of such claims (*Lutheran Church of Missouri-Synod v. FCC*, 1998). However, enhancing the diversity of pro-gramming does fall within the bounds of the FCC's "public interest" mandate (see Busterna, 1976; Kleiman, 1991; McGregor, 1984; Napoli, in press-a), and this goal was what the Commission proffered as its motivation for the EEO policies (*Lutheran Church of Missouri-Synod v. FCC, 1998*).

The courts have even questioned whether diversity of programmers or outlets are, alone, valid regulatory objectives. The courts have isolated diversity in programming as the "critical form of diversity" (*Schurz Communications v. Federal Communications Com-mission*, 1992, p. 1054). Whether this particular hierarchy of values is appropriate has been debated (see Owen, 1978). However, the judicial uncertainty about the value of source diversity helps explain why policies designed to enhance source diversity have been typically promulgated with the explicit intention of enhancing the diversity of content available to audiences. Such expressed motivations appear more likely to receive favorable judicial treatment.

Despite the common assertion of a causal relationship between source diversity and content diversity, policy and legal decisions have often been made without empirical evidence supporting the existence of such a relationship. In many instances, however, this empirical vacuum has undermined these policy decisions. As described above, the assumption of a source-content diversity relationship was implicit in the FCC's EEO policies designed to foster workforce diversity.

This presumed relationship recently came under attack (*Lutheran Church-Missouri Synod v. Federal Communications Commission*, 1998). Specifically, the EEO policy was challenged by the Lutheran Church, which held licenses for two radio stations in the town of Clayton, Missouri. One station was a noncommercial, religious station. The other was a commercial station that broadcast classical music, as well as some religious programming. The church's license renewals were designated for a hearing by the FCC as a result of findings that the stations' personnel did not sufficiently reflect the demographic diversity within the local market area. The church argued that the stations' religious and classical programming required personnel to have a background in the Lutheran doctrine, classical music, or both. Consequently, certain demographic groups were significantly less likely to be qualified for available positions. As a result, the personnel make-up of the stations lacked the necessary demographic diversity. The FCC countered the church's position with the argument that it was unnecessary for personnel such as receptionists, secretaries, engineers, and business managers to have knowledge of the Lutheran doctrine in order for the stations to maintain their Lutheran focus (see *Lutheran Church-Missouri Synod v. Federal Communications Commission*, 1998).

The FCC's argument provides the focal point for the court's eventual decision in favor of the church's challenge to the rules. Specifically, the court recognized the contradiction inherent in the Commission's argument that, according to its EEO policy, a Lutheran background was not necessary to generate Lutheran content, but racial and ethnic diversity among all levels of employees was necessary to foster diverse programming (*Lutheran Church-Missouri Synod v. FCC*, 1998). Obviously, such contradictory reasoning undermined the presumption of a relationship between workforce diversity and content diversity. This presumption was further undermined by the Commission's failure to produce any evidence supporting the existence of such a relationship. The court noted in its decision that the FCC did not introduce a single piece of evidence linking low-level employees to programming content.

Similarly, the courts rejected the presumed but unsubstantiated relationship between the gender of broadcast station owners and broadcast content. In *Lamprecht v. Federal Communications Commission* (1992), the D.C. Circuit ruled that the FCC's policy of granting preferences to female owners in its broadcast licensing decisions violated the Fifth Amendment. A key factor in this decision was the Commission's failure to provide any empirical evidence that female licensees program their stations differently than male licensees. As the court stated, "the Commission's brief cites nothing that might support its predictive judgment that women owners will broadcast women's or minority or any other underrepresented type of programming at any different rate than will men. Nor is there any proof in the administrative record" (p. 395).

This decision contrasts sharply with the Supreme Court's decision in *Metro Broadcasting Inc. v. Federal Communications Commission* (1990). In this latter case, the Court ruled that minority licensing preferences were an acceptable means of promoting broadcast content diversity. A primary reason for the court's decision was what it described as "a host of empirical evidence" supporting the relationship (p. 580). However, according to Spitzer (1991), much of the evidence relied upon by the court was either methodologically flawed or did not directly address the causal relationship between minority ownership and minority content. Indeed, the dissenting Justices found the empirical evidence to be completely unconvincing (*Metro Broadcasting v. Federal Communications Commission*, 1990).

In 1995, the Supreme Court overruled the *Metro* decision on the basis of a failure on the part of the circuit court to apply the appropriate "strict scrutiny" standard, which provides that any racial classifications "are constitutional only if they are narrowly tailored measures that further compelling governmental interests" (*Adarand Constructors, Inc., v. Pena*, 1995, p. 227). According to the majority opinion, written by Justice O'Connor, the lower court's reliance on the less stringent "intermediate scrutiny"[4] standard in the *Metro* decision deviated from precedent and thus represented an "unjustified break from previously established doctrine" (p. 231). The weak empirical evidence presented in the *Metro* decision and Chairman Kennard's (1998) recent call for empirical research on this issue suggest that minority licensing preferences would not, at this point, meet the more rigorous "strict scrutiny" standard.

A final example of communications policymakers' failure to demonstrate the assumed relationship between source and content diversity can be found in the 7th Court of Appeals's rejection of the FCC's revised Fin-Syn rules (*Schurz Communications v. Federal Communications Commission*, 1992). In its decision, written by Judge Posner, the court found the revised rules to be arbitrary and capricious, due, in part, to the fact that the FCC never explained how the rules would accomplish its stated goal of enhancing diversity of programming. At the heart of this decision was Judge Posner's skepticism that increases in source diversity could be presumed to lead to increases in program diversity (*Schurz Communications v. Federal Communications Commission*, 1992, pp. 1054–1055). The FCC provided no information to alleviate this skepticism. As Posner concluded, "How all this [the revised Fin-Syn rules] promotes programming diversity is mysterious, and was left unexplained in the Commission's opinion" (p. 1055).

The *Lutheran Church, Lamprecht*, and *Schurz* cases effectively illustrate the empirical vacuum that has frequently accompanied FCC decisions pertaining to diversity policy. Note that the courts' decisions to overrule the EEO policies, gender licensing preference, and Fin-Syn rules were not made because evidence undermined their presumptions. Rather, the policies in question were overturned because of a failure to produce empirical evidence of any kind supporting the hypothesized relationships. The courts' demand for evidence suggests that these policy premises should be approached as testable hypotheses rather than as shared, unquestionably valid assumptions.

Given this situation, it is discouraging that recent policy decisions have continued to neglect the assessment of content diversity. In its decision to relax and ultimately sunset the Fin-Syn rules, the FCC outlined an empirical plan for the continued monitoring of the effectiveness of the revised policies during the 2 years leading to their complete elimination. The FCC's stated objective was to determine whether the relaxed rules indeed achieved their predicted effects. Consequently, the FCC identified several factors for continued monitoring, including the relative change in the number of independent producers selling television shows to the networks, each network's share of the first-run syndicated programming domestic market, concentration of ownership in the program production industry, and mergers and acquisitions of networks, studios cable systems, and other program providers (Evaluation of the Syndication, 1993a, pp. 3340–3341). These factors clearly reflect the Commission's interest in monitoring the Fin-Syn rules' effects on competition and ownership diversity. However, nowhere in its list of factors did the FCC express any intention to monitor the policies' effects on diversity of programming. Despite the fact that increasing program diversity was one of the primary objectives of the Fin-Syn modifications outlined in its report and order, the FCC ignored program diversity in its plans to monitor the effectiveness of its decision.

Fortunately, the empirical vacuum surrounding the source-content diversity relationship is not quite as great as these examples suggest. In the following section I highlight several instances in which this relationship has been investigated. As will become clear, the expectation that increased diversity of sources leads to increased diversity of content is far from a certainty.

## Content Diversity

Content diversity can be seen as the second link in the diversity chain. As the previous section illustrated, policies designed to enhance source diversity are generally implemented under the assumption that increased source diversity will increase content diversity. This rather indirect approach reflects a common strategy in communications policy, one in which policy objectives are pursued via *structural* regulation (regulation affecting the nature of the sources), as opposed to *behavioral* regulation (regulation directed at the actions of the sources). Thus, the structural changes brought about by the policies are only an intermediate point on the way to achieving more far-reaching policy objectives. Theoretically, these objectives are achieved via an approach that is sufficiently "content neutral" to avoid running afoul of the First Amendment (see *Turner Broadcasting System v. Federal Communications Commission*, 1994, 1997).

### Format or Program-Type Diversity

This component of content diversity refers to the category designations given to radio formats, cable channel formats, and individual television programs. Generally speaking, then, an example of program-type diversity might be the range of different types of television shows from which a viewer can choose during an hour of prime time. If the viewer has a choice of six different situation comedies and three made-for-TV movies, then this is not likely to be seen as a very diverse program mix—at least at the level of the program types. However, perhaps on another night this same viewer has a choice of two situation comedies, two dramas, two news programs, a made-for-TV movie, a variety program, and a talk show. Clearly, within the confines of the same number of channels, there is a much higher level of program-type diversity. Policymakers have generally valued this kind of diversity.

Of course, for these program type or format designations to matter, it is essential that they tap genuine distinctions in audience preferences and, subsequently, behavioral distinctions in viewing patterns. Ideally, individuals have preferred program types, and these program-type preferences are meaningful and powerful predictors of viewing behavior. Thus, a person who lists science fiction programs as his or her most preferred program type is more likely to watch a science fiction program when it is available than a person who lists situation comedies as his or her preferred program type. The existence of such behavioral patterns underscores policymakers' desire for a diversity of program types, given that such diversity increases the likelihood of maximizing the satisfaction of more categories of viewers and hence serves the public interest.

Unfortunately, research on program types has been inconsistent in terms of the degree to which program-type classifications effectively differentiate viewer preferences (Ehrenberg, 1968; Frank, Becknell, & Clokey, 1971; Kirsch & Banks, 1962; Lehman, 1971; Levin, 1980; Rao, 1975). However, in assessing this body of research, Webster and Wakshlag (1983) stated that the "conclusion to be drawn from this succession of studies is that conventional 'common sense' program types . . . bear some systematic relationship to program preference" (p. 436). Perhaps the safest conclusion that can be drawn at this point, then, is that program-type categories do serve as meaningful, if not perfect, predictors of a person's viewing behavior.

*Assessing program-type diversity.* Within all the primary components of diversity and their related subcomponents, empirical assessments of program-type or format diversity have been the most common. Unfortunately, researchers have seldom relied on the same typology of program categories, limiting our ability to draw comparisons across studies. In some instances, researchers have developed their own program typologies (Dominick & Pearce, 1976; Grant, 1994; Lin, 1995; Litman, Hasagawa, Shrikhande, & Barbatsis, 1994). In other instances, they have relied on the program typologies used by ratings organizations, such as A. C. Nielsen and Arbitron (Napoli, 1997; Wakshlag & Adams, 1985), or industry publications (Litman, 1979). Even these institutionally developed program typologies have been internally inconsistent over the years, as they have evolved to account for new program formats and types.

The methodological differences between these various diversity assessments extend well beyond differences in their program typologies. These studies also differ in how they compute their diversity indexes (see Kambara, 1992). One common method is the "top three" index first used by Dominick and Pearce (1976). With this approach, the percentage of the total amount of television programming accounted for by the top-three program types is computed. This percentage thus serves as the measure of diversity, with higher percentages of the total amount of programming accounted for by the top-three program types indicating lower levels of diversity. Although this approach provides a simple and useful measure of the degree of concentration among the top-three program types, the overall amount of information provided by such a measure is limited because it provides no information about the distribution among the remaining program types (Kambara, 1992).

A second commonly used measure is the "relative entropy" measure. This measure is derived from work by Shannon and Weaver (1963) dealing with the measurement of information quantity and variety. Unlike the top three measure, this measure takes into account both the number of different categories offered and the concentration of material within those categories. Mathematically, it is expressed as follows: $H = -\Sigma p_i \log_2 p_i$, where H equals variety and $p_i$ equals the probability of seeing program type i (see Wakshlag & Adams, 1985).

Finally, perhaps the most common method used within diversity assessments is a modification of the Herfindahl-Hirschman Index (HHI) of concentration used by the U.S. Department of Justice in assessing concentration in an industry. This measure involves summing the squared market shares of every firm in a market. Scores below 1000 indicate an unconcentrated market, scores between 1000 and 1800 indicate moderate concentration, and scores above 1800 indicate high levels of concentration (Baseman & Owen, 1982, pp. 33–34). This measure has been adapted to the measurement of program-type diversity by summing the squares of each program type's share of the total number of available programs or total hours of available programming (Litman, 1979, p. 408). It should be emphasized, however, that specific HHI scores have no inherent meaning (e.g., an HHI of 1000 equals moderate diversity) within program-diversity assessment contexts, unlike in antitrust contexts, where score ranges have been empirically associated with the behavior of firms in markets.

*What do these diversity assessments tell us?* The program diversity assessment literature to date can essentially be divided into two categories. The first category primarily consists of descriptive studies. These studies focus on assessing program-type diversity trends over time or on comparing diversity levels across distribution sources (e.g., cable vs. network vs. syndication). Longitudinal analyses of program-type diversity have focused on network prime-time television (Dominick & Pearce, 1976) and on cable television (DeJong & Bates, 1991). Comparative studies have focused on comparing program-type diversity across distribution forms (e.g., Litman, et al., 1994). Although these studies are useful for determining whether specific trends exist over time, and for identifying those programming sources that provide the greatest levels of diversity, from a policy standpoint, the greater concern is with understanding the factors that affect levels of diversity.

The second category of studies includes those that have attempted to investigate the causal factors pertaining to program-type diversity. There have been very few of these studies, but they represent the direction that diversity research must pursue if it is to be of use to communications policymakers. For example, Litman (1979) conducted a program-type diversity assessment for the 1974–1979 time period. He found an increase in network program diversity. This pattern was a reversal of the downward trend identified in a longitudinal assessment of the previous 30 years (Dominick & Pearce, 1976). Litman attributed this sudden up-surge in program-type diversity to increased industry competition and turbulence—specifically, the rise of ABC—during the mid-1970s (p. 403). Long (1979) found that network program diversity suffered after the death of the DuMont network in the 1950s (p. 343), suggesting again a relationship between network competition and program-type diversity. Wakshlag and Adams (1985) found a sharp decline in network program diversity that coincided with the introduction of the Prime Time Access Rule (PTAR) in 1971, a rule that was intended to increase diversity (McGregor, 1984, p. 834). Finally, Levin (1971) found that, within individual television markets, diversity of program types increased with the number of television channels available.

Levin's (1971) research fits well with the concept of "diversity elasticity" (Greenberg & Barnett, 1971), which can be defined as a measure of the proportional change in diversity resulting from a proportional change in the number of channels. Levin's findings are, however, contradicted by the results of a more recent analysis of 41 U.S. broadcast and cable networks (Grant, 1994). Grant found that increasing the number of channels of a particular type did not lead to increased diversity of program types. This finding raises questions about any assumption of a positive relationship between the number of outlets and content diversity. Clearly, it is possible that new outlets may choose to distribute programs that duplicate already available program types (Owen & Wildman, 1992).

In addition, the research suggesting a positive relationship between competition and program-type diversity has been contradicted by recent research by Lin (1995), who found a relatively constant level of program-type diversity in prime-time network television during the 1980s. The increased competition during this period from alternative delivery sources such as cable, satellite, and home video was expected to lead the networks to offer a greater diversity of programs. Instead, however, program-type diversity within the networks remained constant, suggesting that the networks did not consider increasing diversity a necessary strategy for withstanding competition from alternative program sources.

In sum, the research on the determinants of program-type diversity suggests a possible relationship between source diversity and program diversity. However, the evidence at this point is qualified, to say the least, and even contradictory to a certain degree. Research in this area has thus not yet definitively answered the causality question. However, this research should be taken as a starting point for increased efforts on the part of policy analysts to reach a more sophisticated understanding of the factors affecting program-type diversity.

At the same time, however, it is important to recognize that assessing program-type diversity alone does not provide a thorough approach to the concept of content diversity. Indeed, "not all public affairs shows are alike, just as all westerns are not alike. There may be as much 'diversity' *within* traditional program types as *among* program types" (Owen, 1978, p. 44). Certainly, program-type categorizations represent a rather superficial measure of content diversity. They have remained prevalent, however, perhaps because they represent the only reasonably simple and objective method of tapping into content differences within media products. It is important to recognize, however, that content differences in media products extend much deeper than differences in their program-type designation. This fact is reflected in the concepts of demographic and idea diversity.

### Demographic Diversity

Content diversity has also been approached in terms of the racial, ethnic, and gender diversity of the people featured within electronic media programs. Thus, a typical concern among those focusing on the issue of demographic diversity has been whether minority groups and other demographic groups are portrayed on television in reasonable proportion to their prevalence in society. This dimension of diversity has seldom been a point of focus among policymakers. However, recent statements by FCC Chairman Kennard have suggested that demographic diversity merits inclusion within this discussion of diversity policy. Kennard (1998) has argued for the importance of diversifying portrayals of women on television and "creating roles which better reflect the diversity of the population" (p. 2). He has also argued that increasing such diversity "is not unrelated to the increasing presence of women in the industry" (p. 2). Thus, a source-content relationship has once again been asserted. With Kennard's statement, and the Commission's recent commitment to diversity analysis, demographic diversity has become a relevant component of content diversity within the policy arena and merits attention from researchers conducting diversity assessments.

*Assessing demographic diversity.* Despite the recent addition of demographic diversity to the communications policy agenda, assessments of this component of content diversity have been taking place for some time. These studies have often illustrated how certain demographic groups, such as children, the aged, African Americans, and Hispanics, have been underrepresented in television programming (for a useful review of this literature, see Kubey, Shifflet, Weerakkody, & Ukeiley, 1995). Typically, these studies have involved content analyzing a sample of television programming in terms of the race, gender, age, and even occupational characteristics of the characters that appear. These raw numbers are then transformed into percentages (e.g., 89% of all characters in the sample are Caucasian) that can be compared across categories (e.g., male vs. female representation), or compared to census data on the actual demographic breakdowns within the population as a whole (Kubey et al., 1995). Operationalizing demographic diversity in this way suggests whether the electronic media provide an accurate representation of the actual demographic diversity that exists within the population. Unfortunately, research in this area has not investigated structural factors that might affect levels of demographic diversity within electronic media content.

*Idea-Viewpoint Diversity*

Idea diversity represents perhaps the most elusive component of content diversity. Idea diversity refers to the diversity of viewpoints and of social, political, and cultural perspectives represented within the media. This type of content diversity is perhaps most central to the marketplace of ideas metaphor and its relationship to effective democratic self-governance. As Entman and Wildman (1992) stated,

> the more distinct thoughts, analyses, criticisms, and the like that are available on issues of social and political importance, the better off society is. Discussion of the media's performance in offering diverse ideas generally focuses on its contribution to the requirements for good governance in a democratic society, such as a well-informed citizenry.
>
> (p.8)

The concept of idea diversity, and its place in communications policy, are perhaps best represented by the Fairness Doctrine. Initially established in 1949, the Fairness Doctrine required that broadcast licensees present opposing viewpoints on issues of public importance (Editorializing, 1949). The Fairness Doctrine allowed licensees to retain "discretion to choose the substantive content of programming and broadcast formats"; however, broadcasters still had to provide a reasonable opportunity for the presentation of all positions on matters of public importance (Lentz, 1996, p. 276). Thus, increasing the diversity of ideas was the central motivation behind the imposition and enforcement of the Fairness Doctrine. Indeed, the protection of the public's right of access to a diversity of ideas was the central rationale behind the Supreme Court's upholding of the Fairness Doctrine (*Red Lion Broadcasting Co. v. Federal Communications Commission*, 1969). In this case, diversity of content was once again emphasized as a central component of a robust "marketplace of ideas."

Ironically, the same rationale that led to the creation of the Fairness Doctrine also contributed to its elimination as the FCC became concerned that the burdens of Fairness Doctrine compliance were leading broadcasters to provide less coverage of controversial issues than they might otherwise provide (Inquiry, 1985). From an idea diversity standpoint, what is perhaps most important about the Fairness Doctrine saga is that decisions about its effectiveness and ultimate elimination never hinged upon hard empirical evidence of its effects on the overall diversity of viewpoints presented. In its decision to eliminate the Fairness Doctrine, the FCC cited factors it believed contributed to a "significant danger" of a chilling effect (Inquiry, 1985, p. 169), such as a few anecdotal statements from broadcasters that the doctrine affected its decisions about public affairs programming (see Aufderheide, 1990). Ultimately, the primary empirical guidance for the decision came in the form of evidence that competition in the media marketplace had increased sufficiently that the Fairness Doctrine was no longer necessary (Inquiry, 1985, pp. 208–217). Thus, no meaningful assessment of idea diversity accompanied the evaluation of a policy for which the primary objective was to achieve greater idea diversity.

The issue of a possible chilling effect highlights the fact that the Fairness Doctrine represented an increasingly rare instance of an overtly behavioral approach to promoting diverse content (as opposed to the more common structural approach). That is, to a certain degree, the nature of broadcast content was being regulated directly, with the source diversity link in the diversity chain being by-passed entirely. It is therefore not surprising that the Fairness Doctrine faced a strong First Amendment challenge (see *Red Lion Broadcasting v. Federal Communications Commission*, 1969), and that the FCC eventually concluded that, in light of changes in the media landscape, the Fairness Doctrine likely violated the First Amendment and, therefore, would no longer be enforced (Inquiry, 1985).

The FCC has generally avoided assessing idea or viewpoint diversity, concluding that it is virtually impossible to measure effectively (Cusack, 1984, pp. 629–631). Instead, the FCC often has operationalized content diversity purely in terms of program types (Evaluation of the Syndication, 1993a) and has "traditionally equated an increase or decrease in outlet diversity with a corresponding change in viewpoint diversity" (Review of the Commission's Regulations, 1995, p. 3550). However, recent statements have indicated that idea diversity now also falls within the FCC's bounds of empirical concern. In describing the analytical framework for its 1998 biennial review of broadcast regulations, the FCC emphasized "viewpoint diversity" as a key objective (1998 Biennial Regulatory Review, 1998). The Commission defined viewpoint diversity in terms of "a wide range of diverse and antagonistic opinions and interpretations" (1998 Biennial Regulatory Review, 1998, p. 11283). Within this same notice, the Commission asserted a relationship between source diversity and viewpoint diversity, reflecting the type of nexus that the Commission is now particularly interested in subjecting to empirical analysis (Kennard, 1998). Thus, viewpoint diversity has become one of the central criteria for determining the effectiveness and continued viability of the Commission's broadcast regulations (1998 Biennial Regulatory Review, 1998).

*Assessing idea diversity.* As the above discussion suggests, empirical analyses of idea diversity have seldom been conducted by communications policymakers or academics. This is no doubt due, in part, to the high levels of subjectivity involved in categorizing media content according to criteria such as political or ideological perspective. The development of an objective and meaningful method of assessing idea diversity is a daunting task. The enormity of the challenge is well-reflected in Entman and Wildman's (1992) question: "How do we distinguish 'The Cosby Show,' with its frequent overt and covert messages about racial prejudice, from the nightly news in terms of idea content?" (p. 13).

Although many studies have investigated issues such as the effects of different types of ownership, or of competition, on content (more often in print media than in electronic media contexts), these studies typically have addressed narrower dependent variables than the broader construct of idea diversity. Typical dependent variables have included editorial positions, amount of public affairs programming, or amount of local programming (e.g., Busterna & Hansen, 1990; Gormley, 1976; Lacy, 1991). As Compaine (1995) pointed out, "measuring diversity is more difficult than tracking differences in programming, but presumably more to the point of concerns" (p. 771). Perhaps the best example of a systematic effort to measure idea diversity can be found in Busterna's (1988) analysis of the effects of television and newspaper cross-ownership on the diversity of issues covered in the news (the results indicated no significant relationship).

Ultimately, the best place to turn for guidance on how to assess idea diversity empirically may be the extensive literature on the measurement of "bias" in the electronic media (see Gunter, 1997). The negative connotation frequently associated with the term "bias" is a bit misleading, for, as Gunter (1997) pointed out, analysis of bias includes everything from the analysis of presentation formats, patterns in the use of sources, framing techniques, and the range and diversity of topics covered. Thus, the measurement of bias should not be perceived purely in terms of the measurement of distortion, misinformation, or one-sidedness. Instead, the techniques of measuring bias can likely be applied to the construction of measures of, idea diversity in the electronic media, because bias measures are fundamentally concerned with issues of diversity of viewpoints and perspectives.

## Exposure Diversity

Exposure diversity is, in many ways, the neglected diversity dimension. However, it is as central to communications policy (if not more so) as either source or content diversity because of its relevance to the marketplace of ideas metaphor. What exactly is meant by exposure diversity? McQuail (1992a) provided a useful description. He distinguished diversity of content "as sent" from diversity of content "as received." The latter "identifies a different universe of content than that sent—what the audience actually selects" (p. 157). It is this idea of the diversity of content "as received" that is central to the notion of exposure diversity. Analyses of exposure diversity would thus seek to answer questions such as: How many different sources are audiences exposed to in their media use? Are audiences exposing themselves to a wide range of political and social views? Are they exposed to diverse types and formats of programming? Finally, and perhaps most importantly, what factors affect the levels of exposure diversity among audiences? Unfortunately, such questions about the diversity of content as received have received much less attention from policymakers, policy analysts, and academics than questions related to the diversity of content as sent (McQuail, 1992a, pp. 158–159).

At first glance, it might not seem apparent how questions of exposure diversity have relevance from a policy perspective. Some within the policy area have stressed that questions of audience exposure are beyond the bounds of diversity policy and diversity assessment (e.g., Entman & Wildman, 1992). As Baseman and Owen (1982) argued, "it is the number of voices among which the consumer can choose, and not the actual distribution of consumer choices, which is the magnitude of importance" (p. 43). However, when we return to the diversity principle's origins within the marketplace of ideas metaphor, the relevance of exposure diversity to communications policy decisions becomes clear. Specifically, implicit within the "marketplace of ideas" model is the assumption that audiences provided with a diversity of content options consume a diversity of content. That is, for the marketplace to function effectively, "individuals must fairly and equally consider all ideas through a process of rational evaluation" (Ingber, 1984, p. 15). It is this consumption of diverse ideas, sources, and perspectives that facilitates the well-informed decision-making that is central to the democratic notion of effective self-governance (see Meiklejohn, 1948/1972; Sunstein, 1993). From this standpoint, the marketplace ideal is not satisfied simply by the provision of a diversity of content. Diversity of exposure must exist as well. For any of the broader social goals commonly associated with the marketplace of ideas to be accomplished, citizens must take advantage of the information from "diverse and antagonistic sources" that is made available to them.

Clearly then, policymakers concerned with fulfilling the objectives inherent within the marketplace of ideas metaphor need to concern themselves with the degree to which audiences are actually exposing themselves to a diversity of information products and sources. Consequently, audience exposure must be an integral part of the conventional diversity framework and must receive greater attention in diversity research. This will allow diversity policy decisions to emerge from a better understanding of exactly how audiences respond to changes in the level of diversity of their media offerings. Economic policymakers typically do not set prices on goods and services in order to achieve their desired objectives. However, they do make policies designed to affect prices and purchasing habits. These decisions are made with an informed understanding of how consumers and industries will respond to these changes. Similarly, although communications policymakers cannot—and should not—make policies that directly affect consumption habits, it is certainly within the bounds of their responsibility to make policies that promote exposure to a diversity of sources and a diversity of content (Sunstein, 1993). For a communications policymaker not to have a sophisticated understanding of how audiences respond to changes in media offerings is equivalent to an economic policymaker not knowing how consumers respond to changes in prices.

*Assessing Exposure Diversity*

In the previous section I argued that exposure diversity is a fundamental component of the marketplace of ideas metaphor, and that, as an outgrowth of this metaphor, diversity-enhancing policies are ultimately concerned with increasing exposure to a diversity of sources and ideas. Consequently, assessing exposure diversity within the electronic media is essential to gauging the degree to which the ultimate objectives of a free, accessible, and diverse media system are being achieved, regardless of whether the onus of failure lies with policymakers or with the audience. As Sunstein (1993) stated,

> it is hardly unrealistic to assess a system of free expression by examining whether it generates broad and deep attention to public issues, and whether it brings about public exposure to an appropriate diversity of views. These are not utopian goals.
>
> (p. 22)

The obvious question, then, is how do we go about empirically assessing and tracking exposure diversity? Although far less common than assessments of source or content diversity, there have been several efforts to develop measures of exposure diversity that would allow for the tracking of exposure diversity and investigating its key determinants. Specifically, the methodological approaches to the concept focus on either *horizontal exposure diversity* or *vertical exposure diversity*. These categories have been adapted from Entman and Wildman's (1992) discussion of assessing content diversity *within* individual channels (vertical diversity) versus *across* all available channels (horizontal diversity). In the exposure context, horizontal exposure diversity refers to the distribution of audiences across all available content options, whereas vertical exposure diversity refers to the diversity of content consumption within individual audience members (Napoli, 1997).

Horizontal exposure diversity can be seen as related to the concept of audience fragmentation, which focuses on the breaking of the mass audience into smaller and smaller segments (Webster & Phalen, 1997, p. 39). Thus, horizontal exposure diversity focuses on the question of how the mass audience distributes itself across available content options at particular points in time. From such an analytical standpoint, the content variable (e.g., program or format type) is the point of focus. However, the analysis then focuses on the distribution of audience shares or dollars across these categories, as opposed to simply the distribution of available categories (as would be the case in a content diversity assessment).

An example of this approach can be found in Hellman and Soramaki's (1985) analysis of diversity in the videocassette industry. That study conceptualized diversity as each videocassette genre's share of the total number of cassettes appearing on *Billboard* magazine's sales and rental charts. In that case, then, the video-cassette genre was the unit of analysis and diversity was conceptualized in terms of the degree to which different videocassette genres were consumed (given the focus on the most frequently purchased and rented offerings), as opposed to simply the diversity of genres available. Similarly, Rothenbuhler and Dimmick's (1982) analysis of diversity in the popular music industry measured diversity as "the rate of turnover in the top slots on the popularity charts" (p. 143). Finally, Napoli (1997) focused on the distribution of ratings points for primetime network programs in investigating whether audiences consumed program types in proportion to their availability (the results suggested a very strong positive relationship). In each of these examples, diversity of consumption of the mass audience was being assessed, because the researchers relied on gross audience measures, rather than data on the consumption patterns of individuals. As Webster and Phalen (1997) stated about audience fragmentation, "It is a gross measure of media use that reveals little about how intensively individual channels are used over time" (p. 110). However, this type of information is useful for macrolevel analyses of the relationship between the media system and the mass audience.

Vertical exposure diversity refers to measures that focus on the exposure patterns within the individual audience member over time, as opposed to on the distribution of audience ratings or dollars across content options. Vertical exposure diversity can be seen as analogous to the concept of audience polarization, which focuses on "the tendency of individuals to move to the extremes of either consuming or avoiding some class of media content" (Webster & Phalen, 1997, p. 110). Researching the diversity of the consumption patterns of individual audience members requires drawing upon cumulative audience measures, which track individual behaviors, as opposed to gross measures (see Webster & Lichty, 1991, pp. 147–150).

An example of such individual-level analysis can be found in Heeter's (1985) analysis of cable subscribers' channel-viewing behavior. Heeter modified the Herfindahl-Hirschman method of assessing program-type diversity to construct a concentration index of cable subscribers' degrees of channel exposure (p. 143). This approach provided a measure of the individual's level of exposure diversity, in terms of exposure to different program outlets (in this case, cable channels). Similarly, Webster (1986) and Youn (1994) focused on program type and channel exposure at the level of individual users. Webster used Arbitron diary data to track individuals' exposure levels to broadcast and cable channels. Youn used questionnaires to track the diversity of program types consumed by individuals in different media environments.

*What We Know About Exposure Diversity: Implications for the Marketplace Ideal*

Research is relatively sparse in the area of audience consumption and the factors that affect the degree to which audiences consume a diversity of content. However, the scant research does suggest that increases in the diversity of content can lead to decreases in the diversity of exposure. If this is indeed the case, then the objectives inherent in the marketplace of ideas metaphor may actually be undermined, rather than fulfilled, by policies designed to increase the diversity of content options available to audiences (Webster & Phalen, 1994).

This possibility has received support within a variety of studies. Webster (1986) found that users of specialized cable channels (e.g., music video, sports, and news channels) devoted from 12 to 15 times more attention to those services than did the larger cable audience (p. 88). This trend toward the "polarization" of the audiences is reflected in more recent findings, which show a steady decline in the number of overlaps within the 10 most popular programs for African American and Caucasian audiences (Wilke, 1998). It is important to note that this phenomenon is largely attributable to the vastly increased viewing options provided by cable television and to the fact that the diffusion of cable television has allowed for the development of additional national networks (e.g., FOX, UPN, and WB) that target more narrowly tailored demographic segments.

The effects of cable television on viewing behavior were also central to research by Youn (1994), which focused on comparisons of viewing behavior between cable subscribers and nonsubscribers. Youn found that an increase in program-choice options facilitated program choice based on program-type preferences. Among cable subscribers, about 50% of all program consumption coincided with program-type preferences, compared with approximately 25% for non-subscribers (Youn, 1994, p. 472). Thus, although the diversity of program options available to these viewers increased, thereby expanding viewers' opportunities for exposure diversity, the diversity of what they actually chose to expose themselves to declined significantly.

Wober (1989) reported even more extreme findings. These findings suggest that increasing the availability of certain underrepresented program types can actually decrease audience consumption of those program types (pp. 100–101). What is perhaps most distressing is the nature of the program types for which this phenomenon occurs. News, religious, and general information programs all exhibit this trait, suggesting that exactly the type of socially valuable content that policymakers would most like to promote via their diversity policies is being increasingly neglected as viewing options multiply. Wober characterized these program types as "less efficient" and "demand inflexible" due to their inability to attract audiences in proportion to their availability (pp. 103–104).

The implications of these findings are just as important to questions of diversity in media as any findings detecting a decrease in content diversity. They suggest that an increasingly diverse electronic media marketplace could lead to audiences exposing themselves to a less diverse diet of programming. Consequently, the ideals of a well-functioning marketplace of ideas would not be met, and the ultimate objective of much media regulation would be undermined. As Webster and Phalen (1994) pointed out, "If increasing diversity of content means that each individual is actually exposed to less diversity of expression, it's hard to see how such a result facilitates the marketplace of ideas" (p. 35).

In the end, "media policy analysts should be aware that availability and use are not synonymous" (Ferguson & Perse, 1993, p. 43). Consequently, a key shift in analytical orientation needs to take place within the context of diversity policy, one in which the exposure dimension of diversity is placed on more equal footing with the source and content dimensions. Without greater empirical attention to the exposure dimension of diversity, policymakers are guilty of dangerously uninformed decision-making and engaging in an incomplete application of the marketplace of ideas metaphor. Policies need to be assessed and critiqued not only from the perspective of how they contribute to the diversity of content available, but how they contribute to the diversity of content consumed. In the end, it may be that increases in content diversity should be considered essentially meaning-less from a policy perspective if the additional content is ignored by the audience (see Haddock & Polsby, 1990, pp. 349–350).

## Conclusion

Assessing diversity in the electronic media has recently become a paramount concern for communications policymakers. In light of this recent empirical commitment, this essay has deconstructed the diversity principle into its empirically assessable components and has outlined the relationships that policymakers have frequently presumed exist between these components. These relationships between diversity components must receive the greatest attention in future diversity research. Unfortunately, diversity research has been largely descriptive, as opposed to predictive. Researchers have devoted far too little attention to factors affecting the various diversity components and to the possible cause and effect relationships between components. The existence of these relationships is central to the validity of many diversity policies. The lack of evidence supporting these relationships has frequently undermined these policies when they have been subjected to judicial scrutiny.

Thus, diversity policy needs to be better informed about issues such as the effects of economic and structural factors on source and content diversity, the dynamics of the relationship between source and content diversity, and both the structural and individual determinants of exposure diversity (see Litman, 1992). Research in these areas will give policymakers a better understanding of the media environment in which their policies are intended to function, and a better sense of whether specific policies are achieving both their intermediate and ultimate objectives.

Of course, the complexities inherent in a concept such as diversity suggest that any measurement efforts are likely to neglect certain important aspects or to over-simplify in their measurement processes. Such is the nature of the constructs that require measurement (see Napoli, in press-b). These oversimplifications and omissions do not preclude the usefulness of such empirical assessments as analytical tools for policymakers. Economic analyses are filled with a range of simplifying assumptions that undermine the degree to which they accurately reflect real world behavior. They remain very useful, however, as indicators of general tendencies and likely outcomes. Diversity assessments should be considered along the same lines—not as complete representations of objective reality, but as simplified representations of more complex processes.

These simplified representations can be useful decision-making tools, particularly for comparative or longitudinal analyses, in which the data need function only as relative, as opposed to absolute, measures. Certainly, the methodological difficulties in conducting diversity research are substantial. However, the potential for diversity research to inform important policy issues has not yet been reached.

## Questions for Consideration

1    Who do you think should ultimately be held responsible for content diversity in broadcasting—media producers, station owners, or the government? Why?

2    In a highly fragmented media world, why should we care specifically about diversity in broadcasting?

## Notes

1.    On occasion, the FCC has argued that decreases in source diversity can result in increases in content diversity (e.g., Review of the Commission's Regulations, 1995; Revision of Radio Rules, 1992).

2.    Of course, it is possible that concentration in media markets can stem from homogeneity of audience preferences for certain sources of information (see Baseman & Owen, 1982, p. 43).

3.    For a discussion of the theoretical justifications underlying this assumption, see Spitzer (1991).

4.    According to the intermediate scrutiny standard, a racial classification must satisfy an important government objective and be substantially related to the achievement of that objective (see *Metro Broadcasting v. Federal Communications Commission*, 1990, p. 565).

## References

Abrams v. United States, 65 S. Ct. 1416 (1919).

Adarand Constructors, Inc. v. Pena et al., 115 S. Ct. 2097 (1995).

Amendment of Part 73 of the Commission's Rules and Regulations with Respect to Competition and Responsibility in Network Television Broadcasting, 23 FCC 2d 382 (1970).

Associated Press v. United States, 326 U.S. 1 (1945).

Aufderheide, P. (1990). After the Fairness Doctrine: Controversial broadcast programming and the public interest. *Journal of Communication, 40*(3), 47–72.

Bagdikian, B. H. (1997). *The media monopoly* (5th ed.). Boston: Beacon Press.

Baseman, K. C., & Owen, B. M. (1982). *A framework for economic analysis of electronic media concentration issues.* Prepared for the National Cable Television Association for submission in FCC docket no. 82–434. Washington, DC: Economists Inc.

Besen, S. M., Krattenmaker, T. G., Metzger, R. A., Jr., & Woodbury, J. R. (1984). *Misregulating television: Network dominance and the FCC.* Chicago: University of Chicago Press.

Bhagwat, A. (1995). Of markets and media: The first amendment, the new mass media, and the political components of culture. *North Carolina Law Review, 74,* 141–217.

Bilingual Bicultural Coalition on Mass Media, Inc. v. FCC, 595 F.2d 621 (D. C. Cir. 1978).

Bloustein, E. J. (1981). The origin, validity, and interrelationships of the political values served by freedom of expression. *Rutgers Law Review, 33,* 372–396.

Blumler, J. G. (1992). Public service broadcasting before the commercial deluge. In J. G. Blumler (Ed.), *Television and the public interest: Vulnerable values in West European broadcasting* (pp. 7–21). Newbury Park, CA: Sage.

Busterna, J. C. (1976). Diversity of ownership as a criterion in FCC licensing since 1965. *Journal of Broadcasting, 20*, 101–110.

Busterna, J. C. (1988). Television station ownership effects on programming and idea diversity: Baseline data. *Journal of Media. Economics, 1*(2), 63–74.

Busterna, J. C., & Hansen, K. A. (1990). Presidential endorsement patterns by chain-owned newspapers. *Journalism Quarterly, 67*, 286–294.

Chan-Olmsted, S. (1991). Structural analysis of market competition in the U.S. TV syndication industry, 1981–1990. *Journal of Media Economics, 4*(3), 9–28.

Compaine, B. M. (1995). The impact of ownership on content: Does it matter? *Cardozo Arts & Entertainment Law Journal, 13*, 755–780.

Compaine, B. M., Sterling, C. H., Guback, T., & Noble, J. K., Jr. (1982). *Who owns the media? Concentration of ownership in the mass communications industry* (2nd ed.). White Plains, NY: Knowledge Industry Publications.

Complaint of Syracuse Peace Council Against Television Station WTVH Syracuse, New York, 3 F.C.C.R. 2035 (1988).

Cusack, D. M. (1984). Peanuts and potatoes: The FCC's diversification policy and antitrust laws. *Comm/Ent, 7*, 599–645.

DeJong, A. S., & Bates, B. J. (1991). Channel diversity in cable television. *Journal of Broadcasting & Electronic Media, 35*, 159–166.

Department of Justice and Federal Trade Commission. (1992). 1992 horizontal merger guidelines, 57 Fed. Reg. 41552.

Dominick, J. R., & Pearce, M. C. (1976). Trends in network prime-time programming, 1953–74. *Journal of Communication, 20*(1), 70–80.

Editorializing by Broadcast Licensees, 13 F.C.C. 1246 (1949).

Ehrenberg, A. S. C. (1968). The factor analytic search for program types. *Journal of Advertising Research, 8*(1), 55–63.

Entman, R. M., & Wildman, S. S. (1992). Reconciling economic and non-economic perspectives on media policy: Transcending the "marketplace of ideas." *Journal of Communication, 42*(1), 5–19.

Equal Employment Opportunity Processing Guidelines for Broadcast Renewal Applicants, 45 Fed. Reg. 16335 (1980).

Evaluation of the Syndication and Financial Interest Rules, 8 F.C.C.R. 3282 (1993a).

Evaluation of the Syndication and Financial Interest Rules, 73 Rad. Reg. 2d 1452 (1993b).

Ferguson, D. A., & Perse, E. M. (1993). Media and audience influences on channel repertoire. *Journal of Broadcasting & Electronic Media, 37*, 31–47.

Fowler, M. S., & Brenner, D. L. (1982). A marketplace approach to broadcast regulation. *Texas Law Review, 60*, 1–51.

Frank, R. E., Becknell, J. C., & Clokey, J. D. (1971). Television program types. *Journal of Marketing Research, 8*(2), 204–211.

Glasser, T. L. (1984). Competition and diversity among radio formats: Legal and structural issues. *Journal of Broadcasting, 28*, 127–142.

Gormley, W. T. (1976). *The effects of newspaper-television cross-ownership on news homogeneity*. Chapel Hill, NC: Institute for Research in Social Science.

Grant, A. E. (1994). The promise fulfilled? An empirical analysis of program diversity on television. *Journal of Media Economics, 7*(1), 51–64.

Greenberg, E., & Barnett, H. J. (1971). TV program diversity: New evidence and old theories. *American Economic Review, 61*(2), 89–93.

Gunter, B. (1997). *Measuring bias on television*. Bedfordshire, UK: University of Luton Press.

Haddock, D. D., & Polsby, D. D. (1990). Bright lines, the Federal Communications Commission's duopoly rule, and the diversity of voices. *Federal Communications Law Journal, 42*, 331–364.

Handling of Public Issues Under the Fairness Doctrine and the Public Interest Standards of the Communications Act, 48 F.C.C. 2d 1 (1974).

Heeter, C. (1985). Program selection with abundance of choice: A process model. *Human Communication Research, 12*, 125–152.

Hellman, H., & Soramaki, M. (1985). Economic concentration in the videocassette industry: A cultural comparison. *Journal of Communication, 35*(3), 122–134.

Ingber, S. (1984, February). The marketplace of ideas: A legitimizing myth. *Duke Law Journal, 1984*, 1–91.

Inquiry into Section 73.1910 of the Commission's Rules and Regulations Concerning the General Fairness Doctrine Obligations of Broadcast Licensees, 102 F.C.C. 2d 145 (1985).

Kambara, N. (1992, March). Study of the diversity indices used for programming analysis. *Studies of Broadcasting, 28*, 195–206.

Kennard, W. E. (1998, September 11). Remarks to American Women in Radio and Television, Washington, DC. Available: http://www.fcc.gov/Speeches/Kennard/spwek826.html

Kirsch, A. D., & Banks, S. (1962). Program types defined by factor analysis. *Journal of Advertising Research, 2*(3), 29–31.

Kleiman, H. (1991). Content diversity and the FCC's minority and gender licensing policies. *Journal of Broadcasting & Electronic Media, 35*, 411–429.

Krattenmaker, T. G., & Powe, L. A. (1994). *Regulating broadcast programming*. Cambridge, MA: MIT Press.

Kubey, R., Shifflet, M., Weerakkody, N., & Ukeiley, S. (1995). Demographic diversity on cable: Have the new cable channels made a difference in the representation of gender, race, and age? *Journal of Broadcasting & Electronic Media, 39*, 459–471.

Lacy, S. (1991). Effects of group ownership on daily newspaper content. *Journal of Media Economics, 4*(1), 35–47.

Lamprecht v. Federal Communications Commission, 958 F.2d 382 (D.C. Cir. 1992).

LeDuc, D. R. (1982). Deregulation and the dream of diversity. *Journal of Communication, 32*(4), 164–178.

Lehman, D. R. (1971). Television show preference: Application of a choice model. *Journal of Marketing Research, 8*(1), 47–55.

Lentz, C. S. (1996). The fairness in broadcasting doctrine and the Constitution: Forced one-stop shopping in the "marketplace of ideas." *University of Illinois Law Review, 1996*, 271–317.

Levin, H. J. (1971). Program duplication, diversity, and effective viewer choices: Some empirical findings. *American Economic Review, 61*(2), 81–88.

Levin, H. J. (1980). *Fact and fancy in television regulation: An economic study of policy alternatives*. New York: Russell Sage Foundation.

Lin, C. A. (1995). Diversity of network prime-time program formats during the 1980s. *Journal of Media Economics, 8*(4), 17–28.

Litman, B. R. (1979). The television networks, competition, and program diversity. *Journal of Broadcasting, 24*, 393–409.

Litman, B. R. (1992). Economic aspects of program quality: The case for diversity. *Studies of Broadcasting, 28*, 121–156.

Litman, B. R., Hasegawa, K., Shrikhande, S., & Barbatsis, G. (1994). Measuring diversity in U.S. television programming. *Studies of Broadcasting, 30*, 131–153.

Long, S. L. (1979). A fourth television network and diversity: Some historical evidence. *Journalism Quarterly, 56*, 341–345.

Lutheran Church-Missouri Synod v. Federal Communications Commission, 141 F.3d (D.C. Cir. 1998).

McGregor, M. A. (1984). Importance of diversity in controversy over financial interest and syndication. *Journalism Quarterly, 61*, 831–834.

McQuail, D. (1992a). *Media performance: Mass communication and the public interest*. Newbury Park, CA: Sage.

McQuail, D. (1992b). The Netherlands: Freedom and diversity under multichannel conditions. In J. G. Blumler (Ed.), *Television and the public interest: Vulnerable values in West European broadcasting* (pp. 96–111). Newbury Park, CA: Sage.

Meiklejohn, A. (1960). *Political freedom: The constitutional powers of the people*. New York: Harper & Brothers. (Original work published 1948)

Meiklejohn, A. (1972). *Free speech and its relation to self-government*. Port Washington, NY: Kennikat Press. (Original work published 1948)

Metro Broadcasting, Inc. v. Federal Communications Commission, 497 U.S. 547 (1990).

Napoli, P. M. (1997). Rethinking program diversity assessment: An audience-centered approach. *Journal of Media Economics, 10*(4), 59–74.

Napoli, P. M. (in press-a). *Foundations of communications policy: Principles and process in the regulation of electronic media*. Cresskill, NJ: Hampton Press.

Napoli, P. M. (in press-b). The unique nature of communications regulation: Evidence and implications for communications policy analysis. *Journal of Broadcasting & Electronic Media*.

1998 Biennial Regulatory Review: Review of the Commission's Broadcast Ownership Rules and Other Rules Adopted Pursuant to Section 202 of the Telecommunications Act of 1996, 13 F.C.C.R. 11276 (1998).

Nondiscrimination in the Employment Policies and Practices of Broadcast Licensees, 54 FCC 2d 354 (1975).

Owen, B. M. (1975). *Economics and freedom of expression: Media structure and the First Amendment*. Cambridge, MA: Ballinger.

Owen, B. M. (1977). Regulating diversity: The case of radio formats. *Journal of Broadcasting, 21*, 305–319.

Owen, B. M. (1978). The economic view of programming. *Journal of Communication, 28*, 43–50.

Owen, B. M., & Wildman, S. S. (1992). *Video economics*. Cambridge, MA: Harvard University Press.

Peterson, R. A. (1994). Measured markets and unknown audiences: Case studies from the production and consumption of music. In J. S. Ettema & D. C. Whitney (Eds.), *Audiencemaking: How the media create the audience* (pp. 171–185). Thousand Oaks, CA: Sage.

Rao, V. R. (1975). Taxonomy of television programs based on viewing behavior. *Journal of Marketing Research, 12*, 355–358.

Red Lion Broadcasting Co. v. Federal Communications Commission, 395 U.S. 367 (1969).

Redish, M. H. (1982). The value of free speech. *University of Pennsylvania Law Review, 130*, 591–645.

Review of the Commission's Regulations Governing Television Broadcasting; Television Satellite Stations Review of Policy and Rules, 10 F.C.C.R. 3524 (1995).

Revision of Radio Rules and Policies, 7 F.C.C.R. 2755 (1992).

Rothenbuhler, E. W., & Dimmick, J. W. (1982). Popular music: Concentration and diversity in the industry, 1974–1980. *Journal of Communication, 32*(1), 143–149.

Schurz Communications v. Federal Communications Commission, 982 F.2d 1043 (7th Cir. 1992).

Shannon, C. E., & Weaver, W. (1963). *The mathematical theory of communication*. Urbana: University of Illinois Press.

Spitzer, M. L. (1991). Justifying minority preferences in broadcasting. *Southern California Law Review, 64*, 293–360.

Sunstein, C. R. (1993). *Democracy and the problem of free speech*. New York: Free Press.

Turner Broadcasting System v. Federal Communications Commission, 114 S. Ct. 2445 (1994).

Turner Broadcasting System v. Federal Communications Commission, 117 S. Ct. 1174 (1997).

Wakshlag, J., & Adams, W. J. (1985). Trends in program variety and the prime time access rule. *Journal of Broadcasting & Electronic Media, 29*, 23–34.

Webster, J. G. (1986). Audience behavior in the new media environment. *Journal of Communication, 36*(3), 77–91.

Webster, J. G., & Lichty, L. W. (1991). *Ratings analysis: Theory and practice*. Hillsdale, NJ: Erlbaum.

Webster, J. G., & Phalen, P. F. (1994). Victim, consumer, or commodity? Audience models in communication policy. In J. S. Ettema & D. C. Whitney (Eds.), *Audiencemaking: How the media create the audience* (pp. 19–37). Thousand Oaks, CA: Sage.

Webster, J. G., & Phalen, P. F. (1997). *The mass audience: Rediscovering the dominant model*. Mahwah, NJ: Erlbaum.

Webster, J. G., & Wakshlag, J. J. (1983). A theory of program choice. *Communication Research, 10*, 430–446.

Wilke, M. (1998, April 6). Blacks' fave TV shows don't dent overall top 10. *Advertising Age*, p. 18.

Wilson, L. C. (1988). Minority and gender enhancements: A necessary and valid means to achieve diversity in the broadcast marketplace. *Federal Communications Law Journal, 40*(1), 89–114.

Wober, J. M. (1989). The U.K.: The constancy of audience behavior. In L. B. Becker & K. Schoenbach (Eds.), *Audience responses to media diversification: Coping with plenty* (pp. 91–108). Hillsdale, NJ: Erlbaum.

Youn, S. (1994). Program type preference and program choice in a multichannel situation. *Journal of Broadcasting & Electronic Media, 38*, 465–475.

# Chapter 16

## DAVID HENDY

# RADIO AND MODERNITY
## Time, Place and "Communicative Capacity"

**I**T'S IMPORTANT TO NOTE THAT this piece about radio is told from primarily a British perspective. David Hendy, who teaches media at the University of Westminster, London, wrote it as part of a larger book, *Radio in the Global Age*, published in 2000. Hendy does reflect a bit on differences between the highly commercial radio system of the U.S. and the extreme public-service orientation of the British Broadcasting Corporation in the days of Lord Reith, the visionary founder of the BBC. However, a larger theme to emerge from Hendy's essay is radio's role in structuring our lives—both temporally and socially. As you read it, compare the ideas of time and place that Hendy says radio creates in the listener with your own experience of the way radio works on your sense of time and space.

Throughout this discussion of talk and music on radio, I have frequently touched on two underlying themes which now deserve more direct examination: time and place. Researchers have hinted at some of the ways in which the physical distances between broadcasters and listeners are tackled in order to establish feelings of intimacy with the medium—the "simulating co-presence" that Montgomery talks of, for instance, or the sense of community engendered by the medium more generally that we saw in our discussion of radio listening in chapter 3. This suggests that creating a *sense of place* is one recurring theme of radio's meaningfulness in modern life. And as well as a sense of place, there is also our sense of *space* to be considered: that in transmitting its signals over many hundreds of miles, and in allowing us in our domestic lives to be "connected" to events and people beyond physical reach, radio somehow transforms our sense of space *between* different places. Many discussions also hinted at the central role in producing meaningfulness, not so much of individual programmes (or elements of programmes), but of the longer patterns of radio output over time—the way in which the time at which a record is played is perhaps more significant than the lyrics it contains, or the way in which listeners come to associate particular shows and styles of output with particular times of day. This suggests that a second recurring theme should be the ways in which radio's *temporal rhythms*—its narrative structures, hourly cycles and daily and weekly schedules—connect with the temporal rhythms of our everyday lives. In viewing radio from the twin perspectives of "time" and of "place", we do not necessarily escape the contradictions of the medium—how in one sense it may contribute (along with other mass media) to the much discussed phenomenon of social alienation, and how in other ways it may, to use Scannell's phrase again, "rekindle" social life. Even so, without offering a unifying "theory" of radio, I will make some attempt to explore what may underlie these paradoxes and relate them to some of the concepts of modernity—the patterns of contemporary life—that have been applied to the media more generally. I propose to do this through developing the notion of radio's "communicative capacity".

## Time

In arguing that radio's real "text" is the "clock on the studio wall", Garner (1990) was suggesting that the individual elements making up a radio programme only become fully meaningful when heard in their precise temporal context. We can extend this further. Radio is, to state a truism, a time-based medium. Its texts—its programmes—emerge in a linear flow of time, whether measured in seconds (as in commercials or jingles), hours (individual radio shows), or even weeks (in the case of series or whole advertising campaigns). Indeed, as Crisell reminds us, whereas television can deliver its messages pictorially across the space of the television screen as well as over time, radio has *only* the passage of time in which to do its work (1994: 5–6). A programme's identity, although clearly shaped by the voice of its presenter and the choice of its music, is therefore also to be found in the way it orders its content, say, for example, in the course of each hour. Morning programmes, broadcast when most listeners want to "get up and get on", arrange their content in a relatively hectic narrative of many short pieces of speech and music; early-afternoon programmes deliberately achieve a more relaxed tempo through fewer and longer segments of sound. Producers, as we saw in chapter 2, construct radio programmes on the basis of a "clock format": a recurring pattern of sounds and themes arranged in a certain order each hour, with news bulletins, weather reports, sports news and phone-in features at certain fixed times. A programme's clock format is a useful template for producers, but it is also founded on the needs of listeners, who cannot choose the order in which they hear radio, and can only pick and choose what to hear by associating certain programme elements with certain times of the day, and tuning in at the times which allow them to catch them. Of course, no-one can tune in at exactly the right moment, and broadcasters wish to keep their audiences listening for as long as possible. So the clock format is not enough: the "messages" are, as we know, evanescent, and the past and future are always intangible, and there needs therefore to be a constant "signposting" back and forwards, with listeners being reminded incessantly about who is talking and what they are talking about, or what the station is that they are listening to, and what is about to happen, in both the immediate and more distant future. This aural signposting is designed to enable listeners to get their bearings quickly, but its net effect is also to create a sense in which the narrative, though recurring and familiar, is also evolving and never-ending—that something worthwhile (whether a chance to win a dream holiday or the chance to hear the latest single by a particular band) could be missed by turning off. The various means by which radio establishes the beginnings and endings of programmes—verbal motifs, jingles, silence and so on—have been described as "frame" conventions (Goffman 1980: 162–5) or "boundary rituals" (Fiske and Hartley 1978: 166–7). But in fact, very few radio stations still offer discrete programmes of contrasting genres, preferring longer "sequence" shows of two or three hours and even then preferring to propel listeners as swiftly and unobtrusively as possible from one programme to the next. Frame conventions and boundary rituals undoubtedly exist, so that, for example, we know from the short "stab" of a particular jingle that a news bulletin has ended; but framing is rarely expressed in a way which provides an opportunity for listeners to switch off or change stations—they must be encouraged to stay.

In studies of television, the concept of "flow" has been used to explain the way in which the medium is experienced by viewers, not so much as individual programmes but as a sequence of programmes. Raymond Williams (1974) pointed out that we tend to say we're "watching television" rather than watching a *particular* TV programme: it is an indication of the way in which dramas, news, adverts and trails—genres which, though different, often imitate each other in form, and which collide with barely marked boundaries between them—are experienced in one sitting as a single flow. Several authors have suggested that this flow should be understood, not as a smooth uninterrupted process, but an essentially discontinuous and fragmented one. Ellis (1982) describes how television's continuity is punctuated by adverts and trails, and how each individual programme is in turn composed of smaller (and often unrelated) building blocks. As Abercrombie makes clear, "Williams's flow actually takes place across groups of segments" (1996: 16). Such flow is fractured further, as viewers usually change channels many times in the course of an evening's viewing: through zapping, each viewer in effect composes his or her own unique "flow" of images, sounds and feelings.

Are there parallels in radio? Certainly, listeners rarely "tune in" for particular programmes: as we noted in chapter 3, they listen *to the radio*, just as Williams' viewers *watch television*. There is a subtle difference, however. Since radio programme schedules are listed less prominently than television schedules in the press, and retuning a radio set has traditionally been more difficult than changing channels on television, listening to the radio is generally a much less promiscuous affair than watching television: listeners do not "zap" from one station to another in the way they might flick through the channels on television. The "flow" of sounds experienced by listeners to radio is therefore usually composed of the more coherent and *predetermined* flow of a single station for the entire duration of any one listening session. This may not always be the case in the near future. We saw in chapter 1 how technological developments— the arrival of push-button digital radio sets—will soon allow what one broadcaster described as new and "scary" levels of listener promiscuity. We also saw that the technology of audio on-demand creates the possibility of listeners constructing their own schedules—their own unique flow—of programmes. Yet for the time being at least, listeners to radio are less able to subvert a given radio station's own constructed pattern of output over time, and they either accept the schedule of programming offered or switch off altogether.

Even so, while radio's flow is *less* fragmented than that of television's because it is habitually experienced through just one station at a time (rather than many channels), it is simultaneously *more* fragmented than television flow because of the intrinsically more segmented nature of even a single station's output. If radio broadcasts are highly formatted, programme segments are much smaller and more rapid in succession than those that television usually offers. Recall the discussion in chapter 2 of the "acoustic beads" which Crisell describes as constituting the building blocks of programme making. In fact, he makes explicit a comparison with Ellis" "segmentation" concept:

> Commercial radio output typically consists of a string of acoustic beads, a sequence of records interspersed with commercial breaks, presenter's talk, news, weather information and so on—each "bead" of approximately similar length to the others and lasting no more than a few moments. For this kind of output I shall borrow the term "segmentation" which has been coined in relation to television programming (Ellis 1982: 116–26). It is true that Ellis sees almost all broadcast output as segmented— ultimately divisible into "bites" consisting of a scene in a play, an advert, a statement from an interviewee, and so on: but the term seems particularly useful here because the segments which make up talk and music sequences on the radio are much more apparent, more discrete and detachable, than those which co-operate in a "built" programme such as a play or documentary. To a far greater extent they can be added, subtracted or reordered without discernible damage to the whole.
>
> (1994: 72)

Compare this with Kaplan's interpretation of MTV—a music-television channel striking for its adoption of an essentially *radio*-based temporal rhythm:

> The channel hypnotizes more than others because it consists of a series of extremely short (four minutes or less) texts that maintain us in an excited state of expectation. The "coming up next" mechanism that is the staple of all serials is an intrinsic aspect of the minute-by-minute MTV watching. We are trapped by the constant hope that the next video will finally satisfy and, lured by the seductive promise of immediate plenitude, we keep endlessly consuming the short texts. MTV thus carries to an extreme a phenomenon that characterizes most of television.
>
> (1987: 4)

MTV might be viewed as "extreme" in the context of television, but its "extremely short texts" and "coming up next mechanism" for enticing the viewer to keep watching is directly comparable to the *bulk* of mainstream radio's output, with its "acoustic beads" and constant signposting. If so, the concept of flow is even more pertinent in studying radio than it has been for analysing television, though with one important qualification: since radio flow is not quite as fractured across several channels in the way that television flow tends to be, its precise tempo and pattern, along with its content, apparently lies more under the control of the broadcasters themselves than with the listeners.

Higgins and Moss, as we noted earlier, see great ideological significance in this ability of broadcasters to control the flow of sounds over periods of time. Their studies of Australian radio suggested that the apparent haphazardness with which seemingly disparate snippets of news, commercials, personal narratives, songs and comments come together on radio conceals a quite deliberate "sequence of signs and images whose purpose is to transmit certain cultural messages" (1982: 33). It is not the individual elements of programming which carry meaning so much as their coalescence into a unified message through the planned use of a recurrent temporal pattern: callers' personal narratives around the theme of life-as-being-tough being *followed* by—and *overwhelmed* by—the brash positivism of commercials offering a better future (1982: 37). Higgins and Moss' use of the concept of flow raises a question here, though: why should radio listeners be quite so passively accepting of the consumerist ideology with which they identify? Berland finds one possible answer in the tempo of radio output itself. Radio, she argues, is not a sequence of discontinuous items but a "motivated" flow of rapid and predictable items in a continuous sequence. The rapidity of the flow is as "carefully managed" as the predictability of its pattern, and it creates a "continuous rhythm of sound . . . more powerful than any single item enveloped in its progression". In this way, radio teaches us "addiction and forgetfulness": it induces—is *intended* to induce—passive listening, a form of listening which, precisely because it is passive, is accepting and hence vulnerable to any form of persuasion. Listeners, in effect, are simply not given the time to stop and think, because the "text" they are "reading" is fast-moving, continuous and—unless one switches off completely—unstoppable (1993b: 210–11).

The issue of time itself is actually taken one stage further by Berland. She argues that mainstream music radio is actively reconstructing—and, in particular, *quickening*— both the rhythms of our daily lives and our sense of historical change. She makes the point that if a station wished to change format, from for example, MOR (Middle of the Road) to CHR (Contemporary Hit Radio), it would—among other changes, such as a brisker presentation style—adopt a smaller playlist with a higher weekly rotation and faster turnover of hits:

> Like the radio schedule itself, with its strict markers of the hour, its subtly clocked rotation of current and past hits, its advanced promotion of a new release, the music playlist functions as a kind of meta-language of time. The playlist offers a grammar of temporality which draws in the listener and produces him or her (economically, as a commodity; experientially, as a listener) as a member of a stylistic community defined, more and more, in inexorably temporal terms, rather than in relation to geographic or more explicitly substantive identification—assembled that is, in terms of the preferred speed and rate of musical consumption.
>
> (1993a: 113–14)

In mainstream music radio, Berland suggests, time is "speeded-up and broken into contemporaneous moments"; radio marks historical time through music, and where its music is turned-over more rapidly, it "creates a new sense of time, not directly parallel to previous kinds" (1993a: 114).

Radio's relationship with time, and specifically with the rhythms of our daily and weekly lives, has been a central concern of Scannell's analysis of radio (1988, 1996). Here, though, the power relationship between broadcasters and audiences is more evenly balanced, with radio output seen to have a much more sensitive relationship with the pre-existing rhythms of modern life. I mentioned in chapter 3 Scannell's suggestion that broadcasters know their output must adapt itself to, and seek to enter into, the contexts in which it is being heard. These everyday contexts are defined largely by our domestic timetables, the humdrum activities we perform at given moments in the day—getting up, preparing ourselves for work, doing the housework, getting ready for bed, and so on. Radio does not just adapt to these routines and structure its output accordingly across the daily schedule, it also helps *over time* to "thematize" our days. By marking off each *part* of the day as somehow different—"breakfast time", "drive time"—and by marking off each day *as a whole* as a *new* day with fresh events and topics to be discussed (and yet somehow also a day rather like any other), *radio* time chimes with *our* time. Or, as Scannell himself puts it, "Broadcasting, whose medium is time, articulates our sense of time" (1996: 148–52).

It is also the familiarity of certain patterns of radio output *over time*, that helps accumulate a particular programme's identity—an identity defined above all by its recurrent part in our daily lives. We take for granted the daily presence of shows like the *Today* programme on BBC Radio 4, or Radio 1's *Breakfast Show*, or K-Rock's *Howard Stern Show*, because over time we have come to trust that they will be there and to understand what they will entail. In radio advertising too, commercials are rarely one-offs. Campaigns are based on a given number of "Opportunities to Hear" ("OTHs") over a period of several weeks: only *over time* will the listener "get" the message (RAB 1998a, 1998b). If this is so, then formats and schedules are not just tools of production—as we viewed them in chapter 2—or ways of bending to the listeners' own demands and tastes—as we viewed them in chapter 3—but also devices which over time make radio *itself* an ordinary, routine part of our lives:

> A single programme has no identity. . . . For output to have the regular, familiar routine character that it has, seriality is crucial. . . . The net effect of all these techniques is cumulative. In and through time programme output, in all its parts and as a whole, takes on a settled, familiar, known and taken-for-granted character.
>
> (Scannell 1996: 10–11)

So: it is not *just* that radio takes the "stuff of ordinary life" to make "public, communicable, pleasurable" programmes out of it and "revalue" private life by bringing it into the public domain. It is also a matter of time—the way this ordinary everyday experience unfolds *temporally* in a way that parallels the "endless continuum of day-to-day life" (Scannell 1988b: 19). Take radio soap operas, where time in the fictional world invariably runs in precise parallel with the real world: if it is Tuesday in *The Archers* it is usually Tuesday in the real world. And if so:

> it follows that the lifetime of . . . listeners unfolds at the same rate as the lives of the characters in the story. Thus one stands in the same temporal relation to them as one does to one's own family, relatives, friends and everyday acquaintances.
>
> (Scannell 1996: 159)

Time, then, and the familiarity engendered over time, is one of the foundations upon which radio's intimacy is built. And not just its intimacy, but its sociability too. Recall Douglas' idea in chapter 3, that it is the *simultaneity* of the listening experience which turns individual listeners into communities of listeners: we rarely tape a radio programme in the way that we might record a favourite television programme—so, like everyone else, we have to be listening *at the time* to catch a particular programme. And if we are listening at the same time, that means that we have something in common: our lives stand in the same temporal relation to other listeners as much as they stand in the same temporal relationship to the programmes we hear.

So: radio time "chimes" with our time in a way that generates intimacy and sociability. Yet "our time" is itself influenced by "radio time". Influenced a great deal, Berland implies, since we often listen to radio stations which mark us off by our "preferred speed and rate of musical consumption", which generally quicken the pace of our lives and threaten to overwhelm us with the unceasing torrent of their output. Influenced a little less, Scannell implies, if only because radio output has to accommodate itself to the domestic routines within which it is consumed. This is not an unbridgeable gulf in interpretation. Scannell certainly acknowledges that radio has helped us "thematize" our daily lives by making us aware of what others are doing and *when* each day. This picks up a thread from our earlier discussion of audiences in chapter 3, where I suggested that radio might well be gratifying needs which it has in some sense helped to create. Radio, then, does not just work to time, it also mediates our sense of it. Or, rather, our senses of it. For we must also remember that the fragmentation of radio listening into tighter niche markets means that the "simultaneity" of radio which Douglas sees as central to its sociable dimension is experienced in ever smaller communities nowadays. We do not have to construct a grand theory of a fractured, alienated society in order to recognize that we do not all live our lives at the same pace and to the same daily pattern, and that different radio stations now offer us several different temporal rhythms with which to live our lives.

## Place

Let us turn now to radio's sense of place. Those working as radio producers are frequently urged to use sound to "take" the listeners to a particular place: they assemble location recordings of aural "actuality" into atmospheric "soundscapes" that evoke certain locales. These soundscapes, as Crisell and Shingler and Wieringa remind us, are not accurate reflections of the sounds of the world, but clearly selective and stylized. Nevertheless, the urge to create this sense of place is common, not just to radio drama or features, but also to radio news, and much of the talk scattered through music radio. It is the same urge to "take" listeners out of their real listening environments that prompts so many outside broadcasts, at concerts, music festivals, sports events, ceremonies, public rallies and so on: they have the virtue of presenting radio stations as not being isolated from the world beyond their studios, and they are presented simultaneously to listeners as a chance for them to take part in an event that they might never be able to attend in person. Television, of course, does much the same, so that we can say that broadcasting as a whole offers some form of window on the world, some access to the ongoing public life that takes place beyond the domestic environments in which we watch TV and listen to the radio. If so, we can argue that while broadcasters use the technology of transmission and networking to send their signals across ever larger distances—"shrinking" global space—conversely, listeners can use broadcasting to *expand* their horizons.

These horizons, though, are not always expanded in entirely uncomplicated ways. For one thing, an individual item on the radio might seek to create a particular sense of place when dealing with a particular story, but the radio "text" as a whole is made up of many items—a flow of many different senses-of-place. Format radio gives us, say, a record by an American artist followed by a news report from the Balkans, some sports commentary from Europe and a travel bulletin from the nearest town. As Berland reminds us, radio joins together "geographically and philosophically unrelated items" in new juxtapositions—it literally splits "sound from source" (1993b: 210).

All this juxtapositioning takes place in a public "space"—but a space nevertheless defined by broadcasters rather more than by listeners. Brand and Scannell, in their study of the Tony Blackburn show, suggested the programme's identity lay precisely in its ability to straddle the public institutional space from which the radio presenter speaks and the private, domestic or work spaces from which callers speak. Yet to "enter" the studio as a caller is "to cross a threshold, to enter a social environment that creates its own occasions, discursive and performative rules and conventions" (1991: 222–3): all listeners are entitled to enter, but they are there to supply—to co-produce—a pretty strictly defined sense of "fun" (or, in the case of current affairs phone-ins, "news"). The public space offered to listeners by radio is therefore one with strictly limited horizons, even if listeners accept that and collude with it in order to simply pass the time in an entertaining way. Ultimately, implies Scannell, if such *sociability* has been achieved, then broadcasting has done its work.

Sociability is, here, a *virtual* coming together—a coming together of listeners with broadcasters, callers and other listeners, in which other people, other cultures, other musics, are "revealed" through broadcasting. As such, it is at the heart of radio's ability to affirm our sense of place in the world in human terms, and underlies all the medium's claims to a special form of intimacy. But what sort of "sociability" does radio actually present to us? We know that listeners feel "close" to *presenters* with whom they are allowed to become familiar. But the overriding characteristic of radio seems to be its ability to make us aware of *other listeners*. Montgomery's study of "Our Tune", and both Hobson's and Coward's studies of the relationships forged through listening to DJs, return us time and time again to radio presenting the audience back to itself: we are spoken to as individuals and the personal crises of individuals are described, but a community of shared interests is invoked, "not the family, or the neighbourhood, or even the nation as such, but rather the radio audience itself" (Montgomery 1991: 175–6).

This radio audience is often defined as specifically tied to a place, it is *local*—and indeed radio, as we saw in chapter 1, is much more highly localized than television. But we also know that the audience definition is constantly shifting, not just between stations but also moment-by-moment within a single station's output: sometimes it is defined by musical taste, at other times by age, by occupation, even by star sign. These definitions promise to draw us out of our geographical and domestic isolation, and offer us membership of new communities of *interest* much less tied to geographical place. Yet, as we also know from our survey of the radio industry in chapter 1, audiences are being packaged into ever smaller "fragmented" interest groups, and globalization—which the media contribute to and reflect—can simultaneously make this enlarged world a flatter, more homogenized, one: the news agenda, the music we hear, and the style of pro-gramming we hear it packaged in, is everywhere superficially different but almost everywhere essentially the same. This makes the sense of place and community engendered by radio a rather contradictory affair.

Take three examples, drawn in turn from southern Africa, Western Australia and

North America. Scannell (1997) looked at patterns of radio listening in Zimbabwe, and showed how, even though many more people listened to the state-broadcaster's "Radio 2" station than to the more international, Afropop-dominated "Radio 3", they were poorer and there was something of a stigma attached to it:

> The station [Radio 2] was "weird", "not modern", "country stuff", "African". I was told by a friend that some people would switch off Radio 2 before visitors or neighbours came in, so as not to be found listening to the station.
>
> (1997: 10–11)

The two stations, both ostensibly serving a national audience, clearly catered for two different musical "taste publics", but it is noticeable that ZBC's Radio 2 lacked the aspirational quality that attached to its Radio 3. A similar "pull" towards urban life was detected in Green's study of broadcasting in the Western Australian outback (1998). Here, until the advent of commercial television via Intelsat in 1986, many isolated farmsteads had no television or radio services at all, while other communities received only public-service broadcasts supplied by the Australian Broadcasting Corporation (ABC)—broadcasts which suffered from an image as "worthy but dull". Green's study found that, without the adverts—and the glamour, fashion, gossip, music and style that such adverts embodied—listeners felt excluded from membership of a common, popular, *consumerist* culture. Some listeners who took occasional trips to Perth began to make illegal cassette recordings of programmes on 96FM—the city's main commercial pop station—to be brought back for endless replaying once home in the outback. Many of those replying to questionnaires distributed by Green were adamant that what they really wanted from their "local" radio or television was "entry" to the cosmopolitan, consumerist lifestyle enjoyed by those living in Perth. In the short term, this could only be achieved by travelling long distances, and capturing on tape the sleek, polished output of someone else's radio station.

One predictable *longer-term* solution to these listeners' demands would no doubt be for their "local" service to adopt a more "sophisticated"—that is, "urban"—style for itself. We saw in chapter 1 how, by repackaging syndicated material beamed across whole networks, many radio stations are becoming the "localizers" of national or even international content. What's more, as Berland points out in one of her studies of Canadian radio (1993a), where there is a particularly big urban centre its stations seem to act as "magnets" to listeners in outlying smaller towns. And since these magnet stations are increasingly likely to belong to a branded chain, they are also quite likely to have tighter formats playing a narrower range of mostly nationally and internationally distributed music than their small town competitors; they are likely to belong to a branded chain. In this way, the dominant means by which urban radio formats its own output "delocalizes" and "recentralizes" space. Berland therefore draws a parallel with Harold Innis's original thesis about how "space-binding" media, in permitting more rapid dissemination of information across ever larger spaces, also "erode local memory and the self-determination of peripheral groups" (Berland 1993a: 111).

What makes radio different to television here is what Berland calls the "psychic investment" radio listeners—unlike television viewers—make in "local space", despite its underlying "recentralizing" tendencies. "People's feelings about community, about territory, work and weekends, roads and traffic, memory and play, and what might be happening across town" are seized by radio so that it can "map our symbolic and social environment". Radio therefore distinguishes itself from television through "highly conventional and elaborated strategies of representation"—strategies which actively draw attention to the radio station as a live and local entity—which provide a local "feel" that attracts both listeners and advertisers in the face of competition from television.

> In this context the DJ serves to personalize and thus locate the station as more than an abstract mediation of records, advertisers and listeners. DJs are increasingly disempowered in terms of programming, and make fewer and fewer decisions about music and other content. But it falls to the DJ's voice to provide an index of radio as a live and local medium, to provide immediate evidence of the efficacy of its listeners' desires. It is through that voice that the community hears itself constituted, through that voice that radio assumes authorship of the community, woven into itself through its jokes, its advertisements, its gossip, all represented, recurringly and powerfully, as the map of local life.
>
> (1993a: 116)

Radio, then, seems to offer us a more Janus-faced text than television: in spatial terms, at least, it appears to be "omnisciently 'local' without arising from or contributing to local cultures" (1993a: 112). This is where radio provides a particularly striking variation on the broader debate about globalization. It has been transnational in scope for much longer than other electronic media, and it has contributed heavily to the widespread cultural diffusion of Anglo-American pop music. However, through various forms of local stations, micro radio, pirates, and special-interest community stations, commentators suggest that it "has also been an important instrument of localism" (Held et al. 1999: 351). Yet if Berland is right, this localism is often illusory. Or to put it another way, it gives a highly local "feel" to a "text" which, despite its frequent concern with particular soundscapes, is in many respects as a whole largely place-*less*. Radio, as Fairchild concludes, is now more than ever "deterritorialized" (1999).

## "Communicative Capacity"

This comes across as a rather more pessimistic conclusion than Scannell's vision of a medium which "rekindles the life and fire of the world" (1996: 164–5). But they are not irreconcilable views. Berland herself acknowledges radio's central paradox in a passage I have already drawn upon in the first chapter, but which bears repeating here:

> It is a space-binding medium, ensuring the rapid, broad distribution of changing texts without restriction to an originary space or a cultural elite. On the other hand, it is aural, vernacular, immediate, transitory; its composite stream of music and speech, including local (if usually one-way) communication, has the capacity to nourish local identity and oral history, and to render these dynamic through contact with other spaces and cultures. This capacity for mediating the local with the new defines its styles of talk and construction of station identity.
>
> (1993: 112).

The important phrase here is *capacity*. Radio has certain capabilities, but they are not always exercised. Perhaps then radio is not communicative as such, it merely has what I shall call "communicative capacity"—a capacity only sometimes fulfilled. What do I mean by this? We know it is a much more varied phenomenon than television, scattered more widely, and adopting a wider range of forms, from pirate, underground and community stations through to local, national and international stations, and networked chains, some being commercial, others public service. It should be no surprise, therefore, if radio fulfils its communicative capacity in different ways and with varying degrees of success: no single, unifying theory can accommodate its range. Beck (1998) has remarked on radio's essential "hybridity"—its ability to adapt and change, sometimes drawing on the forms of other mass media like television, at other times exhibiting a fully deployed range of "radiogenic" features. Even so, some underlying patterns can be discerned. I argued in chapters 1 and 2 that the broad distinction between commercial radio and public-service radio remains meaningful, and if this is so it must manifest itself in the radio text as much as in the structures of the industry. It is significant that, for example, while Scannell and Montgomery—who can perhaps both be described as "optimists" over radio's communicative powers—focus on case studies drawn from the public-service sector, Higgins and Moss address *commercial* radio, and Berland's focus is quite specifically *music* radio stations in the commercial sector. This is not to suggest that public-service radio everywhere and always nourishes a constructive relationship between its different audiences while commercial radio does not. But it may be that the commercial or public-service status of a radio station does affect the extent to which its communicative capacity is reached.

Rothenbuhler (1996) even argues that commercial radio, on the American model at least, is best understood as lacking any communicative goals *at all*. It communicates, but only as a means to non-communicative (in this case economic) ends; it cares little about the messages it transmits so long as the audience is there to bring in advertising revenue. Rothenbuhler starts by accepting the definition of communication as an act meaningfully orientated to others. There are four elements to this: communicators must have

- A purpose for communication;
- Some idea to express;
- Some means to express it;
- Someone to whom to express it.

Communicating successfully "requires artful expression adapted to the purpose, the idea, the medium, and the audience" (1996: 130). We normally expect communication to follow rules of "quantity and quality"—in other words, we expect each other to say neither more nor less than is needed and to say what is relevant and true (Grice 1989). But where communication becomes an instrument for a non-communicative purpose—to make money, rather than to educate, inform or entertain for its own sake—any "message purpose" becomes subordinate to the "money purpose":

> If we think of radio stations as trying to communicate with their audiences, as really trying to say something, then changes in format, such as from country to oldies or from rock to all talk, make no sense. They are irrational changes of mind. That is because these communicators are not

communicators in the normative sense; they are instrumental communicators, and, as such, their expression is not substantively but instrumentally
motivated. They will say anything if it will likely make money. . . . In
addition to having chosen their medium without regard for any communicative purpose . . . [they] have done so without any act of invention, that is
without any thought of anything to say. . . . When business people choose
the radio for business reasons, they also choose a medium of expression,
but not for expressive reasons.

(Rothenbuhler 1996: 132–3)

In this interpretation, when disc jockeys prattle and news bulletins stick to their full
duration on a "quiet" news day, it is because *they have nothing to say but still need to say
something*: the station must go on broadcasting, because there will always be people
within reach of a station's signal who just might be converted into a commercial
audience of potential consumers. To have to have something to say 24 hours a day—
even if it is rather banal—is what drives radio stations towards tight formats based on
crude audience typifications: they provide decision-making rules which avoid the
near-impossible information-processing task of rapid "message making", deciding every
few minutes who out of the universe of people may be listening and what records, out
of the universe of music, should be played to them (1996: 135).

This picture of commercial "format" radio as a medium stripped of real expressive
content contrasts quite starkly, at first sight, with the avowed communicative intention
of public-service radio. The public-service ethic of broadcasting, as embodied in Reith's
BBC, has historically presented radio as a medium which treats listeners, not so much as
consumers but as rational social beings immersed in a "public sphere" of free and
rational exchange of reasoned opinion. Put like this, such a contrast could explain
the fundamental contradictions we have explored through this chapter: alienating
tendencies emerging from an exploitative commercial sector, and more nurturing
forms of communication emerging from the public service. But it is not quite the case
that we are observing two distinct models of radio communication, one commercial—
and typified by Rothenbuhler's North American model—another public service—and
typified by a Reithian-shaped BBC of noble educative, informative, intentions. Tolson
(1991) reminds us that the search for relaxed, audience-friendly styles of address in
the mass media predates commercialization, and that even public-service operators like
the BBC have long communicated within a "populist", rather than a "paternalist" public
sphere—a modern public sphere, capable of containing everyday language, placing
events and entertainments in a common public domain, and interconnecting the public
and private worlds (Tolson 1991: 195–7). Tolson argues that while there is no single
"communicative ethos", the distinction is therefore not between "paternalist" (public-
service) models and "populist" (commercial) models, but between two contradictory
forces within broadcasting's modern public sphere: a vacillation between "its two
demands for information and entertainment" (1991: 197).

I would argue that, in the specific case of radio, we need to put it slightly differently. Berland wrote of the paradox of radio being a "space-binding" medium
which can nourish local identity through contact with other spaces and cultures, but a
medium too where formats—in industrializing both its relations of production and
its temporal language—squeeze out its "vernacular, immediate, transitory" qualities
(1993a: 112). In other words, where radio is most heavily formatted, the freedom for

truly communicative radio—in Berland's words, radio that renders local identities "dynamic"—is constrained, diminished. Almost all mainstream radio is now format radio to a greater or lesser extent—broadcasting now cares too much about market share and audience size to be otherwise. But it remains true that commercial radio has a *greater* vested interest in formats than public-service radio, so that to some extent our earlier contrast between commercial and public-service models of communication holds true: commercial radio is more formatted than public-service radio, and as the commercial sector grows so too does the dominance of format radio. Rothenbuhler puts the consequences somewhat brutally:

> Over time, commercial interests displace communicative interests, and meaning and aesthetics become subordinate to commercial exploitation. Commercial radio, then, short of giving up its commercial nature, can only damage radio as a system of communication.
>
> (1996: 139)

The vision is apocalyptic, but perhaps more applicable to the mainstream of radio than to radio as a whole. At the end of chapter 1, I argued that the nature of radio still allows for at least some renewal and diversity in the margins of the industry. Low costs, new channels of distribution, and a more individualized production process than is the case in television still allow some creative room for manoeuvre in fulfilling the medium's communicative capacity. Radio, then, is not—or at least, not *yet*—devoid of meaning. What is more, its role in changing our sense of place and of time raises wider issues of social identity:

> as our sense of the past becomes increasingly dependent on mediated symbolic forms, and as our sense of place within it becomes increasingly nourished by media products, so too our sense of the groups and communities with which we share a common path through time and space, a common origin and a common fate, is altered: we feel ourselves to belong to groups and communities which are constituted in part through the media.
>
> (Thompson 1995: 35)

The media in general, then, are not simply involved in reporting on a social world which would, as it were continue very much the same without them. Rather, "the media are actively involved in constituting the social world" (1995: 117). If the radio medium, devoid as it may be of much of its communicative capacity, still helps to define the contours of our social lives, our next task must be to assess the *kinds* of cultures it helps reproduce.

## Questions for Consideration

1   Do the radio stations that you listen to use time and space in ways that David Hendy describes? If not, how are they different?

2   Hendy uses Raymond Williams's concept of "flow" to discuss our experience of radio sounds. Do you find the concept of flow helpful to understanding how you experience radio?

3   Increasingly, people are listening not to traditional radio but to "Internet radio" or to compilations of music that they create for themselves for their iPods and MP3 players. To what extent, and how, do these new ways of listening to music bring up considerations of time and space that are different from those Hendy describes regarding traditional broadcast radio?

# Bibliography

Abercrombie, N. 1996: *Television and Society*. Cambridge: Polity Press.

Adorno, T. W. 1990: On Popular Music. In S. Frith and A. Goodwin (eds), *On Record: Rock, Pop and the Written Word*. London: Routledge, 301–14.

Adorno, T. W. 1991: On the Fetish Character in Music and the Regression of Listening. In J. M. Bernstein (ed.), *The Culture Industry: Selected Essays on Mass Culture by Theodor Adorno*. London: Routledge, 26–52.

Albrow, M. 1996: *The Global Age*. Cambridge: Polity Press.

Anderson, B. 1991: *Imagined Communities: Reflections on the Origins and Spread of Nationalism*. New York: Verso.

Arbitron 1999: *The Arbitron Internet Listening Study: Radio in the New Media World*. http://www.arbitron.com/studies/20nmw.htm

Armstrong, C. B. and Rubin, A. M. 1989: Talk Radio as Interpersonal Communication. *Journal of Communication*, 39 (2), 84–94.

Arrow-FM 1999: *Rates*. http://www.arrowfm.co.uk/rates.html

Attali, J. 1985: *Noise: The Political Economy of Music*. Minneapolis and London: University of Minnesota Press.

Barboutis, C. 1997: Digital Audio Broadcasting: The Tangled Webs of Technological Warfare. *Media, Culture & Society*, 19, 687–90.

Barnard, S. 1989: *On the Radio: Music Radio in Britain*. Milton Keynes: Open University Press.

Barnes, K. 1990: Top 40 Radio: A Fragment of the Imagination. In S. Frith (ed.), *Facing the Music*, London: Mandarin, 8–50.

Barnett, S. and Morrison, D. 1989: *The Listener Speaks: The Radio Audience and the Future of Radio*. London: HMSO.

Barnett, S. and Curry, A. 1994: *The Battle for the BBC: A British Broadcasting Conspiracy*. London: Aurum Press.

Barrie, C. 1999: News report in *The Guardian*, 3 February 1999.

Barthes, R. 1973: *Mythologies*. London: Vintage.

Barthes, R. 1975: *S/Z*. London: Jonathan Cape.

Barthes, R. 1977: *Image-Music-Text*. London: Fontana.

Bauman, Z. 1992: *Intimations of Postmodernity*. London: Routledge.

Bauman, Z. 1998: *Globalization: The Human Consequences*. Cambridge: Polity Press.

BBC 1992: *Extending Choice: The BBC's Role in the New Broadcasting Age*. London: BBC.

BBC 1998: *Annual Report and Accounts 97/98*. London: BBC.

BBC CDR 1997: *BBC Digital Radio: clearing the way for radio's future*. CD-Rom. London: BBC.

BBC DRRF 1998: *BBC Digital Radio Research Findings*. London: BBC.

BBC ENPSN 1997: *BBC ENPS Newsletter*, April 1997. London: BBC.

BBC NRRA 1996: *BBC Network Radio Research and Analysis: Tomorrow's Listener*. Data presented to Radio Academy Conference, Birmingham, July 1996.

BBC Radio 1 1997: *BBC Radio 1 Commissioning Strategy 1997/8*. London: BBC.

BBC Radio 4 1998: *BBC Radio 4 Commissioning Guidelines 1998/9*, 2nd edn. London: BBC.

Beck, A. 1998: Rezoning Radio Theory (A draft book in electronic form), *Sound Journal*, http://speke.ukc.ac.uk/sais/sound-journal/index.html

Bennett, A. 1997: Village greens and terraced streets: Britpop and representations of Britishness. *Young: Nordic Journal of Youth Research*, 5 (4), 20–33.

Bennett, T., Frith, S., Grossberg, L., Shephard, J. and Turner, G. (eds) 1993: *Rock and Popular Music: Politics, Policies, Institutions*. London and New York: Routledge.

Bensman, J. and Lilienfeld, R. 1979: *Between Public and Private*. New York: Free Press.

Berland, J. 1993a: Radio Space and Industrial Time: The Case of Music Formats. In S. Frith et al. (eds), *Rock and Popular Music: Politics, Policies, Institutions*. London: Routledge, 104–18.

Berland, J. 1993b: Contradicting Media: Toward a Political Phenomenology of Listening. In N. Strauss (ed.), *Radiotext(e)/Semiotext(e)*. 6 (1), 209–17.

Blumler, J. 1991: The New Television Marketplace: Imperatives, Implications, Issues. In J. Curran and M. Gurevitch (eds), *Mass Media & Society*, 1st edn. London: Edward Arnold, 194–215.

Blumler, J. and Gurevitch, M. 1982: The Political Effects of Mass Communication. In M. Gurevitch, T. Bennett, J. Curran and J. Woollacott (eds), *Culture, Society and the Media*. London: Methuen, 236–67.

Bourgault, L.M. 1995: *Mass Media and Sub-Saharan Africa*. Bloomington: Indiana University Press.

BPI 1998: *Statistical Handbook*. London: British Phonographic Industry Limited.

Brand, G. and Scannell, P. 1991: Talk, Identity and Performance: The Tony Blackburn Show. In P. Scannell (ed.), *Broadcast Talk*. London: Sage, 201–26.

Brecht, B. 1932: Der Rundfunk als Kommunikationsapparat. In *Blattaer der Hessischen Landestheaters*, Darmstadt 16. Reprinted and translated in N. Strauss (ed.), *Radiotext(e)/Semiotext(e)*. 6 (1) (1993), 15–17.

Briggs, A. 1995: *The History of Broadcasting in the United Kingdom*, (5 volumes). Oxford: Oxford University Press.

Browne, D. R. 1990: Aboriginal Radio in Australia: From Dreamtime to Prime Time? *Journal of Communication*, 40 (1), 111–20.

Browne, D. R. 1992: *International Radio Broadcasting: The Limits of a Limitless Medium*. New York: Praeger.

Cairncross, F. 1997: *The Death of Distance: How the Communications Revolution will Change our Lives*. London: Orion Business Books.

Cantril, H. 1940: *The Invasion from Mars: A Study in the Psychology of Panic*. Princeton, NJ: Princeton University Press.

Carlton 1998: *Annual Report and Accounts 1998*. London: Carlton Communications PLC.

Carroll, R. L., Silbergleid, M. I., Beachum, C. M., Perry, S. D., Pluscht, P. J. and Pescatore, M. J. 1993: Meanings of Radio to Teenagers in a Niche-Programming Era. *Journal of Broadcasting & Electronic Media*, 37 (2), 159–76.

Cashmore, E. and Rojek, C. 1999: *Dictionary of Cultural Theorists*. London: Arnold.

CIN 1998: *Presspack*. London: Chart Information Network.

Chapple, S. and Garofalo, R. 1977: *Rock "n" Roll is Here to Pay: The History and Politics of the Music Industry*. Chicago: Nelson Hall.

Chrétien, J., Dupaquier, J., Kabanda, M., Ngarambe, J. and Reporters Sans Frontières 1995: *Rwanda: Les médias du génocide*. Paris: Karthala.

Classen, C. 1993: *Worlds of Sense: Exploring the Senses in the History and Across Cultures*. London: Routledge.

Collins, J. 1992: Some Anti-Hegemonic Aspects of African Popular Music. In R. Garofalo (ed.), *Rockin' the Boat: Mass Music and Mass Movements*. Boston: South End Press, 185–94.

Coward, R. 1984: *Female Desire*. London: Paladin, Grafton Books.

Crisell, A. 1994: *Understanding Radio*, 2nd edn. London: Routledge.

Crisell, A. 1997: *An Introductory History of British Broadcasting*. London and New York: Routledge.

Croteau, D. and Hoynes, W. 2000: *Media/Society: Industries, Images, and Audiences*, 2nd edn. Thousand Oaks, CA: Pine Forge Press.

Curran, J. and Seaton, J. 1997: *Power Without Responsibility: The Press and Broadcasting in Britain*, 5th edn. London and New York: Routledge.

de Mateo, R. 1997: Spain. In B. S. Østergaard (ed.), *The Media in Western Europe: The Euromedia Handbook*, 2nd edn. London: Sage, 194–209.

Digital One 1998: *Press Release: Digital One Gets the Go Ahead to take Radio into the Digital Age*, 12 October 1998.

Digital One 1999: *Press Release: Digital One begins Test Transmissions*, 16 April 1999.

Donovan, P. 1997: *All Our Todays: Forty Years of Radio 4's "Today" Programme*. London: Jonathan Cape.

Douglas, S. J. 1999: *Listening In: Radio and the American Imagination, from Amos "n" Andy and Edward R. Murrow to Wolfman Jack and Howard Stern*. New York and Toronto: Random House.

Drew, R. 1996: Narration Can be a Killer. In K. MacDonald and M. Cousins (eds), *Imagining Reality: The Faber Book of Documentary*. London and Boston: Faber and Faber, 271–3.

Dunnett, P. J. S. 1990: *The World Television Industry*. London: Routledge.

Dyson, F. 1994: The Genealogy of the Radio Voice. In D. Augaitis and D. Lander (eds), *Radio Rethink: Art, Sound and Transmission*. Canada: Walter Phillips Gallery, 167–86.

Elliott, P. 1974: Uses and Gratifications Research: A Critique and a Sociological Alternative. In J. Blumler and E. Katz (eds), *The Uses of Mass Communications*. London: Sage, 249–68.

Ellis, J. 1982: *Visible Fictions*. London: Routledge.

Ellison, M. 1999: Post-rock Radio Daze. In the *Guardian*, 18 October 1999, G2 16.

Fairchild, C. 1999: Deterritorializing Radio: Deregulation and the Continuing Triumph of the Corporatist Perspective in the USA. *Media, Culture & Society*, 21, 549–61.

Fathi, A. and Heath, C. L. 1974: Group Influence, Mass Media and Musical Taste among Canadian Students. *Journalism Quarterly*, 51, 705–9.

FCC 1999: *Federal Communications Commission Audio Services Division: Broadcast Stations Total*, 31 March 1999. http://www.fcc.gov/mmb/asd/totals/bt990331.html

Feld, S. 1994: *Sound and Sentiment: Birds, Weeping, Poetics, and Song in Kaluli Expression*, 2nd edn. Philadelphia: University of Pennsylvania Press.

Fiske, J. 1987: *Television Culture*. London: Methuen.

Fiske, J. 1989: Moments of Television: Neither the Text nor the Audience. In E. Seiter, H. Borchers, G. Kreutzner and E.-M. Warth (eds), *Remote Control: Television, Audiences, and Cultural Power*. London: Routledge, 56–78.

Fiske, J. 1990: *An Introduction to Communication Studies*, 2nd edn. London: Routledge.

Fiske, J. and Hartley, J. 1978: *Reading Television*. London: Methuen.

Fornatale, P. and Mills, J. E. 1980: *Radio in the Television Age*. Woodstock, NY: Overlook Press.

Frith, S. 1978: *The Sociology of Rock*. London: Constable.

Frith, S. 1987: Towards an Aesthetic of Popular Music. In R. Leppert and S. McLary (eds), *Music and Society: the Politics of Composition, Performance and Reception*. Cambridge: Cambridge University Press, 133–49.

Frith, S. 1996: *Performing Rites: On the Value of Popular Music*. Oxford: Oxford University Press.

Gallagher, M. 1982: Negotiations of Control in Media Organizations and Occupations. In M. Gurevitch, T. Bennett, J. Curran and J. Woollacott (eds), *Culture, Society and the Media*. London: Methuen, 151–73.

Garfield, S. 1998: *The Nation's Favourite: The True Adventures of Radio 1*. London: Faber and Faber.

Garfinkel, H. 1984: *Studies in Ethnomethodology*. Cambridge: Polity Press.

Garner, K. 1990: New Gold Dawn: The Traditional English Breakfast Show in 1989. *Popular Music*, 9 (2), 193–202.

Garnham, N. 1986: Contribution to a Political Economy of Mass-Communication. In R. Collins, J. Curran, N. Garnham, P. Scannell, P. Schlesinger and C. Sparks (eds), *Media, Culture & Society: A Critical Reader*. London, Beverly Hills, Newbury Park and New Delhi: Sage, 9–32.

Garnham, N. 1992: The Media and the Public Sphere. In C. Calhoun (ed.), *Habermas and the Public Sphere*. Cambridge, MA: MIT Press, 359–76.

Garnham, N. 1994: The Broadcasting Market and the Future of the BBC. *Political Quarterly*, 65 (1), 11–19.

Garofalo, R. 1992: Introduction. In R. Garofalo (ed.), *Rockin' the Boat: Mass Music and Mass Movements*. Boston: South End Press, 1–13.

Gell, A. 1995: The Language of the Forest: Landscape and Phonological Iconism in Umeda. In E. Hirsch and M. O'Hanlon (eds), *The Anthropology of Landscape: Perspectives on Place and Space*. Oxford: Clarendon Press, 232–54.

Giddens, A. 1984: *The Constitution of Society*. Cambridge: Polity Press.

Giddens, A. 1991: *Modernity and Self-Identity: Self and Society in the Late Modern Age*. Cambridge: Polity Press.

Gillet, C. 1988: *Making Tracks: the Story of Atlantic Records*. London: Souvenir.

Glasser, T. L. 1984: Competition and Diversity among Radio Formats: Legal and Structural Issues. *Journal of Broadcasting*, 28 (2), 127–44.

Goffman, E. 1980: The Radio Drama Frame. In J. Corner and J. Hawthorn (eds), *Communication Studies*. London: Edward Arnold.

Goffman, E. 1981: *Forms of Talk*. Philadelphia: University of Pennsylvania Press.

Goodlad, L. M. E. 1999: Packaged Alternatives: the Incorporation and Gendering of "Alternative" Radio. Unpublished paper, University of Washington.

Goodwin, P. 1998: *Television Under the Tories: Broadcasting Policy 1979–1997*. London: BFI.

Gough, D. 1999: Soaps in Front Line of Battle against Aids. News report in *The Guardian*, 4 January 1999.

Graham, A. 1998: Broadcasting Policy and the Digital Revolution. In J. Seaton (ed.), *Politics and the Media: Harlots and Prerogatives at the Turn of the Millennium*. Oxford: Blackwell Publishers, 30–42.

Graham, J. 1999: Personal interview with Jefferson Graham, Independent Radio Group, 28 May 1999.

Green, L. 1998: Constructing Community through Broadcasting Communications in Remote Western Australia. Paper delivered to Radio Studies Network, Third Annual Association of Media, Cultural and Communication Studies Conference, Sheffield, 11–12 December 1998.

Green Paper 1998: *Regulating Communications—Approaching Convergence in the Information Age*. London: Department of Culture, Media and Sport, July 1998.

Grice, P. 1989: *Studies in the Way of Words*. Cambridge, MA: Harvard University Press.

Grierson, J. c. 1934–6, 1996: First Principles of Documentary. In K. MacDonald and M. Cousins (eds), *Imagining Reality: The Faber Book of Documentary*. London and Boston: Faber and Faber, 97–102.

Guralnick, P. 1991: *Sweet Soul Music: Rhythm and Blues and the Southern Dream of Freedom*. London: Penguin.

Gurevitch, M. 1996: The Globalization of Electronic Journalism. In J. Curran and M. Gurevitch (eds), *Mass Media and Society*, 2nd edn. London: Methuen, 204–24.

Gustafsson, K. E. and Hultén, O. 1997: Sweden. In B. S. østergaard (ed.), *The Media in Western Europe: The Euromedia Handbook*, 2nd edn. London: Sage, 210–28.

GWR 1998: *Annual Report and Accounts 1997/98*. http://www.gwrgroup.musicradio.com

Habermas, J. 1989: *The Structural Transformation of the Public Sphere*. Cambridge: Polity Press.

Hachten, W. A. 1974: Broadcasting and political crisis. In S. W. Head (ed.), *Broadcasting in Africa: A Continental Survey of Radio and Television*. Philadelphia: Temple University Press, 395–8.

Hamm, C. 1991: "The constant companion of man": Separate Development, Radio Bantu and Music. In *Popular Music*, 10 (2), 147–73.

Hamm, C. 1995a: Privileging the Moment of Reception: Music and Radio in South Africa. In C. Hamm (ed.), *Putting Popular Music in its Place*. Cambridge: Cambridge University Press, 249–69.

Hamm, C. 1995b: Music and Radio in the People's Republic of China. In C. Hamm (ed.), *Putting Popular Music in its Place*. Cambridge: Cambridge University Press, 270–305.

Handel, S. 1989: *Listening: An Introduction to the Perception of Auditory Events*. Cambridge, MA: MIT Press.

Hardy, J. 1997: Julian Hardy of Capital Interactive, speech to "Radio Meets the Web" Radio Academy Conference, London, November 1997.

Harris, R. 1997: Dick Harris, speech to "News Radio" Radio Academy Conference, London, 1997.

Hartley, J. 1982: *Understanding News*. London: Methuen.

Harvey, D. 1989: *The Condition of Postmodernity*. Oxford: Blackwell Publishers.

Head, S. W. and Sterling, C. H. 1990: *Broadcasting in America: A Survey of Electronic Media*, 6th edn. Boston: Houghton Mifflin.

Held, D., McGrew, A., Goldblatt, D. and Perraton, J. 1999: *Global Transformations: Politics, Economics and Culture*. Cambridge: Polity Press.

Hendy, D. 1994: Radio Five Live—Is it Too Fast for its Own Good? *British Journalism Review*, 5 (2), 15–17.

Hendy, D. 2000a: A Political Economy of Radio in the Digital Era. *Journal of Radio Studies*, 7 (1) 213–34.

Hendy, D. 2000b: Pop Music in the Public Service: BBC Radio 1 and New Music in the 1990s. *Media, Culture & Society* 22 (6) November 2000.

Hennion, A. and Meadel, C. 1986: Programming Music: Radio as Mediator. *Media, Culture & Society*, 8 (3), 281–303.

Hesmondhalgh, D. 1996: Flexibility, Post-Fordism and the Music Industry. *Media, Culture & Society*, 18 (3), 469–88.

Higgins, C. S. and Moss, P. D. 1982: *Sounds Real: Radio in Everyday Life*. St Lucia, London and Sydney: University of Queensland Press.

Higgins, C. S. and Moss, P. D. 1984: Radio Voices. *Media, Culture & Society*, 6 (4), 353–75.

Hirsch, P. 1990: Processing Fads and Fashions: An Organization-Set Analysis of Cultural Industry Systems. In S. Frith and A. Goodwin (eds), *On Record: Rock, Pop and the Written Word*. London: Routledge, 127–39.

Hobson, D. 1980: Housewives and the Mass Media. In S. Hall, D. Hobson, A. Lowe and P. Willis (eds), *Culture, Media, Language*. London: Routledge, 105–14.

Hochheimer, J. L. 1993: Organizing Democratic Radio: Issues in Praxis. *Media, Culture & Society*, 15, 473–86.

Hutchby, I. 1991: The Organization of Talk on Talk Radio. In P. Scannell (ed.), *Broadcast Talk*. London: Sage, 119–37.

Kaplan, E. A. 1987: *Rock Around the Clock*. London: Methuen.

Katz, E., Gurevitch, M. and Haas, H. 1973: On the Use of Mass Media for Important Things. *American Sociological Review*, 38 (2), 164–81.

Katz, E. and Wedell, G. 1978: *Broadcasting in the Third World: Promise and Performance*. London: Macmillan.

Keith, M. C. 1997: *The Radio Station*, 4th edn. Boston: Focal Press.

Kellow, C. L. and Steeves, H. L. 1998: The Role of Radio in the Rwandan Genocide. *Journal of Communication*, 48 (3), 107–28.

Lazarsfeld, P. and Field, H. H. 1946: *The People Look at Radio*. Chapel Hill: University of North Carolina Press.

Ledbetter, J. 1997: *Made Possible By . . . The Death of Public Broadcasting in the United States*. London and New York: Verso.

Levin, M. 1987: *Talk Radio and the American Dream*. New York: Lexington Books.

Lewis, P. M. and Booth, J. 1989: *The Invisible Medium: Public, Commercial and Community Radio*. London: Macmillan.

Lewis, T. 1993: Triumph of the Idol—Rush Limbaugh and a Hot Medium. *Media Studies Journal*, 7 (3), 51–62.

Lloréns, J. A. 1991: Andean Voices on Lima Airwaves: Highland Migrants and Radio Broadcasting in Peru. *Studies in Latin American Popular Culture*, 10, 177–89.

Longhurst, B. 1995: *Popular Music & Society*. Cambridge: Polity Press.

Lowery, S. and De Fleur, M. L. 1983: *Milestones in Mass Communication Research: Media Effects*. New York and London: Longman.

McChesney, R. 1997: *Corporate Media and the Threat to Democracy*. New York: Seven Stories Press.

McCourt, T. and Rothenbuhler, E. 1987: Commercial Radio and Popular Music: Processes of Selection and Factors of Influence. In J. Lull (ed.), *Popular Music and Communication*. Beverly Hills: Sage, 101–15.

McCourt, T. and Rothenbuhler, E. 1997: Soundscan and the Consolidation of Control in the Popular Music Industry. *Media, Culture & Society*, 19, 201–18.

McLeish, R. 1994: *Radio Production*, 3rd edn. Oxford: Focal Press.

McLuhan, M. 1994: *Understanding Media: The Extensions of Man*. Boston: MIT Press.

McQuail, D. 1983: *Mass Communication Theory*. London: Sage.

MacDonald, K. and Cousins, M. (eds) 1996: *Imagining Reality: The Faber Book of Documentary*. London and Boston: Faber and Faber.

Manaev, O. 1991: The Influence of Western Radio on the Democratization of Soviet Youth. *Journal of Communication*, 41 (2), 72–91.

Mann, R. (ed.) 1999: *The Blue Book of British Broadcasting*, 25th edn. London: Tellex Monitors.

Marr, W. 1999: *An Investigation into the Role of Music Radio Producers*. Unpublished BA Media Studies dissertation, University of Westminster, London.

Matic, V. 1999a: Letter from Belgrade. News report in the *Guardian*, 5 April 1999.

Matic, V. 1999b: Will the real Radio B92 please stand up! Email received from Belgrade, 13 April 1999, via B92 support group in the Netherlands. http://helpb92.xs4all.nl

Media Research Limited 1998: *Credentials: Broadcast Analysis Examples*, mimeograph press-release, Radio Academy Conference, London.

Mendelsohn, H. 1964: Listening to Radio. In L. A. Dexter and D. M. White (eds), *People, Society, and Mass Communications*, New York: Free Press of Glencoe, 239–49.

Montgomery, M. 1986: DJ Talk. *Media, Culture & Society*, 8, 421–40.

Montgomery, M. 1991: Our Tune: a study of a discourse genre. In P. Scannell (ed.), *Broadcast Talk*. London: Sage, 138–77.

Mosco, V. 1996: *The Political Economy of Communication*. London: Sage.

Moy, S. 1998: *The Renaissance of Radio 1 and British Music*. Unpublished BA Media Studies dissertation, University of Westminster, London.

Mulholland, S. 1998: Stephen Mulholland, BBC Digital Radio, speech reported in *Radio Academy Festival Report 1998*. London: Radio Academy.

Murdock, G. 1981: Organising the Imagination: Sociological Perspectives on Radio Drama. In P. Lewis (ed.), *Radio Drama*. London and New York: Longman, 143–63.

Murroni, C., Irvine, N. and King, R. 1998: *future.radio.uk: public policy on the future of radio*. London: IPPR.

*Music Week*: various editions. Published weekly, London: Miller Freeman / United News and Media.

Negus, K. 1992: *Producing Pop: Culture and Conflict in the Popular Music Industry*. London: Edward Arnold.

Negus, K. 1993: Plugging and Programming: Pop Radio and Record Promotion in Britain and the United States. *Popular Music*, 12 (1), 57–68.

Negus, K. 1996: *Popular Music in Theory*. Cambridge: Polity Press.

Negus, K. 1998: Cultural Production and the Corporation: Musical Genres and the Strategic Management of Creativity in the US Recording Industry. *Media, Culture & Society*, 20, 359–79.

NERA 1998: *Report on UK Commercial Radio's Future: Final Report*. London: National Economic Research Associates.

New York Times 1999: The Glow at the End of the Dial. In *New York Times Magazine*, 11 April 1999, 68–77.

O'Connor, A. 1990: The Miners' Radio Stations in Bolivia: A Culture of Resistance. *Journal of Communication*, 40 (1), 102–110.

Østergaard, B. S. (ed.) 1997: *The Media in Western Europe: The Euromedia Handbook*, 2nd edn. London: Sage.

Page, B. I. and Tannenbaum, J. 1996: Populistic Deliberation and Talk Radio. *Journal of Communication*, 46 (2), 33–54.

Page, T. (ed.) 1990: *The Glenn Gould Reader*. New York: Vintage.

Parker, M. 1991: Reading the Charts—Making Sense with the Hit Parade. *Popular Music*, 10 (2), 205–17.

Pease, E. C. and Dennis, E. E. 1993: Radio the Forgotten Medium: Preface. *Media Studies Journal*, 7 (3), xi–xix.

Performing Rights Society 1999: *Welcome to Radio: Payment Comparison*, Mimeograph. London.

Pickering, M. and Shuker, R. 1993: Radio Gaga: Popular Music and the Radio Quota Debate in New Zealand. *New Zealand Sociology*, 8 (1), 21–59.

Plowright, P. 1999: Interview with Piers Plowright, former Chief Producer, BBC Radio Features, 24 June 1999.

Poulantzas, N. 1978: *State, Power and Socialism*. London: New Left Books.

Powell, Adam Clayton, III 1993: You Are What You Hear. *Media Studies Journal*, 7 (3), 71–6.

Powell, M. 1997: Is it Live? Does it Matter? Mike Powell, Chief Executive UKRD, 28 July 1997. http://www.vru.co.uk/Live.htm.

RAB 1998a: *Effective Radio Weights: A Guide to What Constitutes an Effective Weight of Radio Advertising*. London: Radio Advertising Bureau.

RAB 1998b: *Media Planning on Radio: A Guide to Best Practice in Radio Media Planning*. London: Radio Advertising Bureau.

RAB (US) 1999: Radio Ad Sales Surpass $15 Billion in 1998. Press Release, US Radio Advertising Bureau 8 February 1999. http://www.rab.com/pr/dec98rev.html

Radio and Records Online 1999: *Arbitron Ratings: New York, June 1999*. http://www.rronline.com/Subscribers/Ratings/Homepage.htm

Radio and Records 1999: Radio & Records Directory: Ratings, Industry Directory & Program Supplier Guide, vol. 2. Los Angeles: Radio and Records.

Radio Academy 1998: *Radio Festival Report*. London: Radio Academy.

Radio Authority 1998: *Radio Authority Pocket Book, June 1998*. London: Radio Authority.

Radio Authority 1999: *Radio Authority Pocket Book, June 1999*. London: Radio Authority.

RAJAR 1999a: *Rajar 99*. London: Radio Joint Audience Research Limited.

RAJAR 1999b: *Quarterly Summary of Radio Listening: Survey Period Ending 28th March 1999*. London: RAJAR-Ipsos-RSL.

Rehm, D. 1993: Talking Over America's Electronic Backyard Fence. *Media Studies Journal*, 7 (3), 63–9.

Ross, S. 1993: Music Radio—The Fickleness of Fragmentation. *Media Studies Journal*, 7 (3), 93–104.

Rothenbuhler, E. 1996: Commercial Radio as Communication, *Journal of Communication*, 46 (1), 125–43.

Rothschild-Whitt, J. 1979: The Collectivist Organization: An Alternative to Rational-Bureaucratic Models. *American Sociological Review*, 44, 509–27.

Sakolsky, R. and Dunifer, S. (eds) 1998: *Seizing the Airwaves: a Free Radio Handbook*. San Francisco and Edinburgh: AK Press.

Scannell, P. 1988a: The Communicative Ethos of Broadcasting. Paper presented to the International Television Studies Conference, British Film Institute, London.

Scannell, P. 1988b: Radio Times: The Temporal Arrangements of Broadcasting in the Modern World. In P. Drummond and R. Paterson (eds), *Television and its Audience*. London: BFI, 15–31.

Scannell, P. 1991: The Relevance of Talk. In P. Scannell (ed.), *Broadcast Talk*. London: Sage, 1–13.

Scannell, P. 1996: *Radio, Television and Modern Life*. Oxford: Blackwell.

Scannell, P. 1997: Radio and the music industry in Zimbabwe. Unpublished paper, Centre for Communication and Information Studies, University of Westminster, London.

Scannell, P. and Cardiff, D. 1991: *A Social History of British Broadcasting, volume 1: 1922–1939*. Oxford: Blackwell Publishers.

Schlesinger, P. 1978: *Putting 'Reality' Together: BBC News*. London and New York: Routledge.

Schulman, M. 1988: Radio and Cultural Identity: Community and Communication in Harlem, USA. *RTV Theory and Practice*, Special Issue 3, 185–214.

Seymour-Ure, C. 1991: *The British Press and Broadcasting since 1945*. Oxford: Blackwell Publishers.

Shapley, O. 1996: *Broadcasting A Life*. London: Scarlet Press.

Shingler, M. and Wieringa, C. 1998: *On Air: Methods and Meanings in Radio*. London: Arnold.

Sieveking, L. 1934: *The Stuff of Radio*. London: Cassell.

Silverstone, R. 1985: *Framing Science: The Making of a BBC Documentary*. London: BFI.

Silvey, R. 1974: *Who's Listening?* London: George Allen and Unwin.

Smith, R. B. 1998: Absolute Talk on the Radio. *Media Studies Journal*, 12 (2), 72–9.

Smythe, D. 1977: Communications: Blindspot of Western Marxism. *Canadian Journal of Political and Social Theory*, 1 (3), 1–27.

Soley, L. 1993: Clandestine Radio and the End of the Cold War. *Media Studies Journal*, 7 (3), 129–38.

Soley, L. and Nichols, J. S. 1987: *Clandestine Radio Broadcasting: A Study of Revolutionary and Counter-revolutionary Electronic Communication*. New York: Praeger.

Sparks, C. 1998: *Communism, Capitalism, and the Mass Media*. London: Sage.

Stavitsky, A. 1993: Ear on America. *Media Studies Journal*, 7 (3), 77–92.

Stokes, M. 1994. Introduction: Ethnicity, Identity and Music. In M. Stokes (ed.), *Ethnicity, Identity and Music: The Musical Construction of Place*. Oxford: Berg, 1–27.

Stoller, P. 1989: *The Taste of Ethnographic Things*. Philadelphia: University of Pennsylvania Press.

Storr, A. 1992: *Music and the Mind*. New York: Free Press.

Synott, A. 1993: *The Body Social: Symbolism, Self and Society*. London: Routledge.

Thompson, J. B. 1995: *The Media and Modernity: A Social Theory of the Media*. Cambridge: Polity Press.

Thompson, M. 1999: Interview with Matt Thompson, Producer, Loftus Productions, 26 October 1999.

Thorn, R. 1997: Hearing is Believing: the evidence. *Sound Journal*. http://speke.ukc.ac.uk/sais/sound-journal/index.html

Tolson, A. 1991: Televised Chat and the Synthetic Personality. In P. Scannell (ed.), *Broadcast Talk*. London: Sage, 178–200.

Tran, M. 1999: Yahoo nets broadcast.com in $5.7bn multi-media deal. News report in The *Guardian*, 2 April 1999.

Trappel, J. 1997: Austria. In B. S. Østergaard (ed.), *The Media in Western Europe: The Euromedia Handbook*, 2nd edn. London: Sage, 1–16.

Troldahl, V. C. and Skolnik, R. 1968: The Meanings People have for Radio Today. *Journal of Broadcasting*, 12, 57–67.

Tusa, J. 1993: Live Broadcasting: The keynote address. In N. Miller and R. Allen (eds), *It's Live But is it Real? Proceedings of the 23rd University of Manchester Broadcasting Symposium*, London: John Libbey, 6–14.

Tyler, B. and Laing, D. 1998: *The European Radio Industry: Markets and Players*, 2nd edn. London: Financial Times.

UKDRFN 1998: *UK Digital Radio Forum Newsletter*, Issue no. 4, July 1998.

Valentine, C. A. and Saint Damian, B. 1988: Gender and culture as determinants of the "ideal voice". *Semiotica* 71, 3 (4), 285–303.

Wall, T. 1999: The Meanings of Black and Dance Music in Contemporary Music Radio. Paper delivered to Third Triennial British Musicological Societies' Conference, University of Surrey, Guildford, July 1999.

Wallis, R. and Malm, K. 1990: Patterns of Change. In S. Frith and A. Goodwin (eds), *On Record: Rock, Pop, and the Written Word*. London and New York: Routledge, 160–80.

Wallis, R. and Malm, K. 1993: From State Monopoly to Commercial Oligopoly. European Broadcasting Policies and Popular Music Output Over the Airwaves. In T. Bennett, S. Frith, L. Grossberg, J. Shephard and G. Turner (eds), *Rock and Popular Music: Politics, Policies, Institutions*. London and New York: Routledge, 156–68.

Weintraub, N. T. 1971: Some Meanings Radio has for Teenagers. *Journal of Broadcasting*, 15, 147–52.

White, I. 1998: Auntie Catches Up with the Net. News report in *Broadcast*, 20 February 1998.

Wilby, P. and Conroy, A. 1994: *The Radio Handbook*. London and New York: Routledge.

Williams, R. 1974: *Television: Technology and Cultural Form*. London: Fontana.

Williams, R. 1983: *Towards 2000*. London: Hogarth Press.

Winston, B. 1998: *Media Technology and Society: A History, from the Telegraph to the Internet*. London and New York: Routledge.

Wolfe, K. 1984: *The Churches and the British Broadcasting Corporation, 1922–1956*. London: SCM Press.

Woolf, M. and Holly, S. 1994: *Radio Survey: Employment Patterns and Training Needs 1993/4*. London: Skillset.

World DAB Forum 1998: *Country Progress Reports, July 1998*. London: World DAB Forum.

# Chapter 17

## JANIS IAN

## FALLOUT
## A Follow Up to "The Internet Debacle"

I N MAY 2002, BEFORE THE widespread popularity of iTunes, *Performing Songwriter Magazine* published an article titled "The Internet debacle" by the songwriter and performer Janis Ian. Ian had lambasted the recording industry's move to condemn the then-popular free music sharing site Napster and ultimately have the court shut it down. As she wrote,

> Please note that I am *not* advocating indiscriminate downloading without the artist's permission. I am *not* saying copyrights are meaningless. I am objecting to the RIAA spin that they are doing this to protect "the artists," and make us more money. I am annoyed that so many records I once owned are out of print, and the only place I could find them was Napster. Most of all, I'd like to see an end to the hysteria that causes a group like RIAA to spend over 45 million dollars in 2001 lobbying "on our behalf," when every record company out there is complaining that they have no money . . .
>
> As artists, we have the ear of the masses. We have the trust of the masses. By speaking out in our concerts and in the press, we can do a great deal to damp this hysteria, and put the blame for the sad state of our industry right back where it belongs—in the laps of record companies, radio programmers, and our own apparent inability to organize ourselves in order to better our own lives—and those of our fans. If we don't take the reins, no one will.

Ian's essay struck a chord among music artists and fans at the same time that it raised the anger of Hillary Rosen, then head of the Record Industry Association of America (RIAA), and of executives from the major recording firms that support the RIAA. All that caused Ian to post a second essay on her web site about the reactions to her piece. That essay, "Fallout," is reproduced below. Many would say it is prescient about the directions that the music industry, online music, and performers would take in the years following its August 2002 publication.

## I Am Out of My Depth

Quite frankly, when I spent three months researching and writing "The Internet Debacle" for *Performing Songwriter Magazine*, I wasn't planning to become part of a "cause". I assumed that some of the magazine's 35,000 subscribers might read it, and a few might email me about it. I'd been writing articles for "Perfsong" since its inception, and had never gotten more than a couple of emails in response to any of them. So I went into it blind.

I had no idea that a scant month later, the article would be posted on over 1,000 sites, translated into nine languages, and have been featured on the BBC, in *USA Today*, and a host of other press.

The article came out eight weeks ago, and once we saw the reaction, we posted it on my own website soon after. In the past twenty days I've received over 2,200 emails from unique senders (people who've never been to my site before). I've answered every one myself, getting an education I never intended to get in the process. I've corresponded with lawyers, high-schoolers, state representatives, executives, and hackers. And I've felt out of my depth for a good portion of it.

I am in no way qualified to answer most of the questions I received, though I did my best, or referred them to someone else for discussion. The issues here are much, much bigger than I can encompass. I only wrote about downloading, record companies, and music consumers; within a few days, I found myself trying to answer questions like "Who owns the culture?" for myself. Length of copyright, fair use on the web, how libraries are being affected—these are all things I hadn't given much thought to before.

When I began researching the original article, I was undecided as to whether downloading was wrong, but the more I researched, the more I reached the conclusions stated in "The Internet Debacle". I've had only a few weeks since the first article was published, and I've been on the road the entire time, so I haven't had the opportunity to research most of these questions. I want to thank Jim Burger and other attorneys and fans who kindly sent me articles and court cases to read off-line, while I was sitting in the car en route to the next city.

Do I still believe downloading is not harming the music industry? Yes, absolutely. Do I think consumers, once the industry starts making product they *want* to buy, will still buy, even though they can download? Yes. Water is free, but a lot of us drink bottled water because it tastes better. You can get coffee at the office, but you're likely to go to Starbucks or the local espresso place and bring it back to the office with you, because that coffee tastes better. When record companies start making CD's that offer consumers a *reason* to buy them, as illustrated by Kevin's email at the end of this article, consumers will buy them. The songs may be free on line, but the CD's will taste better.

## My Current Conclusions

In an article for *Newsweek*, Steven Levy writes:

> "So why are the record labels taking such a hard line? My guess is that it's all about protecting their internet-challenged business model. Their profit comes from blockbuster artists. If the industry moved to a more varied ecology, independent labels and artists would thrive—to the detriment of the labels . . . The smoking gun comes from testimony of an RIAA-backed economist who told the government fee panel that a dramatic shakeout in Webcasting is 'inevitable and desirable because it will bring about market consolidation'."
>
> *("Labels to Net Radio: Die Now", Steven Levy in Newsweek, July 15, 2002.)*

There are, as I see it, three operative issues that explain the entertainment industry's heavy-handed response to the concept of downloading music from the Internet:

### 1. Control

The music industry is no different from any other huge corporation, be it Mobil Oil or the Catholic church. When faced with a new technology or a new product that will revolutionize their business, their response is predictable:

a.    Destroy it. And if they cannot,
b.    Control it. And if they cannot,
c.    Control the consumer who wishes to use it, and the legislators and laws that are supposed to protect that consumer.

This is not unique to the entertainment industry. This mind-set is part of the fabric of our daily lives. Movie companies sued consumers and hardware manufacturers over VCR manufacturing and blank video sales, with Jack Valenti (Motion Picture Association of America chairman) testifying to Congress that "the VCR is to the movie industry what the Boston Strangler is to a woman alone at night"—and yet, video sales now account for more industry profit than movies themselves!

When Semelweiss discovered that washing your hands before attending a woman in childbirth eliminated "childbed fever", at a time when over 50% of women giving birth in hospitals died of it, he was ridiculed by his peers, who refused to do it.

No entrenched model has ever embraced a new technology (or idea) without suffering the attendant death throes.

### 2. Ennui

The entertainment industry is still operating under laws and concepts developed during the 1930's and 1940's, before cassettes, before boom boxes, before MP3 and file-sharing and the Internet. It's far easier to insist that all new technologies be judged under old laws, than to craft new laws that embrace *all* existing technologies. It's much easier to find a scapegoat, than to examine your own practices.

As they say, "You can't get fired for saying no."

## 3.  *The American Dream*

The promises all of us are made, tacitly or otherwise, throughout our lives as Americans. The dream we inherit as each successive generation enters grade school—that we will be freer than our grandparents, more successful than our parents, and build a better world for our own children. The promises made by our textbooks, our presidents, and our culture, throughout the course of our childhoods: Fair pay for a day's work. The right to leave a job that doesn't satisfy, or is abusive. Freedom from indentured servitude. The premise that every citizen is allowed a vote, and no one will ever be called "slave" again. The promise that libraries and basic education in this country are free, and will stay so.

These are not ideas I came up with on the spur of the moment; this is what we're taught, by the culture we grow up in.

And of everything we are taught, one issue is always paramount—in America, it is *the people* who rule. It is *the people* who determine the government. *We* elect our legislators, so they will pass laws designed for *us*. *We* elect and pay the thousands of judges, policemen, civil servants who implement the laws we elect our officials to pass.

It is the promise that our government supports the will of *the people*, and not the will of big business, that makes this entire issue so damning—and at the same time, so hope-inspiring.

When Disney are permitted to threaten suit against two clowns who dare to make mice out of three balloons and call them "Mickey" as part of their show, the people are not a part of it. When Senator Hollings accepts hundreds of thousands of dollars in campaign contributions from entertainment conglomerates, then pretends money has nothing to do with his stance on downloading as he calls his own constituents "thieves," the people are not involved. When Representatives Berman and Coble introduce a bill allowing film studios and record companies to "disable, block or otherwise impair" your computer if they merely *suspect* you of file-trading, by inserting viruses and worms into your hard drive, it is *the people* who are imperiled. And when the CEO of the RIAA commends this behavior as an "innovative approach to combating the serious problem of Internet piracy" *[Hilary Rosen, in a statement quoted by Farhad Manjoo, Salon.com June 2002]*, rather than admitting that it signifies a giant corporate step into a wasteland even our government security agencies dare not enter unscathed, *the people* are not represented.

## A Hopeful Thought

> "If classroom copying is sharply curtailed, if we give someone a software patent over basic functions, at some point the public domain will be so diminished that future creators will be prevented from creating because they won't be able to afford the raw materials they need. An intellectual property system has to insure that the fertile public domain is not converted into a fallow landscape of walled private plots."
>
> (*James Boyle in the* New York Times, *March 31, 1996*)

I said that the research and information I've received over the past three weeks has made me hopeful, and I meant it. Because I know that although RIAA and their supporting companies can afford to spend 55 million dollars a year lobbying Congress and in the courts, they cannot afford to alienate every music buyer and artist out there. At that point, there will be a general strike, make no mistake. Just one week of people refusing to play the radio, buy product, or support our industry in any way, would flex muscles they have no idea are out there.

And I know that although businesses can spend unlimited dollars on campaign funding, only *the people* can elect a government. I believe that to a politician, no amount of lobbying money is worth the price of being voted out of office.

That, my friends, is why I have hope. Because I know that in America, votes count. Because I know that if enough people understand this issue, and vote accordingly, right will win. Legislation will be enacted that takes the will of the people into consideration, and favors their right to learn over Disney's right to control. Internet radio, currently in peril, will go offshore and out of the country if necessary, so audiences can hear thousands of songs instead of a narrow playlist. The RIAA will become a small footnote in the pages of Internet history, and the people will have triumphed—again.

## A Modest Proposal for an Experiment That Might Lead to a Solution

> The record companies created Napster by leaving a void for Napster to fill.
> (*Jon Hart and Jim Burger,* Wall Street Journal *www.WSJ.com April 2, 2001*)

*1. All the record companies get together and build a single giant website, with everything in their catalogues that's currently out of print available on it, and agree to experiment for one year.*

This could be the experiment that settles the entire downloading question once and for all, with no danger to any of the parties involved. By using only out of print catalogue, record companies, songwriters, publishers and singers won't be losing money; the catalogue is just sitting in storage vaults right now. And fans can have the opportunity to put their money where their mouths are; if most people really *are* willing to pay a reasonable price for downloaded music, traffic on this site should be excellent. If most people really are downloading from sites like Napster because there's so much material unavailable in stores, traffic on this site should be unbelievably good.

*2. The site offers only downloads in this part of the experiment.*

Since all the items on my proposed site are unavailable on CD, there's no need to invest time and money linking to sites (or building record company sites) where consumers can buy them on a CD. This will also ensure that the experiment stays pure, and deals with only downloading. It would also preclude artists like myself from offering downloads of material available on CD's, skewing the results.

3. Here's where the difficult part comes in. *All the record companies agree that, for the sake of the experiment, and because these items are currently dead in the water anyway, they're going to charge a more-than-reasonable price for each download.*

By "reasonable" I'm not talking $1.50 per song; that's usurious when you can purchase a brand-new 17-song CD for a high price of $16.99, and a low price of $12.99. I mean something in the order of a *quarter per song*. I read a report recently showing that in the heyday of Napster, if record companies had agreed to charge just a *nickel* a download, they would have been splitting *$500,000 a day, 24 hours a day, 52 weeks a year.*

Record companies would have to agree that there'd be no limits on how many songs you could download, so long as you were willing to pay for each one; this is a major reason their own sites haven't been more successful.

Keeping the rate that low would:

(a)    Encourage consumers to use the site, even those of us for whom downloading with a modem is time-consuming and tedious.

(b)    Spread a lot of great old music around—and music, like all art, stands on the bones of those who've gone before. One of the big problems with so much catalogue out of print is that whole generations are growing up never having heard the "originals", but only the clones. It's always better to build on the real thing.

(c)    Do a great deal to repair the record companies' credibility in the eyes of consumers—in fact, it could be made to look like a gift of gratitude for all the support consumers have shown over the years! And while I know this may not seem important to the corporate model right now, it will become increasingly important as the world continues to shrink, mistrust of large business grows, and more and more people go back to "brand loyalty". If Sony are being reasonable, and BMG are not, sooner or later the Sony brand will conquer the market, and BMG will have to fall into line or fall out. That's capitalism at its best, isn't it?

5. *Last but not least, the monies received would be portioned out fairly. I'm no economist, but the model might read something like this:*

(a)    The record companies would bear the brunt of the costs involved in creating the site. There are plenty of ways for them to make money from this experiment, whether it works or not, and the massive exposure of their out of print catalogue, with a little attention to which albums receive the most downloads, could create a whole new sub-industry in a short time. It's good for them to share, and to pool their resources; if nothing else, it will stop their constant bickering for a while.

(b)    A reasonable (there's that word again) amount would be deducted off the top of each download to pay for costs. This deducted amount would *not*, as is traditional, be borne completely by the artists or their heirs. It would be shared by all parties concerned—companies, singers, writers. Limits would be put on costs, so companies couldn't divert funds to pay their normal operating costs. And the accounts would be published *on the website monthly*, open for inspection by anyone. If you did this, they could even set up the initial experiment as a non-profit, and deduct the cost of putting up the site! Record companies would not be allowed to charge for storage fees, artwork, free goods to Guam; consumers could begin to trust them again.

(c)    From that point on, share and share alike. Let the record company, the artist, the songwriters and the publishers split the take equally. Don't laugh! The costs of that album have already been paid, no matter what they tell you, and the only cost associated with this is putting the stuff on line, then maintaining the site itself. And again, the stuff was just sitting in storage; they weren't expecting any earnings from it. The songwriters, who traditionally get paid more than the singers, would be fairly compensated and have nothing to complain about. And the singers, for once, would be paid for the works they'd recorded.

(d)   In an ideal world, several different types of downloading formats would be available——.wav files, MP3 files, Ogg Vorbis files. Maybe you'd charge a tiny bit more for a higher sampling rate. And like the record companies, any companies owning the software for these downloads would donate their software for the sake of this experiment, with future terms to be negotiated later if it succeeds.

What a great way for consumers to decide which one they like! What a great way for software companies to prove that theirs is better!

There are all kinds of other protocols you could implement once you knew whether this worked. For instance:

- Imagine an Internet where there's one giant music site, easily accessible to anyone with a modem and computer. The site offers downloads at reasonable prices for everything and anything ever recorded, and links you back either to direct sales, or to other sites where you can purchase the music in CD, DVD, or other formats. Wouldn't it be great to search under an artist's name and literally be able to hear everything they ever did?

- Links could be made from the artist and their work to press articles, streaming videos (I know, I know, but until we can all copy a stream to DVD as easily as we can from the TV to a video, it's a non-issue), special artwork, interviews, movies, concert footage, even guitar lessons.

Live cams could show artists' concerts, from anywhere in the world, giving fans who can't go to Japan the opportunity to see how the concert is different there. Venues that maintain live cams could have their own sub-websites, and charge a fraction of the cost of going to a concert for these. They could even be coupled with tours of the surrounding area, interviews with local fans and artists, and the like. Who knows—the music industry might actually wind up educating an entire global generation. It won't affect concert sales, because people who go to a concert know they're getting something very different from sitting at home watching it on a screen. Otherwise, MTV and VH1 would have put theaters out of business years ago.

- Last and most important, artists and consumers could feel like they were a part of something bigger than themselves, and actually become *partners* with the music industry. And that industry, instead of responding with Draconian measures and safeguards, could feel like they were actually a part of the community—helping to further the artistic and intellectual resources of this country, and of the world.

America has always exported its culture; that's our number one route into the hearts of the rest of the world. Instead of shutting that down, let's run with the new model, and be the first and the best at it. It's a brave new world out there, and somebody's going to grab it.

And now, on to the fun stuff:

Emails received on this subject: 1,268 as of July 30, 2003 (does not include message board posts)

Number of times the article has been translated into other languages: 9. (French, German, Chinese, Japanese, Italian, Spanish, Portuguese, Russian, Yugoslavian.)

Times AOL shut my account down for spamming, because I was trying to answer 40–50 emails at a time quickly and efficiently: 2

Winner of the *Put Your Money Where Your Mouth Is* award: Me. We began putting up free downloads around a week after the article came out.

Change in merchandise sales after article posting (previous sales averaged over one year): Up 25%

Change in merchandise sales after beginning offering free downloads: Up 300%

Offers of server space to store downloads: 31

Offers to help me convert to Linux: 16

Offers to help convert our download files from MP3 to Ogg Vorbis: 9

Offers to publish a book expose of the music industry I should write: 5

Offers to publish a book expose of my life I should write: 3

Offers to ghost-write a book expose of my life I shouldn't write: 2

Offers of marriage: 1

Number of emails disagreeing with my position: 9

Number of people who reconsidered their disagreement after further discussion: 5

Interesting things about the emails: All but 3 were coherent. Of those, one only seemed to be incoherent, but was in fact written by someone who spoke no English, and used Babblefish.com as a translator. (Sample: "I love your articles and play your music for my babies" became "I love babies and want to touch your articles.")

Silliest email: A disagreeing songwriter who said he was going to download all my songs, burn them to CDs, and give them away to all his friends. Thank you!

Biggest irony: I'm writing this on a Sony Vaio laptop that came with my first ever CD burner, and easy instructions on how to copy a CD or download a file.

And from the emails:

> "Several years ago the music industry reached an agreement with CD manufacturers to receive a royalty on blank, recordable CDs to compensate for the effects of copying music . . . the recording industry is receiving a royalty for the 'Audio' CD so that it can be used for copying music, taking the money, and then turning around and complaining that the CD is being used to make 'unauthorized' copies. Now what is up with that? Make up your mind!"
>
> (bohannon)

> ". . . America On Line became so prominent by sending out CDs of their product via direct mail. Their growth rate quickly exceeded the capacity of their infrastructure, but that problem does not affect the music industry: they have the infrastructure. Why in the world do they not sign more small artists to a one-record deal, with 'first-dibs' rights guaranteed to the record companies, for a comparatively small fee to the artist for the first record? They could send out CDs just the way AOL does, except with maybe 20 cuts per CD, of different artists, mailed quarterly? Eighty good artists per year, in your mailbox. If only one catches fire, the record company exercises their 'first dibs' option, the artists can't bolt to a different label, and they get signed for a more standard record deal. Anyone who doesn't catch on gets dropped after one CD . . . at least they

got a shot. Would the cost of this positive publicity really be any more than the cost of fighting file sharing?"

(henry 1)

". . . they should take a tip from the movie industry and modern DVDs, which so overload the consumer with clear and compelling value that even those who wouldn't bat an eye about downloading a CD and not paying for it . . . have no motivation to spend dozens of hours downloading and piecing together all the value and quality available in a $25 DVD. I've bought DVDs for $20 where the movie was the tip of the iceberg—music tracks, documentaries, interactive presentations, audio tracks, stills, screen tests, and on and on. . . . They can fight with compelling value—whether it's built in videos, computer games, free tickets, unique passwords to go download bonus tracks, demo tracks and dance mixes . . . karaoke tracks for each song, alternate vocal takes. . . . Who could, or would, want to spend the time reproducing all that via downloading? As long as the consumer experience of a music CD can be duplicated with an hour or two of downloading and a quick burn to CD, they aren't going to convince anybody who might actually buy the CDs (but aren't, because they can download them) to do so . . . Rather than do things to alienate the current base of consumers that regularly buy their product, they should focus on adding value to their product."

(kevin)

## A Final Note

Our representatives are not in Congress or the Senate because they want to make a better living. They're there because they want power, and influence. Without the office, they have neither.

If they believe their actions will cause large amounts of the population to vote against them, no amount of money will be sufficient to buy their cooperation. If you let your representatives know, en masse, that you will not vote for them if they support ridiculous measures such as the bill allowing media companies to spread viruses on the computer of anyone "suspected" of file-sharing, and if enough of you tell them so, they will NOT work hand in glove with the RIAA.

We cannot possibly match the monies the record companies can devote to litigation, but we CAN threaten to vote those representatives who are in bed with them out of office. And ultimately, it's the votes they care about.

---

### Questions for Consideration

1   Do you agree with Janis Ian that illegal downloading is not harming the music industry? Find articles through Nexis or Factiva that help you make a case that agrees or disagrees with her.

2   Ian wrote her essay in 2002. In what ways is today's digital music situation different, and in what ways is it similar?

# Chapter 18

# JANET WASKO

# PROMOTING THE INDUSTRY

**P**ROMOTIONAL ACTIVITIES FOR THE SUMMER 2008 blockbuster *The Dark Knight* were underway well before the summer flicks of 2007 hit theaters and included the usual candy company tie-ins, billboards, and trailers, as well as an elaborate "viral" marketing campaign (named because it quickly spreads through social networks like a virus). This sort of hoopla may cause you to wonder when and how marketing promotions came to play such a significant role in the motion picture industry. In this essay, excerpted from the 2003 book *How Hollywood Works*, Janet Wasko traces the recent history of movie marketing and explores some of the most popular promotional tactics of film companies.

Hollywood companies succeed year after year in dominating film markets around the world for a variety of reasons, but it must be stressed that these companies do not simply rely on the strength of their products competing in these markets. As Samuel Arkoff once claimed, "No picture has ever been made that is good enough to sell itself" (Donahue, 1987, p. 82).

Film companies spend massive amounts of money on advertising and promotion to ensure that consumers are aware of their products. In addition, Hollywood encourages press coverage of their activities, not only through film reviews, but various kinds of publicity associated with films and film celebrities. Films also receive attention at festivals and markets, as well as through yearly awards given out by industry and non-industry groups.

Promotion draws attention to the industry's products but Hollywood also employs various strategies to protect its interests, both within the US and internationally. These efforts are carried out by industry organizations that often call upon the US government for assistance and support. This chapter will present an overview of the ways that Hollywood both promotes and protects its business.

## Movie Marketing

The film that is often credited with changing how movies are distributed and marketed was *Jaws*—the first movie to open at a thousand theaters and to use network television to support it. Before that, what are now called marketing departments were publicity departments. In addition, much less money was spent on advertising, with more attention given to publicity and trailers.

After the *Jaws* experience in the 1970s, publicity departments gradually evolved into "multi-disciplined" marketing departments, which include specific divisions for publicity, creating advertising, media buying, and promotion (including product placement and tie-in activities). More recently, a specific area has been developed for Internet promotion. Film companies attempt to keep these activities coordinated and moving together to put out a single message. As one marketing executive explains:

> [I]t's sort of like planning a military invasion. You can't plan to have your air force do something, your artillery do something, and your infantry do something, without any knowledge of their power. So you have to assess the power of each one of your organizations to implement a program before you can design a battle plan.
>
> (PBS, 2001)

Not surprisingly, each company arranges marketing activities somewhat differently. The same marketing executive cited above explains:

> It's very different from company to company. There are companies that will not put a movie into production without the endorsement of the marketing department. They are as involved in reading scripts, making the decisions on whether that movie is going to get made as is the production element. [But] some companies really could care less what the marketing department says.
>
> (ibid.)

If the average movie costs around $28 million to market, about $3 to $5 million dollars of that is for the production of materials and running the marketing campaign; the balance is the cost of media (ibid.). Although the studios use in-house marketing personnel, outside companies or individuals can also be employed to create specific parts of the campaign, such as the trailers, television commercials, or print material. This process of using outside vendors may be contributing to increasing marketing expenditures, an issue that is considered in the next section.

## Issue: Marketing Madness

It might be useful to ask why the marketing costs for films continue to grow. Some industry observers argue that a fear of box office failure and a never-ending cycle of "hyper-competition" have developed as the studios try to outspend each other in promoting their big films. Based on reports on marketing research and competition, more and more money is poured into advertising campaigns and other efforts to boost box-office numbers.

Of special importance is the amount of television advertising that is assumed to be needed to support big, blockbuster films. Certainly, this process has contributed to the further commercialization of the industry, not to mention the waste involved in the massive amounts of money poured into such efforts. But it also has apparently shifted power within marketing departments, and even within the studios themselves. Levin (2000) observes that "people who are more involved in how you put together television commercials—the creative folks who do that kind of work—have risen in importance in these marketing departments. The publicity people have been diminished a little bit against the creative people, and the budgets have soared."

There is so much emphasis on marketing in general that a commonplace assumption in the industry is that if a movie is successful, it was a great movie, but if it was a failure, it was because of weak marketing. In addition, the emphasis on the initial opening, or first weekend, has become intense. The marketing department becomes responsible for a big opening, which, it is argued, "becomes critical for the entire life of the movie" (ibid.). Films that do not manage to attract big bucks during their opening weekend are considered losers, and are relegated to the home video market rather quickly. Thus, marketing campaigns become crucial to the success of major Hollywood films. More details about this process follow in the next few sections.

## Marketing Strategies

A wide range of considerations is involved in designing marketing plans. In addition to the usual marketing factors, when the film will be released and the competition influence these decisions. The design of the marketing also will take into account the genre, the plot, and the cast. For instance, how much publicity is possible from the film's stars may influence how dependent the marketing campaign needs to be on advertising versus publicity. Promotional partners also may be possible, thus "other people's money" can be used to promote the film.

## Marketing Research

For many, many years, Hollywood has attempted to use research to foretell a film's success in the marketplace. But it is still a tricky business, as evidenced by the stories that industry people tell about the films that were rejected based on supposedly solid research. For instance, Universal passed on *Star Wars*, Columbia gave up on *E.T.: The Extra Terrestrial* after extensive development, and all of the major studios passed on *Raiders of the Lost Ark* except for Paramount.

As one industry insider explains, "Motion picture research attempts to predict what audiences want to see, when they want to see it, and the best means of motivating them to go to the film" (Donahue, 1989, p. 98). Sometimes it works, but more often it doesn't. Hollywood seems to have mixed feelings about marketing research, especially when it attempts to assess moviegoers' awareness of future movies and their likelihood of seeing them, especially in international markets. As a *Variety* reporter concludes, "Companies are eager for the information, but occasionally skeptical about its reliability."[1]

Nevertheless, filmmakers and distributors still employ outside companies to provide research on which to make decisions. While numerous companies offer such services, the dominant firms are interestingly connected to the industry's trade publications. National Research Group (NRG) dominates the domestic market for film research and has a virtual international monopoly on such services. NRG is owned by VNU, the same company that owns the *Hollywood Reporter*.

In 1997 VNU acquired NRG, which was recently integrated into its Nielsen Entertainment unit. Nielsen offers a range of movie-marketing services, including box office tracking, focus-group testing and surveys, and includes a number of companies that provide information, marketing solutions, and analytical tools to the entertainment industry. Nielsen Entertainment is especially important in measuring box office results, but also tracks music, video/DVD, and book sales. In addition to NRG, the companies involved are Nielsen EDI, Nielsen ReelResearch, Nielsen VideoScan, Nielsen Entertainment Marketing Solutions (EMS) and others.

Domestically, NRG's chief competitor is MarketCast, which is owned by *Variety*'s parent company, Reed Business Information. MarketCast provides market research for motion picture studios, production companies, film exhibitors, television networks, and Internet content providers, supporting them in the development of marketing strategies for movies, television and Internet programming. (More background will be presented on Reed below in the section on the trade press.)

Various methods are used to pre-test concepts, titles, etc., as well as to guide marketing campaigns before and after a film is produced. Market surveys may be used to identify features of a film that have the widest consumer appeal, or that reveal a target audience. Research methods may include "intercept" techniques (pedestrians asked to respond to questions about concepts, stars, or advertising copy). Interviews also are used to elicit responses to advertising.

Test screenings may involve the screening of either a rough cut, the final cut, the trailer or television commercials, followed by questionnaires that attempt to identify what segment of the audience is attracted to the film and why. A test screening can lead to changes in the film, reediting or even reshooting. But information gleaned from test screenings also is used to develop a marketing strategy, often focussing on a target audience. Focus group sessions also are utilized, especially after a target audiences is identified.

Film companies also attempt to use marketing segmentation techniques to target consumers in their advertising and promotional campaigns. For instance, the following scheme is presented on a film company website as a way to categorize American movie audiences:

*Gen Y Audiences*. Approximately 28 percent of American society aged 14 to 26, and of primary interest to traditional movie marketers. Gen Y actually ranges from 7 to 26 in three distinct waves.

*Gen X Audiences*. Baby Busters—now tagged Generation X approximately 18 percent of American society, aged 26 to 42. Strong audience for independent films, goes their own way, seeks out the unknown and undiscovered.

*Boomer Audiences*. The strong new audience segment, approximately 32 percent of American society, 43 to 56 years old, empty-nesters with time and money and strong appetites for interesting films.

(filmprofit.com)

Marketing research also continues after a film opens, sometimes utilizing exit interviews to find out how audience members responded to the film. Subsequent advertising, as well as changes in the release pattern, may be altered based on the findings of such research.

## Issue: Marketing to Children

Early in 2002, the Federal Trade Commission reported that the entertainment industry deliberately targeted children and teenagers with advertising for R-rated films, as well as using them in focus groups to test such movies.[2] An example from the documents used in the study showed that MGM/United Artists had tested commercials for the horror film *Disturbing Behavior* on children as young as 12, while using children 9 to 11 to research ideas for another horror movie.

During a later Senate hearing, film executives admitted to being guilty of "competitive zeal" in marketing violent movies to children and offered varying acts of contrition. However, they were divided over whether to end the practice. Some of the companies pledged to alter their policies of advertising adult-rated movies to schools and youth groups, as well as on television shows, websites, and in magazines with primary audiences under age 17. They also agreed to expand their rating systems to help parents better evaluate films, with Warner Bros. planning to add the designations L for profane language, S for sex and V for violence. And all the executives said that their studios had stopped using children in focus groups for R-rated films, unless accompanied by adults. How serious these efforts will be remains to be seen, but represents an attempt by government representatives to place pressure on the industry.

The next sections will present overviews of specific marketing activities, such as publicity, advertising, trailers, and the Internet, followed by some attention to film festivals and markets, critics and reviewers, film awards, and the trade press. Promotional activities such as product placements, merchandising and tie-ins also contribute to the marketing of a film, but were discussed in the last chapter.

## Publicity

Publicity can be defined as unpaid media attention, as opposed to paid promotion or advertising, and includes a wide range of activities, including critics' reviews and film festivals, which will be discussed separately below. Media coverage of a film is not fortuitous, nor is it typically initiated by media outlets. Publicity for Hollywood films is the result of deliberate and calculated planning by publicists and public relations specialists.

Publicity begins even before production, usually after a film receives a green light, but accelerates during the principal photography. A unit publicist or public relations firm is assigned at this time and stays with the film through its release.

Again, publicity on the set is not accidental, but carefully planned by publicists who prepare press releases, invite the press on the set and arrange interviews with talent. Publicists may arrange for video to be shot during production for electronic press kits, music videos, and featurettes or the making-of-the-movie programs, as well as coordinating photos and talent interviews. Publicists also get involved in script and editing changes as well as market research.

As the film nears completion, publicists try to create a buzz for a film in whatever way possible. One way is to get other media to cover the film, including cover stories in national magazines, television programs (news, talk shows, entertainment programs, etc.), as well as other media outlets. The aim is to stimulate coverage of a film outside of the entertainment section of the news media by staging events, drawing attention to stars, etc.

One recent example was the media blitz that accompanied the James Bond release, *Die Another Day*, in November 2002. The film's stars appeared across the media, accompanied by a myriad of cross-promotional advertisements of the branded products in the film. *Time* magazine's coverage was a seven-page color spread, while *Newsweek* devoted four pages to the new release. Numerous other magazine covers featured the images of the film's stars, who also traveled the talk show circuit.

Traditional means of film publicity include press kits or books which supply advertising material for exhibitors (and later, home video companies, etc.) and the press (magazines, newspapers and television) from 6–8 weeks before a film opens. The kit may include story description, photos, star bios, sample stories, etc. Other theater material includes posters, standees or stand-ups, window cards, etc. Electronic press kits include video interviews, behind-the scenes footage, the trailer, perhaps a music video and other material that can be used to publicize the film. Promotional items such as t-shirts, buttons, key chains, and music are also included with press kits, as well as being used as giveaways to the public.

A few months before a film's release, it is shown to the trade (mostly exhibitors) and to the press, as well as to audiences in a few theaters (usually in Los Angeles). In addition to audience information, sneak previews are intended to enhance word of mouth about the film as well as to elicit responses to the film from preview cards. However, previews also can become profitable for blockbuster films when shown at numerous theaters. For instance, during one weekend in November 2002, *Harry Potter and the Chamber of Secrets* was shown at sneak previews in 522 theaters in Britain and gathered $12.5 million, while in Japan the film was sneaked at 777 screens for one day and yielded $3.7 million.

Stars also participate in media junkets and other publicity events. Appearances on talk shows, features on entertainment programs, and most recently, special cyber-space events and chat sessions, can be invaluable in terms of "free" advertising. As films also need to be sold to exhibitors, stars are often requested to attend exhibitors' conventions or other events. Star appearances are especially important in foreign countries, where marketing campaigns are designed separately and revenues can surpass those from the US market. For instance, Vin Diesel, the star of *XXX*, did a 12-country, two-month tour to promote the film, thus upping the gross receipts to over $150 million by the end of 2002.

Distributors also use "fieldmen" to promote a film in major cities around the USA. These employees (or independent agencies) make sure that the film receives local attention in the press, as well as arranging promotional events, contests and giveaways at department stores, radio stations, and other sites.

## Advertising

Advertising costs for a film can be more than the cost of production and, as noted above, have grown dramatically over the last few decades. The MPAA reported that the average for new feature films by member companies was $27.3 million in 2002. Again, advertising campaigns and budgets vary for each Hollywood film, but a few common practices still prevail. Advertising is aimed at the film industry itself (especially exhibitors, but also other sectors), as well as consumers in the various markets where a film will be sold.

Trade advertising involves ads in trade papers (*Variety* and *The Hollywood Reporter*) before, during and after production, for various purposes. Distributors typically arrange such advertising, in addition to national campaigns.

Other advertising efforts are aimed at the national and local level. The amount of money and where it is spent are often related to a film's release pattern. However, national advertising has become increasingly important, as big films open in wide releases across the country. Network television has become common and has driven up the costs of advertising campaigns. *Variety* reported that movie studios increased their spending on television ads in 2001 over the previous year by 55 percent on network television and 74 percent on cable. Films also are advertised in other outlets, including newspapers, radio, magazines, and billboards. The major distributors and exhibitors often work with advertising agencies when purchasing such media time and space. The studios' media buyers, together with their advertising agencies, claim to know the appropriate level and extent of advertising for each film. As one marketing executive explains: "With their budget they plan the strategy as to whom to buy, when to buy and how to buy, so that the result reaches the target audience for each movie with the greatest economy" (Squire, 1992, p. 299). One may wonder, then, why some films are not successful at the box office and why advertising costs keep rising.

Cooperative advertising has come to mean mostly local advertising. Although this expense may be shared by the exhibitor and distributor, there is a good deal of variation depending on the location, the companies involved and the specific film. For instance, New York represents a significant market that can contribute as much as 10 percent of a film's domestic theatrical revenues. However, it also represents high advertising costs and the potential for negative reviews (see especially Donahue, 1987).

*      *      *

## Trailers

Trailers (or movie previews shown in theaters) can be traced back to the 1920s, if not earlier, when they were outtakes or uncut footage. Trailers originally ran at the end of a film showing, but because people were leaving before the trailers were finished, they were moved to before the featured film.

Prior to the 1970s, trailers were produced and distributed to theaters by a company called the National Screen Service (NSS), along with other items such as posters, photos, and material for local advertising. In fact, the National Screen Service has an interesting history that indicates the extent that Hollywood has changed its promotional habits.

NSS was created in 1920 to produce and distribute trailers, which were an important part of the studios' marketing campaigns. NSS prepared trailers for several major studios, and eventually also became involved in distributing "movie paper" (also called standard accessories), which included 8″ × 10″ press stills, lobby cards, half sheets, inserts, one sheets, three sheets, six sheets and twenty-four sheets.

Most of the majors arranged for NSS to handle these materials, together with its affiliate, Advertising Accessories Inc. By the mid-1940s most of the majors used NSS, which continued to be the center for movie paper advertising until the mid-1980s. After this point, the business became more dispersed, although NSS continued to handle approximately 15–20 percent of the advertising paper. In September, 2000, the NSS offices were bought by Technicolor, Inc., which now provides these services, with particular emphasis on the one-sheet.[3]

Today, trailers can range in length from 30 seconds to 4.5 minutes, but average 2.5 to 3 minutes. Shorter teasers can appear as much as a year in advance of a film's opening, serving as an announcement and rarely featuring much actual film footage as the movie is often in production. For instance, during summer 2002, teasers for *The Hulk* were shown, although the film was not scheduled to open until summer 2003.

More than ever, trailers are crucial to a successful film these days. In fact, trailers are probably the most important, effective, and cost-efficient way of marketing a new film. A 2002 survey by *Variety* and Moviefone found that ticket buyers cited trailers as the biggest influence on their movie choices, followed by television, newspapers and Internet.

In addition, trailers have become important with the proliferation of wide releases of films that rely on opening weekends to set their value. "We'll spend five months to a year obsessing about them, every single cut and every single moment that we use," says David Sameth, DreamWorks' head of creative advertising. "That's indicative, I think, of how intense the pressure is on creating the right piece."

Trailers can be produced within the studios, although companies specializing in this type of production also are employed and have proliferated recently. For instance, The Ant Farm is a Los Angeles-based motion picture advertising company that worked on *Lord of the Rings: The Fellowship of the Ring* and *The Sixth Sense*, among others. One of its representatives explained that, "You have to find what is unique in each movie and figure out a way to highlight that and get the audience excited about it."

In light of the significance of trailers, their placement has become particularly important. For instance, because of an agreement between George Lucas' Lucasfilm and Pixar Animation Studios, trailers for *Star Wars: Episode II—Attack of the Clones* were included before *Monsters, Inc.* However, the studios distributing the films (Twentieth Century Fox and Disney, respectively) apparently were not involved or consulted about the decision. The deal prompted some concern at the studios, where (as *Variety* reported), there is "fear of losing control of a valuable element of the Hollywood marketing machine." The issue put into question who has control of the space before the movie—the theater, the studio, the producer or even a star?

## Internet Promotion

As noted in Chapter 3, Hollywood companies now utilize the Internet to promote their products. Most films have Internet sites which open long before the movie appears in theaters, primarily to promote the film, but also to gather information about fans.

The technology offers new possibilities for "one-to-one marketing," using databases of moviegoers with preferences and profiles, and targeted email promotions. The sites also can be used to "build communities." An early example: Sony Tristar's *Starship Troopers* site featured "Mobile Infantry" that users could employ to join the battle against the giant alien bugs, while Trooper ID screens provided links to other users' sites. The *Starship* site had attracted over 30,000 users by summer 2000, thus providing free promotion for the film. By 1997, 40 percent of the movie sites online had interactive attributes, such as games or quizzes, and 30 percent had community features (Chowdhury et al., 1997).

Movie sites also may feature product placements or companies that have promotional tie-ins. For instance, the 2002 site for *Die Another Day* featured links to 24 "007 partners," including Finlandia Vodka, Bollinger Champagne, Talisker Scotch Whiskey, and Heineken Beer, as well as Ford, Jaguar, and Aston Martin. The site also offered numerous versions of the film's trailer, music, and videos, in addition to production notes, downloadable screen savers, information about the film's production and release, and photos and material on past Bond films.

## Press Coverage and Film Critics

### Hollywood and the Press

Hollywood has always had an interesting relationship with the press, as the film industry is a source for popular newspaper content as well as a customer for its advertising services. Press coverage of Hollywood involves everything from film reviews to features on film stars' personal lives. During the last decade, it may seem that more press attention has been given to the business of Hollywood, with box office returns regularly reported in local newspapers and a plethora of "entertainment news" programs.

Interestingly, the same companies that own film companies own some of the more popular entertainment news sources. Examples would include periodicals such as *Entertainment Weekly* (AOL Time Warner), as well as television shows such as *Entertainment Tonight* (Paramount). While this type of "entertainment news" sometimes includes stories about the film business, it is mostly fan-oriented with an emphasis on Hollywood celebrities and movie reviews.

One estimate is that there are over 2,000 journalists in the USA who write about Hollywood films. At least, that is the number of press kits that studios often send out for new films (Squire, 1992, p. 300). Another indication of the extent of press coverage is represented by the Hollywood Foreign Press Association (HFPA), a non-profit organization with members representing magazines and newspapers in some 55 countries with a claimed combined readership exceeding 250 million.

The HFPA's background can be traced to the formation of the Hollywood Association of Foreign Correspondents in 1928. A competing group of foreign journalists was organized in 1943 as the Hollywood Foreign Press Association. In 1955, the HFPA united members from the two groups and established definite requirements for membership. Currently, members must submit recent by-lined articles for active status and participation in the association's activities. These include interview opportunities with motion picture talent, plus visits to sets, press days, and film festival events.

But the press does not always need to arrange these events on their own, as noted earlier in the discussion of Hollywood publicity. Studios and other film companies actively court press coverage of upcoming and new films, especially, but also Hollywood activities, in general.

## Film Critics

The term "critics" (or *Variety*'s term, "crix") refers to "persons usually employed by newspapers, television stations or other media who screen newly released movies and provide their subjective views and comments on the movie for the public's information" (Cones, 1992, p. 120).

Over the years, some newspaper columnists and reviewers have developed extremely close relationships with Hollywood. While well-known columnists such as Hedda Hopper and Louella Parsons became Hollywood celebrities themselves, some feel that they were much more manipulated by the studio system than movie critics are by today's media system.

Critics and film reviewers still play a special role in the Hollywood system. Studios regularly schedule critics' screenings in advance of a film's release, hoping to receive favorable reviews. However, if negative reviews are expected, the studio may decide not to screen a picture, hoping to delay the bad publicity as long as possible (although this strategy may backfire as critics may be harsher in their reviews because of the delay).

However, the studios have been known to woo key critics in various ways. In addition to supplying information and material about upcoming films, they may wine and dine critics at previews, arrange special interviews with stars or other key talent, or provide a variety of other special considerations or favors. Marketing and advertising campaigns also sometimes feature quotes from well-known critics, thus improving their reputation and (possibly) encouraging them to make more favorable comments to get their name in film advertisements.

It is assumed, therefore, that movie critics are able to influence the box office success of a film. A "powerful critic theory" is also prevalent in other industries where reviews are often thought to make or break commercial properties such as Broadway plays, books, etc., but the relationship between film critics and Hollywood seems to have become particularly entangled. As one movie marketing executive explains: "Critics . . . I think we've made them important to us. We quote them all the time. We use excerpts from their reviews in our advertising. But we're probably doing that because we don't have enough confidence in our own good work to not use them" (Brouwer and Wright, 1990, p. 520).

Another commonplace assumption by many in the industry is expressed as follows: "if it's not a good movie, gets poor reviews and opens poorly, it might be saved. If it's not a review-driven movie, such as an action or teenage movie, and opens poorly, it probably can't be saved" (Squire, 1992, p. 302).

A number of academic studies have attempted to assess the influence of critics' reviews on motion picture selection, however, with mixed results. Eliashberg and Shugan (1997, p. 77) reviewed these studies and observe that:

> In sum, research evidence on critics' reviews and their effect seems inconclusive. It suggests that the role critics (or movie experts) play may be interpreted as influential, in shaping movie-goers' interest in attending movies. It also suggests a moderate, and possibly different, impact for positive and negative reviews . . . Finally, it suggests that the reviews may only indicate movie-goer tastes.

In their own study, Eliashberg and Shugan found that critical reviews may influence late and cumulative box office receipts but do not have a significant impact on early box office revenues. In other words, critics serve more as leading indicators than as opinion leaders.

Meanwhile, in a recent study, MarketCast reported on a national random sample of moviegoers that found friends' opinions and quotes in ads more important than critics' opinions. Furthermore, over 50 percent of participants in the study reported that they ignore what critics say about a film, feeling that critics can't relate to normal audiences or misled them about movies.

In a more recent study, *Variety* polled four dozen filmmakers in Hollywood and New York in 2000 and found that industry insiders have mostly negative views about critics. A typical opinion was the following: "I can't name one critic that I trust. If there was ever an art to it, it's been lost." The report concluded that "There's a hunger for quality criticism that once played a key role in American filmmaking; moviemakers are angry that it's been replaced by blurbmeisters, report cards, one-to-four-star rankings and thumbs (aloft and below)."[4]

Some filmmakers felt that reviewers in the past had more passion and that, "Now it's about soundbite criticism." However, they also felt that's not always the fault of critics. Now, there are few films that lend themselves to impressive reviews, plus "They're being hit on by the studios to a much greater extent, and they're being hyped." In addition, there was some sympathy for reviewers who are faced with a huge number of films for review these days.

Filmmakers were especially contemptuous of the "most heavily blurbed" TV critics. One filmmaker observed, "If there ever was an art to film criticism, it was lost. It all started with the televising of *Siskel* & *Ebert*. People stopped reading." One of the key reviewers in the USA, Roger Ebert, illicited a love-hate response from filmmakers. Ebert, with his late partner, Gene Siskel, seems to have created the most familiar image of today's film critic. (Perhaps, ironically, the duo established their name in television through a program produced by one of the majors.)

Jowett and Linton have offered another assessment of the critic-industry relationship:

> While the producer-distributors would prefer to have good critical reviews than bad ones, even the latter will be accepted if the audience has good things to tell its peers about the movie. Such a discrepancy simply adds support to movie-makers' contention that critics are cultural eunuchs who know nothing about the business—let alone the art of making movies.

(1989, p. 70)

Some industry people realize that critics are necessary for the business and try to use them to their benefit. As one of the filmmakers interviewed in the *Variety* poll mentioned above explained: "the key to following a critic is knowing how to interpret his tastes for your own needs." Others in Hollywood still wage bitter battles with reviewers, and sometimes those conflicts are quite public. One recent example was director James Cameron's infamous response to Kenneth Turan's negative comments in the *Los Angeles Times* about Cameron and his film *Titanic*. More recently, Castle Rock decided not to screen *The Adventures of Pluto Nash* to critics prior to its release because negative comments on the Internet revealed a "predisposition by reviewers to pan it." Release of the film, which stars Eddie Murphy, had already been delayed for nearly two years for various reasons.

And then there was the group of French filmmakers who were tired of attacks by French film critics and issued a public directive against their attackers. The French directors proposed that negative reviews be suppressed until after opening weekend, an idea that attracted a good deal of attention, but little hope of success.

It is probably not surprising that there are associations for film critics, similar to other professional groups associated with the film industry. Critics have organized groups in many major US cities, including Los Angeles, New York, Chicago, Dallas, Fort Worth and San Francisco. The National Society of Film Critics was formed in 1966 by a group of magazine writers who had been refused admittance to the New York Film Critics, which was comprised exclusively of newspaper writers.

Meanwhile, critics groups are organized in foreign cities (London, for instance) and countries (Australia, for instance) and the International Federation of Film Critics claims to "defend the rights and interests of professional film critics and the improvement of conditions in which they carry out their work." More recently, an Online Film Critics Society has also been formed.

*     *     *

## Film Festivals and Markets

Marketing and promotional possibilities for films also are presented by film festivals and markets, which have multiplied at a rather fast rate over the past few decades. Over 600 festivals of one kind or another were reported worldwide by *Variety* in 2002, however, the exact number of festivals is difficult to estimate. For instance, in 2000, the European Coordination of Film Festivals reported over 150 festivals in Europe alone (Turan, 2002).

The attention given to some festivals and the awards they give to individual films can be alluring and advantageous for some film-makers and companies. Some of the key festivals have also added markets to their events, offering further opportunities for buying and selling products and making industry contacts. These events have become especially important for smaller or independent films as press and audience attention can generate invaluable word-of-mouth promotion. Again, festivals may be particularly lucrative for smaller or independent films, as positive attention may attract distributor attention and ultimately affect a film's success, especially in international markets.

Yet, some filmmakers and distributors are wary of festivals, fearing the potential damage of a negative response. There also can be relatively high expenses associated with participation, including the cost of travel. Some of the major Hollywood blockbusters may not need to be screened at festivals and thus avoid these additional expenses.

*Los Angeles Times* reviewer Kenneth Turan has categorized film festivals as those with aesthetic, business or geopolitical agendas. He identifies and discusses Havana, Sarajevo and Midnight Sun as having geopolitical goals, while Pordenone, Lone Pine and Telluride are examined for their primarily aesthetic goals. Meanwhile, Cannes, Sundance and ShoWest represent festivals with distinct business agendas (Turan, 2002). Only a few of the more prominent festivals and markets are discussed briefly here.

The *Cannes Film Festival* is actually the Festival International du Film and has been organized on a regular annual basis since 1951. The event is probably the best-known film festival, and, in fact, has been called the world's largest yearly media event: "a round-the clock cinematic billboard that in 1990 attracted 3,893 journalists, 221 TV crews, and 118 radio stations representing 81 countries" (Turan, 2002, p. 14). But Cannes also includes a film market where as many as 600 films are screened in hopes of attracting buyers. Cannes is said to have a love-hate relationship with Hollywood, yet has been known to give major Hollywood films important awards that are then used in marketing pitches.

Meanwhile, the *Sundance Film Festival* was started 1978 in Salt Lake City, growing to become "the flagship of the burgeoning American independent film movement" after being adopted by Robert Redford's Sundance Institute in 1985 and relocated to Park City, Utah. However, the event has become increasingly useful for the major studios, as well. Redford's explanation is an example of how the mainstream film industry catches up with and eventually encompasses the independent, the marginal or the peripheral:

> When the first studio people showed up, I dragged them off the street and into the screening rooms. . . . Eventually—and this caught me by surprise—people began flocking here because they were interested in the wonderful, diverse menu of films we were screening that started with *El Norte* and gained steam with *Sex, Lies, and Videotape*. Sundance was suddenly so cool that Hollywood simply couldn't ignore it. In fact, Hollywood wanted to be "in" with it. When Hollywood came, the merchants came. And when the merchants came, fashion came. And when fashion came, the media came and voted, Sundance was a part of the mainstream.[5]

\*        \*        \*

### Festival Choices

The selection process at film festivals often relies on personal trust, long-time friend-ships, and subjective opinion. While there are usually festival selection committees, gatekeepers or political lobbyists have emerged on the festival circuit. These characters operate between filmmakers and festival heads, influencing the films that are offered and chosen. While big titles by well-known directors or films from the US majors rarely are affected by these maneuvers, international exposure can be crucial for smaller or independent films.

Festivals have distinct images and getting a film into the right festival is also crucial for smaller films, especially. The biggest industry exposure is said to come from around ten of the top festivals: Rotterdam, Berlin, Cannes, Locarno, Montreal, Venice, Toronto and San Sebastian, plus Annecy for animation and Amsterdam for documentaries. As a *Variety* reporter explains:

Getting the wrong fest—or even the wrong section of a fest—can be counterproductive to a movie's launch. Is it too small for the giant screen of Locarno's Piazza Grande or too populist for its competition? Is it edgy enough for Berlin or too cutting edge for Cannes? Will a nice but unflashy Euro pic be lost in a U.S.-dominated fest like Sundance; would it be better appreciated at Venice?[6]

Sometimes production companies or distributors hire a full-time person just to coordinate festival entries. In fact, some companies have asked festivals to pay service fees to cover these additional costs.

## Festival Sponsorship

Even film festivals are becoming more commercialized, as more businesses are offering sponsorship for the events. Because the presumed impact of traditional advertising is weakening, festivals offer companies with expensive products access to an ideal audience. In other words, festivals attract educated middle-aged consumers with above-average incomes. For example, a recent printed program from the Sundance Film Festival included advertisements from over 125 corporate sponsors.

Corporate funding has been typical for many festivals, but primarily in the form of charitable donations. Recently, however, a more intense partnership has developed between sponsoring companies and festivals, involving marketing departments and advertising agencies. Companies have become interested in a more active and visible role, while these corporate alliances provide festivals with additional funds for promotion.

## Film Awards

Hollywood companies attempt to draw attention to their products through press coverage and critical reviews. But attention and acclaim also can be generated through various awards that originate both from inside and outside the film industry.

### Academy Awards

The best-known film awards are presented by the Academy of Motion Picture Arts and Sciences, or in other words, by the industry itself. The Academy Awards were first organized in 1929 and have grown to become benchmarks for filmmaking, as well as playing an important economic role for the industry.

Regular awards are presented for outstanding individual or collective efforts in 24 categories. Up to five nominations are made in most categories, with balloting for these nominations restricted to members of the Academy branch concerned; directors, for instance, are the only nominators for Achievement in Directing. Nominations for awards in the foreign language and documentary categories are made by large committees of members drawn from all branches. Best Picture nominations and final winners in most categories are determined by the entire membership.

Nomination ballots are mailed by the Academy in January to its members (there were over 5,600 voting members in 2002). The secret ballots are sent to Pricewater-houseCoopers, the professional services firm formerly known as Price Waterhouse. The results of nomination balloting are announced in early February. Then, final ballots are mailed in early March and members have two weeks to return them. After ballots are tabulated, only two partners of PricewaterhouseCoopers are claimed to know the results until the envelopes are opened on stage during the Awards Presentation in March. The Academy Awards Presentation program is itself a media event, attracting worldwide audiences and extensive media coverage.

The nominations and awards are considered some of the best ways to promote a film and can potentially lead to a substantial increase in revenues. Dodds and Holbrook (1988) evaluated the impact of Academy Awards on film revenues, and found significant effects of Best Picture, Best Actor, and Best Actress awards on post-award revenues. Another study found that theatrical revenue can increase 5–10 percent if a film is nominated, while actually receiving an award can enhance a film's value for cable and network television by 50–100 percent (Donahue, 1987, p. 81).

Thus, receiving a nomination and ultimately an award are seen as adding value to a film commodity. Serious efforts are made to attract these honors and expensive campaigns to influence voting begin in November each year. In the past, elaborate strategies have been used involving targeted advertising and promotional gimmicks. Studios, independent distributors, and publicists use various strategies to make sure that the Academy members view their film. Special screenings are held, free admissions are offered to commercial runs of a film or video cassettes are shipped to the voters. For several years, the Academy has aggressively monitored campaigning and has issued guidelines that limit company mailings to those items that "actually assist the members in their efforts to assess the artistic and technical merits of a film."

However, at least one author and film critic believes that the campaigns around the Academy Awards have become "nastier, more aggressive, more expensive and more sophisticated." Emanuel Levy, chief film critic for *Screen International* and the author of *Oscar Fever: The History and Politics of the Academy Awards*, notes that "aggressive campaigns have been run for Oscars as far back as the 1940s."[7]

The campaigning may indeed affect the outcome, as over the years there have been some classic examples of films that won (or didn't win) because of political and/or economic reasons. For instance, in 1941 *Citizen Kane*, directed by Orson Welles and based on newspaper mogul William Randolph Hearst, lost to *How Green Was My Valley*. It was widely suggested Hearst's influence in Hollywood had much to do with ensuring that Welles did not triumph. In 1959 screenwriter Ned Young failed to win an Oscar for *The Defiant Ones* because he was blacklisted. His pseudonym, Nathan E. Douglas, won it instead. More recently, in 1998, intense and heavy spending by Miramax was believed to have helped *Shakespeare In Love* defeat *Saving Private Ryan*, widely regarded as the favorite.

### Other Awards

There are a huge number of awards made yearly that involve Hollywood films.[8] While many of these are relatively insignificant, a few important awards are given by organizations or associations connected to the industry. The Hollywood Foreign Press

Association presents the Golden Globe Awards at the end of January every year, while the Los Angeles, New York and London Film Critics Associations also present yearly accolades.

Awards also are given by the Hollywood guilds. What has been called Hollywood's pre-Oscar Final Four—the quartet of guild award shows the first two weekends of March—includes trophies from the Producers Guild, the Writers Guild, the Screen Actors Guild, and the Directors Guild.

Meanwhile, the National Board of Review hands out awards that often serve as "signposts" to the winning Oscars. The organization was created as a censorship group in 1909, but its current board is composed of around 150 members from varying professions, including educators, doctors, lawyers, historians, and few former industry insiders. The membership is said to be a mystery to most people in the film business. Although the group's selections tend to favor the specialty market, with an emphasis on breakthrough performances and emerging talent, the board's choice has agreed with 41 percent of the Academy's best picture choices since 1980.

While the artistic and creative merit of these various awards can be disputed endlessly, the promotional and potential financial benefit is less debatable. Any kind of nomination or award is typically used extensively in advertising and promotional activities, and often boosts a film's overall revenues.

*     *     *

## Questions for Consideration

1   Why and how might film companies use different promotional strategies based on their considerations of the audiences?

2   Choose a recently released big-budget movie and, using a periodical database such as Nexis or Factiva, find out as much as you can about the promotional activities that the studio and its marketing agencies orchestrated. How different is the range of activities from the picture that Wasko described?

## Notes

1.   For instance, in September 2002, United International Pictures announced it would drop National Research Group's tracking service, though the international distributor will have a continuing relationship with the firm for other sorts of overseas research.

2.   F. Fiore, "Hollywood Admits Marketing Violent Movies to Young Kids," *Los Angeles Times*, 29 September 2000, p. C-1.

3.   http://www.learnaboutmovieposters.com/NewSite/INDEX/ARTICLES/nss_history.asp

4.   J. Bing, "PIX NIX CRIX SHTICKS: Reviewers Get Thumbs-Down from Filmmakers," *Variety*, 13 March 2000, p. 1.

5.   "Turning an Industry Inside Out: A Conversation with Robert Redford," *Harvard Business Review*, May 2002, Vol. 80, Issue 5.

6.   D. Elley, "Underground Network Plays Politics with Pix," *Variety*, 26 Aug 2002, p. 1.

7.   D. Campbell "Hollywood Knives are Out as Oscars get Nasty," *The Guardian*, 16 March 2002.

8.   For an extensive list of awards and festivals, see http://www.imdb.com/Sections/Awards/Events.

# Chapter 19

## MATTHEW P. McALLISTER, IAN GORDON, AND MARK JANCOVICH

# BLOCKBUSTER MEETS SUPERHERO COMIC, OR ART HOUSE MEETS GRAPHIC NOVEL?

## The Contradictory Relationship between Film and Comic Art

*BATMAN, SUPERMAN, THE HULK*, AND *X-MEN* are but a few of the many superheroes who have successfully transitioned from the comic book pages to the big screen over the years. Indeed, there is a long history between the film and comic book industries, and each industry has been influenced by these relations. Yet communication researchers Matthew P. McAllister, Ian Gordon, and Mark Jancovich suggest in their 2006 article that there is more to this relationship than meets the eye. Particularly significant are the ways in which both industries have responded to what the authors call a "commercialistic blockbuster mentality." What emerges then, is the question of how to balance the tension between financial and creative control—an issue many industries continue to grapple with.

Summer 2006 was a telling season for the often polarized nature of comic book-related movies, as a comparison of two U.S. releases indicates. A major studio "tentpole" release—a high-profile film with the economic potential to singlehandedly boost a studio's financial profile for the year (Prince 5)—was *X-Men: The Last Stand* (*X3*). Based on characters owned by Marvel Entertainment, the largest U.S. comics publisher with approximately 37% of the market, *X3* demonstrated the huge amount of money involved in producing a Hollywood blockbuster. *X3* cost over $200 million to make, showed in more than 3,700 U.S. theaters, and set a Memorial Day box office record with an intake of $122 million in four days (Kaltenbach 1).

Equally symbolic of modern Hollywood, however, was the film's 67% box-office drop in its second weekend. *X3*, a Twentieth Century Fox release, had the full promotional power of Rupert Murdoch's News Corp. behind it, which included tie-ins with popular Fox network programs *American Idol*, *The Simpsons*, and *Family Guy*; local promotional news stories on television affiliates; and an *X3* page on the

NewsCorp-owned Web site MySpace.com (Angwin B3; Johnson). The movie's reviews were mixed, with one common criticism being its conformity to an oft-cited shortcoming among blockbusters: its emphasis on explosions over character development (Denby 90). The number-two comics publisher, DC, controlling about 33% of the comics market and not far behind in movie revenue, continued its comeback later that summer with the much-hyped *Superman Returns* (Box Office Mojo; Steinberg B1).

On the other hand, the release of the modestly budgeted *Art School Confidential* during the same time period offers another facet of the relationship between the two institutions. This Terry Zwigoff-directed movie is a scornful look at art and life, based on a graphic novel story by Daniel Clowes, who also wrote the screenplay. Distributed by Sony Pictures Classics (Sony's art film distributor), and coproduced by Mr. Mudd (actor John Malkovich's production company), the movie was shown at several film festivals before its theatrical release in fewer than 800 U.S. theaters and earned less than $4 million at the box office. Although the movie received mixed notices, a common complaint by reviewers was not regarding its "Hollywoodness," but rather its overly dark and cynical tone (Kleinschrodt 10); one positive reviewer, though, noted that it was "a bitter, witty college picture unlike any other" (Phillips 1; Box Office Mojo).

Such is the seemingly yin-yang nature of the relationship between comic art to motion pictures. Comic book-related films have done much to both establish the action-oriented mega-blockbuster and the thematically and/or visually innovative art film, even if particular examples do not easily fall along a neat alternative-mainstream continuum. This article will briefly examine these relations and posit potential developments for both film and comic books given this relationship.

## Comic Books and the "Popcornization" of the Hollywood Blockbuster

As Stringer points out, although the definition of a film blockbuster is diverse and even contentious, "size" seems to be a central concept (3). Big casts, big costs, big distribution, big spectacle, and big revenue—or at least some combination—are implied as necessary conditions in many discussions of the blockbuster. The idea of the high publicity, expensive, and revenue-generating "tentpole" picture is an important strategy for the modern major film studios. As Schatz notes, "In terms of budgets, production values and market strategy, Hollywood has been increasingly hit-driven since the early 1950s" (15). This immediate postwar establishment of the prestige A picture, however, emphasized big-budgeted epics like *The Ten Commandments* (1956), *Around the World in Eighty Days* (1956), *Lawrence of Arabia* (1962), and *Cleopatra* (1963); not all of these films were successful at the box office, with *Cleopatra* being notorious in this regard.

Schatz and others have noted that specific manifestations of blockbusters are historically specific. By the end of the 1980s, the blockbuster A picture was defined by many in the industry differently than in earlier eras: still big budgeted, but with a much larger advertising budget (especially targeting television) involving cross-promotional partners; a wide theatrical release pattern that includes the global market; the goal of a publicity-generating, huge opening weekend; the search for franchise-friendly premises and characters; and, in terms of genre, the dominance of the action-adventure, special effects-oriented "popcorn" thriller. Comic art—especially comic books—has played a key role in this evolution of the Hollywood blockbuster, especially in the narrowing of narrative genres and industrial strategies that characterize post-1980 blockbusters.

One early way that comics-based films have contributed to this development is that comic strips and books were key materials for the motion picture serial in the 1930s and 1940s. In these serials, audiences would see a chapter each week of an unfolding action narrative, usually drawn back by chapter-ending cliffhangers (sometimes literally, as burned in popular memory by silent film cliffhangers like *The Perils of Pauline* [1914]). Comics-licensed serials from this era included the very influential serial *Flash Gordon* (1936), as well as *Superman* (1948), *The Adventures of Captain Marvel* (1941), *Dick Tracy* (1937), *Spy Smasher* (1942), *The Phantom* (1943), and *The Batman* (1943). Aside from their visibility in the movie industry in the 1930s and 1940s and their role as early, usually economically successful, attempts at adopting comic books/strips to film, one could argue that the style and format of these movies—perhaps exploiting the serialized narrative structure and visual modalities of comics—indirectly influenced the episodic and cliffhanger nature of the action film genre, some of them self-consciously so, such as *Raiders of the Lost Ark* (1981).

More important, modern comic book-based films have helped establish the industrial formula of the Hollywood popcorn blockbuster: fantastic action movie as cultural event. Comic book materials attract a youthful moviegoing demographic, appeal to nostalgic older audiences, and offer thrills and well-defined archetype characters, especially heroes who also have well-established track records for popularity, licensing, and sequel potential. With the soundbite simplicity of high-concept blockbuster films (i.e., the economy of the titles *Batman Begins* [2005] and *Superman Returns* [2006]), branded advertising and marketing is facilitated, an increasingly emphasized factor in an era of big media promotion (McAllister). Illustrating the degree to which these factors are now culturally engrained, the second season of HBO's Hollywood satire *Entourage* depicts character Vincent Chase's apex of blockbuster stardom through his casting as the lead in the faux Warner Brothers-distributed and James Cameron-directed *Aquaman*. (One episode in this storyline depicts the obsession of Chase and his buddies with *Aquaman* topping the opening weekend box-office gross of then-champ *Spider-Man*.) Also no doubt contributing to this synergistic mix of properties is Time Warner's ownership of HBO, Warner Brothers Films, and DC Comics (including the character Aquaman). This mix is symbolically reified in *Entourage* despite public claims in summer 2006 by Time Warner President Jeffrey Bewkes that synergy is "bullshit" (Karnitschnig A1).

Looking at specific films, any list of the most influential films for this strategy would include such noncomic book-related movies as 1975's *Jaws* (Gomery), and 1977's *Star Wars* (Kapell and Lawrence). But in addition to these, *Superman* (1977), *Superman II* (1980), and *Batman* (1989), all DC-based Warner Brothers films, contributed significantly as well. Acquiring National Periodical Publications (DC Comics) in 1967 and then Warner Brothers-Seven Arts in 1969, Steve Ross, the early architect of the company that would later become Time Warner, valued National because of its success in merchandising DC Comics' characters and other figures, including James Bond (Bruck; Jones; "Kinney Plans").

*Superman*, budgeted in 1977 at a whopping (for that era) $55 million, established several precedents for the popcorn blockbuster, not the least of which was the idea of hiring big stars in action genres that previously were made under mostly B-picture budgets. Marlon Brando was hired early in the film's production to earn it popular

publicity and industrial credibility; Gene Hackman's hiring soon followed. Foreshadowing later efforts at coordinated licensing, Warner set up 1,000 retail displays and 12,000
floor displays in bookstores to sell Superman-related merchandise through the Warner
subsidiary Licensing Corporate of America. *Superman*'s pre-1970s status as a globally
appealing character (Gordon) is also relevant. The fact that *Superman*'s non-U.S. box
office was larger than its U.S. box office was an early precursor to the globalization of
Hollywood and illustrated the appeal of superhero movies to a worldwide audience
(boxofficemojo.com), illustrating a global mind-set, the inclusion in international
venues such as Cannes (Stringer, "Neither One Thing" 203).

Following up these characteristics was its sequel, *Superman II* (1980–1981). It
heightened the global importance of big films by its theatrical release in Australia and
Europe several months before debuting in the United States. It also added to the
commercial dimensions of the modern blockbuster formula (for a discussion of the
commercialization of modern film, see Wasko). The strategic filming of much of
this sequel during the making of the original *Superman*—following the supposedly
accidental simultaneous filming of the mid-1970s films *The Three Musketeers* and *The Four
Musketeers*—set a precedent for later planned film series franchises such as *The Lord of the
Rings* and *The Matrix* (Russo N20). More than a year before *E.T.: The Extra Terrestrial*'s
(1982) well-publicized Reece's Pieces partnership, *Superman II* was a visible contributor
to the institutionalization of product placement in high-profile films. It featured several
paid placements, including the prominence of Marlboro logos and cigarettes (especially
used by Lois Lane in the film) for a fee of over $42,000, a figure that eventually became
notorious when revealed during the U.S. Congress's investigation of youth marketing
by tobacco (Segrave 182).

*Batman* (1989), aside from its enormous box office and cultural visibility before
and during its wide release, illustrated the importance of corporate synergy and widespread licensing, as Meehan has argued. In this case, unlike *Star Wars*, the licensing and
merchandising (e.g., soundtracks, novelization) was largely in-house via the parent
company, then-titled Warner Communications, Inc., and was strategically planned and
distributed in stages as part of the film's publicity and subsidiary revenue. The company
used strategic publicity appearances and announcements associated with the film at
the fan meeting Comic-Con in San Diego to turn around the initial negative reaction
to Michael Keaton's casting as Batman (Martin and Broeske 20). The studios now
routinely use Comic-Con for even noncomic book films to generate early fan interest
and buzz; the strategy is an institutionalized part of a larger cultivation of fans by the
entertainment industry. Finally, Jack Nicholson's eventual $50 million payday from
*Batman*—a result of a landmark point participation deal for not just a percentage of the
gross box office revenue but also toys and other products bearing his likeness (Warren
3)—significantly increased star compensation and, therefore, blockbuster movie
budgets.

The film and comic book industries have been profoundly affected by the connection between the two institutions, and industry discourse frequently acknowledges
this connection. The success of both *Fantastic Four* in 2005 and *X-Men 3* in 2006 were
publicly credited with turning around (if only temporarily) a stale box office, for
instance. This success has been generalized by the film industry to include the suitability
of comic book films for modern blockbusters. One box-office analyst noted about
*Fantastic Four*'s performance that "comic book movies, if properly marketed, are exactly
what mainstream audiences want to see in their summer movies" (qtd. in Germain 2).

In fact, post-1990s comic book films have raised the stakes on the commercial block-buster. With the need for big stars and an emphasis on increased special effects in such films, budgets continue to reach sky-high levels. The price tag of *Superman Returns* was purported to be upward of $260 million, while *Spider-Man 3* (2007) cost as much as $300 million (Marr and Kelly A1). In addition to putting pressure on film financing, such trends also encourage a growing involvement of investment companies, and the accompanying bottom-line mentality and heightened emphasis on track record and formula. One example is Legendary Pictures, which exists to "make consistent, reliable returns in the inconsistent movie business" by investing in "lots of studio-financed movies" that follow the blockbuster formula (Mehta 120). The first two films Legend-ary Pictures financed were *Batman Begins* and *Superman Returns*.

Increasingly, comic book companies see themselves in the character-licensing business (at the very least) and perhaps even more specifically in the filmed entertain-ment industry. Given the decline in comic book sales—from a high of nearly $1 billion in the mid-1990s to less than half that in 2005 (Gustines 8)—comic book publishers are, ironically, de-emphasizing the medium of comics. DC Comics, of course, is part of the Time Warner empire, the largest media conglomerate in the world, including Warner Brothers Films, a coproducer of virtually all DC-related films. Marvel Enter-tainment has moved into film development and production, after years of poor returns on licensing revenue from external studio-produced films based on their properties. In what has been called by a trade journalist "one of the most radical business-model overhauls in Hollywood history," Marvel is redefining itself as "an independent film studio" that makes its own movies (Hammer 112). Avi Arad, Marvel Studio's former chief executive officer who brokered many of the high-profile Marvel-licensed films, resigned in 2006 but remained involved with the film production unit ("Marvel Studios' Arad [. . .]" B7). Borrowing more than $500 million from Merrill Lynch and securing a distribution deal with Paramount, Marvel is planning several theatrical releases beginning in 2008. In the worst-case scenario, if the films significantly underperform, Marvel would actually lose control of its characters to Merrill Lynch. However, Marvel's plan is to maximize box-office marketing and predictability by making the central characters as commercial as possible, which may not be critically aligned with character complexity. About a possible Hulk sequel, Arad said, referencing the under-performing but dark and interesting Ang Lee-directed *Hulk* (2003), "the Hulk movie was a study of anger, and people wanted a popcorn movie [. . .] Our Hulk will be a diet Hulk. Lighter. Focusing on the love story, Hulk as hero, and his battle with the villain" (qtd. in Hammer 112). Similarly, Johnson argues that the complexity of a character like Wolverine—multifaceted as manifested in the comic book versions—becomes more circumscribed and simplistic when the character becomes defined as a visible and valuable multimedia brand.

## Graphic Novels as Filmic Inspiration

The contribution of comic art to films is not just its role in the Hollywood blockbuster. Other smaller and, often innovative, U.S.-released films have been directly influenced by comics, especially graphic novels. These "alternative comics," which frequently com-bine certain aesthetic and political attributes of the underground comics of the 1960s and the economic stability and narrative continuity of mainstream comic book companies like Marvel and DC, were cultivated by the direct sales comic books shops that developed in the 1970s (Hatfield; Sabin; Witek). Not bound by the superhero genre, the corresponding male adolescent market, or typically by a smooth integration into large media corporate synergy, these forms often deal graphically with adult themes (in ways that may be better tolerated in drawn rather than photographic forms) and stretch the potential of the comic book medium as a combined visual and verbal form of communication. Graphic novels and other types of alternative comics may be visually and/or thematically innovative, and films that are based on these novels may stretch the industrial and technological boundaries of their medium in attempt to mimic their source material. Until relatively recently, Hollywood's attraction to underground/alternative comics was limited to the very occasional animated curiosities such as *Fritz the Cat* (1972) and *Heavy Metal* (1981). Since the 1990s, however, graphic novels have become a significant source of cinematic influence, including many live-action adaptations.

For example, we see discussions about the role of violence in people's lives in movies based on graphic novels, such as *A History of Violence* (2005), *The Road to Perdition* (2002) and *V for Vendetta* (2005). Although these movies may sometimes reveal their "comic book" roots (the protagonist in the purportedly realistic *A History of Violence* is a hypertalented killer), they still encourage a reflection that is striking for mainstream film. *A History of Violence* and its exploration of violence's instrumentality and effect on everyday life was labeled as "subversive" by critics from *Film Comment*, the *Los Angeles Times*, *Rolling Stone*, and the *Village Voice* (Lim; Taubin). Much of this praise is no doubt due to changes in the story made by director David Cronenberg and the adapted screenplay by Josh Olson, particularly in its portrayal of a changed relationship between the married couple in the story. Nevertheless, the basic premise and themes of the story (the implications of a violent past for an ordinary life) came from the graphic novel by John Wagner and Vince Locke.

*V for Vendetta*, the most superhero-oriented of the three films mentioned above, translates the original Alan Moore-created critique of Thatcher-era conservatism to filmic symbolism more closely related to the recognizable, well-circulated iconography of the era of George W. Bush, Abu Ghraib, and Guantanamo Bay. The film deals metaphorically with a Gordian knot reminiscent of Iraq in a way that few other fictional films have to date; the fact that the hero was a sympathetic "terrorist" was, to say the least, unusual for that time, and clearly struck a controversial note with critics (see Giles; Els). Although the original graphic novel was commenting on a different and quite specific historical context, Moore's use of allegory to explore contemporary political abuses and the role of violence as resistence facilitated the story's application to post-9/11 society. "The fact that the film version was not produced until well over 20 years after the original version debuted speaks to the uncomfortable political nature of the source material for Hollywood" (Els 86).

The nature of representation and identity is another theme for which graphic novel-based movies may be especially well positioned. *American Splendor* (2003), using Harvey Pekar's autobiographical comics as a guide, mixes animation, acted portrayals, and documentary-style interviews to convey an ordinary man's view of self and the world; in doing so, it presents a self-reflective version of film, much as the comic itself does, and a critique of corporate media and the accompanying devaluation of ordinary life in such media (Hatfield). Similarly, *Ghost World*'s (2001) bleak take on teen identity and consumerism contrasts significantly with the typical Hollywood teen film (see Hight; Flanagan).

*American Splendor* also brought an unusual visual style to its film, with its mix of animation and real-life representation, clearly profoundly influenced by Pekar's varied comic looks. *From Hell* (2001) also was apparently visually influenced by its dirty, detail-oriented source material and its unflinching views of horrific mutilation.

One of the most stylistically faithful movies to its graphic novel origin was *Sin City* (2005), so much so that it literally broke Hollywood rules. Calling the film a "translation" rather than an adaptation, codirector Robert Rodriguez attempted to mimic—virtually shot by shot—the distinctive angles, visual tone and color schemes of Frank Miller's graphic novel stories. In fact, the artistic influence of Miller on the film was so important to Rodriguez that he insisted Miller be given codirector status and that the film be publicized as *Frank Miller's Sin City*. The codirector status got Rodriguez in trouble with the Directors Guild, as it went against standard crediting practices (Olsen). The result is a uniquely stylized film that uses color, makeup, digital cameras, green screen backgrounds, and camera angles in striking ways (even if its attitude toward gender, once again, reflects a stereotypical comic book sensibility).

## Problematizing Polarization: Complex Cross-Industry Flows

Similar to most cultural categories, the distinctions between indie/cult and commercial/mainstream are easy to theorize, but become complicated in application; the use of the phrases "cult" and "mainstream" may have political and promotional uses by both fans and industry players, for instance (Jancovich). This is also true for both film and comic books. Many studios and media conglomerates have more "art-house" film production and distribution units (such as Time Warner's independent distributor, Picturehouse) and most send representatives and films to supposedly alternative festivals like Sundance. Comic book companies, similarly, have more adult-targeted, "alternative-esque" imprints like DC's Vertigo, and smaller companies often merge to get involved in heavily licensed properties. Dark Horse, the fourth-largest U.S. comic book publisher, has its own film production company involved in the making of films such as *The Mask* (1994) and *Hellboy* (2004). It has recently created a cooperative production company with Image Entertainment (a licensing and distribution company, different from Image Comics) to form Dark Horse Indie, a new film production company.

Many of these "new wave" graphic novel adaptations were relatively "safe" parodies or differently imagined versions of the superhero genre like *The Mask, Mystery Men* (1999), and *Men in Black* (1997). Similarly, some mainstream superhero comics and blockbuster films are more edgy and psychologically/thematically interesting than their graphic novel-art house film equivalent; compare, for example, *Hulk,* based on the most fight-oriented of Marvel comics, with *The League of Extraordinary Gentleman* (2003), adapted from the work of comic book auteur Alan Moore. Both *Hulk* and *Dick Tracy* (1990) explicitly attempt to copy the unique medium characteristics of comics; like *Sin City,* they bring unique color motifs and frame compositions to film (Cohen).

Mainstream films may also use the credibility of alternative comics, which could further erode the independent-mainstream polarization. The 1989 *Batman*'s darker vision of the superhero, especially when compared with the campy TV version, was not only encouraged by the alternate/adult market for comics, but also by the Frank Miller *Dark Knight* version produced by DC in the mid-1980s. Meehan argues that, via this graphic novel, Warner "essentially test marketed a dark reinterpretation of *Batman* with an adult readership" that would lead the way for the Tim Burton-directed version (53). That a major subplot of this film involved Joker-created terrorism via product tampering, not exactly a conducive environment for heavy product placement, also may have indicated that the film's dark tone prevented it from being the ideal commercial blockbuster. With its themes of infanticide (via Penguin) and sadomasochism (via Catwoman), the "Dark Knight" trope continued with *Batman Returns*, much to the discomfort of cross-promotional partners like McDonald's. The two later versions, *Batman Forever* and *Batman and Robin*, more distant from their graphic novel influences but more connected to a corporate blockbuster model, "sanitize[d] the Dark Knight, making him more kid-friendly and wooing back corporate sponsors in the process" (Terrill 494).

## Conclusion

Both films and comic books have been influenced by their dealings and interactions with each other. With comic books, for example, there is evidence that the larger comics companies could be moving in a medium-redefining direction with their additional focus on filmmaking, and their deemphasis on the nuts-and-bolts of comics creation. As they dig deeper for movie characters without resources devoted to cultivating new characters, the future of the mainstream comic book industry may be in doubt. One comic book industry analyst asked in a pessimistic article in *Variety*, "Where are the next DC and Marvel characters coming from?"; another remarked, "Marvel and DC talk about all these characters they have, but some of them are so old they have no built-in audience" (Zeitchik 5).

Films, on the other hand, look to comics as inspiration for additional commercial and aesthetic inspirations. In some ways, this has encouraged or at least facilitated a movement toward the commercial blockbuster, where the main focus is on economic predictability and long term licensing potential. On the other hand, comics–both adult graphic novels and the superhero fanboy variety–may lead to cinematic innovations, visual and thematic, as one medium is translated into another.

However, the relationship of Hollywood to graphic novels and other more sophisticated comics forms may be a double-edged sword. A hypercommercial Hollywood seems to tolerate sex and violence more than political edginess and character complexity. As film adaptations become a more institutionalized part of graphic novels and other alternative comic productions, one wonders if Hollywood's flirtation could also bring unfortunate lessons about the dangers of seduction.

### Questions for Consideration

1   Do you think that a "commercialistic blockbuster mentality among Hollywood studios" is a problem for society? Why or why not?

2   The authors quote a comic book analyst who remarked, "Marvel and DC talk about all these characters they have, but some of them are so old they have no built-in audience." What do you think is meant by "built-in audience"? Do you agree with this person's take on the comic book industry?

# Works Cited

Angwin, Julie. "News Corp. Wields Powers for *X-Men*." *Wall Street Journal* 26 May 2006: B3.

Box Office Mojo. 7 June 2006 <http://www. boxofficemojo.com/>.

Bruck, Connie. *Master of the Game: Steve Ross and the Creation of Time Warner*. New York: Simon, 1994.

Cohen, Michael. "Panel Beating: Drawing a Comic Aesthetic in *Dick Tracy*." Gordon, Jancovich, and McAllister.

*Contra Costa Times*. "Getting Graphic; Filmic Adaptations Boost Popularity of Comic Novels." *Chicago Tribune*, 3 Apr: 2006: 36.

Denby, David. "Violent Times: The Current Cinema." *New Yorker*, 5 June 2006: 90.

Denison, Rayna. "It's a Bird! It's a Plane! No, It's DVD!: *Superman*, *Smallville*, and the Production (of) Melodrama." Gordon, Jancovich, and McAllister.

Els, Frik. "Remember, Remember *V for Vendetta*." *Finweek* 23 Mar. 2006: 86.

Flanagan, Martin. "Teen Trajectories in *Spider-Man and Ghost World*." Gordon, Jancovich, and McAllister.

Germain, David. "*Fantastic Four* KO's Hollywood Doldrums." *Houston Chronicle* 11 July 2005: 2.

Giles, Jeff. "Anarchy in the UK: V for Vendetta 'Tries Talkin' about a Revolution." *Newsweek* 20 Mar. 2006: 69.

Gomery, Douglas. "The Hollywood Blockbuster: Industrial Analysis and Practice." *Movie Blockbusters*. Ed. Julian Stringer. London: Routledge, 2003. 72–83.

Gordon, Ian. "Nostalgia, Myth and Ideology: Visions of Superman at the End of the 'American Century'," *Comics and Ideology*. Ed. Matthew P. McAllister, Edward H. Sewell, Jr., and Ian Gordon. New York: Peter Lang. 2001. 177–193.

Gordon, Ian, Mark Jancovich, and Matthew P. McAllister, eds. *Film and Comics*. Jackson: UP of Mississippi (forthcoming).

Gustines, George Gene. "Even Superheroes Can Use Some Buffing of the Brand." *New York Times* 9 May 2005: 8.

Hammer, Susanna. "Is Marvel Ready for Its Close-up?" *Business 2.0* May 2006: 112.

Hatfield, Charles. *Alternative Comics: An Emerging Literature*. Jackson: UP of Mississippi. 2005.

Hight, Craig. "*American Splendor*: Translating Comic Autobiography into Drama Documentary." Gordon, Jancovich, and McAllister.

"Hoping to Soar with Superman." *Business Week* 11 Dec. 1978: 147, 151.

Jancovich, Mark. "Cult Fictions: Cult Movies, Subcultural Capital and the Production of Cultural Distinctions." *Cultural Studies* 16.2 (2002): 306–22.

Johnson, Derek. "Will the Real Wolverine Please Stand Up?" Marvel's Mutation from Monthlies to Movies." Gordon, Jancovich, and McAllister.

Jones, Gerard. *Men of Tomorrow: Geeks, Gangsters, and the Birth of the Comic Book*. New York: Basic, 2004.

Kaltenbach, Chris. "Long Weekend Marks 'X-Men' as a Box-Office Superhero." *Knight-Ridder Tribune Business News* 31 May 2006: 1.

Kapell, Matthew Wilhelm, and John Shelton Lawrence, eds. *Finding the Force of the Star Wars Franchise: Fans, Merchandise, and Critics*. New York: Peter Lang, 2006.

Karnitsching, Matthew. "That's All Folks": After Years of Pushing Synergy, Time Warner Inc. Says Enough." *Wall Street Journal* 2 June 2006: A1.

"Kinney Plans to Acquire National Periodical in Exchange of Stock." *Wall Street Journal*, 24 July 1967: B1.

Kleinschrodt, Michael. H. "Cynicism Mires 'Art School' in Mediocrity." *New Orleans Times Picayune* 12 May 2006: 10.

Lim, Dennis. "The Way of the Gun." *Village Voice*, 21–27 Sept. 2005: 34–35.

Marr, Merissa. and Kate Kelly. "Budget Buster." *Wall Street Journal* 12 May 2006: Al.

Martin, Sue, and Pat. H. Broeske "Batmanjuice." *Los Angeles Times* 11 Sept. 1988: 20.

"Marvel Studios Arad Steps Down as CEO." *Wall Street Journal* 1 June 2006: B7.

McAllister, Matthew P. "From Flick to Flack: The Increased Emphasis on Marketing by Media Entertainment Corporations." *Critical Studies in Media Commercialism*. Ed. Robin Andersen and Lance A. Strate. New York: Oxford UP, 2000. 101–22.

Meehan, Eileen. " 'Holy Commodity Fetish, Batman!': The Political Economy of a Commercial Intertext." *The Many Lives of the Batman: Critical Approaches to a Superhero and His Media.* Ed. Roberta E. Pearson and William Uricchio. New York: Routledge, 1991, 47–65.

Mehta, Stephanie N. "Money Men." *Fortune* 29 May 2006: 120–24.

Olsen, Mark. "Sneaks '05." *Los Angeles Times* 16 Jan. 2005: E12.

Phillips, Michael. " 'Art School' Tinted with a Dark Palette." *Chicago Tribune*, 12 May 2006: 1.

Prince, Stephen. "Introduction: World Filmmaking and the Hollywood Blockbuster." *World Literature Today* 77.3–4: 3–7.

Russo, Tom. "Sequels Ahead of Their Time." *Boston Globe* 2 Feb. 2003: N20.

Sabin, Roger. *Adult Comics: An Introduction.* New York: Routledge. 2003.

Schatz, Thomas. "The New Hollywood." *Movie Blockbusters.* Ed. Julian Stringer. London: Routledge, 2003. 15–44.

Segrave, Kerry. *Product Placement in Hollywood Films: A History*, Jefferson: McFarland, 2004.

Steinberg, Brian. "Look—Up in the Sky! Product Placement!" *Wall Street Journal* 18 Apr. 2006: B1.

Stringer, Julian. Introduction. *Movie Blockbusters.* Ed. Julian Stringer. London: Routledge, 2003. 1–14.

—— "Neither One Thing Nor the Other: Blockbusters at Film Festivals." *Movie Blockbusters.* Ed. Stringer. London: Routledge, 2003, 202–13.

Taubin, Amy. "Model Citizens." *Film Comment* 41.5 (2005): 24–28.

Terrill, Robert E. "Spectacular Repression: Sanitizing the Batman." *Critical Studies in Media Communication* 17.4 (2000): 493–509.

Warren, James. "Some Stars Demand, 'Show Me the Money.' " *Chicago Tribune* 3 Mar: 2000: 3.

Wasko, Janet. *Hollywood in the Information Age: Beyond the Silver Screen.* Austin: U of Texas P. 1994.

Witek, Joseph. *Comic Books as History: The Narrative Art of Jack Jackson, Art Spiegelman, and Harvey Pekar.* Jackson: UP of Mississippi, 1989.

Zeitchik, Steven. "Kryptonite for Comic Pics?" *Variety* 28 Jan. 2006: 5.

# PART FOUR

# The Digital Media

# INTRODUCTION

CONSIDER, FOR A MOMENT, HOW many times you have heard the phrase "new media." Have you ever stopped to consider what this means and how "new" media differ from existing forms of mass communication? First of all, it is important to realize that "new" is a relative term; television, radio, and even newspapers were considered "new" during the era in which they emerged. Instead of new media, then, we will talk here about "digital media," which is commonly understood to include the Internet, mobile phone, and video game industries. When people say *digital*, it is a quick way of referring to digits—1s and 0s—which computers use to carry out their functions. These digits can be manipulated to produce an astonishing array of possibilities, many of which you encounter during your day-to-day activities. If you go to the bank, shop at the supermarket, or even drive in your car, you are coming into contact with computers—and digits—in one way or another.

Digital media can be distinguished from traditional ("analog") media in two important ways. First, because they use content encoded in computer bits, digital media can accept content from other digital media much more easily than can analog media. So, for example, you can move a song encoded as a digital MP3 file from the Internet to your computer hard drive and your portable MP3 player. This is an example of media convergence. Media convergence also takes place when companies move the same content across many media boundaries. Digital media allow such movements to take place far easier than in the past.

A second distinguishing feature of digital media is their ability to allow audiences to interact with their content. For example, readers of print magazines cannot write back to the editors instantly, while Web readers typically can. In fact, media companies have been using the interactive capabilities of digital media—from the Internet to the mobile device to video games—to encourage their audiences to talk back to them, talk to each other, and even create new materials and load them onto web sites. The last-mentioned form of creation even has a term connected to it: user-generated content (UGC). Firms encourage UGC on their websites in the hope that their audiences will develop a loyalty that will keep them coming back. User-generated materials are also relatively inexpensive ways to populate web sites, and some firms are even making these part of their marketing campaigns.

The essays in this section will help you to learn more about these activities and may prompt you to consider what they mean for the future of media. We have chosen essays that bring these features into larger conversations about the nature of democracy, privacy, and creative expression in the twenty-first century. You might well be familiar with many of the products and technologies discussed in these essays, and we hope that these readings will allow you to think more critically about them.

# Chapter 20

# CHRIS ANDERSON

# THE LONG TAIL

MOST MEDIA BUSINESS HAVE TYPICALLY gone after very large audiences as a requirement for making a profit. This might be trying to create a hit song, a blockbuster film, a top-rated TV program, or a best-selling book. Yet in an era of digital media storage and distribution, *Wired* magazine editor-in-chief Chris Anderson believes there is a value to selling specialized products to small, niche audiences. That is because there are so many of them and because this can be profitable in the digital age. Anderson calls this approach "The Long Tail," and, in this 2004 article, he describes how the approach has been successfully adopted by companies like NetFlix, iTunes, and Amazon. His argument might also explain why on the Web many mainstream media companies are selling "the non-hits" as well as the "hits." As you read this, consider the ways that "The Long Tail" is impacting not only media companies and audiences, but also creators and advertisers.

In 1988, a British mountain climber named Joe Simpson wrote a book called *Touching the Void*, a harrowing account of near death in the Peruvian Andes. It got good reviews but, only a modest success, it was soon forgotten. Then, a decade later, a strange thing happened. Jon Krakauer wrote *Into Thin Air*, another book about a mountain-climbing tragedy, which became a publishing sensation. Suddenly *Touching the Void* started to sell again.

Random House rushed out a new edition to keep up with demand. Booksellers began to promote it next to their *Into Thin Air* displays, and sales rose further. A revised paperback edition, which came out in January, spent 14 weeks on the *New York Times* bestseller list. That same month, IFC Films released a docudrama of the story to critical acclaim. Now *Touching the Void* outsells *Into Thin Air* more than two to one.

What happened? In short, Amazon.com recommendations. The online bookseller's software noted patterns in buying behavior and suggested that readers who liked *Into Thin Air* would also like *Touching the Void*. People took the suggestion, agreed wholeheartedly, wrote rhapsodic reviews. More sales, more algorithm-fueled recommendations, and the positive feedback loop kicked in.

Particularly notable is that when Krakauer's book hit the shelves, Simpson's was nearly out of print. A few years ago, readers of Krakauer would never even have learned about Simpson's book—and if they had, they wouldn't have been able to find it. Amazon changed that. It created the *Touching the Void* phenomenon by combining infinite shelf space with real-time information about buying trends and public opinion. The result: rising demand for an obscure book.

This is not just a virtue of online booksellers; it is an example of an entirely new economic model for the media and entertainment industries, one that is just beginning to show its power. Unlimited selection is revealing truths about what consumers want and how they want to get it in service after service, from DVDs at Netflix to music videos on Yahoo! Launch to songs in the iTunes Music Store and Rhapsody. People are going deep into the catalog, down the long, long list of available titles, far past what's available at Blockbuster Video, Tower Records, and Barnes & Noble. And the more they find, the more they like. As they wander further from the beaten path, they discover their taste is not as mainstream as they thought (or as they had been led to believe by marketing, a lack of alternatives, and a hit-driven culture).

An analysis of the sales data and trends from these services and others like them shows that the emerging digital entertainment economy is going to be radically different from today's mass market. If the 20th- century entertainment industry was about hits, the 21st will be equally about misses.

For too long we've been suffering the tyranny of lowest-common-denominator fare, subjected to brain-dead summer blockbusters and manufactured pop. Why? Economics. Many of our assumptions about popular taste are actually artifacts of poor supply-and-demand matching—a market response to inefficient distribution.

The main problem, if that's the word, is that we live in the physical world and, until recently, most of our entertainment media did, too. But that world puts two dramatic limitations on our entertainment.

The first is the need to find local audiences. An average movie theater will not show a film unless it can attract at least 1,500 people over a two-week run; that's essentially the rent for a screen. An average record store needs to sell at least two copies of a CD per year to make it worth carrying; that's the rent for a half inch of shelf space. And so on for DVD rental shops, videogame stores, booksellers, and newsstands.

In each case, retailers will carry only content that can generate sufficient demand to earn its keep. But each can pull only from a limited local population—perhaps a 10-mile radius for a typical movie theater, less than that for music and bookstores, and even less (just a mile or two) for video rental shops. It's not enough for a great documentary to have a potential national audience of half a million; what matters is how many it has in the northern part of Rockville, Maryland, and among the mall shoppers of Walnut Creek, California.

There is plenty of great entertainment with potentially large, even rapturous, national audiences that cannot clear that bar. For instance, *The Triplets of Belleville*, a critically acclaimed film that was nominated for the best animated feature Oscar this year, opened on just six screens nationwide. An even more striking example is the plight of Bollywood in America. Each year, India's film industry puts out more than 800 feature films. There are an estimated 1.7 million Indians in the US. Yet the top-rated (according to Amazon's Internet Movie Database) Hindi-language film, *Lagaan: Once*

*Upon a Time in India*, opened on just two screens, and it was one of only a handful of Indian films to get any US distribution at all. In the tyranny of physical space, an audience too thinly spread is the same as no audience at all.

The other constraint of the physical world is physics itself. The radio spectrum can carry only so many stations, and a coaxial cable so many TV channels. And, of course, there are only 24 hours a day of programming. The curse of broadcast technologies is that they are profligate users of limited resources. The result is yet another instance of having to aggregate large audiences in one geographic area—another high bar, above which only a fraction of potential content rises.

The past century of entertainment has offered an easy solution to these constraints. Hits fill theaters, fly off shelves, and keep listeners and viewers from touching their dials and remotes. Nothing wrong with that; indeed, sociologists will tell you that hits are hardwired into human psychology, the combinatorial effect of conformity and word of mouth. And to be sure, a healthy share of hits earn their place: Great songs, movies, and books attract big, broad audiences.

But most of us want more than just hits. Everyone's taste departs from the mainstream somewhere, and the more we explore alternatives, the more we're drawn to them. Unfortunately, in recent decades such alternatives have been pushed to the fringes by pumped-up marketing vehicles built to order by industries that desperately need them.

Hit-driven economics is a creation of an age without enough room to carry everything for everybody. Not enough shelf space for all the CDs, DVDs, and games produced. Not enough screens to show all the available movies. Not enough channels to broadcast all the TV programs, not enough radio waves to play all the music created, and not enough hours in the day to squeeze everything out through either of those sets of slots.

This is the world of scarcity. Now, with online distribution and retail, we are entering a world of abundance. And the differences are profound.

To see how, meet Robbie Vann-Adibé, the CEO of Ecast, a digital jukebox company whose barroom players offer more than 150,000 tracks—and some surprising usage statistics. He hints at them with a question that visitors invariably get wrong: "What percentage of the top 10,000 titles in any online media store (Netflix, iTunes, Amazon, or any other) will rent or sell at least once a month?"

Most people guess 20 percent, and for good reason: We've been trained to think that way. The 80–20 rule, also known as Pareto's principle (after Vilfredo Pareto, an Italian economist who devised the concept in 1906), is all around us. Only 20 percent of major studio films will be hits. Same for TV shows, games, and mass-market books—20 percent all. The odds are even worse for major-label CDs, where fewer than 10 percent are profitable, according to the Recording Industry Association of America.

But the right answer, says Vann-Adibé, is 99 percent. There is demand for nearly every one of those top 10,000 tracks. He sees it in his own jukebox statistics; each month, thousands of people put in their dollars for songs that no traditional jukebox anywhere has ever carried.

People get Vann-Adibé's question wrong because the answer is counterintuitive in two ways. The first is we forget that the 20 percent rule in the entertainment industry is about *hits*, not sales of any sort. We're stuck in a hit-driven mindset—we think that if something isn't a hit, it won't make money and so won't return the cost of its production. We assume, in other words, that only hits deserve to exist. But Vann-Adibé, like executives at iTunes, Amazon, and Netflix, has discovered that the "misses" usually make money, too. And because there are so many more of them, that money can add up quickly to a huge new market.

With no shelf space to pay for and, in the case of purely digital services like iTunes, no manufacturing costs and hardly any distribution fees, a miss sold is just another sale, with the same margins as a hit. A hit and a miss are on equal economic footing, both just entries in a database called up on demand, both equally worthy of being carried. Suddenly, popularity no longer has a monopoly on profitability.

The second reason for the wrong answer is that the industry has a poor sense of what people want. Indeed, we have a poor sense of what we want. We assume, for instance, that there is little demand for the stuff that isn't carried by Wal-Mart and other major retailers; if people wanted it, surely it would be sold. The rest, the bottom 80 percent, must be subcommercial at best.

But as egalitarian as Wal-Mart may seem, it is actually extraordinarily elitist. Wal-Mart must sell at least 100,000 copies of a CD to cover its retail overhead and make a sufficient profit; less than 1 percent of CDs do that kind of volume. What about the 60,000 people who would like to buy the latest Fountains of Wayne or Crystal Method album, or any other nonmainstream fare? They have to go somewhere else. Bookstores, the megaplex, radio, and network TV can be equally demanding. We equate mass market with quality and demand, when in fact it often just represents familiarity, savvy advertising, and broad if somewhat shallow appeal. What do we really want? We're only just discovering, but it clearly starts with *more*.

To get a sense of our true taste, unfiltered by the economics of scarcity, look at Rhapsody, a subscription-based streaming music service (owned by RealNetworks) that currently offers more than 735,000 tracks.

Chart Rhapsody's monthly statistics and you get a "power law" demand curve that looks much like any record store's, with huge appeal for the top tracks, tailing off quickly for less popular ones. But a really interesting thing happens once you dig below the top 40,000 tracks, which is about the amount of the fluid inventory (the albums carried that will eventually be sold) of the average real-world record store. Here, the Wal-Marts of the world go to zero—either they don't carry any more CDs, or the few potential local takers for such fringy fare never find it or never even enter the store.

The Rhapsody demand, however, keeps going. Not only is every one of Rhapsody's top 100,000 tracks streamed at least once each month, the same is true for its top 200,000, top 300,000, and top 400,000. As fast as Rhapsody adds tracks to its library, those songs find an audience, even if it's just a few people a month, somewhere in the country.

This is the Long Tail.

You can find everything out there on the Long Tail. There's the back catalog, older albums still fondly remembered by longtime fans or rediscovered by new ones. There are live tracks, B-sides, remixes, even (gasp) covers. There are niches by the thousands, genre within genre within genre: Imagine an entire Tower Records devoted to '80s hair bands or ambient dub. There are foreign bands, once priced out of reach in the Import aisle, and obscure bands on even more obscure labels, many of which don't have the distribution clout to get into Tower at all.

Oh sure, there's also a lot of crap. But there's a lot of crap hiding between the radio tracks on hit albums, too. People have to skip over it on CDs, but they can more easily avoid it online, since the collaborative filters typically won't steer you to it. Unlike the CD, where each crap track costs perhaps one-twelfth of a $15 album price, online it just sits harmlessly on some server, ignored in a market that sells by the song and evaluates tracks on their own merit.

What's really amazing about the Long Tail is the sheer size of it. Combine enough nonhits on the Long Tail and you've got a market bigger than the hits. Take books: The average Barnes & Noble carries 130,000 titles. Yet more than half of Amazon's book sales come from *outside* its top 130,000 titles. Consider the implication: If the Amazon statistics are any guide, the market for books that are not even sold in the average bookstore is larger than the market for those that are. In other words, the potential book market may be twice as big as it appears to be, if only we can get over the economics of scarcity. Venture capitalist and former music industry consultant Kevin Laws puts it this way: "The biggest money is in the smallest sales."

The same is true for all other aspects of the entertainment business, to one degree or another. Just compare online and offline businesses: The average Blockbuster carries fewer than 3,000 DVDs. Yet a fifth of Netflix rentals are outside its top 3,000 titles. Rhapsody streams more songs each month *beyond* its top 10,000 than it does its top 10,000. In each case, the market that lies outside the reach of the physical retailer is big and getting bigger.

When you think about it, most successful businesses on the Internet are about aggregating the Long Tail in one way or another. Google, for instance, makes most of its money off small advertisers (the long tail of advertising), and eBay is mostly tail as well—niche and one-off products. By overcoming the limitations of geography and scale, just as Rhapsody and Amazon have, Google and eBay have discovered new markets and expanded existing ones.

This is the power of the Long Tail. The companies at the vanguard of it are showing the way with three big lessons. Call them the new rules for the new entertainment economy.

## Rule 1: Make Everything Available

If you love documentaries, Blockbuster is not for you. Nor is any other video store— there are too many documentaries, and they sell too poorly to justify stocking more than a few dozen of them on physical shelves. Instead, you'll want to join Netflix, which offers more than a thousand documentaries—because it can. Such profligacy is giving a boost to the documentary business; last year, Netflix accounted for half of all US rental revenue for *Capturing the Friedmans*, a documentary about a family destroyed by allegations of pedophilia.

Netflix CEO Reed Hastings, who's something of a documentary buff, took this newfound clout to PBS, which had produced *Daughter From Danang*, a documentary about the children of US soldiers and Vietnamese women. In 2002, the film was nominated for an Oscar and was named best documentary at Sundance, but PBS had no plans to release it on DVD. Hastings offered to handle the manufacturing and distribution if PBS would make it available as a Netflix exclusive. Now *Daughter From Danang* consistently ranks in the top 15 on Netflix documentary charts. That amounts to a market of tens of thousands of documentary renters that did not otherwise exist.

There are any number of equally attractive genres and subgenres neglected by the traditional DVD channels: foreign films, anime, independent movies, British television dramas, old American TV sitcoms. These underserved markets make up a big chunk of Netflix rentals. Bollywood alone accounts for nearly 100,000 rentals each month. The availability of offbeat content drives new customers to Netflix—and anything that cuts the cost of customer acquisition is gold for a subscription business. Thus the company's first lesson: Embrace niches.

Netflix has made a good business out of what's unprofitable fare in movie theaters and video rental shops because it can aggregate dispersed audiences. It doesn't matter if the several thousand people who rent *Doctor Who* episodes each month are in one city or spread, one per town, across the country—the economics are the same to Netflix. It has, in short, broken the tyranny of physical space. What matters is not where customers are, or even how many of them are seeking a particular title, but only that some number of them exist, anywhere.

As a result, almost anything is worth offering on the off chance it will find a buyer. This is the opposite of the way the entertainment industry now thinks. Today, the decision about whether or when to release an old film on DVD is based on estimates of demand, availability of extras such as commentary and additional material, and marketing opportunities such as anniversaries, awards, and generational windows (Disney briefly rereleases its classics every 10 years or so as a new wave of kids come of age). It's a high bar, which is why only a fraction of movies ever made are available on DVD.

That model may make sense for the true classics, but it's way too much fuss for everything else. The Long Tail approach, by contrast, is to simply dump huge chunks of the archive onto bare-bones DVDs, without any extras or marketing. Call it the Silver Series and charge half the price. Same for independent films. This year, nearly 6,000 movies were submitted to the Sundance Film Festival. Of those, 255 were accepted, and just two dozen have been picked up for distribution; to see the others, you had to be there. Why not release all 255 on DVD each year as part of a discount Sundance Series? In a Long Tail economy, it's more expensive to evaluate than to release. Just do it!

The same is true for the music industry. It should be securing the rights to release all the titles in all the back catalogs as quickly as it can—thoughtlessly, automatically, and at industrial scale. (This is one of those rare moments where the world needs more lawyers, not fewer.) So too for videogames. Retro gaming, including simulators of classic game consoles that run on modern PCs, is a growing phenomenon driven by the nostalgia of the first joystick generation. Game publishers could release every title as a 99-cent download three years after its release—no support, no guarantees, no packaging.

All this, of course, applies equally to books. Already, we're seeing a blurring of the line between in and out of print. Amazon and other networks of used booksellers have made it almost as easy to find and buy a second-hand book as it is a new one. By divorcing bookselling from geography, these networks create a liquid market at low volume, dramatically increasing both their own business and the overall demand for used books. Combine that with the rapidly dropping costs of print-on-demand technologies and it's clear why any book should always be available. Indeed, it is a fair bet that children today will grow up never knowing the meaning of out of print.

## Rule 2: Cut the Price in Half. Now Lower It

Thanks to the success of Apple's iTunes, we now have a standard price for a downloaded track: 99 cents. But is it the right one?

Ask the labels and they'll tell you it's too low: Even though 99 cents per track works out to about the same price as a CD, most consumers just buy a track or two from an album online, rather than the full CD. In effect, online music has seen a return to the singles-driven business of the 1950s. So from a label perspective, consumers should pay more for the privilege of purchasing à la carte to compensate for the lost album revenue.

Ask consumers, on the other hand, and they'll tell you that 99 cents is too high. It is, for starters, 99 cents more than Kazaa. But piracy aside, 99 cents violates our innate sense of economic justice: If it clearly costs less for a record label to deliver a song online, with no packaging, manufacturing, distribution, or shelf space overheads, why shouldn't the price be less, too?

Surprisingly enough, there's been little good economic analysis on what the right price for online music should be. The main reason for this is that pricing isn't set by the market today but by the record label demi-cartel. Record companies charge a wholesale price of around 65 cents per track, leaving little room for price experimentation by the retailers.

That wholesale price is set to roughly match the price of CDs, to avoid dreaded "channel conflict." The labels fear that if they price online music lower, their CD retailers (still the vast majority of the business) will revolt or, more likely, go out of business even more quickly than they already are. In either case, it would be a serious disruption of the status quo, which terrifies the already spooked record companies. No wonder they're doing price calculations with an eye on the downsides in their traditional CD business rather than the upside in their new online business.

But what if the record labels stopped playing defense? A brave new look at the economics of music would calculate what it really costs to simply put a song on an iTunes server and adjust pricing accordingly. The results are surprising.

Take away the unnecessary costs of the retail channel—CD manufacturing, distribution, and retail overheads. That leaves the costs of finding, making, and marketing music. Keep them as they are, to ensure that the people on the creative and label side of the business make as much as they currently do. For a popular album that sells 300,000 copies, the creative costs work out to about $7.50 per disc, or around 60 cents a track. Add to that the actual cost of delivering music online, which is mostly the cost of building and maintaining the online service rather than the negligible storage and bandwidth costs. Current price tag: around 17 cents a track. By this calculation, hit music is overpriced by 25 percent online—it should cost just 79 cents a track, reflecting the savings of digital delivery.

Putting channel conflict aside for the moment, if the incremental cost of making content that was originally produced for physical distribution available online is low, the price should be, too. Price according to digital costs, not physical ones.

All this good news for consumers doesn't have to hurt the industry. When you lower prices, people tend to buy more. Last year, Rhapsody did an experiment in elastic demand that suggested it could be a lot more. For a brief period, the service offered tracks at 99 cents, 79 cents, and 49 cents. Although the 49-cent tracks were only half the price of the 99-cent tracks, Rhapsody sold three times as many of them.

Since the record companies still charged 65 cents a track—and Rhapsody paid another 8 cents per track to the copyright-holding publishers—Rhapsody lost money on that experiment (but, as the old joke goes, made it up in volume). Yet much of the content on the Long Tail is older material that has already made back its money (or been written off for failing to do so): music from bands that had little record company investment and was thus cheap to make, or live recordings, remixes, and other material that came at low cost.

Such "misses" cost less to make available than hits, so why not charge even less for them? Imagine if prices declined the further you went down the Tail, with popularity (the market) effectively dictating pricing. All it would take is for the labels to lower the wholesale price for the vast majority of their content not in heavy rotation; even a two- or three-tiered pricing structure could work wonders. And because so much of that content is not available in record stores, the risk of channel conflict is greatly diminished. The lesson: Pull consumers down the Tail with lower prices.

How low should the labels go? The answer comes by examining the psychology of the music consumer. The choice facing fans is not how many songs to buy from iTunes and Rhapsody, but how many songs to buy rather than download for free from Kazaa and other peer-to-peer networks. Intuitively, consumers know that free music is not really free: Aside from any legal risks, it's a time-consuming hassle to build a collection that way. Labeling is inconsistent, quality varies, and an estimated 30 percent of tracks are defective in one way or another. As Steve Jobs put it at the iTunes Music Store launch, you may save a little money downloading from Kazaa, but "you're working for under minimum wage." And what's true for music is doubly true for movies and games, where the quality of pirated products can be even more dismal, viruses are a risk, and downloads take so much longer.

So free has a cost: the psychological value of convenience. This is the "not worth it" moment where the wallet opens. The exact amount is an impossible calculus involving the bank balance of the average college student multiplied by their available free time. But imagine that for music, at least, it's around 20 cents a track. That, in effect, is the dividing line between the commercial world of the Long Tail and the underground. Both worlds will continue to exist in parallel, but it's crucial for Long Tail thinkers to exploit the opportunities between 20 and 99 cents to maximize their share. By offering fair pricing, ease of use, and consistent quality, you can compete with free.

Perhaps the best way to do that is to stop charging for individual tracks at all. Danny Stein, whose private equity firm owns eMusic, thinks the future of the business is to move away from the ownership model entirely. With ubiquitous broadband, both wired and wireless, more consumers will turn to the celestial jukebox of music services that offer every track ever made, playable on demand. Some of those tracks will be free to listeners and advertising-supported, like radio. Others, like eMusic and Rhapsody, will be subscription services. Today, digital music economics are dominated by the iPod, with its notion of a paid-up library of personal tracks. But as the networks improve, the comparative economic advantages of unlimited streamed music, either financed by advertising or a flat fee (infinite choice for $9.99 a month), may shift the market that way. And drive another nail in the coffin of the retail music model.

## Rule 3: Help Me Find It

In 1997, an entrepreneur named Michael Robertson started what looked like a classic Long Tail business. Called MP3.com, it let anyone upload music files that would be available to all. The idea was the service would bypass the record labels, allowing artists to connect directly to listeners. MP3.com would make its money in fees paid by bands to have their music promoted on the site. The tyranny of the labels would be broken, and a thousand flowers would bloom.

Putting aside the fact that many people actually used the service to illegally upload and share commercial tracks, leading the labels to sue MP3.com, the model failed at its intended purpose, too. Struggling bands did not, as a rule, find new audiences, and independent music was not transformed. Indeed, MP3.com got a reputation for being exactly what it was: an undifferentiated mass of mostly bad music that deserved its obscurity.

The problem with MP3.com was that it was *only* Long Tail. It didn't have license agreements with the labels to offer mainstream fare or much popular commercial music at all. Therefore, there was no familiar point of entry for consumers, no known quantity from which further exploring could begin.

Offering only hits is no better. Think of the struggling video-on-demand services of the cable companies. Or think of Movielink, the feeble video download service run by the studios. Due to overcontrolling providers and high costs, they suffer from limited content: in most cases just a few hundred recent releases. There's not enough choice to change consumer behavior, to become a real force in the entertainment economy.

By contrast, the success of Netflix, Amazon, and the commercial music services shows that you need *both* ends of the curve. Their huge libraries of less-mainstream fare set them apart, but hits still matter in attracting consumers in the first place. Great Long Tail businesses can then guide consumers further afield by following the contours of their likes and dislikes, easing their exploration of the unknown.

For instance, the front screen of Rhapsody features Britney Spears, unsurprisingly. Next to the listings of her work is a box of "similar artists." Among them is Pink. If you click on that and are pleased with what you hear, you may do the same for Pink's similar artists, which include No Doubt. And on No Doubt's page, the list includes a few "followers" and "influencers," the last of which includes the Selecter, a 1980s ska band from Coventry, England. In three clicks, Rhapsody may have enticed a Britney Spears fan to try an album that can hardly be found in a record store.

Rhapsody does this with a combination of human editors and genre guides. But Netflix, where 60 percent of rentals come from recommendations, and Amazon do this with collaborative filtering, which uses the browsing and purchasing patterns of users to guide those who follow them ("Customers who bought this also bought . . ."). In each, the aim is the same: Use recommendations to drive demand down the Long Tail.

This is the difference between push and pull, between broadcast and personalized taste. Long Tail business can treat consumers as individuals, offering mass customization as an alternative to mass-market fare.

The advantages are spread widely. For the entertainment industry itself, recommendations are a remarkably efficient form of marketing, allowing smaller films and less-mainstream music to find an audience. For consumers, the improved signal-to-noise ratio that comes from following a good recommendation encourages exploration and can reawaken a passion for music and film, potentially creating a far larger entertainment market overall. (The average Netflix customer rents seven DVDs a month, three times the rate at brick-and-mortar stores.) And the cultural benefit of all of this is much more diversity, reversing the blanding effects of a century of distribution scarcity and ending the tyranny of the hit.

Such is the power of the Long Tail. Its time has come.

## Questions for Consideration

1    Can you think of companies that have recently adopted a Long Tail approach?
2    How might an independent recording artist benefit from the Long Tail?

# Chapter 21

# YOCHAI BENKLER

# PEER PRODUCTION AND SHARING

**I**F YOU HAVE EVER USED the online encyclopedia Wikipedia, you know that its success depends on the collaborative efforts of individuals who are willing to devote their time and energy to the production of information. This is known as peer production and also includes practices like the development of free or open-source software, the creation of virtual worlds like Second Life, and the production of news projects like Slashdot. In this essay, excerpted from Harvard Law School professor Yochai Benkler's 2006 book *The Wealth of Networks: How Social Production Transforms Markets and Freedom,* Benkler uses these and other examples to understand how new technologies are causing a fundamental shift in the creation of information, knowledge, and culture.

\*     \*     \*

At the heart of the economic engine of the world's most advanced economies, we are beginning to notice a persistent and quite amazing phenomenon. A new model of production has taken root; one that should not be there, at least according to our most widely held beliefs about economic behavior. It should not, the intuitions of the late-twentieth-century American would say, be the case that thousands of volunteers will come together to collaborate on a complex economic project. It certainly should not be that these volunteers will beat the largest and best-financed business enterprises in the world at their own game. And yet, this is precisely what is happening in the software world.

\*     \*     \*

The term "peer production" characterizes a subset of commons-based production practices. It refers to production systems that depend on individual action that is self-selected and decentralized, rather than hierarchically assigned. "Centralization" is a particular response to the problem of how to make the behavior of many individual agents cohere into an effective pattern or achieve an effective result. Its primary attribute is the separation of the locus of opportunities for action from the authority to choose the action that the agent will undertake. Government authorities, firm managers, teachers in a classroom, all occupy a context in which potentially many individual wills could lead to action, and reduce the number of people whose will is permitted to affect the actual behavior patterns that the agents will adopt. "Decentralization" describes conditions under which the actions of many agents cohere and are effective despite the fact that they do not rely on reducing the number of people whose will counts to direct effective action. A substantial literature in the past twenty years, typified, for example, by Charles Sabel's work, has focused on the ways in which firms have tried to overcome the rigidities of managerial pyramids by decentralizing learning, planning, and execution of the firm's functions in the hands of employees or teams. The most pervasive mode of "decentralization," however, is the ideal market. Each individual agent acts according to his or her will. Coherence and efficacy emerge because individuals signal their wishes, and plan their behavior not in cooperation with others, but by coordinating, understanding the will of others and expressing their own through the price system.

What we are seeing now is the emergence of more effective collective action practices that are decentralized but do not rely on either the price system or a managerial structure for coordination. In this, they complement the increasing salience of uncoordinated nonmarket behavior. The networked environment not only provides a more effective platform for action to nonprofit organizations that organize action like firms or to hobbyists who merely coexist coordinately. It also provides a platform for new mechanisms for widely dispersed agents to adopt radically decentralized cooperation strategies other than by using proprietary and contractual claims to elicit prices or impose managerial commands. This kind of information production by agents operating on a decentralized, nonproprietary model is not completely new. Science is built by many people contributing incrementally—not operating on market signals, not being handed their research marching orders by a boss—independently deciding what to research, bringing their collaboration together, and creating science. What we see in the networked information economy is a dramatic increase in the importance and the centrality of information produced in this way.

## Free/Open-Source Software

The quintessential instance of commons-based peer production has been free software. Free software, or open source, is an approach to software development that is based on shared effort on a nonproprietary model. It depends on many individuals contributing to a common project, with a variety of motivations, and sharing their respective contributions without any single person or entity asserting rights to exclude either from the contributed components or from the resulting whole. In order to avoid having the joint product appropriated by any single party, participants usually retain copyrights in their contribution, but license them to anyone—participant or stranger—on a model that combines a universal license to use the materials with licensing constraints that make it difficult, if not impossible, for any single contributor or third party to appropriate the project. This model of licensing is the most important institutional innovation of the free software movement. Its central instance is the GNU General Public License, or GPL. This requires anyone who modifies software and distributes the modified version to license it under the same free terms as the original software. While there have been many arguments about how widely the provisions that prevent downstream appropriation should be used, the practical adoption patterns have been dominated by forms of licensing that prevent anyone from exclusively appropriating the contributions or the joint product. More than 85 percent of active free software projects include some version of the GPL or similarly structured license.[1]

Free software has played a critical role in the recognition of peer production, because software is a functional good with measurable qualities. It can be more or less authoritatively tested against its market-based competitors. And, in many instances, free software has prevailed. About 70 percent of Web server software, in particular for critical e-commerce sites, runs on the Apache Web server-free software.[2] More than half of all back-office e-mail functions are run by one free software program or another. Google, Amazon, and CNN.com, for example, run their Web servers on the GNU/ Linux operating system. They do this, presumably, because they believe this peer-produced operating system is more reliable than the alternatives, not because the system is "free." It would be absurd to risk a higher rate of failure in their core business activities in order to save a few hundred thousand dollars on licensing fees. Companies like IBM and Hewlett Packard, consumer electronics manufacturers, as well as military and other mission-critical government agencies around the world have begun to adopt business and service strategies that rely and extend free software. They do this because it allows them to build better equipment, sell better services, or better fulfill their public role, even though they do not control the software development process and cannot claim proprietary rights of exclusion in the products of their contributions.

*      *      *

## Peer Production of Information, Knowledge, and Culture Generally

Free software is, without a doubt, the most visible instance of peer production at the turn of the twenty-first century. It is by no means, however, the only instance. Ubiquitous computer communications networks are bringing about a dramatic change in the scope, scale, and efficacy of peer production throughout the information and cultural production system. As computers become cheaper and as network connections become faster, cheaper, and ubiquitous, we are seeing the phenomenon of peer production of information scale to much larger sizes, performing more complex tasks than were possible in the past for nonprofessional production. To make this phenomenon more tangible, I describe a number of such enterprises, organized to demonstrate the feasibility of this approach throughout the information production and exchange chain. While it is possible to break an act of communication into finer-grained subcomponents, largely we see three distinct functions involved in the process. First, there is an initial utterance of a humanly meaningful statement. Writing an article or drawing a picture, whether done by a professional or an amateur, whether high quality or low, is such an action. Second, there is a separate function of mapping the initial utterances on a knowledge map. In particular, an utterance must be understood as "relevant" in some sense, and "credible." Relevance is a subjective question of mapping an utterance on the conceptual map of a given user seeking information for a particular purpose defined by that individual. Credibility is a question of quality by some objective measure that the individual adopts as appropriate for purposes of evaluating a given utterance. The distinction between the two is somewhat artificial, however, because very often the utility of a piece of information will depend on a combined valuation of its credibility and relevance. I therefore refer to "relevance/accreditation" as a single function for purposes of this discussion, keeping in mind that the two are complementary and not entirely separable functions that an individual requires as part of being able to use utterances that others have uttered in putting together the user's understanding of the world. Finally, there is the function of distribution, or how one takes an utterance produced by one person and distributes it to other people who find it credible and relevant. In the mass-media world, these functions were often, though by no means always, integrated. NBC news produced the utterances, gave them credibility by clearing them on the evening news, and distributed them simultaneously. What the Internet is permitting is much greater disaggregation of these functions.

## Uttering Content

NASA Clickworkers was "an experiment to see if public volunteers, each working for a few minutes here and there can do some routine science analysis that would normally be done by a scientist or graduate student working for months on end." Users could mark craters on maps of Mars, classify craters that have already been marked, or search the Mars landscape for "honeycomb" terrain. The project was "a pilot study with limited funding, run part-time by one software engineer, with occasional input from two scientists." In its first six months of operation, more than 85,000 users visited the site, with many contributing to the effort, making more than 1.9 million entries (including redundant entries of the same craters, used to average out errors). An analysis of the quality of markings showed "that the automatically-computed consensus of a large number of clickworkers is virtually indistinguishable from the inputs of a geologist with years of experience in identifying Mars craters."[3] The tasks performed by clickworkers (like marking craters) were discrete, each easily performed in a matter of minutes. As a result, users could choose to work for a few minutes doing a single iteration or for hours by doing many. An early study of the project suggested that some clickworkers indeed worked on the project for weeks, but that 37 percent of the work was done by one-time contributors.[4]

The clickworkers project was a particularly clear example of how a complex professional task that requires a number of highly trained individuals on full-time salaries can be reorganized so as to be performed by tens of thousands of volunteers in increments so minute that the tasks could be performed on a much lower budget. The low budget would be devoted to coordinating the volunteer effort. However, the raw human capital needed would be contributed for the fun of it. The professionalism of the original scientists was replaced by a combination of high modularization of the task. The organizers broke a large, complex task into small, independent modules. They built in redundancy and automated averaging out of both errors and purposeful erroneous markings—like those of an errant art student who thought it amusing to mark concentric circles on the map. What the NASA scientists running this experiment had tapped into was a vast pool of five-minute increments of human judgment, applied with motivation to participate in a task unrelated to "making a living."

While clickworkers was a distinct, self-conscious experiment, it suggests characteristics of distributed production that are, in fact, quite widely observable. We have already seen how the Internet can produce encyclopedic or almanac-type information.

The power of the Web to answer such an encyclopedic question comes not from the fact that one particular site has all the great answers. It is not an *Encyclopedia Britannica*. The power comes from the fact that it allows a user looking for specific information at a given time to collect answers from a sufficiently large number of contributions. The task of sifting and accrediting falls to the user, motivated by the need to find an answer to the question posed. As long as there are tools to lower the cost of that task to a level acceptable to the user, the Web shall have "produced" the information content the user was looking for. These are not trivial considerations, but they are also not intractable. As we shall see, some of the solutions can themselves be peer produced, and some solutions are emerging as a function of the speed of computation and communication, which enables more efficient technological solutions.

Encyclopedic and almanac-type information emerges on the Web out of the coordinate but entirely independent action of millions of users. This type of information also provides the focus on one of the most successful collaborative enterprises that has developed in the first five years of the twenty-first century, *Wikipedia*. *Wikipedia* was founded by an Internet entrepreneur, Jimmy Wales. Wales had earlier tried to organize an encyclopedia named Nupedia, which was built on a traditional production model, but whose outputs were to be released freely: its contributors were to be PhDs, using a formal, peer-reviewed process. That project appears to have failed to generate a sufficient number of high-quality contributions, but its outputs were used in *Wikipedia* as the seeds for a radically new form of encyclopedia writing. Founded in January 2001, *Wikipedia* combines three core characteristics: First, it uses a collaborative authorship tool, Wiki. This platform enables anyone, including anonymous passersby, to edit almost any page in the entire project. It stores all versions, makes changes easily visible, and enables anyone to revert a document to any prior version as well as to add changes, small and large. All contributions and changes are rendered transparent by the software and database. Second, it is a self-conscious effort at creating an encyclopedia—governed first and foremost by a collective informal undertaking to strive for a neutral point of view, within the limits of substantial self-awareness as to the difficulties of such an enterprise. An effort to represent sympathetically all views on a subject, rather than to achieve objectivity, is the core operative characteristic of this effort. Third, all the content generated by this collaboration is released under the GNU Free Documentation License, an adaptation of the GNU GPL to texts.

The shift in strategy toward an open, peer-produced model proved enormously successful. The site saw tremendous growth both in the number of contributors, including the number of active and very active contributors, and in the number of articles included in the encyclopedia (table 21.1). Most of the early growth was in English, but more recently there has been an increase in the number of articles in many other languages: most notably in German (more than 200,000 articles), Japanese (more than 120,000 articles), and French (about 100,000), but also in another five languages that have between 40,000 and 70,000 articles each, another eleven languages with 10,000 to 40,000 articles each, and thirty-five languages with between 1,000 and 10,000 articles each.

The first systematic study of the quality of *Wikipedia* articles was published as this book was going to press. The journal *Nature* compared 42 science articles from *Wikipedia* to the gold standard of the *Encyclopedia Britannica*, and concluded that "the difference in accuracy was not particularly great."[5] On November 15, 2004, Robert McHenry, a former editor in chief of the *Encyclopedia Britannica*, published an article

**Table 21.1** Contributors to *Wikipedia*, January 2001–June 2005

|  | Jan. 2001 | Jan. 2002 | Jan. 2003 | Jan. 2004 | July 2004 | June 2005 |
|---|---|---|---|---|---|---|
| Contributors* | 10 | 472 | 2,188 | 9,653 | 25,011 | 48,721 |
| Active contributors** | 9 | 212 | 846 | 3,228 | 8,442 | 16,945 |
| Very active contributors*** | 0 | 31 | 190 | 692 | 1,637 | 3,016 |
| No. of English language articles | 25 | 16,000 | 101,000 | 190,000 | 320,000 | 630,000 |
| No. of articles, all languages | 25 | 19,000 | 138,000 | 409,000 | 862,000 | 1,600,000 |

\* Contributed at least ten times; ** at least 5 times in last month, *** more than 100 times in last month.

criticizing *Wikipedia* as "The Faith-Based Encyclopedia."[6] As an example, McHenry mocked the *Wikipedia* article on Alexander Hamilton. He noted that Hamilton biographers have a problem fixing his birth year—whether it is 1755 or 1757. *Wikipedia* glossed over this error, fixing the date at 1755. McHenry then went on to criticize the way the dates were treated throughout the article, using it as an anchor to his general claim: *Wikipedia* is unreliable because it is not professionally produced. What McHenry did not note was that the other major online encyclopedias—like *Columbia* or *Encarta*—similarly failed to deal with the ambiguity surrounding Hamilton's birth date. Only the *Britannica* did. However, McHenry's critique triggered the *Wikipedia* distributed correction mechanism. Within hours of the publication of McHenry's Web article, the reference was corrected. The following few days saw intensive cleanup efforts to conform all references in the biography to the newly corrected version. Within a week or so, *Wikipedia* had a correct, reasonably clean version. It now stood alone with the *Encyclopedia Britannica* as a source of accurate basic encyclopedic information. In coming to curse it, McHenry found himself blessing *Wikipedia*. He had demonstrated precisely the correction mechanism that makes *Wikipedia*, in the long term, a robust model of reasonably reliable information.

Perhaps the most interesting characteristic about *Wikipedia* is the self-conscious social-norms-based dedication to objective writing. Unlike some of the other projects that I describe in this chapter, *Wikipedia* does not include elaborate software-controlled access and editing capabilities. It is generally open for anyone to edit the materials, delete another's change, debate the desirable contents, survey archives for prior changes, and so forth. It depends on self-conscious use of open discourse, usually aimed at consensus. While there is the possibility that a user will call for a vote of the participants on any given definition, such calls can be, and usually are, ignored by the community unless a sufficiently large number of users have decided that debate has been exhausted. While the system operators and server host—Wales—have the practical power to block users who are systematically disruptive, this power seems to be used rarely. The project relies instead on social norms to secure the dedication of project participants to objective writing. So, while not entirely anarchic, the project is nonetheless substantially more social, human, and intensively discourse—and trust-based— than the other major projects described here. The following fragments from an early version of the self-described essential characteristics and basic policies of *Wikipedia* are illustrative:

> First and foremost, the Wikipedia project is self-consciously an encyclopedia—rather than a dictionary, discussion forum, web portal, etc. Wikipedia's participants commonly follow, and enforce, a few basic policies that seem essential to keeping the project running smoothly and productively. First, because we have a huge variety of participants of all ideologies, and from around the world, Wikipedia is committed to making its articles as unbiased as possible. The aim is not to write articles from a single *objective* point of view—this is a common misunderstanding of the policy—but rather, to fairly and sympathetically present all views on an issue. See "neutral point of view" page for further explanation.[7]

The point to see from this quotation is that the participants of *Wikipedia* are plainly people who like to write. Some of them participate in other collaborative authorship projects. However, when they enter the common project of *Wikipedia*, they undertake to participate in a particular way—a way that the group has adopted to make its product be an encyclopedia. On their interpretation, that means conveying in brief terms the state of the art on the item, including divergent opinions about it, but not the author's opinion. Whether that is an attainable goal is a subject of interpretive theory, and is a question as applicable to a professional encyclopedia as it is to *Wikipedia*. As the project has grown, it has developed more elaborate spaces for discussing governance and for conflict resolution. It has developed structures for mediation, and if that fails, arbitration, of disputes about particular articles.

The important point is that *Wikipedia* requires not only mechanical cooperation among people, but a commitment to a particular style of writing and describing concepts that is far from intuitive or natural to people. It requires self-discipline. It enforces the behavior it requires primarily through appeal to the common enterprise that the participants are engaged in, coupled with a thoroughly transparent platform that faithfully records and renders all individual interventions in the common project and facilitates discourse among participants about how their contributions do, or do not, contribute to this common enterprise. This combination of an explicit statement of common purpose, transparency, and the ability of participants to identify each other's actions and counteract them—that is, edit out "bad" or "faithless" definitions—seems to have succeeded in keeping this community from devolving into inefficacy or worse. A case study by IBM showed, for example, that while there were many instances of vandalism on *Wikipedia*, including deletion of entire versions of articles on controversial topics like "abortion," the ability of users to see what was done and to fix it with a single click by reverting to a past version meant that acts of vandalism were corrected within minutes. Indeed, corrections were so rapid that vandalism acts and their corrections did not even appear on a mechanically generated image of the abortion definition as it changed over time.[8] What is perhaps surprising is that this success occurs not in a tightly knit community with many social relations to reinforce the sense of common purpose and the social norms embodying it, but in a large and geographically dispersed group of otherwise unrelated participants. It suggests that even in a group of this size, social norms coupled with a facility to allow any participant to edit out purposeful or mistaken deviations in contravention of the social norms, and a robust platform for largely unmediated conversation, keep the group on track.

A very different cultural form of distributed content production is presented by the rise of massive multiplayer online games (MMOGs) as immersive entertainment.

These fall in the same cultural "time slot" as television shows and movies of the twentieth century. The interesting thing about these types of games is that they organize the production of "scripts" very differently from movies or television shows. In a game like Ultima Online or EverQuest, the role of the commercial provider is not to tell a finished, highly polished story to be consumed start to finish by passive consumers. Rather, the role of the game provider is to build tools with which users collaborate to tell a story. There have been observations about this approach for years, regarding MUDs (Multi-User Dungeons) and MOOs (Multi-User Object Oriented games). The point to understand about MMOGs is that they produce a discrete element of "content" that was in the past dominated by centralized professional production. The screenwriter of an immersive entertainment product like a movie is like the scientist marking Mars craters—a professional producer of a finished good. In MMOGs, this function is produced by using the appropriate software platform to allow the story to be written by the many users as they experience it. The individual contributions of the users/co-authors of the story line are literally done for fun—they are playing a game. However, they are spending real economic goods—their attention and substantial subscription fees—on a form of entertainment that uses a platform for active coproduction of a story line to displace what was once passive reception of a finished, commercially and professionally manufactured good.

By 2003, a company called Linden Lab took this concept a major step forward by building an online game environment called Second Life. Second Life began almost entirely devoid of content. It was tools all the way down. Within a matter of months, it had thousands of subscribers, inhabiting a "world" that had thousands of characters, hundreds of thousands of objects, multiple areas, villages, and "story lines." The individual users themselves had created more than 99 percent of all objects in the game environment, and all story lines and substantive frameworks for interaction—such as a particular village or group of theme-based participants. The interactions in the game environment involved a good deal of gift giving and a good deal of trade, but also some very surprising structured behaviors. Some users set up a university, where lessons were given in both in-game skills and in programming. Others designed spaceships and engaged in alien abductions (undergoing one seemed to become a status symbol within the game). At one point, aiming (successfully) to prevent the company from changing its pricing policy, users staged a demonstration by making signs and picketing the entry point to the game; and a "tax revolt" by placing large numbers of "tea crates" around an in-game reproduction of the Washington Monument. Within months, Second Life had become an immersive experience, like a movie or book, but one where the commercial provider offered a platform and tools, while the users wrote the story lines, rendered the "set," and performed the entire play.

## Relevance/Accreditation

How are we to know that the content produced by widely dispersed individuals is not sheer gobbledygook? Can relevance and accreditation itself be produced on a peer-production model? One type of answer is provided by looking at commercial businesses that successfully break off precisely the "accreditation and relevance" piece of their product, and rely on peer production to perform that function. Amazon and Google are probably the two most prominent examples of this strategy.

Amazon uses a mix of mechanisms to get in front of their buyers of books and other products that the users are likely to purchase. A number of these mechanisms produce relevance and accreditation by harnessing the users themselves. At the simplest level, the recommendation "customers who bought items you recently viewed also bought these items" is a mechanical means of extracting judgments of relevance and accreditation from the actions of many individuals, who produce the datum of relevance and by-product of making their own purchasing decisions. Amazon also allows users to create topical lists and track other users as their "friends and favorites." Amazon, like many consumer sites today, also provides users with the ability to rate books they buy, generating a peer-produced rating by averaging the ratings. More fundamentally, the core innovation of Google, widely recognized as the most efficient general search engine during the first half of the 2000s, was to introduce peer-based judgments of relevance. Like other search engines at the time, Google used a text-based algorithm to retrieve a given universe of Web pages initially. Its major innovation was its PageRank algorithm, which harnesses peer production of ranking in the following way. The engine treats links from other Web sites pointing to a given Web site as votes of confidence. Whenever someone who authors a Web site links to someone else's page, that person has stated quite explicitly that the linked page is worth a visit. Google's search engine counts these links as distributed votes of confidence in the quality of the page pointed to. Pages that are heavily linked-to count as more important votes of confidence. If a highly linked-to site links to a given page, that vote counts for more than the vote of a site that no one else thinks is worth visiting. The point to take home from looking at Google and Amazon is that corporations that have done immensely well at acquiring and retaining users have harnessed peer production to enable users to find things they want quickly and efficiently.

The most prominent example of a distributed project self-consciously devoted to peer production of relevance is the Open Directory Project. The site relies on more than sixty thousand volunteer editors to determine which links should be included in the directory. Acceptance as a volunteer requires application. Quality relies on a peer-review process based substantially on seniority as a volunteer and level of engagement with the site. The site is hosted and administered by Netscape, which pays for server space and a small number of employees to administer the site and set up the initial guidelines. Licensing is free and presumably adds value partly to America Online's (AOL's) and Netscape's commercial search engine/portal and partly through goodwill. Volunteers are not affiliated with Netscape and receive no compensation. They spend time selecting sites for inclusion in the directory (in small increments of perhaps fifteen minutes per site reviewed), producing the most comprehensive, highest-quality human-edited directory of the Web—at this point outshining the directory produced by the company that pioneered human edited directories of the Web: Yahoo!.

Perhaps the most elaborate platform for peer production of relevance and accreditation, at multiple layers, is used by Slashdot. Billed as "News for Nerds," Slashdot has become a leading technology newsletter on the Web, coproduced by hundreds of thousands of users. Slashdot primarily consists of users commenting on initial submissions that cover a variety of technology-related topics. The submissions are typically a link to an off-site story, coupled with commentary from the person who submits the piece. Users follow up the initial submission with comments that often number in the hundreds. The initial submissions themselves, and more importantly, the approach to sifting through the comments of users for relevance and accreditation, provide a rich example of how this function can be performed on a distributed, peer-production model.

First, it is important to understand that the function of posting a story from another site onto Slashdot, the first "utterance" in a chain of comments on Slashdot, is itself an act of relevance production. The person submitting the story is telling the community of Slashdot users, "here is a story that 'News for Nerds' readers should be interested in." This initial submission of a link is itself very coarsely filtered by editors who are paid employees of Open Source Technology Group (OSTG), which runs a number of similar platforms—like SourceForge, the most important platform for free software developers. OSTG is a subsidiary of VA Software, a software services company. The FAQ (Frequently Asked Question) response to, "how do you verify the accuracy of Slashdot stories?" is revealing: "We don't. You do. If something seems outrageous, we might look for some corroboration, but as a rule, we regard this as the responsibility of the submitter and the audience. This is why it's important to read comments. You might find something that refutes, or supports, the story in the main." In other words, Slashdot very self-consciously is organized as a means of facilitating peer production of accreditation; it is at the comments stage that the story undergoes its most important form of accreditation—peer review ex-post.

Filtering and accreditation of comments on Slashdot offer the most interesting case study of peer production of these functions. Users submit comments that are displayed together with the initial submission of a story. Think of the "content" produced in these comments as a cross between academic peer review of journal submissions and a peer-produced substitute for television's "talking heads." It is in the means of accrediting and evaluating these comments that Slashdot's system provides a comprehensive example of peer production of relevance and accreditation. Slashdot implements an automated system to select moderators from the pool of users. Moderators are chosen according to several criteria; they must be logged in (not anonymous), they must be regular users (who use the site averagely, not one-time page loaders or compulsive users), they must have been using the site for a while (this defeats people who try to sign up just to moderate), they must be willing, and they must have positive "karma." Karma is a number assigned to a user that primarily reflects whether he or she has posted good or bad comments (according to ratings from other moderators). If a user meets these criteria, the program assigns the user moderator status and the user gets five "influence points" to review comments. The moderator rates a comment of his choice using a drop-down list with words such as "flamebait" and "informative." A positive word increases the rating of a comment one point and a negative word decreases the rating a point. Each time a moderator rates a comment, it costs one influence point, so he or she can only rate five comments for each moderating period. The period lasts for three days and if the user does not use the influence points, they expire. The moderation setup is designed to give many users a small amount of power. This decreases the effect of users with an ax to grind or with poor judgement. The site also implements some automated "troll filters," which prevent users from sabotaging the system. Troll filters stop users from posting more than once every sixty seconds, prevent identical posts, and will ban a user for twenty-four hours if he or she has been moderated down several times within a short time frame. Slashdot then provides users with a "threshold" filter that allows each user to block lower-quality comments. The scheme uses the numerical rating of the comment (ranging from −1 to 5). Comments start out at 0 for anonymous posters, 1 for registered users, and 2 for registered users with good "karma." As a result, if a user sets his or her filter at 1, the user will not see any comments from anonymous posters unless the comments' ratings were increased by a moderator. A user can set his or her filter anywhere from −1 (viewing all of the comments) to 5 (where only the posts that have been upgraded by several moderators will show up).

Relevance, as distinct from accreditation, is also tied into the Slashdot scheme because off-topic posts should receive an "off topic" rating by the moderators and sink below the threshold level (assuming the user has the threshold set above the minimum). However, the moderation system is limited to choices that sometimes are not mutually exclusive. For instance, a moderator may have to choose between "funny" (+1) and "off topic" (−1) when a post is both funny and off topic. As a result, an irrelevant post can increase in ranking and rise above the threshold level because it is funny or informative. It is unclear, however, whether this is a limitation on relevance, or indeed mimics our own normal behavior, say in reading a newspaper or browsing a library, where we might let our eyes linger longer on a funny or informative tidbit, even after we have ascertained that it is not exactly relevant to what we were looking for.

The primary function of moderation is to provide accreditation. If a user sets a high threshold level, they will only see posts that are considered of high quality by the moderators. Users also receive accreditation through their karma. If their posts consistently receive high ratings, their karma will increase. At a certain karma level, their comments will start off with a rating of 2, thereby giving them a louder voice in the sense that users with a threshold of 2 will now see their posts immediately, and fewer upward moderations are needed to push their comments even higher. Conversely, a user with bad karma from consistently poorly rated comments can lose accreditation by having his or her posts initially start off at 0 or −1. In addition to the mechanized means of selecting moderators and minimizing their power to skew the accreditation system, Slashdot implements a system of peer-review accreditation for the moderators themselves. Slashdot accomplishes this "metamoderation" by making any user that has an account from the first 90 percent of accounts created on the system eligible to evaluate the moderators. Each eligible user who opts to perform metamoderation review is provided with ten random moderator ratings of comments. The user/metamoderator then rates the moderator's rating as either unfair, fair, or neither. The metamoderation process affects the karma of the original moderator, which, when lowered sufficiently by cumulative judgments of unfair ratings, will remove the moderator from the moderation system.

Together, these mechanisms allow for distributed production of both relevance and accreditation. Because there are many moderators who can moderate any given comment, and thanks to the mechanisms that explicitly limit the power of any one moderator to overinfluence the aggregate judgment, the system evens out differences in evaluation by aggregating judgments. It then allows individual users to determine what level of accreditation pronounced by this aggregate system fits their particular time and needs by setting their filter to be more or less inclusive. By introducing "karma," the system also allows users to build reputation over time, and to gain greater control over the accreditation of their own work relative to the power of the critics. Users, moderators, and metamoderators are all volunteers.

The primary point to take from the Slashdot example is that the same dynamic that we saw used for peer production of initial utterances, or content, can be implemented to produce relevance and accreditation. Rather than using the full-time effort of professional accreditation experts, the system is designed to permit the aggregation of many small judgments, each of which entails a trivial effort for the contributor, regarding both relevance and accreditation of the materials. The software that mediates the communication among the collaborating peers embeds both the means to facilitate the participation and a variety of mechanisms designed to defend the common effort from poor judgment or defection.

## Value-Added Distribution

Finally, when we speak of information or cultural goods that exist (content has been produced) and are made usable through some relevance and accreditation mechanisms, there remains the question of distribution. To some extent, this is a nonissue on the Internet. Distribution is cheap. All one needs is a server and large pipes connecting one's server to the world. Nonetheless, this segment of the publication process has also provided us with important examples of peer production, including one of its earliest examples—Project Gutenberg.

Project Gutenberg entails hundreds of volunteers who scan in and correct books so that they are freely available in digital form. It has amassed more than 13,000 books, and makes the collection available to everyone for free. The vast majority of the "e-texts" offered are public domain materials. The site itself presents the e-texts in ASCII format, the lowest technical common denominator, but does not discourage volunteers from offering the e-texts in markup languages. It contains a search engine that allows a reader to search for typical fields such as subject, author, and title. Project Gutenberg volunteers can select any book that is in the public domain to transform into an e-text. The volunteer submits a copy of the title page of the book to Michael Hart—who founded the project—for copyright research. The volunteer is notified to proceed if the book passes the copyright clearance. The decision on which book to convert to e-text is left up to the volunteer, subject to copyright limitations. Typically, a volunteer converts a book to ASCII format using OCR (optical character recognition) and proof-reads it one time in order to screen it for major errors. He or she then passes the ASCII file to a volunteer proofreader. This exchange is orchestrated with very little super-vision. The volunteers use a Listserv mailing list and a bulletin board to initiate and supervise the exchange. In addition, books are labeled with a version number indicating how many times they have been proofed. The site encourages volunteers to select a book that has a low number and proof it. The Project Gutenberg proofing process is simple. Proofreaders (aside from the first pass) are not expected to have access to the book, but merely review the e-text for self-evident errors.

Distributed Proofreading, a site originally unaffiliated with Project Gutenberg, is devoted to proofing Project Gutenberg e-texts more efficiently, by distributing the volunteer proofreading function in smaller and more information-rich modules. Charles Franks, a computer programmer from Las Vegas, decided that he had a more efficient way to proofread these e-texts. He built an interface that allowed volunteers to compare scanned images of original texts with the e-texts available on Project Gutenberg. In the Distributed Proofreading process, scanned pages are stored on the site, and volunteers are shown a scanned page and a page of the e-text simultaneously so that they can compare the e-text to the original page. Because of the fine-grained modularity, proofreaders can come on the site and proof one or a few pages and submit them. By contrast, on the Project Gutenberg site, the entire book is typically exchanged, or at minimum, a chapter. In this fashion, Distributed Proofreading clears the proofing of tens of thousands of pages every month. After a couple of years of working independently, Franks joined forces with Hart. By late 2004, the site had proofread more than five thousand volumes using this method.

*    *    *

## Questions for Consideration

1   Why does Benkler consider peer production to be in conflict with the current economic model?

2   While some writers laud the idea of the peer-production model of media, others believe that audiences ultimately will want media content created by experts and professional media practitioners. Where do you stand, and why?

## Notes

1.   Josh Lerner and Jean Tirole, "The Scope of Open Source Licensing" (Harvard NOM working paper no. 02–42, table 1, Cambridge, MA, 2002). The figure is computed out of the data reported in this paper for the number of free software development projects that Lerner and Tirole identify as having "restrictive" or "very restrictive" licenses.

2.   Netcraft, April 2004 Web Server Survey, http://news.netcraft.com/archives/web_server_survey.html.

3.   Clickworkers Results: Crater Marking Activity, July 3, 2001, http://clickworkers.arc.nasa.gov/documents/crater-marking.pdf.

4.   B. Kanefsky, N. G. Barlow, and V. C. Gulick, *Can Distributed Volunteers Accomplish Massive Data Analysis Tasks?* http://www.clickworkers.arc.nasa.gov/documents/abstract.pdf.

5.   J. Giles, "Special Report: Internet Encyclopedias Go Head to Head," *Nature*, December 14, 2005, available at http://www.nature.com/news/2005/051212/full/438900a.html.

6.   http://www.techcentralstation.com/111504A.html.

7.   Yochai Benkler, "Coase's Penguin, or Linux and the Nature of the Firm," *Yale Law Journal* 112 (2001): 369.

8.   IBM Collaborative User Experience Research Group, History Flows: Results (2003), http://www.research.ibm.com/history/results.htm.

# Chapter 22

## STEVEN JOHNSON

# YOUR BRAIN ON VIDEO GAMES
## Could They Actually be Good for You?

**T**HE LARGE BODY OF RESEARCH on the negative effects of video games is more than two decades in the making, and it recalls many of the early concerns on the harmful effects of television. Yet in recent years, researchers have found evidence that video games, including violent ones, can be beneficial. Steven Johnson's article from a 2005 issue of *Discover* magazine introduces us to some of the most provocative findings, including those which suggest that video games enhance the thinking and learning processes. As you read this piece, think critically about *what* research was presented as well as *how* it was presented to appeal to a specific audience.

James Gee, a Professor of Learning Sciences at the University of Wisconsin, was profoundly humbled when he first played a video game for preschool-age kids called *Pajama Sam: No Need to Hide When It's Dark Outside*. Gee's son Sam, then 6, had been clamoring to play the game, which features a little boy who dresses up like his favorite action hero, Pajama Man, and sets off on adventures in a virtual world ruled by the dastardly villain Darkness. So Gee brought *Pajama Sam* home and tried it himself. "I figured I could play it and finish it so I could help Sam," says Gee. "Instead, I had to go and ask *him* to help *me*."

Gee had so much fun playing *Pajama Sam* that he subsequently decided to try his hand at an adult video game he picked at random off a store shelf—an H.G. Wells-inspired sci-fi quest called *The New Adventures of the Time Machine*. "I was just blown away when I brought it home at how hard it was," he says. "I thought, 'You can't tell me that people go to the store and pay fifty dollars and buy this!' Then I found out that there are billions spent each year on these games."

Gee's scholarly interest was also piqued. He sensed instantly that something interesting was happening in his mind as he struggled to complete the puzzles of *The Time Machine*. "I hadn't done that kind of new learning since graduate school. You know, as you get older, you kind of rest on your laurels: You learn certain patterns, you know your field, and you get a lot of experience. But this requires you to think in a new way. I saw that the excitement of this is the challenge and the difficulty and the new learning. That's what makes it fun!"

Gee's epiphany led him to the forefront of a wave of research into how video games affect cognition. Bolstered by the results of recent laboratory experiments, Gee and other researchers have dared to suggest that gaming might be mentally enriching. These scholars are the first to admit that games can be addictive, and indeed part of their research explores how games connect the reward circuits of the human brain. But they are now beginning to recognize the cognitive benefits of playing video games: pattern recognition, system thinking, even patience. Lurking in this research is the idea that gaming can exercise the mind the way physical activity exercises the body: It may be addictive because it's challenging.

All of this, of course, flies in the face of the classic stereotype of gamers as attention deficit-crazed stimulus junkies, easily distracted by flashy graphics and on-screen carnage. Instead, successful gamers must focus, have patience, develop a willingness to delay gratification, and prioritize scarce resources. In other words, they *think*.

One of the most popular video games ever created is called *Tetris*. It involves falling tile-like tetrominoes that a player must quickly maneuver so they fit into space at the bottom of the screen. In the early 1990s, Richard Haier, a professor of psychology at the University of California at Irvine, tracked cerebral glucose metabolic rates in the brains of *Tetris* players using PET scanners. The glucose rates show how much energy the brain is consuming, and thus serve as a rough estimate of how much work the brain is doing. Haier determined the glucose levels of novice *Tetris* players as their brains labored to usher the falling blocks into correct locations. Then he took levels again after a month of regular play. Even though the test subjects had improved their game performance by a factor of seven, Haier found that their glucose levels had decreased. It appeared that the escalating difficulty of the game trained the test subjects to mentally manipulate the *Tetris* blocks with such skill that they barely broke a cognitive sweat completing levels that would have utterly confounded them a month earlier.

Nearly a decade after Haier's study, Gee hit upon an explanation. He found that even escapist fantasy games are embedded with one of the core principles of learning— students prosper when the subject matter challenges them right at the edge of their abilities. Make the lessons too difficult and the students get frustrated. Make them too easy and they get bored. Cognitive psychologists call this the "regime of competence" principle. Gee's insight was to recognize that the principle is central to video games: As players progress, puzzles become more complex, enemies swifter and more numerous, underlying patterns more subtle. Most games don't allow progress until you've reached a certain level of expertise.

This is exactly the model of how *Tetris* works: When you first launch the game, the blocks fall at a leisurely pace, giving you plenty of time to rearrange them as they descend so they'll fit the spaces where they fall and gradually build up a wall that fills the screen. As you get better at manipulating the blocks, the game starts dropping them at increasing speeds.

To understand why games might be good for the mind, begin by shedding the cliché that they are about improving hand-eye coordination and firing virtual weapons. The majority of video games on the best-seller list contain no more bloodshed than a game of *Risk*.

The most popular games are not simply difficult in the sense of challenging manual dexterity; they challenge *mental* dexterity as well. The best-selling game of all time, *The Sims*, involves almost no hand-eye coordination or quick reflexes. One manages a household of characters, each endowed with distinct drives and personality traits, each cycling through an endless series of short-term needs (companionship, say, or food), each enmeshed in a network of relationships with other characters. Playing the game is a nonstop balancing act: sending one character off to work, cleaning the kitchen with another, searching through the classifieds with another. Even a violent game like *Grand Theft Auto* involves networks of characters that the player must navigate and master, picking up clues and detecting patterns. The text walk-through for *Grand Theft Auto III*—a document that describes all the variables involved in playing the game through to the finish—is 53,000 words long, the length of a short novel. But despite the complexity of these environments, most gamers eschew reading manuals or walk-throughs altogether, preferring to feel their way through the game space.

Gee contends that the way gamers explore virtual worlds mirrors the way the brain processes multiple, but interconnected, streams of information in the real world. "Basically, how we think is through running perceptual simulations in our heads that prepare us for the actions we're going to take," he says. "By modeling those simulations, video games externalize how the mind works."

Among all popular media today, video games are unique in their reliance on the regime of competence principle. Movies or television shows don't start out with simple dialogue or narrative structures and steadily build in complexity depending on the aptitude of individual viewers. Books don't pause midchapter to confirm that their reader's vocabularies have progressed enough to move on to more complicated words. By contrast, the training structure of video games dates back to the very origins of the medium; even *Pong* got more challenging as a player's skills improved. Moreover, only a fraction of today's games involve explicit violence, and sexual content is a rarity. But the regime of competence is everywhere.

Even if Gee is right and games are learning machines, one question remains: Do the skills learned in the virtual world translate into the real one?

In the spring of 2003, a research assistant in the cognitive sciences at the University of Rochester named Shawn Green began helping cognitive science professor Daphne Bavelier with a project investigating visual perception. Contrary to conventional wisdom, Bavelier's lab had found that people born deaf do not show better-than-average visual skills across the board; instead, they have very specific skills, including the ability to monitor their peripheral field. So Bavelier and Green began developing computerized tests to track these abilities. But a strange thing happened as they worked on the software. When Green took the tests himself, he scored off the charts. "Since I was an avid action video-game player," he says, "we decided to test the hypothesis that experience with action video games was the origin of the observed differences."

Green and Bavelier devised an experiment involving a series of quick visual-recognition tests, such as picking out the color of a letter or counting the number of objects on a screen. The study revealed dramatic perceptual differences between gamers and non-gamers that were far more pronounced than the differences between hearing and deaf individuals. When Green tweaked the tests to make them challenging enough so the gamers wouldn't have perfect scores, the nongamers sometimes performed so poorly that their answers might as well have been random guesses. The researchers also debunked the premise that visually intelligent people were more likely to be attracted to video games in the first place. They had a group of nonplayers spend a week immersed in the World War II game *Medal of Honor* and found that the group's skills on the visual test improved as well. The evidence was overwhelming: Games were literally making people perceive the world more clearly.

Green did the initial research as part of his honors thesis. After graduation, he and Bavelier continued the study. *Nature* published the results in 2003. "The learning induced by video-game playing occurs quite fast and generalizes outside the gaming experience," Green says. "Our tests are quite dull and very unlike gaming itself. They require subjects to perform the same highly specialized task over and over on boring displays using geometrical shapes or letters. There is no character, no plot story, no goal, and no challenge to raise the stakes. But clearly, whatever it is that gamers learn transfers to situations that use different tasks and stimuli."

The premise that games teach generalized skills that apply in real-world situations has been corroborated by recent studies. James Rosser, director of the Advanced Medical Center at Beth Israel Medical Center in New York City, found that laparoscopic surgeons who played games for more than three hours a week made 37 percent fewer errors than their nongaming peers, thanks to the improved hand-eye coordination and depth perception. A recent book published by the Harvard Business School Press looked at studies of three distinct groups of white-collar professionals: hard-core gamers, occasional gamers, and nongamers. The research the authors surveyed contradicts nearly all the received ideas about the impact of games. The gaming population turned out to be consistently more social, more confident, and more comfortable solving problems creatively. They also showed no evidence of reduced attention spans compared with nongamers.

The U.S. military has long supported the premise that learning through games can prepare soldiers for the complex, rapid-fire decision making of combat. In 2002 they released their own game, *America's Army*, designed to provide a profile of a soldier's occupational abilities. Recruits can now submit their game score when they sign up for service, helping what Army enlistment brochures tout as "the best possible match between the attributes and interests of potential soldiers and the attributes of career fields and training opportunities." A growing recognition that game skills carry over into real-world skills has also prompted the establishment of private research teams, including an MIT-sponsored group called the Education Arcade and an international consortium of scholars called the Serious Games Initiative, which are exploring how to incorporate the positive effects of gaming in traditional educational environments.

In the fall of 2003, two media researchers at the University of Southern California set up a study to look at the patterns of brain activity triggered by violent video games. Peter Vorderer and René Weber booked time on an fMRI machine, loaded a popular game called *Tactical Ops* on an adjoining computer console, and watched one test subject after another pretend to be part of a special forces team trying to prevent a terrorist attack. Each test subject inserted his head three feet into the cavity at the center of the fMRI, where a small mirror positioned directly above his eyes made it possible to view the computer screen. During the course of the game, the scanner tracked the blood flow to different parts of the brain, creating a map of neural activity.

Before Vorderer and Weber even looked at any of the brain scans, they were surprised by the behavior of the dozen or so adults who volunteered for the test. Participating in an fMRI study involves lying for extended periods of time in an extremely confined space. Even a mild claustrophobic will invariably find the experience intolerable, and most people need a break after 20 minutes. But most of the *Tactical Ops* players happily stayed in the machine for at least an hour, oblivious to the discomfort and noise because they were so entranced by the game.

The blithe reaction of the *Tactical Ops* players to being entombed in a cacophonous scanner may prompt some people to jump to a predictable conclusion: Video games are dangerously addictive. But if games challenge the mind as much as this new research suggests, why do people in search of escapist entertainment find them so captivating?

The answer may have to do with the neurotransmitter dopamine. A number of studies have revealed that game playing triggers dopamine release in the brain, a finding that makes sense given the instrumental role that dopamine plays in the way the brain handles both reward and exploration. Jaak Panksepp, a neuroscientist at the Falk Center for Molecular Therapeutics at Northwestern University, calls the dopamine system the brain's "seeking" circuitry, which propels us to explore new avenues for reward in our environment. The game world is teeming with objects that deliver clearly articulated rewards: more life, access to new levels, new equipment, new spells. Most of the crucial work in game interface design revolves around keeping players notified of potential rewards available to them and how much those rewards are needed.

In a sense, neuroscience has offered up a prediction, one that games obligingly confirm. If you a create a system in which rewards are clearly defined and achieved by exploring an environment, you'll find human brains drawn to those systems, even if they're made up of virtual characters and simulated sidewalks. It's likely those *Tactical Ops* players in the fMRI machine were able to tolerate the physical discomfort of the machine because the game environment so powerfully stimulated the mind's dopamine system.

Of course, dopamine is also involved in the addictiveness of drugs. "The thing to remember about dopamine is that it's not at all the same as pleasure," says Gregory Berns, a neuroscientist at Emory University School of Medicine in Atlanta, who looks at dopamine in a cultural context in his forthcoming book, *Satisfaction*. "Dopamine is not the reward; it's what lets you go out and explore in the first place. Without dopamine, you wouldn't be able to learn properly."

The video game cocktail of sleek technology, dopamine-friendly environments, and sensationalist narratives means that some players end up getting too attached to their joysticks. There's no denying that some games place far too much emphasis on gratuitous violence, and others on absurd watered-down Tolkien fantasy. If there is a health problem associated with gaming, it's likely to be the lack of physical exertion that comes from sitting in front of a monitor all day. "The biggest problem we run into, especially from the media, is that everyone wants an answer as to whether a game is good or bad for you just as it stands there on the shelf." Say Gee. "For little kids, *Pokémon* is a great cognitive developer, if it's being scaffolded by the parents and they're getting their kids to talk about it. But if it's just a passive babysitter, then it's no good for you."

I ask Gee what kind of cognitive skills we should expect to find in the *Pokémon* generation. Not surprisingly, he's got a list. "They're going to think well about systems; they're going to be good at exploring; they're going to be good at re-conceptualizing their goals based on their experience; they're not going to judge people's intelligence just by how fast and efficient they are; and they're going to think nonlaterally. In our current world with its complex systems that are quite dangerous, those are damn good ways to think."

Gee's remarks remind me of an experience I had a few years earlier, introducing my 7-year-old nephew to *SimCity 2000*, the best-selling urban simulator that lets you create a virtual metropolis on your computer, building highways and bridges, zoning areas for development, raising or lowering taxes. Based on the player's decisions, neighborhoods thrive or decline into ghettos, streets get overrun with traffic or remain wastelands, criminals prosper or disappear. When I walked my nephew through the game, I gave him only the most cursory overview of the rules; I was mostly just giving him a tour of the city I'd built. But he was absorbing the rules nonetheless. At one point, I showed him a block of rusted, crime-ridden factories that lay abandoned and explained that I'd had difficulty getting this part of my city to come back to life. He turned to me and said, "I think you need to lower your industrial tax rates." He said it as calmly and as confidently as if he were saying, "I think we need to shoot the bad guy."

In a 20-minute tour of *SimCity*, my nephew had learned a fundamental principle of urban economics: some areas zoned for specific uses can falter if the zone-specific taxes are too high. Of course, if you sat my 7-year-old nephew down in an urban studies classroom, he would be asleep in 10 seconds. But just like those *Tactical Ops* players happily trapped for an hour in an fMRI, something in the game world had pulled at him. He was learning in spite of himself.

## Questions for Consideration

1   Which of the findings about video games in this article do you think are most important to parents? Why?
2   Using periodical databases such as Nexis or Factiva, create a catalog of ills that experts have associated with video games. How should parents balance the positive and the negative considerations of the games?

## Resources

John Beck and Mitchell Wade, 2004: *Got Game: How the Gamer Generation Is Reshaping Business Forever*. Harvard Business School Press.

James Paul Gee, 2003: *What Video Games Have to Teach Us About Learning and Literacy*. Palgrave Macmillan.

Steven Berlin Johnson, 2005: *Everything Bad Is Good For You: How Today's Popular Culture Is Actually Making Us Smarter*. Riverhead Books. www.stevenberlinjohnson.com

# Chapter 23

## MICHAEL REAL

# SPORTS ONLINE
## The Newest Player in Mediasport

T HE INTERNET HAS BECOME A hotbed of sports activities, ranging from live-action reporting websites and fantasy football leagues to online gambling sites and fan blogs. As Michael Real points out in the following essay, which was published in *The Handbook of Sports and Media* in 2006, the Internet's popularity among sports enthusiasts stems from its ability to combine the sights of television, the sounds of radio, and the interactivity of video games. Real relates much of his research on the online world of sports to larger trends in the media, including patterns of concentrated ownership and increasing opportunities for audience participation. He encourages us to consider how our own experiences with media can tell us a great deal about the contemporary nature of mass communication.

From its explosive development in the last decade of the twentieth century, the World Wide Web has become an ideal medium for the dedicated sports fanatic and a useful resource for even the casual fan. Its accessibility, interactivity, speed, and multimedia content are triggering a fundamental change in the delivery of mediated sports, a change for which no one can yet predict the outcome. Like an unanticipated child, the newest member of the sports media family has disrupted everything. Family roles, once clearly established, are shifting as the older siblings—newspapers, magazines, radio, television, VCRs, and even computers—adjust to this new invasive presence.

The global technology network of the online Internet, nicknamed "the Web," is not so much a new and separate medium for sports use as it is a new combination of previous media. It offers the textual information and data that have made newspaper sports pages valuable for more than a century. It offers the speed and sound of the live radio broadcast that has produced programs and stars in sports since the Roaring Twenties. The Web can bring to the fan the sights, sounds, and immediacy of the family's previous star sibling, the sports of live-action and prerecorded television, offerings whose presence was vastly multiplied by satellite and cable. The Web even evokes the on-demand control of computers and video games. And, by having all these talents, this mixture of angel and demon offers more than any of the previous media from which it has emerged. Still young and unfocused, the Web is the gifted younger sibling whose promise generates both excitement and threat for all members of the family.

Research on the Internet is understandably yet at an early stage. Internet use for political and social purposes—travel, political campaigns, issue advocacy, dating, pornography—are important and under examination in journals and books. Sports as an interest group, or *genre*, of Internet use offers the opportunity to explore in depth the leisure uses and social dimensions of the Internet. An early study looked at the Web's use for sports history (Cox & Salter, 1998). A look at gender in ABC's online Olympic coverage in 2000 found the same reduction and stereotyping of female atheletes as has been found in other media (Jones, 2004). A more comprehensive look (Beck & Bosshart, 2003) briefly distinguished the Web's role as a sports encyclopedia, an interactive medium for self-publishing, a publicity vehicle for teams and athletes, a betting site, an outlet for neglected sports, and a site of struggle between independent website designers/bloggers and the megamedia conglomerates already dominating sports and media.

From the few studies and from the real world of online sports, many questions emerge. What is the combination of technologies and applications that comprises the world of sports online? What are the real and projected scales and economies of sports on the Web? Who are emerging as the dominant players, the winners and losers, in this complex? What conflicts and controversies have marked the first decade of the growing availability of sports over the Internet? What do answers to these questions tell us of the nature of the Internet? Of sports today? Of media theory? This analysis seeks answers to these questions through a mixture of methods: interviews with producers of Web sports and a focus group of fans, an examination of sports Web history and industry reports, a survey of Internet use by media/sport researchers, and comparisons to traditional theories of media. The picture that emerges from this has some of the blurriness and jumpiness of most online video, but the action on-screen is, in its own way, as exciting as any major sporting event.

## History and Scale: Sports Score Big Online

Noting the popularity and new economic profitability of sports online, the technology editor of *BusinessWeekOnline*, Salkever titled his 2003 report simply "Sports Score Big Online." By that time, annual income from advertising on sports-themed Web sites was expected to approach $2.4 billion, and sports-related electronic commerce was estimated to bring in $4.7 billion. Featuring play-by-play audio plus real-time data, Major League Baseball was charging $14.95 per month to its 300,000 subscribers and netting a profit of nearly $6 million on an income of $80 to 90 million from its 31 Web sites (Holt, 2004). At the same time, 150,000 Nascar.com subscribers were paying $19.95 to receive live audio of the races, along with such extras as telemetry feeds of technical and performance information (brake, throttle, GSP location) of cars on the track and the two-way radio conversations between drivers and pit crews (Salkever, 2003). In a surprisingly short time, sports Web sites had matured from unprofitable labors of love by fanatics to supplemental loss-leaders for leagues, teams, and media corporations to directly profitable enterprises with huge growth potential. Sports fantasy league members were willing to pay $20 or more merely to participate, creating one of many revenue sources for sports Web sites.

By the first decade of the twenty-first century, the biggest sports Web sites were ESPN.com, Yahoo! Sports, AOL Sports, SI.com, and Sportsline.com, each recording more than a million unique visitors each week (Databank Sports, 2001). The success of these sites did not happen overnight or without struggle. The pioneers saw their utopian visions of the 1990s give way a few years later to the dot.com recession. As on the playing field, from this unanticipated challenge the strongest competitors emerged in more dominant positions, but the process had been longer and more arduous than the competitors might have wished.

Sports Web sites have evolved with the Web itself. As Beck and Bosshart (2003) noted, the transmission rates of data over the web and the limited memories of personal computers made the early Internet a very limited resource. It took patience for early adopters to log on, find their way to useful information, and receive it. Transmission of anything other than small blocs of text was impractical. No more. As a result, both production and content have expanded exponentially.

The history of ESPN.com,[1] the leader in the field, indicates the erratic if successful trajectory of the development of the Internet and Web sports. In 1995 ESPN signed a two-year contract with Starwave, a start-up operated by the former partner of Bill Gates at Microsoft, Paul Allen, to develop and operate a Web site for ESPN, the 24-hour sports network that had begun amid great skepticism in 1979 and came to dominate the field. Even the Web site's name was unstable in the early years. After toying with the label "Satchel.com," the first address became "ESPN-net.sportszone.com," but that was reduced a few years later to "ESPNnet.com" and finally to "ESPN.com." A handful of Starwave's employees operated the ESPN site first from Belleville, Washington, and then from Seattle. Beginning in 1999, ESPN.com was moved in stages to the central ESPN complex in Bristol, Connecticut, where, still in its first decade, it employed more than 100 editorial staff and perhaps twice that many technical staff, all in addition to its marketing staff in New York. Before it reached such success, there were more than a few times when its ownership seemed at a loss as to what ESPN.com might be. When the Walt Disney Company bought ABC and ESPN, Disney sold ESPN.com's operating company, Starwave, to Infoseek in Sunnyvale, California. But, rethinking its strategy, Disney then bought Starwave back and incorporated it into its new division, the Walt Disney Internet Group, known as "w.dig." During ESPN.com's rocky evolution, there were conflicts between east and west employee groups, between editorial and advertising interests, and between ESPN.com and ESPN's television and magazine operations.

Sports Web site content was also evolving significantly during this first decade, as changes at ESPN.com reflected. In the early years, ESPN.com featured little more than regularly updated scores and related information from the NFL, MLB, the NBA, and their college counterparts. This information was simply transferred from wire services such as the Scripps Howard News Service, which did not cover all sports; the Associated Press, whose information was available only to ESPN.com premium subscribers; and other sports tickers and services. Gradually the site began to incorporate information on soccer, golf, tennis, and other less dominant sports. The staff labored to include a short nightly feature, "In the Zone," but the site was close to pure data information. Finally, by 2004, the site was offering 10,000 pages of sports items updated continuously.

Even after the move to Bristol, the Web site was not integral to ESPN's larger purposes. ESPN.com was confined to conducting polls in conjunction with television events and offering chat rooms for NFL fans and similar groups. By 2003 this had changed to the point where ESPN.com was named one of the company's six priority areas and was one of the principles in the nightly production meetings of ESPN. ESPN.com also joined the television and magazine components of ESPN in jointly creating and operating an "Enterprise Reporting Team." This investigative unit could manage each outlet for maximum effect in releasing its work. For example, when they were preparing to break the story of association between Ohio State football player Maurice Clarett and a known gambler, they chose to release the story first on the Web site, then on *SportsCenter* that night, and eventually in the magazine. Using the Web site first enabled ESPN to explain the story and its background in sufficient detail so that its release on television that night would be less likely to generate erroneous or misleading pickup by other media. The magazine's two-week production schedule made it impractical for releasing the Clarett story first in the magazine.

ESPN.com added two features in 2004, one providing television clips and the other encouraging personalizing of individual access to ESPN.com. "ESPN Motion" during the night sends several minutes of full-motion video to a subscriber's hard drive, where a single click during the day will bring up a highlight reel with the highest quality video currently available on the Internet. Dunks, touchdowns, and home runs are shown interspersed with 30-second commercials, utilizing a technology developed in-house by ESPN. The second feature, "My ESPN," enables a subscriber to customize his (92% of ESPN.com subscribers are male) or her homepage to highlight teams, sports, and players of most personal interest. Information that might have been three or four menus and clicks away is immediately featured.

## Audience Size and Characteristics: Take Me out to the Webcast

The growth of the number of persons accessing sports sites on the World Wide Web has grown in a manner parallel to the growth of Web production and content, perhaps at even a faster rate. When compared to television numbers, the subscription numbers to leading sports Web sites seem small, but they have been expanding rapidly.

MLB.com's Web sites were making a profit less than two years after the league planned them in 2000, according to a report by Holt (2004). At that time, the baseball owners voted to centralize baseball's Internet operations with one site for the major leagues and one site for each of thirty teams. Bob Bowman, the CEO of MLB.com, a wholly owned subsidiary of Major League Baseball, projected 25,000 subscribers for the first full year of service in 2003. Against the backdrop of Web surfers expecting everything to be available free, MLB.com was asking $79.95 for the season or $14.95 per month. Yet, in its first few weeks, the service achieved its target number and within the year was claiming 300,000 subscribers. In addition to paying that fee for live audio of all games, subscribers could also download the video of "Baseball's Best," the more than 50 games deemed most historic, dating back to the 1936 World Series. MLB.com reported that 2 to 3 million fans each day visited major league sites during the six-month season, and 65 million visitors accessed a total of 560 million page hits on the sites during the 26 days of the playoffs (Holt, 2004).

The 2003 Super Bowl on ABC-TV was viewed in 43.4 million homes in the United States, while only 1,028,000 visitors accessed the official Super Bowl Web site. But that Web number was nearly triple the number from two years earlier. In 2001 only 359,000 persons had accessed the Web site. The numbers are small but the growth is rapid. The same 2003 Super Bowl saw more than 1.4 million unique visitors on the ESPN.com Web site. With both ABC and ESPN owned by Disney, the telecast and Web site could be effectively coordinated.

Like sports on television, the demographics of those accessing sports Web sites are desirable to many commercial sponsors. A majority of ESPN.com users are in the 18 to 34 male demographic. They average 9 minutes per page, while the global average according to Nielsen (2004b) is 45 seconds per Web page. The second-and third-page usage on ESPN.com, where the fan has found what he is most seeking, averages an amazingly sustained 13 minutes. The majority of users are college educated or in college. They are affluent, white-collar types.

Certain sports events are irresistible to the Web sports fan. March Madness features 64 NCAA college teams engaged in basketball games in the same two-day period on a Thursday and Friday. The sheer number of teams and games drives fans to the Internet. Nielsen//NetRatings reports 20 million unique visitors to sports Web sites for those games. Nielsen analyst Ryan explains: "Online tournament brackets, real-time game results, and up-to-the-minute commentary make the Web a huge attraction for March Madness fans" (Nielsen, 2004a, para 3). ESPN.com's audience during the first week of March Madness in 2004 was 4.493 million; Yahoo Sports had 2.396 million; and AOL Sports, SI.com, and Sportsline.com all had more than 1 million unique visitors. Total Web sport site users increased by 13% for that week.

When we expand the picture of Web sports to the world, as in the Olympics, the scale and duration of the attentive, purposeful audience is striking. Nielsen (2004b) reported that the average global user of the Internet engages in 24 to 29 sessions per month, visits 58 domains, and accesses 1,014 pages, each for an average of 45 seconds. The sessions average 48 minutes, totaling more than 23 hours per month. Given what advertisers are willing to pay for access to the viewers of television, it is not surprising that they are beginning to develop successful methods to reach the global Web audience. And Nielsen (2004b) reported that three of every four Americans have access to the Internet, with more than half having broadband access. The two fastest growing sites in the United States in August, 2004, were NBCOlympics.com, the Web site of the television network carrying the Games, and Athens2004.com, the official Web site of the Games. Their number of unique visitors was up more than 12%, making NBC's total more than 2.2 million unique visitors. Nielsen analyst Gotta (Nielsen, 2004c, para 7) noted, "Due to the time zone differences between Athens and the United States, this year's Olympics on the Web has turned out to play a significant role for American fans." With time differences of six hours or more from Athens, Web surfers in the United States, as in many parts of the world, could seek the factual information during the day and watch the television replays in the evening.

## Television and the Web: Enemies or Allies—Who Is Undermining Whom?

The emergence of the Web has triggered debates on whether the hard-copy daily newspaper will disappear and how soon, whether video rentals and video games will migrate to Web delivery systems, whether television networks will be reduced to just another lane on the information superhighway, and whether countries and cultures will blend into the long-anticipated Global Village. But for the Web, most potential rivalries have turned into partnerships, somewhat akin to when an international soccer club entices rival stars onto its roster. The playing field of Web sports is still an open one— there are many independent Web sites—but the trend has clearly been toward consoli- dation of ownership and convergence with other major media entities.

By 1999, warning shots were being fired about how the Web may destroy televi- sion's lucrative world. Burton (1999), a sports marketing expert, warned in *Advertising Age* that the Web could bring about the demise of TV as we know it. Under the inflammatory headline "The Internet Stands Ready to Undermine TV's Costly Sports Empire," Burton noted Nielsen's report that online homes watch 13% less television, about one hour less per day. Sports were the "killer application" that drove the success of radio and television, in Burton's analysis, and will do the same for the Internet (para 5). The huge television contracts of major sport leagues ($17.6 billion for eight years for the NFL) could be threatened by the overly cluttered sports telecasting world and its failure to deliver efficiently the 12- to 24-year-old computer-friendly male target. For Burton, the old broadcasting model faced the new multicasting model. He saw television networks offering sports Web sites as a potentially self-destructive move, one which would contribute to greater Internet usage and undercut television sports rights fees. He cautioned, "The sports circus may cause young males to move from the slow-paced world of TV Town to the infinitely more exciting lure of Digital Depot. That could mean the TV joins the radio in the attic (para 20)."

In 2000, Jordan (2000) continued the argument in *Nieman Reports* by charging that "The Web Pulled Viewers Away From the Olympic Games." His question was "How much longer will exclusive broadcast rights hold sway over the way that viewers take in these events?" His argument was made through the 56 million and 46 million page views, respectively, recorded by the official Olympics Web site and Sports Yahoo during the duration of the Sydney Games. NBC's television ratings were down but its Web site had 66 million page views, an average of more than 4 million daily. In 1996, he noted, NBC had two full-time staff on its Web site for the Atlanta Olympics but had 40 full- time and 100 part-time in Sydney for its Web site. On the television side, the network paid $705 million in rights fees for the lowest rated television Olympics since Mexico City in 1968. It required NBC to pay advertiser buy-backs, but the network still projected profits in the tens of millions of dollars. While television declined at the 2000 Games, the Internet was on the rise. One third of Internet users reported watching less television as a result. Jordan wonders whether a nation of computer-outfitted house- holds will again be content to turn to television for events that ended hours before.

Even as Burton and Jordan were making their nightmare arguments about the future of television, Web sites were successfully exploring webcasting and seeking out partnerships with television networks. Seeing the successful synergy of ESPN and its Web site and CBS and its Web site, SportsLine, the venerable sports publication *The Sporting News* spent years working up a partnership for its Web site, an effort which resulted in its joining forces with Fox television. The benefits shared between Sporting News Online, *Sporting News Magazine*, and Fox Sports included major cross-promotions of each other's offerings and a sharing of columnists/commentators and celebrity features.

At the same time, streaming video technology had forged another bridge uniting television and the Web by making the transmission of television over the Web practical (Krikke, 2004) without the need to download large files before playback. Also, access-on-demand could be coupled with new miniaturized wireless devices for access anywhere. The move from online to television and back became more seamless, and television and computer screens began to be more interchangeable. Consoli (2003) reported that a traditional online corporation, AOL, capitalized on the synergy by advertising in the 2003 Super Bowl that it offered the Super Bowl ads on its Web site. It drew 5.5 million people within 36 hours. AOL also airs video clips from NBA, MLB, and Nascar, and four-minute highlight clips from each NFL game on Sunday nights. A potentially long legal battle emerged between a television recording/playback system and the NFL when the FCC (Cannella & Bechtel, 2004) cleared TiVoGo to allow its users to disseminate programs to remote television sets, thus opening a means to circumvent the NFL's regional and blackout rules. Clearly, television and the Web could be made synergistic allies as easily as blood enemies.

As six major transnational media conglomerates came to own and dominate a large part of the world of media by the early twenty-first century (McChesney, 2004; "Who Owns What," 2004), cross-ownership and operating agreements were erasing the distinctions between previously competing media like television and the Web or newspapers and radio. The high profile Web sites for sports were merely one member of the diverse media family being employed by megacorporations to maximize the publicity and control of media products and information channels. The once unruly youngster, the Web, had been made to line up alongside his siblings in formal family photos and forget former loyalties or antagonisms in the new family unity of commercialism-above-all.

## Sports Gambling and the Web: You Can Bet on It

Gambling and sports have an uneasy relationship at best, from the Chicago "Black Sox" World Series scandal of 1919 to Pete Rose's various acknowledgements and denials. The Internet has the potential to multiply the problem. Web-based gambling is available to anyone anytime, night or day, dressed or not. While illegal in the United States due to the inclusion of the Web under the 1961 Federal Wire Act prohibition of betting over the phone (Angwin, 2004), offshore online sites can be readily accessed by casual betters, children, gambling addicts, and even athletes.

Like sports on the Web, gambling online has grown rapidly, most of it centered on sports. Between 1997 and 2003, the number of gambling Web sites grew from 25 to 1,800 (Weir, 2003). During that time, Internet gambling losses grew from an estimated $300 million to somewhere between $3 billion and $6 billion. Internet gambling addiction increased by 25% over two years and was the number-one gambling problem among college students. A study by the Division on Addictions of the Harvard University Medical School ("The Motivated Scholar," 2002) reported that 5.6% of U.S. college age and young people are pathological in their betting—gambling to recoup losses, spending money they don't have, unable to stop—almost three times the rate among the general adult population. Having it available so effortlessly has made the Internet the primary source for college student betting and sports gambling. White, college-educated males with sports participation backgrounds are the majority among sports gambling addicts. Even prominent athletes have become its victims. Washington Capitals hockey star Jaromir Jagr admitted to running up a $500,000 debt betting through a Belize-based offshore Web site. Cross and Vollano (1999) found 35% of student athletes had gambled on sports and 5% of males had bet on their own games, accepted bribes to play poorly, or provided insider tips for gamblers. A 2000 University of Cincinnati study found 25.5% of Division I basketball and football players gambled on college sports and 3.7% on their own games (Weir, 2003). An NCAA report (2004) found that 6% of male student athletes gambled on the Internet and 21% gambled on college sport; 2% of female athletes gambled on the Web and 6% on college sports. Access to Web gambling exacerbates the problems of both student and student-athlete gambling.

Australia, New Zealand, and the United Kingdom have legalized online wagering, bringing regulation and taxation to the industry. The U.S. approach has resisted legalizing it and has worked with credit card companies to try to prevent it. The MGM Mirage casino operated an offshore gambling Web site until congressional opposition forced it to close. With the gambling industry lobbying for its legalization and gambling counselors and critics opposing it, online gambling is a site for struggle over whether to let anyone be his or her own bookie or to further oppose the industry that dares not meet in the country of its best customers (Richtel, 2004).

## The Active Fan: Web Sites, Blogging, and Fantasy Leagues

The shift in media research and theory away from the passive couch potato of bullet theory to the active user seeking information and gratification finds an ultimate expression and qualifier in the Web sports fan. The qualifying condition is that the Web sports fan is NOT the participating athlete actually playing the game. The average fan still receives and absorbs messages and media, is outside the action, and does not score the dramatic winning touchdown, hit the late-inning home run, or sink the game-clinching long jumper as time runs out. But, given that qualification, the fan today through the Web can be strikingly active, taking a step beyond even the success of sports radio talk shows in the 1980s and 1990s.

Fantasy leagues are now huge businesses in which a fan pays up to $100 to play by selecting players and then working the team through the season. When other Web sites go from free use to a fee charge, subscriptions dry up. But fantasy-league Web sites have performed impressively by achieving better than a 20% successful conversion rate, according to John Bruel, a sports marketing consultant. By 2003 Yahoo Sports claimed 10 million players in its fantasy football league and a growth rate of 40% per year (Salkever, 2003). Other major sports sites have similar fantasy leagues and membership rates. The quantity and depth of information available on the Web enables a fantasy league player to be the well-informed general manager of a complex, seemingly realistic virtual team. Subscribing to specialized Web sites and information sources, constantly exchanging opinions and insights with other fans, tracking down rumors and trivia, developing personnel and game strategies, the diehard player in an online fantasy league is exercising a new option first anticipated in British newspapers for soccer fans, an engrossing, time-consuming chance to "play" with and against the best. And, like gambling or sports channel obsessions, it can be addictive.

The active fan is also present in the creation of the endless number of sports-oriented Web sites and the success of specialized Web services. Most sports teams, leagues, school athletic departments, and other institutional presences in sports have dedicated Web sites. But these tend to be islands of safe, noncontroversial items: schedules, statistics, game stories, personal features. These sites are surrounded by dozens of fan-generated Web sites that express and feed the insatiable appetite of fans for connections to their favorite team or competitor. These scattered sites have, in turn, given rise to large and complex organizations feeding the hunger for team and region information. Layden (2003) found that Rivals.com, for example, from its base in Tennessee, by 2003 had 83 Web sites devoted to college sports and operated by local experts, whether sports journalist or avid fan. TheInsiders.com ran 87 such sites from its base in Seattle, and countless others did likewise. One of Rival.com's sites was Volquest.com. It claimed 2,000 University of Tennessee fans who paid up to $10 per month, accessed 250,000 pages per day, and flooded the site on national football signing day in February with more than one million visits.

Fan Web sites have expanded the traditional watchdog function of the press by having eyes and ears everywhere. In 2003, Iowa State basketball coach Larry Eustachy lost his position because of pictures and stories of him drinking and partying with students after a game in Missouri. The damaging photos were first posted on tigerboard.com three months before they were published by the *Des Moines Register*. Also in 2003, newly appointed Alabama football coach Mike Price was first charged on a rival fan's message board, autigers.com, with throwing money and scandal around at a strip club in Pensacola, Florida. In a few days the story went to the mainstream press and Price was fired (Layden, 2003). While fan Web sites are normally preoccupied with coaching strategy and player recruitment, they actually serve many uses and provide a variety of gratifications. Rivals.com Web sites have a network of analysts that cover each major market in the United States and offer photos, audio and video highlights, message boards, a recruiting database, and more (Clark, 2003).

Sports Web sites have also expanded on the quantity of reporting on sports, even offering real-time running Web logs, or *blogs*, of sporting events while they happen. The Web-based fan can listen to the play-by-play audio of many sports in far-flung places, watch video of some, and read details of each stage of the action both as reported, the news function, and as analyzed, the editorial function. Apropos of this latter function, beginning in 1998 a sports columnist for the *St. Paul Pioneer Press* was providing a play-by-play written commentary on play selection and performance in real-time during Minnesota Vikings games. He was dubbed the "laptop quarterback" (Gray, 2000). Neighborhood blogs on local sports, schools, and politics capitalize on the Web's potential for ultralocal community services by providing localized people-power content (Palser, 2004).

## The Death of Distance in Sports Fandom

As Kevin Jackson (personal communication, April 19, 2004) of ESPN.com put it, "There are no displaced sports fans anymore." Extending a process that began with cable and satellite television featuring teams by subscription from afar, the Web can now make a fan feel local even when hundreds or thousands of miles away. Walker (2003, para 8) reported that 55% of Major League Baseball fans do not live near their favorite team; he dubs them "the long-distance fan." Each morning, a geographically distant fan can read the local press coverage of his team, shop in the team store, satisfy his hunger for debate on the team through message boards, and follow the game action as it happens—all on the Web. He can watch premium-television sports packages, get score updates on his cell phone, and feel as engaged with his team as if he were in that city (Walker, 2003). Also, the one-sport fans can find on the Web just what they want and only that, wherever it may be, whether snowboarding, cheerleading, or the NBA, as our student panel reported (Focus Group, 2004). The internationalism of the Web creates exotic opportunities. Soccer fans in South Africa follow European teams closely, Japanese fans track the careers of their heroes performing in American baseball, franchises buy Chinese players to get access to that huge market, media moguls buy teams and leagues to provide content for their global satellites—and distance disappears.[2]

The stadium-without-walls parallels the online university-without-walls[3] and other institutions that provide access and connection to previously excluded publics. Mass communication first brought accounts of sports events to those not present through the next day's newspaper; then through same-day broadcasts; and now through instantaneous, globally available versions of both, and more.

## Specialized Web Sports Usage: Academics in Cyberspace

How do specialized groups use the Internet for sports? A survey of one group—international academic researchers specializing in sports and media—suggests some patterns (Real & Beeson, 2004). The convenience sample of 22 researchers from 11 countries included 7 females and 15 males. Fifteen of them use the Internet daily to access sports information, three weekly, three monthly, one rarely, but none never. Respondents most sought out information on scores and results, followed closely by events and teams. But they also sought information on athletes, features, chats, and research. All 22 had been obtaining online sports information since at least 2001, 10 from 1997 or earlier. The effect of Web usage on other media usage was spread relatively evenly. It led to reduced newspaper use for five, television for four, radio for three, magazines for three, and personal sources for four. Eighteen of the 22 have sports Web sites bookmarked as favorite sites. The sites varied from country to country and included general sports Web sites; sport-specific Web sites; university sports Web sites; and, in one case, a local hockey team Web site.

The Web serves useful purposes for researchers, but most add notes of caution. Among the comments were[4] "Very, very useful. . . . Mostly, helpful and accurate. . . . Good access to material through official sports clubs websites, e.g., financial data. . . . A wonderful source of information for facts and figures, some discussion rooms are very helpful. . . . Economic information (e.g., ownership) outdates so rapidly that the Internet can be a useful way of updating." Frustrations include "Long search for in-depth information. . . . Methodologically difficult. . . . One difficulty of web studies still is the lack of a standard technique for studying the web, so each study has to develop its own methodological framework." The accuracy of Web information is a common concern of researchers: "It is a fine resource if used appropriately and not relied on exclusively. . . . You can use it for information, but always have a second source. . . . Be sure to double check information to ensure accuracy. . . . Check very carefully every source." One respondent explained, "As is the case with everything Internet related, be careful. General/background information (i.e., Olympic medal winners) is no big deal, and legitimate sources, such as a major newspaper, are fine. But I refuse to consider anything from any source that I am not familiar with. And there are far too many of those out there!" Another respondent was concerned with escalating expectations: "It just keeps getting better although there is an increased expectation in terms of the amount of information one should be able to get and process."

The future of the Web offers both steps and jumps forward in the view of survey respondents:

> Faster, smoother and much more reliable. . . . Ticket booking will become more common on the Web. Live streaming will grow. . . . More audio and video streaming. Soon you will be able to access any sporting event from the Web. . . . Convergence is the way we are going; we'll be able to see more and more—and better quality—pictures on the web. . . . Streams of highlights, more in-depth information, a special site with resources for researchers on sports and mediasport.

One respondent suggested some details:

> Broadband access will increase even further and the IOC will eventually feature online Olympic sports once they get their territorial issues sorted out, to name one example. Also, enhanced digital technology will make our typical current technology categories—such as the web vs. analog TV/radio sets—obsolete, as there will be a fusion of both, particularly via wireless technologies.

## Theoretical Implications: How Different Is the Web?

The emergence of strong centralized Web sites—ESPN.com, Sportsline, Nascar.com, cnnsi.com, MLB.com—confirms the importance of the editorial function of media, that is, the ability to coordinate information and make sense of it. Impossible amounts of information are available somewhere on the Web, but coordinating them into a meaningful, accessible assemblage is the service that makes possible Web *usage* as opposed to random Web wandering. The public looks to Web sites for gatekeeping of information and even agenda setting of its relative importance, although search engines like Google make Web agenda setting more audience-driven than in traditional media. Search engines and user-friendly Web site organization are crucial. Mere access to information means little in the age of information overload.

On the other side, access to *producing* information for the medium sets the Web apart from many traditional media where only professionals could produce newspapers or television and the public could only receive them. This open system recalls the emancipatory structuring of media called for by radical theorists such as Enzensberger (1974). This open structure, however, is constricted as major-media Web sites gain predominance over the quirky individual Web sites left over from the Web's first generation.

Media theories of political economy and globalization are clearly central to gaining an intellectual grasp of the world of Web sports. Globalizing trends are unmistakably evident in the Web itself, the ownership structure of media, and increasingly in the world of sport franchises and leagues. These parallel forces are exploited by the large corporations, many of which own both sports and media properties, including dominant Web sites ("Who Owns What," 2004). For example, the Walt Disney Company had revenues of $25 billion in 2000 from its holdings, which included the professional hockey team, The Mighty Ducks of Anaheim, as well as ABC sports; the nine cable television channels of ESPN; and all or part of ESPN.com, Soccernet.com, NBA.com, NFL.com, and Nascar.com. By 2004, the Time Warner Corporation owned the Atlanta Braves (MLB), Hawks (NBA), and Thrashers (NHL) alongside *Sports Illustrated* and 12 other leading sports magazines, TBS Superstation, Turner Network Television (TNT), and cnnsi.com. Rupert Murdoch, however, has taken this media–sport merger trend the furthest. His News Corporation and News Limited are large in the United States, owning the Fox network, 34 television stations, and the DirecTV satellite service. His News Corporation, in addition, owns 18 Fox Sports regional networks, Madison Square Garden Network, and Fox Sports Radio Network. It owns all or part of the American professional sports franchises the Los Angeles Dodgers, New York Rangers, New York Knicks, Los Angeles Kings, and Los Angeles Lakers. Still, Murdoch's *international* combination of sports and media ownership is more extensive yet. He owns major newspapers in London, New York, and Australia; major international satellites; and the television rights to major sports in many parts of the world. It is no surprise that *The Sporting News* placed Murdoch at the top of its list of the 100 most powerful people in sport for two consecutive years, the first person to repeat (Rowe & McKay, 1999).

Given these trends toward convergence and consolidation of ownership, the likelihood of a Spiral of Silence emerges, one in which fringe, minority voices get less hearing and are gradually brought into conformity. Similarly, as dominance of the Web reverts, as seems to be happening, toward the media monopolies, the hegemony of the privileged over Web content and values will marginalize less powerful groups as it has in other media. The *volume* of a distinct opinion, as in the adamancy of sports and political radio callers, should not be mistaken for *differentness*. As Herbert Schiller (1991) warned, abundance is not the same as diversity. Nations and global forces bent on conformity will find ways to enforce it even with the Web, however much more difficult and imperfect that enforcement may be on the Web compared to earlier centrally controlled media.

McLuhan (1964) remarked that the content of a new dominant medium is the previous dominant medium. The content of the novel was its predecessor, the epic poem. The content of film was the novel, the medium that preceded it historically. The content of television was both radio and film. Projecting in this manner, will the content of the Web turn out to be television, its predecessor as the dominant public medium? That, like so many fascinating questions concerning the Web, will be answered only by time.

## Questions for Consideration

1 How does Real's discussion of television and the Internet relate to the larger phenomenon of convergence?

2 A number of companies are now selling sports video games for use on mobile phones. How would you extend Real's discussion to the mobile phone industry?

## Notes

1. The history of ESPN.com is based on an extensive interview with Kevin Jackson (April 19, 2004, Athens, OH), who has been with the site since its beginning and is now chief desk editor for ESPN.com. Industry trade publications extended and confirmed many of his details.

2. This deterritorialization of sport has been explored by Cornel Sandvoss (2003) in *A Game of Two Halves: Football, Television, and Globalization* (London: Routledge). I have experienced this also in my own life as a fan. In 1971, when I moved from the Midwest to Southern California, I could no longer follow my lifelong team, the Chicago Cubs. Within a decade, I discovered to my surprise that I had, instead, become a San Diego Padres fan; because of local media coverage, when the Cubs visited San Diego, I knew none of the Cubs and all of the Padres. By 2000, when I moved back to the Midwest, this had changed dramatically. I could still follow my San Diego Chargers closely through the NFL Sunday Package on satellite and Web sports sources. If you know the Chargers' record in that period you know what a mixed blessing this was.

3. In 2004, I joined the faculty of an innovative Canadian campus, Royal Roads University. Offering undergraduate and graduate degrees through online instruction and annual three-week residencies, this institution illustrates the new institution-without-walls capabilities available for sports, education, and other sectors.

4. Quotations cited here are from the original responses of survey participants. The elisions in these quotations indicate separate statements from *different* respondents.

## References

Angwin, J. (2004). Could U.S. bid to curb gambling on the web go way of prohibition? *Wall Street Journal—Eastern Edition, 244*(22), B1. Retrieved August 23, 2004, from EBSCOhost Web site: http://epnet.com

Beck, D., & Bosshart, L. (2003). Sports and the Internet. *Communication Research Trends, 22*(4), 14.

Burton, R. (1999). A world wide web of sports. *Advertising Age, 70*(46), 66. Retrieved August 23, 2004, from EBSCOhost Web site:http://epnet.com

Cannella, S., & Bechtel, M. (2004). Under review. *Sports Illustrated, 101*(6), 26. Retrieved August 23, 2004, from EBSCOhost Web site: http://epnet.com

Clark, E. (2003). Rivals.com keeps online sports fans in real time. *Network Magazine, 18*(6), 50. Retrieved August 23, 2004, from EBSCOhost Web site: http://epnet.com

Consoll, J. (2003). AOL rushing for more TV yardage. *Media Week, 13*(34), 4. Retrieved August 23, 2004, from EBSCOhost Web site: http://epnet.com

Cox, W., & Salter, M. (1998). The IT revolution and the practice of sports history: An overview and reflection on Internet research and teaching resources. *Journal of Sports History, 25*(2), 283–302.

Cross, M. E., & Vollano, A. G. (1999). *The extent and nature of gambling among college student athletes.* Ann Arbor, MI: University of Michigan Athletics Department. Retrieved August 23, 2004, from EBSCOhost Web site: http://epnet.com

Databank Sports. (2001). *Advertising Age, 72*(30), 25. Retrieved August 23, 2004, from EBSCOhost Web site: http://epnet.com

Enzensberger, H. (1974). *The consciousness industry*. New York: Seabury Press.

Focus Group. (2004, May 25). [Author conducted group interview with ten Ohio University students.] Athens, Ohio: unpublished data.

Gray, R. (2000). Laptop quarterback. *American Journalism Review, 22*(1), 16. Retrieved August 23, 2004, from EBSCOhost Web site: http://epnet.com

Holt, C. (2004). Major League Video. *Video Systems, 30*(4), 58. Retrieved August 23, 2004, from EBSCOhost Web site: http://epnet.com

Jones, D. (2004). Half the story? Olympic women on ABC news online. *Media International Australia-Incorporating Culture & Policy*, 15. Retrieved August 23, 2004, from EBSCOhost Web site: http://epnet.com

Jordan, G. B. (2000). Web pulled viewers away from the Olympic games: From Sydney, it was a tale of two technologies, yesterday's and tomorrow's. *Nieman Reports, 54*(4), 43. Retrieved August 23, 2004, from EBSCOhost Web site: http://epnet.com

Krikke, J. (2004). "Streaming video transforms the media industry." *IEEE Computer Graphics and Applications. 24*(4), 6. Retrieved August 23, 2004, from EBSCOhost Web site:http://epnet.com

Layden, T. (2003). Caught in the net. *Sports Illustrated, 98*(20), 46. Retrieved August 23, 2004, from EBSCOhost Web site: http://epnet.com

McChesney, R. (2004). *The problem of the media: U.S. communication politics in the 21st century*. New York: Monthly Review Press.

McLuhan, M. (1964). *Understanding media: The extensions of man*. New York: McGraw-Hill.

The motivated scholar: Gambling in college. (2002, December 11). *The Wager. 7*(50). Retrieved August 12, 2004, from http://www.thewager.org/Backindex/vol7pdf/wager750.pdf.

NCAA. (2004, May 12). *Executive summary for the National study on collegiate sports wagering and associated health risks*. Retrieved May 26, 2004, from http://www.ncaa.org/gambling/2003National Study/slideShow

Nielsen//NetRatings. (2004a, March 19). March madness draws college hoops fans online. Retrieved August 24, 2004, from http://www.nielsen-netratings.com/pr/pr_040319.2.pdf

Nielsen//NetRatings. (2004b, August 18). U.S. broadband connections reach critical mass, crossing 50 percent mark for web surfers. Retrieved August 24, 2004, from http://www.nielsen-netratings.com/pr/pr_040818.pdf

Nielsen//NetRatings. (2004c, August 24). The Olympic Games sweep fastest growing sites last week. Retrieved August 24, 2004, from http://www.nielsen-netratings.com/pr/pr_040824.pdf

Palser, B. (2004). The difference a year makes. *American Journalism Review, 26*(1), 58. Retrieved August 23, 2004, from EBSCOhost Web site: http://epnet.com

Real, M., & Beeson, D. (2004, May 29). *Sports and the Internet: A preliminary examination of a new medium*. Paper presented at the International Communication Association, New Orleans.

Richtel, M. (2004). An industry that dares not meet in the country of its best customers. *New York Times, 153*(52852), C4. Retrieved August 23, 2004, from EBSCOhost Web site: http://epnet.com

Rowe, D., & McKay, J. (1999). Field of soaps: Rupert v. Kerry as masculine melodrama. In R. Martin & T. Miller (Eds.), *SportCult* (pp.191–210). Minneapolis: University of Minnesota Press.

Salkever, A. (2003, April 15). Sports score big online. *Business Week Online*. Retrieved August 23, 2004, from EBSCOhost Web site: http://epnet.com

Schiller, H. (1991). *Culture inc: The corporate takeover of public expression*. New York: Oxford University Press.

Walker, S. (2003). The long distance fan. *Wall Street Journal—Eastern Edition, 242*(13), W1. Retrieved August 23, 2004, from EBSCOhost Web site: http://epnet.com

Weir, T. (2003, August 22). Online sports betting spins out of control. *USA Today*. Retrieved August 23, 2004, from EBSCOhost Web site: http://epnet.com

"Who owns what." (2004). *Columbia Journalism Review*. Retrieved March 8–15, 2004, from http://www.cjr.org/tools/owners/

# Chapter 24

## HENRY JENKINS

# QUENTIN TARANTINO'S *STAR WARS*?
## Digital Cinema, Media Convergence, and Participatory Culture

A T THE SAME TIME THAT media conglomerates are trying to move their products across media boundaries, audiences are turning to new technologies to create and distribute their own songs, films, and articles. Think movie scene parodies on YouTube; *Saturday Night Live* skit recreations; and song covers uploaded onto social networking sites. In this case study of the *Star Wars* fan films, Henry Jenkins, a scholar of new media and co-founder of the MIT Comparative Media Studies Program, brings these trends of media convergence and participatory culture into conversation. Jenkins is particularly interested in the ways in which fan-produced *Star Wars* films can be considered both as "alternative" (in contrast to mainstream) and "commercial" concepts which, until very recently, were set in opposition. This essay also raises some broader questions about the nature of expression and control in the twenty-first century.

> For me the great hope is now that 8mm video recorders are coming out, people who normally wouldn't make movies are going to be making them. And that one day a little fat girl in Ohio is going be the new Mozart and make a beautiful film with her father's camcorder. For once the so-called professionalism about movies will be destroyed and it will really become an art form.
>
> (Francis Ford Coppola)

> We're going to empower a writer, somewhere in the world, who doesn't have filmmaking resources at his or her disposal. This is the future of cinema—*Star Wars* is the catalyst.
>
> (Jason Wishnow, maker of the digital film, *Tatooine or Bust*)

Maybe you received [a] digital postcard from someone you know during the height of the Monica Lewinsky scandals. Like so much that circulates on the Net, it came without any clear-cut attribution of authorship. The same image now appears on a variety of Web sites without much indication of its origins. Given such an image's decentralized circulation, we have no way of knowing whether it was seen by more or fewer people than saw the Elian Gonzales spoof of the "Whazzup" commercials or the image of Bill Gates as a Borg from *Star Trek: The Next Generation*. Yet, few of us could be ignorant of the source material it parodies—the Brothers Hildebrants' famous poster for the original release of *Star Wars*. In this contemporary and somewhat off-color version, Bill Clinton thrusts his power cigar skyward as a scantly clad Monica clings to his leg, her black thong undies barely visible through her translucent white robe. The sinister face of Ken Starr looms ominously in the background. Hillary shields Chelsea's eyes from this frightful spectacle.

This grassroots appropriation of *Star Wars* became part of the huge media phenomenon that surrounded first the release of the digitally enhanced original *Star Wars* trilogy in 1997 and the subsequent release of *The Phantom Menace* in 1999. Spoofs and parodies of Star Wars were omnipresent the summer of 1999. The trailer for *Austin Powers II: The Spy Who Shagged Me* toyed with trigger-happy audiences eagerly anticipating their first glimpse of *The Phantom Menace* preview reel. It opened with ominous music, heavy breathing, and a space ship interior, as a voice-over narrator explained, "Years ago, a battle was fought and an empire was destroyed. Now the saga will continue." The chair revolves around to reveal not the anticipated Darth Vader (or his later-day counterpart, Darth Maul), but Doctor Evil, who shrugs and says, "You were expecting someone else?" Bowing before the media phenomenon, Austin Powers was released with the slogan, "If you see only one movie this summer, see . . . *Star Wars*. If you see two movies, see *Austin Powers*." *Doonesburry* did a series of cartoons depicting the "refuge camps" awaiting entry into the *Star Wars* films. Weird Al Yankovich, who had previously been successful with a music video, "Yoda", offered his own prequel with "The Saga Begins." *Mad TV* ran two spoofs — one which imagined Randy Newman composing feel-good music for the film, while another featuring George Lucas as an obnoxious, overweight fan boy who seeks inspiration by dressing in a Ewok costume and who hopes to introduce Jar Jar's aunt "Jar-Jar-Mina" in his next release. David Letterman proposed casting smooth-voiced singer Barry White as Darth Vader. Accepting Harvard's Hasty Pudding Award, Samuel L. Jackson offered his own imitation of how Yoda might have delivered his lines from *Pulp Fiction*. Almost all of us can add many more entries to the list of mass-market spoofs, parodies, and appropriations of the *Star Wars* saga—some directed at the film's director, some at its fans, others at the content of the series itself, with Jar Jar Binks bashing becoming the order of the day.

I begin with reference to these various commercial spoofs of *Star Wars* as a reminder that such creative reworkings of science fiction film and television are no longer, and perhaps never were, restricted to fan culture, but have become an increasingly central aspect of how contemporary popular culture operates. Too often, fan appropriation and transformation of media content gets marginalized or exoticised, treated as something that people do when they have too much time on their hands. The assumption seems to be made that anyone who would invest so much creative and emotional energy into the products of mass culture must surely have something wrong with them. In this essay, I will take a very different perspective—seeing media fans as active participants within the current media revolution, seeing their cultural products as an important aspect of the digital cinema movement. If many advocates of digital cinema have sought to democratize the means of cultural production, to foster grassroots creativity by opening up the tools of media production and distribution to a broader segment of the general public, then the rapid proliferation of fan-produced *Star Wars* films may represent a significant early success story for that movement. Force Flicks, one of several databases for fan film production, lists almost 300 amateur-produced Star Wars films currently in circulation on the web and identifies an even larger number of such works as "in production." There is a tremendous diversity of theme, approach, and quality represented in this sample of the current state of amateur digital filmmaking. Some of the films have developed enormous cult followings. Amazon.com, the on-line bookseller, reports that sales of *George Lucas in Love* were outselling *The Phantom Menace* among their video customers, while *Troops* (which offers a Cops-style behind the scene look at the routine experience of stormtroopers serving their hitch on Tatoine) was featured in a two page spread in *Entertainment Weekly* and its director, Kevin Rubio, was reported to have attracted offers of production contracts from major studios.

In this essay, I will explore how and why *Star Wars* became, in Jason Wishnow's words, a "catalyst" for amateur digital filmmaking and what this case study suggests about the future directions popular culture may take. *Star Wars* fan films represent the intersection of two significant cultural trends—the corporate movement towards media convergence and the unleashing of significant new tools which enable the grassroots archiving, annotation, appropriation, and recirculation of media content. These fan films build on long-standing practices of the fan community but they also reflect the influence of this changed technological environment that has dramatically lowered the costs of film production and distribution. I will argue that this new production and distribution context profoundly alters our understanding of what amateur cinema is and how it interects with the commercial film industry. In the end, I want to propose the fan film aesthetic as a significant middle ground between the commercial focus of the new "dot-coms" and the avant-garde aesthetics of the "low-res" film movement, an approach which facilitates grassroots cultural production by building upon our investments in mainstream culture.

## Media in Transition: Two Models

### Media Convergence

As media critics, such as Robert McChesney, have noted, the current trend within the entertainment industry has been toward the increased concentration of media ownership into the hands of a smaller and smaller number of transmedia and transnational conglomerates. Horizontal integration, that is the consolidation of holdings across multiple industries, has displaced the old vertical integration of the Hollywood studios. Companies such as Viacom and Warners Communication maintain interests in film, cable, and network television; video, newspapers and magazines; book publishing and digital media. What emerged are new strategies of content development and distribution designed to increase the "synergy" between the different divisions of the same company. Studios seek content that can move fluidly across media channels. According to the "high concept" logic which has dominated the American cinema since the 1970s, production decisions privileged films with pre sold content based on material from other media ("books"); simple, easily summarized narrative "hooks;" and distinctive "looks," broadly defined characters, striking icons, and highly quotable lines.

Initially, this "books, hooks, and looks" approach required the ability to construct ancillary markets for a successful film or television program. Increasingly, however, it becomes difficult to determine which markets are ancillary and which are core to the success of a media narrative. The process may start with any media channel but a successful product will flow across media until it becomes pervasive within the culture at large—comics into computer games, television shows into films, and so forth. Marsha Kinder has proposed the term, "entertainment supersystem," to refer to the series of intertextual references and promotions spawned by any successful product. The industry increasingly refers to *Star Trek* or *Star Wars* as "franchises," using a term that makes clear the commercial stakes in these transactions. This new "franchise" system actively encourages viewers to pursue their interests in media content across various transmission channels, to be alert to the potential for new experiences offered by these various tie-ins.

As a consequence of these new patterns of media ownership and production, there is increasing pressure toward the technological integration of the various content delivery systems, what industry analysts refer to as convergence. Technological convergence is attractive to the media industries because it will open multiple entry points into the consumption process and at the same time enable consumers to more quickly locate new manifestations of a popular narrative. One may be able to move from watching a television drama to ordering the soundtrack, purchasing videos, or buying products that have been effectively "placed" within the narrative universe.

Such an approach requires the constant development of media content that can provoke strong audience engagement and investment. For this synergy-based strategy to be successful, media audiences must not simply buy an isolated product or experience but rather must buy into a prolonged relationship with a particular narrative universe, which is rich enough and complex enough to sustain their interest over time and thus motivate a succession of consumer choices. This approach encourages studios to be more attentive to audience interests, and studios are using the Net and the Web to directly solicit feedback as well as to monitor unsolicited fan responses to their products.

The strength of this new style of popular culture is that it enables multiple points of entry into the consumption process; the vulnerability is that if audiences fail to engage with the particular content on offer, then that choice has a ripple effect across all of the divisions of the media conglomerate. For every *Batman* that demonstrates the enormous potential of this franchising process, there is a *Dick Tracy* that just about takes the producing company down with it. In such a world, intellectual property, which has proven popular with mass audiences, has enormous economic value, and companies seek to tightly regulate its flow in order to maximize profits and minimize the risk of diluting their trademark and copyright holdings.

*Star Wars* is, in many ways, the prime example of media convergence at work. Lucas's decision to defer salary for the first *Star Wars* film in favor of maintaining a share of ancillary profits has been widely cited as a turning point in the emergence of this new strategy of media production and distribution. Lucas made a ton of money and Twentieth Century Fox learned a valuable lesson. Kenner's *Star Wars* action figures are thought to have been key in re-establishing the value of media tie-in products in the toy industry, and John Williams's score helped to revitalize the market for soundtrack albums. The rich narrative universe of the *Star Wars* saga provided countless images, icons, and artifacts that could be reproduced in a wide variety of forms and sold to diverse groups of consumers. The serialized structures of the films helped to sustain audience interest across a broad span of time and to provide an opportunity to revitalize it as each new sequel or prequel is released. Despite an almost two-decade gap between the release dates for *Return of the Jedi* and *The Phantom Menace*, Lucasfilm continued to generate profits from its *Star Wars* franchise through the production of original novels and comic books, the distribution of video tapes and audio tapes, the continued marketing of *Star Wars* toys and merchandise, and the maintenance of an elaborate publicity apparatus, including a monthly glossy newsletter for *Star Wars* fans. The careful licensing of the *Star Wars* iconography enabled Lucasfilm to form strategic alliances with a multitude of corporate partners, including fast food franchises and soft drink bottlers, which sought to both exploit and enlarge public interest in their forthcoming release. As a consequence, by spring 1999, it was impossible to go anywhere without finding yourself face to face with the distinctive personas of Darth Maul, Queen Amildala, or Jar Jar Binks.

This climate of heightened expectations also fostered the production of the various commercial *Star Wars* parodies mentioned earlier, as other media producers sought to "poke fun" at the hype surrounding *Star Wars* phenomenon while tapping into audience awareness of the film's impending release. Letterman's spoofs of *Star Wars* were as much a part of the publicity campaign for the movie as were the appearance of Natalie Portman or the other film stars on his program. The good-natured trailer of *Austin Powers* played with audience anticipation of the *Star Wars* trailer and became itself a vehicle for creating media buzz about both works.

## Participatory Culture

Patterns of media consumption have been profoundly altered by a succession of new media technologies which enable average citizens to participate in the archiving, annotation, appropriation, transformation, and recirculation of media content. Participatory culture refers to the new style of consumerism that emerges in this environment. If media convergence is to become a viable corporate strategy, it will be because consumers have learned new ways to interact with media content. Not surprisingly, participatory culture is running ahead of the technological developments necessary to sustain industrial visions of media convergence and thus making demands on popular culture which the studios are not yet, and perhaps never will be, able to satisfy. The first and foremost demand consumers make is the right to participate in the creation and distribution of media narratives. Media consumers want to become media producers, while media producers want to maintain their traditional dominance over media content.

A history of participatory culture might well start with the photocopier, which quickly became "the people's printing press," paving the way for a broad range of subcultural communities to publish and circulate their perspectives on contemporary society. The Video-Cassette-Recorder (VCR) enabled consumers to bring the broadcast signal more fully under their control, to build large libraries of personally-meaningful media content, and increasingly gave them tools which facilitated amateur media production. By the early 1990s, media fans were using the VCR to re-edit footage of their favorite television programs to provide raw materials for the production of music videos which enabled them to comment on the relationships between program characters. The availability of low-cost camcorders, and more recently digital cameras, has empowered more and more people to begin to enter directly into the filmmaking process; the power of the camcorder as a means of documentary production was aptly illustrated by the Rodney King video which placed the issue of police brutality in Los Angeles onto the national agenda. Portable technologies, such as the walkman and cell phone, enabled us to carry our media with us from place to place, to create our own "soundtracks" for our real world experiences, and to see ourselves more and more connected within a networked communications environment. Computer and video games encouraged us to see ourselves as active participants in the world of fiction, to "fight like a Jedi" or to "outshoot Clint Eastwood." Digital photography and audio sampling technologies made it easy to manipulate and rework the sights and sounds of our contemporary media environment, paving the way for new forms of cultural expression, ranging from Photoshop collages to music sampling. These technologies do not simply alter the ways that media are produced or consumed; they also help to break down barriers of entry into the media marketplace. The Net opened up new space for public discussions of media content and the Web became an important showcase for grassroots cultural production. On one of my favorite Web sites, known as the Refrigerator, parents can scan in their children's artwork and place them on global display. In many ways, the Web has become the digital refrigerator for the "Do-It-Yourself" ("DIY") movement. Prior to the Web, amateurs might write stories, compose music, or make movies but they had no venue where they could exhibit their works beyond their immediate circles of family and friends. For example, among those "digital movies" indexed by the various *Star Wars* fan Web sites were Super-8 productions dating back to the original release of *A New Hope* (such as *Star Wars Remake*) but only now reaching a broader audience because of their online circulation. The Web made it possible for alternative media productions of all kinds to gain greater visibility and to move beyond localized publics into much broader circulation.

This ability to exhibit grassroots cultural productions has in turn fostered a new excitement about self-expression and creativity. For some, these grassroots cultural productions are understood as offering a radical alternative to dominant media content, providing space for various minority groups to tell their own stories or to question hegemonic representations of their culture. Groups such as the Goths or the Riot Grrls have been quick to explore these political uses of the Web, as have a variety of racial and ethnic groups. Culture jammers seek to use the power of digital media to call into question the consumerist logic of mass media. Others employ the Web as a means of getting greater visibility, of attracting public notice as a prelude for entering directly into the commercial media world. The Web has become an important showcase for productions of film school students, for example. Still others understand their cultural productions in the context of building social ties within a "virtual community" defined around shared interests. The pervasiveness of popular culture content has made it a particularly rich basis for forming social ties within the geographically dispersed population of the Internet. People who may not ever meet face to face and thus have few real-world connections with each other can tap into the shared framework of popular culture to facilitate communication. Fans were early adopters of all of these media technologies and as a consequence, their aesthetics and cultural politics have been highly influential in shaping public understanding of the relationship between dominant and grassroots media. Such groups seek not to shut down the corporate apparatus of the mass media but rather to build on their enjoyment of particular media products, to claim affiliation with specific films or television programs, and to use them as inspiration for their own cultural production, social interaction, and intellectual exchange.

As more and more amateur works have entered into circulation via the Web, the result has been a turn back toward a more folk-culture understanding of creativity. Historically, our culture evolved through a collective process of collaboration and elaboration. Folktales, legends, myths and ballads were built up over time as people added elements that made them more meaningful to their own contexts. The Industrial Revolution resulted in the privatization of culture and the emergence of a concept of intellectual property that assumes that cultural value originates from the original contributions of individual authors. In practice, of course, any act of cultural creation builds on what has come before, borrowing genre conventions and cultural archetypes, if nothing else. The ability of corporations to control their "intellectual property" has had a devastating impact upon the production and circulation of cultural materials, meaning that the general population has come to see themselves primarily as consumers of— rather than participants within—their culture. The mass production of culture has largely displaced the old folk culture, but we have lost the possibility for cultural myths to accrue new meanings and associations over time, resulting in single authorized versions (or at best, corporately controlled efforts to rewrite and "update" the myths of our popular heroes). Our emotional and social investments in culture have not shifted, but new structures of ownership diminish our ability to participate in the creation and interpretation of that culture.

Fans respond to this situation of an increasingly privatized culture by applying the traditional practices of a folk culture to mass culture, treating film or television as if it offered them raw materials for telling their own stories and resources for forging their own communities. Just as the American folk songs of the nineteenth century were often related to issues of work, the American folk culture of the twentieth century speaks to issues of leisure and consumption. Fan culture, thus, represents a participatory culture through which fans explore and question the ideologies of mass culture, speaking from a position sometimes inside and sometimes outside the cultural logic of commercial entertainment. The key difference between fan culture and traditional folk culture doesn't have to do with fan actions but with corporate reactions. Robin Hood, Pecos Bill, John Henry, Coyote, and Br'er Rabbit belonged to the folk. Kirk and Spock, Scully and Mulder, Hans and Chewbacca, or Xena and Gabrielle belong to corporations.

Fan fiction repairs some of the damage caused by the privatization of culture, allowing these potentially rich cultural archetypes to speak to and for a much broader range of social and political visions. Fan fiction helps to broaden the potential interest in a series by pulling its content toward fantasies that are unlikely to gain widespread distribution, tailoring it to cultural niches under-represented within and under-served by the aired material. In theory, such efforts could increase the commercial value of media products by opening them to new audiences, though producers rarely understand them in those terms.

Consider, for example, this statement made by a fan:

> What I love about fandom is the freedom we have allowed ourselves to create and recreate our characters over and over again. Fanfic rarely sits still. It's like a living, evolving thing, taking on its own life, one story building on another, each writer's reality bouncing off another's and

maybe even melding together to form a whole new creation. . . . I find
that fandom can be extremely creative because we have the ability to keep
changing our characters and giving them a new life over and over. We
can kill and resurrect them as often as we like. We can change their
personalities and how they react to situations. We can take a character
and make him charming and sweet or cold-blooded and cruel. We can give
them an infinite, always-changing life rather than the single life of their
original creation.

Fans reject the idea of a definitive version produced, authorized, and regulated by
some media conglomerate. Instead, fans envision a world where all of us can participate
in the creation and circulation of central cultural myths. What is most striking about the
quote above is that the right to participate actively in the culture is assumed to be "the
freedom we have allowed ourselves," not a privilege granted by a benevolent company.
Fans also reject the studio's assumption that intellectual property is a "limited good," to
be tightly controlled lest it dilute its value. Instead, they embrace an understanding of
intellectual property as "shareware," something that accrues value as it moves across
different contexts, gets retold in various ways, attracts multiple audiences, and opens
itself up to a proliferation of alternative meanings. Giving up absolute control over
intellectual property, they argue, increases its cultural value (if not its economic worth)
by encouraging new, creative input and thus enabling us to see familiar characters and
plots from fresh perspectives. Media conglomerates often respond to these new forms
of participatory culture by seeking to shut them down or reigning in their free play with
cultural material. If the media industries understand the new cultural and technological
environment as demanding greater audience participation within what one media
analyst calls the "experience economy," they seek to tightly structure the terms by
which we may interact with their intellectual property, preferring the pre-programmed
activities offered by computer games or commercial Web sites, to the free-form
participation represented by fan culture. The conflict between these two paradigms—
the corporate-based concept of media convergence and the grassroots-based concept
of participatory culture—will determine the long-term cultural consequences of our
current moment of media in transition.

If *Star Wars* was an important ur-text for the new corporate strategy of media
convergence, *Star Wars* has also been the focal point of an enormous quantity of grassroots media production, becoming the very embodiment of the new participatory
culture. Fans began to write original fiction based on the *Star Wars* characters within a
few months of the first film's release, building on an infrastructure for the production
and distribution of fanzines that had first grown up around *Star Trek*. Fan writers
sustained the production of original *Star Wars* stories throughout the "dark years" when
Lucas had seemingly turned his back on his own mythology and the release of *The
Phantom Menace* provoked an enormous wave of new fan stories on the Web.

Grassroots appropriation and transformation of *Star Wars* has not, however, been
restricted to media fandom per se but has spread across many other sectors of the new
DIY culture. Will Brooker, for example, notes the persistence of *Star Wars* references in
punk and techno music, British underground comics, novels like Douglas Coupland's
*Microserfs*, films like Kevin Smith's *Clerks*, and various punk, thrasher, and slacker zines.
Brooker argues that the rebellion depicted in the *Star Wars* films provides a useful model
for thinking about the coalition-based cultural politics which define this whole DIY

movement. The Empire, Brooker argues, is a "colonizing force" which seeks to impose top-down regimentation and demand conformity to its dictates. The Rebellion is a ragtag coalition of different races and cultures, a temporary alliance based on constant flux and movement from base to base, and dependent upon often decentralized and democratic forms of decision-making.

Encouraged by Lucas's romantic myth about grassroots resistance to controlling institutions, these fans have actively resisted efforts by Lucasfilm to tighten its control over intellectual property. Through the years, Lucasfilm has been one of the most aggressive corporate groups in trying to halt fan cultural production. As early as 1981, Lucasfilm had issued legal notices and warnings to fans who published zines containing sexually explicit stories, while implicitly giving permission to publish non-erotic stories about the characters: "Since all of the *Star Wars* Saga is PG-Rated, any story those publishers print should also be PG. Lucasfilm does not produce any X-Rated *Star Wars* episodes, so why should we be placed in a light where people think we do?" Many fans felt that Lucasfilm was claiming the right to ideologically police their shared "fantasies." Much of the writing of fan erotica was pushed underground by this policy, though it continued to circulate informally. In fall 1997, the Usenet discussion group devoted to *Star Wars* responded to increased traffic sparked by the re-release of the "digitally-enhanced" versions of the original films, creating a separate newsgroup where fans could post and critique original fiction set in the *Star Wars* universe. In a rare action, the Usenet hierarchy vetoed the plan, not even allowing it to be presented for a formal vote, claiming that it promoted "illegal activities," i.e., that net discussions of fan fiction encouraged the violation of Lucasfilm's copyright. Many believe that they made this decision based on a series of "cease and desist" letters issued by Lucasfilm attorneys aimed at shutting down *Star Wars* fan Web sites or blocking the circulation of fanzines. Controversy erupted again when, in a shift of position which some felt was more encouraging to fans, Lucasfilm offered *Star Wars* fans free Web space and unique content for their sites, but only under the condition that whatever they created would become the studio's intellectual property. Fan activists were sharply critical of these arrangements, both on political grounds (insisting that it set a precedent which went directly against their own argument that fan fiction constituted a legitimate exercise of their "fair use" rights) and on economic grounds (concerned that such arrangements would make it impossible for them to profit in the future from their creative efforts, noting that some *Star Trek* fan writers had been able to turn their fan fiction into the basis for professional novels).

Yet if studio legal departments still encourage the rigorous enforcement of intellectual property law as a means of regulating the flow of media materials, their creative departments often display a rather different understanding of the intersection between media convergence and participatory culture. The culture industry has its own reasons for encouraging active, rather than passive, modes of consumption. They seek consumers who are mobile, who move between different media channels, and make meaningful links between different manifestations of the same story. Contemporary popular culture has absorbed many aspects of "fan culture" which would have seemed marginal a decade ago. Media producers are consciously building into their texts opportunities for fan elaboration and collaboration—codes to be deciphered, enigmas to be resolved, loose ends to be woven together, teasers and spoilers for upcoming developments—and they leak information to the media which sparks controversy and speculation. Media producers also actively monitor and, in some cases, directly participate in the fan discussions on the Web as a way of measuring grassroots response to their productions. The products which are emerging within this new media culture, then, are more complex in their reliance on back story and foreshadowing, more dependent on audience member's familiarity with character history, more open to serialization, genre-mixing, cross-overs between different fictional universes, and more playful in their reliance on in-joke references or spoofing of other media content. As such, these media producers rely on audience access to an archive of episodes on videotape and the informational infrastructure provided by various fan-generated Web sites and databases. The most adept producers in this new media environment are, in fact, using the Web to reinforce or expand on the information contained in the commercial material.

The old either–or oppositions (co-optation vs. resistance) which have long dominated debates between political economy and cultural studies approaches to media simply do not do justice to the multiple, dynamic, and often contradictory relationships between media convergence and participatory culture. Approaches derived from the study of political economy may, perhaps, provide the best vocabulary for discussing media convergence, while cultural studies language has historically framed our understanding of participatory culture. Neither theoretical tradition, however, can truly speak to what happens at the intersection between the two. The result may be conflict (as in ongoing legal battles for access to or regulation over intellectual property rights), critique (as in the political activism of culture jammers who use participatory culture to break down the dominance of the media industries), challenge (as occurs with the blurring of the lines between professional and amateur products which may now compete for viewer interest if not revenues), collaboration (as in various plans for the incorporation of viewer-generated materials), or recruitment (as when commercial producers use the amateur media as a training ground or testing ground for emerging ideas and talent). In some cases, amateur media draws direct and explicit inspiration from mainstream media content, while in others, commercial culture seeks to absorb or mimic the appropriative aesthetic of participatory culture to reach hip media-savvy consumers. These complex interrelationships provide the context for public awareness and response to amateur digital cinema production around *Star Wars*. In the next section, I will explore more fully the ways that *Star Wars* fan filmmakers have negotiated a place for themselves somewhere between these two competing trends, trying to co-exist with the mainstream media, while opening up an arena for grassroots creativity.

## "Dude, We're Gonna Be Jedi!"

> Maru pays homage to *Star Wars* and is intended to demonstrate to everyone who spent their entire childhood dreaming of wielding a light saber that inspired personal visions can now be realized using tools that are readily available to all of us. Maru was made using a camcorder and a PC with a budget of about $500. . . . Technology and the new media facilitate the articulation and exchange of ideas in ways never before imagined, and we hope that others will harness the power of these tools as we have in order to share their dreams with the world
>
> (amateur filmmakers Adam Dorr, Erik Benson,
> Hien Nguyen, Jon Jones)

*George Lucas in Love*, perhaps the best known of the *Star Wars* parodies, depicts the future media mastermind as a singularly clueless USC film student who can't quite come up with a good idea for his production assignment, despite the fact that he inhabits a realm rich with narrative possibilities. His stoner roommate emerges from behind the hood of his dressing gown and lectures Lucas on "this giant cosmic force, an energy field created by all living things." His sinister next-door-neighbor, an arch rival, dresses all in black and breathes with an asthmatic wheeze as he proclaims, "My script is complete. Soon I will rule the entertainment universe." As Lucas races to class, he encounters a brash young friend who brags about his souped-up sports car and his furry-faced sidekick who growls when he hits his head on the hood while trying to do some basic repairs. His professor, a smallish man, babbles cryptic advice, but all of this adds up to little until Lucas meets and falls madly for a beautiful young woman with buns on both sides of her head. Alas, the romance leads to naught as he eventually discovers that she is his long-lost sister.

*George Lucas in Love* is, of course, a spoof of *Shakespeare in Love* as well as a tribute from one generation of USC film students to another. As codirector Joseph Levy, a 24-year-old recent graduate from Lucas's Alma Mater, explained, "Lucas is definitely the god of USC. . . . We shot our screening-room scene in the George Lucas Instructional Building—which we're sitting in right now. Lucas is incredibly supportive of student filmmakers and developing their careers and providing facilities for them to be caught up to technology." Yet what makes this film so endearing is the way that it pulls Lucas down to the same level of countless other amateur filmmakers and in so doing, helps to blur the line between the fantastical realm of space opera ("A long, long time ago in a galaxy far, far away") and the familiar realm of everyday life (the world of stoner roommates, snotty neighbors, and incomprehensible professors). Its protagonist is hapless in love, clueless at filmmaking, yet somehow he manages to pull it all together and produce one of the top-grossing motion pictures of all time. *George Lucas in Love* offers us a portrait of the artist as a young geek.

One might contrast this rather down-to-earth representation of Lucas—the auteur as amateur—with the way fan filmmaker Evan Mather's Web site constructs the amateur as an emergent auteur. Along one column of the site can be found a filmography, listing all of Mather's productions going back to high school, as well as a listing of the various newspapers, magazines, Web sites, television and radio stations which have covered his work—*La Republica*, *Le Monde*, *The New York Times*, *Wired*, *Entertainment Weekly*, *CNN*, *NPR*, and so forth. Another sidebar provides up to the moment information about his works in progress. Elsewhere, you can see news of the various film festival screenings of his films and whatever awards they have won. A tongue-in-cheek manifesto outlines his views on digital filmmaking: "*. . . no dialogue . . . no narration . . . soundtrack must be monaural . . . length of credits may not exceed 1 / 20 the length of the film . . . nonverbal human or animal utterances are permitted . . . nonsense sounds whilst permitted are discouraged . . . all credits and captions must be in both English and French whilst the type size of the French title may be no greater in height than 1 / 3 the height of the English . . .*" More than 19 digital films are featured with photographs, descriptions, and links that enable you to download them in multiple formats. Another link allows you to call up a PDF file reproducing a glossy full-color, professionally-designed brochure documenting the making of his most recent work, *Les Pantless Menace*, which includes close-ups of various props and settings, reproductions of stills, score sheets, and storyboards, and detailed explanations of how he was able to do the special effects, soundtrack, and editing for the film. We learn, for example, that some of the dialogue was taken directly from Comm-tech chips that were embedded within Hasbro *Star Wars* toys. A biography provides some background: "Evan Mather spent much of his childhood running around south Louisiana with an eight-millimeter silent camera staging hitchhikings and assorted buggery . . . As a landscape architect, Mr. Mather spends his days designing a variety of urban and park environments in the Seattle area. By night, Mr. Mather explores the realm of digital cinema and is the renown creator of short films which fuse traditional hand drawn and stop motion animation techniques with the flexibility and realism of computer generated special effects."

The self-promotional aspects of Mather's site are far from unique. The Force.Net Fan Theater, for example, offers amateur directors a chance to offer their own com-mentary on the production and thematic ambitions of their movies. The creators of *When Senators Attack IV*, for example, give "comprehensive scene-by-scene commentary" on their film: "Over the next 90 pages or so, you'll receive an insight into what we were thinking when we made a particular shot, what methods we used, explanations to some of the more puzzling scenes, and anything else that comes to mind." Such materials often constitute a conscious parodying of the tendency of recent DVD releases to include alternative scenes, cut footage, storyboards, and director's commentary. Many of the Web sites provide information about fan films under production or may even include preliminary footage, storyboards, and trailers for films that may never be completed. Almost all of the amateur filmmakers have developed their own posters and advertising images for their productions, taking advantage of new Pagemaker and Photoshop software packages that make it easy to manipulate and rearrange images using the home computer. In many cases, the fan filmmakers often produce elaborate trailers, complete with advertising catchphrases.

*   *   *

All of this publicity surrounding the *Star Wars* parodies serves as a reminder of what is one of the most distinctive qualities of these amateur films—the fact that they are so public. Mather, for example, reports, "Since I started keeping track in February 1998, this site has been visited by over a half-million people from all seven continents, including such faraway places as Antarctica, Iran, San Marino . . . and Canada." The idea that amateur filmmakers could develop such a global following runs counter to the historical marginalization of grassroots media production.

In her book, *Reel Families: A Social History of Amateur Film*, Patricia R. Zimmerman offers a compelling history of amateur filmmaking in the United States, examining the intersection between nonprofessional film production and the Hollywood entertain-ment system. As Zimmerman notes, a variety of critics and theorists, including Harry Potempkin in the 1920s, Maya Deren in the 1950s, Jonas Mekas and George Kuchar in the 1960s, and Hans Magnus Enzensberger in the 1970s, had identified a radical poten-tial in broadening popular access to the cinematic apparatus, fostering a new public consciousness about how media images are constructed and opening a space for alterna-tive experimentation and personal expression outside of the industrial context of the studio system. Amateur film production emerged alongside the first moving pictures. Tom Gunning has argued that the Lumiere Brothers' shorts were best understood within a context of amateur photography in France, while Zimmerman points to the ways that amateur theater movements in the United States, as well as a prevailing entrepreneurial spirit, provided a base of support of amateur filmmaking efforts in the

1910s. However, the amateur film has remained, first and foremost, the "home movie," in several senses of the term: first, amateur films were exhibited primarily in private (and most often, domestic) spaces lacking any viable channel of distribution to a larger public; second, amateur films were most often documentaries of domestic and family life rather than attempts to make fictional or avant-garde films; and third, amateur films were perceived to be technically flawed and of marginal interest beyond the immediate family. Jokes and cartoons about the painfulness of being subjected to someone else's home movies are pervasive in our culture and represent a devaluing of the potential for an amateur cinema movement. Zimmerman cites a range of different critical appraisals which stressed the artlessness and spontaneity of amateur film in contrast with the technical polish and aesthetic sophistication of commercial films. She concludes, "[Amateur film] was gradually squeezed into the nuclear family. Technical standards, aesthetic norms, socialization pressures and political goals derailed its cultural construction into a privatized, almost silly, hobby." Writing in the early 1990s, Zimmerman saw little reason to believe that the camcorder and the VCR would significantly alter this situation, suggesting that the medium's technical limitations made it hard for amateurs to edit their films and that the only public means of exhibition were controlled by commercial media-makers (as in programs such as *America's Funniest Home Videos*).

Digital filmmaking alters many of the conditions which Zimmerman felt had led to the marginalization of previous amateur filmmaking efforts—the Web provides an exhibition outlet which moves amateur filmmaking from private into public space; digital editing is far simpler than editing Super-8 or video and thus opens up a space for amateur artists to more directly reshape their material; the home PC has even enabled the amateur filmmaker to directly mimic the special effects associated with Hollywood blockbusters like *Star Wars*. As a consequence, digital cinema constitutes a new chapter in the complex history of interactions between amateur filmmakers and the commercial media. These films remain amateur, in the sense that they are made on low budgets, produced and distributed in noncommercial contexts, and generated by nonprofessional filmmakers (albeit often by people who want entry into the professional sphere), yet, many of the other classic markers of amateur film production have disappeared. No longer home movies, these films are public movies—public in that from the start, they are intended for audiences beyond the filmmaker's immediate circle of friends and acquaintances; public in their content, which involves the reworking of personal concerns into the shared cultural framework provided by popular mythologies; and public in their aesthetic focus on existing in dialogue with the commercial cinema (rather than existing outside of the Hollywood system altogether).

Digital filmmakers tackled the challenge of making *Star Wars* movies for many different reasons. *Kid Wars* director Dana Smith, is a 14 year old who had recently acquired a camcorder and decided to stage scenes from Star Wars involving his younger brother and his friends, who armed themselves for battle with squirt guns and Nerf weapons. *The Jedi Who Loves Me* was shot by the members of a wedding party and intended as a tribute to the bride and groom, who were *Star Wars* fans. Some films—such as *Macbeth*—were school projects. Two high school students—Bivenido Concepcion and Don Fitz-Roy—shot the film, which creatively blurs the lines between Lucas and Shakespeare, for their high school advanced-placement English class. They staged light saber battles down the school hallway, though the principal was concerned about potential damage to lockers; the Millennium Falcon lifted off from the gym, though they had to composite it over the cheerleaders who were rehearsing the day they shot that particular sequence. Still other films emerged as collective projects for various *Star Wars* fan clubs. *Boba Fett: Bounty Trail*, for example, was filmed for a competition hosted by a Melbourne, Australia Lucasfilm convention. Each cast member made their own costumes, building on previous experience with science fiction masquerades and costume contests. The film's stiffest competition came from *Dark Redemption*, a production of the Sydney fan community, which featured a light-saber-waving female protagonist, Mara Jade. Their personal motives for making such films are of secondary interest, however, once they are distributed on the Web. If such films are attracting world-wide interest, it is not because we all care whether or not Bievenido Concepcion and Don Fitz-Roy made a good grade on their Shakespeare assignment; we are unlikely to know any of the members of the wedding party that made *The Jedi Who Loves Me*. Rather, what motivates far-away viewers to watch such films is our shared investments in the *Star Wars* universe. These amateur filmmakers have reframed their personal experiences or interests within the context of a popular culture mythology that is known around the world.

In a very tangible sense, digital filmmaking has blurred the line between amateur and professional, with films made for miniscule budgets duplicating special effects which had cost a small fortune to generate only a decade earlier. Amateur filmmakers can make pod racers skim along the surface of the ocean or landspeeders scatter dust as they zoom across the desert. They can make laser beams shoot out of ships and explode things before our eyes. Several fans tried their hands at duplicating Jar-Jar's character animation and inserting him into their own movies with varying degrees of success. (One filmmaker spoofed the defects of his own work, having Jar-Jar explain that he took on a different accent for his part in Lucas's movie and suggesting that he had recently undergone a nose job.) The light saber battle, however, has become the gold standard of amateur filmmaking, with almost every filmmaker compelled to demonstrate his or her ability to achieve this particular effect. Many of the *Star Wars* shorts, in fact, consist of little more than light saber battles staged in Suburban rec-rooms and basements, in empty lots, in the hallways of local schools, inside shopping malls or more exotically against the backdrop of medieval ruins (shot during vacations).

As amateur filmmakers are quick to note, Lucas and Steven Spielberg both made Super-8 fiction films as teenagers and saw this experience as a major influence on their subsequent work. Although these films have not been made available to the general public, some of them have been discussed in detail in various biographies and magazine profiles. These "movie brat" filmmakers have been quick to embrace the potentials of digital filmmaking, not simply as a means of lowering production costs for their own films, but also as a training ground for new talent. Lucas, for example, told *Wired* magazine, "Some of the special effects that we redid for *Star Wars* were done on a Macintosh, on a laptop, in a couple of hours. . . . I could have very easily shot the Young Indy TV series on Hi-8. . . . So you can get a Hi-8 camera for a few thousand bucks, more for the software and the computer; for less than $10,000 you have a movie studio. There's nothing to stop you from doing something provocative and significant in that medium." Elsewhere, he has paid tribute to several of the fan filmmakers, including Kevin Rubio (the director of *Troops*) and Joe Nussbaum (the director of *George Lucas in Love*).

Lucas's rhetoric about the potentials of digital filmmaking seems to have captured the imaginations of amateur filmmakers, and they are struggling to confront the master on his own ground. As Clay Kronke, a Texas A&M University undergraduate who made

*The New World*, explained, "This film has been a labor of love. A venture into a new medium. . . . I've always loved light sabers and the mythos of the Jedi and after getting my hands on some software that would allow me to actually become what I had once only admired at a distance, a vague idea soon started becoming a reality. . . . Dude, we're gonna be Jedi." Kronke openly celebrates the fact that he made the film on a $26.79 budget with most of the props and costumes part of their pre-existing collections of *Star Wars* paraphernalia, that the biggest problem they faced on the set was that their plastic light sabers kept breaking after they clashed them together too often, and that those sound effects he wasn't able to borrow from a *Phantom Menace* PC game were "follied around my apartment, including the sound of a coat hanger against a metal flashlight, my microwave door, and myself falling on the floor several times."

The amateur's pride in recreating professional quality special effects always seems to compete with a recognition of the enormous gap between their own productions and the big-budget Hollywood film they are mimicking. Scholars and critics writing about third world filmmaking have productively described those films as an "imperfect cinema," noting the ways that filmmakers have had to deal with low budgets and limited access to high tech production facilities, making it impossible to compete with Hollywood on its own terms. Instead, these filmmakers have made a virtue out of their limitations, often spoofing or parodying Hollywood genre conventions and stylistic norms through films that are intentionally crude or ragged in style. The abruptness in editing, the roughness of camera movement, the grittiness of film stock, and the unevenness of lighting have become markers of authenticity, a kind of direct challenge to the polished look of a big budget screen production. These amateur filmmakers have also recognized and made their peace with the fact that digital cinema is, in some senses, an "imperfect cinema," with the small and grainy images a poor substitute for the larger-than-life qualities of Lucas's original films when projected on a big screen with Dolby Surroundsound. The trailer for the *Battle of the Bedroom* promises "lots of dodgy special effects," while the team that made *When Senators Attack* chose to call themselves Ultracheese Ltd. In some cases, the films are truly slapdash, relishing their sloppy special effects, embarrassing delivery, and salvage store costumes. *The Throne Room*, for example, brags that it was shot and edited in only thirty minutes, and it shows. Two hammy adolescents cut-up in home movie footage clearly shot their living room and inserted into the *Throne Room* sequence from *A New Hope* to suggest their flirtation with Princess Leia. In others, the productions are quite polished, but the filmmakers still take pleasure in showing the seams. Setting its story in "a long, long time ago in a galaxy far cheaper than this one," Keri Llewellyn's technically-accomplished *Star Wars* reproduces the assault on the Death Star, using origami-folded paper TIE fighters and a basketball painted white as a stand-in for the Death Star. As The Death Star bursts into flames, we hear a loud boink as the elastic string holding it in space snaps, and it falls out of the frame.

\*      \*      \*

We are witnessing the emergence of an elaborate feedback loop between the emerging "DIY" aesthetics of participatory culture and the mainstream industry. The Web represents a site of experimentation and innovation, where amateurs test the waters, developing new practices, themes, and generating materials which may well attract cult followings on their own terms. The most commercially viable of those practices are then absorbed into the mainstream media, either directly through the hiring of new talent or the development of television, video, or big screen works based on those materials, or indirectly, through a second-order imitation of the same aesthetic and thematic qualities. In return, the mainstream media materials may provide inspiration for subsequent amateur efforts, which, in turn, push popular culture in new directions. In such a world, fan works can no longer be understood as simply derivative of mainstream materials but must be understood as themselves open to appropriation and reworking by the media industries.

This process is aptly illustrated by considering the work of popular artists like Kevin Smith, Quentin Tarantino, Mike Judge, Matt Groening, and Kevin Williamson, whose films and television series reflect this mainstreaming of fan aesthetics and politics. Their works often deal explicitly with the process of forming one's own mythology using images borrowed from the mass media. One of the protagonists of *Pulp Fiction*, for example, decides at the end that he wants to "wander the earth" like Kane in television's *Kung Fu*. *Reservoir Dogs* opens with a five-minute discussion of the erotic connotations of Madonna's "Like A Virgin," defining the characters first and foremost through their relationships to popular culture. Characters in *Chasing Amy* engage in animated debates and speculations about the sexuality of the various teens in the *Archie* comics, while *Dazed and Confused* opens with the scene of high school students trying to recall as many different episodes of *Gilligan's Island* as they can, before one of the women offers a devastating critique of how the series builds upon the iconography of male pornography. Kevin Smith's films make recurring in-joke references to *Star Wars*, including a debate about the ethical obligations of the independent contractors who worked on the Death Star (*Clerks*), a comic episode when Silent Bob becomes convinced that he can actually perform Jedi mind tricks (*Mall Rats*), and a long rant about the "blackness" of Darth Vader (*Chasing Amy*); Smith devotes an entire issue of his *Clerks* comic book to various characters' attempts to corner the market on collectible *Star Wars* action figures.

The protagonist of Williamsons's television series, *Dawson's Creek*, decorates his room with posters for Steven Spielberg films, routinely discusses and critiques classic and contemporary films with the other characters on the series, and draws inspiration from them for the creation of his own videos. Tarantino's whole aesthetic seems to have emerged from his formative experiences working at a video store. In such an environment, older and newer films are more or less equally accessible; some movie is always playing on the monitor and providing a background for everyday interactions. These video store experiences encourage a somewhat scrambled but aesthetically productive relationship to film history. Tarantino, Smith, Williamson, and their contemporaries make films that attract the interests of other video store habitues, much as earlier generations of filmmakers—the French New Wave or the American Movie Brats—made movies for other cineastes. Much as the cineaste filmmakers set scenes in movie theatres or made whole movies centering around their protagonist's obsessions with the filmgoing experience, these newer filmmakers frequently cast video store clerks as protagonists (*Clerks, Scream*), celebrating their expertise about genre conventions or their insightful speculations about popular films. This video store aesthetic mixes and matches elements from different genres, different artistic movements, and different periods with absolute abandon. Tarantino's tendency toward quotation runs riot in the famous Jack Flash restaurant sequence in *Pulp Fiction*, where all of the service personnel are impersonating iconic figures of the 1950s and the menu uses different comedy teams to designate different shake flavors. As the John Travolta character explains, "It's like a wax museum with a pulse," a phrase which might describe Tarantino's whole approach to filmmaking. Even his casting decisions, such as the use of *Medium Cool*'s Robert Forrester and blaxploitation star Pam Greers in *Jackie Brown*, constitute quotations and appropriations from earlier film classics.

Not surprisingly, the works of these "video store filmmakers" have been deeply influential on the emerging generation of amateur digital filmmakers—almost as influential in fact as *Star Wars* itself. Jeff Allen, a 27-year-old "HTML monkey" for an Atlanta-based Internet company, for example, made *Trooperclerks*, a spoof of the trailer for *Clerks*, which deals with the drab routine confronted by the stormtroopers who work in convenience stores and video rental outlets on board the death star. The short spoof, which was immediately embraced and promoted by Kevin Smith's View Askew, was later followed by a half-hour animated film based on the same premise, made in response to the news that *Clerks* was being adapted into an animated network series. Allen's focus on *Clerks* came only after he considered and rejected the thought of doing a *Star Wars* parody based on Tarantino's *Reservoir Dogs*. Similarly, Allen Smith heads a team that is producing a feature-length animated film, *Pulp Phantom*, which offers a scene-by-scene spoof of *Pulp Fiction*, recast with characters from *Star Wars*. At writing, the team has produced more than ten episodes for the Web, taking the story up to the point where paid assassin Darth Maul races the over-dosing Princess Amadala to the home of drug dealer, Hans Solo, frantic lest he get into trouble with her jealous gangland husband, Darth Vader. In a particularly inspired bit of casting, Jar Jar Binks plays the geeky college student who, in a still to be anticipated installment, Maul accidentally blows away in the back of Boba Fett's vehicle. "Fan boy" filmmakers like Smith and Tarantino are thus inspiring the efforts of the next generation of amateur filmmakers, who are, in turn, developing cult followings that may ultimately gain them access to the commercial mainstream. *The Pulp Phantom* Web site, for example, includes a mechanism where loyal fans can receive e-mail each time a new installment of the series gets posted.

This cyclical process has only accelerated since the box office success of *The Blair Witch Project*, which presented itself as an amateur digital film (albeit one which got commercial distribution and challenged *Phantom Menace* at the box office in the Summer of 1999) and had built public interest through its sophisticated use of the Web. *The Blair Witch Project*, in turn, has inspired countless Web-based amateur parodies (including *The Jar Jar Binks Project* and *The Wicked Witch Project*) and has sparked increased public and industry interest in the search for subsequent amateurs who can break into the mainstream, while the bigger budget sequel to *The Blair Witch Project* takes as its central image the explosion of amateur filmmakers who have come to Birkerts, Maryland in hopes of making their own documentaries on the mysterious deaths.

## Conclusion

> I personally find the opportunity to explore this new form of entertainment and creative expression both stimulating and liberating. While much of what we have learned throughout our careers will apply, I am also certain that new and unusual aesthetic values will quickly evolve—shaped by the medium itself, the public and the creative collaborations which this company will encourage.
>
> (Ron Howard)

> Just as MTV introduced a new entertainment forum for music videos, we think this new enterprise will offer a new form of entertainment for the rapidly growing population of Internet users. POP.com has the capability not only to offer a variety of entertainment options, but to tap into an as-yet-undiscovered talent pool that is as global as the Internet itself.
>
> (Jeffrey Katzenberg)

What is the future of digital cinema? One position sees digital cinema as an extension of avant-garde filmmaking practices, opening a new space for formal experimentation and alternative cultural politics and offering experimental artists access to a broader public than can be attracted to screenings of their works at film festivals, museums, or university classes. Another position, represented by the founders of Pop.com above, sees the digital cinema as a potential new site for commercial developments, an extension of the logic of media convergence, a kind of MTV for the 21st century. In this vision, established filmmakers, such as Steven Spielberg or Tim Burton, can produce shorter and riskier works, emerging talents can develop their production skills, and works may move fluidly back and forth between the Web, television, film, and computer games. Interestingly, both groups want to tap into the hipness of "DIY" culture, promoting their particular vision of the future of digital cinema in terms of democratic participation and amateur self-expression, pinning their hopes, as Coppola suggests, on the prospect that a "little fat girl" from the midwest will become the "Mozart" of digital filmmaking. Both visions have inherent limitations: the "low-res" movement's appeals to avant-garde aesthetics, its language of manifestos, and its focus on film festival screenings may well prove as elitist as the earlier film movements it seeks to supplant, while the new commercial version of the digital cinema may re-inscribe the same cultural gatekeepers who have narrowed the potential diversity of network television or Hollywood cinema.

The *Star Wars* fan films discussed here represent a potentially important third space between the two. Shaped by the intersection between contemporary trends toward media convergence and participatory culture, these fan films are hybrid by nature—neither fully commercial nor fully alternative, existing as part of a grassroots dialogue with mass culture. We are witnessing the transformation of amateur film culture from a focus on home movies toward a focus on public movies, from a focus on local audiences toward a focus on a potential global audience, from a focus on mastering the technology toward a focus on mastering the mechanisms for publicity and promotion, and from a focus on self-documentation toward a focus on an aesthetic based on appropriation, parody, and the dialogic. Coppola's "little fat girl" has found a way to talk back to the dominant media culture, to express herself not simply within an ideolect but within a shared language constructed through the powerful images and narratives that constitute contemporary popular culture. She will find ways to tap into the mythology of *Star Wars* and use it as a resource for the production of her own stories, stories which are broadly accessible to a popular audience and which, in turn, inspire others to create their own works much as Lucas created *Star Wars* through the clever appropriation and transformation of various popular culture influences (ranging from Laurel and Hardy to *Battleship Yomamoto* and *The Hidden Fortress*).

This third space will survive, however, only if we maintain a vigorous and effective defense of the principle of "fair use," only if we recognize the rights of consumers to participate fully, actively, and creatively within their own culture, and only if we hold in check the desires of the culture industries to tighten their control over their own intellectual property in response to the economic opportunities posed by an era of media convergence. At the moment, we are on a collision course between a new economic and legal culture which encourages monopoly power over cultural mythologies and new technologies which empower consumers to archive, annotate, appropriate, and re-circulate media images. The recent legal disputes around Napster represent only a skirmish in what is likely to be a decade long war over intellectual property, a war which will determine not simply the future direction of digital cinema but the nature of creative expression in the 21st century.

## Questions for Consideration

1   What types of media products are most likely to attract audience participation and appropriation?

2   How is the type of amateur participation that Jenkins describes similar to the model of peer production that Yochai Benkler discusses in another reading (Chapter 21)? How is it different?

# Chapter 25

# ETHAN SMITH AND PETER LATTMAN

## DOWNLOAD THIS
### YouTube Phenom has a Big Secret

CONTEMPORARY DISCUSSIONS OF THE VIDEO sharing site YouTube often emphasize its role in helping ordinary people achieve their "15 minutes of fame," recalling much of the talk surrounding reality TV when it emerged on the scene nearly a decade ago. Yet, also like reality TV, some of the so-called ordinary people on YouTube have a team of agents and publicists helping them out. You may recall, for instance, the highly publicized Lonelygirl15 hoax, where teenage blogger Bree turned out to be an aspiring actress. In the following article, which was published in the *Wall Street Journal* in 2007, Ethan Smith and Peter Lattman tell the story of YouTube phenomenon Marie Digby. Although Digby appeared to be an amateur singer posting homemade music videos of herself, she was actually a signed recording artist whose YouTube strategy was developed by her recording company. Not only do cases like these raise ethical issues, but they also point the way toward understanding the new directions of marketing in the twenty-first century.

A 24-year-old singer and guitarist named Marie Digby has been hailed as proof that the Internet is transforming the world of entertainment.

What her legions of fans don't realize, however, is that Ms. Digby's career demonstrates something else: that traditional media conglomerates are going to new lengths to take advantage of the Internet's ability to generate word-of-mouth buzz.

Ms. Digby's simple, homemade music videos of her performing popular songs have been viewed more than 2.3 million times on YouTube. Her acoustic-guitar rendition of the R&B hit "Umbrella" has been featured on MTV's program "The Hills" and is played regularly on radio stations in Los Angeles, Sacramento and Portland, Ore. Capping the frenzy, a press release last week from Walt Disney Co.'s Hollywood Records label declared: "Breakthrough YouTube Phenomenon Marie Digby Signs With Hollywood Records."

What the release failed to mention is that Hollywood Records signed Ms. Digby in

2005, 18 months before she became a YouTube phenomenon. Hollywood Records helped devise her Internet strategy, consulted with her on the type of songs she chose to post, and distributed a high-quality studio recording of "Umbrella" to iTunes and radio stations.

In an August 16 blog posting on her MySpace page, Ms. Digby wrote: "I NEVER in a million years thought that doing my little video of Umbrella in my living room would lead to this. tv shows, itunes, etc!!!"

Ms. Digby's MySpace and YouTube pages don't mention Hollywood Records. Until last week, a box marked "Type of Label" on her MySpace Music page said, "None." After inquiries from *The Wall Street Journal*, the entry was changed to "Major," though the label still is not named.

The artist and her label say there's nothing untoward about the campaign. In interviews, Ms. Digby and executives at the company describe her three-month string of successes as part of a lengthy process of laying the groundwork for the upcoming release of her debut album.

Ms. Digby says she doesn't mention her record label on her Web sites because "I didn't feel like it was something that was going to make people like me."

Ms. Digby certainly isn't the first professional to feign amateur status on YouTube. Last year, "LonelyGirl15" was revealed to be a 19-year-old actress, working with film-makers represented by the Creative Artists Agency.

The fact that a big company supported Ms. Digby's ruse reflects how dearly media giants want in on the viral revolution that's changing how young consumers learn about new entertainment—even if it means a tiny bit of sleight-of-hand. It also reflects how difficult it is for new recording artists to get noticed now that young fans are paying more attention to Web sites such as Google Inc.'s YouTube and News Corp.'s MySpace than to traditional media like commercial radio.

"There are significant challenges in breaking new artists now, but there are also amazing opportunities," says Ken Bunt, Hollywood Records' senior vice president for marketing who helped devise Ms. Digby's campaign. "People get so mired in the difficulties they don't say, 'What opportunities does online present?' This is a great example of an opportunity."

Though all involved say that Hollywood Records' role in her online rise has been limited, label executives say they did nothing to discourage Ms. Digby from conveying the impression that she had stumbled into the spotlight. Ms. Digby says she chose the songs. Hollywood Records bought the Apple Inc. laptop computer and software that Ms. Digby—who lives with her parents in Los Angeles's upscale Brentwood neighbor-hood—used to post her YouTube videos. Her version of "Umbrella" that is being sold at Apple's iTunes Store is a high-quality studio recording made in June by Hollywood Records, which also made it available to radio stations.

Ms. Digby, whose exotic looks reflect her Japanese and Irish heritage, began writing songs as a high-school student and set off in search of a music career during her freshman year at the University of California, Berkeley. She says she found herself flying back to Los Angeles almost every week to play solo gigs at open-microphone nights at clubs. At age 19, she left Berkeley and concentrated full-time on music.

While Ms. Digby won regular bookings at nightclubs, things didn't begin to click until a chance encounter with Barry Krost, a music manager whose past clients have included Cat Stevens. He took her on as a client and in early 2005 secured her a publishing deal with Rondor Music, a publisher that is part of Vivendi SA's Universal Music Group.

In late 2005, Ron Moss, Rondor's executive vice president, connected Ms. Digby to a Hollywood Records executive named Allison Hamamura, who was immediately taken with the singer. Before the year was out, Hollywood Records had signed Ms. Digby. Since then, the label has worked with the singer on her debut album of original songs. The album was produced by Tom Rothrock, who also recorded a recent hit record by British singer James Blunt.

Once the album was completed late last year, Ms. Digby and her label began looking for ways to gain visibility. "I was coming out of nowhere," Ms. Digby says. "I wanted to find a way to get some exposure."

That's when the idea of posting simple videos of cover songs came up. "No one's going to be searching for Marie Digby, because no one knows who she is," Mr. Bunt, the Hollywood Records senior vice president, reasoned. So she posted covers of hits by Nelly Furtado and Maroon 5, among others, so that users searching for those artists' songs would stumble on hers instead. Her version of Rihanna's "Umbrella" proved a nearly instant hit.

As Ms. Digby's star rose, other media outlets played along. When Los Angeles adult-contemporary station KYSR-FM, which calls itself "Star 98.7," interviewed Ms. Digby in July, she and the disc jockey discussed her surprising success. "We kind of found her on YouTube," the DJ, known as Valentine, said. Playing the lucky nobody, Ms. Digby said: "I'm usually the listener calling in, you know, just hoping that I'm going to be the one to get that last ticket to the Star Lounge with [pop star] John Mayer!" The station's programming executives now acknowledge they had booked Ms. Digby's appearance through Hollywood Records, and were soon collaborating with the label to sell "Umbrella" as a single on iTunes.

"We did discover this artist through YouTube," says KYSR Program Director Charese Fruge. The DJ couldn't be reached for comment.

"I don't think we need a television show to find talent in America," crowed NBC late-night talk show host Carson Daly, introducing a performance by Ms. Digby last month. "We have the Internet." Mr. Daly's music booker, Diana Miller, says she booked the singer through Hollywood Records' public-relations department.

At the show's taping, Ms. Digby gave a backstage interview that was posted online by NBC. "I just did this YouTube video two months ago and never, ever imagined that it would actually get me on TV or radio or anything like that," she said. "I just did it in my living room and it blew up first on YouTube and then I guess it got to Star 98.7 and then Carson Daly found me so that's why I'm here."

Most of Ms. Digby's new fans seem pleased to believe that they discovered an underground sensation. A YouTube user posting a message in response to a cover of Linkin Park's "What I've Done" wrote, "you truely have talent! get urself out there . . . if u really wanted im positive u could land some sick record deals!! id buy a CD 4 sure!"

At a concert last week at a Los Angeles nightclub called the Hotel Cafe, Ms. Digby played to a sold-out crowd of young fans. Even with the club's handful of tables reserved for Hollywood Records executives and their guests, Ms. Digby continued to play the ingenue. Introducing "Umbrella," Ms. Digby told the audience: "I just turned on my little iMovie, and here I am!"

**Questions for Consideration**

1    Would you consider what Digby and her record label did ethical? Why or why not?

2    What do the examples of LonelyGirl15 and Digby suggest about the role of marketing in new media environment?

PART FIVE

# Advertising and Public Relations

# INTRODUCTION

THE LATEST STATISTICS ON THE ubiquity of advertising in America are quite staggering. According to a 2007 *The New York Times* article, an average person can encounter up to 5,000 advertising messages a day![1] In addition to their placement in traditional and new media, ads are also appearing in some highly unusual places. As the *Times* article went on to explain, ads are now showing up on everything from supermarket eggs to airline motion sickness bags to the sides of buildings. Further, readily identifiable ads are only part of a wider system of commercial messages. Think of event sponsorship, word-of-mouth campaigns, and product placement. The increase in these activities has led some professionals and scholars to favor the sweeping phrase "marketing communication" to indicate all forms of commercial-message production and distribution in society.

While the sheer presence of so many ads, known in the business as "clutter," is causing advertisers to rethink their practices, technology, too, is a driver of change. As audiences increasingly go online for news, information, and entertainment, advertisers are following. For many advertisers, the Internet and other digital media provide a unique promise: the individualized targeting of messages. For example, if you frequently visit restaurant review web sites, you may start to receive pop-up banners advertising new dining places. As you will read about later, mobile phones may increase such instances of ad customization.

Some people do not like advertising simply because they don't want to be bothered, and they feel that ads bother them. But advertising and marketing communication in today's media environment also raise other types of privacy concerns, as well as big topics such as commercialism and social ritual, and commercialism and democracy. We hope that reading them prompts you to think critically about what the ad-supported system asks of you as a consumer and as a citizen.

## Note

1    Louise Story, "Anywhere the eye can see, it's an ad." *New York Times*, January 15, 2007, www.nytimes.com

# Chapter 26

# JAMES B. TWITCHELL

# THE WORK OF ADCULT

**H**AVE YOU EVER NOTICED HOW many retail outlets seem to have an aisle reserved for holiday merchandise such as Valentine's Day candy, American-flag themed picnic ware, Halloween costumes, and Christmas decorations? Have you ever noticed how far in advance of the holidays this merchandise appears? It is perhaps not surprising that advertisers are eager to reap the financial rewards of holidays and events. What may surprise you, however, is the extent to which advertisers have influenced these rituals over the years. In the following essay, excerpted from James Twitchell's 1997 book *Adcult USA: The Triumph of Advertising in American Culture*, Twitchell traces the history of many popular "festivals of consumption." He also suggests some of the ways in which advertisers' influence continues to shape how we experience these holidays. In doing this, Twitchell prompts us to consider the taken-for-granted ways in which advertisers shape our culture and society.

## When you Care Enough to Send the Very Best: Festivals of Consumption in Adcult

We move through an invisible gel of time. In ancient days we knew where we were in the time flow by the amount of light and dark that occurred each day. And the rhythms of the seasons showed us where we were in our life*time* as we became aware of the cycles of vegetation. To mark these limits we have the light delineations of days, months, and years, as well as the growth delineations of furrowing, planting, tending, and harvesting. To mark these time blocks, we often celebrate some rite of passage.

The rise of the world's great religions saw the co-opting of these demarcations as they became tied to some mythic paradigm, no longer just of light and growth, but of human purpose. This syncretism is nowhere better seen than in the colonizing of ancient time markers by nascent Christianity. Not by happenstance does the birth of

Jesus occur at the winter solstice; not by happenstance does the Resurrection happen in the springtime (on the Sunday following the first full moon after the vernal equinox). Nor do the attendant ceremonies of these time marks, in which we gather together to ask the Lord's blessing, exchange gifts, eat special foods, and sometimes exchange still more gifts, have anything to do with whimsy. These ceremonies tell us where we are in time. The power of Christianity (and of any other enduring organizing system) is that it never does away with the old pattern but continually adapts it to changing needs.

So it is with Adcult. The ancient rhythms of the day, the artificial separation of the week, the solar mandates of the year are remembered in Adcult, as they are in Christianity, with specific services in which we are led from one time zone to another. From morning devotion to evening vespers to nighttime prayer, from Sunday service to Sunday service, through a year punctuated with festivals of thanksgiving and grieving, Christians keep time with their church. The clock is on the church steeple and the church bells ring out these changes. From breakfast and morning news through coffee break to late-afternoon cocktail time to sign-off, from Saturday shopping to Saturday shopping, through a year punctuated by festivals of consumption and sales, modern Adcultists keep time with their advertising. Our clock is no longer on the church but inside the television set. We move in half-hour blocks from morning chat through midday soap operas to late afternoon reruns to the newshour to early prime to prime time to late fringe and finally into late night. During the teleyear we move from the introduction of the new shows in the fall through the sweeps weeks of winter to the reruns of summer. (Or at least we used to, until the chaos of cable.)

We begin our circadian rhythm with a meal called breakfast. Before Messrs. Post and Kellogg this meal consisted of breaking fast by finishing last night's dinner. In fact, if you go to Western Europe where break-fast traditions are still in force, you find the same meat courses of generations ago. Often table scraps were reheated—rashers and bangers and blood pudding. (What we didn't eat then went to the floor as dog food. There was no "dog food" until Ralston Purina's ad agency created it.) The abundant supply of grains, and the technology to treat and package them, led to the advertising claim that "Breakfast is the most important meal of the day." It is an important stop on "the road to Wellville." Cereal at breakfast is a uniquely American custom, embedded by the constant repetition of spurious claims of improved health (just like dog food) and energy (just like patent medicine). Breakfast stuck.

The coffee break, however, took more doing. Here we have a drug, caffeine, which stimulates the nervous system and provides a short-term increase in attentiveness. The producers of coffee, once they were able to grow and cure it in bulk, didn't know where to position their product. Was it a breakfast drink or a dinner drink? Initially it made sense to make coffee time near the end of the workday, and indeed many early ads show coffee being consumed near quitting time.

So too the cocktail hour, a celebration of yet another addictive drug, comes after quitting time in the industrial age. However, drinking alcohol comes during the day in agrarian cultures. In the eighteenth century the rise of first cheap gin, then rum, posed a hazard for the machine age. Although such drinks were not only a triumph of technology but also a sign of agricultural proficiency (because they depend on producing a surplus of rye, corn, wheat, barley, sugar cane, apples, and potatoes), their consumption during the day was a hindrance to orderly production. "Blue Monday," for instance, came about because the culture was unable to separate drunkenness from the workweek. It was resolved, as Witold Rybczynski has argued in *Waiting for the Weekend*

(1991), with the separation of Saturday, not Monday, from the week into the weekend. So too the cocktail hour is the way to separate work and play. Coffee went to the morning, alcohol to early evening.

Although the stars and the planets make the years, months, and days, people make the workweek and the workweek depends on the weekend. Who knows why we separate work from leisure—do we work to have leisure or is leisure a preparation for work?—but we separate it in almost every culture. No one knows how the seven-day cycle developed, but somehow it stuck. Across cultures and through history, dividing time into seven-day chunks is the habit of humans. Some years ago the Ford Foundation calculated that nine days would make more economic sense, as we would work in three shifts of three days with a three-day rest, but as much as machines would profit, humans wouldn't. We like seven days—that's all there is to it. Perhaps this has to do with digestion and food spoilage, or perhaps it is simply that enough work is simply enough; no one knows. But this much is clear. To separate workweeks from each other, cultures need an off-on switch with a day of transition. This rest day gets coded in early modern times with religious sanctions. So, to summarize, the "rest day" is demanded by workers, sanctified by a supernatural force, and reinforced by institutional events. Hence the universal appeal of what we call Sunday. But what about Saturday? Why don't we have six workdays and then rest day?

We did. Until the eighteenth century it was work, work, work, stop, work, work . . . in chunks of six and one. Then a number of interesting developments shifted the rhythm to five and two. These developments are at the heart of Adcult. First, efficient production meant surplus, and surplus means that market day was no longer a time where you *could* exchange stuff but a time when you *had* to exchange stuff. To capture the economies of mass production markets had to be expanded, and to do this the distribution systems had to be enlarged. Second, workers now needed time off to buy the excess goods. Third—and here the fun begins—just as the industrial revolution is providing buyers and sellers of surplus goods and labor, the brewers are making it possible to have not just a cocktail hour but a real bender. This bender occurs naturally enough on Sunday afternoon. It is paid for on Monday. "Keeping Saint Monday" was a common and thoroughly inefficient way of equilibrating work and leisure. It was prized by certain groups, like cobblers, barbers, and tailors who simply started work Monday afternoon. No one much cared about them, but when factory workers started to pay allegiance to Saint Monday, something had to be done. When you fire up a steam engine, everyone should be sober and ready to work.

The Early Closing Society, started in the middle of the nineteenth century, was almost immediately successful in trading Monday for Saturday. It should have been, for almost every important interest group supported it, except, of course, for those cobblers, tailors, and barbers. (Many barbers still take Monday off but aren't sure why.) The church, the leaders of industry, and especially the retailers, all found the relocation of consumption, whether alcohol or piece goods, to Saturday much more to their liking. Some precedent for moving the time off from Monday to Saturday already existed. Printers and some home workers (usually weavers) had only half-Saturday work, either because there were no Sunday papers or because their work was picked up and paid for on Saturday—called reckoning day.

With the advent of trains and the ability to gather either at a country home (for the wealthy) or at a fair (for the working people), the idea of the "week-end" took hold. After World War I construction unions joined the movement to solidify the workweek by pushing for the eight-hour day ("eight hours for work, eight hours for rest, eight hours for what we will"), and the Saturday shutdown switch was installed. Some unions made up of predominantly Jewish workers, like the Amalgamated Clothing Workers of America, had already taken Saturday off. They got no argument from enlightened capitalists like Henry Ford. More time to shop meant more time to buy. Blue laws, those most peculiar edicts written on blue paper in the 1780s, were not repealed, partly because retailers lobbied for them. Close down Sunday, move Monday to Saturday, and open up Saturday for retail. The dance hall revelries and later the movie matiness reinforced the saturnalian quality of Saturday. Whatever Saturday may have been—a method to get rid of food before it spoiled, a way to increase work by organizing Monday, a placebo to counteract boredom, a way to get parishioners to church—we all know what it has become. It has become shopping day at the mall.

To really observe and appreciate the effect of Adcult on our sense of time, however, we need to turn from the circadian and weekly rituals of consumption to the calendric festivals. For here, supplanting such religious and political events that crossed the Atlantic, like Shrove Tuesday, Twelfth Night, Ash Wednesday, Whitsuntide, and even Punkie Night, are a series of holiday events sustained by commercial interests. In the Darwinian struggle for attention these festivals of consumption have outdistanced the ancient festivals of church time. *Holiday*, which derives its meaning from *holy day*, is now more appropriately Consume-like-crazy Day. Festivals may begin in the woods, they may move into the apse, but they end up at Sears.

With the eager help of my students let me take you through the year of a young adult. This thoroughly unscientific study was accomplished with the "instrument" in figure 26.1 and class discussion. Let's start the year at the beginning. New Year's Eve, a festival of enthusiastic drinking eagerly attended by adolescents, is almost always celebrated with the accompaniment of a television set. Else how would they know to sing "Auld Lang Syne" at midnight? Television shows the party goers how to respond when the ball falls and the howling begins. It shows them Times Square, a veritable son et lumière of bill-board art called spectaculars in the trade. Although most of my students have not been to Times Square, they know about the Sony Jumbotron video screen, some twenty-three feet wide and four stories high. They know about these signs and how to respond to them, because they are a fixture of modern sports and concert entertainment. They are what we have for the recitative reading of the church service. Watch the sign. But the real importance of New Year's is not that we have to go to Times Square to celebrate it in accordance with some signs we see on TV. The real importance is that it marks the end of the football bowl season and the preparation for Super Bowl Sunday.

While my students are at home with family for New Year's, they are all together at school for the Super Bowl. All the men and most of the women will watch this game, and although many will not care much for the combat, it is nothing short of amazing how much they care for the advertising. They know new campaigns will break and they know things will move fast, so they pay attention. I have actually observed a student distressed that he missed the Apple 1984 ad that was shown only once during the game. He now watches, hoping to see another such important cultural event. Needless to say, they all know about the Bud Bowl.

The next event in their lives will be Valentine's Day. Here we have an almost pure example of syncretism, as Christianity layered the celebration of the martyrdom of St. Valentine over the Roman Feast of Lupercalia, which in turn hijacked the Greek

The last time each of the following events occurred, what did you do? with whom? where? what special objects were involved?

| Event | ACTIVITY | | | | | | | WHO | | | WHERE | | | | | | SPECIAL OBJECTS | | |
|---|---|---|---|---|---|---|---|---|---|---|---|---|---|---|---|---|---|---|---|
| | T.V. SPECIAL | SPECIAL FOOD | PARTY | GO OUT (VISIT, MOVIE ETC.) | RELIGIOUS | ALCOHOL | ALONE | IMMEDIATE FAMILY | RELATIVES | FRIENDS | OWN HOME | RELATIVES OR FRIENDS HOME | RESTAURANT OR NIGHTCLUB | CHURCH/SYNAGOGUE | PUBLIC PLACES | NOTHING | CARD OR PHONE | DECORATIONS | GIFT(S) |
| NEW YEAR'S | | | | | | | | | | | | | | | | | | | |
| VALENTINE'S DAY | | | | | | | | | | | | | | | | | | | |
| MEMORIAL DAY | | | | | | | | | | | | | | | | | | | |
| 4TH OF JULY | | | | | | | | | | | | | | | | | | | |
| LABOR DAY | | | | | | | | | | | | | | | | | | | |
| BIRTHDAY (OWN) | | | | | | | | | | | | | | | | | | | |
| MOTHER'S DAY | | | | | | | | | | | | | | | | | | | |
| FATHER'S DAY | | | | | | | | | | | | | | | | | | | |
| ANNIVERSARY | | | | | | | | | | | | | | | | | | | |
| GRANDPARENT'S DAY | | | | | | | | | | | | | | | | | | | |
| ELECTION NIGHT | | | | | | | | | | | | | | | | | | | |
| SUPERBOWL | | | | | | | | | | | | | | | | | | | |
| MISS AMERICA PAGEANT | | | | | | | | | | | | | | | | | | | |
| PRO SPORTS | | | | | | | | | | | | | | | | | | | |
| ACADEMY AWARDS | | | | | | | | | | | | | | | | | | | |
| ST PATRICK'S DAY | | | | | | | | | | | | | | | | | | | |
| COLUMBUS DAY | | | | | | | | | | | | | | | | | | | |
| HALLOWEEN | | | | | | | | | | | | | | | | | | | |
| THANKSGIVING | | | | | | | | | | | | | | | | | | | |
| SPRING BREAK | | | | | | | | | | | | | | | | | | | |
| CHRISTMAS/HANUKKAH | | | | | | | | | | | | | | | | | | | |
| LENT/ROSH HASHANAH | | | | | | | | | | | | | | | | | | | |
| SECRETARIES DAY | | | | | | | | | | | | | | | | | | | |
| SATURDAY | | | | | | | | | | | | | | | | | | | |
| SUNDAY | | | | | | | | | | | | | | | | | | | |
| FRIEND'S VISIT | | | | | | | | | | | | | | | | | | | |
| FRIEND'S ILLNESS | | | | | | | | | | | | | | | | | | | |
| FRIEND'S MOVING | | | | | | | | | | | | | | | | | | | |
| DEATH | | | | | | | | | | | | | | | | | | | |
| WEDDING | | | | | | | | | | | | | | | | | | | |
| BIRTH | | | | | | | | | | | | | | | | | | | |
| DIVORCE | | | | | | | | | | | | | | | | | | | |

**Figure 26.1** How Time Is Spent and Events Are Celebrated in Adcult. SOURCE: Adapted from Mihalay Caikszentmihalyi and Eugene Rochberg-Halton, *The Meaning of Things: Domestic Symbols and the Self,* p. 265.

Feast of Pan. With the reduction of postal rates in the late nineteenth century, and the perfection of chromolithography, the day was taken over by card companies. Valentine's Day is second only to Christmas in the number of cards moved through the mails. The card companies have not been alone. To magnify a minor aspect of the pagan ceremony—the drawing of lots for sweethearts—into a central concern, candy makers have confected the day, supplying sweetheart candies for the kiddies. Champagne makers have attempted the same for grown-ups, and of course florists have not been far behind.

Their advertising notwithstanding, champagne can no longer make an Adcult festival. Only beer can. If New Year's Eve were entering the Adcult calendar now, it would be a beer holiday. Beer has clout. About a month after the Washington's Birthday sales comes St. Patrick's Day. In Ireland this day is not unlike what American Christmas used to be: morning in church, afternoon sport (usually Gaelic games like rugby and horse racing), and finally family dinner. Few bars are open. March 17 is a serious day to the Irish, commemorating Patrick, who was kidnapped by the English, converted to Christianity, and returned home to convert the heathens (metaphorically: drive out the snakes). There are parades, yes. But here is what there are not: no green beer, no rivers dyed green, no shamrocks, no leprechauns, no green lines down highways, no Lucky Charms for breakfast, no soaping in Irish Spring showers, no one singing "When Irish Eyes Are Smiling," and especially no massive communal beer drunks. Our brewers have not only made this a day to get drunk, but each has even provided a special beer with which to do it. Killian's Irish Red bills itself as "The O'fficial Beer of St. Patrick's Day," never mentioning that it is brewed by the fine Republican Protestants of Adolph Coors Company of Golden, Colorado. No matter that it far outsells the top Irish import, Guinness Stout (which is owned by the English, but then again so is Bailey's Irish Cream). For those who wish to be Irish without getting drunk, Anheuser-Busch brews O'Doul's, a nonalcoholic brew with the comforting slogan, "It's what the leprechauns drink when they're not drinking beer." Per usual, the card companies are not far behind. Hallmark has 150 kinds of St. Patrick's Day cards, most of them tasteless. Little wonder the Irish have lodged countless complaints against the stereotyping done by the American companies.

At the end of March comes Adult's golden ring—a celebration of the advertising of a commodity by advertising it again. The Academy Awards ceremony is brought to us by the Academy of Motion Picture Arts and Sciences to promote the motion pictures that created the academy to promote the pictures. Well, not quite right. Actually, the Oscars are brought to us by Revlon, Royal Caribbean Cruise Lines, and J. C. Penney under the watchful eye of the motion picture studios, which are themselves minor parts of worldwide entertainment conglomerates like Matsushita, News Corp., Disney, Sony, Time Warner, Viacom, and you know the rest. The Oscars have had such a success in promoting themselves that there are now a handful of such awards, like the Tonys, Grammys, Golden Globes, Ace Awards, and the MTV Music Video Awards, in which the group giving the award is essentially advertising itself.[1]

In the 1930s the studio bosses under Louis B. Mayer sought a way to advertise their wares and swell profits. They also wanted to prevent the newly formed unions from cutting into their profits. So Meyer invented the Academy of Motion Picture Arts and Sciences, invoking all the semiotics of high culture: the academy, the arts, the sciences. Had the word *cinema* been in vogue, he doubtless would have used it instead of *motion pictures*. For advertisers the Oscars are the demographic flip side of the Super Bowl, and the advertising rates reflect this. It is the highest rated show for twenty-five- to forty-nine-year-old women, watched by almost half the households that are watching television. Ad rates are a bit lower than for the football game. If men's products are launched in January campaigns on the Super Bowl, women have to wait a few months. Because no beer is involved, the Oscars are not a central holiday, but many of my students will dress up and pretend to attend, celebrating the kitschiness.

They don't have to pretend for the next calendric event; this one's for them. Around Easter time thousands of adolescents migrate to Florida's beach shrines around Daytona Beach, Panama City, South Padre Island, and California's Palm Springs. Those students with more disposable income, and less ability to pass for drinking age, are off to Mexico, especially Cancún. About 40 percent of the college population will make a trek during spring break. No card companies, please; no florists, no champagne, just beer, more beer, and perhaps a little suntan lotion. As could be predicted when such a demographically pure audience so dedicated to consumption congregates, the sponsors are waiting for them to arrive. Not only does MTV change its programming to bring the events to the melancholy stay-at-homes and younger sibling understudies, but beer companies run continuous ads in campus newspapers alerting all comers to the proper etiquette of getting drunk. Sometimes they make a mistake, as when Miller Brewing ran an ad featuring "4 Surefire Ways to Scam Babes," which was so politically incorrect that Miller had to apologize. So much commercial promotion is now involved in spring break that during a thinly veiled beach entertainment sponsored by a car company, the audience became unruly and three thousand Generation X'ers chanted, "Promo, promo, promo," drowning out the spiel.

Easter barely survives for this generation. A candy holiday can never compete with a beer holiday. In the paper-rock-scissors game of festivals, beer trumps candy, which trumps flowers. The celebration of spring rebirth has so enthused candy manufacturers that they now spend millions to emphasize a minor aspect of a fertility cult, namely, the burdening of the fecund rabbit with tons of heavy eggs. Who cares what a rabbit is doing laying eggs? Who cares how the rabbit gets these eggs, or why he hides them, so long as they are filled with sugary goo and covered with chocolate? The celebration of new life, the sunrise service, the Resurrection, the promise of Eastering is really not germane to a culture that is hermetically sealed off from the rhythms of the seasons. Easter does, however, mark the beginning of Daylight Saving Time, which lengthens the shopping day.

Until Cromwell's mischief had passed, Easter was not really important to the English and was never important to the Puritans. The Puritans detested all ceremonies, which probably explains why they disappeared so quickly. The first industries to see the rebirth potential in Easter were the clothing manufacturers. Although we now buy most new clothing around the back-to-school sales of Labor Day, the English signified a new beginning by buying Easter clothing. In early Adcult it was considered good luck to wear three new articles of clothing on this day, which of course you wore to church. You were seen advertising your prosperity. This tradition moved across the Atlantic. After services at St. Thomas or St. Bartholomew the young sophisticates of Manhattan would parade down Broadway to Canal Street along to the Battery. This was also a time to dress up pets and bring them along. This Easter parade is, alas, almost a thing of the past, because no company wants to sponsor, à la Macy's Thanksgiving Day Parade, such a religion-specific event at the wrong time of the merchandising year.

Not to worry, the kings of candyland, Nestlé, Mars, and Hershey, keep Easter alive and humming. They have been able to own three holidays during which they sell special candy at full retail price. There is Christmas candy (candy canes), Halloween candy (candy corn), and Easter candy (chocolate bunnies and eggs). Seasonal candy accounts for most of these companies' profits, with Easter far in the lead with sales of more than $500 million. The only vestige of Christianity in the modern Easter celebration is the rolling of eggs, which may be a dim analog to the rolling of the stone from Jesus's tomb.

The really interesting April holiday is a restaurant holiday: Professional Secretary's Dayfi (always with the registered trademark symbol, if you please, in all the desktop calendars). May 27 is the busiest lunch day in cities, with overcrowded restaurants often going to double shifts. The greeting card companies, candy makers, and florists are also pleased that April now promises yet another chance to peddle their wares. But the real support for ProSec Day comes from the overnight express deliverers and the airlines. Federal Express sends special greetings to 320,000 secretaries, UPS is not far behind, and the airlines often send trinkets of appreciation. Why? Secretaries make most of the shipping and reservation decisions. According to the *Wall Street Journal*, which cares enough to know about these kinds of things, most professional secretaries hate the day (Duff 1993:Bi). They would prefer a pay raise.

May is also a month of wonderful holidays. The month begins with May Day, a day of such exuberance that youngsters used to "go a-maying" at the crack of dawn "to fetch the flowers fresh." The fairest maid was crowned with a wreath as queen of May. Every village had a maypole on the green that the villagers entwined with flowers and then danced around, celebrating the glory of life renewed. Aside from the Russians, who liked to rumble their rocket launchers through Red Square, and Vassar students, who enjoyed modern dance, and Freudians who delighted in explaining the relationship of the maypole to springtime, no one else really cares about the first day of May. Even April First and its celebration of stupidity has outdistanced May Day.

Perhaps there are too many other holidays in May to be distracted. First, there is Cinco de Mayo, a holiday sponsored by the distillers of tequila and Mexican fast-food restaurants, which has as much to do with Mexican Independence as St. Patrick has to do with Irish Catholicism. Second is the most important holiday in May. It is the day to which all Adcult holidays aspire—Mother's Day. It is a day so filled with guilt that even the hardest heart pays full retail.

In the early years of the twentieth century Anna Jarvis lived with her aged mother outside Philadelphia. Her mother was not an easy person to live with and Jarvis's other siblings quickly left home. The responsibility of caring for Mother fell to Jarvis. After a few difficult years, the woman died, and Jarvis entered a period of what has been uncharitably called "prolonged pathological mourning" (Jones 1980:177). She fashioned a small altar of dried flowers that she tended faithfully. People paid attention to Jarvis. She was so tender and devoted in her never ending mourning, she was so daughterly; she would speak of little other than her mother to anyone who would listen.

Although her siblings found Anna Jarvis tedious, others found her downright inspirational. John Wanamaker, master merchandiser of his self and his store, was transfixed. He encouraged Jarvis to copyright the day to make sure the integrity of her feelings was not compromised. Meanwhile, he ran special full-page ads in the *Philadelphia Inquirer*, incorporating her message of filial thanksgiving, organized an annual program of music and recitations in the store, gave flowers away to customers, and reportedly said that he would rather have been the founder of Mother's Day than the king of England. Not everyone agreed, certainly not Congress, which was petitioned to commemorate the day but demurred. Alas, Anna Jarvis never lived to see either herself as a mother or her Mother's Day enshrined in Adcult.

World War I changed that. What with the boys separated from their moms and all, it seemed the least the government could do was to encourage the lads to write a special May-time message to mom. They did. "The hand that rocks the cradle rules the world" was the rallying cry. Mother's Day cards, called Mother Letters, were expedited past censors in record time and soon became an annual event around May 10. More impor-tant, in the years after the war the cause of mom was taken up by the burgeoning Sunday school Movement. As a way to increase attendance the second Sunday of May was set aside as a time to commemorate in church what the state seemed too timid to admit: moms rule. There was some precedent for this, as "mothering Sunday" had a peculiar history in the early industrial revolution. On mothering Sunday apprentices returned home, attended the mother church for a service in which the biblical story of Hannah was usually related, ate a piece of mothering cake at home, and perhaps had enough momisms to last a year.

As is usual for spring ceremonies, flowers were involved. You wore a red flower if your mother was living, a white one if she was not. In 1934 Postmaster James Farley ordered a commemorative Mother's Day stamp showing Whistler's Mother whiling away the time waiting for Junior to come home. Farley had the engraver crop the painting and insert a vase of carnations in the lower lefthand corner. Persnickety art historians and their fellow travelers were outraged that such a work of art (Whistler's *Mother* was so important that it had been sold to the French in 1891 and was in the Louvre) had been used so crassly as a postage stamp. Farley apologized, but who cared? Mothers would have their day and indeed they did. By 1950 Mother's Day had become the second-largest retail sales holiday. Helped out by AT&T, MCI, and the other phone companies, as well as by the candy makers, florists (especially the carnation growers), and the U.S. Postal Service, we now spend billions of dollars each second Sunday in May to make sure that mom is acknowledged and appreciated—very often from a distance.

My students now enter a long refractory period, from late May to late October. It's summer vacation. To be sure, there is beer drinking on Memorial Day with the running of the Indianapolis 500, and there is Father's Day in early June in which we are supposed to give dad not much, and July 4 and beer, then Labor Day, and return to school. Pity poor Columbus Day. Not only did the day's "hero" inflict all kinds of hardship on the Native Americans, and not only do the Italians make lousy beer, but this is simply the wrong time of year to buy stuff, any stuff. The telephone companies make pathetic attempts to encourage us to "discover" new values by calling home, but we're too smart. We know what's coming up in a month or so.

If you want to see the powers of Budweiser, Miller, and Coors really let loose in Adcult, wait until the end of October. The night used to belong to the Druid, not Michelob. Halloween was yet another pagan festival, this one having to do with the harvest and the coming on of cold weather. Bonfires were lit and chants sung for safe passage through dangerous winter. Bonfire Night was taken over by the church to become All Hallow's Eve, with perhaps a little of Guy Fawkes Day mixed in, accounting for the appearance of prankish games. All we now share with the Druids is the link with dying light, as this time marks our return to standard time and the end of Daylight Saving Time. That we get dressed up in the costumes of characters that may well have scared us, that we demand and get treats, and that mischief is just below the surface all reinforce Halloween as an empowering event for the underaged. To candy makers this kind of subversion is nirvana. After all, this is the nature of candy.

To their brewing brethren, however, this was a time for despair. A night is a terrible thing to waste. What had started as a most somber adult ceremony was been taken over by the kiddies but, thanks to the brewers, it is rapidly becoming an adult, albeit young adult, time again. About ten years ago Halloween became an Oktoberfest event. Go to your grocery store now, and what do you see surrounding the stacks of fully priced candy? Stacks of beer and tons of advertising. This is a holiday in the process of being colonized by Adcult.

So we have Coors Light, "the official beer of Halloween," changing its slogan so that the word *fright* is substituted for *right*, making "It's the fright beer now." Anheuser-Busch has a young woman dressed as a vampire telling celebrants, "I vant to drink your Bud," and Miller pictures the Frankenstein monster under the ambiguous line, "Keep a level head this Halloween." When the National Parent-Teacher Association, the National Council on Alcoholism and Drug Dependence, and the Center for Science in the Public Interest tattled on the beer companies and told the surgeon general what was going on, she scolded the brewers. Representatives of Miller, Anheuser-Busch, and Coors denied that their Halloween ads were aimed at underage consumers. The marketing approach, they said, had been driven by consumer research showing that Halloween had already become a popular occasion for adult parties. Say no more. Case closed.

All these festivals of consumption are just so many Groundhog Days compared to the festival to settle the score, the festival of festivals, the only festival to achieve transcendental status—Christmas. We need not be reminded of its central place in Adcult. Here is the make-it or break-it event, not only of parenthood but of family life for the whole year. Western capitalism depends on it. Uzi owners, cockfight enthusiasts, and militant vegetarians who complain of being marginalized have only an inkling of what Grinches feel during this season.

Christmas season starts during a wonderful holiday. Thanksgiving. Of course, Thanksgiving has nothing whatsoever to do with the Pilgrims and collegial times with Squanto, the affable Indian. It has everything to do with Sarah Josepha Hale's crusade in the 1820s to make a family time for remembering her ancestors who came over on the you-know-what. As editor of the Boston-based *Ladies'Magazine* she had a bully pulpit. After the divisiveness of the Civil War President Lincoln thought it a good idea to celebrate our communal past. He proclaimed the last Thursday in November as a day to give national thanks. And so it continued until 1939, when an Ohio department store owner named Fred Lazarus Jr. proposed that Thanksgiving be moved one week earlier to provide a bit more shopping time. Tired of the depression, FDR agreed. The Republicans and right-thinking people were shocked, and a Joint Resolution of Congress restored the fourth Thursday in 1941. But too late. Macy's parade had already started and Santa was cropping up at stories. Christmas had begun.

Christmas is a great demonstration of the calendric dynamics of Adcult at work. What started as a pagan ceremony celebrating the winter solstice, became a Roman feast day, was pretty much ignored by all (especially by the Puritans, whose anticelebration regulations stood until the late eighteenth century, complete with fines for those who do work on "such days as Christmas"), was for a short time a religious day (the only one sanctioned by the U.S. government), was serendipitously discovered by the department stores as an efficient way of "working off" the end-of-year surplus, and now has been returned full cycle as a pagan ceremony.

The last turn of the Christmas screw was applied December 24, 1867, when R. H. Macy kept his store open until midnight. He set a one-day sales record of more than $6,000. A few years later he was decorating his windows with dolls and trinkets, and it was all over. By the 1870s Christmas sales were double the next best holiday, Mother's Day. In December 1891 F. W. Woolworth was on the bandwagon, exhorting his store managers:

> This is our harvest time. Make it pay. . . . Give your store a holiday appearance. Hang up Christmas ornaments. Perhaps have a tree in the window. Make the store look different. . . . This is also a good time to work off "stickers" or unsalable goods, for they will sell during the excitement when you could not give them away other times. Mend all broken toys and dolls every day.
>
> (Boorstin 1973:159)

By the end of the century Woolworth had done something else to stimulate sales. Quite by accident, to avert a Christmas strike, F. W. gave his workers a bonus. He presented $5 to each employee for each year of employment, not to exceed $25. The multiplier effect was soon felt as other companies followed suit. No good Christmas deed ever goes unpunished, regardless of motive, and by 1951 the National Labor

Relations Board had ruled that the Christmas bonus was no bonus at all but an expected remuneration. To make economic matters still more explosive, banks joined the splurge by marketing Christmas Club savings (read, spending) accounts that matured just in time to pay full retail prices at the department stores. The juggernaut of Christmas, to a considerable degree fueled by Jewish merchants in New York, now couldn't be stopped. In 1946, after years of protesting the singing of Christian carols in the public schools, the Rabbinical Assembly of America realized it couldn't fight what it in part had started. The rabbis solved the problem by elevating a minor holiday of their own, Hanukkah, and slipstreamed it into the calendar. Soon Hanukkah became paganized with not one but eight days of giving. No power resists Adcult.

You can keep Christ out of Christmas but not Santa. This character, a weird conflation of St. Nicholas (a down-on-his-luck nobleman who helped young women turn away from prostitution), and Kriss Kringle (perhaps a German barbarism of *Christ-kintle*, a gift giver) is the apogee of magical thinking. He has become so powerful that when kids are told he doesn't exist, their parents become depressed. Santa Claus was a creation of Clement Clarke Moore and Thomas Nast. In 1822 Moore wrote a poem for his daughters that was reprinted in newspapers and found its way a decade later into the *New York Book of Poetry*. In his poem "A Visit from St. Nicholas" (not "The Night Before Christmas") an elflike creature runs about Christmas Eve delivering presents. He is tiny, small enough to come down the chimney.

> When what to my wondering eyes should appear,
> But a miniature sleigh, and eight tiny rein-deer;
> With a little old driver, so lively and quick,
> I knew in a moment it must be St. Nick.

St. Nick was plumped up into full-sized Santa by the editorial cartoonist Thomas Nast. In 1869 he collected these images from *Harper's Weekly* and published them in a book called *Santa Claus and His Works*. If we have Moore to thank for the reindeer (and all their great reindeer names), we have Nast to thank for fattening up Santa and sending him to the North Pole.

By the end of the nineteenth century Santa was everywhere. He was in newspapers, in magazines, a doll, on calendars, in children's books, and—thanks to Louis Prang—on Christmas cards. He first appears in a suit sketched by Nast but now, with chromo-lithography, colored red. But Santa is not ready for prime time yet. He still needs a little tuck here, a little letting out there. He needs a big belt, he needs those buccaneer boots, he needs a beard trim, he needs shtick. He gets it. The jolly old St. Nick that we know from countless images did not come from Macy's department store, neither did he originate in the imaginations of Moore and Nast, nor did he come from Western European folklore. He came from the yearly advertisements of the Coca-Cola Company.

In the 1920s Coca-Cola was having difficulty selling its soft drink during the winter. The soda execs wanted to make it a cold weather beverage. "Thirst knows no season" was their initial winter campaign. At first they decided to show how a winter personage like Santa could enjoy a soft drink in December. They showed Santa chugalugging with the Sprite Boy (the addled young soda jerk with the Coke bottle cap jauntily stuck on his head). But then they got lucky. They started showing Santa relaxing from his travails by drinking a Coke, then showed how the kids might leave a Coke (not milk) for Santa, and then implied that the gifts coming in from Santa were in exchange for the Coke. Pay dirt. Santa's presents might not be in exchange for a Coke, but they were "worth" a Coke. Coke's Santa was elbowing aside other Santas. Coke's Santa was starting to own Christmas.

From the late 1930s until the mid-1950s Haddon H. Sundblorn spent much of the year preparing his Santas for the D'Arcy Agency in St. Louis. He would do two or three Santas for mass-market magazines and then one for billboards and maybe another for point-of-sale items. They almost always showed Santa giving presents and receiving Coke, sharing his Coke with the kids surrounded by toys, playing with the toys and drinking the Coke, or reading a letter from a kid while drinking the Coke left like the glass of milk. The ad lines read "They knew what I wanted," "It's my gift for thirst," "And now the gift for thirst," or "Travel refreshed." Sundblom was quick to glom on to any passing motif. After Disney made *Bambi* and Gene Autry sang "Here Comes Santa Claus," the reindeer were often worked into the illustration. After all, the provenance of Rudolph the Red Nosed Reindeer was pure Adcult. Rudolph was created by Robert L. May, a copywriter for Montgomery Ward, and his story proved so popular that 2.3 million copies of "Rudolph" were sent out with the catalog in 1939.

It is an axiom of modern merchandising that what you make during Christmas is your profit for the year. One of the most accurate predictors of future spending is what Toys 'R' Us does in December. So important is the figure that the company now makes no public announcements of its Christmas sales until mid-January, lest it roil the markets. Giving—although it can hardly be called *giving* in any traditional sense of the word—is the essence of this festival of consumption. So the key is to make not-giving unspeakably churlish even if, from a retail point of view, as F. W. Woolworth implied, most of what is given is junk.

Not-giving is the mythic responsibility of Scrooge. Whereas Santa is front and center, dispensing his subtle blackmail, his evil twin Scrooge is on hand to be ridiculed for his more sensible behavior. Scrooge says hoard, hoard, hoard; Santa says spend, spend, spend. Our almost totally subversive reading of Charles Dickens's *A Christmas Carol* is a case study of how popular imagination, in consort with Walt Disney and the department store industry, renders meaning in Adcult. Dickens's tale is now every-where. Hundreds of editions are in print—well over 225 adaptations for stage, screen, and radio; it is on records, tape, and CDs; it is a ballet, an opera, a musical, in hundreds of cartoons; its characters are omnipresent in advertising. Scrooge has jumped loose of his text, becoming such characters as Scrooge McDuck for Disney or the Grinch for Dr. Seuss. We willingly—nay, gleefully—have subverted the character of Scrooge and the moral of the story to serve the greater glory of Adcult.

Who cares that *A Christmas Carol* was a potboiler written because Dickens desperately needed to recoup the losses of *Martin Chuzzlewit*? Who cares that the story was not serialized, because Dickens reckoned he could make more by publishing it whole? And especially who cares that Scrooge's redemptive act was most assuredly not to give presents at all but to give succor to the poor? Dickens saw the story as a plea for compassion, a way to relieve the distress of the urban poor, an act of noblesse oblige, a redress of his own miserable childhood. What redeems Ebenezer Scrooge in print is definitely *not* that he gives presents, or a turkey, but that he takes fatherly responsibility for Tiny Tim, the crippled son of his clerk Bob Cratchit. This is what Scrooge means when he says, "I will love Christmas in my heart and try to keep it all the year." When *A Christmas Carol* was published in 1843, Christmas gifts were not exchanged and most companies did not even take the day off. What makes you a Scrooge today is that you refuse to heft your share of "deadweight" gifts.[2] No mention is made of caring for the less fortunate. The paradox is palpable, perhaps instructive.

The *work* of commercial advertising, that it arrests attention long enough for an otherwise overlooked message to be delivered, has mightily altered the cultures it has entered. Not only has it commandeered the media in which it appears, but it has also affected content. That television shows, for instance, are filled with middle-class stories, that these stories often revolve around consumable objects, that they are told in discrete twelve-minute segments, and that they have uniformly happy endings is partially the result of the demands of advertisers.

More profound than the influence of advertising on the form and content of media, however, is its transformation of the audience's sense of time and self. An example is how weddings have been modified in the last half-century as they have become ritualized ceremonies of acquisition. Two generations ago no one had heard of such things as the bridal registry, nonrecyclable wedding garments, an industry of how-to manuals ("on the wedding day they give one another a piece of wedding jewelry—tiny diamond earings or a pearl necklace for her, priced anywhere from $35 to $60,000, and cufflinks or a wrist watch for him" [Baldrige 1992:13A]), elaborate ring exchanges, and even now, as I write this, the development of wedding-day jewelry exchanges between the participants and their in-laws. Spend an hour reading a bride's magazine, or look at the ubiquitous newspaper supplements, and you will see Adcult hard at work making what was once a communal or civil or religious ceremony into a holiday of consumption.

But we now turn to yet another region colonized by advertising, a region long thought immune to the blandishments of the vulgar, the sacred preserve of Highcult and the inner sanctum of Victorian value, a world of value ripe for the plucking—the world of art.

## Questions for Consideration

1   What holidays and/or events are not discussed in Twitchell's essay? Why do you think this is?

2   What are some other ways in which advertisers think about time and the timing of their campaigns?

3   As we move further into the new media environment, do you think marketers will place more or less emphasis on the holidays? Why might this be so?

## Notes

1.   Alas, the advertising industry, which should understand the commercial value of public self-congratulations, has only botched its own. The Clios became almost hopelessly corrupt in the early 1990s, and now a number of fledgling awards like the Effin and the Addie are trying to take its place but without much national acceptance. My favorite? The Cresta, short for "creative standards." The worse? The International Andy Awards, short for who knows what? Only one international award, the Cannes Lion, has any credibility. A radical

idea: instead of advertising agencies getting dressed up and giving each other hundreds of awards for doing what they are supposed to do, why not have consumers judge advertising? A more radical idea: an award for ads that can be shown to sell products.

2.    Economists call lunky objects "deadweight" gifts. Deadweight is short for "deadweight loss," which is the difference between what the gift giver has spent and the value the recipient places on it. Billions of dollars are "wasted" each Christmas as Uncle Louie receives a glow-in-the-dark necktle from his niece to whom he has sent Neef golf clubs. Both parties would be better off exchanging cash. But they don't, and that is what makes the transaction so interesting to economists. In Adcult currency exchange would be unthinkable.

# Chapter 27

## BOB GARFIELD

## "CHAOS SCENARIO"
## A Look at the Marketing Industry's
## Coming Disaster

A S TELEVISION SETS BECAME MORE affordable and accessible in the mid-twentieth century, many people—and many advertisers—flocked to the new medium. The changes adversely affected the radio and magazine industries, until they learned to adjust their approach to advertisers and consumers. We are currently witnessing a similar disruption of consumer media habits with the Internet, and the transformation is causing much concern and confusion in the television industry as well as most other media businesses. In the essay that follows, Bob Garfield, a writer for the trade magazine *Advertising Age*, notes that the transition to a radically different advertising/media system will not happen without effort—even struggle—by advertisers as well as media firms. Garfield wrote his piece in 2005, but the painful readjustments he knew marketing and media practitioners had to make are still taking place.

Meet George Jetson, circa 2020.

He doesn't have a personal hovercraft or a food computer, but the rest of the future is more futuristic than he thought. Spacely Sprockets and Cogswell Cogs are out of business. Digits are the new widgets.

### TV is Gone

Over-the-air network TV is gone, along with program schedules, affiliate stations and hotel demand in Cannes in the third week of June. George, Jane, Judy and Elroy get their entertainment, and their news, any way they wish: TV, phone, camera, laptop, game console, MP3 player. They get to choose from what the Hollywood big boys have funded and distributed, or what the greater vlogosphere has percolated to their attention.

ABC, NBC and CBS are still major brands, but they surely aren't generating radio waves. Three initials never uttered, however, are CPM. They've long since been supplanted not just by ROI, but VOD, video on demand; P2P, the peer-to-peer Napsterization of content; DRM, the allocation of royalties for digital distribution of content; VOIP, Internet telephony; and RSS, the software that aggregates Web content for easy access by the user.

Branded Entertainment has long since been exposed as a false idol, because consumers got quickly fed up with their shows being contaminated by product placements. Satellite radio is a $4 billion 8-track tape player, stored on a high shelf in the garage, pushed aside by podcasting, which is free. The Upfront Market is an exhibit at the Smithsonian. The Super Bowl survived as the No. 1 pay-per-view event. *Survivor* didn't.

The space-age family of the future can still watch *CSI*, any episode they want, whenever they want, but not on any advertiser's dime—unless they choose for their viewing costs to be subsidized. Yet advertisers know everything about them and understand virtually every move they make.

## Marketers aren't Adversaries

And the Jetsons don't fight it. In 2020, consumers understand that marketers aren't adversaries; they're intimates, sharing info for everybody's mutual benefit.

Yesiree, by George, it's a brave and exciting new world that the near future holds, a democratized, consumer-empowered, bottom-up, pull-not-push, lean forward and lean back universe that will improve the quantity and quality of entertainment options, create hitherto unimaginable marketing opportunities and efficiencies and, not incidentally, generate wealth that will make the current $250 billion domestic ad market seem like pin money.

Alas, the future—near or not—doesn't happen till later.

So let's return to contemporary business reality in the digital revolution, already in progress. Because in the intervening 15 years—or 20 years, or five—there are three more initials to consider: SOS.

Because revolutions by their nature are neither seamless nor smooth.

## Collapse of Old Model

Because there is no reason to believe the collapse of the old media model will yield a plug-and-play new one.

On the contrary, there is nothing especially orderly about media's New World Order. At the moment it is a collection of technologies and ideas and vacant-lot bandwidth, a digital playground for visionaries and nerds.

So what happens when 30 Rock and Black Rock and the other towering edifices of network TV are rubble, and the vacant lot has yet to be developed?

Undeveloped and unprepared. Unprepared to lawfully deliver *CSI*. Unprepared to absorb $4 billion ad dollars, much less broadcast's $42 billion. Unprepared legally, technologically and even socially to pick up the pieces of the old world order.

Hold on. Let's change metaphors. Forget the construction site. Make it a space-age treadmill, cycling too fast for George Jetson to keep his footing. "Jane!" he pleads. "Stop this crazy thing!" But Jane can't stop it. Nobody can stop it, and nobody can quite hang on.

Ah, yes. The Chaos Scenario.

## Downward Spiral

The statistics are already getting tiresome, but let's review a few of the more salient ones, shall we?

According to Nielsen, network TV audience has eroded an average of 2% a year for a decade, although in the same period the U.S. population increased by 30 million.

In the last sweeps period, for the first time, cable commanded a larger audience than broadcast.

The cost of reaching 1,000 households in prime time has jumped from $7.64 in 1994 to $19.85 in 2004.

A 2000 Veronis Suhler Stevenson survey showed that Americans devoted an average of 866 hours to broadcast TV annually and 107 to the Internet, a ratio of 8:1. The projection for 2005 had the TV/Internet ratio at 785 hours to 200, or just under 4:1.

U.S. household broadband penetration has gone from 8% in March 2000 to an estimated 56% in March of this year, according to Nielsen/NetRatings.

## 70% of DVR Users Skip Commercials

Five percent of U.S. homes are equipped with TiVo or other digital video recorders, and not only does time-shifting of favorite programs render network schedules irrelevant, 70% of DVR users skip past TV commercials.

Complicating problems, consolidation in the telecom industry and potential re-regulation of DTC drug advertising threaten billions in network ad revenue, jeopardizing the supply–demand quotient that has propped up network prices for five years. Meanwhile, there is the sword of Damocles called "cost." The reality-TV fad has enabled networks to fill their ever-more-irrelevant schedules and cast for hits with cheap programming. But how much longer will they last? Westerns and spy shows, superheroes and hospital dramas all once burned bright. Then they burned out.

What's ominous about that is not the inevitable end of the latest hot genre; it's the inevitable end of the profitability that has gone with it. And the downward spiral could begin at any moment. In fact, to switch metaphors once again, Shawn Burns, managing director of Wunderman, Paris, looks at the 2005 upfront and sees "the last strand of the rope bridge."

Mr. Burns, of course, makes a living preaching the wonders of segmentation and the bankruptcy of mass marketing. No wonder he observes with barely camouflaged glee that the efficiency pendulum has swung. "There's been research," he says, "that real cost of obtaining 30 seconds of the consumer's attention is the same in 2005 as it was *before the invention of television*."

## Fraying Rope

Emphasis his. Yes, he has a vested interest in being a doomsayer. He is by no means, however, the only one who sees the rope fraying.

"I still love and enjoy TV and believe it is very effective for advertisers," says Association of National Advertisers President Bob Liodice. "But we're killing it. We're gradually killing it with cost increases, the level of clutter, the quality of the creative that is out there."

"How can they continue to ask for more and more for fewer and fewer faces?" asks Geoffrey Frost, chief marketing officer of Motorola. "I don't believe that is sustainable. I believe there will be disruption. There's already disruption."

"It's an inevitable kind of slow collapse of the entire mass media advertising market," says J.D. Lasica, author of *Darknet: Remixing the Future of Entertainment* and president of the Social Media Group consultancy. "What we're seeing is that not only does television have to reinvent itself from the content point of view, it has to reinvent itself as an advertising medium."

## Primitive Standards

No mystery as to how, either. As technology increasingly enables fine targeting and interaction between marketer and consumer, the old measurement and deployment standards are primitive almost to the point of absurdity.

"The industry's key currency is basically reach, frequency, exposure and cost per thousand," says Rishad Tobaccowala, president of Internet media shop Starcom IP. "I'm not saying whether it's right or wrong but that's currently the currency. And where the currency ought to be is about outcomes, engagement and effectiveness. Because right now all I'm doing is I'm measuring how cheaply or how expensively I'm buying the pig. I'm not figuring out whether the hot dog tastes good."

None of this is lost on any sentient being in the media and marketing business. Any lingering denial most likely evaporated when Procter & Gamble Global Marketing Officer Jim Stengel—he of the $5.5 billion marketing budget—faced agency heads a year ago at the American Association of Advertising Agencies' Media Conference and declared the existing model "broken." But it's not just the ad model; it's the content model, as well. Writer and former venture capitalist Om Malik looks at TiVo and the video-on-demand horizon and is prepared to call in the backhoes for the institution of the prime-time schedule.

"Hasn't it collapsed already?" asks the author of *Broadbandits: Inside the $750 Billion Telecom Heist*. "Look at their viewership. Isn't it going down every day? I mean, we can pick and choose what foods we eat, what car we drive, what clothes we wear and what colognes we use. And some guy sitting in New York decides how I should watch?"

## Consumer Control

Point taken. As more control has been placed in the hands of the consumer, the consumer has shown every intention of exercising it. Especially in the coveted 18–34 cohort, viewers are fleeing TV and going online, where nobody need have their content dictated to them. But as to Mr. Malik's rhetorical question—hasn't the old model collapsed already—the answer happens to be:

No, it hasn't.

Network TV spending went up in 2004, by 10.7%. According to Jack Myers' Report, last year's upfront market yielded a 15.4% increase across the four majors, and Mr. Myers projects a 4% increase for the top four in 2005. Yes: increase. There are many possible explanations for the phenomenon. One is habit; gigantic institutions tend not to rapidly adapt. Another is greed: the self-interest of the comfortably situated old guard to preserve the status quo. The third is supply and demand, upward pricing pressure from Viagra, et al, which engorged the marketplace with billions in new spending. The main factor, though, is that network TV audiences remain coveted, because—shrinking though they are—they represent the last vestige of mass media and marketing, or, as Motorola's Mr. Frost calls it, "the last surviving conglomeration of human beings in the living room."

Precisely, says David Poltrack, executive vice president of research at CBS, who sees incremental revenue opportunities in video-on-demand, but no end to the dominance of broadcast TV in the foreseeable future. "Unless the advertising community finds something to replace television advertising, I think the relative value of the top-quality inventory is always going to be appreciating relative to all the other options," he says. "Unless someone can come up with a more effective way of introducing a new product than broad-based advertising exposure, I think that business is always going to be there."

Which is why Motorola, whose nifty palm-sized Razr device represents the Jetsons' media future today, mainly used TV to introduce the gizmo to the world. Because there are still a few programs that catch the imagination of enough human beings in enough living rooms to represent a mass-marketing opportunity.

"I still believe in TV," Mr. Frost says. "People still watch it, and I love being associated with the right kind of programming that is different, that is appealing, that embodies the kind of innovation we want to stand for as a company."

## "Teetering Ecosystem"

On the other hand, he acknowledges that the financing of the "right kind of programming"—not to mention the overwhelming majority of flops—depends on network revenue streams that could dry up quickly. "The teetering ecosystem behind all this stuff that allows people like us to sort of cherry-pick" for exceptional programs, he says, "may begin to find itself in serious trouble."

So while the old model hasn't necessarily collapsed, new-media gurus could be forgiven for seeing the beginning—or middle—of the end. Steven Rosenbaum, pioneer of citizen-produced TV and founder of MagnifyMedia, envisions a world of content created by and for individuals over broadband. He snorts at Mr. Poltrack's defense of the status quo.

"These guys," he says, "their job is to postpone the future."

## Viacom Split

Another skeptic apparently is Sumner Redstone, chairman of CBS parent Viacom. One week after Mr. Poltrack spoke to Ad Age, Mr. Redstone announced his plan to split the company in two, presumably to reduce the drain of CBS and its other broadcast properties on the stock value of the company's faster-growing media assets.

So for the moment, let's assume that there is indeed major trouble ahead, that the law of diminishing returns will eventually kick in, that advertisers who've paid more and more for less and less will not pay indefinitely for nothing. Marketers will begin to abandon network TV. Ad prices will fall. Profitability will disappear. Program development will suffer, leading to more advertiser defection, and so on in a consuming vortex of ruin. But wait. The network refugees will not flee empty handed. They'll draw carts bearing steamer trunks stuffed with a quarter trillion dollars.

Then what? In the short run, obviously, more boom times for cable, and then: Payday for the New World Order.

"A bit of it will go to this new emerging network which will be on the mobile phones," says Mr. Malik. "The next thing you will see is the emergence of more Internet-based video advertising. . . . There's going to be a lot of hit-and-miss in this but I think that's another area you'll see a lot of progress made. A third channel is . . . Internet-enabled cable services. They're not home runs by any means but they're definite solid singles and doubles."

## Economics of Scale

No dingers? So what? The whole point of new media is small ball. Quit playing for the three-run homer and amass the singles and doubles. Because, says Starcom's Mr. Tobaccowala, "the key thing is economics of scale is going to disappear. That's really what the issue is. Our business has been built on the economics of scale. And instead we're going to go into the economics of re-aggregation. Which is how do you get 10, 20, 30, 40 thousand people instead of taking in 250 million and making them into 12 and 30 million dollar segments. How do you re-aggregate one at a time into the tens of thousands?"

Fragmentation, the bane of network TV and mass marketers everywhere, will become the Holy Grail, the opportunity to reach—and have a conversation with—small clusters of consumers who are consuming not what is force-fed them, but exactly what they want. Producers and broadcasters capitalized with billions of dollars will be on approximately equal footing with podcasters and video bloggers capitalized with $399.99 12-months same-as-cash from Best Buy. And just as DailyKos, Instapundit, Wonkette and Wil Wheaton have coalesced large followings in the cacophony of the blogosphere, some of the citizen-video programmers will find not just a voice but an audience.

Wait. Did I Say "Will Find?" Make That "Are Finding."

"All of that is happening," says Drazen Pantic, founding member of videologging Web site unmediated.org, "In the last two or three years, we've had a silent revolution of consumer electronics. And broadband is coming. It's a huge proliferation in the last two years. And so people are going to start broadcasting from home and so on. You will have zillions of people, broadcasting for the audience of 10."

Except when it's much bigger than 10. A month ago, a little girl named Dylan Verdi posted a home movie on her father's Web site. PressThink.org's Jay Rosen dubbed her the world's youngest vlogger. The link went viral and, as her father Michael reports on his own videolog, "24 hours later 2,000 people had downloaded her video." It would have been much more, but he had to shut his site down so he wouldn't wind up penniless from bandwidth charges.

## Web Proves it can Outdraw TV

The Internet has also demonstrated its ability to outdraw TV. JibJab satirical animations have been downloaded by the millions, for instance. And even TV programming has drawn better online than in its native habitat—such as when comedian Jon Stewart went on CNN's *Crossfire* to assassinate Tucker Carlson live on cable.

"That episode got, what, 400,000 viewers maybe on big old powerful CNN?" says Jeff Jarvis, president of Advance.net, the online arm of Advance Publications, and author of the media blog BuzzMachine.com. "Well that same segment was copied onto the Internet, where it got at least 5 million views. So what's more powerful, the network CNN owns or the network no one owns? So now suddenly the distribution is exploded. Now on the Internet we can all swim in the same pool as content created by, you know, Universal or Disney. The tools are cheap and easy."

It is a beautiful thing: the total democratization of media, combined with the total addressability of marketing communications. We, the people, cease to be demographics. We become individuals again.

"Choice is a good thing," Mr. Jarvis says. "Choice is a proxy for power. The more choice we have the more power we have. The most important invention in the history of media was not the Guttenberg Press, it was the remote control. It gave us control over the consumption of media. Then came the cable box and the VCR and the TiVo and now come the means of creating content. Now I can create a radio show and put it on the Internet. Nyah, nyah, nyah."

Maybe it's "nyah, nyah, nyah—take that Big Media." Or maybe it's "tra la, tra la— what an empowering new world." Either way, it's underway.

## Straight-to-Internet Campaigns

On the advertising side, Google last year generated $3 billion in revenue, about the same as The New York Times Co. No surprise that Vonage, the Internet telephony carrier, is using the Internet to find subscribers, but Procter & Gamble put its money where Jim Stengel's mouth is by launching Prilosec OTC with 75% of its budget allocated off TV. American Express allocates 80% of its budget off the airwaves. The new Pepsi One campaign will use no TV whatsoever. (Not Capital One. Not Purina One. Pepsi One.) In the new-media laboratory called South Korea, where universal broadband is social policy and its penetration exceeds 80%, the Internet's share of ad spending is twice that of the U.S. TV, meanwhile, accounts for only 34.4%.

In the wake of BMW films, such diverse U.S. marketers as Amex, Burger King, Lincoln-Mercury and Motorola have created an ever-expanding universe of content/advertising hybrids, Webisodic short films to reach younger prospects online.

Mercury's "The Lucky Ones" is so barren of product and brand messages it is scarcely advertising at all.

Netcasting, of course, also delivers pure programming, too. From the top down was the streaming, on Yahoo, of Kirstie Allie's new show, *Fat Actress*. From the bottom up, video logs—or vlogs—like Dylan Verdi's are being generated every day. At Rocketboom.com, chirpy, irreverent host Amanda Congdon delivers oddball news and snarky observations in a primitive studio (or maybe a one-bedroom). At J.D. Lasica's alpha Web site Ourmedia.com, citizen journalists and producers post their own news reports, animations, music videos and whatever else amuses them free of charge.

So that should be the answer: the seamless transition from TV to online, from mass media to micro media, from mass marketing to permission marketing. But not so fast. George Jetson does his vlogging in 2020. Om Malik says he believes the scenario could just as easily take place by 2010. But this is 2005. What if the rope bridge finally snaps, say, next year? Or the next?

It better hadn't. Because the future isn't quite ready.

Think: Yugoslavia.

Perhaps you are familiar with it. It used to be a country, ruled by an authoritarian criminal. Then it began to fragment. There went Slovenia, and Croatia next. Then Bosnia. Kosovo made its move, and in the ensuing madness, the regime collapsed. The unshakeable Slobodan Milosevic, who had fomented four wars in the name of Greater Serbia, was overthrown. Democracy! Empowered individuals! A new model!

And, five years later, unemployment is 32%. The average monthly income is $336. The prime minister was assassinated by organized criminals and the country's most notorious war-crimes suspect is at large. Unmediated.org's Mr. Pantic, formerly of Belgrade's freedom-fighting radio station B92, is only too familiar with the problem.

"There is no way," he says, "to make the transition into anything that is different or new or whatever without chaos. Because as with democracies you need five or six newly elected parliaments, you need to replace people who have ties with the old regime."

## Change Doesn't Happen Overnight

Likewise, he says, in the transition from old media to new: "The new paradigm is not going to be established overnight." There are too many obstacles.

> **BROADBAND PENETRATION** It has catapulted to nearly 60%, but that is still a long way from 100%. In South Korea, where penetration exceeds 80%, online advertising does indeed have twice the share of the U.S. online industry, but it is still less than 5%.

> **CAPACITY** "I don't think the interactive community has sufficient capacity to handle a seismic change in a transition from network to online," says the ANA's Mr. Liodice. "I don't think that's gonna happen." Online-marketing consultant Joseph Jaffe agrees. The author of the forthcoming *Life After the 30-Second Spot* doesn't believe there will ever be a dollar-for-dollar transfer of TV money to the Internet. But even 10% of all money now allocated to TV would more than double the total online

spending. "You've got a handful of publisher properties that may be able to kind of cope initially," Mr. Jaffe says, "and then be able to at least kind of sustain that increased demand. But for the most part, when the tsunami hits, all hell's gonna break loose."

**QUALITY** Dylan Verdi is a cute little girl, but once the novelty of world's-youngest-vloggerdom wears off, there is no reason for anyone outside of her immediate family to watch her iMovies. "I mean you can put a lot of bad video clips that you shoot with your camera phone on the Web," says Mr. Malik, "but how many people want to watch that? If you're going to create a product for passive consumption it has to be good. I mean look at all the shows that fail. There is very low tolerance for bad television."

**FINANCING** "Where," Mr. Malik asks, "does the money come from to produce the programming of high enough quality to reach the audiences that are obviously going to be smaller than the status quo?" In a video-on-demand universe, networks may send along free samples of new shows to paying customers of existing ones, but absent vast reservoirs of ad revenue, the risk of program development may well be prohibitive. A collapse of the old model could create a Hollywood dustbowl.

**LEGISLATION** Peer-to-peer software such as BitTorrent, which permits affordable transfer of large video files, also enables video piracy, and could be legislated or litigated into oblivion by a beleaguered Hollywood desperate to preserve the value of its backlist. Sen. Orrin Hatch, R-Utah, last year introduced an anti-P2P bill called the Inducing Infringement of Copyright Act of 2004 (Induce Act).

**COST** As pricing in the search business has amply demonstrated, any influx of spending into the online space will drive prices upwards, potentially erasing the efficiencies promised by even the most ultra-targeted media buy. The metrics of reach may change radically, but not necessarily those of frequency. As Mr. Tobaccowala puts it, "Millions of people arrive at the Yahoo Homepage. What people don't realize is that they arrive one at a time."

**SUITABILITY** Content will be enormously diverse, agrees Forrest Research research director Chris Charron, but will it constitute a legitimate advertising medium? "A lot of people talk about these social networks and blogs and the blogosphere as being great ways to attract consumers and attract eyeballs and potentially good advertising opportunities, but history shows that is not the case, even recent history. Remember GeoCities? I think they were bought by Yahoo for $3 or $4 billion. Well, it never became a very viable advertising outlet and that's because it wasn't a great context for people to place ads. Advertisers weren't interested in putting it on a personal homepage for Chris Charron for my friends and relatives to see."

**CONTENT DIVIDE** Convergence means not only technological and economic disruption; it means social disruption. Cost of broadband and VOD programming will surely exceed $100 per month for each household, and most likely twice that, disenfranchising tens of millions of Americans and changing the dynamics of a shared popular culture. The idea of a vast digital underclass mocks the Internet's promise of the democratization of media.

Then, of course, there is the biggest monkey wrench in the works: the absurd lack of preparedness for anything other than the most deliberate evolution into a Jetsonian future.

"Even if all the technology were in place and scaled up to size," says Mr. Tobaccowala, "what isn't ready really is either clients, agencies, or the media companies. Because in effect what we have to change is the way we do business."

Oh, preparations are underway. Earlier this year, Rupert Murdoch's News Corp. retained McKinsey & Co. to figure out how to transition to this Internet thing—which is something like nailing plywood to the windows when the hurricane makes landfall. News Corp. no doubt feels safe enough, because Fox network customers are still lining up to buy, partly because they know how to do that. GRPs are buggywhips that just feel so familiar and reassuring in their hands. No wonder Mr. Stengel is showing up at the 4A's revival tent preaching salvation: "If we believe that there's life beyond the 30-second spot," he demanded, "why are we still dependant on reach, frequency and advertising pre-market scores?"

## Yahoo's Gambit

So don't storm the Bastille just yet. Even the revolutionaries aren't quite organized for the revolution. Among those not quite ready for the end of prime time is Yahoo, which hired ABC programming chief Lloyd Braun to develop whatever content will be when content will come from the likes of Yahoo.

"The key for us," he told an iMedia Brand Summit in February, "is to be able to come up with that unique, signature, compelling content for the Internet, the way television has been able to do over the years."

Duh. As to what that might look like, he was a little bit fuzzy.

"What I'm not saying is that we're just going to be doing television shows on Yahoo, and we're going to be streaming them, so we're going to do our version of *Lost*, or our version of *Alias*. There's going to be a big place for video streaming and all of that, don't get me wrong, but I don't believe ultimately that the future of Internet content is by doing on the PC, or on mobile devices, what you can already get on your living room television set. We have to really get our arms around what those expectations are. What is the audience looking for when they go on the Internet?"

Yes, that would seem to be the question. But nobody has definitively answered it. That's why there are hand-wringing Cassandras like Jim Stengel and giddy opportunists like Wunderman's Shawn Burns.

But what if you are a direct marketer in what promises to be the Golden Age for direct marketing and a historic opportunity knocks and you lack the manpower to answer the door? Under the current circumstances, Mr. Burns says he'd first advise clients to scale up their Web capabilities by a factor of 10. But he concedes that in a Gold Rush economy, he doesn't know where all the Web designers would come from to do the work. That, of course, is the essence of the Chaos Scenario—a critical shortage of resources and infrastructure.

It's almost comical to hear Starcom's Mr. Tobaccowala talk about the marketing landscape of the very near future.

"Expect to see a lot of event and store-based marketing," he says. "Expect people to actually go completely away from electronic media to experiential media, if you can call it that. So expect for instance Starbucks, bars, all kinds of things—bathrooms, OK?"

Bathrooms? Jim Stengel has $5.5 billion burning a hole in his pocket, and he's supposed to invest it in bathrooms?

"That's exactly the point," says John Hayes, chief marketing officer for American Express. "There isn't the off-the-shelf capacity today. You have to create it. You have to build them. You have to come up with the ideas. To access the talent, you have to basically construct solutions."

Hence Amex's Jerry Seinfeld/Superman Webisodes and sponsored concerts Webcast to prospects. If the old model is broken, Mr. Hayes can't just sit around waiting for somebody else to fix it.

"As in any industry," he says, "those who are unprepared for change will obviously suffer the consequences."

That warning has to be pried from Mr. Hayes' lips, but it is a warning nonetheless—sort of a reciprocal to another sort of warning. David Poltack, of CBS, may or may not be the spokesman for the status quo, but you can't miss the "You'll be sorry" quality to his caution about his notion of the chaos scenario should marketers abandon network TV.

## An Economic Downfall?

"If they do," he says, "then the entire marketing system that perpetuates this economy will be weakened. And this is not a problem for just the broadcast television networks. This is a major problem for everyone who markets a product to the consumers in this country. Because there has been and there is not currently on the horizon anywhere near as effective a way to market products to the mass consumer marketplace. And if in fact that current system deteriorates to the point that advertisers and marketers abandon it, I don't see anything that's going to replace it and the entire marketing infrastructure and the economy is going to be diminished. And that's a lot bigger problem than just a network television program."

In other words, what's good for CBS is good for America.

The other possibility is the opposite: that what's bad for CBS, and for ABC and NBC and Fox and Conde Nast and the Gannett Co. is very good for America, because what emerges from the ruins will be superior in every way to what it replaced. Better for marketers, better for the economy and especially better for Mr. Jetson, who won't have a robot maid but very likely will have a million-channel universe.

As Rishad Tobaccowala elegantly concludes, "Those who come to destroy TV are those who are eventually going to save it."

And the world will rejoice, happily awash in electrons. But before the liberté, fraternité and egalité, beware. This is revolution, and first we will be awash in the blood of the old guard.

## Questions for Consideration

1    How might the chaos scenario play out in other traditional media industries?

2    In what ways might the sorts of marketing activities Garfield describes be beneficial and/or detrimental to people as customers for goods and as audiences for media material?

# Chapter 28

## JOSEPH TUROW

# RETHINKING TELEVISION IN THE DIGITAL AGE

**THE WAYS IN WHICH YOU** watch and experience television are very different from those of just a decade ago. The spread of digital recording devices, the rise of on-demand services, and the shift to digital platforms has led to more power in the hands of audiences. Perhaps not surprisingly, these changes are highly problematic for television executives and the advertisers who support them. In this recent essay, Joseph Turow, a professor of communication at the University of Pennsylvania, explores how those in the television and advertising industries are responding to these challenges and what this suggests about the future of television. His description of a move toward customizable and targeted programming is already beginning to be realized. The piece urges consideration of the social implications of this trend, including those related to issues of privacy.

For many U.S. media and marketing executives the appearance of the digital video recorder marked the beginning of the end of television as they had known it. Essentially a computer with a large hard dive, the DVR acted like a video cassette recorder in enabling its owners to record programs and to view them at other times. Unlike a VCR, the technology marketed to the public by TiVo and other firms was connected to an updatable guide that made finding programs across more than one hundred channels easy. Also unlike a VCR, in some versions made by Replay TV (and in "hacked" versions of TiVo) it allowed viewers to skip ahead 30 seconds at a time without at all viewing what was skipped. That, advertisers knew, would be commercials. In fact, Replay TV used its PVR's facility for skipping over commercials as a selling point in its early ads.

But the concern that marketing and TV executives had around DVRs ran deeper than viewers' ability to skip commercials. It reflected a broader worry that digital devices that would remake television to give consumers the kind of control over what and when they watched was already emerging on the internet. With the worry that consumers could really push away ads better than ever before, and that consumers were increasingly turning to the internet and other digital media and that they were often poaching TV materials without their associated commercials, major marketers began to change their own advertising strategies so as to ensure as much as possible that they could follow, and influence, the consumers they wanted to reach wherever they went. As they did that, they were in effect helping to bring an end to television as we have known it.

Well into the first decade of the 21st century, the domestic box we call "television" is in the U.S. becoming merely one node in advertisers' attempts to reach desirable individuals as they move across different media. Moreover, the logic of marketer-media concerns points to even greater changes in the decades to come. A variety of overlapping developments suggest a future in which the presentation of news, entertainment and advertising is customized to the individual backgrounds of audience members and available virtually everywhere through both stationary and mobile media. In addition to a variety of social issues posed by the rise of database marketing, the developments raise the question of what television really means today and whether not too long from now it will be a useful label at all.

## Coming to Terms with Digital Media

Those who at the start of the century said the fear of digital video recorders was exaggerated pointed out that sales were rather small. One trade article in 2002 called the DVR "a technology in search of a business model."[1] Others disagreed strongly. They pointed out that the sales rate of branded DVRs was increasing and that home satellite firms and cable systems were beginning to integrate unbranded versions into set-top boxes. They noted TiVo's admission that 60 percent to 70 percent of people watching via its technology were skipping commercials. And they admonished that whatever accommodation advertisers would make with DVR firms, it would undercut the by-then-traditional approach of mounting 15- or 30- second commercials within shows.

Of course, marketers have long been irked by the power that intended audience members hold to not pay attention to—and even dismiss the value of—the marketers' ads, especially when the ads pay for content or activities that the consumers value. Stories in and out of the trade press have pointed out that people talk, visit the kitchen or used the bathroom during TV commercial breaks. Television executives saw as their major task to help advertisers draw and keep attractive audiences, as determined by the Nielsen company's ratings. Exactly what "attractive audiences" meant, and how to draw and keep them, were ideas that changed over the decades in network and local TV. From the early 1950s through the late 1990s network executives took pains to convince advertisers that beyond intuition they were developing systematic survey and program-analyzing techniques to guide the choice of shows as well as tactics such as least objectionable programs, lead-ins, lead-outs and hammocking to array the programs for optimal audience flow through the prime time schedule.

The arrival of TiVo and other DVRs threatened to upend the routines of predictable scheduling and advertising placement that had become the verities upon which commercial U.S. television was based. Moreover, the explosion of channels to the consumer via the web, cable TV, satellite television, and handheld media, with their transformation from analog to digital, led advertisers to question longstanding ways to reach audiences. As an *Advertising Age* columnist noted in 2007, "Digital media—pretty much on an hourly basis these days—seems to throw out a new way to disrupt the traditional pathways to the consumer."[2] In this environment of swirling change, advertising executives began to question the verities of media planning and television's central position in them. The consensus began to develop past mid-decade that the way to consumers, particularly young consumers, could not be through traditional television commercials. If TV commercials were to be used at all, they had to be created with the goal of making them so buzz-worthy as to be sparks to discussions among members of the target groups that might even involve sending versions of the commercials on the internet or cell phone or elsewhere. "The world is digital," noted the world CEO of the huge Universal McCann media buying division of Interpublic, "and we must adapt to take full advantage of that as an industry."[3]

One way marketers have come to terms with the digital challenge has been to integrate their products into non-advertising media content with the hope of getting more attention than traditional advertising would. An early version of this approach was "product placement," the act of trading or buying an item's position within media content. The practice can be traced back to at least the silent movies and became a frenzied TV phenomenon in the wake of marketers' first concerns about DVRs. Many marketers have realized, however, that simply mentioning or inserting a product into part of a program would rarely get them far in demonstrating the item or building its personality.

So the next step involved integrating the item or service directly into the TV action to bring out its brand character. Yet ad executives soon concluded that this approach too was self-limiting in an era where their target consumer's attention was fleeting and often far from particular programs and even from the traditional TV set. Marketers' current strategy is therefore to create a mix of advertising and product integration that provocatively piques the interest of the target audience so that they visit the marketer's website to see more, share the ideas about it virally via the web and move it across a variety of media platforms, including television.

The Super Bowl provides the optimal service for advertisers looking to use television as one element in a multimedia promotion. In the mid 2000s, the season-ending American football match was still a place on sponsored network TV to find young adult men in huge numbers. Rather than adopting the pre-TiVo goal of aiming thirty second commercials at them with the hope that the ads will enhance brand identities and sales, recent Super Bowl advertisers have seen the game commercial as a way to engage the audience weeks before its airing and far after it. The website naming company Godaddy.com, for example, worked to cultivate a reputation for creating Super Bowl commercials that network executives consider unacceptably sexual. In the months before the event it whipped up young-adult interest in the commercials it is trying to get past the censors. Then it used the steamy spot that the network accepted to drive the core audience to its website where they can see ones that did not make it through, enjoy racier versions of the accepted one, and learn about the company. "We can't get across what we do in a 30-second spot," noted the company's CEO "so we have to run a spot that is polarizing enough to get people to come to our website to see more."[4]

Anheuser-Bush, the largest Super Bowl advertiser, took an even more drastic tack. Apart from encouraging discussion about its spots in the weeks prior to the CBS show, the beermaker used its in-game commercials to kick off Bud.TV, what can only be described as a clear acknowledgement that the end of traditional TV is at hand for the company's core twentysomething consumers. "What cable and satellite were to the last generation, digital is to this generation," said the firm's vice present of global media. Pitching the site as a full-service entertainment network on the web, the company promised to limit product placement drastically and instead offer up a place where Bud drinkers could find collegial entertainment that would generate buzz offline and on. "What they're offering up is bigger than integration," opined an executive from the marketing communication giant Omnicom. Its branded entertainment arm was involved in the project. He explained: "They're offering up a destination, a community for their audience, and I think that's even a bigger idea than placing products in shows."[5]

Part of marketers' goal of creating a website that is highly trafficked by its target users relates to a second strategy for a post-television world: channeling the audience's involvement in "user-generated content" into activities that will enhance their identification with company products. User-generated content is a term that characterizes the digital video, blogging, podcasting, mobile phone photography, software and wikis that millions of people are creating as technologies of production and distribution become more accessible and affordable than in previous decades. Wikipedia says the term "came into the mainstream in 2005," but a Nexis search of *Advertising Age* reveals that it was already on marketers' radar in 2000 as a way to bring people closer to companies.[6] The popular press celebrated Facebook, YouTube, MySpace and similar social media sites as the incarnation of (in Wikipedia's words) "collaboration, skill-building and discovery" by "end-users as opposed to traditional media producers, licensed broadcasters, and production companies." Marketers, for their part, saw the phenomenon as a way to bond consumers to them by giving them the incentive, and sometimes even the tools, to create advertisements about them. While some advertisers sneered—one suggested that user-generated commercials involved the inmates taking over the asylum—many others mounted multimedia ad-making contests with prizes and fame as the rewards.

Television emerged as one node in a multi-channel extravaganza that focused on generating excitement in young male adults around user-generated ad messages. The 2007 Super Bowl gave these activities a particularly high profile, as Frito Lay, General Motors, and the National Football League announced contests for audience-created commercials with the winning ones to be shown during the game. The companies' websites accepted thousands of submissions, and blogs and other commentaries around the internet buzzed with discussions about the commercials. All three firms themselves pumped hoopla around the submissions as well the final selection in ways that clearly linked the user-generated strategy to the strategy of using TV as only one node—albeit a central node—in a multi-channel strategy.

## Early Versions of Television Interactivity

Advertising executives who implement the multiplatform and user-generated strategies are convinced that traditional television—the long-dominant static domestic box—increasingly will have to be used together with other media if it is to be an effective marketing tool in the twenty-first century. The TV industry had worked with analog versions of interactivity via the telephone during the pre-digital era of the 1950s through 1990s. A few widely-promoted cases involved entertainment: the three broadcast networks hyped viewers' interest by encouraging them to phone and vote for plot endings. More common, however, was the use of the phone for direct marketing. With the rise of 800 numbers, advertisers invited viewer contact through individual commercials; in longform "infomercials" at odd hours on broadcast or cable channels; at the end of programs to hawk videos and tie-ins (such as selling a necklace from a soap opera) at the end of network shows; and, beginning 1982, with entire shopping shows and even shopping networks.[7]

Attempts to get viewers involved in programming on a more continual basis than through phone or web votes necessitated actual tinkering with TV equipment. In the early 1970s engineers started sending data through the vertical blanking interval (VBI) of the analog signal. The VBI is the black stripe at the top and bottom of the TV picture. Broadcasters can use part of it to send data that viewers can receive using a special decoder. In the U.S. the most common application was for text captions often used by deaf viewers. But two VBI technologies that together made inroads into more than a million cable and DBS homes in the late 1990s were Wink and WebTV. Both used the vertical blanking interval to send what Wink called "enhanced broadcasting." Viewers saw commercials during pauses in the shows, at the end of shows, or in their own shows or channels (which in essence tried to make the commercials the entertainment). Available by 2003 in over five million cable and direct broadcast satellite homes, Wink and WebTV enabled marketers to go well beyond a 30-second TV spot. Consumers could request more information on a product or service, participate in polls, sweepstakes and promotions.

The first steps cable, satellite and broadcast TV executives took with the rise of digital technology was to directly translate what had been awkward attempts at interactivity into more fluid, though similar, activities. Now voting on entertainment could take place easily via text messages from cell phones—and entire programs (such as American Idol) could be built around them. Products from TV shows—and even the shows themselves—could be sold on the programs' websites. And using the internet or the DVR with a phone line (depending on whether the provider was a cable or satellite system), a content supplier could offer far more interactivity more quickly than the vertical blanking interval would allow. US trade magazines pointed out that in the U.K. News Corp's BSkyB satellite operation pushed set-top-box interactivity to the point that the "red button" on the remote became part of the national consciousness. It could provide up to eight simultaneous windows on the TV screen, allowing people to watch the news with sound while looking at a weather forecast and viewing a football game.[8]

Some marketers, though, wondered whether U.S. viewers wanted that kind of interactivity around products while watching television. Stating that interactive TV commerce had not been terribly successful on BSkyB, a U.K. analyst opined in late 2002 that "[f]or many, the TV remains a 'lean-back' medium, though which people want to be entertained." The vice president of business development at Visible World, a new-technology advertising company, offered in 2005 that Americans felt the same way as the Brits about interactive entertainment. Research showed, he said, that capabilities such as the instant replay of football action on digital video recorders gets high use when consumers first encounter them. After a short while they lose interest and simply view what comes at them.[9]

At the same time, marketing and media executives often added at conferences, in one-on-one conversations and in the trade press that consumer interest might well change with future generations of viewers. Turn-of-the-century 18 to 55 year olds were stuck in an old model of TV viewing. Their children, and their children's children, seemed much more comfortable using media in a multitasking, constantly-clicking way.

"The issue for us and others [in interactive television]," said a TiVo executive in 2004, "is getting past the inertia of how people watch TV. It hasn't changed . . . our whole lives. What we've learned is that all of the advertisers we've worked with have accepted that sometime in the future, the consumer will be in charge. Once you see that, you see there are more opportunities than barriers."[10]

## Encouraging Digital Interactivity

Among the opportunities marketers tried to exploit were ways to bring audiences to meet up with commercials that they would actively want to watch. Two approaches stand out. The "targeted pull" approach aims to provide motivated viewers with a place to actually find commercials they want to watch. The "customized push" tack sends to viewers commercials that appear to be traditional but are really tailored to their background as a result of database analysis. Both these methods can be combined to yield "pull" commercials that are customized. Moreover, current technology makes customized and interactive product placement possible. A key question is whether—or more likely, when—marketing and media practitioners will spend the sizeable amount of money needed to roll out some of the more high-tech of these activities.

TiVo—whom ad people saw initially as the Darth Vader of TV commercials—was actually an important force behind the pull approach. TiVo executives concluded that it needed revenue from advertisers if their company were to survive. The DVR firm's ability to tinker with the TV signals that its million-plus viewers receive also gave it the ability to point them from regular commercials to its Showcase, a space for watching commercials "on demand." So, for example, investment firm Charles Schwab & Co. paid TiVo to link a thirty second network spot starring golfer Phil Mickelson to Showcase via a special symbol on TiVo-attached sets. The symbol signaled to viewers that if they clicked they could see more; it turned out to be a four-minute video about the company and three segments with the golf pro. Viewers of the Showcase could also order information from Schwab via the TV set. They could then return to the program they were watching at the exact point they were watching.[11] As the director of operations at the agency that oversaw the Schwab presentation noted, this use of the DVR marked a "TV-plus approach" that "gave us great response from the hand raisers, as far as a direct-response medium."[12]

The idea spread beyond TiVo. Linking its set-top DVR with its satellite delivery system, EchoStar's Dish Network in 2004 started offering advertisers similar packages to around 9 million of its subscribers.[13] Another version of this targeting of potential hand-raisers involved video-on-demand (VOD) cable services. Video on demand refers to programs that are stored digitally on huge servers at a cable company and sent to a person's television via the digital cable box when the person presses a button on the remote to receive it. The advertising piece involves placing long-form commercials directly at the end of VOD programs that seem to resonate with particular advertisers.

On Comcast cable systems, for example, a VOD program from the Discovery Science Channel in early 2005 was preceded by a message from General Motors Corp. that urged viewers to stay tuned at the end of the program for a video about a new Corvette. That 15-minute video at the end of the program was a documentary-style message from GM highlighting the advanced technology in the car, a message that might be interesting to the kind of people who would select a science program on VOD.

Borrowing from the experience of VBI virtual ad channels and TiVo Showcase, GM also worked with Comcast to develop a VOD channel called the GM Showcase, where viewers could select similar programs about other GM products and ask for more information. "The thing about selling new cars and trucks is that in any given market, only about 1.5 percent of the population is looking for a new vehicle," agreed the general director of media operations for GM. The VOD world's advantage over linear television, she said, is it allows marketers to reach exactly those people.[14]

## Adding Personalization to Interactivity

For those consumers who might not be motivated to pull ads to them, Comcast and other cable operators were experimenting with variations on the traditional push approach. The aim was to link database marketing capabilities to thirty second commercials during the programs. In one sense, it was still traditional because it assumed a "lean back" consumer who didn't have to change behavior in the face of ads. At the same time, it marked the drive toward digital marketing discrimination in the TV world.

Comcast, for example, promoted its ability to send different commercials to different areas based upon distinctions that it and its advertisers found between those areas. With a service it called Adtag, the same car dealer could add different voiceovers to an ad based on geographic location. From one viewpoint what Comcast was offering advertisers was nothing more than the ability to target to zones based around the distribution equipment—the "head ends"—of their local systems.[15] Because the systems covered fewer homes than broadcast signals, advertisers could discriminate between smaller areas based on data from geodemographic research companies such as Claritas that provide information about the wealth, lifestyles and purchasing habits based on postal ZIP codes. Yet this kind of targeting encouraged greater differentiation among neighborhoods by television advertisers than was previously possible. The Visible World technology that powered it, though, had far greater capability. Backed by such huge ad players as WPP Group and Grey Global, the small startup's Intellispot system could create and deliver TV commercials that change message and creative elements in real time.[16] It did that by creating different layers for parts of the commercial that will be changed digitally. At cable system head-ends, the commercial was placed on servers jointly run by the cable firm and Visible World. The layered nature of the commercials allowed the advertisers to change the message for that zone based on anything from the weather to the time of day to the day of the week without delivering multiple tapes.

A Visible World executive said people in homes receiving the commercials would not know (unless told) that they were getting messages targeting to their area. He added that the customization could easily be integrated with interactivity. Visible World could work with interactive advertising firms to allow people who receive the customized commercial to click on elements of the commercial to learn more or request information.[17]

A bit further under the Intellispot hood the possibility of even greater customization appeared. The software could implement thousands of versions of a commercial in seconds by changing features from music to voiceover to characters to graphics. In the case of a car commercial, for example, one layer might involve the vehicle; another, the driver, a third, the kind of highway; yet another, the song played in the background.

Based on database instructions to software in household set-top boxes, Visible World could create commercials customized to different individuals homes, not just head-end zones.

Although it was technically quite feasible for cable systems to implement household-customized commercials in 2005, it wasn't happening except in scattered tests. One reason was the relatively sparse use of the digital set top boxes needed to process the commercials. Gerrit Niemeijer, Visible World's chief technology officer, noted in 2005 that cable firms were loath to spend the dollar or more per box that would be required to give a digital box the ability to process his firm's layered commercial. A dollar seemed like a small amount, he pointed out, but for a multiple system operator it added up to substantial money; Comcast, for example, has over twenty million subscribers in 2005.[18]

Niemeijer offered an additional hurdle: privacy concerns. He said he has heard cable system executives express worries that the kinds of personal-information issues that swirled about the web would hit them. Yet he firmly expressed the opinion that the Cable Television Act of 1984 doesn't prohibit cable firms from sending customized commercials to households. No one seems to contest that point, despite the complexity of the Act's privacy section. Using the same kinds of tortured clauses and possible escape hatches common to corporate website privacy policies, the section seems to first take away and then return to cable firms the right to give marketers ways to discriminate among subscribers. The section seems also to say that cable systems cannot sell personally identifiable information to marketers—except that they can sell basic "mailing list" information. That means the names and addresses of individual subscribers. The section also gives cable systems the right to collect a lot more data about subscribers for their own uses if subscribers give "prior written or electronic consent"—or if it is "necessary to render a cable service or other service provided by the cable operator to the subscriber." One such "other service" may well be advertising.[19]

Spotlight managing director Hank Oster stated his belief that privacy laws prevent his Comcast division from selling subscriber names and addresses to advertisers. Spotlight does collect loads of demographic and viewing information about households in head-end zones and then aggregates the data in order to interest sponsors. Spotlight will also take data from individual advertisers about individual addresses that they want to target and confirm the percentage of the zone's households they represent. So, for example, the cable ad marketer will confirm to Kraft that 25% of the homes in an area are addresses that Kraft knows buy the company's cheeses. That high percentage might encourage Kraft to advertise in that Comcast zone—or purchase Showcase programming—because it is higher than the national average.

A Visible World executive added that often the advertiser is more active than the cable firm in bringing substantial household data to the marketing situation. In the future, he predicted the advertiser would download personal information to the cable box that would help create the custom-layers for the target. The information would disappear after the commercial was created. Because neither the cable firm nor Visible World would share that information, it all would be quite legal and potentially very powerful for sending different commercial offers to households—and possibly eventually even people in those households—based on what marketers conclude about them.

Behind such goals is an awareness that much of the digital media world is moving in the direction of database-driven approaches to audiences and content. Advertising and television executives see the internet, now the most interactive of electronic media, as a test bed for gathering and analyzing information about particular members of the audience in the interest of better persuading them. U.S. television executives could hardly stand by and watch the growth of the new forms of database marketing without realizing its importance to the survival of their industry. They also knew, however, that traditional domestic television at mid-decade had nothing like the interactive capabilities and personalization technologies that were needed to execute comparable approaches to advertising and selling.

"This is the future of TV advertising," contended a venture capitalist with an investment in Navic Networks, a startup firm competing with Visible World. "If I were to factor what TV advertising may be like in three to five years, I think today's concept of producing blanket TV ads will be analogous to dropping leaflets out of an airplane."[20] Backing up his claim, Forrester Research had found a high percentage of database-marketing executives for major financial, telecom, and retail firms very interested in household-level TV ad targeting. Their desire to reach the right people was so high that they said they would pay between fifty and sixty cents for each ad delivered to a household. It means spending as much as $600 to reach one thousand viewers at a time when conventional prime time television charged between $30 and $40 per thousand. "That's off the chart," exclaimed a Forrester analyst.[21]

The collection of data about viewers, the complex analysis of the data, and the implementation of messages based on them is still in its relative infancy on the web—and even more so in the traditional TV industry. Nevertheless, tailored communication to database-driven niches is moving forward according to an industrial logic that marketing and media executives repeat often: To get consumers to pay attention to commercial messages, marketers must know as much as possible about them and interact with them whenever and wherever they can convince consumers to find them relevant. The recipe involves attempting to take charge by attempting to inculcate a strong sense of brand trust while gathering information with which to decide whether and how a customer is worth engaging in customized digital relationships. Six inter-related activities form the heart of the logic: screening consumers for appropriateness, interacting with them electronically, targeted tracking of them, data mining, mass customization of advertising messages, and the cultivation of relationships based on the knowledge gained.

Visible World was, in fact, working along these lines to make that idea as attractive as possible by making it easy for advertisers to find the households they wanted. They turned to Teradata, a Dayton, Ohio-based company owned by NCR that sells consumer behavior data to advertisers such as Travelocity. The advertisers were using it to target consumers with tailor-made ads on the Internet. The idea was to do for TV what it does online: to deliver TV ads that are not just tailor-made to people who live in certain neighborhoods, but are also tailored to suit individual interests. "Our end-game is to mass customize commercials as granular as you can get," a Visible World executive told *Advertising Age* in connection with its Teradata project. "We envision the day—in three to five years—when consumers will actually request commercials [customized for them], and that is the ultimate relevance."[22]

The notion that commercials can be tailored—as well as made interactive—for particular households and even individuals is such an attractive idea to marketing and new media practitioners that they often discuss it as the ultimate antidote to ad-skipping. Their expectation is that viewers will pay attention when people see and hear products and claims that speak directly to their interests. An obvious addition to this armamentarium is customized product integration directly into programs.

Asked about the possibilities of customized product placement, executives from marketing and technology firms say that while possible today it would be even harder to implement than customized commercials. Gene Dwyer, Director of Technology for Princeton Video Imaging (PVI), said that his company has the capability to custom-insert products into shows during real time. He added, however, that the desire to carry out customized ad versions of these activities surrenders at this point in time to the demands such household-level customizations make on the set-top box. Database-driven product placement requires even more computing power in the digital set-top box than does the Visible-World type commercial creation. The reason is that while creating a thirty second commercial requires the combination of layers, the customized product placement requires that plus integration of the material into the flow of ongoing programming.

## The Rise of many "Televisions"

It is, however, a pretty sure bet that within the next decade and a half the customization of all sorts of commercial messages will prove both quite feasible and competitively essential. At this point, the biggest logjam with cable is technical: there are not enough digital set-top boxes in the approximately-70% of U.S. homes that get their TV via cable, and the boxes that do exist are too primitive to accommodate real-time customization. But the situation is very fluid. Cable firms already see strong reason to pepper their subscribers' homes with digital set-top boxes as well as add substantial computing power to them. The particular motivation is strong competition from satellite and phone companies (telcos) that aim to compete with cable firms to provide a "triple play" of voice, video and data. Consumer electronics companies such as Apple, HP, Sony and Phillips also stand ready to compete with all these firms in the "home entertainment" space.

The nation rollout in the US of digital television by large phone companies such as Verizon and AT&T using internet protocol technology is beginning to ramp up the need by cable firms to deploy smarter interactive capabilities. Ed Grazyk, marketing director at Microsoft TV, Verizon's technology supplier, noted that all subscribers would get HDTV, DVR, VOD and an interactive electronic program guide (EPG) as part of his firm's service. He added that the telcos will, over time, easily add various advanced, internet-based interactive services to the offering. In fact, technologies already available from Microsoft (the Xbox 360) Apple (Apple TV) and Oracle (via various Linksys products) allow viewers to personalize the program guide and to conduct programming searches and schedule recordings from PCs and other connected devices. They also allow individuals to incorporate internet content and personal media into the viewing experience, allowing viewers, for example, to view on the TV digital photos stored on a networked PC. Most important, from an advertising standpoint, they allow for sending of new forms of commercials to the home and even the individual on the home television set. One rapidly growing example involves the integration of brands into internet-linked video games. Companies such Massive (owned by Microsoft) and Double Fusion aim to dynamically change the commercial messages seen in the games depending upon what the game provider knows about the users.

But the arrival of an interactive, customizable domestic TV set is just the start of transformations in television technology that promise to further reshape programming and advertising. Although the internet and the domestic TV set will increasingly be integrated, the standalone PC will increase as a vehicle for accessing professionally- and amateur- created programming. Despite some employers' displeasure, the workplace has become a venue of major importance to advertisers who want to reach huge numbers of people who troll through the web and buy products at times when their employers would rather they work. While some workplaces block the viewing of IPTV, in many places employees do go online to watch during the day. Media firms and their sponsors see the potential for customized programming and commercials in that space based upon what they learn about their audiences. Already researchers are beginning to note differences in the video-on-demand programming people choose to consume, depending whether they are watching on the web or on cable.[23] As data about differences in viewing based on video platforms (and location) become part of the industry belief system, it will affect the kinds of audiovisual entertainment and targeted advertising that are presented in different venues.

And while new ways to merge advertising and programming on the home set and internet are major concerns of programmers, technologists, and marketing executives, the newest buzz centers on the "third screen"—the mobile phone. In Japan, Korea, and parts of Europe, developments in both programming and marketing have outpaced those in the United States, where 3G and other broadband mobile technologies are not as developed. The new audiovisual age is just beginning, but major media conglomerates are jockeying alongside entrepreneurial upstarts to decide what programming will work best on handhelds, how to repurpose contemporary materials for mobile audiences, and how to create search engines that help people find what they want to watch at the time they want it. Not only are media firms and marketers deciding the best avenues for return on investment in this new area, they are confronting mobile phone companies that have a strong monetary interest in controlling access to their customers in order to charge media firms that want to reach them and to get cut a cut of advertising. Tensions among wireless firms, media companies, and marketers around these issues are likely to increase.

One valuable bit of information about customers that the mobile providers hold is their location as they move through the day. Media firms and marketers do have other ways to reach their favorite customers as they travel. People can text-message their postal address or postal code, for example; they can scan a barcode in a store; or they can point their blue-tooth enabled phone to a transmitter on a billboard. Whatever the method, being able to follow known individuals who agree to receive programming, information and discounts in places that matter to them takes the personalization of messages to an entirely new level. It's likely that people who agree to these sorts of relationships will knowingly or unknowingly offer up enormous amounts of information about their interests, backgrounds and movements in time and space. This is information marketers can use as they travel with consumers down the aisles of supermarkets, electronics stores, and other retail outlets. It is here, at the point of product selection—what Procter and Gamble executives have called the "first moment of truth"—that marketers might find the ability to send coupons or engage in other tailored incentives particularly compelling media buys.

The ability to move customized audiovisual advertising via handhelds directly to the point of purchase may lead some advertisers to lessen their purchase of space and time on traditional media. It also seems likely that what media firms learn about the habits of individual consumers via out-of-home tracking may affect far more than decisions about the materials and ads they serve them in the mobile space. What they learn might well have implications for the spectrum of audiovisual news, information, entertainment—and the embedded marketing messages—that they confront at home as well.

Just a bit into the twenty-first century, then, advertising and media practitioners see "television" as part of a cross-platform activity that is part of the process of meeting the needs of marketers who want to be able reach customers at every turn. The traditional domestic television box is in the short term being used as a way to move target audiences to the internet where marketers can engage directly with them through the medium's increasing interactivity, targeted tracking, data mining and the cultivation of relationships. In the medium and long term, media and marketing executives aim to migrate these capabilities to the domestic TV box as well as other large and small screens in and out of home. Whether all—or any—of these audiovisual technologies should be called "television" will actually be one of the smaller issues confronting media and marketing practitioners as well as the researchers who study the social implications of their work. The rethinking of television is both causing and reflecting changes in the way society relates to itself. It is an ongoing process that deserves close attention.

---

## Questions for Consideration

1   What are some benefits of customizable programming and ads for the individual? What are some costs of customizable programming and ads for the individual? In your mind, do the benefits outweigh the costs?
2   With all the changes taking place in the ways people watch audiovisual news and entertainment, some people might argue that it is difficult to know what "television" means today. Do you agree? Why?

---

## Notes

1. Bradley Johnson, "TiVo, ReplayTV View for Uncertain Prize," *Advertising Age*, November 4, 2002, p. 42.
2. [No author], "Are Media Agencies Ready for Convergence?" *Advertising Age*, March 1, 2007.
3. Nick Brien, quoted in [No author], "Are Media Agencies Ready for Convergence?" *Advertising Age*, March 1, 2007.
4. Bob Parsons, quoted in Bruce Horovitz, "Marketers Set Up a Screen Play," *USA Today*, February 2, 2007.
5. Gail Schiller, "Bud.TV Hops to it With Originals," *Hollywood Reporter*, February 2, 2007.
6. "User-generated Content," Wikipedia (http://en.wikipedia.org/wiki/User-Generated_Content), accessed on February 5, 2007; and Patricia Riedman, "Dot-com slump crimps marketing," *Advertising Age*, May 29, 2000, p. 66.
7. Roy M. Speer and Lowell W. Paxson created the first television shopping show, *Home Shopping*, in the Tampa Bay area of Florida in 1982, and in other parts of the country three years later. See Andrew Feinberg, "Picking Up the Pieces in Home Shopping," *New York Times*, September 28, 1988, Section 3, p. 4.

8.    Martha Bennett, "Interactive Television: Moving Forward, at a Snail's Pace," *Forrester IdeaByte*, November 1, 2002.

9.    Interview with Pat Ruta, VP Business Development, Visible World, February 11, 2005.

10.    Brodie Keast, quoted in Tobi Elkin, "Madison + Vine: Getting viewers to opt in, not tune out," *Advertising Age*, November 4, 2002, p. 10.

11.    Anne M. Mack, "Interactive Quarterly," *AdWeek*, September 20, 2004, via Nexis.

12.    Jason Kuperman of Tequila, Los Angeles, quoted in Anne M. Mack, "Interactive Quarterly," *AdWeek*, September 20, 2004, via Nexis.

13.    Anne M. Mack, "Interactive Quarterly," *AdWeek*, September 20, 2004, via Nexis.

14.    Tony Gnoffo, "Technology forces television advertisers to re-evaluate methods," *Philadelphia Inquirer*, January 23, 2005, p. E-01.

15.    Conversation with Dana Runnells, Senior Marketing Manager, Comcast Spotlight, February 11, 2005.

16.    Jack Neff, "Addressable TV meet with agency and marketer resistance," *Advertising Age*, March 15, 2004, p. 12.

17.    Interview with Pat Ruta, VP Business Development, Visible World, February 11, 2005.

18.    Interview with Gerrit Niemeijer, February 14, 2005.

19.    See Cable TV Privacy Act of 1984, Section 551, "Protection of Subscriber Privacy" part c. http://www.epic.org/privacy/cable_tv/ctpa.html

20.    Dan Nova, quoted in Janet Whitman, "New ad technology tailors TV ads to specific viewers," *Marketing News*, November 15, 2004, p. 35.

21.    Eric Schmitt of Forrester Research quoted in Janet Whitman, "New ad technology tailors TV ads to specific viewers," *Marketing News*, November 15, 2004, p. 36.

22.    Richard Linnett, AdAges, *Advertising Age*, March 4, 2004, p. 36.

23.    Joe Mandese, "On-Demand Video Data Reveals Online, Cable Users Go To It Differently," *Online Media Daily*, March 29, 2007.

# Chapter 29

## INGER L. STOLE

# PHILANTHROPY AS PUBLIC RELATIONS
## A Critical Perspective on Cause Marketing

YOU MAY HAVE NOTICED THE abundance of pink products for sale in stores and online during the month of October. As part of Breast Cancer Awareness Month, many businesses—from cosmetic companies to food manufacturers to appliance retailers—offer rose-hued merchandise with a portion of the sales going to support breast cancer research. While these companies cite this as an act of social responsibility, Inger Stole takes a different perspective in this essay, published in 2008. Stole, a professor of communication at the University of Illinois at Urbana-Champaign, notes that companies attach themselves to particular causes to get favorable publicity. The problem with this, she contends, is that marketing-friendly social issues get most media attention and critical but more controversial social problems have a very hard time breaking through into media and public consciousness.

It is generally understood by scholars and practitioners that effective public relations (PR) campaigns are not developed in response to a crisis. On the contrary, the best public relations strategies take a long-term approach and work hard to establish any client as a contributing and trusted pillar of its community. Well thought-out strategies can prevent crises from happening, or, if crises are unavoidable, they can certainly mitigate damages. The implicit objective of PR is often framed as protection of businesses from public attacks and the establishment of enough goodwill to protect them from hostile government regulations. This may be true, but it is just as accurate to characterize the purpose of PR in less hallowed light. PR's community work is beneficial, and its governmental reaches are designed to allow businesses to receive and maintain favorable licenses, privileges, subsidies and regulations from the government without any counterproductive public "interference." Accordingly, the pioneers of many PR techniques came from industries like electric utilities, broadcasting and telecommunication, whose entire business models were based on getting and keeping government monopoly franchises on lucrative terms (Fones-Wolf, 2006; Stole, 2006;

McChesney, 1993). The less the public questioned the legitimacy of private power in these government-created industries, the better. PR was not optional, but built right into the heart of the enterprise. It has since come to play a major role for nearly all large enterprises in the economy.

In order for a PR strategy to be successful, these goals cannot be explicitly revealed to the public. Due to their self-serving purpose, PR campaigns are generally presented under the guise of furthering some other more altruistic objective. In recent years, PR has increasingly merged with advertising in an effort to not only protect the political prospects of a firm, its public image and long-term profitability, but also to expand sales and profits in the short-term (Ries & Ries, 2002).

This article discusses how cause marketing, a rapidly growing form of corporate philanthropy, has emerged as a public relations tool-of-choice in many business circles. As the name suggests, cause marketing fuses the traditional PR function with a concern for pushing sales in the short-term. Cause marketing comes in many forms, but the most common—the one explored in this article—is the use of "purchase-triggered" donations. This is where a business or corporation will donate a sum or percentage from a commercial transaction to a social cause. Often, a corporation will explicitly team up with a nonprofit partner for a cause-marketing campaign. As such, cause marketing provides companies with an excellent tool to improve their public image, build closer relationships with consumers, and ultimately boost sales and profits.

While cause marketing, or the practice of pegging consumer purchases to philanthropic donations, may seem to be a perfect solution to aid a series of social ills and problems, this article argues that it also raises a host of troubling dilemmas for scholars and for society—issues we have barely begun to consider. Perhaps foremost, the practice of cause marketing suggests that businesses may leverage the existence of dire social problems to improve their public images and profits while distracting attention from their connections as to why these social problems continue to exist.

*　　*　　*

## From Corporate Charity to Strategic Philanthropy

For nearly a century, American businesses have relied on public relations in one form or another. The goal behind the majority of these effort have been to defuse, impress, or evade critics in order to create a business-friendly atmosphere and prevent laws or regulations opposed by businesses from gaining popular support. (Or, as mentioned in the introduction, the corollary to this is that businesses use PR to receive and maintain lucrative licenses, subsidies and regulations from the government.) This trend came of age in the late 19th century when rapid industrial growth and a wave of corporate mergers caused public uneasiness about big business and unregulated corporate power (Ewen, 1996; Marchand, 1987; Marchand, 1998). An arrogant attitude among industry leaders combined with an unwillingness to acknowledge the public's concerns fueled a view of American corporations as "soulless" and uncaring (Marchand, 1998). Instead of changing their conduct and affecting their bottom lines, corporations attempted to change the public's perception of their behavior and it was in this capacity that they enlisted help from PR professionals. Businesses like International Harvester, U.S. Steel, and AT&T were quick to recognize the value of institutional advertising and favorable press to project their socially responsible side to the public. A prominent employer of these techniques was John D. Rockefeller, who made PR history by hiring the famous press agent, Ivy Lee, to help change his public image from that of an infamous robber baron to that of a caring philanthropist. Breaking with contemporary norms, Lee encouraged Rockefeller to widely publicize his philanthropic bent instead of making his charitable donations in anonymity. It did not take long before this strategy—which effectively "branded" Rockefeller, and implicitly his business endeavors, as benign and caring—was emulated by others (Marchand, 1987; Marchand, 1998; Ewen, 1996; Chernow, 1998). Beyond this incident, Lee's work for Rockefeller helped develop one of the most fundamental PR strategies to date and one that PR practitioners still use: philanthropic involvement to silence their client's critics or to appease public interest groups, their consumer base, or stakeholders. Thus, companies' efforts are frequently rooted in self-preservation and a need to polish their images (Hicks, 2000). What businesses have learned over time, however, is that the most effective PR campaigns are not developed in response to a crisis. On the contrary, the best PR strategies require a long-term approach with hard work to establish any client as a contributing and trusted pillar of its community. This might not only insulate business from public attacks and government regulations but also serve to increase customer confidence in the company's goods and services to help raise its profits. Cause marketing provides an excellent example of how a marketing technique can serve this dual goal simultaneously.

*　　*　　*

Defined as "a business strategy that integrates a social issue or cause into brand equity and organizational identity to gain significant bottom-line impacts" (Cone/ Roper, 1999, p. 18), cause marketing aims at linking corporate identities with non-profits, good causes, and significant social issues through cooperative marketing and fundraising programs (File & Prince, 1998). If well executed, cause marketing can help a business build a civic identity and bolster public loyalty to a brand or institution. A close association with a nonprofit cause may also increase employee satisfaction and loyalty. Last but not least, by donating time and money to nonprofits, business might ward off criticism and underscore pressure from groups and individuals who believe corporate America should help pay for public services through higher taxes (Polonsky & Wood, 2001; Fox, 1999). It is no wonder, then, that businesses consider cause market-ing "a powerful tool to be used in a calculated program of public relations and long-term investing" (Marconi, 2002).

Cause marketing traces its official start to 1983, when American Express launched a much-acclaimed campaign to help restore the Statue of Liberty and Ellis Island. Promising to contribute 1 cent for every card transaction and $1 for every new card issued during the last quarter of 1983 to the cause, the credit card company collected $1.7 million for the restoration effort. But the monuments were not the only beneficiaries. The effort generated fantastic publicity in the forms of news and television stories about the effort, and the 28% increase in use of the American Express cards that followed was obviously a big plus for the company.[1] The newly minted strategy was not lost on others and the practice, referred to as cause marketing, was born. By the early 1990s, U.S. businesses had undertaken cause marketing on a grand scale. Between 1990 and 1998, the amount spent on this form of marketing rose from $125 million to over half a billion dollars annually (Bishoff, 2000/2001), and in 1999, American businesses spent $630 million on cause marketing (Good Deeds, 1999). Six years later, the amount had increased to well over $1 billion dollars, and, in 2007, experts predict the amount to exceed $1.4 billion (The Growth of Cause Marketing, 2006; Cause Marketing's Power, 2006).

## Cause Marketing and Cause Branding

Although there are several sub-categories of cause marketing, this article focuses on purchase-triggered donations, the practice pioneered by American Express in 1983.[2] The practice where a company pledges to contribute a percentage or set amount of a product's price to a charitable cause or organizations is the most widely used and recognized form of cause marketing. A few examples may be helpful.

Founded in 1982 to "eradicate breast cancer as a life-threatening disease," the Susan G. Komen Foundation has become one of the most visible fundraising organizations for cancer research, as well as a favorite charity for cause marketers (King, 2006). Its annual "Race for the Cure"—a five-kilometer run/walk—is the largest ongoing sports/ fundraising event in the country. More than most nonprofits, the Komen Foundation is actively involved in marketing its event to companies in search of cause marketing ventures; business is more than forthcoming. In 2006, some 20 large companies including Kellogg's, Yoplait yogurt, Pier 1 Imports, Re/Max Real Estate, and American Airlines, were members of Komen's Million Dollar Council. In addition to paying a million dollars for the right to serve as official sponsors of the annual race, each company had separate cause marketing efforts that showcase their connections to the cause. Yoplait, for example, pledged to donate 10 cents to the Komen Foundation for each of the first 30 million yogurt lids it received from customers. Not to be outdone, Kellogg's sent a pink ribbon heart-pin to every customer who donated $5 to the Komen Foundation and mailed proof of the contribution along with two purchase labels from specially marked cereal boxes. Also partnering with Komen was BMW. The automaker developed an elaborate scheme to benefit the foundation—and possibly itself. As part of a campaign called "Ultimate Drive," BMW donated $1 for each mile of test driving during a particular period, and pledged a percentage from the sale of its "Pink Ribbon Collection" of watches, T-shirts, and notebooks to the Komen Foundation (Susan B. Komen, 2006).

For anyone doubting a cause marketer's interest in breast cancer awareness, a trip to any department store or a thumbing through any woman's magazine during October, "the official Breast Cancer Awareness month," is suggested. The sheer number of manufacturers who adorn their products with pink ribbons with an offer to donate a share of their sales to the cause is nothing short of astonishing.

In addition to the obvious promotional value that businesses receives from association with some nonprofits, cause marketing efforts can also be read as subtle strategies for the undermining of government-funded programs in sector such as health and educational sectors by providing private alternatives. Upromise, for example, is a program involving major companies like, Coca-Cola, and New York Life Insurance. Each time a parent, grandparent, or other caring adult patronizes one of the more than 20,000 grocery or drug stores, 40,000 retail stores and services, 8,000 restaurants and 350 online retailers affiliated with the program; rents a car from Avis; or buys or sells a home with an affiliated real estate company, he or she can request that a portion of the amount be deposited in a college savings account established in a child or grandchild's name. The size of the contribution varies. While a few participants pledge as much as 10% of the purchasing price, most donate 1%. Thus, in order to earn $1,000 for college, relatives and friends must purchase $100,000 of goods and services, while providing the participating companies with a great deal of valuable demographic information (Upromise, 2006). As new technologies emerge, marketing efforts follow.

One example is the "giving malls" that have sprung up on the Internet (Ridge, 1999). Since 1997, iGive.com has offered customers the opportunity to buy from more than 400 affiliated merchants and to direct up to 39% of every purchase (although the typical donation is 3%) to any of more than 18,000 nonprofits, often local chapters of large national nonprofit organizations. The chance to be associated with a good cause is not lost on retail giants like Amazon.com, L.L Bean, Barnes & Noble, Office Max, eBay and Dell. During its nine years of existence, iGive.com helped distribute nearly $2 million to a total of 30,000 charitable causes (iGive, 2006). Sometimes a company ties its identity so closely with its cause marketing efforts that, by design or pure coincidence, it appears to be a nonprofit itself. Working Assets, a for-profit company headquartered in San Francisco, is one example. A self-described "socially responsible long distance telephone and credit card company," it donates 1% of customers' telephone charges and 10 cents for each credit card transaction it processes to nonprofit organizations working for peace, human rights, economic justice, or the environment. An annual ballot listing participating organizations is sent to Working Assets customers to determine how the unrestricted general-support grants are allocated. During its first year (1986), Working Assets donated $32,000 to nonprofit organizations. In 1997, donations totaled nearly $3 million and by 2005, donations had increased to $4 million. By 2006, the company claimed to have donated a total of $50 million to various causes through its cause marketing program (Working Assets, 2006).

Although it is difficult to assess the participating rate in the many cause-related efforts, consumers report a high degree of satisfaction. A Cone/Roper study conducted between 1993 and 1994 found that 84% of the respondents had a more positive image of a company if it did something "to make the world better." Seventy-eight percent of adults said that they would be more likely to buy a product associated with a cause they cared about, and 66% indicated that they would switch brands in order to support a cause they found to be important. Sixty-two percent of the respondents said they would switch retail stores to support a cause they believed in and 64% of those asked thought that cause marketing should be a standard part of a company's activities. Cause marketing was found to have its strongest impact on people who had attended at least some college and earned more than $30,000 annually (Cone/Roper, 1999). A follow-up survey among young people conducted in 2006 showed an even stronger consumer endorsement of cause marketing. Eighty-nine percent of the interviewed indicated a preference for a brand associated with a good cause if the product didn't differ in terms of price and quality from its competitors, and 83% claimed to have more trust in a company that came across as socially and environmentally responsible (Civic-Mined Millennials, 2006).

## Cause Marketing: Who Really Benefits?

As the government sector is increasingly pushed to the sideline, the decision over which groups gets to dominate the philanthropic landscape is increasingly left to private initiatives. At first glance, cause marketing appears to be a win–win situation for businesses and nonprofit organizations alike. The latter garner their funds needed, while businesses get to bask in the glory of having performed good deeds. Judging from the increase in cause marketing, business has clearly embraced the concept and few nonprofit organizations are turning the private sector away. This, however, does not mean that the practice of merging marketing and social causes is without its problems. While cause marketing may do a wonderful job of collecting funds for the affiliated charities, it should not be forgotten that social causes, in desperate need of funding, may venture into partnerships that are far from equal and sometimes hold the potential of causing more harm than good (Andreasen, 1996). Because cause marketing is an attempt to increase a firm's return on its investment, it goes without saying that causes are not always selected on the basis of the potential good that can be achieved but, rather, on the free publicity and increased sales that a particular affiliation might bring to a company. In fact, and this is particularly true when it comes to business alliances with the larger nonprofits, a cooperation can produce free publicity and many PR opportunities, thus saving advertising and promotional expenses for the business involved. The latter may also gain access to the nonprofit's clientele, staff, trustees, and donors, all of whom are potential customers. Such access makes nonprofits with large memberships especially attractive to many companies (Andersen, 2001). In their eagerness to reach affluent consumers and impress them, companies have started to poll this group in order to determine their charitable preference and, consequently, where to focus future cause marketing efforts. In February 2006, for example, the Luxury Institute, a research group claiming to represent "the sole independent voice of the wealthy consumer," surveyed households with over $5 million in personal wealth and $200,000 in annual income to identify their favorite nonprofit organizations. Habitat for Humanity, America's Second Harvest and St. Jude's Hospital topped the list, followed by many health- and research-related charities (Luxury Institute, 2006). In this setup, nonprofit groups that serve valid social functions but fail to fit a corporate profile or appeal to the customer groups that businesses want to reach risk being ignored, while other causes, because they serve as better marketing vehicles, receive a disproportionate amount of interest (Polonsky & Woods, 2001, p. 16). A practice of leaving support for social causes to a market-driven system where the support for these causes hinges on their capability to complement a sales message leaves much to be desired and yields business too much power.

A serious problem associated with cause marketing, according to Alan Andresen (2001), is deception. Most cause-related campaigns tend to highlight the cause and downplay the business objective. All too frequently, the true nature of business's contribution is not explained to the public. How, for example, is "a portion of the profits" translatable into dollars and cents for the cause? Who, in other words, benefits more from a transaction, the business or the nonprofit organization? A cause-marketing campaign sponsored by Philip Morris (now Atria) illustrates the problem. In the late 1990s, the tobacco giant's effort to combat domestic abuse and aid its victims raised an impressive $60 million. Unbeknownst to the public, however, was the fact that Philip Morris spent an additional $100 million—$40 million more than it was giving away— to promote its own generosity (Bischoff, 2000/2001).

A more recent example raises some of the same concerns. In fall of 2006, several large manufactures joined a cause marketing effort to raise money for a British based nonprofit organization called Global Fund. The group works to alleviate AIDS, tuberculosis and malaria in Africa. As corporate partners in project "Red," companies like Motorola, Armani, Apple, and The Gap designed the color red or red-labeled products and promised to donate an average of 50% of net profits from the "Red" items to the cause. While Global Fund faced the prospect of some much needed funds from the project, manufacturers stood to gain as well. Even with 50% of the profit pledged to the cause, each "Red" T-shirt or cashmere bikini (sold at $100), provided a handsome profit for The Gap. Likewise, Apple's donations from the sale of its specially designed "Red" iPods and Motorola's contributions from selling "Red" cellphones helped benefit the companies' bottom line (Product Red, 2007). Donations varied by licensing contract. Motorola chipped in 8 to 10% from the sale of its $165 "Red" MotoRazr and its $60 to $70 Bluetooth H500 headsets while Converse, the footware company, pledged between 10 and 15% from the sale of its "Red" products (Spethmann, 2007).

As an added benefit to the involved companies, free and extensive media exposure as well as a high public profile was given to "Red" by Bono, the musician and philanthropist and also a "Red" cofounder. In October 2006, Bono appeared on the *Oprah Winfrey Show* to launch "Red" in America. For the better part of the hour-long show, viewers followed Oprah and Bono as they shopped at The Gap, Apple, Motorola and Armani Stores along Michigan Avenue in Chicago, where a gushing Oprah bought 10 of most items. Although it is impossible to estimate the publicity value of such product placements, the media exposure certainly exceeds the cost of donating a percent of profits from "Red" product sales to charity. But this was, of course, not discussed as all emphasis was placed on the positive work being generated by the participating companies. "This show today is about getting medicine to people who need it," announced Oprah. "So by just buying a T-shirt, a pair of jeans, even a cellphone, you can actually begin to save lives. I think the people will be amazed at how little money it really takes to provide AIDS drugs" (Harpo Productions, 2006, p. 4).

Unbeknown to many, however, is the fact that "Red" is not a charity but a brand created by a commercial company called Persuaders that oversees licensing agreements for the participating companies. The undertaking, in other words, is little more than sophisticated cause marketing. In order to be associated with "Red" and Bono, companies agree to several years of ongoing donations from the sale of select products to the cause and to develop a line of high quality products. Each sponsor is granted product exclusivity, meaning that none of their direct competitors will be accepted to the program (Frazier, 2007; Spethmann, 2007).

Due perhaps to its strong commercial overtones, "Red" has attracted its share of criticism. Within its first year of existence, the campaign was reported to have had raised a total of $18 million for the Global Fund. This, however, paled in comparison with the estimated $100 million in combined promotional budgets that The Gap, Motorola, and Apple had spent to publicize their participation in the campaign (Frazier, 2007). Although spokespeople for "Red" dispelled the numbers as "wrong on all counts," they failed to produce convincing evidence to the contrary and The Gap and Apple declined to comment (Rush & Rush Molly, 2007; Red Charity Disputes, 2007).

Another and quite unfortunate problem that sometimes arises from cause marketing schemes is harm to the nonprofit group. Because the corporate motive behind cause marketing is influenced not by pure altruism but largely by financial self-interest, nonprofit groups should think twice before entering into cause-related partnerships with business (Andreasen, 1994; File & Prince, 1998). "Cause marketing is controversial because of its emphasis on self-interest rather than altruism and because it threatens to commercialize nonprofits," argue File and Prince (1998, p. 1531). Heeding this advice, the American Heart Association categorically turns down requests for cause-marketing ventures with businesses out of fear that such partnerships may harm its credibility (File & Prince, 1998). The botched pact between the American Medical Association (AMA) and Sunbeam Corporation serves as an example for caution. In the summer of 1997, the AMA agreed to endorse nine products in Sunbeam's "Health at Home" line, including blood pressure monitors and thermometers. In return, Sunbeam would pay a percentage of sales to the AMA, in the form of "royalties," for AMA's research and education programs. Sunbeam hoped that the AMA seal of approval would provide a competitive advantage that could significantly boost sales. Both consumer groups and medical professionals voiced their protest. The former questioned whether the AMA would be honest in its evaluation of Sunbeam's products and worried that consumers could be misled into buying Sunbeam products that were more costly but not necessarily better, than competing brands. Consumers might see the AMA name on a product and conclude that Sunbeam was a philanthropic donor to the AMA, instead of a participant in a marketing deal. Some worried that the AMA would be violating its own code of ethics by recommending a product in which it had a financial interest (Caratan, 1997). Days after the deal was announced, the chair of AMA's board of trustees revoked it due to lack of board approval. Not easily dismissed, Sunbeam sued the AMA for breach of contract and the company was awarded $9.9 million in court (AMA Settles).

Companies with deep pockets and questionable environmental records are all too eager to form cause-marketing relationships with environmental groups. While the money may be tempting for the financially strapped organizations, they also know that one oil spill, environmental disaster or embarrassing disclosure (none of which they have any control over) could very well cost them their credibility.

Another concern facing partnerships between nonprofits and businesses is the risk of spreading corporate values into the nonprofit arena. This is well-illustrated by the aggressive attempts that fast-food producers, the bottling industries, and any industry selling products to children have made to establish their presence in the nation's schools. The practice of paying financially-strapped schools for displaying their products and paying sales commissions on items sold are examples of how advertising and cause marketing has made a presence in schools across the U.S. (Molnar, 1996; Klein, 1999; Barber, 1998).

## Business Considerations

The decision whether or not to become involved with a particular nonprofit organization rests with business interests that understandably fear that affiliation with certain organizations might cause a consumer backlash or result in poor publicity. Thus, organizations advocating gay and lesbian causes; those working in the fields of health or welfare reform; and groups such as Planned Parenthood with its pro-choice agenda do not have corporations lining up at their doorsteps (Andreasen, 2001; Silver, 1997; Till & Novak, 2000). Because of their association with brand name products and the desire not to repel desired consumers, cause marketers are very sensitive to groups or causes that might prove even slightly controversial. In 2004, for example, MasterCard decided to retire an affinity card bearing the iconic image of three firefighters raising the U.S. flag amid the World Trade Center rubble because it feared public criticism and accusations of exploiting the September 11, 2001 tragedy. The card had been launched at the request of a September 11-related charity, with a sum from each card application going to help victims and their families. Perhaps not coincidentally, the credit card company's announcement came immediately after families of September 11 victims accused President Bush of exploiting a similar image in his re-election campaign (MasterCard cancels, 2004).

At times, however, ill-conceived cause marketing efforts slip through the cracks (Andreasen, 2001) and there are those times when even the promotional industry believes that businesses have "crossed the line" of good taste. There is a certain amount of risk involved, and firms do what they can to minimize it. In the summer of 1999, for example, Procter & Gamble began a cause marketing campaign with Give Kids the World, an organization that helps terminally ill children and their families take vacations, as its nonprofit partner. Campaign commercials showed terminally ill children playing in the Florida sun and explained how viewers, through purchase-triggered donations, could help sustain the program. For every pack of Pampers it sold, Procter & Gamble would contribute a sum to Give Kids the World. To some, this was just another run-of-the-mill campaign, but for others, including *Advertising Age*, the effort left a bad taste. "Somehow, over the past decade, the industry and the consumer have come to accept, even embrace, various kind of cause marketing," stated the trade journal. "Nobody seems too troubled that the supposed corporate philanthropy isn't philanthropy at all; it is a licensing agreement, a promotional tie-in tying into rain forests and hunger and sick kids in place of 'Tarzan' and 'Star Wars.'" The campaign, according to *Advertising Age*, not only exploited the emotions of the families involved, it exploited the emotions of the viewers, because "using the image of terminally ill children to get a spike in diaper sales is unspeakably perverse, no matter who benefits" (Garfield, 1999, p. 47).

Sometimes the hypocrisy is more difficult to detect and the cause-marketing efforts by the Wisconsin-based corporation, Kohl's, serve as an excellent example. As is the case for the majority of Wisconsin-based corporations, Kohl's Corporation pays no state income tax. Instead, it has devised is own program to help pay for education and children's health care in Wisconsin and in other states where it operates (Pitsch, 2006). Through its Kohl's Cares for Kids® program, the company has devised a cause marketing program called Kohl's Cares for Kids' Merchandise. This offers customers a chance to buy a toy or book from Kohl's with the assurance that 100% of the net profits will be donated to "support programs designed to meet the needs of children" in their community (Kohl's Corporation, 2006). By supporting its "children's health initiative" and offering various scholarships, Kohl's projects a caring image and a concern for children's wellness while consumers, some of them not able to pay for their own health insurance, help foot the bill.

Some campaigns are ill-conceived to the point of backfiring on businesses and nonprofits alike. Why, for example, would fast-food giant Wendy's donate proceeds from sales of its French fries to Denver's Mercy Medical Center, an institution that daily admits patients with nutrition-related illnesses, and why would the medical center accept (Meyer, 1999)? Similarly confusing was a cause-related campaign by the Coors brewery, designed to benefit literacy (McChesney, 1995).

Poorly conceived and hypocritical efforts may foster public cynicism against cause marketing. The public may not believe that a business is interested in helping terminally sick children, support anti-cancer causes, aid the educational system, or fight hunger in Africa (to use a few of the examples discussed above) but view the effort as just another attempt to sell diapers, cell phones, shoes, fast food, and Armani clothing (Andreasen, 2001). Is, in fact, asks a critic of the "Red" campaign, "the rise of philanthropic fashionistas decked out in 'Red' T-shirts and iPods really the best way to save a child dying of AIDS in Africa?" Shouldn't people, if they really want to help, donate to the Global Fund directly (Frazier, 2007)?

There are indications that some consumers are beginning to question business's motives. A Roper poll conducted in December 2006, for example, revealed that only 12% found corporate donation claims to be "completely credible" and the 17% did not believe marketers claims of non profit donations "at all" (Frazier, 2007). Although the findings may put business on the alert and force them to be less transparent, it is quite unlikely that the practice will subside in the near future. Cause marketing fills a function, not only as a promoter of products and producer of consumer goodwill, but in an important tool in the neo-liberal struggle for greater privatization of welfare and social services.

## Conclusion

By increasingly leaving the task of funding the nonprofit sector to business, we now face a situation where the survival and success of many charities depend on their ability to fit a business profile. While losing funding for government-sponsored programs in the social sector, we have been sold on a corporate version of how to run social services, one that emphasizes profits and offers spare change as a way to deal with problems of structural magnitude. For example, while cause marketers have latched on to illiteracy as an issue (Pringle & Thompson, 2001), none has stepped forward to raise awareness about the more fundamental issue of poorly funded schools and the social and economic conditions that often cause kids to underperform in educational settings. Likewise, while businesses may eagerly solicit funds for breast cancer research, they do not devote much attention to the evidence that link certain industry practices with cancer (Marshall, 2007). Thus, in most instances, cause marketing is merely a cleverly disguised ploy to mask some of the fundamental problems for which the very same marketing forces are directly or indirectly responsible.

In addition to these macro-concerns, there are also fundamental problems with cause marketing as such. Because firms leverage their giving activities and only give if there is consumer action, cause marketing schemes commercialize the philanthropic process (Polonsky & Wood, 2000). Funding to the nonprofit sector is increasingly pegged to our behavior as consumers and this is problematic (Hutten, 2001). One of the latest trends in the world of cause marketing includes workshops that train nonprofits on how to market themselves and their causes to potential businesses. For example, a course offered by Cause Marketing Forum, which is one of the leading business organizations in this area, promises "critical background on cause marketing fundamentals with special insights into what motivates corporations to partner with nonprofits" and provides a step-by-step guide to help nonprofit organizations make themselves more attractive to business partners (CM 101 for Nonprofits, 2006). Thus, it is no longer business looking to do good, but nonprofits desperate for funding trying to appear good in the eyes of business. Adding to the nonprofit's challenge is that fact the companies have an economic inventive to consider the demographic profile of their target audience (Wilson, 2000).

Traditional forms of product marketing have sought a (white) middle- or upper-middle-class, and predominantly female, audience and have avoided controversy at all costs. Advertisers also tend to act on the assumption that certain emotions put consumers in a purchasing mood and that others serve as deterrents. It is for this reason that airlines, for example, request that their ads be pulled in the event of a major plane crash, and that tobacco companies have traditionally withdrawn advertising from mass media that insist on publicizing the harmful effects of smoking. Following this line of reasoning, it is easy to see why the more controversial nonprofit groups may fail to attract sponsors while well established and less controversial ones attract many.

Few can deny that problems such as teen pregnancy, incest, child abuse, sexually transmitted diseases, drug abuse, and alcoholism are serious social problems worthy of attention. But while corporate sponsors flock to a popular cause such as the Komen Race for the Cure in support of the fight against breast cancer (Peepeles, 2002; King, 2006), few of the more controversial causes attract cause marketing partners. Quite often, however, the most controversial charities, with the least chance of being adopted for cause-related schemes, conduct important pioneering work. Think, for example, what a difference it might have made if, in addition to selling cars, cornflakes and collecting yogurt container lids to fund breast cancer research, companies would highlight the basic lack of health care, a situation that prevents many from detecting this terrible disease in its early and most curable stage. But, as George Monbiot, states so eloquently, "as companies appear to fill the gaps they have helped create, they can present themselves as indispensable vehicles for social provision, enabling them to argue for a further reduction in state services" (Monbiot, 2001, p. 2). Recently, the new and drastic budget cuts combined with increasing privatization of social service operations under President George W. Bush has helped to accelerate this process (Koulish, 2007).

By transforming the generosity, compassion and charitable inclinations of Americans into a well-functioning branding strategy, companies have arrived at a very successful formula. On the surface, many American corporations have managed to rid themselves of the "soulless," uncaring image of the past. But looks, as we know, can be deceiving. The practice of hinging important issues such as health care and education on vagaries of marketing trends is not entirely satisfactory. As scholars and citizens, we must address the question: Is the emerging system of cause marketing and commercially-driven philanthropy the most rational way for society to address fundamental social issues? This article is intended to contribute to further research and debate on exactly that question.

## Questions for Consideration

1   What responses do you think cosmetic or appliance retailers that use cause marketing would give to Ingrid Stole? Would you agree with them or with Stole?

2   In closing, Stole suggests that companies seem to exploit "the generosity, compassion, and charitable inclinations of Americans." Do you think this is an accurate description of those who support cause related marketing? Why or why not?

## Notes

1.   In 2003, American Express launched yet another cause marketing involving the Statue of Liberty. Following the same strategy as 20 years earlier, the credit card company promised to pledge 1 cent for each purchase made the American Express Card up to $2.5 million and to give a direct donation of $500,000 to help pay for critical security measures and enable the Statute, which has been closed since September 11, 2001, to once more accommodate visitors. In addition to the above strategy, American Express also offered to facilitate cardholders' donation of American Express Reward Points to help the restoration effort and to help assist cardholders to make direct payments to the same (American Express, 2003).

2.   In addition to purchase-triggered donations, there are six other main types of cause marketing arrangements. The first four relate to standard corporate practices. These are: *advertising*, in which a business aligns itself with a particular cause and uses ads to communicate the cause's message; *public relations*, in which a business calls press and public attention to a strategic partnership between itself and a nonprofit group; *sponsorship*, in which a business helps fund a particular program or event; *licensing*, in which a business pays to use a charity logo on its products or services, and *co-branding* where both a business and a nonprofit raise funds to build brand awareness. A sixth type of cause marketing is *facilitated giving*, where a business facilitates customer donations to a charity (Adkins, 2000).

## References

Adler, S. M. (2006). *Cause for Concern: Result-Oriented Cause Marketing*. Ohio: Thompson Higher Education.

Adkins, S. (2000). *Cause-Related Marketing: Who Cares Win*. Oxford, Auckland, Boston, Johannesburg, Melbourne, New Delhi: Butterworth-Heinemann.

AMA Settles Sunbeam Fiasco. Retrieved December 21, 2006, from http://www.quackwatch.org/04ConsumerEducation/News/sunbeam.html

American Express (2003 November 25). American Express Launches National Campaign to Re-open the Statue of Liberty: Pledges Minimum of $3 Million with Cardmember Support. Current News Release. Retrieved March 2004 from http://home3.americanexpress.com/corp/latest news/statue-of-liberty.asp

Andreasen, A. R. (1996 November–December). Profits for Nonprofits: Find a Corporate Partner. *Harvard Business Review*, 47–50.

Andreasen, A. R. (2001). *Ethics in Social Marketing*. Washington, D.C.: Georgetown University Press.

Barber, B. R. (1998). *A Place for Us: How to Make Society Civil and Democracy Strong*. New York: Hill and Wang.

Bishoff, D. (2000 December/2001 January). Consuming Passions. *Ms. Magazine*, 63.

Bronn, P. S., and Vrioni, A.B. (2001). Corporate Social Responsibility and Cause-related Marketing: An Overview. *International Journal of Advertising*, Vol. 20 (1), 207–222.

Caratan, F. B. (1997). American Medical Association Apologizes for Commercial Deal. Retrieved August 30, 2006 from http://www.bmj.com/cgi/content/full/315/7107/501/c

Cause Marketing's Power Shown in MediaLab Study. Retrieved October 30, 2006, http://www.causemarketingforum.com/page.asp?ID = 192

Chernow, R. (1998). *Titan: The Life of John D. Rockefeller Sr*. New York: Random House.

Civic-Minded Millennials Prepared to Reward or Punish Companies Based on Commitment to Social Causes. Retrieved October 30, 2006 from http://www.coneinc.com/pages/pr_45.html

Collins, C. and Yeskel, F. (2000). *Economic Apartheid in America: A Primer on Economic Inequalities & Insecurity*. New York: The New Press.

Cone/Roper. (1999). *Cause Related Marketing Trend Report: The Evolution of Cause-Related Branding*. New York: Cone/Roper.

CM 101 for Nonprofits Teleclass Series, 2006. Retrieved October 30, 2006. from http://www.causemarketingforum.com/teleclass_detail.asp?ID = 469

Ewen, S. (1996). *PR! A Social History of Spin*. New York: Basic Books.

File, K. M., and Prince, R. A. (1998 October). Cause-Related Marketing and Corporate Philanthropy in the Privately Held Enterprise. *Journal of Business Ethics*, 1 (14), 1525–1539.

Fellman, M. (1999 April). Wirth Cause Marketing Takes a Strategic Turn. *Marketing News*, 33 (9), 4.

Fones-Wolf, E. (2006). *Waves of Opposition: Labor and the Struggle for Democratic Radio*. Urbana: University of Illinois, Press.

Fox, R. (1999 September). Employees and Consumers like Cause Marketing. *Incentive*, 173 (9), 16.

Frazier, M. (2007 March 5). Costly Red Campaign reaps Meager $18M; Bono & Co spend up to $100 on Marketing; Incur Watchdog's Wrath. *Advertising Age*, 78(1), 1.

Friedman, M. (1962). *Capitalism and Freedom*. Chicago: University of Chicago Press.

Garfield, B. (1999 July 26). Manipulative Tactic Leaves a Sour Taste. *Advertising Age*, 70 (31), 47.

Gobe, M. (2001). *Emotional Branding: the New Paradigm for Connecting Brands to People*. New York: Allworth Press.

Good Deeds Attract Customers and Workers (1999 August). *USA Today*, 128 (2651), 15–16.

Glyn, A. (2006). *Capitalism Unleashed: Finance, Globalization, and Welfare*. New York: Oxford University Press.

Harpo Productions Inc. (2006). Oprah and Bono Paints the Town "Red." The Oprah Winfrey Show October 13, 2006. Livingston, NJ: Burrelle's Information Services, LLC (Written transcripts).

Hertz, N. (2003). *The Silent Takeover: Global Capitalism and the Death of Democracy*. New York: Harper Collins.

Hicks, T. (2000 June 26). Do the Right Thing. *Sporting Goods Business*, 1533 (10), 15.

Hutton, J. G. (2001). Narrowing the Concept of Marketing. In Michael T. Ewing (Ed.), *Social Marketing*. Binghamton NY: The Haworth Press, 5–24.

iGive.com. Retrieved March 14, 2004 from http://www.igive.com/htlm/body_pressrelease8.cfm

Kelly, M. (2001). *The Divine Right of Capital: Dethroning the Corporate Aristocracy*. San Francisco: Berrett-Koehler Publishers, Inc.

King, S. (2001 winter). All Consuming Cause: Breast Cancer, Corporate Philanthropy, and the Market for Generosity. *Social Text*, 19 (4), 115–143.

King, S. (2006). *Pink Ribbons Inc.: Breast Cancer and the Politics of Philanthropy*. Minneapolis: University of Minnesota Press.

Klein, N. (1999). *No Logo: Taking Aim at the Brand Bullies*. Picador: New York.

Knittel, M. (2003). Corporate Average Tax Rates: Overview and Recent Trends. National Tax Association—Tax Institute of America. Proceedings of the Annual Conference on Taxation. Washington, 240–51. Retrieved July 14, 2007 from http://proquest.umi.com

The Kohl Corporation, Kohl's Cares For Kidsfi. Retrieved December 21, 2006 from http://www.kohlscorporation.com/CommunityRelations/Community01.hm

Korten, D. C. (1999). *The Post-Corporate World: Life after Capitalism*. San Francisco: Berrett-Koehler Publishers, Inc.

Korten, D.C. (2001). *When Corporations Rule the World*. San Francisco: Berrett-Koehler Publishers, Inc. 2nd edition.

Kotler, P., and Lee, N. (2005). *Corporate Social Responsibility: Doing the Most Good for Your Company and Your Cause*. Hoboken, NJ: John Wiley & Sons.

Koulish, R., Conservatives Waging War on Nonprofits. Retrieved March 6, 2007 from http://www.commondreams.org/views07/0216–20.htm

LeRoy, G. (2005). *The Great American Job Scam: Corporate Tax Dodging and the Myth of Job Creation*. San Francisco: Berrett-Koehler Publishers, Inc.

Luxury Institute Nonprofit Survey. Retrieved November 1, 2006 from http://www.causemarketingforum.com/page.asp?ID = 434

Marchand, R. (1987 Winter). The Fitful Career of Advocacy Advertising: Political Protection, Client Cultivation, and Corporate Morale. California *Management Review*, 29 (2), 128–157.

Marchand, R. (1998). *Creating the Corporate Soul: The Rise of Public Relations and Corporate Imagery in American Big Business*. Berkeley, Los Angeles, and London: University of California Press.

Marshall, L. (2007 January 23). Is Breast Cancer Awareness a Marketing Sham? AlterNet. Retrieved on January 30, 2007 from http://www.alternet.org/envirohealth/46813/

Marconi, J. (2002). *Cause Marketing: Build Your Image and Bottom Line through Socially Responsible Partner-ships, Programs, and Events*. Chicago: Dearborn Trade Publishing.

Mastercard Cancels 9/11 Credit Card (2004 March 6). *The News Gazette* (Champaign, Illinois), E1.

McIntyre, R. and Nguyen, C.T.D. (2004, November). Freeloaders: Declining Corporate Tax Payments in the Bush Years. *Multinational Monitor*, 14–17.

McChesney, R. (1993). *Telecommunications, Mass Media, and Democracy: The Battle for the Control of U.S. Broadcasting, 1928–1935*. New York: Oxford University Press.

McChesney, S. (1995 April). Champions of a Cause. *Electric Perspectives*, 20–24.

Meyer, H. (1999 December). When the Cause is Just. *Journal of Business Strategy*, 20 (6), 27–31.

Miller, W. H. (1982 February 22). Push Yet to Come? Industry isn't Rushing into Social Activism. *Industry Week*, 18.

Mizerski, D., Mizerski. K., and Sadler, O. (2002). A Field Experiment Comparing the Effectiveness of "Ambush" and Cause-related Ad Appeals for Social Marketing. *Social Marketing*, Ewing, D. ed. The Haworth Press, Inc., 25–45.

Molnar, A. (1996). *Giving Kids the Business: The Commercialization of America's Schools*. Boulder, CO: Westview Press.

Monbiot, G. (2001 July 31). Superstores Brand Us to Ensure We Belong to Them: Caring Corporates are Filling the Gaps They Create Themselves. Retrieved July 14, 2007 from http://www.guardian.co.uk/Archive/Article/0,4273,4231008,00.html.

Mullen, J. (1997 summer) Performance-based Corporate Philanthropy: How "Giving Smart" Can Further Corporate Goals. *Public Relations Quarterly*, 61 (3), 42–48.

Phillips, R. (2000 summer). The Corporate Community Builders: Using Corporate Strategic Philanthropy for Economic Development. *Economic Development Review*, 17 (1), 1–7.

Peeples, Carol. (2002 July). Avon's Calling. *The Progressive*, 23–26.

Pitch, M. (2006 December 6). 2 of 3 Companies Pay No State Income Tax: Report Looks at Businesses that Filed Wisconsin Tax Returns in 2003. *Wisconsin State Journal*, A1. Retrieved December 21, 2006 from http://www.madison.com/archives/read.php?ref=/wsj/2006/12/05/0612050025.php

Polonsky, M., and Wood, G. (2001 June). Can Overcommercialization of Cause-related Marketing Harm Society? *Journal of Macromarketing*, 21 (1), 8–22.

Pringle, H., and Thompson, M. (2001). *How Cause-related Marketing Builds Brands*. Chichester, New York, Weinheim, Brisbane, Singapore and Toronto: John Wiley & Sons.

Product Red. Retrieved February 2, 2007 from http://www.joined.com/

Red Charity Disputes Marketing Budget (2007 March 5). CNNmoney.com. Retrieved July 2 from http://web.lexis-nexis.com

Ridge, P. S. (1999 December 23). A Special Background Report on Trends in Industry and Finance. *The Wall Street Journal* (eastern edition), A1.

Ries, A., and Ries, L. (2002). The Fall of Advertising and the Rise of PR. New York: Collins.

Rush, G., and Rush Molloy, J. (2007 March 8). Bono's Red Campaign Says it's Raised Lots of Green, *Daily News* (New York). Retrieved July 2, 2007 from http://web.lexis-nexis.com

Silver, R. (1997 October). Playing it Too Straight: Cause Marketing that Puts Too Much Emphasis on "Safe" Charities may Insult Key Customers. *Marketing Magazine*, 102, 44.

Spethmann, B. (2007 January 1). The Red Brigade. *Promo*, 18.

Steckel, R., Simons, R., Simons, J., and Tanen, N. (1999). *Making Money While Making a Difference: How to Profit with a Nonprofit Partner*. Homewood Illinois: High Tide Press.

Stole, I. (2006). *Advertising on Trial: Consumer Activism and Corporate Public Relations in the 1930s*. Urbana: University of Illinois Press.

Susan B. Komen Foundation. Retrieved March 23, 2006 from www.komen.org

The Growth of Cause Marketing. Retrieved October 30, 2006 from http://www.causemarketingforum.com/page.asp?ID=188

Till, B.D., and Nowak, L.I., (2000) Toward Effective Use of Cause-related Marketing Alliances. *Journal of Brand Management*, 9(7), 427–484.

Upromise. Retrieved March 14, 2004 from http://www.upromise.com/nspage?su=9960

Working Assets. Retrieved November 1, 2006 from http://workingassets.com

Webb, D. J., and Lois A. M. (1998 Fall). A Typology of Consumer Responses to Cause-Related Marketing: From Skeptics to Socially Concerned. *Journal of Public Policy & Marketing*, 17 (2), 226–238.

Weeden, C. (1998). *Corporate Social Investing: The Breakthrough Strategy for Giving and Getting Corporate Contributions*. San Francisco CA: Berrett-Koehler Publishers, Inc.

Welsh, J. C. (1999 September-October). Good Cause, Good Business. *Harvard Business Review*, 21.

Wilson, M. (2000 August). More than Just Causes. *Chain Store Age*, 76 (8), 37–40.

Yankelovich, Daniel (2006). *Profit with Honor: The New Stage of Market Capitalism*. New Haven: Yale University Press.

# Chapter 30

# DEEPA KUMAR

# MEDIA, WAR, AND PROPAGANDA
## Strategies of Information Management During the 2003 Iraq War

**W**HICH MEDIA SOURCES DO YOU turn to for news and information about current events? Can you trust these sources to provide you with credible information? Deepa Kumar's 2006 essay explores the issue of journalistic credibility within the context of the Iraq War. Taking a highly critical perspective on the relationship between the military and the press, Kumar suggests that mainstream media supported the government's 2003 decision to go to war through the circulation of pro-war arguments. Kumar considers this to be a form of propaganda resulting from concentrated media ownership and an advanced system for government information management. Her analysis prompts her to question whether or not the present media system is fulfilling its role in a democratic society.

Today, few would disagree that the Bush administration resorted to propaganda in order to justify its war on Iraq and that the news media simply presented as fact information that they should have carefully scrutinized. Some media outlets have even admitted to this. An editorial on May 25, 2004 in *The New York Times* states that in a number of instances, their coverage of the Iraq war "was not as rigorous as it should have been" and that "information that was controversial then, and seems questionable now, was insufficiently qualified or allowed to stand unchallenged."[1] Several scholars such as Orville Schell have argued that the news media not only accepted but actively embraced information based on spurious intelligence. The result was that dissenting voices were "buried on back pages, ignored on op-ed pages, or confined to the margins of the media, and so denied the kinds of 'respectability' that a major media outlet can confer."[2] This raises disturbing questions for democracy and the role of the media in facilitating the widest possible exchange of ideas.

Highlighting the crisis of democracy in the twenty-first century, Douglas Kellner argues that the media have become the "arms of conservative and corporate interests," due to the concentration of ownership.[3] Thus, instead of acting in the interests of the public, they advance the interests of political and economic elites. There is also an abundance of research that shows that the mainstream media have a long history of supporting the efforts of the government during war.[4] At least since the Spanish–American war of 1898, which marked the entry of the US onto the global stage of imperial conquest and rivalry, the news media have played an important role in winning public consent for war.[5] An explosion on the *USS Maine* led many newspapers, particularly those owned by William Randolph Hearst, in coordination with pro-war voices in government, to accuse Spain without a shred of proof and beat the drums of war.[6] If the *Maine* became the rallying cry for war with Spain, the Johnson administration, in a replay of history, concocted the "Gulf of Tonkin" incident in 1964. They claimed that the *Maddox*, an American destroyer, was fired at by the North Vietnamese in an unprovoked incident. This turned out to be untrue, but it gave Johnson the congressional resolution he needed to prosecute the Vietnam War.[7] The media were willing partners in this deception.[8] More recently, during the 1991 Gulf war, the first Bush administration rallied behind the fabricated story of Kuwaiti babies torn from incubators by Iraqi troops as one of the key justifications for war.[9] Given this history, it is hardly surprising that the Bush administration would resort to similar mechanisms and that the media would be complicit in their efforts. What is significant about the Iraq war is the depth and scope of duplicity.

In this paper, I analyze media coverage of the 2003 war on Iraq, both in the build up to war and during the war, in order to delineate media and government strategies that ensured a preponderance of pro-war arguments. The mechanisms of information control were successful, I argue, due to two co-existing factors: the development and testing of government information control strategies over the last three decades, and the emergence of a for-profit giant conglomerate media system that lends itself to propaganda due to its structural limitations. The convergence of these two trends has seen a further integration of the media into the military industrial complex, building upon existing Cold War relationships. As the "War on Terror" continues, we can expect the growth of more sophisticated methods of information control and the further curtailment of diversity and debate, unless significant challenges are posed by an informed public. We have seen steps in this direction in the aftermath of the war with the growth of public skepticism towards the corporate media. I conclude by arguing that dissenting voices in the academy have a responsibility to challenge the logic of this new age of empire, not only through our research but also through our participation in social movements.

## The Evolving Propaganda Machine: Historical and Structural Factors

The current system of war information management derives from strategies devised by political elites and military planners over the last 30 years which built upon those of the Cold War. After the Vietnam War, sections of the political elite came to believe that it was media coverage of the war that led to US defeat. Among other things, they argued that television distorted the war by showing graphic images of the dead, turning Americans against the war. While television did show some images of casualties, it was nowhere near the claimed volume. Between 1965 and 1970, only about 3 percent of all evening news reports from Vietnam showed heavy fighting with dead or wounded.[10]

Additionally, TV war stories featuring images of casualties were brief and were a minority of all reports filed.[11] Right up to 1968, media coverage of war was consistent with the official line. However, despite the reality, future war planners would conclude that they could never again risk uncensored media coverage of wars.

Through trial and error, a system of media control was devised over the 1980s. The first real attempt was during the US invasion of Grenada in 1983. Media control was so successful that there was a virtual black out of this war because journalists were prevented from going to Grenada. In response to protests, the National Media Pool was created which included a small number of trusted reporters who could be taken to the scene of war at short notice. This was put into practice in the next major US invasion, Panama in 1989. During this war, then Secretary of Defense Dick Cheney insisted on a Washington-based pool, which meant that the most knowledgeable reporters—those with some experience and knowledge of Panama—would not be in the region. He then decided not to inform the press of the invasion until a few hours before it began. As a result, as with Grenada, journalists could not reach Panama on time. Once they arrived, they were held captive by the military for another five hours. Ultimately, journalists found that they had little information and no pictures other than what the Pentagon had provided them, and this is what they reported.[12] Military planners had finally devised a system of media control: restrict access to the battlefield and thus minimize coverage of casualties, provide the media with military approved images of the war, create a "pool" of trusted journalists who could be relied upon, and drum up patriotism.[13]

By the time of the Gulf War of 1991, the system of media censorship had been all but perfected. As Dick Cheney, one of the contributors to this system, would state after the war: "Frankly, I looked on it [the media] as a problem to be managed. The information function was extraordinarily important. I did not have a lot of confidence that I could leave it to the press."[14] The pool system allowed the military to control the movement of journalists and to restrict where they went and what they saw. Journalists were taken to selected sites and not allowed to interview soldiers without a military minder present. Additionally, reporters were not allowed to pass on stories until they were inspected by the military. In the absence of direct access to the war, reporters were treated to press briefings with images of precision bombing and laser-guided missiles hitting their target.

Even the language used to discuss the war assumed Orwellian forms: bad became good and night day. As Kellner argues, "Euphemisms concealed the lethality of the destruction and the effects of the bombing and provided a false picture of surgical, precision bombing."[15] While the dominant images and language suggested that the war was being fought with precision guided bombs, in reality only 7 percent of the ordinance was the "smart" bombs. Furthermore, 70 percent of the smart bombs missed their targets. In all, both conventional and smart technology weapons killed an estimated 200,000 or more and destroyed the infrastructure including electrical power, water, sanitation, and communication facilities. But the pool system prevented journalists from covering this destruction. When journalists Jon Alpert and Maryann DeLeo managed to obtain video footage of the destruction, NBC and CBS refused to air their videotapes. The media also squelched reports of "friendly fire" casualties.

In the 2003 war on Iraq, many of the same characteristics of war coverage can be observed. Additionally, as I will discuss below, several new facets of censorship were incorporated, making the system more sophisticated. In part, this evolution and perfecting of the media–military industrial complex propaganda system is voluntary and conscious. For instance, Bush advisers Karl Rove and Mark McKinnon met with the heads of Viacom, Disney, MGM and others after 9/11 to discuss how the media could "help" the government's efforts. Before the start of the Iraq war, CNN set up a system of "script approval" where reporters had to send their stories to unnamed officials in Atlanta before they could be run. This would ensure that if the military made any errors, CNN monitors would act as the second layer of filtering. Rupert Murdoch of News Corporation took an active role in setting the tone of his news media outlets, so that, not coincidentally, all 175 editors of Murdoch's worldwide newspaper empire took a position in support of the war.[16] Fox, also owned by News Corporation, took this support to the extreme, going so far as to ridicule antiwar protesters.

The convergence of media and government interests in war propaganda derives from shared economic and political interests. In order for US-based media conglomerates such as AOL—Time Warner, Disney, Viacom etc., to continue to be profitable and to extend their reach, they rely on the government to protect their interests domestically and internationally. Domestically, policies like the Telecommunication Act of 1996 have allowed for unprecedented media concentration. Internationally, the US government, through institutions like the World Trade Organization, pries open foreign governments for US media investments. In the case of Iraq, the conquest of that country and the strengthening of US control in the region allows US-based media conglomerates and telecommunications giants to be better positioned to dominate Middle East markets.

In addition to cooperation between media and political elites, another element that has allowed the emergence of the current system of war propaganda arises from the structural limitations of the corporate media system. The pressure to increase profit, felt quite acutely by giant media conglomerates, has led to methods of operation that have compromised journalist ethics. The "Fox effect" shows how this works. The Fox news channel emerged, over the course of the war on Iraq, as the most watched source of news on cable. Fox's approach to the war was self-consciously biased in favor of war, and it sought to tap into a conservative niche market. Anchors and reporters openly chided antiwar voices and abandoned any pretence of neutrality and objectivity. Despite the obvious violations of journalistic integrity, Fox received high ratings, and disturbingly other channels took steps to emulate Fox.[17]

Additionally, there are more long-term structural weaknesses that allow the media to be manipulated. There has been much scholarship on the nature of the corporate media, and in the interests of space I will highlight only a few factors: excessive reliance on government and corporate sources, professional journalism's deference to official sources, the lack of funding for investigative journalism, the marginalization of dissenting voices, and mechanisms that promote self-censorship. Over the last two decades, in order to keep costs low, media conglomerates have downsized and laid off journalists. The result is that they have become more reliant on cheap or free sources of information. The two main sources of such information are corporate public relations departments and the government. Vast amounts of information reach the news media through these two sources. The Pentagon alone employs thousands of people, and spends millions of dollars on its public relations every year.[18] When combined with the "beat" system, where reporters are sent to established locations such as the White House, the Pentagon, the State Department, and so on to routinely cover events, the extent of media reliance on government information becomes clear. The outcome of this dependency is that government (and corporate) sources acquire enormous power to manipulate the news.[19]

Furthermore, the logic of "professional journalism" encourages reporters to accept this status quo. As Robert McChesney argues, the standards of professional journalism work to legitimate and prioritize corporate profit-making journalism over partisan public-service journalism.[20] One consequence of this is the tendency to view those in positions of authority, such as government officials or CEOs, as "credible" and reliable sources of information. Brent Cunningham, managing editor of *Columbia Journalism Review*, argues that the pursuit of objectivity has exacerbated the tendency to rely on official sources making journalists passive recipients of the news.[21] This reliance on official sources, combined with cost-cutting measures that have dried up resources for investigative reporting, has resulted in the practice of running unverified government-issued information as news. Political elites have learnt how to use this to their advantage. During the Iraq war, many "facts" and pieces of evidence were stated as truth, only to be recanted later when their veracity was called into question. In another context, Peter Teeley, a press secretary of George H. W. Bush, explained this strategy: "You can say anything you want during a debate, and 80 million people hear it." If it happens to be untrue, "so what? Maybe 200 people read [the correction] or 2,000 or 20,000."[22]

While official sources are treated deferentially, those who do fall outside the accepted gamut of legitimate sources are dismissed. This logic serves to limit diversity. For instance, when the Chicago-based pacifist group *Voices in the Wilderness* invited the American news media to cover a visit by American antiwar teachers to an Iraqi school, the media declined. Norman Solomon, who was present when this took place, explained this incident as follows:

> I was there when Kysia [a member of Voices in the Wilderness] handed the press release to a TV crew. As soon as he left, the crew didn't even bother to read the entire press release before declaring that it was propaganda. They considered Voices to be outside the reign of legitimate sources, and therefore it could be safely ignored.[23]

This is not to say that there are not journalists who want to report on wars in ways that are more inclusive of diverse opinions. However, they are restricted by in-built systems of discipline and rewards. During the war on Iraq, even celebrity journalists like Peter Arnett would be disciplined for crossing the line. Arnett was fired by NBC and National Geographic for stating on Iraqi TV that US war aims had failed to proceed as planned. The effect of this form of disciplining is one of self-censorship. As Dan Rather stated in a BBC interview in 2002: "What we are talking about here—whether one wants to recognize it or not, or call it by its proper name or not—is a form of self-censorship. I worry that patriotism run amok will trample the very values that the country seeks to defend."[24] The atmosphere of charged patriotism after 9/11 not only promoted self-censorship but also squelched debate. In subtle and not-so-subtle ways, the range of acceptable political discussion was made clear. For instance, network and cable television channels incorporated logos that prominently featured the American flag. They also adopted names for their war coverage that bore a strong resemblance to the Pentagon's language. Fox and MSNBC went with "Operation Iraqi Freedom," the Pentagon's name for the Iraq operation, CBS opted for "America at War," and CNN used "Strike on Iraq." With titles and logos that in no uncertain terms establish "us" and "them" in news coverage, it was almost a foregone conclusion which side would receive favorable coverage and which would not.

In sum, the emergence of the system of information management in effect during the 2003 war on Iraq is the product of post-Vietnam military strategy combined with the willing cooperation of media elites operating within a conglomerated system that lends itself to propaganda. While the media have been a part of the military industrial complex since the Cold War, this integration was strengthened post-Vietnam. In the following sections, I discuss how the war on Iraq was covered. In particular, I show how the propaganda efforts of the pro-war side were able to find an echo, and even amplification, in the mainstream media, while dissenting views were muffled.

## War Rhetoric: The Bush Administration's Case for War

Well before 9/11, the neoconservatives associated with the Bush administration had developed ways in which to shape US foreign policy in the post-Cold War era. September 11 presented them with an opportunity to campaign publicly for their vision of world politics. This vision is exemplified in the documents of the Project for a New American Century (PNAC), founded in 1997 by many individuals in high positions in the Bush administration. A partial list of PNAC founders includes Vice President Dick Cheney, his chief of staff Lewis Libby, Chief Pentagon adviser Richard Perle, Secretary of Defense Donald Rumsfeld, and his deputy Paul Wolfowitz.[25] In September 2000, a PNAC document argued that the US should use overwhelming military force to take control of the gulf region. The report called for "maintaining global US preeminence . . . and shaping the international security order in line with American principles and interests."[26] But in order to realize this goal, the report went on to add, it was necessary to have "some catastrophic event—like a new Pearl Harbor."[27] This event presented itself one year later in the form of 9/11, and the neoconservatives would use this opportunity to launch a propaganda campaign to win support for war with Iraq.

The case for war on Iraq, as I show below, consisted of at least two key arguments: that Iraq was in some way connected with the events of 9/11, and that the Iraqis possessed weapons of mass destruction (WMDs), had used them in the past, and were willing to use them against the US. In trying to make this case to the public, the neoconservatives in the Bush administration were assisted by several like-minded individuals and groups/think tanks, which when combined with the complicit corporate media, can be seen to constitute an "axis of deception."

### Iraq and 9/11

While the war on Afghanistan seemed easy to justify from the Bush administration's point of view, tying Iraq to 9/11 and to al Qaeda proved to be a challenge. Yet the efforts to find this connection, as Richard Clarke the former counterterrorism czar reveals in his book *Against All Enemies*, began almost immediately after 9/11. Clarke mentions an incident where President Bush took a few people aside, including himself, and said to them: "I know you have a lot to do and all . . . but I want you, as soon as you can, to go back over everything, everything. See if Saddam did this. See if he's linked in any way."[28] To carry out this mission, James Woolsey, former director of the CIA and a founding member of PNAC, was sent to Europe to find the evidence. In Europe, Woolsey "discovered" that Czech intelligence had information that Mohammed Atta, the alleged leader of the September 11 attacks, had met with an Iraqi agent in Prague in April, 2001. The report was dismissed as not credible by US, British, French, and Israeli intelligence agencies.[29] However, this did not stop Woolsey from appearing on several talk shows and writing op-ed pieces in major newspapers. Even though these allegations were discredited, the limited range of information meant that the public did not have adequate access to both sides of the story. Polls taken at the end of 2002 and in early 2003 reflect the misconceptions surrounding this issue: almost half of all Americans believed that there was a connection between Iraq and 9/11, and many believed that several of the hijackers were Iraqi, though none were.[30]

Woolsey was not alone in making the connection between 9/11 and Iraq. His arguments were reinforced by several members of the Bush administration. For instance, Cheney stated on NBC:

> *Cheney*. That's been pretty well confirmed, that he [Atta] did go to Prague and he did meet with a senior official of the Iraqi intelligence service in Czechoslovakia last April, several months before the attack. Now, what the purpose of that was, what transpired between them, we simply don't know at this point. But that's clearly an avenue that we want to pursue.
>
> *Tim Russert (Anchor)*. What we do know is that Iraq is harboring terrorists. . . .
>
> *Cheney*. Well, the evidence is pretty conclusive that the Iraqis have indeed harbored terrorists.[31]

The pattern used to establish an Iraq–al Qaeda link was to assert the connection, sometimes accompanied with caveats of uncertainty as in the quote above, only to be later recanted placing the blame on faulty intelligence. Cheney would later state that the intelligence regarding the Atta–Prague incident was not conclusive. If so, then one wonders why Cheney would argue that this meeting was "well confirmed" and why he would prematurely make public inconclusive intelligence. Another associated strategy was to hide behind the excuse of "classified" information. For instance, when Paul Wolfowitz was asked during a congressional hearing to confirm the Atta–Prague story, he replied that he could not since "this gets into a lot of classified areas." He went on to add that "[a]lmost everything that's important is shrouded in uncertainty. Nothing is black or white."[32] Wolfowitz and others could rely on the media to accept this line of argument because of the credibility that official sources are granted by the journalist apparatus.

In addition to the Atta story, the connection between Iraq and al Qaeda was made through the method of establishing guilt-by-suggestion. By mentioning Iraq and al Qaeda in the same breath, and by constantly repeating this connection, the link was established. Thus, Bush would state that "the [Iraqi] regime has longstanding and continuing ties to terrorist organizations. And there are al Qaeda terrorists inside Iraq."[33] The implication is that Iraq must support al Qaeda. While Iraq may have had ties to organizations that the US considers to be "terrorists," and while there may have been al Qaeda stationed in Iraq, by juxtaposing these two sentences it sent the message that Iraq supported al Qaeda and encouraged them to set up camp in Iraq. Hence, the suggestion of a connection rather than the explicit linking of the two served to establish guilt without the accuser having the burden of proof or accountability. When asked to provide evidence of such links, administration figures like Donald Rumsfeld would evade the question. At a news conference, Rumsfeld said, "I suppose that, at some moment, it may make sense to discuss that [evidence of al Qaeda in Iraq] publicly." He went on to add, "It doesn't today. But what I have said is a fact—that there are al Qaeda in a number of locations in Iraq."[34]

Another rhetorical strategy was to establish guilt-through-speculation. Bush administration officials argued that an Iraq–al Qaeda collaboration could pose a serious threat to the US. Thus, Cheney would state:

> *Cheney.* But that's one of the reasons—it takes us back into the axis of evil speech the president made at the State of the Union, our concerns about Iraq, our concerns about the possible marriage, if you will, between the terrorist organization on the one hand and a state that has or is developing weapons of mass destruction on the other. And *if* you ever get them married up—that is *if* somebody who has nukes decides to share one with a terrorist organization, with the expectation they'll use it against us, obviously we've got another problem.[35]

The entire argument is based around constructing hypothetical scenarios. When there was no concrete evidence to suggest that terrorist organizations were acting in concert with "rogue" nations, the argument was based on constructing imaginary connections. Bush would reinforce this logic when he argued that the "danger is, is [sic] that they work in concert . . . the danger is, is [sic] that al Qaeda becomes an extension of Saddam's madness and his hatred and his capacity to extend weapons of mass destruction around the world."[36] In short, al Qaeda *might* work with Iraq which *could* then pose a grave danger in some foreseeable future.

It is interesting that on the same day that Bush could only speculate about connections between al Qaeda and Iraq, the Defense Secretary had evidence of this connection. Rumsfeld stated on CNN that "[w]e have what we consider to be credible evidence that al Qaeda leaders have sought contacts in Iraq who could help them acquire weapons of mass destruction capabilities. We do have, I believe, *it's one report*, indicating that Iraq provided unspecified training relating to chemical and/or biological matters for al Queda members."[37] This "one report" could prove to be false, but it leaves the door open for Rumsfeld to claim that he had faulty intelligence.

As the war drew closer, Bush and Cheney would drop the aforementioned strategies and go on to directly accuse Iraq of having ties to al Qaeda.[38] In a radio address on February 8, 2003, Bush would state "Saddam Hussein has longstanding, direct and continuing ties to terrorist networks. Senior members of the Iraqi intelligence and al Qaeda have met at least eight times since the early 1990s. Iraq has sent bomb-making and document forgery experts to work with al Qaeda. Iraq has also provided al Qaeda with chemical and biological weapons training."[39] Cheney would also make similar statements.

Overall, the connection between Iraq and 9/11 was made through three strategies. The first was to present facts attached with a disclaimer of uncertainty, so that when the evidence was proved false, the credibility of the source could still be maintained by blaming faulty intelligence or claiming that the information was classified. This strategy continues to be used as a way to explain the absence of WMDs. The second strategy was to establish guilt through suggestion. This involved mentioning al Queda and Iraq in the same sentence as a way to imply, rather than assert as fact, a connection between the two. And the third strategy was to establish guilt through speculation, which consisted of projecting imaginary scenarios of what a possible alliance between al Qaeda and Iraq could mean. In addition to tying Iraq to 9/11, the pro-war advocates argued that Iraq was an immediate threat to the US. In an effort to promote a campaign of fear, they argued that Iraq had weapons of mass destruction and was willing to use them.

### Iraq and WMDs

The argument about WMDs began in earnest in September, 2002 when British Prime Minister Tony Blair and Bush, in a joint press conference, declared that the International Atomic Energy Agency (IAEA) had issued a new report stating that Iraq had revived its nuclear weapons project. "I would remind you," Bush insisted, "that when the inspectors first went into Iraq and were denied—finally denied access [in 1998], a report came out of the Atomic—the IAEA that they were six months away from developing a weapon." He added, "I don't know what more evidence we need."[40] Three weeks after this press conference, Mark Gwozdecky, the chief spokesperson of the IAEA, stated that no such report exists.[41]

Later that month, Blair argued that not only did Iraq possess WMDs, but it was capable of deploying them in forty-five minutes. On September 24, Blair released a 50-page "dossier" on Iraq's weapons program. This was reinforced by at least two other pieces of "evidence" furnished by the neoconservative camp. The first was that Iraq had purchased aluminum tubes in order to build nuclear weapons in a matter of six months. And the second was that Iraq had tried to buy uranium from the African country, Niger. The proof of these allegations was based on a series of letters that the administration claimed was the "smoking gun." It was in this context that Bush was able to win a congressional resolution on October 11, 2002 giving him a blank check for war on Iraq. Shortly after this resolution, the truth began to surface.

On December 6, *60 Minutes* broadcast an interview with former UN weapons inspector David Albright, who stated that the aluminum tubes were most likely meant for conventional weapons.[42] One month later, Mohammed El Baradei, head of the IAEA, confirmed this report and declared that the tubes had no relation to a nuclear program. In February 2003, the British *Channel 4 News* revealed that large chunks of the Blair dossier were plagiarized, simply cut and pasted, from a University of California graduate student's thesis.[43] In early March, nuclear weapons experts revealed that the letters demonstrating that Iraq had bought uranium from Niger were hoaxes. These forged letters were even disowned by the CIA; the agency also stated that they had communicated this information to the administration as far back as 2001.[44] When Joseph Wilson, a US diplomat, publicly criticized the Bush administration claims about Iraq seeking uranium from Niger, the White House, apparently, leaked the name of his CIA undercover operative spouse as punishment. Despite evidence to the contrary, the Bush administration insisted that the Niger forgeries were proof that Iraq has WMDs. And on March 7, 2003, Colin Powell went before the UN Security Council and repeated the discredited aluminum tubes story. Hans Blix, executive director of UNMOVIC who supervised inspections in Iraq, also speaking before the Council that day contradicted several pieces of intelligence about Iraq's weapons. For instance, he pointed out that there was no evidence to indicate that Iraq had mobile chemical weapons production units. However, he also expressed uncertainty about Iraq's weapons, stating that more inspections were necessary.[45] But this assessment would not halt the US drive to war. Blix would later speculate in his book, *Disarming Iraq*, that the decision by the US to overthrow Hussein was made much in advance and would have proceeded regardless of UN inspections, which several figures in the Bush administration did not hold in high regard.[46]

Overall, the approach was that faulty and unverified information was repeated often enough until, in true Orwellian fashion, falsehoods came to be accepted as truth. In order to keep these lies alive in the public imagination, the administration relied on the support of several well-funded think-tanks with easy access to the media. In addition to PNAC, several associations such as the American Enterprise Institute, the Center for Strategic and International Studies, the Washington Institute for Near East Policy, Middle East Forum, the Hudson Institute, the Hoover Institute, and the Committee for the Liberation of Iraq, were involved in the propaganda efforts.[47] These organizations went through Benador Associates, a media relations company, to ensure that their arguments found a space in the media. Benador was successful in booking several Middle East and terrorism "experts" from these associations on television programs and placing op-ed pieces in prominent newspapers. A Lexis-Nexis search with the terms "Iraq" in the headline and just one of the groups mentioned above, the "American Enterprise Institute" in the full text, came up with 620 hits in major newspapers and 655 hits on television during the years 2002–2003. Thus, overwhelmingly, as we shall see in the following section, pro-war voices dominated the framing of this issue.

## Media and War Propaganda

With few exceptions, the bulk of media coverage on the front pages of major newspapers and headline news on television simply parroted the administration's line before and during the war. This spirit is best captured in Dan Rather's statement: "George Bush is the president, he makes the decisions, and, you know, as just one American, whenever he wants me to line up, just tell me where."[48] Even though there was enough evidence to suggest that the case for war was fraught with contradictions, the media chose to present certain "facts" and ignore others. While there are differences in how various sections of the media covered the war, and I take great care in this paper to point to instances where the mainstream media uncovered information critical of the war, the overall tone, as I show below, was weighted decisively in favor of war.

The key strategy was omission. For instance, in the weeks leading up to the crucial Security Council vote on the war, US officials listened in on phone conversations and read the emails of UN Security Council representatives from Angola, Cameroon, Chile, Bulgaria, Guinea and Pakistan who were stationed in New York. A media system that behaves as the "watchdog" of the government would have reported this incident as a major story. However, a media system that is complicit with the larger program of the military industrial complex acts to silence and marginalize contradictory information. After the British newspaper, the *Observer*, broke the story in early March, 2003, a study of US media treatment of this story shows that the *LA Times* and the *Washington Post* did their best to play down the significance of the matter while other media, including the networks, did not even cover the story.[49]

In October, 2002, when Czech president Vaclav Havel stated that there was no evidence that Atta had met with an Iraqi official or that he was in the country during the alleged meeting, mainstream media again downplayed this information. It is significant that while several media outlets carried stories on Atta's alleged meeting with Iraqi officials, only three newspapers and three television news sources had stories that focused on the denial of such a meeting.[50] In short, while the original accusations were featured prominently, the retractions or refutations were barely addressed. As *The New York Times* would later admit, articles "based on dire claims about Iraq tended to get prominent display, while follow-up articles that called the original ones into question were sometimes buried. In some cases, there was no follow-up at all." The *Times* was not alone in this practice, but it was one of the few media sources that would take responsibility for it.

Coverage of the claims that Iraq had WMDs was similar to coverage of the alleged links between al Qaeda and Iraq. Despite abundant evidence to the contrary, such as the interviews with former weapons inspector Scott Ritter who had stated repeatedly that Iraq was 90–95 percent disarmed, the media chose to bury questions about WMDs deep inside a story or to ignore it all together. Perhaps the most egregious example of this attitude was the approach taken towards the *Newsweek* exclusive with an Iraqi defector run on March 3, 2003.[51] The article stated that Hussein Kamel, the highest-ranking Iraqi official ever to defect from Saddam Hussein's inner circle, had told CIA and British intelligence officers in 1995 that after the Gulf War, Iraq had destroyed all its chemical and biological weapons. However, as a study notes, Bush, Powell, and other administration officials had repeatedly cited "Kamel's defection . . . as evidence that (1) Iraq has not disarmed; (2) inspections cannot disarm it; and (3) defectors such as Kamel are the most reliable source of information on Iraq's weapons."[52] It is significant that testimony that could throw into doubt the key argument made by the Bush administration was largely ignored by the rest of the media and buried.[53] Some media outlets would even take a hostile tone towards those who disagreed with the US position on WMDs. Even Hans Blix was attacked by *The New York Times* in an article that questioned his integrity, claiming that he was "more interested in pleasing all sides than stating the facts."[54]

The media also ignored the historical connections between the US and Iraq. It is well known that Saddam Hussein was an ally of the US, and that the US supplied Iraq with chemical and biological weapons during the 1980s, but with few exceptions, the media developed collective historical amnesia on this question. One of the exceptions was a *Washington Post* story that stated clearly that US involvement with Iraq "included large-scale intelligence sharing, supply of cluster bombs through a Chilean front company, and facilitating Iraq's acquisition of chemical and biological precursors."[55] The article went on to add that the "administrations of Ronald Reagan and George H. W. Bush authorized the sale to Iraq of numerous items that had both military and civilian applications, including poisonous chemicals and deadly biological viruses, such as anthrax and bubonic plague," and that this practice continued even after Iraq used chemical and biological weapons against the Kurds. At the very least, the article threw into question the sincerity of the Bush administration's denunciation of Hussein's use of chemical weapons against "his own people," i.e., the Kurdish population. But this history was largely downplayed.[56]

In addition to downplaying or omitting facts that would refute the administration's case for war, the media also went out of their way to create a climate supportive of the war. They did so in two ways—first, by stacking the deck with pro-war guests and "experts" and, second, by firing or intimidating reporters and talk-show hosts who upset this scenario. Additionally, several media outlets refused to accept anti-war ads. A study of PBS and the three networks' evening news shows conducted over a two-week period in February, 2003, found that 76 percent of the guests were either current or former government or military officials, of which all but one person advocated a pro-war stance. On the other hand, less than 1 percent of the guests were associated with the antiwar movement, even though large demonstrations involving hundreds of thousands had already taken place in the US.[57]

Additionally, Phil Donahue's show was cancelled by MSNBC because, according to a leaked internal report, the show presented "a difficult public face for NBC in a time of war."[58] The report went on to add that Donahue "seems to delight in presenting guests who are antiwar, anti-Bush and skeptical of the administration's motives." While the official excuses for dropping the show had to do with ratings and profits, in reality Donahue's show averaged 439,000 the month before it was cancelled, which made it the top-rated show on MSNBC, outperforming *Hardball with Chris Matthews*.[59]

The message to journalists was clear: either censor yourself or face disciplining. This message came not only from the elites who run the mass media, but also from the White House. As journalists Russell Mokhiber and Robert Weissman note, White House press passes are hard to come by if you are known to be a reporter who asks tough questions.[60] A vivid display of the results of these tactics was to be found at Bush's prime time news conference on March 6, 2003. The press conference was so tightly controlled that even compliant White House journalists were irate. Bush called only on reporters he wanted from a pre-determined list, while following a tight script, emphasizing 9/11 and repeating the same points again and again. Bush had gone too far in exposing the degree of media subservience, and some journalists were annoyed.[61] But not much would change during the actual war on Iraq.

## Reporting the War on Iraq

Donald Rumsfeld described the coverage of the war in classic Orwellian terms: "I don't think . . . there has ever been the degree of free press coverage as you have seen in this instance."[62] The illusion of freedom comes from the fact that unlike the 1991 Gulf War, when journalists were not allowed to witness the war first hand, this time "embedded" journalists were allowed onto the frontlines. However, in order to be an embed, reporters had to sign a contract with the military agreeing to a 50-point program that stated what they could and could not report. A close reading of this program shows that it had in-built mechanisms of scrutiny, which would reveal themselves as the war progressed. In all, there were about 900 reporters, mainly US and British, embedded with the troops. Those who were not embedded were termed "unilaterals" and did not have access to transportation and other facilities. Perhaps most important, embeds were protected by the military while unilaterals were on their own. Arguably, this distinction between embeds and unilaterals was less about protection and more about issuing a threat—a threat that the military would soon act upon.

While reporting from the scene of battle is not new, what was new about this war was the live footage from the actual battles. Far from making the war more realistic, it positioned viewers, quite literally, to witness the skirmishes from the point of view of the military. If you shoot the action from the side of the US and British forces, it becomes very clear who the "good guys" and "bad guys" are and whom to support. Far from objective reporting, the embedded reporters were telling the story both physically and ideologically from the vantage point of the US and British troops. Ideologically, the journalists seemed to identify with the soldiers. This would seem natural; after all, they ate with them, they slept together, and they even wore the same clothes. As Pamela Hess, a UPI reporter, would state, "Reporters love troops. Put us with these 18-year-old kids . . . we just turn to jelly."[63] When setting this system up, it must have been clear to the war planners that this situation would create identification with the soldiers and lead to voluntary self-censorship by the journalists.

However, this system could also backfire. For instance, already at the start of the war, a significant minority of soldiers had expressed disagreement with the war. Had the war dragged on, leading to more US casualties and fatalities, this sentiment is likely to have become more generalized as it did in Vietnam after 1968 when large numbers of soldiers turned against the war. Since the official end of war on May 1, the occupation of Iraq has had an impact on the consciousness of soldiers. Many have articulated the view that they are not there to liberate the people of Iraq, but instead to occupy that country. As one angry sergeant put it, "If Donald Rumsfeld was here, I'd ask him for his resignation."[64] A growing number of military personnel and their families have started to speak out against the occupation leading to the formation of coalitions like "Bring the Troops Home Now" and "Military Families Speak Out" which consist of thousands of military families. Had this happened during the war, embedded journalists would have been positioned to report on this discontent. But as it worked out, the official war was short, and journalists left before these sentiments could manifest themselves. Thus, the footage of the actual battlefield served to promote identification with the soldiers, thereby bolstering the "support the troops" argument.

To add to this, reporters saw only what the troops did and lacked the mobility to travel elsewhere or to witness the havoc created in the aftermath of an attack. The result was images of sophisticated machinery, bombs, and wreckage, but little of the human consequences. We did not see the horrific pictures of Iraqi casualties, the dead, and the destruction of their homes and cities or those of dead or injured US soldiers either. As discussed earlier, this is consistent with the model of information management agreed upon by the military and media elite. Just like the Gulf war, even though the footage was available to network executives, they declined to air it. And like the Gulf war, the military and the White House ensured clean war coverage.

What was different this time was that embedded journalists were allowed to show real images of the action and the superior fire power and artillery of the US and British troops, unlike the military simulations of the 1991 war or the fireworks-like display in the night sky. This shift was motivated in large part by advances in the Pentagon's psychological warfare program and the move to enlist the media in the US "shock and awe" operation. As Michael Ryan, a former editor for *Time*, observed, the "American media, essentially, have become an extension of the military psychological operations, with Rumsfeld hoping they can help to scare the daylights out of Iraq."[65] In April 2003, using technology capable of overriding domestic media broadcasts, the US re-broadcast news programs featuring Tom Brokaw and Peter Jennings to the Iraqi population.[66]

A large part of the psychological operations was the spread of misinformation. The constant demand for new information on the 24-hour news channels, and the credibility associated with official sources, meant that often military claims would be relayed without taking the time to check the facts. An update from a military official would receive wide publicity, only to be retracted or modified later. The British newspaper, *The Guardian*, and the BBC tracked these claims and counter-claims.[67] The extent of the deception is stunning. As one senior BBC news source commented, "We're absolutely sick and tired of putting things out and finding out they're not true. The misinformation in this war is far and away worse than any conflict I've covered, including the first Gulf War and Kosovo."[68]

On the first day of war, military spokespersons claimed that Iraq had fired scuds into Kuwait. This story received much play in the media. Three days later, US General Stanley McChrystal stated that no scuds had been fired. On March 21, Admiral Sir Michael Boyce and Donald Rumsfeld reported that Umm Qasr had fallen to "coalition" forces. This was not true. In fact, Umm Qasr was officially reported "taken" *nine times* before it was actually taken.[69] On March 27, Tony Blair in a joint press conference with Bush declared that two British soldiers had been executed by the Iraqis and that this was proof of Saddam Hussein's "depravity." The next day, the prime minister's spokesperson stated that there was no "absolute evidence" that the soldiers were executed.[70] On March 29, an explosion in a market in Baghdad killed at least 50 civilians. The official spokespersons for the US and UK, who both seemed to share a similar media strategy, claimed that they had nothing to do with the incident. The media ran this story without question. A few days later, Robert Fisk, of the British *Independent* newspaper, found shrapnel that identified the cause of the explosion as a US missile. Over the course of the war, there were a series of claims that troops had found evidence of weapons of chemical and biological weapons, only to declare shortly after that there were no such weapons. Even the story of rescued POW Jessica Lynch on April 1, 2004, it was later revealed, was based on faulty information.[71]

Some have argued that these claims and counter-claims were genuine mistakes made in the heat of war. This would be disingenuous. The history of using the mainstream media in psychological operations is both long and well documented. As Lieutenant Commander Arthur A. Humphries, an advocate of press control, argued over two decades ago, "The news media can be a useful tool, or even a weapon, in prosecuting a war psychologically, so that the operators don't have to use their more severe weapons."[72] The spread of misinformation is part of a calculated plan whose rationale is to plant a story for a specific goal, regardless of the truth of the story.

Cynically, some in the military tried to blame the misinformation on reporters. Richard Gaisford, an embedded BBC reporter, replied to this charge as follows, "We have to check each story we have with [the military]. And the captain, who's our media liaison officer, will check with the colonel, and they will check with the Brigade headquarters as well."[73] Unwittingly, Gaisford revealed the extent to which the embedded system was under military control. What this quote also reveals is the willingness of media organizations to be part of such a system of censorship.

In addition to the direct censorship on the battlefield, there was another coordinating organization that played a key role in orchestrating the war propaganda. The White House set up an institution known as the Office of Global Communication which acted as a public relations agency for the Bush administration. Its tasks included issuing daily talking points to US spokespersons around the world. Its role was to coordinate the messages from the Pentagon, the State Department, and the military officials in the Middle East, so that the comments from these sources were approved in advance by the White House and were consistent with the official line. The Office also trained and provided former military personnel to be interviewed by the media. *Chicago Tribune* reporter Bob Kemper notes that so "controlled is the administration's message that officials from Bush on down often use identical anecdotes to make their points."[74] Even the choice of words was thought out. For instance, the office sent directives to the military spokespersons not to refer to Iraqi troops loyal to Saddam Hussein as the "Fedayeen," since this term held a positive association. Instead, they were asked to refer to these troops as "terrorists," "death squads," or "thugs."[75]

Even the best designed public relations campaign, however, can fail if other sources of information that contradict the official line are allowed to flourish. Thus, when the war on Iraq proved not to be a cakewalk in its first several days, journalists who pointed that out had to be disciplined. Peter Arnett, the Pulitzer Prize winning journalist, was fired from MSNBC for admitting on Iraqi television that things were not going as planned for the US. The Iraqi television station in Baghdad, which had contradicted many of the claims made by US and British officials, was bombed. Rather than express horror at this bombing, many reporters at Fox, CNN, MSNBC, and other media outlets supported the bombing. Fox News's John Gibson wondered: "Should we take Iraqi TV off the air? Should we put one down the stove pipe there?" On CNBC, Forrest Sawyer offered tactical alternatives to bombing: "There are operatives in there. You could go in with sabotage, take out the building, you could take out the tower."[76] What these quotes illustrate is that nothing close to balance was being maintained on the channels.

Journalists also became targets in this war. The biggest assault on reporters who did not toe the US line began on April 8 when a US missile hit the Baghdad office of Al-Jazeera, which had devoted considerable coverage to the deaths of Iraqi civilians. The attack killed Tareq Ayub, a 34-year old Jordanian journalist. The same day, the US fired at the Palestine Hotel where most foreign journalists not embedded with the military were staying, killing two more journalists. Sections of the media, such as *The New York Times*, were forced to admit that these events raise "concerns" and "bring accusations" that the military was deliberately targeting journalists.[77] Arguably, this was part of the plan. Weeks before this incident, veteran BBC reporter Kate Adie was told by a senior Pentagon official that if unilateral broadcast satellite links were detected, they would be targeted, even if the journalists were still at the intercepted location.[78] More recently, the British newspaper *The Daily Mirror*, citing a leaked memo of a conversation between Blair and Bush in April, 2004, claimed that Blair convinced Bush not to bomb Al-Jazeera's headquarters.[79]

It appears that the overall media strategy of the war makers had several fronts: the use of embedded journalists; the spread of misinformation; threats, bombings, or even death for journalists and media outlets hostile to the US, and a central propaganda-coordinating mechanism, i.e., the Office of Global Communication. This level of planning and strategizing is not new; rather, as discussed earlier, it is the culmination of a decades-long process to strengthen the media–government nexus.

## Conclusion

In this paper, I have argued that the propagandistic coverage of the war on Iraq reveals the extent to which the media are complicit with the aims of the military industrial complex. Yet, this relationship is sometimes strained in the interests of maintaining credibility. In democratic societies, the media have to maintain a semblance of independence so as not to appear to be obviously subservient to elite interests. In the months following the war when the reality blatantly contradicted war propaganda, such as when WMDs were not discovered, the media were forced to acknowledge this discrepancy. A slew of such events/facts then kept up the pressure on the media—from the growth of the liberation movement in Iraq to the revelations of the Abu Ghraib prison torture scandal. To add to this, as more "respectable" official sources, such as Democratic politicians like Howard Dean and Dennis Kucinich, and later Republicans such as John McCain and Chuck Hagel, as well as former officials like Richard Clarke and Joseph Wilson, came forward to voice their criticisms, the space for questioning expanded.

This was not uniformly true of all media. Thus, while Fox continued to insinuate, a full year after the official end of warfare, that WMDs might still be found in Iraq, *The New York Times* ran the 9/11 commission report of 2004, which established that there was no connection between Iraq and al Qaeda, as front-page news. Finally, the media also had to respond to the anti-war movement whose arguments were vindicated in the aftermath of the war. The combination of three factors—an avalanche of empirical evidence that threw war claims into question, the pressure of domestic and international movements, and the emergence of skeptical official sources—forced large sections of media to take a more adversarial role in order to maintain credibility.

However, despite their best efforts, the public only seems to have grown more skeptical of the media. In the lead up to the war, even though close to 60 percent held mistaken views about the war, the remaining resisted the propaganda.[80] A Zogby poll taken a month before the outbreak of war found that just over half of the population supported war, while a substantial 41 percent opposed it.[81] The numbers against the war and occupation would increase as incidents like Abu Ghraib, as well as the various falsehoods, began to be revealed. It would appear that along with the rejection of war propaganda, there has been a growing distrust of the mainstream media. Since the start of the Iraq war, significant numbers of Americans began to rely on British media for information about the conflict.[82] The audience for the BBC World News bulletins aired on PBS increased by almost 30 percent during the first weeks of the war, and the BBC's website saw a dramatic increase in the number of Americans visiting the site. About 40 percent of *The Guardian* newspaper's online readers are located in the United States. Christian Christensen concludes that this preference for British media is due to a growing gap between the public's expectation of fair and accurate information and the American media's failure to deliver. He adds that what seems to have disappointed Americans most of all is that the media have covered scandalous events in a "relatively timid and uncritical" way.

This search for alternative sources of information is visible in another mediated sphere: weblogs. Over the first half of 2004, left-wing blogs experienced a significant increase in traffic.[83] Matthew Klam explains that partisan blogs have seen this growth due to the public's increased sense of crisis and the inability to tolerate the "once-soothing voice of the non-ideological press" (p. 45). However, as I have shown in this paper, the media are far from non-ideological. Additionally, it is important to note that it is not simply partisan blogs that are being sought after but *left-wing* blogs, i.e., those critical of the status quo. This trend is also visible in documentary films. Michael Moore's *Fahrenheit 9/11* drew millions and set a box office record for documentaries. The documentary *Outfoxed*, a critique of the Fox channel and an expose of its rightwing, pro-Republican bias, was originally intended to be sold as DVDs. However, after more than 50,000 copies were sold within the first ten days of its release, it began to be distributed in theatres.

What these examples demonstrate is an increased politicization of the American citizenry and an enormous potential to rebuild the anti war movement. At the same time, there has also been a hardening of the pro-war side, leading many to characterize the 2004 election year as one marked by polarization. However, while the pro-war and conservative segment of the population has been given political expression by the Republican Party, the absence of a viable political party to the left of the Democratic Party meant that the anti-war potential remained largely unorganized. There were few demonstrations that expressed the disgust that the majority of Americans felt towards the Abu Ghraib incidents. Instead, progressives threw their support behind the Democratic presidential candidate, arguing for the logic of "Anybody but Bush," even though John Kerry promised to continue the occupation of Iraq. At the end of the day, despite the differences between the two major parties, they were both agreed on the right of the US to intervene militarily around the globe and to craft the new imperial project of the twenty-first century.[84]

In this context of growing public skepticism, the failure of the media to meet the democratic needs of this society, and the absence of significant anti-war and anti-imperialist voices in the public sphere, intellectuals bear an enormous responsibility. Dissenting voices in the academy, with access to institutional resources, have a role to play in producing scholarship critical of the new imperialism. However, to be practically effective, this research needs to be placed at the service of progressive movements and to be tied to the project of rebuilding an anti-imperialist movement.

## Questions for Consideration

1    Using a database such as Nexis or Factiva, review the way newspapers covered the U.S. government's decision to go to war in 2003. Do you agree with Kumar's argument that press coverage during 2003 was largely propagandist?

2    Some people would say that in the age of the Internet, people can to look online for many sides of arguments and not be guided only by mainstream newspapers and television news programs. Would this viewpoint change your view of Kumar's conclusions about the failure of the media system to fulfill its democratic role? Why or why not?

## Notes

1. *The New York Times*, "The Times and Iraq," 26 May 2004, sec A.
2. Orville Schell, "Why the Press Failed," *ZNet*, 14 July 2004, http://www.zmag.org/content/showarticle.cfm?SectionID=21&ItemID=5883 (accessed 5 September 2004).
3. Douglas Kellner, "The Media and the Crisis of Democracy in the Age of Bush-2," *Communication and Critical/Cultural Studies* 1 (2004): 31.
4. See, for instance, John McArthur, *Second Front: Censorship and Propaganda in the Gulf War* (New York: Hill & Wang, 1992); Noam Chomsky, *Media Control: The Spectacular Achievements of Propaganda* (New York: Seven Stories Press, 2002); Marcus Wilkerson, *Public Opinion and the Spanish-American War: A Study in War Propaganda* (New York: Russell & Russell, 1967); Philip M. Taylor, *War and the Media: Propaganda and Persuasion in the Gulf War* (New York: Manchester University Press, 1992); Hamid Mowlana, George Gerbner, and Herbert I. Schiller, ed., *Truimph of the Image: The Media's War in the Persian Gulf—A Global Perspective* (Boulder: Westview Press, 1992); Daniel Hallin, *The Uncensored War: The Media and Vietnam* (Berkeley: University of California Press, 1989); and Douglas Kellner, *The Persian Gulf TV War* (Boulder: Westview Press, 1992).
5. Wilkerson.
6. A 1976 investigation by Admiral Hyman Rickover concluded that the explosion was caused not by an external mine but by spontaneous combustion of the ship's coal bins—though some historians still dispute his findings. See Hyman G. Rickover, *How the Battleship Maine Was Destroyed* (Washington: Department of the Navy, Naval History Division, 1976).
7. Howard Zinn, *A People's History of the United States* (New York: HarperPerennial, 1995).
8. Hallin.
9. John MacArthur, "An Orwellian Pitch: The Inner Workings of the War-Propaganda Machine," *LA Weekly* 21–27 March 2003, www.laweekly.com/ink/03/18/features mcarthur.php (accessed 10 April 2003).
10. MacArthur.
11. Hallin.
12. Trevor Thrall, *War in the Media Age* (New Jersey: Hampton Press, 2000).
13. MacArthur.
14. Patrick Sloyan, "Hiding Bodies," *Rolling Stone* 20 March 2003, 47.
15. Kellner, *Persian Gulf TV War*, 239.
16. Roy Greenslade, "Their Master's Voice," *The Guardian* 17 February 2003, media.guardian.co.uk/mediaguardian/story/0,7558,896864,00.html (accessed 4 April 2003).
17. Jim Rutenberg, "Cable's War Coverage Suggests a New 'Fox Effect' on Television Journalism," *New York Times* 16 April 2003, B9.
18. Edward Herman and Noam Chomsky, *Manufacturing Consent: The Political Economy of the Mass Media* (New York: Pantheon Books, 1988).
19. Deepa Kumar, *Outside the Box: Corporate Media, Globalization, and the UPS Strike* (Urbana Champaign: University of Illinois Press, 2006).
20. Robert W. McChesney, *The Problem of the Media: U.S. Communication Politics in the 21st Century* (New York: Monthly Review Press, 2004).
21. Brent Cunningham, "Re-thinking Objectivity," *Columbia Journalism Review* July/August 2003.
22. MacArthur.
23. Norman Solomon, *Target Iraq: What the News Media Didn't Tell You* (New York: Context Books, 2003), 15.
24. Quoted in Solomon, *Target Iraq*, 23.
25. Sheldon Rampton, and John Stauber, *Weapons of Mass Deception: The Uses of Propaganda in Bush's War on Iraq* (New York: Jeremy Tarcher/Penguin, 2003).
26. Project for a New American Century, *Rebuilding America's Defenses: Strategy, Forces and Resources For a New Century*, 2000, http://www.newamericancentury.org/publicationsre ports.htm, ii (accessed 25 March 2003).
27. Project for a New American Century, 51.
28. Richard A. Clarke, *Against All Enemies: Inside America's War on Terror* (New York: Free Press, 2004), 32.

29. Jim Lobe, "Watch Woolsey," *Asia Times* 8 April 2003, http://www.atimes.com/atimes/Middle_East/ED08Ak05.html (accessed 15 May 2003).

30. This is not to suggest that media coverage directly caused this level of misconception. However, it is not a coincidence that public knowledge and opinions coincided with the media's one-sided narrative.

31. Dick Cheney, interviewed by Tim Russert, *Meet the Press*, NBC, 9 December 2001. Transcript available at: http://www.washingtonpost.com/wp-srv/nation/specials/attacked/transcripts/cheneytext_120901.html (accessed 3 April 2003).

32. Walter Shapiro, "It's No Secret that 9/11 Report is Stingy on Answers," *USA Today* 20 September 2002, sec. A, 6A.

33. Judy Woodruff, *CNN Inside Politics*, CNN, 26 September 2002.

34. Bradley Graham, "Al Qaeda Presence in Iraq Reported," *Washington Post* 21 August 2002, sec A, A1.

35. Tim Russert, *Meet the Press*, NBC, 19 May 2002, my italics.

36. Mike Allen, "Bush Asserts That Al Qaeda Has Links to Iraq's Hussein," *Washington Post* 26 September 2002, sec. A, A29.

37. Judy Woodruff, *CNN Inside Politics*, CNN, 26 September 2002, my italics.

38. For a series of these quotes, see *The New York Times*, "President's Political Thorn Grows Only More Stubborn," 17 June 2004, sec A, A15.

39. George Bush, President's Weekly Radio Address, The Whitehouse, http://www.whitehouse. gov/news/releases/2003/02/ (accessed 3 April 2003).

40. Joseph Curl. "Agency Disavows Report on Iraq Arms," *Washington Times* 27 September 2002, http://www.washtimes.com/national/20020927–500715.htm (accessed 3 April 2003).

41. Curl.

42. CBS News, "Selling the Iraq War to the US," *60 Minutes*, www.cbsnews.com/stories/2002/12/06/60minutes/main532107.shtml (accessed 3 April 2003).

43. Gary Gibbon, "No. 10 Admits Dossier Blunder," *Channel 4 News*, 7 February 2003, www.channel4.com/news/2003/02/week_1/07_dossier.html (accessed 3 April 2003).

44. Chris Smith, "A Spurious Smoking Gun," *Mother Jones* 25 March 2003, http://www.motherjones.com/news/update/2003/13/we_338_01.htm (accessed 15 May 2003).

45. Hans Blix, "Oral Introduction of the 12th Quarterly Report of UNMOVIC," UN Security Council meeting, 7 March 2003, http://www.un.org/Depts/unmovic/SC7asdelivered.htm (accessed 15 May 2003).

46. Hans Blix, *Disarming Iraq* (New York: Pantheon Books, 2004), 12–13.

47. Stauber and Rampton, 2003.

48. Jim Rutenberg, and Bill Carter, "Draping Newscasts with the Flag," *New York Times* 20 September 2001, sec. C, C8.

49. Fairness and Accuracy in the Media, *Times, Networks Shun UN Spying Story*, 11 March 2003, http://www.fair.org/activism/un-observer-spying.html (accessed 15 May 2003).

50. A Lexis-Nexis search with the terms "Atta" and "Czech" in the full text for the period of October and November, 2002, reveals that only three newspapers had stories not including editorials (*New York Times, Boston Globe,* and *St. Petersburg Times*) and three television sources (ABC, CNNfn and NBC) carried the 21 October story denying the connection.

51. John Barry, "Exclusive: The Defector's Secrets," *Newsweek* 3 March 2003, http://stacks.msnbc.com/news/876128.asp (accessed 15 May 2003).

52. Fairness and Accuracy in Reporting, *Star Witness on Iraq said weapons were destroyed: Bombshell revelation from a defector cited by White House and press*, 27 February 2003, http://www.fair.org (accessed 15 May 2003).

53. While the media did finally start to question the Bush administrations claims regarding weapons of mass destruction when none were found months after the end of the war, this move arguably has less to do with their role as an adversarial press and more to do with saving face and holding on to their credibility.

54. Cited in Blix, *Disarming Iraq*, 216.

55. Michael Dobbs, "US Had Key Role in Iraq Buildup," *Washington Post* 30 December 2002, sec. A, A1.

56. So far, many of the examples cited in this essay that contradict the pro-war case come from the mainstream media. I specifically chose these examples, passing up several scholarly books and journal articles that could make the same points, in order to shed light on a media system that is complicit in the propaganda war. It is not the case that media organizations were manipulated by the government to carry false information; rather, despite full access to information that contradicted the pro-war arguments, the media chose to be willing partners in the propaganda campaign.

57. Fairness and Accuracy in Reporting, *In Iraq Crisis, Networks are Megaphones of Official Views*, 18 March 2003, http://www.fair.org/reports/iraq-sources.html.

58. Howard Krutz, "Protest Letters to Donahue draw Savage Response," *The Washington Post* 5 March 2003, sec C, C01.

59. Bill Carter, "MSNBC Cancels Phil Donahue," *The New York Times* 28 February 2003, http://www.nytimes.com/2003/02/26/business/media/26PHIL.html?ex=1133758800&en=760a6baa2f12e8ab&ei=5070 (accessed 3 April 2003).

60. Russell Mokhiber and Robert Weissman, "Too Much," *Corp-Focus*, 2003, lists.essential.org/pipermail/corp-focus/2003/000146.html (accessed 16 May 2003).

61. Michael Crowley, "Bush Rats the Press," *NY Observer* 12 March 2003.

62. Quoted in Michael Ryan, "In this Ear We Report What They Decide," *Tompaine.com*, 24 March 2003, http://www.tompaine.com/feature.cfm/ID/7477 (accessed 16 May 2003).

63. Quoted in Ryan.

64. Quoted in Peter Jennings, *World News Tonight with Peter Jennings*, ABC, 15 July 2003.

65. Ryan.

66. Nancy Snow, *Information War: American Propaganda, Free Speech and Opinion Control since 9–11* (New York: Seven Stories Press, 2003).

67. Annie Lawson, Lisa O'Carroll, Chris Tryhorn and Jason Deans, "War Watch: Claims and Counter Claims During the Media War over Iraq," *The Guardian* 11 April 2003, media.guardian.co.uk/iraqandthemedia/story/0,12823,921649,00.html (accessed 16 May 2003). *BBC News*, "Iraq War: Unanswered Questions" 17 April 2003, http://news.bbc.co.uk/1/hi/world/middle_east/2929411.stm#return (accessed 3 April 2003).

68. Quoted in Ciar Byrne, "BBC Chiefs Stress Need to Attribute War Sources," *The Guardian* 28 March 2003, www.guardian.co.uk/Iraq/Story/0,2763,924172,00.html (accessed 3 April 2003).

69. Lawson et al.

70. *BBC News*, "Iraq War."

71. Deepa Kumar, "War Propaganda and the (Ab)uses of Women: Media Constructions of the Jessica Lynch Story," *Feminist Media Studies* 4, no. 3 (November 2004).

72. Quoted in MacArthur.

73. John Pilger, "The War for Truth," *Znet* 7 April 2003, http://zmag.org/weluser.htm (accessed 16 May 2003).

74. Bob Kemper, "Agency Wages Media Battle: Team makes sure war message is unified, positive," *Chicago Tribune* 7 April 2003, http://www.chicagotribune.com/news/chi-0304070189apr07,1,4382383.stoy (accessed 15 May 2003).

75. Mike Allen and Karen DeYoung, "White House is Revising its War Message," *Washington Post* 3 April 2003, sec. A, A32.

76. Fairness and Accuracy in Reporting, *US Media Applaud Bombing of Iraqi TV*, 27 March 2003, http://www.fair.org/activism/iraqi-tv.html (accessed 20 May 2003).

77. Jacques Steinberg, and Jim Rutenberg, "Deaths of Journalists Bring Accusations and Concerns," *New York Times* 9 April 2003, sec. B, B2.

78. David Miller, "Eliminating Truth: The Development of War Propaganda," *Znet* 28 March 2003, http://www.zmag.org/content/showarticle.cfm?SectionID=21&ItemID=3346 (accessed 20 May 2003).

79. Alan Cowell, "Bush Spoke of Attacking Arab News Channel, British Tabloid Says," *The New York Times* 23 November 2005, A1.

80. Clay Ramsey, Stefan Subias, Evan Lewis, and Phillip Worf, *Americans On Terrorism: Two Years After 9/11*, 2003, published by the PIPA/Knowledge Networks Poll, http://www.pipa.org/OnlineReports/Terrorism/FindingsTerr9.03.pdf (accessed 10 March 2004).

81.  *Zogby*, "Overall Support for War Drops. 2003," 21 February 2003, www.zogby.com (accessed 20 May 2003).

82.  Christian Christensen, "For Many, British is better," *British Journalism Review* 15, No. 3 (2004): 23–28.

83.  Matthew Klam, "Fear and Laptops on the Campaign Trail," *The New York Times Magazine* 26 September 2004, 43–49.

84.  Kerry and sections of the Democratic Party are influenced by the views of the Progressive Policy Institute. The Institute's view of foreign policy, known as "progressive internationalism," shares much in common with Bush's National Security Strategy. The report states that while "some complain that the Bush administration has been too radical in recasting America's national security strategy, we believe it has not been ambitious or imaginative enough. We need to do more, and do it smarter and better to protect our people and help shape a safer, freer world." See http://www.ppionline.org/ppi_ci.cfm?knlgAreaID = 124& subsecid=900020&contentid=252144 (accessed 30 March 2004).

# Chapter 31

## STUART EWEN

# THE PUBLIC AND ITS PROBLEMS
## Some Notes for the New Millennium

CONSIDER, FOR A MOMENT, THE significance of the term *public* in public relations. Does the public relations industry respond to the needs of a citizenry hoping to make better informed decisions? Or, rather, does the industry perceive the public as impressionable and highly susceptible to persuasive techniques? This essay, excerpted from the coda of Stuart Ewen's 1996 book, *PR! A Social History of Spin*, attempts to bring these contradictory perspectives into conversation around the issue of democracy. Ewen is particularly concerned with the future of democracy in an era of highly concentrated media ownership, PR spin, and rapid technological change. The issue is as relevant now as when Ewen wrote about it.

In March 1995, as this book neared completion, Edward L. Bernays died in Cambridge, Massachusetts, at the age of 102.[1] Present at the beginning, so to speak, his life (1892–1995) spanned the history that is explored in this book. It is perhaps fitting, then, that just as we opened our quest standing at Bernays's doorstep, so we shall conclude with him.

When I visited with Bernays in the autumn of 1990, I encountered two different people. On the one hand, I met a man who—as witnessed in his nostalgic recollection of Dumb Jack—understood public relations as a necessary response to a society in which expanding democratic expectations were forcefully combating the outmoded assumptions of an old, hierarchical social order. According to this Bernays, the modern belief in universal rights and popular struggles for democracy had confronted elites with a profound question: How could they preserve their social, economic, and political advantages in an age when the idea of a privileged class was coming under mounting attack from below? This first Bernays understood the "public sphere" as contested ground and public relations as a historic response to the vocal demands of a conscious, and increasingly critical, public.

Yet as he described his life and his profession, I glimpsed another Bernays. This one saw the public as a malleable mass of protoplasm, plastic raw material that—in the hands of a skilled manipulator—could be manufactured at will. According to this Bernays, the public mind posed little danger and could be engineered through dexterous appeals to its instinctual and unconscious inner life. This Bernays was the paradigmatic "expert" in a world where "expertise" often refers to a scientifically trained individual's capacity to monitor, forecast, and influence the ideas and/or behavior of others.

This dichotomy characterized Bernays's thinking over a lifetime. In the pivotal years of the late 1940s, for example, Bernays evinced two dramatically dissimilar perspectives on the tasks faced by public relations specialists in a potentially hazardous postwar world.

At one end, in 1947, Bernays maintained that corporate public relations must answer to the ultimatums of a public that had—over the preceding decade and a half—become resolutely aware of its social and economic rights. Toward this goal, Bernays argued, "slogans" and "incantations" would be insufficient. Business must champion and establish policies that would lead to stable employment; adequate old-age pensions; social security; and other forms of insurance, including group accident, sickness, hospital, and life. These concessions, Bernays understood, were necessitated by a public arena that is shaped, at times, by the ideas and actions of ordinary people and by the social expectations they bring to the historical stage. Embedded within this side of Bernays's thinking was an understanding that, willy-nilly, powerful institutions were not always able to govern the dynamics—or the origins—of public expression. The mobilizations of the 1930s had actively punctuated that fact.

At the same time as Bernays was recommending substantive programmatic proposals, however, he was also ordaining the "engineering of consent" as an indispensable instrument of rule. This Bernays was the painter of mental scenery, the fabricator of captivating "pseudo-environments" designed to steer the public mind furtively toward the agendas of vested power. He was a master of stagecraft, shaping "news" and "events" with a hidden hand. Beside the democrat stood the demagogue, a nimble master of illusions, a man who sought to colonize the public sphere on behalf of entrenched managerial interests.

It would be a misconception, however, to see Bernays's contradictions as particular to the man. The ambiguities of his perspective—the murky dissonance separating one who is *responding to* from one who seeks to *manage* the public mind—have marked the history of public relations throughout the twentieth century.

*        *        *

Today, with a powerful machinery of opinion management deeply entrenched—and little coherent opposition heard from below—the meaning and realization of democracy have become more and more elusive. The extent to which power and influence are routinely employed to assemble "phantom publics" on behalf of any purpose challenges us to rethink the structures of social communication and to imagine again the ways by which democratic participation may be accomplished.

Some may argue, looking back on the history recounted in this book, that present circumstances are transient—that, as in the past, the force of democratic expression will undermine and ultimately transgress the engineering of consent. For those who are used to looking at American history as a "pendulum" swinging back and forth between conservatism and liberalism, such an eventuality may seem preordained.

But if one examines other developments chronicled in this book, this interpretation is significantly flawed. Looking at the historical development of public relations as a force in American society, one sees that a consequential change has taken place, one that throws simplistic pendulum theories into question. Coinciding with recurrent swings between public relations as a response to democratic mobilizations and as an attempt to colonize the horizons of public expression, there has been a parallel development. Over the course of this century, while arenas of public interaction and expression have become scarce, the apparatus for molding the public mind and for appealing to the public eye has become increasingly pervasive, more and more sophisticated in its technology and expertise. Economic mergers in the media and information industries, in particular, are only reminders that though many are touched by the messages of these industries, fewer and fewer hands control the pipelines of persuasion.

At the dawn of a new millennium, particularly in the face of this communications imbalance, pivotal questions become more urgent:

- Can there be democracy when the public is a fractionalized audience? When the public has no collective presence?
- Can there be democracy when public life is separated from the ability of a public to act—for itself—as a public?
- Can there be democracy when public agendas are routinely predetermined by "unseen engineers?"
- Can there be democracy when public opinion is reduced to the published results of opinion surveys, statistical applause tracks?
- Can there be democracy when the tools of communication are neither democratically distributed nor democratically controlled?
- Can there be democracy when the content of media is determined, almost universally, by commericial considerations?
- Can there be democracy in a society in which emotional appeals overwhelm reason, where the image is routinely employed to overwhelm thought?
- What developments will emerge to invigorate popular democracy this time around? What will move us beyond prevailing strategies of power that are aimed at managing the human climate?

These are big questions. Their answers, if they are to come, lie beyond the scope of any book. For those who continue to cherish democratic ideals, however, these questions point to an agenda for the future.

In thinking about ways to reawaken democracy, we must keep in mind that the relationship between publicity and democracy is not essentially corrupt. The free circulation of ideas and debate is critical to the maintenance of an aware public. The rise of democratic thinking, in fact, cannot be explained apart from the circulation of pamphlets, proclamations, and other literary documents that provided a basis for public discussion and helped to transform once-heretical ideas into common aspirations.

Publicity becomes an impediment to democracy, however, when the circulation of ideas is governed by enormous concentrations of wealth that have, as their underlying purpose, the perpetuation of their own power. When this is the case—as is too often true today—the ideal of civic participation gives way to a continual sideshow, a masquerade of democracy calculated to pique the public's emotions. In regard to a more democratic future, then, ways of enhancing the circulation of ideas—regardless of economic circumstance—need to be developed.

We need to imagine what an active public life might look like in an electronic age.

We need to discover ways to move beyond thinking of public relations as a function of compliance experts and learn to think of it as an ongoing and inclusive process of discussion. Ordinary people need to develop independent ways and means of understanding and airing public problems and issues and of acting on them.

In 1927—just as public relations and the modern media system were coming of age—John Dewey remarked that "[o]ptimism about democracy is to-day under a cloud." With its bounteous amusements, he argued, a modern consumer culture was deflecting people from the functional responsibilities of citizenship. While "we have the physical tools of communication as never before," he maintained, the public had minimal access to them and was "so bewildered that it cannot find itself."[2] "There is too much public, a public too diffused and scattered and too intricate in composition."[3]

To move beyond this predicament and to rediscover itself as a social force, Dewey asserted, the public must move beyond its status as an audience of consumers and learn to communicate actively with itself.

> Without such communication, the public will remain shadowy and form-less, seeking spasmodically for itself, but seizing and holding its shadow rather than its substance. Till the Great Society [then a common phrase for mass industrial society] is converted into a Great Community, the Public will remain in eclipse. Communication can alone create a great community.[4]

To a disturbing extent, Dewey's speculations on "the public and its problems" continue to resonate. In our commercial culture, the extent to which the public engages in an ongoing and dynamic process of communication—unassisted by the methods and devices of opinion experts—is virtually nil. To move beyond this circumstance, a number of changes need to be made.

Present inequities regarding *who has a say? who gets to be heard?* need to be corrected. The vast power of the commercial communications system today lies in its unimpeded control over the avenues of public discussion. For this situation to change, the public sphere—currently dominated by corporate interests and consciously managed by public relations professionals—must revert to the people.

Though camouflaged by business as usual, the capacity to make such a change happen is within sight. Ironically, the enormous authority of a business-centered world-view is derived from the fact that large corporations have been permitted to occupy and impose upon public properties—such as the broadcast spectrum—without paying any significant rent to the public. For a negligible licensing fee, private corporations harvest an incessant windfall of public influence.

If this practice was to change—if a fund to support public communication, for example, regularly received a fair rent from those who were permitted to exploit public properties commercially—funding for noncommercial venues of expression and for noncommercial arenas of public education would be plentiful. If 15 to 25 percent of all advertising expenditures in the United States were applied this way, the crisis in funding for public arts and education would evaporate. New visions would flourish. Locally based community communications centers—equipped with up-to-date technologies and opening new avenues for distribution—would magnify the variety of voices heard. Schools could more adequately prepare their students for the responsibilities of democratic citizenship.

This issue of education is pivotal, since it has often been a casualty of public relations reasoning. In 1947, Bernays acknowledged this danger when he proclaimed that "[u]nder no circumstances should the engineering of consent supersede or displace the functions of the educational system." Then—contradicting his own admonition—he added that in most situations, an educated public will only interfere with leaders' ability to act. Leaders "cannot wait for the people" to understand issues fully. To harvest public support efficiently, he advised, it is crucial for leaders to arm themselves with the implements of "mass persuasion" and look to the engineering of consent as a strategy of first resort.

Epitomizing public relations doctrine that had been germinating since the First World War, this perspective has had dire consequences for the caliber of public discourse in the United States, particularly in the decades since the end of the Second World War. Inasmuch as public relations is rarely intended to inform the population about the intricacies of an issue and is more often calculated to circumvent critical thinking, it has meant that much of what is put forth for public consumption is intentionally indecipherable on a conscious level. The growing primacy of the image—as the preferred instrument of public address—is predicated on the assumption that images work on people enigmatically, that they affect people without their even realizing that a process of persuasion is going on.

The implications of this predilection, particularly for the ways in which we think about education, are considerable. We live in a world where the modern media of communication are everywhere and inescapable. Instrumental images vie for nearly every moment of human attention. Therefore, it is essential for our schools to move toward the development of critical media and visual literacy programs from the early grades onward.

The systematic examination of media institutions and the forces that influence them will encourage students and teachers to look behind the messages they receive, to uncover what, today, is a predominantly secret world. A better understanding of public relations practices will allow students to see that conventional categories, such as "news" and "entertainment," do not adequately describe the forces at play within them.

In a society where instrumental images are employed to petition our affections at every turn—often without a word—educational curricula must also encourage the development of tools for critically analyzing images. Going back some time, the language of images has been well known to people working in the field of opinion management. For democracy to prevail, image making as a communicative activity must be understood by ordinary citizens as well. The aesthetic realm—and the enigmatic ties linking aesthetic, social, economic, political, and ethical values—must be brought down to earth as a subject of study.

The development of curricula in media and visual literacy will not only sharpen people's ability to decipher their world, but it will also contribute to a broadening of the public sphere. Literacy is never just about reading; it is also about writing. Just as early campaigns for universal print literacy were concerned with democratizing the tools of public expression—the written word—upcoming struggles for media literacy must strive to empower people with contemporary implements of public discourse: video, graphic arts, photography, computer-assisted journalism and layout, and performance. More customary mainstays of public expression—expository writing and public speaking—must be resuscitated as well.

Media literacy cannot simply be seen as a vaccination against PR or other familiar strains of institutionalized guile. It must be understood as an education in techniques that can democratize the realm of public expression and will magnify the possibility of meaningful public interactions. Distinctions between publicist and citizen, author and audience, need to be broken down. Education can facilitate this process. It can enlarge the circle of who is permitted—and who will be able—to interpret and make sense of the world.

One last point. As a precondition for other changes, we need to question demographic categories of identity that, at present, divide the public against itself and separate people who—when viewed from a critical distance—may share common interests. Demographics is a powerful tool of divide and rule. To combat it, we need to rediscover a sense of social connectedness. Beyond looking out for ourselves—as individuals or as members of a particular group—we must also learn to rediscover ourselves in others, to see our concerns and aspirations in theirs.

At present, the champions of vested power insolently claim to be acting in the name of public opinion. Engineers of consent—armed with sophisticated demographic tools—continue to dictate public agendas. For this situation to change, we need to rethink those habits of mind within ourselves that disunite ordinary Americans along lines of class, race, ethnicity, gender, and persuasion, encouraging us to fight it out over increasingly insufficient crumbs. Until a sense of difference is balanced by a sense of commonality, a democratic public will be unattainable. *For the greater good to prevail, we need to imagine ourselves as a greater public.*

## Questions for Consideration

1   Which of Ewen's concluding arguments and suggestions seem most important to you? Why?
2   What do you think Ewen means when he equates public relations with "spin"? Is it possible to conduct public relations without getting involved in spin?

## Notes

1.   Bernays and I corresponded with each other for some time after our autumn 1990 meeting. I sent him a copy of Chapter 1, "Visiting Edward Bernays," when it was completed in late 1994. Unhappily, he passed away before he was able to respond to my narrative of our encounter.
2.   John Dewey, *The Public and Its Problems* (Athens, Ohio, 1927), p. 137.
3.   Ibid., p. 142.
4.   Edward Bernays, "The Engineering of Consent," *Annals of the American Academy of Political and Social Science* 250 (March 1947), pp. 114–15.

# Index